FRANK STILWELL

POLITICAL ECONOMY

THE CONTEST OF ECONOMIC IDEAS

THIRD EDITION

OXFORD
UNIVERSITY PRESS
AUSTRALIA & NEW ZEALAND

OXFORD
UNIVERSITY PRESS

Oxford University Press is a department of the University of Oxford.

It furthers the University's objective of excellence in research, scholarship, and education by publishing worldwide. Oxford is a registered trademark of Oxford University Press in the UK and in certain other countries.

Published in Australia by
Oxford University Press
253 Normanby Road, South Melbourne, Victoria 3205, Australia

First published 2002
Second edition published 2006
Third edition published 2012
Reprinted 2012 (twice), 2013, 2014, 2016 (twice)

National Library of Australia Cataloguing-in-Publication data

Stilwell, Frank J. B.
Political economy : the contest of economic ideas/Frank Stilwell.
3rd ed.

9780195575019 (pbk.)

Includes index.
For first or second year undergraduate students.
Economics.
Comparative economics.

330

Edited by Bruce Gillespie
Typeset in India, by diacriTech, chennai
Proofread by Jamie Anderson
Indexed by Neale Towart
Printed by Sheck Wah Tong Printing Press Ltd

Contents

List of Boxes, Figures, and Tables

Boxes

Figures

Tables

Preface

This book provides an overview of political economy and a scholarly contribution to its further development. Political economy deals with issues that are fundamental to our individual and collective well-being. How wealth is created and used, the inequalities between rich and poor, and the tensions between economic growth and the environment are important illustrative concerns. Conventional economic theory is limited in its capacity to illuminate these issues, so a more coherent and constructive political economic alternative is needed.

Political Economy emphasises the desirability of seeing the big picture right from the outset, by coming to grips with how economic concerns connect with social and political concerns. It focuses on the diversity of viewpoints on economic issues and the principal analytical tools and value judgments associated with each school of economic thought. This is an invitation to controversy.

A broad overview of political economy and some application to contemporary issues can be obtained by reading half of this book: the chapters in the first two parts, the first chapter only in each of the next five parts, and then all chapters in the last two parts. That would mean 21 chapters rather than the full 42. You would be introduced to the ideas of leading personalities in the historical development of economic analysis: Adam Smith, Karl Marx, Alfred Marshall, Thorstein Veblen, and John Maynard Keynes. You might then feel inclined to go back and flesh out your understanding of political economy—and the contributions of some other outstanding scholars—by reading the remaining 21 chapters. Either way, whether you tackle the book as a whole or take the short cut, I hope it leads you to delve deeper into this fascinating field of enquiry.

The approach to studying political economy developed here reflects my participation in the political economy program at the University of Sydney and the influence of my political economy colleagues there. The excellent research assistance of Tim Roxburgh has been invaluable in producing this third edition of the book. Special thanks are also due to Ann Grealis for her continuing personal encouragement and for her tolerance of my preoccupation with political economy, not to mention jazz, blues, and rock'n'roll.

Frank Stilwell

Acknowledgments

The author and the publisher wish to thank the following for photographs:

Corbis/Bettmann, p. 214; Getty/Hulton Archive, p. 198; photolibrary/Alamy/Interfoto, pp. 153, 225; photolibrary/AP, pp. 230, 265; photolibrary/AP/A J Mast, p. 44; photolibrary/AP/ Eddie Adams, p. 307; photolibrary/AP/Marty Lederhandler, p. 245; photolibrary/Mary Evans, p. 102; Sydney Morning Herald picture by David Porter, p. 252.

Every effort has been made to trace the original source of copyright material contained in this book. The publisher will be pleased to hear from copyright holders to rectify any errors or omissions.

Glossary

(135 terms commonly used in political economy)

affluenza

a tendency sometimes said to affect modern societies, where the pursuit of material wealth overwhelms other personal, social, and environmental concerns, usually with disappointing results for human happiness.

aggregate demand

the total expenditure on goods and services within a community (generally a nation); according to Keynesian economics, it is the sum of expenditure on consumption, investment, government spending, and exports less expenditure on imports.

aggregate supply

the capacity (or potential) of the economy to produce goods and services.

alienation

a division or lack of wholeness in the human condition, especially arising because employees do not have control over the nature of the work that they do nor over the products of that work.

barriers to entry

impediments restricting new firms from setting up in an industry.

barter

direct exchange of goods and services without the use of money.

bond

financial asset, the purchase of which entails making a loan to a government or a corporation, entitling the owner of the bond to the receipt of regular interest payments.

Bretton Woods

the place in the USA where an international conference was held in 1944 to consider arrangements for the management of international economic relationships. The governments represented at the conference agreed to establish a regime of fixed exchange rates, with the US dollar as the major reserve currency, convertible for gold, and new international institutions, such as the International Monetary Fund and the International Bank for Reconstruction and Development (part of what is called 'the World Bank').

budget deficit (surplus)

government spending more than (less than) government revenue; a surplus or deficit may be planned or unintended.

capital

a widely used term that normally refers to capital goods (for example, factories, trucks, machinery, tools) that are used in the production of other goods and services. The term may also be used to mean money capital—that is, stocks of money generated by past savings or borrowing (which can be used, *inter alia*, for the purchase of capital goods). A third use of the term is to refer to capital as a social relation (involving command over labour and other resources). In this third sense, reference may be made to a capitalist class.

capital accumulation

the process whereby capital is increased. This is a major impetus for economic growth. A slowing in the rate of capital accumulation is typically followed by an economic crisis.

capitalism

the particular type of economy based on private ownership of the means of production and the pursuit of profit. The term 'monopoly capitalism' may be used where there are large concentrations of ownership and control of capital. 'Competitive capitalism' or 'free market capitalism' are terms usually implying a wider spread of enterprise throughout the economy.

capitalist class

those who own and control the main economic institutions of capitalism.

casualisation

the process whereby proportionately more jobs come to be under a casual employment contract, and thus lack security of employment.

circular and cumulative causation

the process whereby the political economic conditions at a point of time shape subsequent political economic changes, causing greater divergence from the initial conditions. Small differences thereby become magnified and economic inequalities relentlessly increase.

class

the division of society according to economic circumstances. Different views of class in political economy associate it with inequalities of property ownership, power, and income.

commodity

any good or service produced for sale rather than for personal consumption by its producer.

comparative advantage

the principle, developed by David Ricardo, whereby countries are said to benefit mutually by specialising in the production of different types of commodities, then trading with each other. Absolute advantage exists if a country produces a commodity more cheaply than another.

Comparative advantage exists where a country produces everything more cheaply, but some things relatively more cheaply than others; that then forms the basis for its specialisation in production and trade.

competition

a process of rivalry in economic behaviour; for example, between firms seeking to expand their respective market shares of the same or similar products.

concentration and centralisation of capital

a term used in Marxist economics to denote the processes transforming competitive capitalism into monopoly capitalism. Concentration results from the growth of individual business enterprises, whereas centralisation means that the enterprises combine into fewer units, usually through mergers and takeovers.

conglomerate

a company that has economic activities in many industries. Note that the development of conglomerates undermines the coherence of the notion of 'industry' as a means of classifying firms.

conspicuous consumption

consuming goods and services in a manner intended to impress, so that satisfaction derives from the effect on other people, rather than from the utility of the good or service itself.

consumer sovereignty

the view that consumers are independent and free to choose, thereby exercising economic power, because how they spend their incomes determines what products will be produced. This proposition is subject to critique by political economists, some arguing that producer sovereignty (whereby firms mould consumer preferences to suit their own corporate goals) is more characteristic of the modern economy.

consumption

the largest item in national expenditure, comprising the total spending by consumers on goods and services. Consumption may also refer to the actual process of using a good or service; for example, consuming a chocolate bar, or consuming the service of a house by living in it.

corporate power

the capacity of large corporations to use their economic resources to serve their own corporate goals.

corporation

a particular form of business organisation that takes advantage of the laws that allow a corporation to be treated as an individual person and limit the personal liability of its owners for any damages that it may inflict or losses that it may incur.

cost–benefit analysis

the attempt to put money values on the relative advantages and disadvantages to society arising from a particular policy or project; for example, the construction of a new road, hospital, or port.

countervailing power

the power of one group (for example, government, trade unions) to match and resist the power of other groups (for example, corporations).

currency

the notes and coin that are the current medium of exchange in a country.

current account deficit (or surplus)

where payments flowing out of a nation are greater than (or less than) payments flowing in. Payments flowing out typically comprise expenditure on imports plus interest and dividends paid to overseas lenders and investors. Payments flowing in typically comprise revenues from exports plus interest and dividends paid by overseas borrowers and recipients of investment. The current account is to be distinguished from the capital account, which accounts for transactions in financial assets.

demand, law of

generally, the inverse relationship between the price of a commodity and the quantity of it that consumers purchase. One should always be sceptical about 'laws' in economics, since human behaviour seldom, if ever, conforms to universal principles without exceptions.

deregulation

the reduction or removal of state regulations on privately owned businesses. Such regulations may involve, for example, requirements concerning environmental standards, working conditions, occupational health and safety, or the reporting of information about business finances.

derivatives

financial assets whose market value depends on the movements in market prices of other assets.

disarticulation

the severing of economic linkages between industries or regions.

discrimination

unequal treatment of individuals or social groups (regarding, for example, housing, employment, wages, or promotion) on inappropriate grounds (for example, race, sex, religion, or political conviction).

division of labour

the specialisation of workers in particular parts or operations of a production process. It means that different workers are doing different types of jobs. The division of labour may (but does not necessarily) increase economic efficiency and thus enable the production of greater volumes of output. The international division of labour extends the process beyond individual nations, leading to a situation in which countries specialise in different types of employment (for example, farming, mining, manufacturing, provision of services). As a result of the processes of globalisation, the character of the international division of labour is changing.

ecological sustainability

the compatibility of the economy with the physical environment, which requires that ecological systems are not irreversibly degraded by economic activities. The extent to which an economic system is ecologically sustainable is a criterion (along with efficiency and equity) by which it can be evaluated.

economic crises

collapses in investment that cause interruptions to economic growth. Depending on their severity (and the preference of the writer), crises may alternatively be described as slumps, depressions, and recessions.

economic growth

an increase in the value of goods and services produced. Economic growth is commonly measured in terms of gross domestic product (GDP), but it is increasingly widely recognised that GDP is poorly correlated with national well-being.

economic rationalism

the belief that economic goals should have priority over social goals, and that such goals are better served by markets than by the state, because markets ensure the convergence of private goals and the social good.

economic surplus

the excess of the value of production over the cost of simply reproducing the economy. How the surplus is used shapes the form of economic development.

economies of scale

the cost advantages of large-scale production, arising where expansion of productive capacity causes total production costs to rise less than proportionately.

economy

a system for organising the production of goods and services, the distribution of income and wealth, and the exchange of commodities. Economics is the study of the economy. Political economy broadens the study of the economy by recognising the interconnections between the economy, the society, and political processes. The term 'political economy' can refer either to the system or to the study of it.

efficiency

the effectiveness with which economic resources (land, labour, capital) are used to achieve given social ends. Note that because efficiency concerns means, not ends, it is always important to ask: what end? efficient in achieving what? One may refer, for example, to the efficiency of a firm in producing particular outputs.

elasticity

the responsiveness of one economic variable to changes in another. The price elasticity of demand is the responsiveness of demand for a commodity to a change in its price, whereas the price elasticity of supply is the responsiveness of supply of a commodity to a change in its price. The income elasticity of demand is the responsiveness of change in demand for a commodity to changes in the income of consumers.

entrepreneur

a person generating new business activity, usually entailing risk and implementing innovation.

equilibrium

a situation in which the forces making for change in opposite directions are in balance, so there is no tendency to shift from the current position. A market is in equilibrium if, for example, the quantity supplied at the prevailing price exactly equals the amount consumers want to buy at that price.

equity

fairness (for example, in the distribution of income). This definition of equity is different from the meaning of the term in finance, where equity means the shareholders' stake in the ownership of a corporation.

exchange rate

the rate at which different national currencies can be exchanged for each other—that is, the ratio of values or prices of two currencies.

exploitation

according to Marxist economics, exploitation is the process whereby surplus value is generated in a capitalist economy. More generally, it refers to the situation in which one class derives income from the labour undertaken by another class. This differs from the popular use of the term to describe the practices of particularly ruthless employers who pay exceptionally low wages to their workers.

externalities

costs or benefits affecting people other than those directly engaged in market exchange of a particular commodities. Referred to as 'spillover effects', these may be positive (external economies of production and consumption) or negative (external diseconomies of production and consumption).

factors of production

inputs into the process of producing goods and services: land, labour, and capital. Neoclassical economists commonly model the firm as if it were an economic agent combining these factors of production. The concept of factors of production depersonifies land, labour, and capital, and effectively denies their social dimensions.

financialisation

the process of making more economic activities valued and exchanged according to financial or monetary criteria.

fiscal policy

the adjustment made by government to revenues and expenditures in order to affect the level of national income, output, and employment.

Fordism

the organisation of the economy on the principles pioneered by the Ford Motor Company, which subsequently became widespread in industrial capitalist economies in the twentieth century. Fordism's distinctive features are mass production, standardised products, and the control of workers in closely regulated and supervised labour processes.

gender

the division of society according to the differential circumstances of men and women. Whereas sex is biologically determined, gender is socially constructed; it can, for example, be seen in the gender division of labour in household work and in paid work.

genuine progress indicator (GPI)

an estimate of the well-being of a nation's citizens, calculated by including factors that are overlooked in estimates of GDP and GNI, such as income distribution, the costs of land degradation, and the value of household work. Although GPI is a broader measure than GDP and GNI, it does not include all factors that influence human well-being, and is limited to those that can be estimated in monetary terms.

global financial crisis (GFC)

the sudden shock to the world economy that developed in 2007–08, beginning in financial markets in the United States, leading to corporate collapses and generating a recession that rapidly spread to many other countries.

globalisation

the process whereby the significance of national boundaries is eroded as international interconnections proliferate and intensify. Globalisation has economic dimensions (for example, trade in commodities, international investment, and finance) and social and cultural dimensions (for example, globalisation of environmental consciousness, of consumerism, and of activity concerning human rights).

green economics

an alternative to orthodox economics, emphasising the principles of ecological sustainability, social justice, participatory democracy, and community development.

gross domestic product (GDP)

the total market value of goods and services produced within a nation in a given period, after deducting the cost of goods and services used in the production process, but before making deductions for the depreciation of capital goods. GDP refers to the value of goods and services produced within a nation's borders, irrespective of the nationality of the production entity.

gross national income (GNI) (formerly *gross national product*, or *GNP*)

the aggregate value of income that accrues to people and institutions as a consequence of their involvement in production processes or ownership of assets that may be used in production. GNI includes incomes earned by a nation's citizens working overseas and returns on Australian investments abroad, but excludes incomes earned by foreigners employed in domestic production and returns accumulated by foreign capital.

ideology

a system of belief. Ideologies, embodying particular value judgments about the economy and society, commonly give legitimacy to a particular economic or social order; for example, neoliberal ideology as a justification for free-market capitalism.

imperialism

the political economic processes whereby strong classes in some nations dominate over the people of poorer nations. Imperialism's hallmarks are empire building, territorial expansion, and domination of the weak by the strong on an international scale. Lenin called it 'the highest stage of capitalism'.

industry

comprises the firms making broadly similar products; for example, the car industry, the steel industry.

inflation

rising prices. Inflation is normally measured by a consumer price index (CPI), which indicates how the price of a typical basket of goods varies over time.

investment

a significant item in national expenditure, comprising spending on capital goods, usually undertaken by firms and governments. This definition is different from the use of the term in everyday language, where it means the purchase of any asset, such as a government bond, a share in a company, or a piece of real estate.

labour

normally means work done by human beings, contributing to the production and exchange of goods and services. Wages and salaries are its usual reward. 'Labour' may also refer to the class of people who depend for their livelihood on income from work; that is, the working class.

labour power

people's capacity, whether by mental or manual labour, to produce useful goods and services. Converting labour power into labour is a principal concern of capitalist management—hence its need to control the labour process.

labour process

how work is organised and done.

labour theory of value

the view that the value of a commodity depends on the amount of labour that goes into making it (given that the latter reflects what is current best practice or socially necessary).

laissez-faire

a phrase borrowed from the French that indicates an economy left alone to reflect, without involvement by the state, the decisions of free enterprises in markets.

land

most simply, the part of the earth's surface that is not covered by water. Economically, it also refers to the gifts of nature, such as minerals and soil fertility. Land provides space and physical resources. Owners of land may receive payments in the form of rent, depending on its economic value, without necessarily expending any effort. This is sometimes referred to as 'unearned income'.

liquidity preference

people's desire to hold their assets as money rather than in some other (more illiquid) form, such as bonds, shares, or real estate.

marginal cost

according to neoclassical economics, the marginal cost is the increase in total costs of production that results from increasing the volume of output by one unit.

marginal efficiency of capital

according to Keynesian economics, this is the expected rate of return on an additional item of investment expenditure. Firms can be expected to rank investment projects according to their marginal efficiency of capital and undertake those with the highest value first.

marginal product

the increase in output that results from increasing the quantity of a variable factor of production by one unit. According to the principle of diminishing marginal productivity, marginal product declines as more of the variable factor is put into production.

marginal productivity theory

the view, in neoclassical economics, that factors of production are rewarded in proportion to their respective marginal products.

marginal propensity to consume

the proportion of an additional increment of income that is consumed, not saved.

marginal revenue

the increase in the total revenue of a firm when it sells one more unit of its output.

marginal utility

the increase in a person's satisfaction that results from consuming one more unit of a good or service. The principle of diminishing marginal utility, which is central to neoclassical economics, implies that marginal utility declines as more units are consumed.

market

where buyers and sellers exchange commodities or assets that can be held as private property. The term may be used to describe a place (the marketplace) or, more generally, a process of exchange.

market failure

the recognition that, in particular circumstances, markets do not ensure beneficial economic outcomes. Market failures may involve the inadequate supply of public goods, or distortions arising from externalities, or from imperfect competition. Neoclassical economists acknowledge these problems but disagree over their relative importance.

merger

the voluntary combination of two or more firms into one.

mode of production

how the economy is organised for the purpose of producing goods and services. It involves the use of tangible forces of production, comprising the raw materials, capital goods, labour power, and technology. It also involves particular relations of production, concerned with how people are organised (for example, whether by authoritarian, hierarchical means or in democratic, participatory ways). This concept is widely used in Marxist economics.

monetarism

the view that government policy should be restricted to a steady increase in the money supply at a rate just sufficient to match the growth in the volume of goods and services produced. This view of monetarism is different from the discretionary use of monetary (or fiscal) policy to even out economic booms and slumps, a policy approach known as demand management, or macroeconomic fine-tuning.

monetary policy

the adjustment of the supply of money or the price of money (the rate of interest) in order to affect the level of national income, output, and employment.

money

anything that is generally acceptable as a means of exchange and a means of settling debt. It normally consists of currency on issue (notes and coin) and deposits or credit with financial institutions that is obtainable on demand (through an ATM, for example).

monopolistic competition

a market in which there are very many sellers but where they can influence the price of their own products because of some product differentiation or geographical fragmentation of the market.

monopoly

strictly speaking, monopoly means there is only one firm in an industry. But the term is also used more broadly to denote an economy in which the power of big business is dominant, that is, monopoly capitalism.

multiplier

a measure of the effect on national income of a change in one of the components of aggregate demand. If, for example, an increase in investment expenditure of $1 leads to an increased national income of $3, then the multiplier is 3.

national income

the total value of the flow of goods and services produced in a nation over a specified period, for example, one year (*see also* Gross national income).

neoliberalism

the ideology that seeks to justify the restructuring of the economy to increase opportunities for private profit, often couched in such language as 'market freedoms' and 'individual choice'.

oligopoly

a market in which there are only a few sellers. Strategic interdependence shapes the behaviour of the firms in such market conditions.

opportunity cost

what is forgone by using economic resources in one way rather than another. The opportunity cost of unemployment, for example, is the goods and services the unemployed people would have produced if they had jobs. The opportunity cost of attending a university lecture is an hour that you might otherwise spend in the library, a café, or playing sport.

organic composition of capital

a term used in Marxist economics to refer to the relative values of the constant capital and variable capital used in the production of goods and services. A high organic composition of capital in general usually indicates a production process that is quite mechanised, using a high proportion of capital goods relative to labour.

Pareto criterion

a basis for making judgments about how community well-being is affected by the allocation of economic resources. If a reallocation of resources makes at least one person better off without making anyone worse off, it is said to be a Pareto improvement. The term derives from the development of this concept by the Italian theorist Vilfredo Pareto.

perfect competition

the state of affairs in a market in which there are very many sellers providing identical products, so that none can effect the price of its own product, and many buyers, so that none can effect the price it pays. All buyers and sellers have perfect information about all relevant products and their prices. This theoretical model has a central place in neoclassical theory.

Phillips curve

the inverse relationship said to exist between the rate of unemployment and the rate of inflation.

positional goods

goods whose supply is inherently limited, becoming either more expensive or more degraded as rising incomes lead more people to compete to acquire them.

power

in general, the possibility of imposing your will on the behaviour of other people. Economic power refers more specifically to the capacity of individuals or, more typically, institutions to exert influence (over, for example, prices, wages, or government policies) because of their command over economic resources.

praxis

the integration of theory and practice. This linking of analysis and activism is a distinctive feature of the Marxist method in political economy.

privatisation

the sale of government-owned enterprises to private owners; the opposite of nationalisation. The term 'privatisation' is also loosely applied to any shift of emphasis in the economy from the public sector to the private sector.

production

making goods and services.

profit

the excess of revenue over costs. The nature and origin of profit has been a focal point for debates on political economy.

public goods

items whose consumption is inherently collective. They therefore are not produced in sufficient quantity (if at all) in a market economy.

rate of interest

the price of borrowed money. It may also be regarded as the price of liquidity (that is, the opportunity cost of holding assets in a liquid form, as money, rather than in a form that earns interest).

Banks make profits by charging higher interest rates to borrowers than they pay to depositors. In practice, there are many different rates of interest. When economists talk about the rate of interest they usually mean an average of the various rates prevailing in the markets for loans and deposits, or a particular base rate of interest, such as the cash rate set by the central bank.

realisation of surplus value

according to Marxist economics, the conversion of surplus value into profit as a result of capitalist firms selling the commodities they have produced.

rent

payments to landowners for the use of their land. Rent also has a broader meaning in economics, to refer to payments to any factor of production over and above what is necessary in order to maintain it in its current use.

reserve army of labour

a Marxist term used to denote the most marginalised elements of the workforce. It has nothing to do with military conscription. Marx saw the reserve army of labour as having three parts: a floating form, comprising workers displaced by technological change or the concentration and centralisation of capital; a stagnant form, comprising people in irregular employment; and a latent form, comprising workers displaced from agriculture by the encroachment of the capitalist mode of production.

resource allocation

how society's resources—human, natural, and manufactured—are distributed between the competing uses to which they may be put.

savings

income that is not spent on consumption.

Say's Law

the belief that, because producing goods generates the incomes necessary to buy them, there need not be recessions resulting from a glut of unsold products. The idea was developed by the classical economist J. B. Say and later challenged by economists such as J. M. Keynes.

shares

financial assets, traded on the stock exchange, the holding of which confers part ownership in the corporation to which they relate. Shareholders are entitled to vote at shareholders' meetings and to receive such dividend payments as the corporation determines to make each year.

social capital

features of a society that tend to enhance its economic productivity. These features may include trust, the density of personal networks, and the prevalence of social institutions in which people are actively engaged.

socialism

an alternative system of economic organisation, contrasting with capitalism in that it emphasises the collective ownership of the means of production and social control of the economic surplus.

soulful corporation

the view of the corporation as a body serving community interests, or at least tempering its own economic self-interest with responsibilities to the broader community.

speculation

buying and selling assets with a view to making a profit later when prices have changed (that is, a capital gain) without making any productive contribution to the economy.

stagflation

simultaneous unemployment and inflation.

state

the institutions of national administration, including the government, the public service, the judiciary, the police, and the armed forces. It is in analysing the state that the study of political economy connects with the study of government, or political science.

surplus value

that part of the value created by labour that is not returned to workers as wages, but is instead appropriated by capitalist employers. This is a key concept in Marxist economics. Absolute surplus value denotes surplus value obtained by lengthening the working day (or week). Relative surplus value denotes surplus value obtained by increasing the productivity and/or intensity of labour.

sustainability

the capacity of a system to reproduce itself. Economic sustainability requires that worn-out equipment needed for producing goods and services be replaced by new investment. Ecological sustainability requires that natural resources not be depleted for the short-run purposes of a growth-orientated economy.

takeover

the acquisition of one firm by another.

tariff

a tax on imported goods. Tariffs have the effect of partially protecting firms in a nation from overseas competition.

taxation

revenue collected by government for the purpose of financing its expenditures. Taxes may be levied on people (poll tax), their incomes (income taxes), their expenditures (for example, goods and services tax), and their assets (for example, land tax, wealth tax, estate tax).

technology

the technique for producing goods and services, based on the current state of scientific knowledge.

technological change

advance in scientific knowledge and its application to industry. This may involve the production of new goods and services or new methods of producing existing goods and services.

technostructure
Galbraith's term for those who can shape the operations of modern capitalist economic institutions because they control information and organisation. The term usually connotes middle management and skilled employees with technical expertise, rather than a more traditional capitalist class.

trade
exchange of goods and services, either by barter or, more commonly, through the use of money as a medium of exchange. International trade is exchange that crosses national boundaries.

transnational corporation
a company that has affiliate or subsidiary companies in at least one other country than that in which its headquarters are located. This term is used interchangeably with 'multinational corporation', although the former term may imply that the company has more completely transcended its national origins.

unemployment
underutilisation of labour because people who wish to work cannot get jobs. The unemployment rate is normally measured as the percentage of the total workforce who are seeking work but are not currently employed. There are debates about the proportion of measured unemployment that is involuntary and about whether official unemployment statistics indicate the full extent of underutilised labour.

utility
the usefulness of a good or service or, in the neoclassical economic sense, the satisfaction or pleasure derived from consuming it. The estimation of utility is essentially subjective, varying from person to person according to their particular tastes.

value
the worth attributed to a good or service. This may refer objectively to its intrinsic properties, such as the amount of labour, materials, or energy that go into making it. It may be a more subjective notion, referring to the utility the good or service yields to the person who owns or consumes it. Alternatively, it may simply be regarded as its market price. Debates about these competing interpretations of value have been a recurrent feature in political economy. Value may also be defined as the multiple of price and quantity (as in the total value of output, or value added).

wealth
the assets held by individuals, businesses, or by whole societies. Wealth may take the form of money, financial assets such as shares, or other tangible assets, such as houses, cars, boats, or capital goods.

working class
those who derive their income principally from the sale of their labour power, whether it involves manual or mental labour.

PART I

Current Economic Processes and Problems

1 What is Political Economy?

What problems does political economy address?

What questions does it ask?

On what analytic foundations does it build?

Modern political economy provides an accessible approach to the study of economic issues. It seeks to 'illuminate the world in which we live so that we may act in it intelligently and effectively'.[1] This introductory chapter explains how this ambition can be achieved. It suggests three ways of defining political economy:

- in terms of the real-world problems on which it focuses

- in terms of how these problems are analysed

- in terms of the currents of economic thought from which it draws.

It also indicates how political economy can generate more interest than is usual in the study of economics.

Relevance to real economic problems

Economic concerns beset us individually in our everyday lives—earning a living, managing our incomes, and making decisions about spending and saving. They also beset us collectively, generating political choices about how to balance economic growth against environmental concerns, how to redistribute income through taxes and government spending, and how to deal with national and global imbalances in international trade and economic development.

How these issues have been addressed in economic analysis and policy has been strongly influenced by one particular economic theory, neoclassical economics, which emerged in the late nineteenth century and is still the dominant economic orthodoxy today. This theory stresses the beneficial effects of competitive markets as a means of allocating economic resources. From the neoclassical viewpoint, the role of government is, at most, that of an adjunct to the free-market economy. The underlying view is that the capitalist economy is a stable, self-equilibrating system.

A frequently recurring charge against this economic orthodoxy is that the theoretical model of market exchange under competitive conditions fails to illuminate the world in which we actually live.[2] However, the theory has had a strong influence on economic policies in practice, and therefore does have an awesome relevance, for better or worse. This has been particularly evident in the last four decades. Orthodox economic reasoning has given rise to particular policy prescriptions, such as the liberalisation of trade, the deregulation of financial markets, and the privatisation of public enterprises. It is as if the real world is being reconstructed in the image of a particular economic theory. Major political economic problems have resulted, most obviously the dramatic worldwide economic crash that began in 2007–08. The resulting global economic crisis has made necessary a fundamental reconsideration of orthodox economic theory and policies.[3]

Modern political economy provides an alternative that seeks to deal directly with the current political economic problems and policy issues. In addition to the lessons from the global financial crisis, there are many other contemporary concerns: the challenge posed by the power of multinational corporations, the tension between economic growth and ecological sustainability, the economic insecurity and inequality intensified by contemporary structural economic changes, the proliferation of speculative financial activities and their adverse consequences for economic stability and productivity, and the continuing problems of promoting balanced economic and social development, especially in poorer nations.

The immediate appeal of the political economic approach is its direct engagement with these big issues. A link is thereby established between studies in economics and what is reported in the daily newspapers and on radio and television current affairs programs. Simultaneously, links are created with other areas of study, such as geography, history, social studies, political science, and industrial relations. Indeed, this interdisciplinary character of political economy is one of its strengths. Real-world phenomena do not fit neatly into boxes labelled 'economic', 'social', 'political', or 'cultural'. Those categories have been constructed for academic convenience, and the disciplinary divisions—between economics, sociology, and political science, for example—can impede a full understanding. Political economic analysis is enriched by drawing from these other disciplines, leading towards a more holistic approach to social science.[4]

The political economic questions

Major explorations require an orderly procedure. In the case of political economy, this means interrogating each issue systematically by posing basic political economic questions such as:

- What is happening?
- Why?
- Who gains and who loses?
- Does it matter?
- If so, what can be done and by whom?

First, to assess 'What is happening?' requires a stocktaking of the facts of the matter. This sounds simple, but is seldom straightforward, because judgment is usually necessary in deciding which aspects are most important and which are relatively inconsequential. The 'Why?' question shifts attention to the analysis of causal factors: the forces, people, or institutions driving the political economic processes in question. Taking stock of winners and losers requires careful study of how the various participants in the economic drama are affected. The question 'Does it matter?' introduces more explicitly evaluative considerations. This provides the link between the analysis of problems and the discussion of responses, leading into the final question about remedial policies and strategies. We are not simply passive observers of political economic change: as active participants, our effectiveness depends on how we address the strategic question of what can be done. Box 1.1 illustrates these five steps applied to the analysis of 'globalisation'.

BOX 1.1   GLOBALISATION

It is commonly asserted that our lives are now being radically changed by the integration of economic activities on a global scale. Globalisation is said to be breaking down the territorial boundaries that used to limit the opportunities (and threats) that we experienced. According to this view, technological and economic changes are transforming society and culture. We fail to adjust at our peril, individually and collectively.

Is this really so? Asking the five key political economic questions listed on p. 3 can reveal a more sophisticated story.

First, to answer 'What is happening?' requires important distinctions to be made between the globalisation of finance and trade, of culture, of environmental concerns, and of human rights. Focusing on the globalisation of business activities, for example, requires careful study of the changing patterns of international trade in goods and services, international investment, and/or international finance (including the proliferation of speculative activities worldwide).

Answering the question 'Why?' requires analysis of the drivers of change, including the complex interactions between the forces external to nation states and the forces nurtured within them. The influences of consumerism, technology, and government policies towards multinational corporations, for example, come into the spotlight.

The question 'Who gains and who loses?' is equally complex. The changing international distribution of jobs and incomes needs to be considered. Large multinational companies, seeking to take advantage of differential labour costs, have often relocated parts of their manufacturing activities to developing nations. As a result, significant numbers of workers in those countries have gained industrial employment previously unavailable to them; however, although usually better paying than the traditional occupations, these jobs are frequently associated with particular health and environmental risks. Whether the industrialisation, often localised in enclaves called 'export-processing zones', has trickle-down benefits for the rest of the society is also uncertain: it depends on how and where the extra income is spent and on whether the companies pay significant amounts of money in local taxes. Meanwhile, the employees in more affluent nations face pressures for wage reduction in order to try to keep the local manufacturing businesses competitive, or face unemployment if the firms go under.

Does globalisation matter? Certainly, the political economic changes have major social and environmental implications. The advantages for consumers of being able to shop in the global marketplace need to be balanced against the greater economic insecurity that many workers face. The socially destabilising effects of changing patterns of economic inequality demand attention. And the environmental impacts of worldwide sourcing of raw materials, increasingly extensive transport, and use of non-renewable energy sources are further sources of tension.

So, what is to be done? Is the capacity for national economic management undermined by the greater mobility of capital? To what extent, and in which policy fields, are governments able to shape the terms on which nation states engage with the global economy? If governments are losing their managerial capacity, to which other institutions—local, non-governmental, or supranational—can we instead look to control the processes of change? Can labour, environmental, or consumer movements, for example, go global in order to counteract the globalisation of business and finance? These are the kinds of big, strategic questions that globalising processes generate for modern political economists.

Contributory conceptual currents

Describing political economy as a means of understanding a changing world is a down-to-earth beginning to our explorations ... The contest of economic ideas then enters the story, when we recognise that for any economic issue there are competing explanations. Among the different schools of economic thought that have developed during the last two and a half centuries, the following have most obvious relevance in the construction of modern political economy.

Classical political economy

Scholars such as Adam Smith and David Ricardo wrote about economic affairs when capitalism was emerging from feudalism to become the dominant economic system in Western Europe. Although the economy then looked very different from today's—with less sophisticated production and transport technologies, and smaller businesses that usually served only local markets—Smith's and Ricardo's insights into economic interests and political processes are of enduring relevance. The notion of an economic system producing goods and services surplus to what is required for social reproduction remains valuable. Understanding how that surplus may be expanded—whether through trade and an increasingly complex division of labour, for example—is central to the analysis of economic growth. Understanding how the surplus is generated also leads to an explanation of how incomes are distributed—among capitalists, workers, and landowners, for example. Classical political economy is generally held to have conservative political implications, but the underlying conceptions of economic production, distribution, and economic growth can be given a progressive, modern twist. The emphasis on the troublesome issue of land and land ownership, ignored by much economic theorising over the last century, is particularly important.

Marxist economics

Marxist economics also warrants careful consideration. Its roots are in the tradition of classical political economy, but it provides a quite different, more critical, interpretation of capitalism. It emphasises the basis of the capitalist economy, in particular property relations, class structures, and the relentless drive for amassing wealth. Marxist analysis asserts that the source of the economic surplus is the exploitation of labour. The resulting class conflict creates the potential for radical political economic change. Marxist economic analysis can help to understand dramatic shocks to the economic system, such as financial crises, and the persistence of poverty in affluent societies. However, like all economic theories, Marxist analysis needs to be critically reevaluated to test its applicability to the modern economy. Generally, though, the holistic character of Marxian political economy and its emphasis on the conflicts and contradictions driving economic change have evident resonance in the current context. Globalisation, for example, can be interpreted from this perspective as the drive by capitalist business interests to break through the constraints on their growth formerly imposed by national boundaries.[5]

Institutional economics

Institutional economics is another tradition that contributes significantly to modern political economy. It emerged from the German historical school of the nineteenth century and flourished in the twentieth century, partly as a reaction to the abstract character of much orthodox economic theory. Its leading exponents, from Thorstein Veblen to J. K. Galbraith, have persistently emphasised the need to come to terms with the changes in institutional form associated with the ongoing development of capitalist economies. The focus is on economic evolution. Distinctive themes are the growth of big business, transnational corporations, the varied governmental economic activities that occur in different nations, and the influence of trade unions. Although coming from politically diverse positions, the institutional economists have provided powerful ideas for shaping economic reform. A particular focus is the potential for more extensive interventions by the state to reduce the inequality and instability of free-market capitalism.

Keynesian economics

Keynesian economic analysis also has continuing importance. John Maynard Keynes was probably the most significant economist of the twentieth century. He explained why capitalism cannot guarantee full employment, and identified the necessary remedial policies at a time when more conventional economic prescriptions had failed. He showed that the economy did not function simply as the aggregation of economic markets and that, without enlightened government intervention, unemployment would recur. So, too, could the problem of inflation. Orthodox economists responded to the ideas of Keynes by producing a 'neoclassical synthesis',[6] combining a microeconomics emphasising market freedoms with a macroeconomics emphasising the necessity of government intervention. This lacked coherence, both analytically and politically. The assault by monetarists and other new classicists on Keynesian economic interventionism during the last quarter of a century produced a more consistent capitalist free-market ideology. But it spurned the practical insights that Keynes made. As post-Keynesians remind us, there is much in the original work of Keynes about the inherent instability of a monetary economy and about policies conducive to long-run expansion of productive capacity that is worth rescuing.[7] Moreover, the global financial crisis showed how important Keynesian policies are in coping with the instability of modern capitalism.

Neoclassical economics

The role of neoclassical economic theory is more problematic. As already noted, it has been the dominant economic orthodoxy. As such, it needs to be carefully understood. But much of the impetus for modern political economy comes from the quest for an alternative. One approach is to consider neoclassical economics pragmatically, as a possible source of contributions to the modern political economist's tool kit. Some elements within neoclassical economics can be salvaged for this purpose. Later chapters in this book will look at, for example, the analysis of 'externalities' and the measurement of demand and supply elasticities as illustrations of this pragmatic approach. However, the problem is that neoclassical theory also embodies a distinctive ideology—presenting a particular image of a free market capitalist economy serving societal preferences. It is this ideological character of neoclassical theory that makes it difficult to 'mix and match' with other currents of economic analysis that present a more critical view of capitalism. These orthodox economic ideas are better understood when treated comparatively with classical, Marxist, institutional, and Keynesian views. This is the essence of the liberal educational principle applied to the study of economic issues.

Modern political economy

Modern political economy is not a return to the economic ideas that prevailed before neoclassical economics became dominant. Focusing on the conditions for the broad progress of the economy and society is certainly more in tune with the classical tradition than with the narrower, neoclassical focus on market equilibrium. However, modern political economy also draws on the currents of economic thought that have been developed by subsequent scholars, including Joseph Schumpeter, Joan Robinson, Nicholas Kaldor, Michal Kalecki, Paul Sweezy, and Gunnar Myrdal, as well as Veblen, Galbraith, and Keynes. Institutional, Keynesian, and post-Keynesian ideas thereby exert a strong contemporary influence. A common theme is the desire for a down-to-earth approach that addresses real political economic problems and makes values explicit.

Political economy is the study of the economy from a social science perspective. It also extends the subject to embrace environmental concerns. Indeed, probably the greatest challenge for us in the twenty-first century is to reconcile the economic with the ecological. There are some relevant concepts that can be drawn from existing economic analyses for this purpose. Neoclassical economists, for example, commonly concede that recurrent market failures occur when 'environmental goods' such as clear air and water are not properly priced. This leads them to advocate policies of extending private property rights to those environmental goods so that their use can be better controlled through markets. Other social scientists argue instead for a fundamentally different 'ecological economics'.[8] That means seeking not only to build on, but also to transcend, the legacy of existing currents of economic analysis. A similar stance is appropriate in relation to other contemporary challenges, such as the concerns with gender inequalities, work–life balance, and the political economy of human rights. Creative application of existing currents of thought within political economy has to be blended with continued reformulation of the discipline.

Studying political economy is not easy; indeed, the emphasis on competing currents of economic thought and their association with rival political philosophies adds complexity to the subject. But this engagement with controversial issues creates more intellectual excitement than the narrow, seemingly technical, treatment of orthodox economic analysis. The link between political economy and current affairs, as discussed in newspapers, and on radio and television, is also more explicit. There are theories to be studied, of course, but their relative plausibility can be discussed with reference to real-world observations. For all these reasons, the approach of political economy can have substantial appeal for students who are interested in how they fit into the world around them, and how they might contribute to changing it for the better.[9]

Conclusion

There is considerable continuity in the economic activities in which people engage—using natural, human, and manufactured resources to produce goods and services, and distributing the fruits of those endeavours according to the relative economic power of the participants. There is also considerable change, particularly in the present period of rapid technological innovation, global integration, structural economic adjustment, and ecological stresses. In political economic analysis, a similar dualism exists: continuity comes from building on the existing stock of economic knowledge, but change comes through adapting and extending it to deal with the evolving political economic problems and new challenges. The need for creative political economic thinking is evident and urgent.

KEY POINTS

- Political economy addresses real-world concerns in a way that emphasises the connections between economic problems, social structures, and political processes.

- There is a rich heritage of economic thought from which modern political economy draws, including classical political economy, Marxist economics, institutional economics, and Keynesian economics.

- Neoclassical economic analysis also needs to be carefully considered because of its major influence on orthodox economic theory and government policies. The challenge for political economy is to go beyond critique to the formulation of effective alternatives.

2 The Personal is Political Economic

> *Who makes economic decisions?*
>
> *What is the current political economic context in which those decisions are made?*
>
> *What are the principal political economic challenges we face?*

Many people come to the study of economics expecting that it will offer guidelines for getting rich. They are usually disappointed to find that it is about how the economic system works, rather than how the system can be worked for personal advantage. The former may help the latter, of course, because people are likely to make more astute financial decisions if they know about the economic, social, and political forces shaping the business and financial environment. Concurrently, it is also to be hoped that understanding how the economy works will stimulate more concern with strategies to achieve better social outcomes.

Generally, the study of economics should serve the needs of intelligent citizens who wish to make sense of the world around them. This is particularly important in the current era of economic uncertainty, when individuals have to cope with major changes to their material circumstances, often with little understanding of what is driving those changes and the potential to change direction.

The economic context: risk and uncertainty

We live in exciting if unsettling times. Dramatic changes in technology are transforming the way goods and services are produced and, particularly, the way information is transmitted. The barriers once imposed by the tyranny of distance and national boundaries, though still significant, are being eroded. This process has cultural and political, as well as economic, dimensions, but its most notable feature is the growing economic power of transnational corporations. Some of these companies have budgets larger than national economies. Understandably, many individuals feel dwarfed and powerless in these circumstances. The capacity of the democratic institutions within nation states to exercise control over the enormously powerful private corporations is under challenge; in many cases, governments do not even seem to have the will to exercise such control.

Meanwhile, the nature of work is also rapidly changing. A significant proportion of the potential workforce is excluded from making a direct, productive contribution, even when economic growth is taking place. Solving this problem of persistent unemployment is one of the continuing political economic challenges. For those who are in work, the emphasis is now increasingly on casual, part-time, or contract employment. In the advanced industrial nations the number of manufacturing jobs relative to service-sector jobs continues to shrink. More women are in the waged workforce, but the overall allocation of household tasks according to gender has not changed correspondingly. The proportion of older people in the population continues to grow, albeit slowly, posing the challenge of developing appropriate mechanisms for intergenerational income transfers. The capacity of governments to manage these and other processes of income redistribution is impaired by their reluctance to raise taxation to generate the necessary revenue.

Increased income inequalities, within and between nations, are a predictable feature of these circumstances. They repeatedly undermine the conditions for effective cooperation in seeking solutions. The presence of glaring economic inequalities within a nation is not conducive to the cooperative behaviour necessary for the simultaneous achievement of higher productivity and social cohesion. Similar problems exist on an international scale. Imbalances of trade and debt between rich and poor countries accentuate the long-established problem of economic inequality. Some of the poorer nations, most notably China and India, have achieved impressive economic growth rates in the past two decades, but others, especially in sub-Saharan Africa, have been slipping even further behind.

Meanwhile, in the wealthier nations the economic exuberance of the early 2000s has been replaced with a more troubled economic outlook. The capitalist system has always been prone to a cyclical pattern of boom and bust, but the global financial crisis that began in 2007–08 was a particularly harsh reminder of this systemic flaw. Even more worrying for the long term, because of the constraints imposed by the physical environment, is the increasingly unsustainable character of economic growth on a global scale. How to harmonise economy, society, and ecology most effectively is a question to which there is, as yet, no agreed answer.

It is not surprising that many individuals feel overwhelmed by these developments and problems. Therein lies the twin challenge for political economy: to analyse the underlying forces and to posit some effective solutions.

ECONOMIC DECISIONS

Our day-to-day lives involve many economic decisions. Most of these are fairly small scale and short term and of no apparent significance to anyone beyond our immediate family and friends. In the aggregate, they shape the economic environment in which we live. Some such decisions, illustrating our various social and economic roles, are described below.

- As students, we are investing in our economic future as well as—hopefully—pursuing personal development. How much education we undertake and how many qualifications we acquire are likely to have a bearing on our future economic opportunities.
- As consumers, we make daily decisions about which of the sometimes baffling array of products we will buy with our income. We also make decisions, if only by default, about how much we are prepared to forgo the immediate gratification of consumption in order to accumulate personal savings.
- As workers, we are faced with constrained choices about the jobs we seek and the hours we work. We also have to make periodic decisions, individually or collectively, about the strategic stances to take in negotiations with our employers about wages and conditions of work.
- Meanwhile, business decision-makers make their own strategic decisions about employment and wages payments. They also periodically review the methods they use for producing goods and services, how much they will invest in new production facilities, the prices they will charge for their products, and their sales promotion practices.
- Speculators continually review their portfolio of assets, deciding what to buy and sell according to their judgments about future price movements and the possibility of capital gains. When media commentators refer to how 'the markets' respond to economic news or government policy initiatives, it is the behaviour of these speculators to which they are referring.
- Banks decide about making loans to their clients, usually according to set guidelines. They also make decisions about the interest rates offered to depositors and charged to borrowers. The margins between these borrowing and lending rates are a principal source of banks' profits, and so they are kept under continual review.
- Government ministers, especially those in key departments such as Treasury and Finance, also make frequent adjustments to economic policies. They do so in response to changing economic conditions in national and global markets, and to political pressures (including the speculative sentiments of the markets). These public policy positions are also significantly influenced by prevailing economic theories.

Micro decisions: macro outcomes

There is a link between micro personal choices and macro societal choices. Individuals' economic decisions affect and are affected by broader political economic forces. Indeed, it is reasonable, as a first approximation, to see what is happening in the economy as the outcome of the sum of individual decisions. So, whether the economy is functioning well or not—whether the overall economic conditions are buoyant or stagnant, for example—is the result of whether the numerous interdependent decisions mesh effectively. There is, of course, much scope for inconsistency, conflicts of interest, and contradictory elements.

As political economists, we can step back from the individual choices and short-term decisions to see the bigger picture. This can help us understand the political economic structures that shape and constrain our options. It can also help to reveal the forces that change the context within which individual economic decisions are made.

Three trilogies

A simple device for considering some basic political economic principles is shown in Figure 2.1 (overleaf).[1]

The first diagram depicts the relationship between market, state, and community. It shows the three different ways in which economic activity can be organised: market, state, and community. Goods and services may be produced for exchange in the *market*. Many are. Alternatively, the production and distribution of goods and services may be organised by a central coordinating agency such as the *state*. The state may be responsive to the wishes of the society through democratic processes, or it may be authoritarian in character. The third possibility is that the production and distribution of goods and services results directly from *community* provision. People produce goods and services for themselves and their neighbours, and benefit from reciprocal relationships.[2] The community may be quite small—perhaps just a household—or it may comprise a larger group of people whose voluntary cooperation results in purposeful economic activity without the need for markets or a state.

These three different ways of providing for our material needs and wants normally coexist in any society, but their relative importance varies, and there are recurrent tensions between them. The same diagram illustrates the boundary tensions in terms of the balance between public and private sectors of the economy, the choice between voluntary and government welfare provision, and the extent to which social life is structured by market processes.

The second diagram in Figure 2.1 shows the spatial scales at which economic activities can be organised and coordinated: local, national and global. Local production can be for *local* consumption. Much is. *National* coordination of productive activity is also commonly attempted. The markets for some products are nationwide, and governments usually try, more or less successfully, to manage national economies. The *global* dimension is becoming increasingly important, however, as global markets, and even some embryonic forms of a global state, have developed. The articulation of these three spatial scales and the balance between them are key issues. As suggested in the second diagram in Figure 2.1, tensions may occur in relation to national sovereignty, the development of global cities, and regional development. Here is a gentle reminder of the importance of the spatial dimension in political economy. All economic activity—indeed, all of life—takes place in both time and

FIGURE 2.1 THREE TRILOGIES: INSTITUTIONS, SPATIAL SCALES, AND SYSTEMS space, so we need analytical structures that pay due attention to these coordinates of our behaviour.

The third trilogy shown in Figure 2.1 depicts the relationship between economy, society, and ecology. Economic activities always depend on certain social and ecological preconditions—the availability of labour and natural resources, for example—and they have major social and environmental consequences. Political economy necessarily focuses on these connections. It looks at how the balance between economic, social, and ecological concerns is affected by the relationships between market, state, and community, and between local, national, and global scales of economic organisation. In practice, balance is seldom achieved, and the resulting contradictions are manifest in ongoing concerns about distributional equity, ecological sustainability, and the quality of life.

These three trilogies shown in Figure 2.1 draw attention to social choices. Do we want our economic arrangements to be mainly market orientated, increasingly global in character, and prioritising the pursuit of economic growth? Would it be better to have a greater role for the state, and more emphasis on planned national economic development and the pursuit of social and/or environmental goals? Or would we prefer more focus on the role of the community and localised forms of political economic organisation? What combination of these arrangements would be best? How can we seek to achieve that outcome? These are fundamental questions facing us all as citizens. They are issues that political economy seeks to illuminate.

Conclusion

As individuals, we all participate in the political economic drama. The personal is political economic. However, our roles in the drama are not predetermined. As actors, we can improvise, even tear up the script. It helps to know what is going on and what our options are, individually and collectively. We need an understanding of the political economic processes and possibilities. We have to identify what can be done to produce political economic futures consistent with our individual and collective needs and aspirations.

We need, therefore, to understand the capabilities and limitations of markets as means of organising and integrating economic activities. We need to explore appropriate economic roles for community and government that are desirable and feasible in an increasingly global political economic context. We need to devise the most effective means for securing economic progress, and balancing concerns about economic efficiency with social justice and ecological sustainability. And we need to evaluate alternative strategies for the pursuit of greater economic security, stability, and equity.

To address these concerns we must look beyond the short-term, day-to-day economic decisions we make as consumers, workers, investors, or business managers. We need to deepen our understanding of the political economic forces shaping our lives.

KEY POINTS

- Political economy emphasises the context within which an array of individual decisions are made: decisions about the production of goods and services, work and wages, consumption choices, savings and investment, and economic and financial management.

- Economic activities can be organised in different ways, involving various combinations of market, state, and community decision-making. They can be organised at various scales: local, national, or global. The nature of these arrangements has a major bearing on the social and ecological impacts of economic activities.

- The current political economic context features substantial uncertainty and risks.

3 Structural Economic Changes

What major political economic changes have taken place in the past two decades?

To what extent do they have common purposes?

Do they have contradictory characteristics?

In the complex array of political economic changes taking place in the world around us, it is sometimes difficult to see patterns. This has been especially true in the last couple of decades, when the changes have been particularly rapid and diverse. This chapter considers six interlocking dimensions of these structural economic changes:

- the application of new technologies
- the reorganisation of businesses through mergers and takeovers
- the globalisation of production
- the reorganisation of employment conditions
- changes in the economic role of governments
- changes in prevailing economic ideologies.

The application of new technologies

It is usually in the interest of businesses to implement new technologies that cut the costs of production. This often involves labour displacement; that is, producing more outputs of goods and services with fewer workers. Such has been the case throughout the history of industrial society when particular sectors of economic production have been transformed through technological innovation. The microelectronic revolution that began in the 1970s heralded a particularly dramatic wave of change in technologies of production and information dissemination, and computers have since permeated all aspects of design and manufacturing. Today, communications technology continues to reshape economic processes, as commercial transactions, previously reliant on physical, 'bricks and mortar' locations like retail stores, are increasingly conducted over the internet or other computer networks.

What are the implications for employment? Job losses frequently follow technological changes, but structural unemployment has not previously been a major long-term problem. Of course, workers have frequently lost their jobs as a result of technological change. Workers employed in making wagons and carts, for instance, lost their jobs when the technology for making motor cars arrived. However, new technologies have opened up many more markets and avenues for economic growth. Jobs for car workers exceeded the number of jobs displaced in the manufacture of horse-drawn vehicles. For the most part, structural unemployment has, therefore, been only a problem of transition between the old and new structures.

What is different now is that the new technologies are affecting sectors that have absorbed the labour displaced by technological change in the past. We can visualise the process of technological change as a series of overlapping waves. The first wave affected farming. Workers displaced by the mechanisation of agriculture moved to the cities, where they found jobs in manufacturing industries. Then, technological change in manufacturing displaced these workers. This second wave saw the major job growth occurring in the growing services sector. One wit coined the term 'McDonald's law' to describe this situation, positing that, for every job lost in steel mills and car plants, a new job opened up in fast food provision. But the technological changes associated with computerisation and information technologies are now having an impact on the service industries, too. The interesting question arises: Where is there left to go? Some argue that technology will continue to be job-creating as the information economy sector expands. Others express growing concern about the possibility of jobless growth; that is, growth in the output of goods and services unmatched by growth in employment.[1]

So, while the application of new technologies has a strong logic from the business perspective, there is a potentially significant social fallout. A similar dualism is evident in the other dimensions of contemporary structural economic change.

Mergers and acquisitions

The reorganisation of businesses through mergers and acquisitions has been a notable feature of the past two decades. Like the introduction of new technology, there is nothing particularly novel about this. The voluntary combination of firms into larger units (merger) or the takeover of one firm by another (acquisition) is commonly driven by the pursuit of higher profitability. If the larger business unit can achieve economies of scale in the production and/or distribution of its products, it may be able to reduce costs. Indeed, political economists have noted that this type of business reorganisation is a predictable response to a period of economic difficulties. Inefficient production units are weeded out in order to enhance the overall efficiency with which capital is used. Such processes of corporate rationalisation commonly follow successful mergers or acquisitions. The social costs of dislocation are painful for those who lose their jobs or their businesses, but, on this reasoning, the process may be functional for the economic system as a whole.

The tension between private interests and social costs is yet more striking when mergers or acquisitions are undertaken primarily to secure market dominance. This would normally be conducive to higher business revenues or wider profit margins, but there is a strong likelihood that consumers' interests will be violated if the outcome is greater corporate monopoly power. How that power is used or abused becomes a key matter of political concern. The traditional assertion that 'What is good for General Motors is good for the USA' has a decidedly hollow ring in these circumstances. Business interests are not synonymous with social interests.

Not surprisingly, herein lies one of the most frequently recurring economic policy debates: whether to regulate the processes leading to the growth of big business or whether to permit freedom of the marketplace. Traditionally, economists have usually seen competition as preferable to monopoly and have argued the case for public policies to defend and promote it. However, another view favours the use of public policy to foster the growth of large businesses as 'national champions' in a world of competitive, international trade. This latter view reflects growing concerns about how to prosper in the global economy.

The globalisation of production

Globalisation opens up wider economic opportunities but poses particular threats. As noted in Chapter 1, this is one of the key issues of the present time. Globalisation breaks down the impediments to economic interaction that arise from distance and from regulations imposed by nation states (impeding the movement of goods, labour, or capital across national boundaries, for example). With the economic integration of nations comes greater social and cultural integration, too.[2]

Focusing simply on the globalisation of production, it is not difficult to discern the basic logic behind international business. If corporations can shop around the globe for the cheapest raw materials and cheapest labour, they can minimise their costs of producing goods and services. If they can find, or create, new markets for their products in distant lands, that will also increase their revenue. If they can locate their activities in the nations with the lowest tax rates—or at least make it appear that their profits are generated there—that helps them maximise their after-tax profits. Similarly, they may shop around for the countries that apply the least restrictive environmental regulations to their activities. Through all these means, globalisation serves business interests. The outcome is the dramatic geographical reorganisation of the activities of transnational corporations that has proceeded apace in recent decades.

However, the politics of globalisation is contestable. The very changes that have served business interests have generated significant economic and social problems. There is commonly said to be a 'race to the bottom' in wage rates, tax rates, and environmental standards as nations compete to attract transnational corporations. Living standards for workers are threatened. The capacity of governments to finance infrastructure and social services is impaired. Our collective ability to achieve more ecologically sustainable development is a further casualty of the process. How to balance the potentially progressive aspects of globalisation against these real dangers is one of the key issues of the present time.

BOX 3.1   CONTESTING GLOBALISATION

The twenty-first century began with widely publicised anti-globalisation protests. Thousands of demonstrators took to the streets in cities around the world where meetings were being held by the World Trade Organization, the World Economic Forum, and the G8 (comprising the political leaders of the eight most powerful nations). It has since become common for anti-globalisation protestors to congregate whenever and wherever these bodies meet. The concerns of the demonstrators include the concentration of power in the hands of transnational corporations, the trend towards greater economic inequality, the excesses of consumerism, problems of environmental damage, and the undermining of working conditions, human rights, and the rights of Indigenous peoples.

Struggle in the streets is only the visible face of a broad and persistent social movement of people opposed to globalisation. It can be interpreted as a global movement with diverse local and national focal points. Targeting the antisocial behaviour of particular corporations is one strategy; for example, the 'Sweating for Nike' campaign, which exposed the exploitation of low-wage footwear manufacturing workers in developing nations. Challenging the processes by which international agreements are made is a second theme; for example, pressing for the insertion of labour and human rights clauses in trade agreements or opposing proposed agreements, such as the Trans Pacific Partnership Agreement, that would extend the power of international businesses relative to national governments.[3] Building a progressive transnational consciousness is a yet more ambitious aim, seeking to link Indigenous peoples, environmental groups, and other activists in different nations so that they can learn from one another about feasible alternatives to the current form of global capitalism.

In some respects, the anti-globalisation label is inappropriate for this movement. What it stands in opposition to is the globalisation of capital. It seeks to combat corporate globalisation with a more progressive grass-roots globalisation, taking advantage of modern technologies, such as email and the internet, to exchange information among activist groups. It has had significant successes in challenging the removal of national controls over trade and pushing for debt relief for the poorest nations. Annual meetings of the World Social Forum are now held to share information, build networks, and coordinate the activities of the numerous non-governmental organisations (NGOs) involved in challenging the globalisation of capital.

The struggles continue …

The reorganisation of employment conditions

The way in which work is organised within individual workplaces has also been subject to dramatic changes in the past couple of decades. In part, this is a consequence of changes in production and information technologies that require different types of labour, with different skills. In part, it is a consequence of the reassertion of managerial prerogatives, reflecting an ongoing power struggle between employers and employees as classes with competing interests. In part, it is also the product of the drive for more flexibility in the workplace as a means of achieving higher rates of profit.

These pressures are manifest in the greater emphasis on casual, part-time, and contract labour, which give firms more flexibility in varying the number of workers they employ, responding to fluctuations in the level of economic activity. Such arrangements also open up opportunities for increasing the intensity of labour: speeding up or increasing the work employees have to do. A more attractive prospect is working smarter rather than simply harder, but the realisation of that potential for higher productivity depends on workers' commitment to employers, which may be undermined by the erosion of job security. Indeed, greater economic insecurity is the most obvious social fallout of these changes in employment conditions, which place the costs of adjustment squarely on the shoulders of the workforce.

Some contend that these changes in the organisation of work have transformed a Fordist economic system to a post-Fordist one. Fordism, named after Henry Ford (who pioneered the mass production of motor vehicles), required large numbers of workers to engage in routinised tasks to produce standardised products for mass markets. According to the proponents of post-Fordism, those arrangements are now tending to be replaced by smaller and more flexible workforce teams that have relative autonomy and produce more diverse products for niche markets. Whether such a shift to post-Fordism is indeed taking place, and, if so, whether it is more beneficial for employers or employees is a matter of ongoing debate.[4]

Changes in the economic role of governments

Governments have played an active role in facilitating the four dimensions of structural economic change already described in this chapter. They have set the 'rules of the game' for businesses, prescribing particular forms of conduct and proscribing others. However, the rules have been changing. Increasingly, governments have asserted the need for more emphasis on market processes rather than planning. At least that is the declared aim of neoliberalism (sometimes called economic fundamentalism or economic rationalism).[5] The core belief is that giving freer reign to market forces will produce more efficient economic outcomes. Hence, the push for deregulation, privatisation, and the liberalisation of trade and capital movements in most of the major industrial nations in the past three decades. The declared goal has been to create the conditions for the reinvigoration of free-enterprise capitalism.

Deregulation involves the removal of government regulations on businesses: regulations that control their pricing policies, environmental impacts, or employment practices, for example. Privatisation involves the transfer of businesses from public ownership to private ownership, usually through the sale of shares in these former public enterprises. Trade liberalisation involves the reduction of tariffs on imported goods and other impediments to international commerce. Other related policies (anti-policies, one might say) are the removal of government controls over financial institutions and over the flow of capital into and out of countries, and the lowering of business tax rates as means of increasing the material incentive for economic activity. The common theme has been the restoration of the vitality of the capitalist economy, which neoliberals claim had previously been curtailed by excessive government intervention.

In practice, the outcomes have been much less clear-cut. The onset of the global financial crisis in 2007–08 was traumatic for the neoliberal policy stance. It showed that a relatively unregulated market economy is highly unstable. But the neoliberal rhetoric has not matched the actual role of government anyway. The economic activities of government have not been reduced, only reorientated towards more directly serving the interests of business; they have become correspondingly less concerned with progressive income redistribution and with the amelioration of social problems arising from the operations of the market economy. Predictably, winners and losers result. The removal of regulations protecting employment conditions creates more unevenness of employment practices and greater wage disparities. The relaxation of environmental controls leads to more environmentally degrading activities. And the withdrawal of redistributive policies leads to growing problems of economic inequality and poverty. Not surprisingly, in these circumstances neoliberalism, economic rationalism, and economic fundamentalism have become pejorative terms for many people.

Changes in economic ideologies

The viability of any institution depends on the widespread acceptance of its legitimacy. So it is with economic systems. They depend on ideologies that embody beliefs about how the economy operates and the social values that it serves. Neoliberalism serves that function for modern capitalism. As a political practice, it is closely linked to, arguably dependent on, the ideology of free-market economics. At its core is the emphasis on individualism, the belief in the primacy of the individual as the basic unit of society. As Margaret Thatcher, Conservative prime minister of the UK between 1979 and 1990, once put it: 'There is no such thing as society; there are only individuals ...'[6] Those individuals are assumed to be self-interested, rational, and acquisitive, and it is through their interaction in a free-market economy that economic progress is assured. So the argument runs. In the extreme, 'greed is good' appears to be the central tenet.

Such economic ideologies have been vigorously disseminated in the last three decades, effectively countering and undermining the beliefs (such as those associated with Keynesian economics) about the need for a more extensive role for government in the pursuit of social goals. Vigorously promoted by business-funded 'think tanks', they have also provided a head-on challenge to socialist and social democratic beliefs about the desirability of developing institutions to satisfy collective needs.[7] However, ideologies face fundamental challenges when real-world conditions become adverse, such as happened with the onset of the global financial crisis. The need for 'interventionist' responses, such as those associated with Keynesian economics, was recognised again. The policies and ideologies of neoliberalism have been plagued by the recurrent problems of internal contradiction. Even the neoclassical economists, from whose theories the general claims about the efficiency of the market economy derive, have substantial reservations. The more punctilious among them stress the gulf between the strict assumptions underpinning their theoretical propositions and the messy conditions prevailing in the real world. However, the test of an ideology is not its sophistication, but its effectiveness in conveying a simple and seemingly persuasive story. According to that test, the neoliberal ideologies associated with free-market economics continue to be a significant force.

Ideological struggles are seldom, if ever, concluded. Rival beliefs stressing social justice, communitarian values, and ecological sustainability vie with the dominant orthodox economic ideologies. Indeed, because the other dimensions of structural economic change reviewed in this chapter have recurrently unsettling consequences, these rival ideologies are continually reinvigorated. To the extent that ideologies based on competitive individualism undermine social cohesion, they create fuel for a collectivist alternative. To the extent that they pave the way for environmental decay, they stimulate the development of more ecologically based viewpoints. Therein lies much of the source of the social dynamic underpinning the ongoing public contest of economic ideas.

Conclusion

Economic organisation is constantly changing, which is why an historical, rather than mechanistic, approach is necessary in studying how the economy works. 'History versus equilibrium' is former Cambridge economics professor Joan Robinson's characterisation of the two types of approach to studying economics, the former being less elegant but more realistic and useful.[8] History in this context does not simply mean the past: it means the continuous unfolding of events in real historical time. As political economists, we need a dynamic approach to analysing the world around us, illuminating the forces provoking and steering the processes of change. A static view of the economy functioning according to eternal laws of motion sits too uncomfortably with the unstable conditions in the real world.

This reasoning also indicates why seeking quick-fix solutions to economic problems is unlikely to be successful. Because economic problems, such as periodic recessions, economic insecurity, or economic inequality, have complex roots, they are not easily solved with simple remedies. Indeed, as some of the reasoning in this chapter has foreshadowed, governments as well as businesses may pursue strategies that are themselves at the root of our individual and collective economic difficulties. Posited solutions can compound the problems. Our principal task as political economists is to try to make sense of this complexity.

KEY POINTS

- Structural economic changes have been a major feature of the current era: globally, nationally, and locally. They result from new technologies that have been developed for producing goods and services, business reorganisation through mergers and takeovers, geographical relocations of economic activities, and changes in employment conditions.

- These structural economic changes are driven by the pursuit of profit by businesses, buttressed by the institutions of government, and legitimised by ideologies such as neoliberalism.

- Contradictions arise in the processes of structural economic change because the profit-seeking drivers of change commonly generate social, political, and environmental conflicts.

4 Political Economic Challenges

Have structural economic changes produced beneficial outcomes?

What political economic problems need to be addressed now?

Are solutions possible?

Do recent structural economic changes, such as those described in the preceding chapter, provide the basis for a coherent new political economic order? In the broad sweep of history, one might surmise that this is their common purpose. The political economic changes have indeed been wide-ranging and dramatic. However, the notion of a new world order implies prosperity, stability and sustainability. This chapter identifies some pervasive political economic difficulties that stand in the way of that seemingly desirable outcome.

Uneven development

Economic development on a global scale continues to be remarkably lopsided. The gulf in economic prosperity between the affluent and the poor nations remains and, in some instances, continues to grow. This is the essence of what is commonly called the 'North–South problem' (although this terminology is problematic, in that there are some poor nations in the northern hemisphere and some rich ones in the southern).[1]

Which are the most affluent nations, and which are the poorest? Table 4.1 on the next page shows a selection of them ranked according to two different economic and social indicators. The first indicator is gross domestic product (GDP) per head. This is the conventional measure of the value of goods and services produced in each year, divided by the number of people in the country. For the countries shown in this table, it is highest for tiny Liechtenstein, then Norway, the United States, and the Netherlands, followed by Switzerland, Australia, and Canada.

TABLE 4.1 ECONOMIC PERFORMANCE AND HUMAN DEVELOPMENT 2010: SELECTED COUNTRIES

HDI rank		Gross national income (GNI) per capita (PPP* US$ 2008) 2010	Human Development Index (HDI) value 2010
Rich countries			
1	Norway	58 810	0.938
2	Australia	38 692	0.937
3	New Zealand	25 438	0.907
4	United States	47 094	0.902
5	Ireland	33 078	0.895
6	Liechtenstein	81 011	0.891
7	Netherlands	40 658	0.890
8	Canada	38 668	0.888
9	Sweden	36 936	0.885
10	Germany	35 308	0.885
11	Japan	34 692	0.884
12	Korea (Republic of)	29 518	0.877
13	Switzerland	39 849	0.874
14	France	34 341	0.872
15	Israel	27 831	0.872
16	Finland	33 872	0.871
17	Iceland	22 917	0.869
18	Belgium	34 873	0.867
Some poorer countries			
73	Brazil	10 607	0.699
89	China	7258	0.663
108	Indonesia	3957	0.600
110	South Africa	9812	0.597
119	India	3337	0.519
125	Pakistan	2678	0.490
137	Papua New Guinea	2227	0.431
168	Congo (Democratic Republic of the)	291	0.239
169	Zimbabwe	176	0.140

* Purchasing power parity (PPP) accounts for price differences across countries, enabling international comparisons of real output and incomes. It takes account of the exchange rate between the currencies and differences in cost of living, so it provides a better indication of real material living standards in different countries than simply GDP per capita.

Source: United Nations, Human Development Report, UNDP, Geneva, 2010.

The second indicator shown in Table 4.1 is a human development index (HDI), which takes account of national standards in health, housing, education, environmental quality, and equity in income distribution. This measure is the basis on which the countries are ordered in Table 4.1. Norway tops the table, with Australia, New Zealand, the United States, and Ireland close behind.

The developing nations are in a different league. Some formerly poor countries have certainly experienced significant industrialisation and economic modernisation over the past couple of decades. South Korea, Singapore, Hong Kong, and Taiwan—the so-called 'four Asian tigers'—achieved particularly rapid growth in per capita incomes in the last two decades of the twentieth century, while others, such as Malaysia and Thailand, also had rapid increases in national prosperity (although, as the regional economic crisis of the late 1990s reminded us, what goes up can come down, too). India and the People's Republic of China, the world's two most populous nations, have also recorded dramatic increases in overall economic performance during the last two decades, although major socioeconomic problems remain. Elsewhere, particularly in Africa south of the Sahara, the achievement of economic development seems as elusive as ever. The bottom of Table 4.1 shows a selection of some of these desperately poor nations. Brazil and the Republic of South Africa sit above the other countries in this group in terms of their GDP per capita because of the presence of affluent elites alongside the majority of poor people.

The persistence of these glaring economic inequalities on a global scale is not conducive to a stable world economic order. The challenge is to establish more effective mechanisms to narrow the gap between rich and poor, developed and underdeveloped. Indeed, to the extent that economic disparities—and the perception that they are the product of imperialism—underpin international conflict, including terrorism, then the systematic reduction of those disparities has to be a priority.

BOX 4.1   THE POLITICAL ECONOMY OF TERRORISM

On Tuesday, 11 September 2001, in the USA, terrorists hijacked four United Airlines passenger planes. Two were flown into the twin towers of the World Trade Center in New York, causing both huge buildings to collapse. Another was crashed into the Pentagon in Washington, headquarters of the US military. Over 3000 people were killed. Stunned by this atrocity, political commentators said at the time that the world would never be the same again.

The economic impact was less dramatic than many expected. The demand for airline travel, and tourism more generally, slumped immediately, causing widespread redundancies. More generally, the confidence of investors and consumers was badly affected, particularly in the USA. But US President George W. Bush urged American consumers to keep shopping, and the Federal Reserve Bank announced a series of interest rate cuts in order to give some stimulus to consumption and investment spending. The tendency to recession was further offset by the surge of spending on security and by military expenditure, as the US government prepared for some sort of counterattack.

Many other terrorist acts, including suicide bombings, which caused widespread loss of life, had occurred before 11 September 2001. Terrorism had become a feature of the Palestine–Israel conflict, the struggle for a unified Ireland, and the movement for Basque separatism in Spain, for example. But the September 11 attacks were directed against the USA, the world's political, economic, and military superpower, and the deaths of innocent people were so numerous. The US President responded in a manner that has, indeed, made the world a different place since that woeful day.

The so-called Bush doctrine was established to justify waging war, not just on suspected terrorists, but also on any state suspected of harbouring them. So Afghanistan was bombed and invaded by the US military, supported by British and Australian troops among others, because it was thought that the terrorist Osama bin Laden, responsible for the September 11 attacks, was sheltering there. This invasion toppled the Taliban government of Afghanistan, a government that the USA had earlier helped to establish. The invasion forces didn't leave, though: more than a decade later they were still there. Osama bin Laden was eventually killed by US soldiers in May 2011—in neighbouring Pakistan.

The Bush Doctrine was also extended to military assaults on other nations where a potential threat was perceived. The US administration invaded Iraq in 2003 as a preemptive strike against the supposed threat of weapons of mass destruction (which were never found) and purported links between the Iraq government and terrorist organisations (which most independent analysts say never existed). President Bush also named Iran and North Korea as countries that sponsor terrorism, arguing that, along with Iraq, they formed an 'axis of evil' that threatened the USA and its international allies.

Critics of the US strategy have deplored the use of military intervention as a first rather than last resort, the reluctance to explore more peaceful means of pursuing social justice, and the unwillingness to work through the established institutions of the United Nations and the international courts. The Bush doctrine opened up the possibility of other countries claiming legitimacy in following similar procedures. Not surprisingly, the policy has not reduced the incidence of terrorism.[2]

Indeed, this century has seen incidents of international terrorism occurring with disturbing frequency. Western interests have been targeted in bombings in Bali, Jakarta, Madrid, Istanbul, and London. The perpetrators have sometimes claimed their actions to be in retaliation for the US-led war on Iraq and the US-led occupation of Afghanistan. Other related political economic concerns include the imperialist character of US foreign policy and the failure of international institutions to address adequately the massive economic inequalities that exist between nations. The US-led 'war on terrorism' has done nothing to address these fundamental concerns.

Bush's successor as US President, Barack Obama, was awarded the Nobel Peace Prize in 2009, because of his commitment to find more effective solutions. Yet there remains the seemingly insuperable difficulty of turning around both the reality and perception of the US administration being at the core of the problem rather than the solution.

Trade imbalances and debt

Uneven development is partly a product of trade imbalances and cumulative debt. Trade deficits are understandably the norm among the poorer nations. Their exports are, typically, primary products—the produce of farming, forestry, fishing, and mineral extraction—while their imports are characteristically manufactured goods. The extreme case is a so-called banana republic—a country that faces enormous difficulties in exporting sufficient produce to pay for the imported goods that it needs.

Nations with trade deficits can finance them by the inflow of foreign investment or the accumulation of debt. Both have the effect of accentuating economic dependency. The latter often has particularly pernicious effects. Debt, of course, can be economically advantageous. A carpenter who borrows money to buy some tools may then be able to earn sufficient income to pay the interest on the debt and eventually repay the principal of the loan. In such a case, debt aids economic development on a personal scale. However, if the income generated is insufficient to repay the interest on the loan, and if the carpenter then has to borrow more in order to meet those interest payments (or, in the extreme, sell the tools in order to do so), then disaster looms. This is the debt trap. It is the sort of situation into which, on a larger scale, many of the poorer nations have slipped. Paying a quarter, or even more, of their earnings from exports to meet their interest payments is not uncommon among these nations. Such debt impedes economic development.

The central role played by the International Monetary Fund (IMF) and the World Bank in these processes has led to growing demands for their reform, even for their abolition. These institutions were set up by the richer nations at the Bretton Woods conference in 1944, ostensibly to facilitate economic security and development. However, their critics note that more has been taken out of the poorer nations in debt repayments than has been put in to promote economic development. Drawing on World Bank data, one book on globalisation notes that most of the increase in the debt of the poorer nations was generated to pay interest on existing loans, rather than to tackle poverty or to finance productive investment, resulting in a transfer of wealth from the poor South to the rich North.[3] Since 2000, there have been significant initiatives to 'forgive' the debt of the most heavily indebted nations; that is, to no longer require that all the debt be repaid. It is increasingly recognised that this is a price the rich countries must pay in order to secure their own interests in expanding markets as well as aiding economic development.

Speculation and financial instability

Different economic challenges face the more affluent nations. One thorny problem is the prevalence of speculation. Speculative activities are those that offer the possibility of substantial individual material gain (or loss), depending on future asset price movements, but do not add to collective wealth and well-being. There are numerous focal points for speculation, ranging from the buying and selling of tangible assets, such as works of art, antique furniture, stamp collections, real estate, and precious metals, to the buying and selling of financial assets, such as national currencies, shares in corporations, futures, and other derivatives. The increases in the volume of speculative transactions in national currencies and financial instruments has been particularly dramatic.

The result is what has been called 'casino capitalism', driven by the quest for 'profits without production'.[4] Casino capitalism has a rationality of sorts. Investment in establishing and expanding industrial enterprises takes time and technical knowhow. Speculation offers the prospect of quicker and more spectacular returns for people with the necessary wealth, the nerve, and, preferably, some inside information on factors likely to affect asset price movements. However, for the economy as a whole, the result can be counterproductive. An economy in which speculation is rife also tends to be more unstable, because speculative markets are renowned for their volatile prices. 'Follow-the-leader' swings in speculative behaviour lead to alternating booms and slumps.

A speculation-orientated economy also tends to be less productive in the longer term. Some financial markets are a useful adjunct to productive economic activity, but the proliferation of speculative activities in those markets tends to have a capital-diverting effect. It certainly has a personal energy-diverting effect. Entrepreneurial activities come to be focused more on paper games of speculative trading than on the real economy in which tangible goods and services are made. This tendency, like the problems of uneven development, trade imbalance, and debt, also bodes ill for generalised prosperity within the capitalist economy in the years ahead unless ways are found to encourage the redirection of funds from speculative to productive purposes.

BOX 4.2   THE GLOBAL FINANCIAL CRISIS

The global financial crisis (GFC) that began in 2007–08 was the biggest shock to the capitalist economy since the Great Depression that originated in 1929. The crash in asset values, particularly share market values, sent shock waves through the global economy. An economic recession developed in many nations, with falling incomes and rising unemployment.

The warning signs of a coming crash became evident during the emergence of the 'sub-prime crisis' in the United States in 2007. The egregious business practices of a range of financial institutions were the immediate cause of the problem. The financial institutions had been making loans to low-income people wishing to buy houses: these were known as 'sub-prime' loans because there was a relatively high probability that the borrowers would default. Indeed, both borrowers and lenders would become losers when the US housing price bubble burst and prices started to fall.

A devastating transmission process ensued. The problem of mortgage defaults spread because the debts had been repackaged as securities called 'collateralised debt obligations'. Other banks, companies, and governments had bought the securities, believing them to be less risky than proved to be the case. The false confidence was partly because inappropriate reassurances were given by the big credit ratings agencies, Moody's and Standard and Poors. Holding mortgage-backed securities came to be recognised as a much more hazardous process than those ratings agencies had indicated.

When the extent of the actual risks was revealed, financial institutions wanted to sell these mortgage-backed securities. As in any market, when there are lots of sellers but few buyers, prices inevitably fall. The stock market values of the institutions themselves also fell, because they were holding securities that were worth less (if not completely worthless). With the collapse of some of these major financial institutions, particularly in the US and the UK, a financial crisis emerged.

So what originated as a sub-prime crisis of largely US origin became generalised as a global financial crash. The long period of economic growth shuddered to an end, as it inevitably had to sooner or later. The growth of the 1990s and early 2000s had been based on debt-fuelled consumerism, speculation, and the quest for unlimited capital gains, rather than sound finance and sustainable economic production.

Not even government bailouts following the onset of the GFC were able to restore the confidence necessary for the failing financial institutions to resume normal trading with each other. The downturn spread from speculative financial markets to the 'real' economy in which goods and services are produced, leading to the onset of a severe and prolonged global recession in many countries.

Not surprisingly, economists have been divided over how to analyse what fundamentally caused the GFC and what policy responses are appropriate. A common theme in political economic analyses has been that neoliberal economic ideas and policies facilitated the creation of such a crisis-prone situation. Certainly the GFC was a major blow to the claims of mainstream economists that 'free markets' would produce continually efficient outcomes. We need to recognise that economic instability is rife, perhaps even endemic, in the capitalist system. The role of the state in crisis management and the creation of more long-term stability becomes a particularly contentious issue in these circumstances.

Unemployment

Meanwhile, millions of people remain unemployed in various parts of the world economy. In 2009, following the GFC, the International Labor Organization estimated global employment at 212 million people.[5] Therein lie massive personal costs—the lack of income, the absence of occupationally defined social position, and the absence of work-related social networks. Major social costs, such as the costs of ill-health and crime, are also associated with the incidence of significant unemployment. There is also a massive opportunity cost: that is, the goods and services that society forgoes because the unemployed or underemployed are not engaged in socially valued productive activities.

The causes and possible remedies for this problem are the focal point of much political debate, as subsequent chapters of this book indicate. Whether a faster rate of job creation is feasible or desirable is one of the key issues. If that implies a faster rate of economic growth, is that ecologically sustainable? The question of the redistribution of work is also contentious. Is it better to find mechanisms to spread the work around more equitably rather than try to increase the total number of full-time jobs? Or is it more important to redefine socially useful employment in order to include activities not currently valued in capitalist labour markets, and to find some mechanisms for redistributing the pattern of rewards accordingly?

Until such issues have been resolved, it cannot be said that a sound basis for our collective economic future has been established. On the contrary, it seems that the persistence of the unemployment problem, and its concentration in particular localities and among particular minority groups, is giving rise to greater social divisions. Some describe this in terms of the growth of an 'underclass' more or less permanently excluded from the economic mainstream of society. It bodes ill for social cohesion.

Economic inequality

Social cohesion within individual countries is also fractured by persistent economic inequalities. Table 4.2 provides some illustrative data on income inequalities in selected nations, based on the latest available United Nations figures. The ratio of the income received by the richest 10 per cent of people to the income of the poorest 10 per cent is a good summary measure. For the USA, this is about 16:1, for Australia it is over 12:1. In the European nations, the ratio is typically less than 10:1, and in the Scandinavian nations it is around 6:1, indicating the egalitarian effects of social democratic policies. At the other extreme, some South American nations, such as Brazil, have ratios of over 40:1. South Africa is about 35:1, partly because of the legacy of racial discrimination from the apartheid era. In some of the other poorer nations (such as Indonesia, Pakistan, and Burundi) there are wealthy elites, but the data indicate that greater equality of poverty generally prevails.

TABLE 4.2 ECONOMIC INEQUALITIES WITHIN NATIONS: SELECTED COUNTRIES

	Share of income or expenditure (%)		
	Poorest 10%	Richest 10%	Richest 10% to poorest 10%
Rich countries			
Norway	3.9	23.4	6.1
Australia	2.0	25.4	12.5
New Zealand	2.2	27.8	12.5
United States	1.9	29.9	15.9
Ireland	2.9	27.2	9.4

Netherlands	2.5	22.9	9.2
Canada	2.6	24.8	9.4
Sweden	3.6	22.2	6.2
Germany	3.2	22.1	6.9
Japan	4.8	21.7	4.5
Korea (Republic of)	2.9	22.5	7.8
Switzerland	2.9	25.9	9.0
France	2.8	25.1	9.1
Israel	2.1	28.8	13.4
Finland	4.0	22.6	5.6
Belgium	3.4	28.1	8.2
Some poorer countries			
Brazil	1.1	43.0	40.6
China	2.4	31.4	13.2
Indonesia	3.0	32.3	10.8
South Africa	1.3	44.9	35.1
India	3.6	31.1	8.6
Pakistan	3.9	26.5	6.7
Papua New Guinea	1.9	40.9	21.5
Burundi	4.1	28.0	6.8
Niger	2.3	35.7	15.3
Congo (Democratic Republic of the)	2.3	34.7	15.1
Zimbabwe	1.8	40.3	22.0

Note: Because data comes from surveys covering different years and use different methodologies, comparisons between countries should be made with caution.

For the rich countries, the data is based on surveys of income distribution; for the poorer nations (except Brazil), the data is based on surveys of consumption. The latter data therefore, tends to be more equally distributed, for poor people generally consume a greater proportion of their income than do rich people.

Source: United Nations, Human Development Report, UNDP, Geneva, 2009.

These economic inequalities seem to be increasing in many nations. Why this should be so is the subject of ongoing controversy. There is some evidence of a shrinking middle in the types of jobs available. The number of highly paid professional and executive positions has increased, and a more than corresponding growth in their remuneration has taken place. Executive salaries of over $2 million a year, sometimes rising to more than five or even twenty times that figure, are now commonplace. At the other extreme, there has been growth in the number of jobs in secondary labour markets: these are usually casual or part time and lowly paid. Between the two extremes, in the advanced industrial nations at least, there are fewer of the traditional, middle-income positions based on skilled employment in manufacturing industries or the public sector. A British commentator described this as the development of a '40:30:30' society: about 40 per cent of the people prosper as a result of technological and structural economic changes, 30 per cent hang on to less secure employment-based incomes, and the other 30 per cent are more or less permanently excluded from participation in regularly remunerated productive activity.[6]

Is this the basis for a sustainable economic order? At best, it seems that it would be one that would depend on the enforcement of social control to maintain order in the face of polarised interests. Therein lie major difficulties. Economic resources have to be diverted to security measures at the expense of other personal and social goals. If the rich take refuge in security-patrolled, gated communities, while the poor are increasingly policed or incarcerated, as is the case in the USA in particular, then order is maintained at a particularly high social cost. Moreover, these trends may ultimately prove counterproductive, even from a narrowly economic perspective, if growing inequality undermines the cooperation that is a necessary precondition for increased productivity.

Environmental stress

Whether economic growth is sustainable raises yet more fundamental issues. There has been growing recognition of the ecological constraints. Some resources, such as oil, are, to all intents and purposes, non-renewable, and there is necessarily concern about their exhaustion.[7] Other potentially renewable resources are being used more rapidly than they are being replaced. Meanwhile, pollutants produced as by-products of economic activities are the source of cumulative, and sometimes irreversible, environmental decay. Climate change—although its intensity is still debated among scientists—may be regarded as the most pervasive manifestation of these problems on a world scale.[8] Locally, in individual cities and regions, environmental problems are also manifest in unhealthy atmospheric pollution, loss of arable land, damage to waterways and marine life, loss of habitat, and the extinction of many species of flora and fauna. These are not features of a sustainable economic system.

As with the other difficulties briefly reviewed in this chapter, there is no shortage of posited solutions. Some are reformist, while some are more radical, even revolutionary, in character. The use of the price mechanism to provide incentives for more ecologically sustainable economic practices is one possibility favoured by neoclassical economists. Other political economists and environmentalists argue that the market economy is the problem rather than the solution because of the rapacious patterns of economic behaviour that it fosters.[9]

Meanwhile, the intensification of environmental stresses interacts with the other problems, such as economic inequality and uneven development. Societies characterised by major economic inequalities are generally less able to control environmentally damaging processes collectively. Their wealthy classes can, to some extent at least, buy their way out by acquiring 'environmental goods' (such as access to relatively unpolluted air and water) that the poor cannot afford. And, internationally, countries with markedly uneven economic development have great difficulty agreeing on the control of further environmental degradation. The poorer nations tend to be resentful of regulatory policies that impede their capacity to achieve the material economic conditions already achieved by the wealthier nations. The higher production and consumption levels of those wealthier nations contribute disproportionately to the problems of global environmental stress.[10]

BOX 4.3 THE ENERGY CRUNCH

All economic systems are underpinned by particular patterns of energy use. The historical development of industrial capitalism was partly propelled by the shift from using water power to the use of coal to produce steam power for railways and other industrial purposes. The use of coal for electricity generation made possible even more widespread economic growth. During the last century these energy sources, along with newer technologies such as nuclear power, have been supplemented by the use of oil. Indeed, it is little exaggeration to say that modern capitalism, in general, runs on oil. Former President George W. Bush famously conceded in his 2006 State of the Union address that the US economy is 'addicted to oil'.

Oil is overwhelmingly the principal energy source for transportation—cars, trucks, trains, planes, and ships—and a major source of energy for industrial production and domestic purposes. But this is not a sustainable state of affairs. Burning oil for energy production is environmentally damaging, albeit a little less so than burning coal. The use of these hydrocarbons as the basis for modern industry and transport is the major cause of global warming, with potentially catastrophic consequences for the future of life on earth. In any case, the oil is running out.

Estimates of how much oil is left vary considerably, but there are strong reasons to believe that we are already approaching the physical production peak—if it has not already passed. Exploration for new oil fields is showing diminishing returns, while annual oil depletion continues to rise exponentially. The huge oil reserves in easy-to-reach fields have already been discovered and much of them already pumped out. Other areas in which untapped reserves may exist, such as the Arctic, pose enormous technological challenges and butt up against concerns about protecting fragile environments.

Meanwhile, the search for alternative energy sources is ongoing. Some technologies using renewable energy sources, such as solar power and wind power, are well established and could be much more widely used, particularly if supported by government policies. Geothermal energy—driving water deep underground into 'hot rocks' and using the resulting steam to drive turbines—also has potential. Hydrogen could be another major component in an energy solution, either in fuel cells or in internal combustion engines converted to burn hydrogen but, to date, the take-up rate of this alternative technology has been very slow. Nuclear power for electricity generation is yet another alternative, but it raises major safety and ecological concerns. Coal reserves are plentiful, but cannot be used for energy production without potentially devastating consequences for global warming and climate change.

Because oil remains so central to energy use, its control is intensely political. The majority of current known reserves are held by the Organisation of Petroleum Exporting Countries (OPEC), a cartel formed to get a better deal for oil-rich countries in the Middle East in particular when selling to Western, especially US, buyers. It was the dramatic price hikes engineered by OPEC in the 1970s that caused the first of the oil shocks, which had an impact on the industrial capitalist economies. Other oil-producing nations, particularly Russia and the other nations of the former Soviet Union, have been providing alternative supplies in recent years, but current estimates indicate that these are dwindling faster than oil from OPEC sources. So the politics of relations between the West, the USA in particular, and OPEC are crucial.

As the oil runs out, will these international relations remain peaceful? Already oil has been an element in international military conflict. Regardless of the officially stated reasons for the US invasion of Iraq in 2003, for example, there can be little doubt that the military assault would have been less likely if Iraq's main export were bananas. More widespread and prolonged energy resource conflicts and wars are an awesome prospect.[11]

Conclusion

Dramatic structural changes have been propelled by businesses and governments intent on creating the conditions for economic expansion and profitability. A political economic perspective can help us to assess whether these conditions provide the foundation for a new era of general prosperity that is stable and sustainable.

Economists are notoriously poor at prediction. However, if we, as political economists, can understand the past and present conditions, we are better able to identify the possibility of repeating the successes and avoiding the problems previously experienced. Of course, some aspects of economic change are historically specific, so the lessons of history may not be readily transferable to other times and places. Understanding the historically contingent character of political economic processes requires sophisticated judgments.

The evidence reviewed in this chapter suggests that optimism about the triumph of capitalism on a global scale must be tempered, to say the least, with a recognition of some deeply entrenched problems. Our task is to understand the problems, to analyse their causes, and to contribute towards their resolution. There are both intellectual and practical aspects to this challenge. This is what the rest of this book is about: understanding the economy and economic analysis so that we can change them for the better.

KEY POINTS

- Major political economic problems impede the achievement of a stable and prosperous world.

- Addressing this challenge requires a deeper understanding of the nature of uneven development, trade and debt, speculation and financial instability, unemployment, economic inequality, and energy and environmental stresses.

- The quest to understand, and to resolve, these problems is made more urgent by the concerns about security: the problems of economic security revealed by the global financial crisis, the problems of resource security such as those arising from the energy crisis, and the problems of personal security that terrorism brings into sharp focus.

PART II

Economic Systems and Economic Theories

5 Economic Systems

What functions must an economy perform?

How is the economy linked to the society?

How can we judge whether the economy is serving the society well?

We now need to establish some principles on which our explorations into political economy can be based. Having reviewed in the preceding four chapters the broad sweep of issues with which contemporary political economists are concerned, it is time for a change of gear. We must consider more carefully the nature of the economic enquiry itself. This means discussing what an economy is and does, what forms economic organisation can take, and how economic activity links with social structure. It also requires some consideration of how we can judge the performance of an economy in meeting social goals. Through looking at these issues we also start to see some of the sources of disagreement and controversy in political economic enquiry.

Economic fundamentals

The economy can be understood most simply as the means whereby goods and services are produced, exchanged, and distributed among the members of a society. Incomes and wealth are generated through these processes of production, exchange, and distribution. These incomes are more or less evenly shared, creating outcomes that can be egalitarian or markedly inegalitarian. The wealth can be more or less wisely used; it can be used for immediate consumption, for reinvestment in increasing the productive capacity of the economy, or for wasteful purposes associated with war or environmental destruction, for example. Over time, the volume and value of the income-generating economic activities may either expand or contract, causing either economic growth or decline.

Looking at the economy in this way draws attention, first and foremost, to the system by which we provide for our needs, individually and collectively. At a minimum, we need food, clothing, and shelter. Providing for those needs is the most basic economic activity; thus, farmers and fishers are more fundamental to economic activity than are financiers. By similar reasoning, making clothes and building houses are also basic economic activities, although many of the products now made—designer wear and suburban 'McMansions'—go far beyond what is necessary to satisfy our basic needs. Indeed, a vast array of products is made in modern economies, manufactured to gratify desires that are psychological rather than physiological. Notwithstanding the difficulty of distinguishing needs from wants in practice, the point remains—that the basic function of the economy is the practical task of 'provisioning'.[1] The processes by which those products are exchanged, and how the resulting incomes and wealth are distributed, may involve complex financial arrangements. That may explain the common perception that economics is 'all about money'. However, as defined here, the more basic and universal feature of all economic systems is the use of tangible resources—natural, human, and manufactured—for making goods and services.

Economics is the discipline that studies these processes. It analyses the production and exchange of goods and services, the distribution of income and wealth, the disposition of that income and wealth, and the material influences on social progress. Economists have always claimed that, by casting light on these matters, they can help us gain more control over the economic factors that shape our existence. The social purpose of studying economics is to contribute to human betterment. By understanding the causes of poverty and recessions, for example, economists can contribute to pushing back at least some of the constraints on our well-being, individually and collectively.

So, wherein lies the distinction between economics and political economy? It rests largely on the claim by contemporary political economists that mainstream economists have, in practice, abandoned this social mission in favour of theories (about 'pure' markets) that reveal little about how the economy actually operates. Political economy is distinguished by its emphasis on the broader view of economic enquiry, its social purpose and its political application. This gives a distinctively interdisciplinary character to political economy, albeit with material economic concerns as the central focus. Political economy also emphasises that the way in which economic issues are analysed cannot be wholly value free. The selection of issues for study, the distinctive assumptions made, and the form of investigation are all pervaded by judgments. The important thing is to make the values explicit, rather than leave them implicit, masked by claims about a scientific status for the discipline. Other features of political economy follow: the emphasis on evolutionary processes rather than on equilibrium; the emphasis on equity and sustainability as well as efficiency; and the emphasis on all the institutions involved in shaping economic outcomes. The focus is on understanding the social character of economic activity.

Economy and society

What shapes the relationship between economy and society? The functioning of the economy does not take place separately from other aspects of life. Political economists have repeatedly stressed the need to study the social embeddedness of the economic system to analyse how it is related to the construction and reproduction of social order.[2] There are at least seven dimensions of this interaction between the economy and society, as follows.

Nature

All economic activity takes place in an environmental context. The availability and quality of natural resources—land, air, and water—is fundamental to life and to all forms of social existence. The particular forms of economic activity associated with modern societies make heavy demands on the natural resource endowment. Land is converted from wilderness to various forms of agricultural, residential, commercial, and industrial uses. Coal, oil, iron ore, bauxite, and a host of other precious mineral products are extracted from beneath the ground and transformed into products for human use. Water is used for irrigation, industrial cooling, and dispersal of wastes. Apart from its use in sustaining life itself, air is used as a receptacle for emissions resulting from economic activities. How these processes of resource use are organised and managed—whether based on a restorative or rapacious relationship to nature—is the most fundamental feature of economy and society.

Markets

How the goods made by applying human resources to nature are produced and distributed also has a major bearing on the economy–society relationship. Production for exchange is a pervasive feature of modern economic activity. Markets are where those exchanges typically occur. Market interactions impose discipline on the participants in the economic system: sellers cannot sell whatever they want for whatever price they like, nor can consumers buy whatever they want for whatever they would like to pay. Exchanges will only occur when they are expected to be mutually advantageous. An effective market mechanism creates the conditions for such outcomes, but it cannot thereby resolve all economic problems. There may, for example, be circumstances in which no goods and services are available because of interruptions to the production process, or because maldistribution of income causes buyers to come to the market with markedly uneven purchasing power. An economy in which markets play a central role depends on certain social underpinnings—an acceptance of commercial contracts as a legitimate and enforceable foundation for personal interactions, for example. In turn, a market economy tends to leave its clear stamp on the prevailing social structures and attitudes, emphasising material acquisition as the key indicator of social worth and social position.

State

Economic processes of production, exchange, and distribution can be organised by the state rather than left to the operation of market forces. The state comprises all the institutions of national and regional administration, including the government, the public service, and the judiciary. Its most direct economic role in production is through public-sector business enterprises—hence the importance of political decisions about the balance between nationalisation and privatisation. Its other regulatory activities and its tax revenue-raising and expenditure functions are also fundamentally important in shaping economic activity in the private sector of the economy. How these aspects of state involvement in the economic system are constructed and blended is an intensely political issue. A society in which economic provision is state centred can be expected to be more collectivist in character than one in which private enterprise dominates. How the state is controlled—whether through democratic or authoritarian processes—then becomes the key issue.

Class

Class relationships are another central feature of the interaction between economy and society. If, for example, some people own the means of production (such as factories, tools, and machines), while others have only their labour to sell, that gives rise to a distinct class divide. It is likely to be associated with sharp differences in income, wealth, and power. These differences may be the source of social conflict, although some degree of cooperation between classes is essential if the economic system is to continue to function. Indeed, it is this uneasy blend of conflict and cooperation that is the hallmark of a class society. It should also be noted that, while class differences are rooted in economic conditions, their social manifestations— differences in social status and social behaviour, for instance—are often very complex.

Gender and ethnicity

Gender and ethnicity commonly interact with class in shaping the economy and society. A sexual division of labour is said to characterise economic arrangements in which men and women characteristically do different jobs. Likewise, people of different ethnic backgrounds are often located in different segments of the labour market. In both cases, this can be the result of discrimination—although it may be deeply rooted in economic and social institutions and not merely the result of personal prejudice by individual employers. Sexism and racism are pervasive ideologies, and sexist and racist practices can be institutionally embedded. They cause inequalities of economic opportunities and economic rewards to be structured according to gender and ethnicity.

Social capital

Some social scientists have argued that the effectiveness of an economy depends significantly on the character of interpersonal relationships within the society. Where there are strong networks of social interaction, fostering social cohesion and trust, there is said to be a high quality of social capital. This tends to be conducive to higher economic productivity than in societies that are more individualised, fragmented, or conflicted. But how to define and measure social capital—indeed, the usefulness of the concept itself—remains controversial.[3] The use of the term 'capital' in this context is particularly contentious, because networks of social relationships are very different from 'capital' as it is more generally used in economics to refer to financial and physical assets used in producing goods and services.

Ideology

Helping the economy and society to maintain stability and continuity are beliefs about the desirability—even 'naturalness'—of all the foregoing arrangements. This is the role of ideologies. These are systems of belief that shape behaviour, individually and collectively. In general, one would expect such ideologies to reflect the existing material economic conditions. The association between consumerist values and an economic system geared to the production of ever more goods and services is an obvious example. However, dominant ideologies are continually challenged by rival, dissident beliefs. Therein lies an important impetus for change in economic and social organisation.

These seven dimensions of the relationship between the economy and society can be regarded as the glue that holds the political economic system together and determines how it works. The relative importance of nature, market, state, class, gender and ethnicity, social capital, and ideology in shaping economic and social order varies enormously, from country to country and over time. How well these different arrangements work is also the focus of endless debate in political economy. The glue can sometimes fail and, when it does, the system comes unstuck.

BOX 5.1

ELINOR OSTROM (1933-)

Elinor Ostrom is perhaps the least well-known person to have won the Nobel Prize for Economic Sciences. When she was given the award in 2009, academic economists around the world were saying 'Elinor who?' So it is ironic that we begin the series of 'thumbnail sketches' of influential economists in this book by paying attention to her work. Is there really any sound basis for setting her in the company of Adam Smith, Karl Marx, J. M. Keynes, and Milton Friedman, for example? Is it just that she was the first female winner of the Economics Nobel, following 62 males? That gender bias in the history of the economics profession is notable—but not immutable, of course. Yet the greater significance, in the context of this chapter in the book, is Ostrom's challenge to the market-state dualism in economic thought.

Much economic discourse is concerned with considering the relative roles of market and state in creating and allocating economic resources. This market-state dualism is particularly evident when economic policies are discussed, advocated, or criticised. Should the use of economic resources be left to individuals in the market place, making personal choices that may serve a self-interest but sometimes violate broader community interests? How much direct responsibility should the state take for the provision of goods and services, allocating them according to social need? A tendency to polarised political positions—libertarian or statist—is commonly evident in such debates, although there are intermediate positions emphasising the need for regulated markets, for example.

Markets and states—and blends thereof—are not the only means through which an economy can be managed, however. As this chapter has already demonstrated, a broader array of social institutions is commonly involved. Indeed, that may be essential for achieving the goals of efficiency, equity, sustainability, and compatibility with broader social goals. Ostrom's work helps us to understand why.

Consider the challenge of managing common resources. It is often discussed by economists in terms of 'the tragedy of the commons'. The usual inference is that collectively owned resources will be overused because, without a price mechanism to charge for personal use, there is a tendency for everyone to take more than their fair share—to the long-run detriment of all. The classic example is those lands in medieval societies where all peasants could freely graze their livestock. According to the commonly cited study by Garrett Hardin,[4] these lands became degraded because they were overused. Only if they could be converted into smaller lots for which there are private property rights would more sustainable outcomes be achieved. It is a powerful and influential story, but it is a misreading of history. The quality of common land was actually maintained for centuries through a complex set of social arrangements shaping customary use. It was the privatisation of other land that created much of the eventual problem, as more people were forced to try to eke out a living on the common land.

Ostrom's approach to studying how common resources can be effectively managed relies on experimental methods as well as historical analysis. She has shown that, when faced with economic circumstances where interdependence of the actors is crucial to the outcome, quite sophisticated ways of addressing and managing that interdependence usually emerge. Political economic possibilities are not reducible to the linear dimension of markets versus states. A broader array of socioeconomic possibilities needs consideration.

Evaluating economic performance

Understanding economic organisation—its different forms, diverse interpretations, and social implications—is the first task of political economy. The second is to evaluate economic performance. If political economy is to contribute to social progress, this essentially normative dimension is necessary in our deliberations. We need to know what works well and what does not. For this purpose, we need reasonably clear criteria of evaluation. The following four are suggested.

Efficiency

Any economic system should make efficient use of the available resources—natural, human, and manufactured. However, what efficiency really means in this context remains open to debate. The avoidance of waste is certainly implied, but what constitutes waste may itself be a matter of judgment. Is it wasteful to use natural resources to make products that are discarded as junk after their short lifespans? Or is it wasteful not to use all resources at our disposal? Economists have conventionally distinguished three dimensions of efficiency. There is efficiency of resource utilisation: not leaving resources unused, as occurs, for example, whenever there is a significant incidence of unemployment in a region or nation. There is efficiency of resource allocation: ensuring, for example, that the goods and services produced are those that the members of the society actually want to consume. There is efficiency of resource creation: fostering the most productive development of the workforce, for example, or of new production technologies through innovation. For each of these three dimensions we need to remember that efficiency implies a means to particular ends: it is not an end in itself.

Equity

The economic system should distribute its fruits in accordance with our social standards of equity. Equity implies fairness. Therein, of course, lies plenty of scope for different interpretation. Some people interpret equity as requiring equality of economic outcomes, such as equal incomes for all members of the population. Others stress the more modest goal of equality of opportunity, accepting major income inequalities as long as all have an equal opportunity to succeed. On either reading, inequalities associated with systemic patterns of social differentiation according to class, gender, or ethnicity violate the equity ideal. For practical purposes, the degree of inequality in the overall distribution of income or wealth is usually taken as a rough primary indicator of the extent of equity in different types of economy.

Sustainability

We also require of an economic system that it be sustainable. In other words, it must be capable of reproducing itself. That means not using non-renewable natural resources, nor using renewable resources at a faster rate than that at which they are replenished. The harmony between the economy and the physical environment is obviously crucial here. Economic growth based on a rapacious relationship to nature clearly fails this environmental sustainability test. Sustainability has its economic and social dimensions, too. Economically, it is crucial that equipment subject to wear and tear through its use in producing goods and services be maintained and/or periodically replaced; consequently, a sustainable economy must involve forgoing some current consumption in order to ensure sufficient productive investment in capital goods. Socially, sustainability also requires that the relationships between classes, genders, and ethnicities be sufficiently stable for people to continue cooperating in economic activity. For this to happen, those relationships must be perceived as legitimate—otherwise, social turmoil, even revolution, may eventuate.

Compatibility with social goals

The ultimate test of an economic system is whether it serves society well. Does it generate the necessary goods, such as the food, clothing, housing, and other material requisites for a contented society? Does it produce the quality health and educational services necessary for a healthy and well-informed citizenry? Generally, is it conducive to personal and community development, to personal freedom, to cultural enrichment, or to the realisation of spiritual as well as material goals? These are the higher social purposes against which the mundane contributions of the economy need to be judged. Therein lies a host of difficulties: identifying the relevant social goals and their relative importance, deciding how they can be measured or otherwise assessed, and learning how political judgments can be made about trade-offs between them. On such contentious matters there can never be unanimous agreement. There are also good reasons to expect that the character of the economic system will itself have a major bearing on the pattern of prevailing social aspirations—so an objective test is elusive. However, if nothing else, such considerations are a reminder of the need to take a broader view of the economy and of economic progress than that based on the conventional economic indicators.

BOX 5.2 | THE POLITICAL ECONOMY OF CLIMATE CHANGE

The nature and causes of climate change are contentious, as are the appropriate responses. Complex scientific analysis, as well as political economic judgment, is required. The scientific community has become increasingly concerned about the existence and severity of the problem. Sceptics remain, of course, but what had emerged in the 1980s as a growing concern with the 'greenhouse effect' and 'global warming' had become a worldwide recognition of the climate change problem by the international summit meeting that was held in Kyoto, Japan in 1997. Since that date the Intergovernmental Panel on Climate Change (IPCC) has represented the increasingly strong scientific consensus, emphasising that the threat arises, in substantial measure, from human activities. Although progress in getting global agreement to tackle the problem has been lamentably slow, the need to do so has now become well established.

Burning of coal, oil and other fossil fuels causes the emission of carbon into the atmosphere. As a consequence, the infrared radiation generated by the Sun's warming of the Earth is impeded on its way out, causing the planet to warm and the climate to change. The amount of those emissions—and hence the intensity of global warming and climate change—depends on the volume and nature of economic activity that is carbon generating.

Put most simply, there are three contributory factors in climate change: people, production, and technology. A larger population, other things being equal, means a greater demand on resources and a bigger volume of economic activity. However, it is the material living standards of those people that is crucial. This is where the second element—the production process—kicks in, because the volume of economic production drives the demand for energy to produce mineral, agricultural, and manufactured goods, and to transport the goods and people. That is why income and the rate of economic growth matters. An extra child in the United States or other affluent nations, for example, adds many times more to the ecological stresses than a child born into a poorer nation. Technology, as the third element, is crucial, too. Technologies for production and transportation that depend on burning fossil fuels are obviously more problematic than those that do not. So dealing with the climate change problem requires attention to these three influences. Some say that a change in technology would be sufficient; others that policies to lower population growth and/or levels of production and consumption are also needed. The character, form, and distribution of economic growth is central to all such concerns.

Solving—or even just reducing—the threat of climate change requires a comprehensive program of economic restructuring and social transition. This is an enormous challenge. It requires consideration of complex ecological, social, economic, political, cultural, and ethical issues. It requires strong commitment to remedial policies. Proponents of making a transition to a sustainable society commonly emphasise that it cannot be just a transition— it must be a just transition. The 'make the polluter pay' principle has particular relevance in this context, since it implies the need to put the costs of adjustment onto the individuals, firms, industries, and nations responsible for the most carbon emissions, rather than 'equality of sacrifice'. The question of who should take the primary responsibility for leading the way towards more environmentally responsible patterns of production and consumption is clearly a political economic rather than a scientific judgment.

Sustainability is the ultimate goal. Its operational definition is tricky, however, because of different economic, social, and ecological conceptions of sustainability. Economic sustainability requires the reproduction of productive capacity, including the replacement of depreciating capital, whether natural or human built. Social sustainability implies the reproduction of acceptable social structures and institutions, producing social cohesion. Ecological sustainability requires the maintenance of biodiversity, ensuring ecological integrity, maintaining the stock of natural capital and providing for intergenerational equity. Putting the three aspects together is necessary but difficult. It is an issue to which we return in Chapter 35 of this book.

What measure of progress?

The overall performance of a national economy is conventionally measured according to gross domestic product (GDP), which is the sum of the market value of all goods and services produced in a country during a year, irrespective of whether they are produced by individuals, private business enterprises, or government institutions. If this sum is greater than the preceding year's, then economic growth is said to have occurred. Conversely, no growth or, worse, a decline, is held to be indicative of relative economic failure. League tables, such as Table 4.1, are commonly constructed on GDP per capita to indicate the ranking of the different countries of the world in any one year according to this performance measure. In principle, the measure can also apply to subnational areas (gross regional product or gross city product) and to the world as a whole (gross planetary product).

Notwithstanding its widespread application, this conventional measure of economic performance is subject to numerous problems.[5]

- It excludes many useful goods and services that are produced directly for personal consumption rather than for sale. Domestic household production—much of it traditionally (and still) performed by women—is of this character.

- It includes expenditure on goods and services whose production is only necessary because of the damage by producing or consuming other things. Expenditures on pollution control devices and vehicle smash repairs are obvious examples. These 'defensive expenditures' add to GDP, but it is doubtful that they make a net contribution to community well-being.

- No account is taken of the rundown in the stocks of environmental resources that may occur in the process of producing marketed goods and services.

- The time and effort involved in producing goods and services does not enter into the calculations. So no account is taken of the leisure that is sacrificed in order to produce the output.

- The distribution of the products is also not considered. The production of frivolous, luxury consumption items for the wealthy counts equally with the production of basic necessities for the poor.

Reflecting on these problems and biases, one critic has described conventional national measures, 'the crown jewels of economic statistics', as 'almost trivial indicators of anything worth measuring'.[6] This is an issue to which we return in the final chapter of this book. Meanwhile, the inference is clear—merely increasing the volume and value of marketed economic products does not reliably constitute progress.

Conclusion

There are various ways in which economic activity can be organised. Identifying nature, the market, state, class, gender, ethnicity, social capital, and ideology as dimensions of economic and social order draws attention to the array of organising principles and institutions. It draws attention to the complexity of the interrelationships between the economy and society.

There are also various ways in which economic performance can be evaluated. Identifying efficiency, equity, sustainability, and compatibility with social goals indicates the most important dimensions. It also draws attention to some of the deficiencies of narrowly constructed conventional economic indicators, such as GDP.

These considerations show why the exercise of judgment is necessary in political economic analysis. Indeed, the scope of political economic enquiry itself is a matter of judgment. While the economy can be reasonably clearly defined—in terms of production, exchange, and distribution—there is no line clearly dividing the economy from society. By similar reasoning, there is no clear separation of economics, as a form of enquiry, from the other social sciences. There are also inescapably normative elements involved in evaluating economic systems. No wonder that views about the nature of the capitalist economy and how well it serves social goals are so diverse.

KEY POINTS

- Economic systems have distinctive functions: producing goods and services, facilitating the exchange of those products, and distributing income and wealth.

- How well the economy serves the society can be evaluated according to criteria such as efficiency, equity, sustainability, and compatibility with broader social goals.

- There is considerable evidence that growth in the production of goods and services and the accumulation of wealth has not been accompanied by a corresponding increase in social well-being.

6 ▶ Capitalism

What systems of economic organisation are possible?

What is special about capitalism?

What are the common features of capitalist economies?

Economic activity can be organised in various ways in the attempt to satisfy the social purposes identified in the preceding chapter. Communal, slave, feudal, capitalist, and socialist systems are the principal alternatives. Capitalism is evidently the predominant system at the present time. A careful definition of this system is required before studying how it works and making judgments about how well it works. This is attempted in this chapter by contrasting capitalism with other ways in which economic activity can be organised and then by looking in more detail at its distinctive features.

Alternative economic systems

Economic activity can be organised communally. In small social clusters, for example, people can gather to decide what they will produce, how the tasks will be shared, and how the fruits of their combined economic effort will be distributed and used. These decisions may be strongly influenced by custom and convention. Such has been the case in many tribal societies, a traditional focus in anthropological studies. The term 'primitive communalism' is applied in this context, although the economic and social processes may be highly sophisticated. Whether such communal organisation constitutes a viable basis for a large-scale, industrial economy is a moot point, but the principles and practices are relevant wherever cooperative behaviour needs to be nurtured.

A second possible means of economic organisation is slavery. Historically, slavery has been of considerable significance. Explicit use of force by one class (slave owners) over another (slaves) is the central organising principle here. Violence (or the threat of it) is the driver of economic activity, determining what gets done, by whom, how, where, and when. Slavery was commonplace in the Mediterranean lands, which were the cradle of modern Western civilisation, but it has also been crucially important in the more recent economic development of a number of countries. No analysis of the USA, for example, could sensibly ignore the role of slavery in its economic development: slaves from Africa were the principal source of plantation labour and, after emancipation, became a major source of labour in industrial cities such as Chicago and New York. A significant part of Great Britain's wealth in the eighteenth century derived from slavery, too. Coerced labour was also important in Australia, where convict labour was used to build infrastructure, laying the foundations for subsequent economic development. Indentured labour from the islands of the South Pacific also supplemented the workforce, especially on the Queensland sugar plantations. Elements of slavery persist today in many other nations: in the coercive aspects of prostitution, and in the use of child labour and prison labour to produce cheap products for global markets.

Feudalism is a third means of economic organisation. It, too, is of considerable historical and contemporary significance. Like slavery, it has coercive elements, but the core principle is mutual obligation. Under feudalism, the different social classes are linked by a system of mutual rights and obligations, usually based on traditional roles and beliefs. Serfs work on the land of landowners in exchange for social protection. This was the norm during the Middle Ages in Great Britain and much of Western Europe. Derivatives of this system continue to shape the economic development in many of the poorer nations today where a landowning class captures a big share of the economic surplus. Social acceptance of what might otherwise be deemed unacceptable inequalities of class, social position, and power may be maintained by cultural and religious ideologies. The demand for land reform is the usual signal of a move to challenge and change the residual feudal arrangements.

Capitalism is different from these other economic systems because financial considerations dominate. Control over capital becomes the key source of class power in this system. The quest for financial reward is the driving force shaping what is done, by whom, how, where, and when. It also determines who gets what in the distribution of rewards. Work is done for wages; business activity is undertaken for profit. The primacy of these pecuniary relationships is the basic defining feature of capitalism. There may be some collective decision-making, coercion, or mutual obligation, but it is the pervasiveness of financial arrangements that shapes the economy, society, and social values.[1]

Socialism may be regarded as the application of more consistently collectivist principles in the context of a modern, advanced economy. The nature of the economic activity performed, who performs it, how it is performed, and where and when it is performed are determined by a planning process. Therein lies much of the appeal of socialism, in principle at least, as a rational, democratic, and egalitarian set of socioeconomic arrangements. There were some twentieth-century experiments inspired by socialist ideals—in the former Soviet Union and in the People's Republic of China, for example—but whether these actually embodied socialist principles in practice is contentious. There is no single model: market socialism in which both planning and markets operate contrasts with a command economy in which the allocation of economic resources is determined by the state. Similarly, socialism may be based on either centralised or relatively decentralised decision-making processes. Whether socialism in any of these forms can be a viable basis for economic organisation in the twenty-first century is an ongoing controversy, but concerns about the sustainability of capitalism keep the quest for some such alternative permanently on the agenda.[2] Meanwhile, capitalism remains the dominant system of economic organisation on a world scale.

Defining capitalism

Capitalism cannot be defined as easily as we may define 'chair' or 'elephant': we do not so readily know it when we see it. It is necessary to define it in terms of a cluster of interconnected characteristics. The following eight features, summarised in Figure 6.1 below, identify what is special about the system. Each is not unique to capitalism, but together they indicate its distinctive character.

FIGURE 6.1 ELEMENTS IN THE CAPITALIST SYSTEM

Private ownership of the means of production

Capitalism is based on a distinctive system of property rights. Economic resources are characteristically owned by private individuals and institutions. Some land, natural resources, or public utilities may be owned by society as a whole. However, the basic capitalist principle is that economic activity is in the hands of private businesses for the purposes of making profit. These businesses may be run by individuals, such as sole proprietors of small firms. Others are run by bigger institutions that are legally recognised as entities, such as corporations owned by shareholders with limited personal liability.

The capacity of these property owners to derive income from their control over the means of production—the factories, offices, machinery, and equipment with which goods and services are produced—identifies them as a distinct class. How that capitalist class is constituted depends on how numerous are the businesses and how widespread are the shareholdings in the larger firms. Its existence as a class does not mean that internal conflicts of interests cannot occur—indeed, the owners of rival business enterprises are usually in competition with each other—but its defining feature is a common interest in the pursuit of profit.

Labour market

Under capitalism, those who do not own the means of production depend for their economic livelihood on the sale of their capacity to work. That requires the existence of a labour market (or, more usually, a set of labour markets, segmented according to region and occupation). The buyers of labour—those who own and control the means of production—interact there with the sellers of labour. Sometimes individual buyers and sellers directly negotiate wages and employment conditions, but the negotiation process is often mediated by trade unions, employer associations, and regulatory institutions that set the rules of the game.[3] It is the dependence of the bulk of the population on the sale of their capacity to work (in either manual or mental labour)—that is, the existence of a working class—that is the common feature.

Under capitalism workers are free in that, unlike slaves or serfs, they are not tied to a particular employer by physical coercion or social convention. However, their freedom is a constrained freedom. It is the freedom, and the necessity, to sell their capacity to work. This is why capitalism is sometimes said to be a system of 'alienated labour', or a system in which labour is treated as a commodity.

Capital market

Those who establish and run capitalist businesses need funds for that purpose. They need financial capital before they can employ the means of production in order to make goods and services. So, an institution (or group of institutions) is necessary for channelling funds from savers into the hands of businesses or people who can then invest those funds productively. Banks carry out that institutional function by making loans to businesses. Indeed, they can lend much more than they have in deposits, effectively creating money in the process. As such, banks are key capitalist institutions, facilitating the conversion of savings into investment as well as being profit-seeking entities themselves.

The most characteristic capital market institution is the stock exchange. This is where shares in companies are sold to the public, and where the owners of those shares can sell them to others. Not surprisingly, the stock exchange is sometimes held to be the ultimate symbol of capitalism. It is a place where fortunes can be made or lost. However, it is really an adjunct to the productive economy, not in itself a place where wealth is created. Indeed, large companies often make such enormous profits that they can finance expansion of their businesses without needing to raise capital on the stock exchange. Capital markets usually continue to exert some discipline on those businesses, though, if only because the threat of takeover becomes more likely if their share price falls.

Land market

Land is of fundamental importance in all types of economic organisation. In rural areas, its fertility and management determines its capacity to contribute that most basic of human needs: food. In an urban context, its use has a major bearing on the effectiveness of cities as focal points of modern economic life. So, how land is owned, allocated, and regulated has major socioeconomic implications.

Under capitalism, land is characteristically privately owned and is usually allocated through market processes—subject to varying degrees of regulation by the state. Land, like labour and capital, is bought and sold in the market. Arguably, this is not essential for capitalism: land could be owned collectively through the state and allocated or leased to households and businesses. As such, the form of land ownership is not such a fundamentally defining feature of the economic system under capitalism as it is under, say, feudalism. However, under capitalism, the very generality of market processes tends to make land yet another tradeable commodity.

Markets for goods and services

Capitalism is a system of generalised commodity production. Goods and services are typically produced for exchange in the market. That is what makes those goods and services commodities: they are items produced for sale rather than for personal use by their producer.

The processes of exchange sometimes involve direct interaction between buyer and seller, but usually they are mediated by the institutions of wholesale and retail trade. Shopping is the name of the game. Indeed, shoppers play a crucial role in the capitalist system as a whole because, if their purchases do not match the volume and array of commodities produced, economic crises can occur. No wonder the emphasis on consumerism is so pervasive under contemporary capitalism, and no wonder so many resources are channelled into marketing and sales promotion.[4]

Distinctive role of the state

The fifth characteristic of capitalism is, at first sight, more surprising. Surely, one might think, if capitalism is primarily a market economy, then there is no significant role for the state. Not so. In all political economic systems other than anarchism, the state has a significant presence. The key point is what form the state presence takes.

Under capitalism, functions of the state relate directly to the prevailing property rights, and market and class relationships. So the state regulates and enforces the property rights on which the capitalist economy is based. It determines the rules underpinning the operation of markets for labour, capital, land, and commodities. It acts as an umpire in respect of rivalries between businesses that might otherwise be sources of economic instability. It usually seeks to redistribute market incomes, at least to the extent necessary to ensure social stability. It may also be directly engaged in the provision of goods and services that are not provided by the market: fire fighting, law enforcement, and defence, for example. The nature and extent of these state activities is, of course, the focus of continued political debate. The main point here is that capitalism is not synonymous with a pure market economy.

Distinctive ideology

All economic systems have prevailing ideologies associated with them: these are systems of belief that make the system seem legitimate. The dominant ideologies are commonly shaped by, or reflect, the structure of the economy. Determining the direction of causation is a highly contentious exercise, but some broad correlations are clear enough. For instance, consumerist ideologies that regard material goods as the source of personal satisfaction and social status are not unique to capitalism, but they seem to reach their zenith in this type of economy. *Homo economicus*, or 'rational economic person', is fostered by capitalist economic interests.

An emphasis on competitiveness is similarly predictable in an economic system based on competing market interests (although monopoly may be as prevalent as competition in actually existing capitalism). By contrast, ideologies emphasising cooperation can be expected to be more prominent where the economic organisation is collectivist in character. Both types of ideology are usually present in uneasy alliance with each other. However, to the extent that ideology gives legitimacy to an economic system, it is not surprising that the predominant capitalist ideology is consumerist and competitive.

Expansionary tendency

Last, it is pertinent to note the dynamic character of capitalism. As a system driven by the quest for profit, it is geared for growth. This is not to say that growth is always achieved. Indeed, the history of capitalism worldwide is one of alternating periods of boom and slump. But this particular type of economic system works best when it is growing. It may be said that, like a bicycle, capitalism requires forward motion for its stability. That is why periods of recession or economic stagnation precipitate dramatic processes of economic restructuring, as described in Chapter 3.

This dynamism is capitalism's most obvious strength, the source of its capacity to reproduce itself, expand, and adapt. It is also the source of fundamental tensions. There is perpetual conflict between the profit-seeking interests and the broader social goals. There is also a fundamental tension between this growth-orientated economy and the finite resources of the planet on which it exists, a tension that is manifest in growing environmental stress.

Conclusion

Defining capitalism in terms of a cluster of key characteristics provides a description of an ideal model. It is not necessarily ideal in the normative sense of being desirable (we consider those pros and cons later), but in the sense of being a simplified abstraction. The question remains: Do economies in the real world approximate this ideal model? In other words, are the economies of the USA, the UK, Australia, Sweden, Singapore, and other capitalist nations essentially the same? Posed in this blunt manner, the question has to be answered in the negative. There are significant differences in the range of economic functions undertaken by the state. There are also differences between those countries in the economic institutions and ideologies that shape how markets for labour, capital, and land operate. In the USA, for example, the state has been more concerned with supporting the interests of capital and the functioning of the capitalist market economy, whereas in Sweden the state has played a substantial role in the redistribution of income and in economic and social planning. On the other hand, the state in the USA is highly interventionist on a world scale, much more so than Sweden (or any other country), because of its role as self-appointed policeman of international capitalism.[5]

These examples illustrate *varieties of capitalism* in different national contexts. The variations are partly explicable in terms of the historical evolution of the countries concerned. They can also be analysed in terms of the relationships between the economy and society discussed in Chapter 5: the distinctive national characters of nature, market, state, class, gender, ethnicity, social capital, and ideology. If we are to understand how different countries' economies work, detailed historical and institutional study is necessary on a case-by-case basis. The distinctive methodological position being argued here—the punchline to this chapter—is that an analysis of *capitalism in general* is a necessary prelude. Once we understand the fundamental features of the system, we can then layer on the details necessary for understanding the complexities of the real world in which we live.

KEY POINTS

- There are many different systems of economic organisation: communal, slave, feudal, capitalist, socialist, and numerous possible blends thereof.
- Capitalism can be defined in terms of its particular characteristics: the private ownership of the means of production, markets for labour, capital, land, and goods, a distinctive role for the state, legitimising ideologies, and an expansionary tendency.
- These systemic characteristics make it possible to analyse capitalism in general, notwithstanding significant national varieties of capitalism in practice.

7 Economic Theories

Why theorise about the economy?

What has shaped the theorising about capitalism?

How have different theories evolved in the history of economic thought?

Having defined capitalism as a distinctive system of economic organisation, our task now is to understand how it works. For this purpose we must theorise. We have to abstract from the complexity of the economy in the real world in order to focus on the essential or core elements. But what are these core elements? Which theory is appropriate? This chapter begins the intriguing process of exploring the competing economic theories about capitalism.

Why theorise?

For many people, 'theory' is a pejorative term. Theory is something to be avoided if possible. This understandably wary attitude is encapsulated in the familiar expression, 'That is all very well in theory, but the reality is different'. The inference is that theory is inferior to the direct study of the 'reality out there'.

To avoid theory, we may elect to undertake a direct empirical examination of the economy in practice. So, we sally forth, armed with clipboard and pencil (or computer notepad), and look around. Where shall we look first? At the shops, the vast array of goods on sale there, the relative prices of the goods, and the fluctuations in demand and supply for them? At the factories where those goods are produced, to study the production technologies, labour relations, wage rates, and other determinants of the costs of production? At the docks and airports, to see which goods are being exported and imported and how their relative prices compare? At the volume and values of transactions on the stock exchange and other financial markets? Or at the array of economic activities undertaken by governments in providing goods and services, redistributing income through taxation and public expenditures, and engaging in myriad regulatory economic functions? The list of possibilities is mind-boggling. The body of evidence we would accumulate would be indigestible. Without guidelines to distinguish between what is important and what is less relevant, the task is unmanageable. We have to rethink our investigative strategy.

In effect, we are forced to accept the need for some simplification. This process of simplification is the essence of theory construction. We select particular key variables for study and set aside the rest as not being of fundamental importance. We are then able to investigate the nature of the relationships between the key variables. We try, thereby, to develop a sequential process of analysis to help us understand the complex world around us. As the distinguished American economist Kenneth Boulding put it: 'Knowledge is always gained by the orderly loss of information, that is by condensing and abstracting and indexing the great buzzing confusion of information that comes from the world around us into a form we can appreciate and comprehend.'[1] To quote another prominent economist: 'Knowing how to simplify one's description of reality without neglecting anything essential is the most important part of an economist's art.'[2] It seems that we cannot avoid theorising. Some degree of abstraction from reality is unavoidable. The question is how can it most effectively be done without losing touch with reality altogether? On which aspects of the economic system should the theory focus? Which aspects can be safely neglected? It is because economists are not agreed on these matters that economics as a discipline is pervaded by competing economic theories.

This is where the story starts to get interesting. We come directly to the central theme of the book: the contest between different ways of seeing the economy. Of course, the existence of competing theories is not unique to economics: it is characteristic of most academic disciplines. Indeed, some would say it is the hallmark of an open society, in which there is freedom to adopt different viewpoints. However, in economics the presence of competing theories is particularly problematic. In part, this is because economic ideas have influence on the behaviour of governments and other economic institutions. In part, it is because of the interconnectedness of economic methodology and political philosophy. The different ways of seeing reflect different political perspectives—conservative, liberal, and radical—on the way in which the economy functions and how it should function. These are the bases of fundamentally different views about capitalism and social progress.

Competing schools of thought

In order to understand the diverse theories about the economy, it is useful to distinguish between competing schools of thought. In effect, this enables us to cluster similar or related theories and thereby reduce the number of competing theories to more manageable proportions. This helps in understanding the history of economic thought and current political economic debates.

This notion of a school of thought has much in common with the concept of a paradigm. The latter term gained particular prominence as a result of a book by Thomas Kuhn, *The Structure of Scientific Revolutions*, in which he described the development, not of economics, but of the physical sciences.[3] The central issue is how new theories may overthrow existing orthodoxies. Kuhn argued that such transformations periodically occur, often in a quite dramatic manner. The belief that the Earth was the centre of the solar system, for example, was challenged in the sixteenth century by upstarts who sought to demonstrate that the Earth actually revolved around the Sun. These dissidents were ridiculed and persecuted, but eventually their view came to replace the earlier one. It proved to be more consistent with empirical observations. The Sun-as-the-centre-of-the-solar-system paradigm replaced the Earth-as-the-centre-of-the-solar-system paradigm.

We can think of a paradigm as a framework of analysis that defines the issues to be studied and the methods to be applied in studying them. Competing paradigms, Kuhn argued, have been common in the physical sciences. At any time, one paradigm tends to predominate. This constitutes a period of 'normal science'. A clear research agenda is set, but at the expense of limiting the questions that the discipline poses. That paradigm eventually becomes a hindrance to further scientific progress, anomalous observations proliferate, and a period of crisis occurs. A new paradigm emerges, resolving at least some of the anomalies, and a new research agenda is set. Thus science evolves, not in a linear fashion but through periodic revolutions that open space for surges in scientific advance.

There are some important differences between the physical sciences and the social sciences, including economics. In the social sciences, the object of the enquiry is constantly changing. Evolution is a feature of the physical world, too, of course, but economic and social conditions are subject to particularly rapid change. Theories that may be appropriate at one time are rendered inappropriate by new circumstances. Capitalism today is not what it was a century ago, or even fifty years ago: its institutional features have changed dramatically, even if its essential character has significant elements of continuity.

Another complication is the interdependence of theories about social phenomena and the behaviour resulting from the application of those theories. To give an obvious example: how we understand the economy influences the economic policies implemented by governments, which then change, at least to some degree, how the economy operates. This problem of interdependence of subject and object also exists sometimes in the physical sciences, but it is particularly prevalent in economics and other social sciences. Even the process of studying people's behaviour can change what happens, because people often act differently when being observed or monitored.[4]

Last, it is pertinent to note that the development of economics, and of the social sciences in general, is permeated by the influence of material interests. Particular theories may suit the interests of particular individuals, classes, or nations. Because they serve a useful function for the vested interests they support, theories can endure in spite of competing arguments and contradictory evidence. The contest of economic ideas is intertwined with the conflict of economic interests.

This last consideration helps to explain why rival schools of economic thought have such durability. They do not slink away when trounced by 'superior' explanations of economic phenomena. Economists are continually modifying their theories—the professional journals are full of such adaptations—but the core principles have remarkable tenacity. The political purposes that economics serves also have to be taken into account in any serious study of the development of schools of economic thought.

An historical overview

The political character of economic thought is most obvious when the subject is studied in historical perspective. Over more than two and a quarter centuries, paralleling the development of the capitalist economy, exponents of rival schools of economic thought have argued about how capitalism works. Figure 7.1 provides a simple summary of the evolving currents of economic analysis.

FIGURE 7.1 THE HISTORY OF ECONOMIC THOUGHT

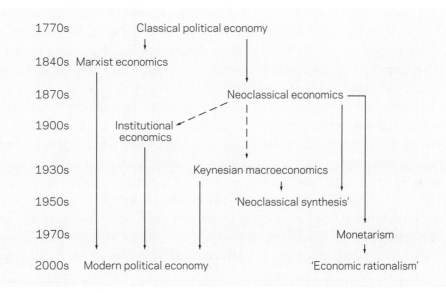

Note: This chart of the main currents of political economic analysis in historical perspective simplifies the complex history of the subject; however, it does draw attention to the principal avenues of continuity (represented by the continuous vertical lines) and discontinuity (represented by the dotted lines). In the former, the new school of thought is a development from the previous one; in the latter, it is a reaction against it.

Each of these competing schools of thought can be understood in terms of the changing economic conditions of the time, the influence of particular economic interests, the influence of prevailing intellectual fashions, and the innovative ideas of great economic thinkers.

Much of the rest of the book is an illustration of these themes. The prefatory remarks in the rest of this chapter set the scene for the more detailed investigations that follow.

It is sensible to begin in the late eighteenth century, when capitalism was clearly emerging from feudalism in Great Britain and, more slowly, in other nations in which capitalist economic relationships were eventually to predominate. This was the period when

Adam Smith wrote his seminal book *An Inquiry into the Nature and Causes of the Wealth of Nations* (usually shortened to *The Wealth of Nations*) and when what we now call classical political economy developed. Of course intelligent people had reflected on the economic conditions before then. However, with classical political economy came the emergence of a specifically capitalist economics.

The classical political economists were concerned with studying the economic character of the society in which they lived. They analysed the capacity of an economic system based on market exchange, rather than customary relationships or state management, to increase national wealth. They believed such a system opened up opportunities for individual initiative, increased productivity, and aided the growth of trade. Some did have grave reservations about whether the mass of the working population would experience rising living standards, but history was on the march, and the development of economic liberalism provided its justification. It continues to have a major influence today.

The neoclassical economists built on the foundations of classical political economy. For more than a century they have been a consistently strong source of support for the view that free markets produce efficient outcomes. Emerging in the late nineteenth century, neoclassical theory provided a formal modelling of equilibrium conditions in competitive markets. This was clearly an attempt to put economics—then newly separated from the study of history and politics—on a more scientific basis. Whether the result was—and is—actually more scientific or more ideological, showing capitalism in an unrealistically favourable light, is a seemingly perpetual controversy.

Meanwhile, Marxist economists, also starting from a basis in classical political economy, developed a markedly different interpretation of capitalism. They contend that it generates pervasive economic inequality, social conflict, and periodic crises. This quite different analysis of the capitalist economy also emerged in the nineteenth century, responding to the economic, social, and political transformations then taking place. The pioneering analysis of Karl Marx, and his collaborator Friedrich Engels, continues as a foundation for radical critiques of the capitalist system, such as those advanced by critics of the current corporate globalisation process and the global financial crisis. On this reasoning, only a fundamental transformation of the political economic system can reconcile economic concerns with social justice and progress.

Between these extremes are reformist perspectives, such as those associated with John Maynard Keynes and with the institutional tradition of economic analysis. These also warrant careful consideration, for they put particular focus on what governments—given the political will—can do to eradicate unemployment, redistribute incomes more equitably, and promote more balanced economic and social development.

Institutional economics was inspired by the critical social analysis of the dissident American economist Thorstein Veblen, writing a century ago. Veblen was deeply critical of capitalism, but his critique was quite different from Marx's, in that he emphasised the social manifestations of business and consumer behaviour rather than the forces for change generated by class conflict. The political tenor of the institutional economics tradition after

Veblen has usually been more concerned with the amelioration of the problems of capitalism than with a revolutionary challenge to the system. The development of the welfare state in the twentieth century was influenced by these institutional economists, as well as by other social reformers.

Keynes, writing between the First and Second World Wars when unemployment was particularly persistent, also saw economic analysis as a means towards reform. He considered the capitalist system 'morally objectionable', but thought it better than the possible alternatives of communism and fascism, support for which was then growing internationally. Understanding the causes of unemployment, and positing solutions for it through economic policy, would, on this reasoning, make a particularly valuable social contribution. As with institutional economics, the Keynesian perspective is one in which the state is central. As historian Eric Hobsbawm put it, Keynes 'wished to save the essentials of a capitalist system but realised that this could be done only within the framework of a strong and systematically interventionist state'.[5] It was in contributing to such reforms, Keynes said, that economists can be the trustees of 'the possibilities of civilisation'.[6]

The ideas of Keynes, reinterpreted in a mechanistic form to make them more compatible with neoclassical theory, became the basis for a new orthodoxy during the three decades after the Second World War. This was the era of the 'neoclassical synthesis', an uneasy blend of Keynesian macroeconomics and neoclassical microeconomics. It coincided with the years of the long boom when, for the advanced industrial capitalist nations at least, there did indeed seem to be continuous economic growth and full employment. The collapse of that long boom in the 1970s led to a major assault on Keynesian economics, both in theory and policy. Western capitalism saw the impact of a resurgent pre-Keynesianism, known as monetarism, which contended that capitalism would work best when government interfered least.

Monetarism led to a general revival in the last three decades of various forms of free-market economics. The ideas of Adam Smith have been blended with propositions from neoclassical theory and neoliberal politics to show the benefits of releasing capitalism from the constraints imposed by trade unions and unwarranted government 'intervention'. This 'new classical economics' sets aside Smith's reservations about markets and businessmen, and overlooks the fundamental differences between capitalism in his time and ours.

Modern political economists express profound reservations about this neoliberal free-market economics. They argue that it fails to provide a coherent means of understanding contemporary capitalism, and that, in practice, its policy prescriptions accentuate economic inequality, instability, and insecurity. They put the case for drawing on the dissident traditions of Marxist economics, institutional economics, and the economics of Keynes, and for building a more critical analysis of capitalism that takes account of contemporary economic problems (as reviewed in Chapter 4).

This, in a nutshell, is the story of the competing schools of economic thought. It is the story of ongoing rivalry—partly methodological and partly political in character—within this contested but highly influential discipline. It illustrates the controversial character of economic ideas about capitalism over more than two centuries.

Have we come a long way? Or are there elements of circularity, repetition, and even regress in the development of economic thought? Has the inherently political nature of economics impeded our understanding of modern capitalism? And, on what basis can future progress be made in understanding the economic system and in changing it for the better? A prerequisite for such progress is understanding how we reached this point. That, essentially, is the rationale for studying political economic analysis in historical perspective. It is the rationale for much of what follows in the rest of this book—teasing out what economic ideas are relevant to understanding the economy and dealing with the political economic challenges that confront us.[7]

Conclusion

Understanding how the capitalist economic system works, for better or worse, is the principal concern of political economy. Even the interpretation of the economy as a system implies an analytical stance, because 'system' implies regularities of behaviour and features that, in principle at least, can be understood and managed.

However, there is no unanimity on how to fashion this understanding. Rather, an economic system such as capitalism can be understood in various ways. Those different ways of seeing exist partly because of methodological differences regarding the best way to construct theory and partly because of differences in value judgments associated with rival political philosophies. Moreover, as an historical analysis of the discipline reveals, there is a strong connection between the contest of economic ideas and the conflict of economic interests.

KEY POINTS

- Theory is essential in understanding the economic system because it enables us to identify key elements and patterns in otherwise intractably complex circumstances.

- Rival economic theories can be characterised as competing schools of thought, interpreting capitalism in markedly different ways and resulting in strikingly different implications for economic policy.

- Understanding classical political economy, neoclassical economics, Marxian economics, institutional economics, and Keynesian economics is an essential foundation for the development of modern political economy.

PART III

Back to Basics

Classical Political Economy

8 Capitalism Emerging

Do the concerns of the classical political economists still matter?

What processes produced the economic system that the classical political economists sought to understand?

Why did they see the emerging capitalist system as progressive?

Classical political economy spanned the period from the late eighteenth century to the late nineteenth century. During this period, significant contributions to economic theory were made by Adam Smith, David Ricardo, Thomas Malthus, Jean-Baptiste Say, James Mill, John Stuart Mill, and many others. Most of these scholars came from relatively privileged backgrounds: the lives of ordinary working men and women permitted no comparable opportunity for leisured study, publication, and social influence.

Why should we be interested now in the ideas of these dead white males? Surely theirs was a different society, with different economic characteristics and problems? Indeed, it would be unreasonable to claim that their analyses can simply be applied today without substantial revision. That said, some familiarity with their contributions is useful for at least three reasons. First, it is interesting in its own right to see how these practical scholars grappled with the workings of the emerging capitalist economy. Second, their work has influenced subsequent economic thought. The major schools of economic analysis, both conservative and radical, are largely developments of, or reactions against, classical political economy; and modern political economy is, in important respects, an extension of the classical tradition. Third, the prescriptions of the classical political economists continue to influence economic policies in the real world, notwithstanding the major economic changes that have taken place over the past two centuries.

The current influence of classical ideas

Many modern economic viewpoints are traceable to classical political economy. Adam Smith (1723–90) is often cited by modern neoliberals in support of the arguments for free-market capitalism, for example. The belief that freedom of exchange and a self-regulating market are the preconditions for social progress is one of the hallmarks of this influential ideology. Promoted vigorously by national and international 'think tanks', this particular economic ideology had a direct connection with the policies of influential politicians in the late twentieth and early twenty-first centuries. Their economic advisers, if not actually tie-wearing members of the Adam Smith Club, have been imbued with a preference for the invisible hand of the market over the visible hand of the state. This preference is revealed in the political rhetoric, if not consistently in the economic policies actually implemented.

The ideas of David Ricardo (1772–1823), another of the leading classical political economists, are also of enduring significance. In his own day, Ricardo was a strong advocate of breaking down the barriers to international trade, arguing that, if each nation specialised in the production of the goods and services for which it was best suited and then traded its surplus with other nations, all would benefit. This is the basis of his famous doctrine of comparative advantage. Proponents of globalisation today generally mount similar arguments—although the term 'competitive advantage' has replaced the Ricardian 'comparative advantage'. An assessment of the cases for and against tariff protection or other impediments to trade can usefully begin with a reconsideration of Ricardo's reasoning.

Or take the case of Thomas Malthus (1766–1834), the gloomy parson, famous for his views on population growth. Malthus argued that there would be a persistent tendency for the rate of population growth to outstrip the rate of growth in food production, leading to famines, illness, and wars, that would prevent the living standards of the mass of the population from rising substantially above subsistence level. There are strong echoes of such concerns in current debates about poverty in developing nations and the environmental constraints on economic growth.[1] On a global scale, high birth rates and poverty remain strongly correlated, although there are grounds for believing that poverty causes high fertility, rather than vice versa. The distinguished economist and former winner of the Nobel Prize in Economic Sciences, Amartya Sen, also argues that the Malthusian 'food availability doctrine' pays insufficient attention to the importance of political factors in explaining and resolving poverty.[2] Many modern environmentalists, stressing the consequences of wasteful production and consumption and the problems arising from the maldistribution between rich and poor nations, are also uncomfortable about a Malthusian 'doomsday' perspective. However, even those who contend that production and consumption levels, rather than population numbers per se, are the root problem tend to couch their concerns in terms of the stresses, and ultimate unsustainability, of growth.

A final illustration concerns the views of French classical political economist Jean-Baptiste Say (1767–1832), who is best known for the so-called 'Say's Law'. This, in a nutshell, is the proposition that supply creates its own demand. Thus, the production of goods and services can be expected to generate the national income that is necessary to purchase those commodities. Hence, there need be no general tendency towards economic recession arising from a shortage of demand. Underconsumption need never be a problem, according to this view. Although the modern free-market economists seldom explicitly cite Say's Law in support of their prescriptions, the legacy lives on. Neoliberals argue that a capitalist economy tends towards its own stable equilibrium, and that government intervention intended to offset recessions by boosting the level of demand is likely to do more harm than good. Even the catastrophic global financial crisis that began in 2007–08, on this reasoning, did not warrant the surge of remedial policies that governments in most capitalist economies felt it necessary to introduce.[3]

BOX 8.1

ADAM SMITH (1723-90)

The outstanding figure in classical political economy was actually a professor of moral philosophy. The study of economic issues was not then separated from the broader study of society and the political ramifications of historical change. The ethical aspects of economic behaviour were regarded as being of paramount importance.

Adam Smith was born in Scotland in 1723. He spent six years as a student at Oxford University, where, as one biographer notes, he 'was dismayed by the low level of intellectual activity and the immorality of his fellow students'.[4] Smith had a pretty low opinion of the professors, too, and surmised that they might be more productive if they were paid according to their performance.

After returning to Scotland he secured a teaching position at the University of Glasgow, before being appointed to the chair of Moral Philosophy. In 1759, he published an important treatise entitled *The Theory of Moral Sentiments* that looked into the social underpinnings, such as trust and empathy, that are conducive to a well-functioning social order. However, it was the 1776 publication of *An Inquiry into the Nature and Causes of the Wealth of Nations* (usually known simply as *The Wealth of Nations*) that really made his name as the leading political economist of the time. The book was an intriguing blend of political judgments, philosophical reflections, and practical observations about commercial activities. It laid the foundation for the systematic study of political economy.

Smith wrote *The Wealth of Nations* after resigning from his professorship to take up a lucrative post as personal tutor to a young nobleman travelling in Europe. Interestingly, he revealed in *The Wealth of Nations* that he was personally quite sceptical of the educational value of extended continental tours for such young men. Other personal contradictions were to follow. He later held the office of 'Comptroller of Customs' for Scotland, in which capacity he managed the tariffs on imported goods—a somewhat awkward role for a proponent of free trade. Smith, although committed to a belief in the progressive role of markets, was a pragmatist. His support for the principles of a market economy was conditional and heavily qualified by ethical concerns. He may well be turning in his grave at some of the extreme laissez-faire ideological positions taken by his modern followers, including some who proudly wear the Adam Smith Club tie.

The ideas of Adam Smith and the other classical political economists are relevant to current debates about market freedoms, the benefits of trade, population growth, recessions, and the appropriate role of government. But are they helpful? They were developed to understand an economic environment quite different from today's. So, in considering the applicability of this intellectual legacy, it is pertinent to consider the historical context in which the ideas originally developed.

The emergence of capitalism from feudalism

The classical political economists were writing at a time when one economic and social order was being replaced by another. Indeed, whether it would actually constitute a new order was a fundamental concern. Smith, Ricardo, Malthus, and Say were observing a dramatic historical transformation that was to culminate in capitalism becoming the dominant economic system. It did not occur overnight, or even over a few decades. Capitalism was the culmination of changes in patterns of economic production and class relationships that had been taking place in Europe from about the eleventh century onwards. By the sixteenth century the rate of change had accelerated, making that century the watershed between the old, decaying, feudal order and the new, emerging, capitalist system. From then, up to the nineteenth century, the 'great transformation' occurred.[5]

Many scholarly works have been written about the nature of this transformation.[6] For our more modest purposes, it will suffice to list some key elements, focusing particularly on the historical conditions in Great Britain. It was there that the capitalist system first took clear shape before it became well developed elsewhere in Europe, was exported to the colonies, and became global in form.[7]

Improvements in agricultural technology were an important foundation. People usually think of capitalism as an urban, industrial economic system, so it is pertinent to note that its origins were rural. Only when a society can adequately feed itself without continuously expending all its labour on producing food do other forms of urban and industrial development become possible. Such potential was already being realised to some extent by the eleventh century. A key contributor was crop rotation and leaving a third of the acreage fallow each year so that the soil's nutrients could be restored, which resulted in higher yields. Horses replaced oxen as the principal sources of traction, enabling more efficient ploughing. Some degree of rural and urban specialisation became possible because of the greater productivity that these changes brought.

The creation of an agricultural surplus facilitated the growth of towns. No longer did all the people need to work on the land in order to subsist. Before the eleventh century, there had been only a few small trade centres among the scattering of villages, but significant towns—albeit still tiny by modern metropolitan standards—were well established by the thirteenth century. The towns that developed in this period can be regarded as the cradles of capitalism; however, this was primarily a merchant capitalism rather than an industrial capitalism.

Craft production was a characteristic economic activity that involved making items for local consumption and, increasingly, trade.

The development of long-distance trade opened up further opportunities for commodity exchange. Some of this trade involved prodigious distances. The Venetian trader Marco Polo, for example, traversed Asia in the thirteenth century. By that time, annual trade fairs, often lasting several weeks, were flourishing in Europe. From about the fifteenth century, fairs were starting to be replaced by permanent commercial centres located in cities that had increasingly sophisticated systems of currency exchange and credit facilities. These places were, in effect, embryos of modern financial centres. They laid the foundations for commercial law, gradually supplementing and then replacing the customary arrangements that formerly prevailed. These developments accelerated the decline of the manorial system. Feudalism was essentially a localised rural economic and social system based on individual manors, each ruled by a lord. This manorial system, the bastion of feudalism, was vulnerable to the spread of monetary exchange relationships. The growth of towns, and of trade between them and the rural manors, began to erode the autonomy and self-sufficiency of the manors. The lords of the manors purchased luxury goods from urban merchants; peasants supplemented their subsistence livelihood by selling some of their produce at local markets. Production for profit, and monetary relations in general, became increasingly widespread.

Meanwhile, the putting-out system was developing. This was a production system in which craftspeople were contracted to manufacture items directly for merchant-capitalists. The merchants provided the raw materials and the craftspeople made the products in their own homes, selling them directly to the merchants for a fee. The putting-out system, well developed by the sixteenth century, was not itself fully capitalist. The workers worked at home, not under the direct supervision of employers, and, significantly, their labour was not wage labour (because they were remunerated for the products made, not for the labour time they expended on making them). However, the system paved the way for capitalist employment. It actually persists in many sectors of modern industry—as outwork in the clothing industry, for example. Indeed, it has become increasingly widespread in computer-based services (such as desktop publishing), which have become modern, hi-tech, cottage industries.

For there to be a fully fledged industrial capitalism, a working class had to be created. Peasants and artisans had to be severed from their traditional livelihoods in order to create pools of wage labour. The enclosure movement was a particularly important means to that end, although its immediate motivation was the acquisition of profits through the privatisation of land. During the eighteenth century, more and more common land—land on which peasants had traditionally grazed their livestock—was fenced off, especially for sheep grazing to produce wool for the expanding textile industry. This accelerated a process of migration from rural areas to towns that had already started in the fifteenth and sixteenth centuries. Peasants, driven from their villages because they no longer had the means to support themselves, frequently became vagrants and moved to the towns in search of whatever livelihood they could eke out. They were the raw material for the formation of an urban industrial working class.

Improvements in transport and production technologies, culminating in the Industrial Revolution, were the final piece in this jigsaw of forces precipitating economic and social change. Technological progress in transportation had resulted in bigger and better sailing ships, and improved navigational aids, which facilitated trade and the establishment of colonies, such as those in the Americas and Australasia. Then, a great burst of technological innovation in the eighteenth and nineteenth century led to dramatic advances in the production of textiles, in coal mining, and in iron and steel. The development of the steam engine was a great leap forward for industrial production and rail transport. These industrial changes took place in a socioeconomic context in which the foundations for capitalism had already been established. The momentum was unstoppable.

A desirable transformation?

The transition from feudalism to capitalism involved changes in class structures, in spatial form, in technological conditions, and in patterns of trade, which provided the material conditions for the new economic and social order. These dramatic changes were accompanied—as dramatic economic changes usually are—by corresponding changes in prevailing ideas. Indeed, some scholars claim that it was the influence of particular ideas conducive to acquisitiveness and material progress that caused capitalism to first take root in Great Britain and then in Europe. The Protestant strain of Christianity is described as providing the accommodating ideology, making the pursuit of personal wealth no obstacle to getting to heaven.[8] But the economic changes themselves precipitated further ideological changes. It was in the context of this great transformation that classical political economy emerged.

The transformation was neither smooth nor uncontested. The erosion of feudal arrangements created considerable insecurity and generated much social conflict. Major changes to traditional economic and social structures always create winners and losers, and the latter can always be expected to resist change. So it was with the changes just described. Peasants' revolts were common from the fourteenth to sixteenth centuries, and there was bitter resistance to the enclosure movement. Some workers, feeling their working conditions threatened by the introduction of new machinery and managerial techniques, formed significant resistance movements, most famously the Luddites. A small group of farm labourers who sought to form themselves into a union to protect their wages and working conditions were found guilty under the Mutiny Act and transported to Australia (although public protest against this harsh sentence eventually succeeded in pressuring the authorities to allow them to return from that dreadful place).[9]

Concerns about the ethical aspects of the transformation to capitalism were also widespread. Would the new economic system be stable? Would it serve society well? Many churchmen worried about the primacy afforded the quest for profit and the implications of putting individual self-interest before social responsibility in economic affairs. It was in assuaging such concerns that classical political economy made its great ideological contribution.

Conclusion

Although the analyses and prescriptions of the classical political economists were diverse, they had a common concern with understanding the emerging socioeconomic system that eventually came to be known as capitalism. They did not see it as a blessing for all humankind, but their teachings generally served as a supporting ideology for the new system. By inference, it was a natural order, compared with which previous systems of economic organisation were underdeveloped precursors.

The class relationships, social customs, and moral beliefs of the feudal era persisted into the age of classical political economy. Disquiet about the ethical implications of embracing a capitalist economy was common. So, there is something rather dubious about taking the analyses developed by classical political economists directly into the modern context, particularly when those ideas are used to justify the extension of capitalist, free-market principles. Nevertheless, as this chapter has argued, there are some significant elements of continuity between the age of classical political economy and today, both in the way capitalist development is interpreted and in the associated dilemmas—moral as well as material. The classical political economic concerns have strong contemporary echoes.

KEY POINTS

- Capitalism took many centuries to emerge from within the previously dominant social and economic structures of feudalism.

- Classical political economy, as an attempt to understand the evolving economic arrangements, was a product of its time, shaped by the material changes and prevailing ethical concerns in Europe in the eighteenth and nineteenth centuries.

- Classical ideas still influence debates about the role of the market, international trade, economic growth, and recessions, notwithstanding the very different political economic conditions prevailing today.

9 Private Vices, Public Virtues

What beliefs about society underpinned classical political economy?

Is it ethical to rely on self-interest as the driver of economic activity?

Do the liberal economic ideas provide a strong case for an unregulated market economy?

Is capitalism a progressive economic system that contributes to social progress? From the time of the classical political economists, this has been a consistently contentious issue. Intellectuals in the eighteenth and nineteenth centuries were deeply concerned with ethical issues, seeing dangers in the breakdown of the old social order as well as opportunities being opened up by the new. Economic liberalism was developed as a reassurance, providing a basis on which most subsequent pro-capitalist ideology relies. It reassured the members of the dominant class that their pursuit of self-interest would drive substantial material progress. However, significant reservations were expressed about whether the mass of the people would similarly benefit. Because of the continuing influence of these ideas—particularly on neoliberalism in recent times—they warrant consideration in the context in which they were developed.

Challenging mercantilism

The ideas of the classical political economists were, first and foremost, a challenge to the prevailing practices and beliefs of mercantilism. Mercantilist doctrines were influential in the seventeenth and eighteenth centuries, as the expansion of business and trade was starting to transform the feudal system. The mercantilist view was that economic progress required a major role for government in managing national economies and regulating international trade. The visible hand of the state was much in evidence. A particular focus was on policies to stimulate exports and minimise imports, thereby ensuring an inflow of gold that would increase the supply of money—and, by implication, the total wealth—in the national economy. The mercantilist regime saw governments granting major monopolistic privileges to the big financial and trading companies in order to promote this goal. These state-sponsored businessmen had a vested interest in preserving the existing economic arrangements.

However, mercantilism had its increasingly influential opponents. Small business people and farmers generally resented the monopolistic privileges accorded to the big trading houses. The taxes levied to finance the national powers—economic, political, and military—also created resentment, especially in the colonies. The slogan 'No taxation without representation' was a central theme of the War of American Independence (1775–83). This resentment against mercantilism, together with the growing interest in liberal economic ideas, began to bode ill for the old order. The classical political economists' call for freedom of the marketplace had growing appeal, particularly to the emergent capitalist class.

Challenging the Christian corporate ethic

There was also a striking clash in the eighteenth and early nineteenth centuries between the new economic ideas and the more conservative social values promulgated by medieval social and religious institutions. As E. K. Hunt writes, it was 'an era in which an outdated economic ideology, the Medieval version of the Christian corporate ethic, came into increasingly sharp conflict with a new social and economic order with which it was incompatible'.[1]

The old order had been based on explicit moral principles. The Christian corporate ethic accepted business enterprise as a means of generating wealth, partly to support charitable acts. 'The rich man, if he does not give alms, is a thief', was one common view.[2] A benevolent paternalism was expected of the upper classes. Greed, selfishness, and covetousness were reviled and denounced. Merchants were regarded as being morally bound to trade at a 'just price' (admittedly an ill-defined concept, but one sharply at odds with charging whatever the market would bear).

By contrast, the new order seemed to require fewer constraints on business activity. Altruism was no longer considered necessary for socially beneficial outcomes: self-interest would suffice. Indeed, self-interest would be heralded as the key driver of economic progress. To quote Hunt, 'The sins that were most strongly denounced within the context of the Christian paternalistic ethic were to become the behavioural assumptions on which the capitalist market economy was to be based'.[3]

Therein lies a tension that has existed in right-wing politics ever since. On the one hand, the 'Tory' view emphasises the paternalistic obligations of the wealthy, the value of charitable works, and the need for economic and social regulation in order to achieve social cohesion. On the other hand, the right-wing libertarian (or neoliberal) view has a greater confidence in the capacity of competitive markets to reconcile conflicting interests and ensure efficient economic outcomes, thereby making social policy less necessary. These are the familiar 'wet' and 'dry' factional positions in modern right-wing political parties.

Did the classical political economists have more in common with the wets or the dries? Adam Smith's position shows the tension. He saw social and economic order arising from people's natural desire to better their lot in life and thereby gain social esteem. However, he also strongly emphasised the social context in which acquisitiveness occurs. His was not the crude 'greed is good' position sometimes espoused by his modern dry disciples. Indeed, Smith, the moral philosopher, had argued in his first major work, *The Theory of Moral Sentiments*, that society is not held together merely by neutral rules, and that sympathy for the plight of our neighbours is important because it leads to a sharing of emotions and sensations. Given these preconditions, he argued, self-interest can then be of positive economic benefit. It is a conclusion summed up in his oft-quoted statement in *The Wealth of Nations* that, 'It is not from the benevolence of the butcher, the brewer or the baker that we expect our dinner, but from their regard to their own interest'.[4]

Here is the classical case for the market as the means by which self-interest can be harnessed for social purposes. Smith's ideological achievement was to show that a new social order could emerge out of the potential chaos of an individualistic society. In his own words:

> each producer intends only his own security; and by directing that industry in such a manner as its produce may be of the greatest value, he intends only his own gain, and he is in this, as in many other cases, led by an invisible hand to promote an end which was no part of his intention. Nor is it always the worse for the society that it was not a part of it. By pursuing his own interest he frequently promotes that of society more effectually than when he really intends to promote it. I have never known much good done by those who affected to trade for the public good. It is an affectation, indeed, not very common among merchants, and very few words need to be employed in dissuading them from it.[5]

Even though the phrase 'invisible hand' is rather buried in this quotation, it has come to symbolise Smith's intellectual legacy. If reliance on the invisible hand is sufficient basis for a thriving economy, no further economic planning or political intervention seems warranted. However, although the notion of an invisible hand implies a general preference for self-regulating markets, Smith saw those markets as requiring social foundations that would shape behaviour in desirable ways. There is an explicitly ethical dimension to the reasoning: the inference that the invisible hand may be the hand of God.

Economic liberalism

In making the case for the greater individual freedom of the marketplace, Smith was in accord with a number of other leading intellectuals of the eighteenth century. A particularly intriguing contribution had been published decades earlier, in 1704. Written by Bernard Mandeville and entitled *The Fable of the Bees*, it was a bestseller. A strange book, it begins with a poem and continues with a number of essays and dialogues. The central theme is how 'private vices' (such as self-interest) can lead to 'public benefits'. Thus, Mandeville argued, individual human actions spontaneously generate orderly social structures such as law, language, the growth of knowledge, and, yes, the market.[6] Selfishness, because of its association with industriousness, would thereby contribute to a thriving economy.

Similar views came from many intellectuals of the era. The emphasis on individual freedom was married to assertions about the need for freedom of trade. The emergent ideology was markedly favourable to capitalist values and practices. It helped sound the death knell of mercantilist doctrines, if not of all mercantilist policies in practice. Moreover, it fitted in with the Protestant theology that emerged from the Reformation—a set of religious beliefs largely free of the moral opprobrium that the Catholic church had heaped on commercial activities. Protestantism held that people would be judged by their faith rather than their works. Acquisitive economic behaviour could be quite compatible with a pure heart and faith in God. Wryly, one might say that a businessman looking into his conscience could readily find 'that God had planted there a deep respect for the principles of private property'.[7]

Economic liberalism draws these ideas together, stripped of the explicitly ethical elements. It is not altogether compatible with political liberalism, which has a broader social agenda, but they share a concern with personal freedom and social order. Economic liberalism establishes a relationship between what is assumed to be people's essential nature and their economic activities. Its distinctive assumptions are:

- *individualism:* the individual is regarded as the basic unit of society, so no sound claim can be made about any social interest that differs from the aggregation of individual interests
- *hedonism:* individuals are driven by self-interest, seeking pleasure, and avoiding pain
- *rationality:* each individual's pursuit of self-interest requires him or her to weigh up the costs and benefits of alternative courses of action and to choose that which promises the most advantageous outcome
- *inertia:* people are basically lazy, remaining inactive unless stimulated by the prospect of personal gain.[8]

If we regard people in this way, it is not difficult to see why the market is a desirable arrangement for dealing with economic matters. Individual preferences for goods and services can be expressed in the marketplace, sending signals to the producers about what is wanted and what is not. Sellers compete with one another to supply the products to meet the demand, and that process of competition keeps prices at a minimum. Not all individual aspirations are necessarily met, but the market mediates between them to achieve effective compromises. Mutually advantageous exchanges occur. Economic resources are efficiently used.

On the other hand …

Although economic liberalism played a key role in legitimising capitalist market relationships, the classical political economists were not unqualified apologists for the emerging capitalist system. That Smith had serious qualms about business practices and an 'ambivalence towards nascent capitalism' is evident from a careful reading of his work.[9] A deep suspicion is evident, for example, in his observation that 'people of the same trade seldom meet together … but the conversation ends in a conspiracy against the public or in some contrivance to raise prices'.[10] What Smith favoured was a process of competition in the market to limit such antisocial business behaviour.

It is also important to note that, although Smith was unsympathetic to governments wielding great economic power, his was not a simple advocacy of laissez-faire. In the lectures on jurisprudence that he delivered at the University of Glasgow, he argued that the chief purpose of government is to preserve justice, and that this would require the state to protect the individual's personal rights, property, reputation, and social relations.[11] In *The Wealth of Nations*, he argued that government must carry out important functions in providing defence against foreign invaders, maintaining public institutions (such as those providing for transport, education, and religion), and protecting citizens against injustices suffered at the hands of other citizens.

Nor was Smith in favour of greater economic inequality. By the general standards of the time, an egalitarian sentiment can be discerned in his writing. His was a vision of society in which all people would be making their personal contributions to economic advancement. In his own words, economic progress would stem from 'the uniform, constant and uninterrupted effort of every man to better his condition'.[12] It would be from the grass-roots effort of the great mass of people, rather than from particular leaders of business or finance, that economic progress would emanate.

It must be borne in mind that Smith was writing about a very different economy from today's. The businesses were usually tiny by modern standards. What Smith saw as desirable was competition, not capitalism per se. He was an opponent, first and foremost, of monopoly. He favoured markets, but saw important roles for government. He emphasised the need to have individual incentives, but did not support increased economic inequality. His views helped to undermine the Christian corporate ethic, but he was deeply concerned about the moral dimension of economic behaviour; as political economist Robert Heilbroner notes, 'Smith was by no means oblivious to the moral costs of acquisitiveness'.[13] These are the reasons why the attempt by modern neoliberals to claim descent from Adam Smith is so problematic. To quote Heilbroner again: 'In Smith's hands the interplay of market forces and moral decline takes the form of a subtle dialectic that invests his work with its remarkable depths. In the hands of his successors the dialectic disappears, and the evaluation of economic growth emphasises its material aspects without any concern as to untoward moral consequences, in terms of either motives or social outcomes'.[14]

BOX 9.1   THE IRISH POTATO FAMINE

In the period 1845–49, a disaster befell Ireland. The potato crop, the staple of the Irish peasants' diet, failed in many parts of the country. Disease caused the potatoes to rot in the ground before they could be eaten. The prospect was widespread starvation. What to do about this appalling situation was a major concern for the British government in London. In this context, classical political economy wielded awesome influence. The British leaders had the capacity to resolve, or at least ameliorate, the Irish crisis by arranging for the supply of food from other sources. However, as the historian Cecil Woodham-Smith notes, their actions (or rather, their inaction) were shaped by a belief in an economic theory that almost every politician of the day held to with religious fervour.

> This theory, usually termed laissez-faire, insisted that individuals should be allowed to pursue their own economic interests and that governments should interfere as little as possible. Not only were the rights of property sacred, but private enterprise was also revered and respected and given almost complete liberty; on this theory, which, incidentally, gave the employer and the landlord freedom to exploit his fellow men, the prosperity of nineteenth-century England had unquestionably been based.
>
> The influence of laissez-faire on the treatment of Ireland during the famine is impossible to exaggerate. Almost without exception, the high officials and politicians responsible for Ireland were fervent believers in non-interference by government, and the behaviour of the British authorities only becomes explicable when their fanatical belief in private enterprise and their suspicions of any action that might be considered government intervention are borne in mind.
>
> The loss of the potato crop was, therefore, to be made good, without government interference, by the operations of private enterprise and private firms using the normal channels of commerce. The government was not to appear in food markets as a buyer, there was to be 'no disturbance of the ordinary course of trade' and 'no complaints from private traders' on account of government competition.[15]

Shops and organisations for importing foodstuffs and distributing them were generally found only in prosperous districts of Ireland: in Ulster in the northeast, Dublin, and in some places in eastern Ireland, including the larger towns such as Cork. In the places where relief would be most needed, in the west and southwest, the means by which it could be distributed rarely existed. It is estimated that over a million people died in the famine, and that a further million emigrated because of it. Some joined the flow of emigrants to Australia; many more went to the USA. The Irish potato famine was a tragic episode in which extreme laissez-faire economics played a major part.

Conclusion

Classical political economy provides the basis on which subsequent economic thought about capitalism has developed. It challenged prevailing mercantilist beliefs about what constituted ordered arrangements of economic activity and social progress. It established economic liberalism as the dominant economic outlook, building on existing views about individualism and acquisitiveness. It flourished at a time when the Christian corporate ethic was starting to be eroded. It seemed to be the modern way of understanding economic activity.

In any period of rapid economic and social change, there are always anxieties and tensions. Now, over two centuries after Adam Smith, many of the anxieties and tensions are different but no less problematic. As one perceptive reviewer of our experience of economic progress warns: 'The essential balance between the collectivist and individualist traditions that has existed for most of the last two hundred years may have been a historical accident ... only possible during the transitional phase between the religious pre-capitalist era and the secular capitalist age. If that is so, the prospects for continued human progress are bleak indeed.'[16] The classical political economic reassurances may have passed their use-by date.

KEY POINTS

- The ideas of classical political economy were widely influential during the late eighteenth and nineteenth centuries, particularly in Great Britain; these ideas became yet more widespread as capitalism developed in other nations and colonies.

- Classical political economy reassured sceptics that an economy based on individual self-interest would not result in chaos, and that the greater freedoms of the marketplace would produce economic progress.

- The leading classical political economists, most notably Adam Smith, were well aware that the general case for laissez-faire had to be qualified because of the dangers of monopoly and the need for good government.

10 Value, Distribution, Growth

What, according to the classical political economists, determines the value of goods and services?

What shapes the distribution of income?

What conditions are conducive to economic growth?

As discussed in the previous chapter, classical political economy has had a powerful influence as capitalist ideology. However, the classical political economists were also deeply concerned with the construction of systematic economic analysis. It is to this aspect that we now turn.

A summary of the main analytical concerns of classical political economy is difficult because significant points of difference separated the leading scholars, such as Smith, Ricardo, and Malthus. However, three common themes can usefully be distinguished: value, distribution, and growth. These raise questions about the economy. What is the value of a commodity and how is it determined? What economic forces shape the distribution of income among the members of a society? How is economic growth generated and why does it sometimes stall? This trilogy of concerns has been central to economic analysis ever since.

Value

What determines the value of different goods and services? You may have personally pondered this issue as you surveyed supermarket shelves or wondered whether you can afford a particular purchase. Why do different brands of car have the prices they do? What determines the relative prices of a cup of coffee and a bar of chocolate? Is the value of something purely a question of its market price? Or, does it reflect some innate characteristic of the product or measure of its intrinsic social worth? Philosophical issues mingle with more down-to-earth, empirical issues in such deliberations.

As a broad generalisation, we can identify three contributions to the analysis of value stemming from the works of the classical political economists. First is the distinction between value in use and value in exchange. The water–diamonds paradox is the standard illustration. Water has more value in use than have diamonds: it is an essential item, necessary for life itself. Diamonds are a luxury item with much more limited uses, but they have the higher value in exchange: their market price by weight or volume is far higher than water's. The obvious explanation for this divergence between usefulness and market price is the differences in supply conditions between the two goods. Water is plentiful and needs little labour to make it available for consumption, while diamonds are scarce and take a great deal of effort (prospecting, mining, cutting, polishing) to make them available. According to classical political economy, these supply conditions are crucial in shaping exchange values.

The second proposition follows from this. Broadly speaking, the value of a commodity reflects its cost of production. Where labour is the sole or principal cost, this means that exchange values depend on the amount of labour expended. As Adam Smith said, 'If, among a nation of hunters, it usually costs twice the labour to kill a beaver which it does to kill a deer, one beaver should naturally exchange for, or be worth, two deer.'[1] It seems natural that what is usually the produce of two days' labour should be worth double the produce of one day's labour. This is the essence of the labour theory of value, which Karl Marx was later to develop as a foundation for his critique of capitalism. For the classical political economists, its more limited role was in explaining the relative prices of different goods and services.

Third, the emphasis was on the 'natural price' of each product. This innate value is not necessarily its actual market price at any particular time. It is a sort of long-term equilibrium price around which day-to-day changes in the market price can be expected to fluctuate. If the actual market price is above the natural price for any significant period of time (because of the scarcity of the item in question, for instance), this will induce the entry of new firms into the market to supply the item, and thereby cause the market price to fall. If the actual market price is below the natural price (because of temporary overproduction relative to demand, say), firms will leave the industry, the glut will be eradicated, and the market price will rise. Thus, in the longer term, the natural price tends to prevail.

These three propositions—about the distinction between use values and exchange values, the role of labour in the determination of value, and the character of natural prices—have given rise to a wide range of subsequent developments. The radical twist given by Marx to the labour theory of value, for example, stands in striking contrast to the neoclassical economists' attempt to refocus the explanation of prices on scarcity and utility. Thus, a common foundation in classical political economy underpins rival views about capitalist exploitation and price determination according to supply and demand. What has dropped out of the picture along the way is the notion of natural price. Even more striking is the abandonment of any concern with a *just* price. In this respect, the attempts by classical political economists to develop a theory of value can be considered as a transition from traditional concerns with ethical aspects of market exchange to modern attempts to refashion economics on a supposedly more scientific basis.

Distribution

What determines the distribution of income and wealth within a society? This second concern of the classical political economists has commanded constant attention ever since. One should hardly be surprised. The question 'Who gets what?' is inherently contentious in any society. Under what circumstances will one individual, or a social class, receive the bulk of the income? Under what circumstances can more equitable outcomes be expected? Is it better to have even or uneven distributional outcomes? According to which criteria? Such questions are among the most politically sensitive issues in economic enquiry.

David Ricardo provided perhaps the most notable of the classical political economists' contributions to this topic. He considered the distribution of income among the classes to be 'the principal problem in political economy'. 'Among the classes' is a key phrase here. Three such classes are identified, each receiving a characteristically different type of income:

- capitalists, who receive profit
- landowners, who receive rent
- workers, who receive wages.

These are classes of real people, not inanimate 'factors of production'. Each gets an income dependent on the nature of their economic contribution.

Profits are identified as the reward for business activity and the necessary condition for capital accumulation. However, the capitalists' economic function is not in amassing wealth for its own sake, but in ploughing profits back into further rounds of business activity in order to increase the value of the capital. Thus, making profits is the *raison d'être* of successful business enterprise. As noted in the preceding chapter, this is the positive face of self-interest, whereby the quest for profits contributes to economic prosperity and expansion. But because profit is a surplus (that which is left over after wages have been paid to workers and rents to landowners), its magnitude crucially depends on the size of those other income claims.

Rent is a payment to landowners, reflecting their capacity to capture part of the economic surplus. In the agricultural context, rent is the difference between the value of output from a piece of fertile land and from a piece of land that is just worth cultivating. As Adam Smith wrote, 'As soon as land becomes private property, the landlord demands a share of almost all the produce which the labourer can either raise or collect from it. His rent makes the first deduction from the produce of the labour which is employed by the land.'[2] The land is necessary for production, but the capacity of landlords to charge a rent for all land other than the most marginal means that the income available to workers and capitalists is correspondingly reduced. For capitalists, this means less capacity for capital accumulation. For workers, it means a reduced possibility of earning higher wages, compounding the forces causing their consignment to a subsistence standard of living.

Wages, according to classical political economists, tend to be kept at the minimum level necessary for workers to reproduce themselves. Were wage increases to encroach on profits, the capital accumulation process would be impeded. So, if workers could not significantly share in the economic surplus, they would have to remain at subsistence level. It was a gloomy prediction for the mass of society that had its most depressing form in the famous doctrines of Thomas Malthus.

According to Malthus, population growth would keep the working class poor. If any rise in wage rates occurred, the population would increase, putting pressure on the capacity for food production and driving living standards down to subsistence level. An equilibrium of sorts would be restored, but it would be a diabolical equilibrium of poverty or near-poverty. Population growth, the inexorable consequence of the 'passion between the sexes', would consign the masses to a life of poverty, despite economic growth. Because 'the power of population is infinitely greater than the power in the earth to produce subsistence for men', any attempt to raise wages would be self-defeating.[3] By the same reasoning, any attempt to help the poor would also be self-defeating, since charity would encourage faster population growth and discourage productive effort. This was a very austere view, especially for a churchman, but Malthus evidently felt his austerity and pessimism to be driven by the logic of the situation. It certainly illustrates the 'freedom from extreme sentimentality' in classical political economy.[4]

Overall, these reflections on what determined the distribution of income between the major classes reinforced the view of economic inequalities as inexorable. The classical political economists' concern with liberty did not imply equality. On the contrary, it was the existence, even the 'naturalness', of the class system that underpinned the different types of income and the associated economic inequalities.

Growth

The third issue addressed by classical political economists had more positive connotations. This is the question of what determines the possibility of economic growth. Like the questions of value and distribution, it is a conundrum that continues to be central to political economic deliberations to this day.

How are economic systems able to expand the production of goods and services and the total flows of income and wealth generated? What conditions are conducive to that expansion? What circumstances are likely to impede it, cause stagnation, or even plunge the economy into depression? Is growth necessary, desirable, and sustainable in the longer term? As with the theories of value and distribution, summarising the diverse views of the classical political economists on these issues is not easy. However, for simplicity, we can identify three main themes:

- the division of labour
- the expansion of trade
- the accumulation of capital.

According to classical political economy, the division of labour is the foundation for growth. Smith was particularly emphatic about this, beginning *The Wealth of Nations* with the famous example of a pin factory in which production levels are increased many times over as a result of workers doing more specialised tasks.[5] The higher output made possible by the complex division of labour would lead to higher profit, which could then lead to the purchase of more tools and equipment, further increasing the productive capacity of the enterprise. A virtuous cycle of expansion would ensue. It would not be virtuous in all respects, though: Smith had significant concerns about its implications for the nature of work itself. This is what we might now call the problem of worker alienation. In Smith's own words, 'The man whose sole life is spent performing a few simple operations ... generally becomes as stupid and ignorant as it is possible for a human creature to become.'[6] There was also the problem of the demand for the product. There would be no point in expanding pin production if there were no growth in the demand for pins. In general, Smith noted, the division of labour is limited by the extent of the market.

The expansion of trade would create the conditions for that increase in demand. This second element in the analysis of growth is closely linked to the theory of comparative advantage developed by Ricardo. This theory seeks to demonstrate that all countries can benefit economically by specialising in producing those items in which they have a relative cost advantage, and then trading with one another in those items. Consider the situation where two countries, A and B, can produce two commodities, X and Y. Even if country A can produce both X and Y more cheaply than country B, the theory of comparative advantage says it should specialise in the one in which it has the greater relative cost advantage, leaving the production of the other to B. International trade will then be to each country's mutual advantage.

Ricardo used the theory of comparative advantage to support the repeal of the Corn Laws, which restricted agricultural imports to Great Britain. Nowadays, the same doctrine is used to support the case for trade liberalisation, including the removal of tariffs imposed on imported goods by national governments. It warrants critical consideration. What is the situation, for example, if the transport costs of international trade substantially offset the benefits of lowered production costs? Or to raise an environmental issue, what is the situation if scarce, non-renewable energy resources are used in that transportation process? Are there not benefits for a nation from having diversified industries (ensuring greater national self-reliance in wartime, for example, or a wider range of employment opportunities for local citizens) that need to be set against the gains from specialisation and trade? Such concerns should caution against the extension of comparative advantage theory to more complex modern situations where there may be sound reasons to restrict trade. From the vantage point of Britain in the nineteenth century, comparative advantage theory constituted a convenient rationale for national self-interest. Its status as a general rationale for free trade, however, is contentious, despite its widespread influence.[7]

What about the possibility of continued capital accumulation? As capitalism was establishing its dominance, many people worried that the growth of its productive capacity would outstrip the market demand for the products. If workers' wages were kept down to subsistence levels, as the classical political economists predicted, this was a likely scenario. Would economic slump then occur? The classic reassurance came from the Frenchman Jean-Baptiste Say. His argument (introduced in Chapter 8) was that, because supply creates its own demand, there was no need to fear a general tendency towards depression, at least not because of overproduction. To be sure, temporary overproduction could occur in any particular industry as a result of miscalculation by the producers, but this would be matched by shortage in another industry. The imbalance would be quickly corrected by a falling price of the product in the industry that overproduced and a rising price in the industry that underproduced.

Malthus was not so confident that a general glut was impossible, arguing that wages, because they are not the total cost of production, may not be sufficient to purchase all that is produced. If that causes prices to fall, the incentive to invest also falls and a prolonged slump may ensue. Excessive savings could have a similar effect, reducing the demand for products and causing stagnation.

Ricardo disagreed, taking basically the same position as Say. He argued that lower wages are a cure for slump, not a cause of it, because businesses will hire the idle workers with the capital created by savings. According to this reasoning, savings are not an end in themselves, but a means of generating capital in order to employ labour. The potential imbalance between savings and investment, which Keynes was later to emphasise, was not considered. According to Galbraith, adherence to Say's Law was 'the prime test by which economists were distinguished from crackpots' until Keynes challenged the classical orthodoxy.[8]

Did these doctrines paint a rosy picture for the prospects of capitalist development? At first sight it may seem so. The classical political economists' emphasis on the benefits arising from the division of labour and the expansion of trade, and the general confidence that there need be no problem of overproduction, seemed to bode well for the future of capitalism, even though the workers could not expect a substantial rise in their material living standards. Yet a pessimistic mood prevailed. Yes, the division of labour and the expansion of trade could create conditions for growth in the wealth of nations, but this would lead to population growth, too. Land that was less productive would then need to be brought under cultivation. This would cause food prices to rise, and so the general level of wages, in money terms, would have to rise in order to ensure that workers continued to subsist. That rise in wages would reduce profits, slowing capital accumulation and economic growth.

This slowing of capital accumulation could result in a 'stationary state'. For Ricardo, this prospect of a stationary state was undesirable, because it presaged a situation in which the dynamics of economic growth were not able to operate. The pessimistic nature of this prognosis is reflected in Thomas Carlyle's famous description of political economy as the 'dismal science'.[9] John Stuart Mill, on the other hand, viewed the prospect of a stationary state in a favourable light as the basis for a progressive society, in which people could turn their attention from mundane economic matters to higher cultural and artistic pursuits.

JOHN STUART MILL (1806-73)

John Stuart Mill was widely regarded as the greatest political economist of his day and the successor to Smith and Ricardo. His magnum opus, *Principles of Political Economy*, was published in 1849 and remained the standard reference on the subject for the best part of half a century until it was displaced by Alfred Marshall's *Principles of Economics*.

A child prodigy, Mill was said to have made 'a complete survey of all there was to be known in the field of political economy' when only 13 years old, having already learnt Latin and Ancient Greek, mastered geometry, algebra, and differential calculus, and written a Roman history, a history of Holland, and an abridged version of the *Ancient Universal History*.[10] His father, the historian and philosopher James Mill, had insisted on this childhood of extreme intellectualism, allowing no holidays 'lest the habit of work should be broken and a taste for idleness acquired'.[11]

The wonder is that Mill junior not only avoided being emotionally crippled by his upbringing, but that he also went on to be a notably humane man, combining the principles of political economy with ethical social concerns. He supported democratic reforms and was an advocate for women's rights.

Mill's political economy textbook synthesised the classical ideas. However, he parted company with other classical political economists in one key respect—by emphasising the malleability of income distribution. He argued that, although economic principles govern production, political choices can shape distribution. Thus, once wealth has been produced, we can share it as we collectively choose, untrammelled by any absolute laws of political economy. In his own words, 'The distribution of wealth, therefore, depends on the laws and customs of society'.[12] It is a matter of politics, not economics. This was the basis for a more optimistic view of the prospects for humankind than was to be found in Malthus, in particular, and the work of the 'dismal science' in general.

Mill thought that reason would prevail in public affairs. Once the working classes understood the Malthusian problem of population growth causing food shortage, they would voluntarily regulate their numbers. Eventually, the economy would reach a stationary state, in which there would be plenty of scope for social betterment. The government would create a more equal society by taxing rents and inheritances.

Mill's mild socialism had little in common with the revolutionary socialism that Marx propounded. As Heilbroner describes it, it was 'a doctrine English to the core: gradualist, optimistic, realistic and devoid of radical overtones'.[13] An echo of Mill's views may be discerned today in the claim by orthodox economists that efficiency is an economic concern and equity a political concern. Unfortunately, this usually leads to the concern with equity being set aside. Mill would have been aghast at this tendency.

Conclusion

The classical political economists laid the foundation for understanding capitalist development. They were, in effect, seeking to do for the study of social phenomena what Isaac Newton had done for the study of the physical world. For this purpose, the economy could be likened to a clock: if one could understand the mechanism, then one could explain the regularities in its working. Thus, the quest was to discover the laws of motion in economic life. In Newton's theory there was the law of gravity; in classical political economic theory self-interest was the propulsive element in an essentially 'natural' economic system.

The view of the economy as a means of producing an economic surplus is also central to the classical interpretation. It underpins much of the theory summarised in this chapter. An economic surplus is the excess of the value of production over and above what is merely necessary to reproduce the economy. How it is generated, how it is distributed, and the purposes for which it is used are the key determinants of how the economy works. The concern to understand this economic surplus constitutes an element of continuity between classical political economy and modern political economy, and a point of contrast with neoclassical economics.

The classical political economists were holistic thinkers. They did not artificially separate the study of economic phenomena from history, geography, politics, and the study of society in general. Modern political economy, as we shall see in later chapters, is partly an attempt to regain this position. It seeks to reestablish an interdisciplinary mode of analysis concerned with the study of value, distribution, growth and the economic dimensions of social progress in general.

KEY POINTS

- According to classical political economy, the value of goods and services depends primarily on the cost of producing them.

- Classical explanations of the distribution of income focus attention on the origins of profit, wages, and rents, and on the relationship between capitalists, workers, and landowners as the principal social classes that receive those different incomes.

- Explaining growth requires analysis of how the division of labour lifts labour productivity, how the principle of comparative advantage drives the growth of trade, and how the incomes resulting from production of goods and services flow into purchases of those goods and services.

11 ▶ Land and Economic Surplus

> *Is land economically important?*
>
> *Is the rent of land a drain on economic progress?*
>
> *Should land rent be taxed?*

The analysis of land has a rather shadowy presence in modern economics. In agricultural economics and natural resource economics it cannot, of course, be ignored. Elsewhere it tends to be treated either as a factor of production—on a par with labour and capital—or as part of the backdrop to the real economic action of production, distribution, and exchange. In classical political economy, however, the analysis of land was a central concern.

Why the change? To some extent the neglect of land in recent economic theorising reflects changed material economic conditions. Economic modernisation, particularly over the last century, has caused proportionately fewer people to be directly engaged in farming. Modern technologies have also made more and more industries 'footloose'; that is, not tied to particular geographical locations. All economic and social activities involve the use of land in some way, but the modern economy in general seems less place bound. Neglect of the role that land plays in the economy also has an ideological dimension. Attention is diverted from the economic and social consequences of private land ownership, now seemingly so normal as not to require analysis. Therein lies a significant bias. Its redress requires some reconsideration of what the leading classical political economists had to say about land. It also requires attention be given to the radical variation on the theme of land ownership in the writings and teaching of Henry George. As we will see, these ideas are directly relevant to modern political economy.

The significance of land in different economic systems

From an ecological perspective, it is particularly important that the use of land be carefully considered. Land is fundamentally different from labour and capital because its supply is inherently limited. It is part of our natural resource endowment. Even from a narrowly economic perspective, it is clear that the availability, use, and productivity of land (both in rural and urban contexts) has a major bearing on the capacity for economic growth. From a broader social perspective, land is also special. Some of us enjoy roaming over publicly accessible tracts of land, while others enjoy exclusive use of small parcels of it. Managing the tension between these public and private aspects of land is a key issue for public policy.

There are enormous differences in the ways in which land is allocated and used. Consider, first, the role of land in traditional Aboriginal societies, such as the Aboriginal peoples of Australia or the Native American peoples of North America. Land is integral to subsistence and to community: indeed, it is usually not seen as something separate from life itself. People exist through being in, and of, nature. The land provides the sustenance that makes life possible. The people may be regarded as its custodians, but it makes little sense to think of them individually or collectively owning the land. They no more own the land than it owns them. Land is simultaneously history, geography, and spirituality; it is not a marketable economic asset.

Under feudalism, land also has a crucial, but quite different, role. Command over the disposition of land is a defining feature of the economic and social order. A person's relationship to the land significantly defines his or her social standing. The privileged position of the ruling class depends on control of the large areas of land that its members possess. They call the shots because they control the key resource that enables them to capture the lion's share of the economic surplus. The mass of the people, on the other hand, are in a position of economic dependency and social subordination because their livelihood depends on their access to land that they do not own.

For the classical political economists, the emergence of capitalism from this feudal order needed to be understood. The transition involved a significant change in the distribution of economic power. It saw a switch from landowners being the dominant element in the ruling class to capitalists being the ascendant element—economically, if not socially and politically. The landowners still dominated parliament in Great Britain, for example. Then, as now, changes in the composition of the ruling class tended to lag behind the economic changes.

So it was natural that, in order to understand the economic conditions of their era, the classical political economists should pay particular attention to questions about land: its ownership, how income is derived from it, and the size of that income relative to other incomes derived from labour and capital. Indeed, even before the age of classical political economy, the land question had been central to economic discourse. The French physiocrats, a group of Enlightenment thinkers of the 1760s, argued that land—a gift of nature—was the only real source of wealth, because it enabled agriculture to generate a net product in excess of production costs.[1]

Rent as a brake on economic progress?

Of the classical political economists, David Ricardo made the most well-developed analysis of the role of land in economic progress. Himself a landowner, Ricardo was nevertheless no apologist for the interests of the landowning class. On the contrary, he saw the capacity of landowners to obtain a major share in the economic surplus as an obstacle to economic development. According to Ricardo, the income that landowners derive in the form of rent comes from the incomes that would otherwise go to capitalists and workers. Insofar as it comes from the profit share, rent impedes the process of capital accumulation and thus limits economic growth. It is an argument that is of continuing significance, notwithstanding the greater interpenetration of land and capital ownership in modern capitalism.

Rent has to be carefully defined. We are used to thinking of it as a payment for the use of housing. We commonly talk of 'renting' a house or a flat (or, generally, any commodity for hire, such as a car or a floor-sanding machine). In that popular sense, we are talking of a payment for temporary access to, or use of, the property. It is important to emphasise that, in this chapter, rent is being used in a more specific sense. It refers only to a payment for land: in other words, it is a site rent. What we normally call the rent for a house can be seen as having two components: the site rent for the land and the payment for hiring the house that stands on the land. Only the first of these two components can properly be called rent for the purposes of the current analysis. Defining rent in this way immediately draws attention to its class character: its association with the wealth and power of landowners.

According to Ricardo, 'the interest of the landlord is always opposed to the interest of every other class in the community'.[2] Why is this so? The Ricardian theory is based on two key assumptions. The first is that land differs in its fertility—so all lands can be ranked from the most fertile to the least fertile. The second is that competition equalises the profit rate among farmers who hire land from landowners. Box 11.1 shows how the revenue generated by the economic use of land has to be shared between landowners, capitalists (the tenant farmers in this model), and workers (the farm employees). The general tendency is for profits to be squeezed because landowners capture a share of the economic surplus generated. Indeed, as more land is brought under cultivation (that is, previously submarginal land becomes marginal), the proportion of the total value of production captured by landowners increases. So, even if wages remain at subsistence level, the profit share declines.

Therein lies a deeply troubling paradox. According to this analysis, profits are the source of capital accumulation, the driving force in the capitalist system, but they are increasingly hard to sustain as economic expansion occurs. Growth is stymied by the diversion of the economic surplus into rent payments. 'Do away with the landowners' is an understandable response. As a member of parliament in the midst of other members who represented landowners' interests, Ricardo took a more reformist stance. He thought the problem could be significantly reduced by the removal of the impediments to trade that led to farmers cultivating land of low fertility. He argued forcefully that the repeal of the Corn Laws, which protected local agriculture from competition from imports, would counter the tendency for rents to rise at the expense of profits.

Whether free trade is the appropriate antidote to the power and wealth of landowners remains a contentious point. Restrictions on agricultural trade are still commonly justified by those wanting to protect the interests of rural landholders and regional communities whose economic prosperity depends on such protection. The Japanese government, for example, imposes restrictions on rice imports, seeking to maintain the viability of the local farming sector, whose importance is social and cultural as well as economic. Although the case for such policies is not normally couched in terms of safeguarding landowners' interests at the expense of capital and labour, that is the usual economic effect. It runs counter to the Ricardian argument for squeezing rents by breaking down the impediments to agricultural trade.

The Ricardian view can be considered part of the general case, considered in the preceding chapter, for trade liberalisation based on the principle of comparative advantage. Restrictions such as the Corn Laws impeded the process of specialisation, which free trade is held to encourage. On this reasoning, it is free trade that is the antidote to the power of landowners to capture the economic surplus as rent. It is a chain of reasoning thoroughly in keeping with the classical political economists' view of the extension of markets as a progressive force for economic change.

BOX 11.1   RENT, WAGES, PROFIT: A RICARDIAN VIEW

Figure 11.1, on the next page, depicts how the value of the produce from land is shared between landowners, capitalists, and workers. The vertical axis measures the monetary values of the land and its produce, while the horizontal axis measures the amount of land used (the number of hectares, for instance).

The line showing the value of the additional product (for example, wheat) from each successive unit of land slopes down to the right as less fertile land is brought under cultivation. In other words, the marginal product of land declines as more is used.

The rent is the difference between the value of product generated by each unit of land and the value generated by the marginal unit; that is, the last piece of land brought under cultivation. This is the differential rent. It is the upper limit of what landowners can charge farmers for using their superior quality land (the land that is more fertile than the marginal land). If OA units of land are used, the total rent is the shaded triangular area XYZ.

FIGURE 11.1 INCOMES FROM THE USE OF LAND

How is the rest of the value (that is, the area OAYZ) shared among farmers and those who work for the farmers as employees? If, as the preceding chapter argued, employees' wages are kept at subsistence level (OW in the graph), then the total wage share is shown by the area OAVW, leaving VWZY as the profit share to go to the farmers as a return on their investment of capital and effort.

Now visualise the situation in which the economy has expanded and more land has been brought under cultivation. The share of rent in the total value produced increases. In the extreme, the profit share disappears (when OC land is used). This illustrates the general tendency for profits to be squeezed out between rents and wages. If wages are raised as more land is brought under cultivation, the squeeze is yet tighter. This may occur when food becomes more expensive, because inferior land has to be used and the subsistence wage is consequently increased. In that case, the line showing the wage rate would slope upwards to the right, which would mean that profits would be eliminated even more quickly as additional units of land were cultivated. Under capitalism this would bode ill for the future of economic growth.

A general assault on land rent

The argument so far has been couched mainly in terms of agricultural land. However, similar principles apply if we consider the use of land in an urban context. Instead of thinking of the land as having a capacity to earn differential rent according to its fertility, we can now visualise its capacity to earn differential rent according to its accessibility (to centres of commercial activity). As a city grows, more land is brought into urban use (for housing, industrial purposes, water storage, waste disposal, and so forth). As in the agricultural model, that more extensive land use raises the capacity of existing urban land to earn even higher levels of rent. So, as towns grow, the landowners are the primary beneficiaries, at the expense of capitalists and workers. Some claim that this process is operating in modern cities, with dramatically adverse economic and social consequences.[3] The ideas of the nineteenth-century social reformer Henry George, as well as those of David Ricardo, are pertinent to understanding these contemporary processes.

As George emphasised, land is essentially a gift of nature. Problems start to arise when it becomes privately owned. As more of nature's gift is used for income-generating purposes, a greater share of the society's total income goes to those who have acquired property rights in land. In the development of the USA, for example, the westward movement of the settlers, and their capture of the land from the Indigenous peoples, vastly increased the material wealth of the settler society. With economic growth in general, the increased value of the land is captured for private rather than public purposes. Coupled with the unequal distribution of its ownership, this exacerbates socioeconomic inequalities. Land may often be held idle because it is bought and sold for speculative gain. That speculation then fuels further socioeconomic inequality, as well as diverting funds from productive purposes.

Henry George's analysis of land as a source of these continuing socioeconomic problems deserves careful consideration. As with other political economic doctrines, it is useful to interpret the arguments and their influence in historical context.

BOX 11.2   HENRY GEORGE (1839-97)

Henry George was the founder of a social movement that, in its time, rivalled Marxism as a major force for radical political economic change. George's focus on the inefficiencies and inequities associated with the private ownership of land, and on the simple remedy of land taxation, inspired many social activists. The ideas he pioneered are still of significant contemporary relevance.

Unlike most of the other intellectual giants in the history of political economy, George had no academic credentials. As a young man in the USA, he had various jobs, eventually turning to journalism, running a struggling little newspaper in San Francisco. He visited New York in 1869 to set up a telegraphic news bureau for the paper (unsuccessfully, as it turned out, because of opposition from larger and more powerful press and telegraph monopolies). While in New York—then the epitome of the modern capitalist city—he was dismayed by the gross inequalities that he witnessed between rich and poor. He asked himself why, in a country so blessed by nature, with more than enough resources for all, there should be such maldistribution. By all accounts, the answer—and the remedy—came to him in a blinding flash.

He began writing his analysis of how rents appropriated by landowners were at the root of all such economic and social problems, and how a single tax on land rent could provide the remedy. From a Georgist perspective, the capture of the economic surplus in the form of rent is at the expense of ordinary working people. As George said, 'The increase in land values is always at the expense of labour'.[4] In the Ricardian view, rent is usually at the expense of profits (since wages are destined to remain at a subsistence level anyway).

The Georgist view had more political appeal because most people, it seems, would benefit from redressing this source of social injustice.

George's work appeared in a series of pamphlets, and then in his major book, *Progress and Poverty*, which was published in 1879. *Progress and Poverty* was translated into 15 languages and sold millions of copies. George travelled internationally, preaching his distinctive gospel. In Australia, his public meetings enjoyed massive attendances. George's diagnosis of the injustices associated with the 'land question' had widespread appeal in a frontier economy like Australia, comparable in this respect to the USA.

The strong social movement that Henry George started is no longer the force it once was. Sadly, it seems more people today are concerned with claiming a stake in the land racket than they are with the reform of public policy regarding land. As a consequence, our cities become more expensive to live in and more socially divided, and most of the economic surplus goes into higher land values that yield private rather than public benefits.

The obvious solution to the economic inefficiencies and social injustices arising from private land ownership is public ownership. The collective land resources could then be used according to whatever development plan the society establishes. However, Henry George did not consider this necessary, because he shared the classical political economists' aversion to an extensive role for the state in the direct management of economic resources. He favoured a market-orientated approach, but with a uniform land tax. Other classical political economists, including David Ricardo, favoured substantial land taxes, but George was unique in thinking that a general tax on the site rent of land would be sufficient to finance all the necessary public expenditures of government. A land tax is the best sort of tax, Georgists have consistently argued, because it creates an incentive to use all land for its most productive purpose in order to generate the revenue to pay the tax. By contrast, taxes on labour and capital create disincentives to productive effort. A single tax on land that would replace all personal income taxes, business taxes, inheritance taxes, and taxes on goods and services, is held to be more economically efficient.

Whether a single tax on site rents today could generate sufficient revenue to finance all government expenditures is debatable, given the growth in the array of such expenditures since George's time.[5] But the case for land taxes remains strong. Indeed, local property taxation is widely used as a means of taxing land ownership and generating revenue for local governments. As a matter of political pragmatism, some balance between taxation of land, other assets, income, and expenditure seems inescapable. It also addresses contemporary concerns about the diversion of the economic surplus into the hands of people who make no directly productive economic contribution.[6]

Conclusion

Land is an important topic in political economic analysis. In the era of classical political economy, the central focus was on agricultural land. In the modern economy, urban land warrants comparable attention. Henry George anticipated this over a century ago, when he noted that the contrast between affluence and poverty was most striking in 'the great cities where the ownership of a little patch of ground is a fortune'.[7] That tendency has been multiplied many times over in the intervening period as cities have grown and land prices escalated. Those land prices are a major element in creating divided cities. In conjunction with housing markets, land markets have led to a spatial segmentation of cities into affluent suburbs and poorer areas, the latter sometimes forming ghettos where socioeconomic disadvantage is perpetuated in a vicious circle. As David Harvey, a leading urban geographer, has argued, the rich command space while the poor are trapped in it.[8]

Land, and the intergenerational transmission of its ownership, is a major source of economic and social inequality. This is not a problem of transition between feudalism and capitalism, as it may have been perceived during the age of classical political economy. It is, rather, an enduring feature of a society in which income from property ownership commonly outstrips income from productive effort. However, as the ownership of land has become ever more intertwined with the ownership of capital, there is a need for an analysis of unearned incomes in general (from capital as well as land). In this context the study of Marxist economics is essential.

KEY POINTS

- Although neglected in subsequent economic orthodoxy, the analysis of land and rent was central to classical political economy.
- The capacity of landowners to capture a substantial share of the economic surplus may retard economic progress while also accentuating inequality in the distribution of wealth.
- Land taxation is a means of diverting the economic surplus from landowners to government so that it can then be used to finance social infrastructure and services.

PART IV

The Critique of Capitalism

Marxist Economics

12 Contesting Capitalism

Are Marxist ideas relevant today?

What are the origins of the Marxist critique of capitalism?

What is distinctive about the Marxist method of analysis?

Many different structures have been built on the foundations laid by classical political economy. The neoclassical economists developed their analysis in a conservative direction, maintaining the focus on the beneficial effects of markets, but narrowing the range of social concerns and purging the theory of its explicitly ethical aspects. We look at their work and its influence a little later. Chronologically prior is the contribution of Karl Marx, providing a thorough critique of the capitalist system. It needs careful consideration because of its controversial character and continuing challenges.

Why study Marx?

There is a common view that Marx is dead—not just the man, but his ideas and their relevance to our lives today. It is a view based largely on the problem of constructing a viable alternative to capitalism in practice.[1] The problem with this negative view is that it ignores Marx's central concerns: interpreting the workings of a capitalist economy, understanding economic change, and considering the principles on which alternatives to capitalism might be based. These aspects of Marxism are neither negligible nor passé: they are central to political economy.

There are three reasons to study Marxist political economy. First, it has a key place in the history of economic thought. Marx developed his ideas from classical political economy. The development of subsequent schools of thought in the economics discipline can be interpreted, in large measure, as either extensions of Marx's analysis or reactions against it. Orthodox economist Paul Samuelson once denigrated Marx as a 'minor post-Ricardian'.[2] It is more sensible to see Marx standing centre stage, with the other actors in the drama either challenging him or tiptoeing around pretending he is not there. An understanding of the development of economic ideas would be markedly deficient without some introduction to Marx and Marxism.

Second, Marxist political economy provides a framework for understanding capitalism today. The institutional features of the economy are different in various ways from the economy Marx analysed in the nineteenth century. Yet modern Marxists contend that there are elements of continuity in the fundamental nature of the system: the relationship between capital and labour, the process of capital accumulation, and the contradictions that periodically cause economic crises. These claims warrant careful consideration.[3] Does Marxism indeed have the capacity to explain the persistence of poverty amid affluence and the continuing problems of economic inequality, underdevelopment, and recessions? How can the basic Marxist tenets be updated and revised for this purpose?

Third, Marxism demands attention because it has had such a great influence in the world. It has inspired numerous liberation struggles. Marx's insistence that it is people who make history—albeit in circumstances not of their choosing—has given this current of political economic thought an essentially activist element. This is where many of the problems with interpreting socialism and communism in practice begin, for all sorts of political acts have been carried out in the name of Marxism. Our concern here is with the Marxist analysis of capitalism and, for this purpose, we can largely set aside the experience of trying to construct non-capitalist economies. By concentrating on the analysis of capitalism, we can situate Marx's analysis in relation to the classical political economy that preceded it and the developments in orthodox economics since.

Marx sought to understand capitalism in its entirety: its emergence from feudalism, its internal dynamics and contradictions, and the type of economic system that might follow it. He developed a view of the political economic process as restless, evolutionary, and potentially revolutionary. Marx, in effect, tried to emulate Charles Darwin, whose ideas about biological evolution were so influential. He was looking for the forces that drove economic, social, and political change. He was doing so at a time when dramatic changes were taking place in Britain and Europe, when capitalism was evolving and reshaping society in its own image.

BOX 12.1   KARL MARX (1818-83)

Karl Marx is surely the most controversial figure in the history of political economy. His analysis of capitalism, and his advocacy of a socialist alternative, has had enormous influence.

Marx was born in Trier, in what is now Germany. At university he studied law and mixed with a group of radical intellectuals called the Young Hegelians, who were followers of the philosophy of G. W. F. Hegel (1770-1831). Marx's increasingly critical social and political views found expression in articles he wrote for newspapers. His growing reputation as a dissident eventually led to the closure of the journal he edited.

He took refuge in France and then Belgium, where the authorities also found his presence unwelcome. In Galbraith's words, 'Germany, France and Belgium would all unite in the view that Marx was an excellent resident of some other country'. Marx eventually settled in London with his wife and family. They lived poorly, dependent on the small income generated by Marx's writing for newspapers and on the financial support of friends, particularly Friedrich Engels, with whom he wrote *The Communist Manifesto*.

Marx spent a great deal of time in the reading room of the British Museum, immersing himself in the works of the classical political economists. His radical reinterpretation of their ideas contributed to his analysis of the capitalist economy, which he developed in his own three-volume work *Capital* and in numerous other books and pamphlets. These works stand as the most powerful critique of the capitalist system ever written.

Marx was also concerned with practical matters. He sought to organise the working classes so that they could challenge capitalism. He founded the International Working Men's Association in 1864 and convened its first meeting, known as the First International, in 1866. He did not see the capitalist system overthrown in his own lifetime, although the 1848 uprising in Paris seemed to herald that possibility before it was brutally crushed.

Marx died in 1883 and was buried at Highgate cemetery in North London. The cemetery continues to be visited by his followers and by those who are merely curious about this person who has had so much influence on the world. Entrance to the cemetery was once free; visitors now have to pay to get in.

The historical context

In the first half of the nineteenth century, the Industrial Revolution transformed Great Britain, then Europe and the USA. It was in Great Britain, particularly in rapidly growing industrial towns, that the face of capitalism was most clearly evident. Marx and his collaborator Friedrich Engels did not think it a pretty sight. The views of the classical political economists seemed out of kilter with observable reality. Capitalism in practice seemed to be a dynamic but rapacious system based on the alienation and exploitation of labour. It produced glaring economic inequalities and periodic economic crises.

What were the major changes then taking place? Most obvious was the growth of the factory system, replacing the putting-out system. Instead of workers making products in their own homes and selling them to merchants, they now increasingly went to work at the premises of their employer. They worked in factories, mines, shops, and warehouses for wage payments—usually paid by the hour. Wage labour was not new, of course, but it had now become the norm. It was an arrangement that suited capitalist employers. It gave them more direct control over the workers' time, and more direct control over the quality of the products, than they had under the putting-out system. However, it also raised complex problems, such as the management of larger groups of workers. It created an identifiable industrial working class.

Many businesses continued to be small-scale operations, owned and managed by individuals and families. However, joint stock companies (businesses that were owned by their shareholders) became increasingly common. So a class of absentee owners was able to derive unearned income from business enterprises. The disposition of this income from the ownership of capital became crucial for the growth of the economy. Would it be ploughed back into investment to expand productive capacity or used for luxury consumption purposes? The accumulation of wealth created some significant tensions for capitalist development.

There is debate about whether the material conditions of working people improved during the period of the Industrial Revolution. When compared with the debilitating rural poverty they had previously experienced, living in conditions of urban poverty may have been a small step up for some people. But the general conditions of the labouring masses in the towns were deplorable: child labour was common, as were working days of between 14 and 18 hours; terrible industrial accidents were frequent; and housing conditions were horrendous. There was chronic overcrowding, poor sanitation, and widespread incidence of disease. Life was short and mean.

Capitalism did not seem to be delivering the ordered and progressive outcomes its champions had promised. Here was a situation crying out for a thorough critique. And of critics there was no shortage. The disruptive social consequences of rapid economic change were the target of both conservatives and socialists. Some of the latter sought to design utopian alternatives:

- Frenchman Henri de Saint-Simon argued that government should actively intervene in production, distribution, and commerce in order to promote the welfare of the masses

- Englishman William Godwin, critical of both capitalism and government, emphasised education and reason as the means of ushering in a socialist alternative

- Welsh humanitarian Robert Owen blended visionary utopian thinking with practical measures to improve the living conditions of the workers at his factory in Scotland and in other model communities, such as 'New Harmony' in the USA

- Frenchman Charles Fourier promoted the idea of cooperatives as an alternative to the wastes of capitalism.[5]

Karl Marx thought 'utopian socialism' inadequate because such schemes did not comprehensively address the root causes of class inequality and exploitation. Working in conjunction with Engels, he sought to develop a more comprehensive political economic critique of capitalism that blended analysis of the current economic situation with a political program for systemic change. The analysis pioneered by Marx and Engels was, and is, distinctive in at least three respects: the scope of enquiry, the method of analysis, and the key political economic concepts.

BOX 12.2 — FRIEDRICH ENGELS (1820-95)

Engels is mainly remembered for his working partnership with Karl Marx. It was a remarkable partnership, not least because Engels was a capitalist. He managed his German family's substantial textile business in Manchester, England.

Three aspects of his relationship with Marx are noteworthy. First, as a relatively wealthy person, Engels was able to give financial assistance to the impecunious Marx. Therein lies an irony. The profits from the Engels family business, extracted through the exploitation of labour, helped to finance the production of books and pamphlets exposing the system of exploitation and to organise its overthrow. Engels shared Marx's revolutionary socialist views, and both knew that the system would not be changed by individual employers turning their backs on the process of capitalist commodity production. Better to use some of the profits to foster the development of progressive ideas and political activities.

Second, Engels was a creative thinker and a powerful writer in his own right. He documented the terrible living conditions of the working class in Manchester, which was the epitome of a rapidly industrialising capitalist city. He wrote about the housing question, exploring what was at the root of the appalling housing problems.[6] He also wrote about the role of the family in relation to private property, looking at nuclear family and marriage as institutions that can be oppressive to the individuals within them. Many regard Engels as a clearer writer than the brilliant, but sometimes obscure and disorganised, Marx. *The Manifesto of the Communist Party* is the best known and most polemic of their joint works, but many of their other works also benefited enormously from Engels's clarity of expression.

Third, Engels outlived Marx by 12 years. During that time he assembled many of Marx's unfinished notes and manuscripts and put them into a form suitable for publication. Only the first volume of *Capital* had been published before Marx's death. Engels arranged for the publication of the other two volumes, and thereby contributed mightily to the foundation of the Marxist tradition of radical scholarship.

The remainder of this chapter briefly considers the wide range of concerns addressed by Marxism and the distinctive method used in analysing them. The following five chapters then examine key concepts, such as the mode of production, surplus value, the circuit of capital accumulation, imperialism, and economic crises. In this way we develop a view of what is distinctive about the Marxist approach to political economic analysis.

The scope of Marxism

The following nine themes illustrate the broad range of concerns.

The study of social classes

The emphasis is on people, how the economy structures their interests, and how their conflicting interests are expressed. Marxists deride the tendency for other currents of economic analysis to focus on things, rather than people, as commodity fetishism.

The analysis of exploitation

The relationship between classes under capitalism is not symmetrical. Because capital hires labour, and not vice versa, there is the possibility—indeed, the inevitability—of exploitation. Marxist analysis treats this as a systemic feature, dependent not on the rapacious inclinations of individual employers, but rather on the structural imperatives of the capitalist economy.

The growth of monopoly power

Competitive markets are sometimes held to be the essence of capitalism, but Marxists emphasise the tendency for them to be supplanted by monopolistic enterprises. This further accentuates the disparities of economic power as 'the big fish eat the little fish'.

The expansionary nature of capitalism

Marxist analysis focuses on the reproduction and growth of the economy, emphasising the dynamism of the capital accumulation process. This directs attention to the process of imperialism and, in modern capitalism, to the role of transnational corporations in driving the globalisation of capital.

Uneven development

Capitalism has always been characterised by great variability—spatially and temporally. Its uneven development over space is manifest in the contrast between rapidly expanding cities and economically stagnant regions. Its uneven development over time is manifest in alternating periods of boom and slump. These, too, are focal points of Marxist analysis.

The commodification of social life

It is important to understand how economic forces shape and reshape our social activities. According to Marxists, the expansionary character of capitalism tends, little by little, to transform social pursuits into marketable commodities. Sport, popular music, and education are pertinent contemporary examples.

Alienation

Here, too, is a tendency that Marxists see embedded in the economic structures of capitalism. Alienation arises because workers have no control over their own labour or the products of their labour. However, alienation is not limited to the workplace. According to radical political economists, it extends into other forms: economic, social, political, and environmental.

The role of the state

As stressed in Chapter 6, capitalism is not, in practice, a purely free-market economy. The state plays a major role in relation to competing class interests. In general, Marxists take the view that the state serves capitalist class interests, although there are many variations on that theme.

Social change

The Marxian approach emphasises the processes causing economic and social transformation, sometimes evolutionary and sometimes revolutionary in nature. Capitalism followed other systems of economic organisation, and can be expected, eventually, to be replaced by other arrangements.

The Marxist method

In general, what you see depends on how you look. As just noted, the Marxian perspective is very broad, looking at the interconnections between economic, social, and political issues. In seeking to systematically analyse this broad array of issues, the Marxist method is simultaneously historical, materialist, and dialectical.

To say that the method of Marxism is historical means that the principal focus is on historical processes, on change over time. The obvious point of contrast is with the focus in orthodox economic theory on equilibrium conditions at a particular point in time, as we will see in Part V of this book. The Marxian focus on history follows from the concern to study the evolution of economic systems.

To say that the method of Marxism is materialist requires a rather fuller explanation. In the philosophical context, materialist is the opposite of idealist. It denotes a primary focus on material conditions, such as the prevailing economic structure, as the key factor shaping society. The German philosopher Hegel, whose ideas strongly influenced Marx in his youth, propounded an idealist philosophy that saw the 'totality of natural, historical, and spiritual aspects of the world represented as a process of constant transformation'.[8] Marx is said to have 'stood Hegel on his head' by emphasising the primary importance of material conditions rather than ideas.[9] In his own words, 'It is not the consciousness of men that determines their existence, on the contrary, their social existence determines their consciousness'.[10] That material and ideological conditions interact is widely accepted. The distinctive feature of the materialist position is to regard the material conditions as the leading factor driving social change.

Putting the historical and materialist aspects of Marxist methodology together produces historical materialism; this is the view that material factors, especially economic conditions, drive social change. This is what is sometimes known as the materialist conception of history. When Marx hit on this concept he knew he was on to something really big. It is the claim that the broad sweep of history is not a series of random or independent events, but rather a process that has a structure shaped by economic conditions. This is one of the most controversial claims in the whole of social science.

The third element in the Marxist method—integrated with the historical materialist perspective—is dialectics. To say that the method of Marxism is dialectical means that the focus is on the conflicts and contradictions, internal to the economic system, that propel change. As Marx and Engels wrote at the very beginning of the *Manifesto of the Communist Party*, 'The history of all hitherto existing society is the history of class struggles.'[11] This puts the focus on the conflict of interests; for example, conflict between employers and employees over the organisation of work and its remuneration. It emphasises that it is the contradictory elements within an economic system that create progress. It thereby emphasises the progressive character of class struggle. It has given participants in countless anti-capitalist political activities and liberation movements the dignity of representing a historical imperative.

The activist element brings in the final element of the Marxist method: praxis. Marxism claims to be not merely a method for the analysis of capitalism; it also claims to be simultaneously a tool for transforming it into socialism. This integration of theory and political practice differentiates Marxism from more detached scholarly activities. Marx himself was a scholar, studying the work of the classical political economists and developing detailed critiques, but always with a political purpose. Praxis requires that scholarship be blended with activism.

There are some interesting tensions in all this. If it is material conditions, rather than ideas, that propel social and political change, why bother with the construction of a theory about capitalism? Is not theorising inherently idealist? And, if the structural conflicts and contradictions within capitalism are destined to usher in socialism, why bother to organise a revolutionary movement? Why not just await the inevitable? These seem to be paradoxical aspects of historical and dialectical materialism, considered in the context of Marxist politics. The notion of praxis provides the reconciliation. By emphasising the importance of material interests and ideas—the unity of action and theory—it indicates the holistic character of the Marxist method. As the inscription on Marx's tombstone reads, 'The philosophers have only interpreted the world in various ways: the point however is to change it'.

Conclusion

Marxism provides the basis for a comprehensive critique of capitalism. In his own time, Karl Marx addressed the problems of a rapidly industrialising society in which exploitation and class conflict were increasingly blatant. The scope of the analysis he and Engels developed was similar to classical political economy in its breadth, although quite different in its political implications. The method of analysis emphasised the study of contradictory elements in historical change.

Marxist political economy has always been highly controversial, and continues to be so today. Its emphasis on capitalism's tendencies to inequality, instability, and insecurity gives it a distinctively radical character. For more than a century it has been a rallying point for anti-capitalist sentiments. In studying Marxism, it is important to keep an open mind about the extent to which the analysis needs to be developed, modified, or rejected in the light of changes to capitalism since the time Marx wrote. That requires careful study of one of the most influential thinkers of the last two centuries and an assessment of the relevance of his ideas today.

KEY POINTS

- Marxist economics builds on foundations in classical political economy to develop a comprehensive critique of capitalism.

- Its breath of scope is exceptional, in that it focuses on social classes, exploitation, monopoly power, capitalist expansion and uneven development, commodification and alienation, the state and social change.

- Its method of analysis is historical, materialist, and dialectical. It also emphasises the integration of analysis and activism.

13 The Mode of Production

Does the economy shape the society?

What is distinctive about capitalism as a mode of production?

How are class relationships structured in such an economy?

In grappling with a broad array of social, economic, and political concerns, a systematic and sequential approach is needed. The Marxian inclination is to begin with the study of how production is organised and how wealth is thereby generated. Understanding the characteristics of society as a whole, including its political institutions, then follows. The analysis thereby moves from the study of the economic base to the study of the social superstructure. In a famous passage, Marx said: 'The economic structure of society [is] the real foundation on which rise legal and political superstructures and to which correspond definite forms of social consciousness.'[1] Thus Marx began, as Russian revolutionary Lenin put it, 'by selecting from all the social relations the production relations as being the basic and prime relations that determine all other relations'.[2]

BOX 13.1   BASE AND SUPERSTRUCTURE

Does the economic base shape the social superstructure? A direct link of this kind is not hard to visualise. Take educational institutions, for example. Schools, technical colleges, and universities are an important aspect of the modern social superstructure. Their form is, to a considerable extent, shaped by the needs of the economy. These needs are partly ideological—for a workforce inculcated with values conducive to the acceptance of authority structures in the workplace. The needs are also practical—for a certain number of skilled technicians, for a certain number of semiskilled process workers, labourers, and so on. Schools, technical colleges, and universities are structured in such a way that they produce these 'outputs' in more or less the required proportions. Indeed, in recent years there have been many calls from political leaders for this link to be an even more emphatic policy objective. Rhetoric about the need for the education system to play a more direct role in fostering the development of a 'clever country' or a 'knowledge nation', for example, has a clearly instrumental character. It implies that the education system should be reshaped to meet national economic needs, first and foremost, rather than cater for the personal development or cultural enrichment of the people involved. The greater emphasis on university courses in business and management, relative to more traditional areas of study in arts and sciences, is symptomatic. The application of economic criteria in evaluating the effectiveness of the education system is also more pervasive. The educational institutions themselves have become more entrepreneurial in their own behaviour, especially as the politicians' calls for better economic outputs have not been matched by the necessary public funding.[3] Overall, these superstructural institutions are being shaped and remoulded to serve the economic requirements of contemporary capitalism.

If that were the whole of the story, the base–superstructure model would fit neatly. However, other tensions and contradictions exist. Within educational institutions are strong traditions emphasising the pursuit of the truth and the development of critical reasoning. Such traditions may not sit comfortably with short-run capitalist interests— although they are surely important in fostering innovation and social progress in the longer term. So it makes more sense to think of the base–superstructure relationship as a two-way relationship. In other words, the character of the superstructure affects the base as well as vice versa. Indeed, if that were not so, changes in the economic base would always be quickly followed by corresponding changes in the social superstructure. Changing the economic system from one based on private ownership to one based on public ownership, for example, would necessarily produce a corresponding change in social institutions and dominant ideology. Things are not so simple in practice. The characteristics of the superstructure, including the prevailing ideologies, are shaped by historical and cultural influences, as well as by the prevailing economic arrangements. Political economic transitions are invariably messy.

Production as the primary concern

All societies must produce in order to survive. Food, clothing, and shelter are the basic necessities: once their supply is ensured we can consider producing other luxury goods and services. How these productive activities are organised, however, can vary quite significantly. Some societies organise production through highly mechanised processes; others use more labour-intensive methods of production. Land is sometimes used extensively, sometimes intensively, for productive purposes. Decisions about production may be made through institutional processes that are haphazard or coherent, centralised or decentralised, authoritarian or democratic.

This focus on the organisation of production is a distinctive feature of Marxist political economy. As we shall see in later chapters, the neoclassical economists do not start here: their analytical focus is on exchange rather than production relationships, and on choices between technically feasible combinations of the factors of production, rather than on the socioeconomic processes by which commodities are actually made. The Keynesian focus is also different, putting more emphasis on the determinants of the overall demand for goods and services, rather than on the processes of production. Institutional economists, studying how technology influences and is influenced by economic institutions, come closer to the Marxian orientation. However, taking the mode of production as the central analytical concept is uniquely Marxist.

What is the mode of production? It is the character of the technical and social processes by which goods and services are made. Figure 13.1 provides the simplest depiction of its interrelated components.

FIGURE 13.1 THE MODE OF PRODUCTION

The forces of production are the most tangible elements. These are the means of production, the labour power, and the technology involved in making goods and services. The means of production include raw materials: those useful things such as minerals, coal, petroleum, wood, and water, that come from natural sources. They also include capital goods: the instruments, machines, and tools that are used for extracting or harvesting natural materials, transporting them, and industrially transforming them. Labour power is the human effort: using muscle and brain. How the labour power is combined with the means of production influences the productivity of the processes by which goods and services are made. It depends significantly on the nature of technology: the cumulative contributions of scientific and technological innovation. Technology governs the connection between the inputs and the outputs of the production process. In other words, it sets limits on the goods and services that can be produced with the land, labour, and capital available in the economy; it comes to be embodied in the form of the capital goods and it shapes the form of the production process itself.

The relations of production are the social and organisational aspects of that production process. Whereas the forces of production are tangible and technical, the relations of production concern how people are organised for the purpose of making the goods and services. Relations of production can take various forms. They can be collective and democratic or they can be hierarchical and authoritarian. Imagine a small, isolated community of people, on an island perhaps, deciding how they will cater for their own material needs. They may collectively take stock of their resources (human, natural, and manufactured) and decide how they will allocate them between different types of production (food, housing, clothing, and so on). Who does what, when, and how is likely to be determined by a process of collective choices. These may be democratic decision-making and the application of egalitarian principles, such as the rotation of the less pleasant as well as the pleasant tasks. However, if one person is able to dictate the tasks to the others—perhaps because she or he has acquired monopoly control over the means of production—the nature of interpersonal relationships in the production process is likely to be significantly different. Authoritarian practices will prevail; and egalitarian principles will be less likely to have much influence on who does what, when, and how. Whether the situation is stable will depend on whether the owner of the means of production is able to ensure compliance by his or her underlings, and whether the system works reasonably well in providing for their material needs.

How the forces of production and the relations of production interact shapes the overall character of the mode of production. Here is the interface of the technical and social elements— of technology and class. According to Marx, a historically significant connection between the development of the two aspects is identifiable. A slave mode of production, for example, uses characteristically rudimentary forces of production. The labour performed by slaves, using basic means of production, is the principal input into the production process. The relations of production are correspondingly crude, based on a coercive relationship between slave owners and slaves. The simple threat, 'Work harder or I will punish you', provides the incentive.

Under feudalism, the forces of production are usually a little better developed. The means of production comprise crude agricultural implements, and labour is performed by serfs who work on the land of the feudal lords in exchange for social protection. Elements of physical coercion are sometimes present, but the social aspects of production process are based on mutual obligation between the feudal lords and the lower orders of society. The relations of production exhibit more sophistication than under slavery.

The connection between the forces and relations of production becomes yet more evident with the development of capitalism. The means of production, the quality of labour power, and the nature of technology become increasingly complex. The relations of production centre on the wage relationship, based on buying and selling in the market. This pecuniary orientation then shapes all aspects of capitalist society, leading to an increasingly commercialised and commodified world.

Under socialism, and then communism, Marx anticipated that a new conjunction of the forces and relations of production would prevail. The forces of production, developed under capitalism to the level that makes a materially affluent society possible (but unrealisable for most members of that society because of the problems arising from conflicting class interests), would be carried over and further developed under socialism. Importantly, according to this reasoning, they can then be married to more egalitarian relations of production. Production and distribution can be organised on the principle 'From each according to his ability, to each according to his needs'.[4] A society that is both affluent and democratic becomes achievable for the first time in human history. Affluence is possible because there is no dominant class controlling the economic surplus for its own purposes, while democracy can be extended to the economy (for example, through workers' control of the enterprises in which they work) and need not remain restricted to the sphere of parliamentary elections, as it is under modern capitalism.

This, in bare outline, is how the forces and relations of production can be visualised as interacting through different modes of production. It is a story of the forces and relations of production working in tandem, the development of one making possible the further development of the other. It is a powerful story, providing a strong basis for optimism about economic and social progress. In the extreme, it is the view of history as a sequence of increasingly more sophisticated, and ultimately more liberating, modes of production.

However, Marxism (in its more careful constructions, at least) sees nothing inevitable about the movement through successive modes of production. Yes, the process of technological change and the social tensions in the relations of production do tend to drive change, so modes of production seemingly well established at a point in time (as capitalism is early in the twenty-first century) have no claim to permanency. But the form that sequential changes take is open-ended. Reversals in the sequence may occur. So, too, may jumps between different modes of production. Obvious examples are Russia and China, which were still predominantly feudal societies with only partial and incomplete elements of capitalist development at the time of their socialist revolutions in the twentieth century. Both made radical breaks in seeking to build a socialist mode of production, but leapfrogging capitalism proved profoundly problematic for the achievement of that socialist goal. Both have subsequently shifted towards capitalism, albeit in a corrupted form in Russia and under the auspices of an authoritarian state in China.

A second qualification to the theory of successive modes of production concerns their impurity. Modes of production may coexist. Indeed, different modes of production are normally present in any one country at any one time. Modern societies that we usually think of as capitalist, such as the USA, the UK, or Australia, have vestigial feudal elements and embryonic socialist elements alongside the dominant capitalist mode of production. The organisation of labour in the home, for example, is not characteristically capitalist: some domestic tasks may be done for wages (by hiring a gardener, cleaner, or childcarer, for example), but most are done by household members themselves (usually disproportionately by women). Transfers of income may be involved (between 'breadwinners' and other members of the household), but this is not synonymous with wage labour, the hallmark of capitalism.

Outwork is a second example of the impurity of modes of production in modern economies. It is common in industries such as the clothing industry, where production involves paying for the products of the workers' (typically female) labour rather than for the labour time spent. Such an arrangement is historically more characteristic of the putting-out system that developed under feudalism before capitalism became established.

Alongside vestigial feudal arrangements may be embryonic socialist arrangements, too. For example, business cooperatives commonly exist in the advanced industrial nations, but they do not operate according to purely capitalist principles. Counterculture communities of various sorts also commonly seek to practise collectivist forms of production and distribution, presaging forms of economy and society not yet fully developed but perhaps capable ultimately of transcending capitalism.[5] Whether such aspirations are achievable is debatable, of course. The point here is an analytical one—that what we commonly call capitalist economies are not necessarily capitalist in all respects. Different modes of production may coexist in any given society; so, when we talk of a particular society being capitalist we are referring only to the *dominant* mode of production in that place at that time.

The effect of these qualifications is to scale down the boldness of the claims made for Marx's analysis of the modes of production. It is not a simple stages theory of historical evolution. Rather, it offers a means of interpreting the interactions between economic and social change. As such, it is an analytic framework rather than a specific prediction about the direction of economic development. Perhaps its greatest value is in drawing attention to the characteristics of capitalism as a mode of production that differentiate it from other modes of production.

Capitalism as a mode of production

The significance of defining capitalism as a mode of production can be brought into sharper focus by comparing it with other ways of defining capitalism, as Maurice Dobb did in his book *Studies in the Development of Capitalism*.[6] Five possibilities are considered.

First, capitalism may be defined as a system based on roundabout, or time-using, methods of production. This emphasises the technological aspect of the economy. According to this view, what makes an economy capitalistic is the use of capital in complex production processes. The problem is that, beyond the most primitive, all economies have been capitalistic in this sense, varying only in degree.

Second, capitalism may be defined as a system based on the unfettered operation of the competitive market mechanism. While this fits in with commonly held notions about capitalism as the 'free-market economy', it interprets capitalism so narrowly as to make it almost nonexistent. In few places, other than the UK and the USA in the nineteenth century, have economies conformed closely to such a freely competitive regime, and even the UK and the USA passed quickly into an age of corporate enterprise and monopoly power. The state has always been a significant presence in capitalist development—indeed, usually establishing the preconditions for capitalist development.

Third, capitalism can be defined as a system in which production occurs for distant markets. This emphasises trade as the distinctive feature. It locates the origins of capitalism in the encroachment of commercial dealings on the localised economic system characteristic of the medieval era. It emphasises the breakdown of the craft guilds, which restricted craftspeople to selling their products only in the local town market. Indeed, the opening up of regional, national, and international trade was an important element in the transition from feudalism to capitalism, as noted in Chapter 8. However, production for distant markets was not unknown in the precapitalist period. It has been characteristic of socialist-based economies, too.

Fourth, we may approach the issue rather differently by emphasising the nature of capitalist ideology. Perhaps capitalism can be defined as the economic system resulting from the entrepreneurial spirit, for instance. The role of ideology in shaping society had been emphasised by Hegel who, as previously noted, was a strong influence on Marx. Hegel envisaged the history of civilisation as a succession of epochs marked by the dominance of successive national cultures. But is ideology more an effect than a cause of such historical changes? If it is, it seems inappropriate to define economic systems in terms of the ideologies to which they give rise. That is why Marx 'inverted' Hegel by emphasising the driving force of material economic conditions. What people think, especially about political economic issues, is important, but does not define the economic system itself.

It is the definition of capitalism as a mode of production that most clearly identifies the particular epoch in which capitalism developed and became readily distinguishable from other economic systems. In his own day, witnessing the establishment, expansion, and evolution of the capitalist system, Marx emphasised its three key characteristics:

- the separation of labour from the ownership of the means of production
- the concentration of the ownership of the means of production in the hands of a single class: the bourgeoisie, or capitalist class
- the appearance of a social class dependent for its subsistence on the sale of its labour power: the proletariat, or working class.

The economic and social transformation wrought by capitalism reverberates to this day. Although capitalist institutions have become characteristically larger, using increasingly sophisticated technologies and interacting with the state in complex ways, the essential feature of capitalism as a mode of production exhibits considerable continuity. The system is distinguishable from others largely because of the class relationships associated with how production is organised. Putting the spotlight first and foremost on class, rather than on technology, market structures, trade, or ideology, is the hallmark of this identification of capitalism as a mode of production.

Conclusion

Defining capitalism as a mode of production puts the focus on the relationship between capital and labour. This relationship has a technical economic dimension: capital and labour as inputs into the production of goods and services. It also has a social dimension: capital and labour as classes, as groups of people with potentially conflicting interests. According to Marxist economics, this latter tension is the essential dynamic in capitalism as an economic system.

Rather schematically, we can say that capitalism has been a progressive system in facilitating the development of the forces of production. Industrialisation, mechanisation, and the increased complexity of capital goods have made possible ever greater levels of material productivity (at least until ecological constraints begin to bite). Concurrently, capitalism has a reactionary character, retarding social progress because its relations of production prevent the achievement of a genuinely affluent society in which the wealth is shared by all. Conflicts arising from the relations of production—manifest in worker alienation, industrial disputes, and periodic economic crises—impair the achievement in practice of the prosperity and progress that the forces of production would otherwise make possible.

Understanding these two faces of capitalism is central to Marxist political economy. Capital and labour must cooperate for production to occur and for the system to be reproduced. However, as social classes, capital and labour have conflicting interests. The conflicts concern economic power (who should make the production decisions, for example) and the distribution of the fruits of cooperation (the extent of inequality in the distribution of income and wealth, for example). The need for cooperation sits uneasily with these recurrent tendencies towards conflict. It is rather like a marriage that is on a permanent knife edge, where the husband and wife can neither live apart nor live comfortably together. Coping with conflict and contradiction is the name of the game.

KEY POINTS

- Marxism is concerned with understanding society in its entirety, but focuses on the economy as the starting point for that enquiry.

- The mode of production embodies technical and social relationships that affect how goods and services are produced.

- Because the capitalist mode of production is based on a class relationship between capital and labour, the system is fraught with conflicts related to the organisation of work and the distribution of income.

14 ▸ Labour, Value, Exploitation

> *What is the labour theory of value?*
> *How does this theory explain the values of different commodities?*
> *How does it explain the exploitation of labour?*

Having defined capitalism as a mode of production, the task now is to understand how it works. How does the relationship between labour and capital affect the functioning of the economy? What determines the value of the products that are made? Where do profits come from? These are the questions that Marx sought to answer by adapting the labour theory of value from the classical political economists. Marx gave this theory a radical twist, turning it into a means of understanding the exploitation of labour by capital. To this day, the labour theory of value has been one of the most contentious currents of political economic analysis. It requires careful consideration, both as a means of explaining commodity prices and class conflicts.

Commodities and values

Marxist analysis, like classical political economy, makes an initial distinction between use values and exchange values. Of course, the production of useful things must occur in every society if it is to sustain itself, let alone prosper economically. Such items range from food, housing, and clothing to a vast array of non-essential goods and services. Each has its own use value, but that use value depends on who consumes it. (You may like hamburgers; I don't. You may not want a surfboard; I do.) Use values are inherently subjective. They vary from person to person, and a common unit of comparison is hard to find.

The problem of comparing the usefulness of one thing with another would not matter much in the simplest society where individuals produce items for their own use. People would allocate their working time according to their own preferences for the things they can hunt, grow, or make. Production would be directly for consumption, not for exchange. But few societies now work like that. Even the simplest division of labour makes it possible for people to produce more of some items than they need for their own consumption, and then exchange them in the market for items that they want. This entails the production of commodities; that is, goods and services made for exchange rather than for personal consumption. When commodity production exists an explanation of exchange values is needed.

What determines how much of one commodity will be exchanged for another in the market? Why are surfboards more expensive than hamburgers? Why is a silk shirt more expensive than a cotton one? What determines the price of the countless commodities available for sale? As we have seen, the classical political economists reasoned that relative prices generally reflect the cost of production of each commodity. The greater the labour needed to make the commodity, the higher the value of that commodity. Marx extended this basic insight into a comprehensive explanation of commodity production and markets.

The labour theory of value

Formally, the labour theory of value asserts that the value of a commodity is determined by the amount of labour needed for its production. This deceptively simple proposition requires three supplementary points of explanation. The first concerns the efficiency of the labour process. It is not the amount of labour actually performed that determines the value of a commodity. A chair made in three hours by an efficient carpenter is not worth less than a chair made in five hours by a less efficient carpenter. If both chairs have the same characteristics, they can be expected to sell in the market at the same price. The labour that determines the value is only the socially necessary labour. This socially necessary labour reflects the general standards of productivity and the state of technology prevailing in the economy at any particular time.

Second, account must be taken of the variations in the skill of the workers. Some occupations require many years of training; others do not. A skilled worker or tradesperson usually produces more value in one hour of work than does an unskilled labourer. The concept of abstract labour takes this into account. It gives us a common unit of the value-creating capacity of labour. Thus, we can express the value created by a skilled worker in terms of abstract labour as a multiple of that created by an unskilled worker. The size of this multiple will normally depend on the time taken to acquire the extra skills. If a quarter of a tradesperson's working life is taken up in the acquisition of skills, for example, we might regard his or her work as contributing 1.25 times as much abstract labour per hour as an unskilled worker's. In this way, the existence of diversity of skills among the workforce can be reconciled with a single labour theory of value.

Third is the issue of unproductive workers—not those who are inefficient or relatively unskilled, but those who do not directly produce commodities at all. There are many such workers in a capitalist economy. Supervisors, for example, may be necessary to ensure that other workers work hard, but they do not themselves produce the commodities. According to a strict interpretation of the labour theory of value, their labour time should not be counted as contributing to the value of the products. This does not imply that such jobs are unnecessary. Indeed, supervisors are normally essential in a capitalist economy because employees work for wages rather than directly for the products of their own labour. Supervisors are necessary, but they are not productive, because their labour does not directly add to the value of the products. No judgment about social worth is implied here, but difficult decisions need to be made about the range of jobs that are unproductive in this sense.

Having made these qualifications to the labour theory of value, a workable basis exists for calculating the value of different commodities. One can calculate how much socially necessary labour time goes into making them, measuring the contribution of workers of different skill levels in terms of abstract labour and excluding the time expended by unproductive workers. Still, a basic question remains: Why should only labour add to value? Drawing on the reasoning of Ernest Mandel, three possible proofs of the labour theory of value can be considered.[1]

First is the demonstration by disaggregation. This rests on the proposition that everything that goes into making a commodity can ultimately be traced back to the contribution of labour. Take the example of a wooden chair. What determines its value is not only the time spent by the carpenter in making it, but also the time spent by the timber worker in felling the tree, by the sawmiller in cutting the tree into useable planks, and by the truck driver in transporting the planks to the carpenter's workplace. The workers who made the screws the carpenter uses also have imparted some value to the product, as have, indirectly, the coal and iron ore miners and the foundry workers whose labour made the steel from which the screws were made. And the carpenter's tools—the saw, screwdriver, and chisel—were made by toolmakers using raw materials extracted and transformed by yet other workers. Those tools would not be fully used up in making the chair, but some part of the value embodied in them, which would depend on the degree of wear and tear on them, could be regarded as having been transferred to the chair. According to this chain of reasoning, everything that adds to the value of the commodity is ultimately traceable to labour.

It is a powerful argument. It recognises that capital goods are important in commodity production—indeed, increasingly important in an era of sophisticated mechanisation—but it also emphasises that these capital goods are the products of labour. Similarly, it indicates that, although natural resources are used in the production process, those resources acquire economic value only through the application of labour to their extraction and processing as inputs into the production process. Environmentalists should be reassured that this is not to deny that nature has intrinsic value. The argument is simply that, under capitalism, natural resources only acquire market value when labour is applied to their conversion for commodity production.

A second attempt to justify the labour theory of value involves more abstract reasoning. This is the so-called logical proof. The claim here is that, while commodities may have many common properties (molecular structure, size, weight, and colour, for example), the only common property that provides a basis for their exchange is that they are products of labour. Weight, for example, cannot be the basis for determining value. If it were, a kilogram of butter would have equal value to a kilogram of gold, which would be a patent absurdity. Only their common property as being products of labour can serve as a systematic basis for the determination of their relative value.

A third chain of reasoning rests on imagining an extreme case: a wholly mechanised society in which no labour is used. Machines produce machines, which produce all the goods and services that everybody needs. In such a society, it is argued, there would be no role for market arrangements since scarcity would have been abolished. It is a world of complete abundance. The elimination of labour has eradicated exchange value. There could be no wages system in such an economy either, since nobody would need to work. There would have to be some other means of distributing the goods and services produced, such as their direct allocation by the state. In other words, it would not be a capitalist economy, and the value basis of the capitalist system would no longer exist.

Whether these proofs of the labour theory of value are persuasive is a matter of judgment. The ultimate test of a theory is whether it actually helps in understanding the world around us. So, the practical question is whether the labour theory of value helps to explain the basis of commodity exchange in real market economies.

Values and prices

Marx certainly thought that the relative prices of commodities could be explained by reference to the labour theory of value. In his own words, 'The determination of price by cost of production is equivalent to the determination of price by the labour-time requisite to the production of a commodity.'[2] However, using the labour theory of value to explain prices requires dealing with some tricky problems.

First, actual market prices may be influenced by fluctuations in consumer demand. A commodity will not have a high market value unless it is in demand, irrespective of how much labour goes into making it. But producers will not make it if it is not in demand, you may say. Indeed, but producers do make mistakes, and anticipating changes in demand is seldom easy. Market prices may fluctuate independently of the amount of labour that goes into making the products. A fruitseller may reduce her prices just before packing up for the day, not because of any variation in the amount of labour going into the production of the fruit but because she judges that the fruit might spoil overnight and become unsalable.

Second, by similar reasoning, the state of market competition can have a bearing on actual market prices. Where competition is vigorous, prices will tend to conform more closely to labour values than where elements of monopoly are present. Monopolists can drive up prices by creating artificial scarcity, irrespective of the amount of labour embodied in the products they sell.

Third, where different branches of industry have an unequal degree of mechanisation, there may also be a tendency for relative market prices to deviate from relative labour values for the products concerned. Firms in the technologically advanced sectors will normally be able to secure higher profit margins than firms in the less technologically advanced sectors. If the rate of profit is not the same in all branches of industry, then the relationship between labour values and market prices will not be uniform. This is the essence of the transformation problem, which is the analytical problem of transforming values into prices.[3]

These three considerations cast doubt on the adequacy of the labour theory of value as a means of explaining relative commodity prices in practice. It is on these grounds that many economists reject the theory. However, there is a possible rescue, emphasising its usefulness in explaining long-run price trends. Indeed, over long periods of time, prices of different commodities do broadly reflect the labour that goes into making them, even though the market prices may deviate from labour values in the short run.

Consider a simple illustration comparing the prices of haircuts and watches. Forty years ago, in countries such as the USA, the UK, and Australia, the price of a simple, cheap watch was many times more (perhaps ten in round terms) than the price of a basic haircut for a man. There has been prodigious technological advance in watch production since then, partly as a result of the microelectronic revolution, so that much less labour, direct and indirect, is now needed to make a watch. By contrast, there has been no significant advance in hairdressing technologies: a haircut is still largely a matter of one worker standing beside a person's head with a pair of scissors. Lo and behold—cheap watches now cost less than a professional haircut. Of course, one can spend much more on a watch made with more labour-intensive methods and/or more valuable materials. One can also spend more on a haircut if more complex and time-consuming treatments are required. But the differential rate of technological change in watchmaking and hairdressing have clearly influenced the general pattern of relative prices. One example like this does not prove the labour theory of value, of course. Nor would a longer list of examples (which would not be difficult to construct). What it does suggest, if our concern is with understanding long-term trends in commodity prices, is that a labour theory of value can be a helpful starting point.

According to Marxists, though, the labour theory of value has a more important role than explaining relative prices: it is the key to understanding the class relationships underpinning the production of commodities. It explains the pervasive character of exploitation.

Value and surplus value

> *There are people in this country who work hard every day;*
> *Not for fame and fortune do they strive;*
> *And the fruits of their labour are worth more than their pay.*

This was the jingle in an Australian television beer commercial that showed sweaty workers enjoying a drink or two after their daily efforts. The advertiser's aim was to present ordinary citizens contributing to the advancement of the nation over and above what they are rewarded in wages (and, hopefully, spending some of those wages on the advertised product as well). Ironically, and no doubt unintentionally, the last line of the jingle also summarises the Marxist theory of surplus value: that workers produce value over and above what is returned to them as wages.

Let us build up this theory more systematically. The starting point is the distinction between labour power and labour. Labour power is a person's potential to work. In Marx's words, it is 'the aggregate of those mental and physical capabilities existing in a human being which he exercises whenever he produces a use-value of any description'.[4] Labour, on the other hand, is work actually undertaken. So, the one is a capacity, the other an actual activity. It is rather like the distinction between the power to digest food and the actual process of digestion, or between nuclear strike capacity and nuclear war.

When an employer hires workers (by the hour, week, or year), it is labour power that is being purchased. Labour power is a commodity and, according to Marx, will normally exchange in the market at its value, like any other commodity. That value—the prevailing wage rate—varies from place to place and from time to time, determined historically through processes of class struggle. The average wage rate in Australia for adult workers, for example, is currently around $250 a day for a seven-hour day. Given that prevailing wage rate, employers have to decide whether it is in their interests to hire workers; that is, to purchase labour power in the market. The answer is that it is worth them doing so only when the value of the commodities produced by workers exceeds the wages that must be paid. The capitalist employer does not employ workers because of altruism: the goal is profit. Workers will be hired only when it is expected that they will contribute to the profit of the enterprise by producing more value than they are paid in wages. Formally, this means that the condition for employment is that the value of the commodities produced by labour exceeds the value of labour power.

A division of the working day is implied. For the first part of the working day, the employee is producing just enough commodities to cover his or her own wage. This is called the necessary labour, which is the labour required for producing value equivalent to the wage the worker receives. The rest of the day involves surplus labour. This is the labour expended by the worker that directly benefits the employer. In value terms, this contribution by the worker to the income of the employer is surplus value, the amount of value created by the worker that is not returned as wages.

Surplus value as the source of profits

Who gets the surplus value? The profits of capitalist business enterprises are the most direct manifestation of surplus value in monetary form. In this regard, Marxist economics is in accord with conventional accounting practices. It treats profits as an economic surplus, just as accountants calculate profits as the surplus of revenues over costs. How these profits are then shared between the shareholders (whose interests are in dividend payments and increasing their share prices) and the managers of the capitalist enterprises (whose interests are in their own remuneration packages and the growth of the firms they manage) is a matter of contention. Both have a common interest in maximising the flow of surplus value into profits, however.

There are other claimants to surplus value. Supervisory workers have to be paid their wages and, since they do not themselves directly produce value, their wages must come from the surplus value generated by other workers. It is profitable to employ such supervisors to the extent that they help to ensure that surplus value is extracted from productive workers. So, although they are formally unproductive workers, their employment is not uneconomic. Within the logic of the capitalist economy, they have a claim on surplus value. The size of their share depends, like other workers', on their strength in bargaining over their wage levels with their employers.

Other claimants to surplus value include banks and other financial institutions, who commonly lend money to capitalist businesses. The businesses pay interest payments and other charges that are associated with those loans. These payments are deducted from the surplus value that would otherwise be retained as profits by industrial enterprises. Banks themselves are capitalist businesses and seek profit; but the peculiarity of their position is that their profit involves the transfer of surplus value produced in productive enterprises. Similarly, landowners obtain part of the surplus value. In situations where businesses do not own the property from which their business is conducted, rent has to be paid to landlords.

Governments may also capture part of the surplus value through taxation. Taxes on businesses reduce corporate post-tax profits. In return, governments usually provide services that are useful for business, such as building the basic infrastructure necessary to make commerce possible. So it is not all one-way traffic. Indeed, governments may well expand the scope for capitalist business activity over time. However, at any particular time, the revenues generated by governments from business taxation (usually a small minority of total tax revenue sources) is a claim on surplus value.

It should be evident that many sections of society have an interest, more or less directly, in surplus value. These include capitalist firms, their shareholders and managers, supervisors, financial institutions, landowners, and governments. They have divergent interests in how the surplus value is shared.[5] However, they have a common interest in there being a large total pool of surplus value. In Marxist terms, this means a common interest in the process of exploitation.

Exploitation and class struggle

In Marxist political economy, the term 'exploitation' refers to any situation where one class of people derives income from the labour of another class. It is a pervasive process. Indeed, Marx noted that exploitation, in this sense, existed in all preceding societies. Under slavery, slave owners live off the work done by slaves. Under feudalism, the standard of living of the manorial lords depends on the labour contributed by serfs. What is novel about capitalism is the persistence of exploitation, despite labour becoming 'free'. Indeed, the freedom of workers under capitalism is historically unprecedented. Workers are not tied to a master but are free to work for whomever is willing to hire them. Hence the great puzzle: how can labour be both free and exploited at the same time? The characteristically Marxist response emphasises the constrained character of that freedom: it is the freedom to work for employers who are seeking to extract surplus value.

Not surprisingly, there is a conflict of interests. The employers want the highest possible ratio of surplus labour to necessary labour, or (what amounts to the same thing) the highest possible ratio of surplus value to wages. The employees want the reverse: the highest possible ratio of wages to total value produced. This conflict of interests is structurally embedded. Both sides, predicably, organise to seek the upper hand, employers forming employer associations and workers forming trade unions to give themselves more collective bargaining power.

Struggles over absolute surplus value and relative surplus value ensue. Increases in absolute surplus value arise when workers work longer to produce more value without a corresponding increase in wages. Increases in relative surplus value arise whenever employers are able to capture a larger proportion of the total value produced during a given period of time.

Struggles over the length of the working day put the focus on absolute surplus value. Such class struggles have been of great historical significance in capitalist development: working hours were lengthened; in the early nineteenth century, for instance, fourteen-hour workdays were common. Since then, workers, largely through their organisation into trade unions, have been successful in shortening the length of the normal working day, first to twelve hours, then to ten hours, and eventually to eight hours. By the early twentieth century, the eight-hour workday had become the norm in countries such as the UK and Australia. The push for shorter working hours has stalled significantly over the past half-century and there has been evidence of some reversals, as shown by the growing trend to unpaid overtime. However, a strong push for further reductions in the length of the working week has resumed in recent years. Proponents of 'work–life balance' have given a modern edge to this traditional focus of workers' struggles.[6]

Facing these setbacks in respect of their capacity to generate absolute surplus value, capitalist employers have sought to raise relative surplus value. They have usually done so by increasing the productivity and/or intensity of labour. Raising the productivity of labour can be achieved through enhancing the skills of the workforce, equipping the workers with superior tools or machinery, or eliminating waste from the production process. If workers produce more value during a given time period, and if their wages do not rise correspondingly, surplus value is increased.

Raising the intensity of labour has a yet more direct effect. It means that workers produce more value during a given time period because they are working harder. How to make workers work harder is, of course, the great challenge for capitalist management. What employers buy is labour power—the capacity to work—but their task is to make sure that the maximum amount of labour—actual work—is undertaken. Box 14.1 below summarises some managerial strategies employed for this purpose.

From a Marxist perspective, exploitation is not something imposed by particularly nasty employers, but rather a condition for the normal functioning of the capitalist economy. It is a systemic characteristic, not an aberration. Part of the value produced by workers is taken by capitalist employers—indeed, there would be no point, from an employer's perspective, in employing the workers otherwise. Capitalism needs exploitation for its normal functioning. Some political economists argue that positing this connection between profits, surplus labour, and exploitation does not require a formal basis in value theory.[7] The use of the labour theory of value reflects the influence on Marx of the classical political economists. What is of continuing interest, though, is the link that the theory provides between the analysis of production and the analysis of distribution. This link concerns the class relations involved in producing commodities and the different incomes that those classes receive.

BOX 14.1 — MANAGERIAL STRATEGIES FOR INCREASING THE INTENSITY OF LABOUR

Many workers take pride in their jobs and their own productivity. Some voluntarily perform unpaid overtime. The belief in doing 'a fair day's work for a fair day's pay' is widespread. In various ways, these personal, ethical, and social commitments influence how work is performed. But the basic fact remains: under capitalism, work is done for wages, so the material benefits of harder or faster work usually accrue, in the first instance, to the employer rather than the employee.

In his influential book, *Labor and Monopoly Capital*, Harry Braverman described how employers in the twentieth century sought to raise the intensity of labour by using 'scientific management'. Scientific management is also known as Taylorism, after its pioneer Frederick Taylor (1856–1917). This approach to management, which emphasised managerial control over each and every stage of workers' productive activities, changed the nature of work in many industries and occupations.[8]

Other political economists have pointed out more diverse means by which employers have increased the intensity of labour in practice. Richard Edwards, for example, distinguishes between three strategies: simple control, technical control, and bureaucratic control.[9] Simple control occurs when bosses directly exert their personal authority over workers. 'Work harder or you'll be fired' is the characteristic message. Technical control involves the use of technology as a means of increasing the intensity of labour. Setting the pace of work by setting the pace of machinery is commonplace in many routine factory jobs. Bureaucratic control is the more sophisticated alternative, embedding work incentives in the social-organisational aspects of the enterprise. Its hallmarks are career ladders, bonus payments, and the encouragement of each worker's personal identification with corporate goals.

Political economists also distinguish between 'lean production' and 'team production' in the organisation of work.[10] The former, as a modern form of Taylorism, requires centralised control over the workforce, usually with an eye to cutting out unnecessary labour. The latter entails more decentralised decision-making, giving some degree of autonomy to groups of workers. Team production is often more conducive to productivity, but managers tend to be cautious about its introduction, fearing that the empowerment of workers may threaten managerial prerogatives.

Modern managers also tend to be coy about explicitly admitting to their primary concern of extracting more work from the workers. Human resources management (HRM) is the more acceptable face of capitalist businesses today. It comprehensively extends the process of bureaucratic control throughout the workplace while encouraging worker compliance. The central economic goal remains a higher intensity of labour and a corresponding increase in surplus value.

Conclusion

The twists and turns in the development of Marxist value theory have a dual purpose: to explain the market prices of commodities and to explain the relationship between labour and capital. There is an obvious connection. Because labour power is itself a commodity, its price is determined in the market. The difference between that price and the total value of commodities produced shapes the overall amount of profit that capitalist firms make. Employers and employees have a conflict of interest over the relative size of these wage and profit shares (and a more fundamental conflict of interest about a system that generates such pervasive conflict). This theory explains both the origin of profits in the exploitation of labour and the economic drivers of class struggle.

Marxist political economy also draws attention to the struggle over the economic surplus. All economic systems need some sort of surplus. That surplus is the excess of the value of what the workers produce over what is returned to them in the form of wages. That surplus is needed to replace wornout machinery, to pay for new infrastructure, and to fund innovation. What is distinctive about capitalism—by comparison with the socialist system that Marxists have always advocated—is not the existence of a surplus, but the control of that surplus by a particular class. In this respect, capitalism does indeed have some continuity with slave and feudal modes of production. The size and disposition of the surplus reflect the exercise of the power of the dominant class in each case. Under socialism, Marx anticipated, the size and disposition of the surplus would be a matter for collective determination by the society as a whole.

KEY POINTS

- According to the labour theory of value, the value of a commodity depends on the amount of labour necessary for its production.

- Part of the value produced by labour is captured by employers. This surplus value is the source of capitalist profits, but it also flows to many other sections of the economy and society.

- Conflict over the relative shares of wages and surplus value pervades capitalist economies and gives rises to diverse trade union and managerial practices.

15 Capital Accumulation

What drives the capitalist economy?

Is economic growth inexorable?

How does the economic system change as it grows?

Previous chapters have shown how capitalism can be understood as a mode of production, and how its functioning depends crucially on the character of the relationship between capital and labour. But the economy does not stand still while it is being studied. It reproduces itself. It grows. It changes as it grows. A central concern of Marxist analysis is to understand the process of capital accumulation that shapes these dynamics.

Economic growth and capital accumulation

The great historical achievement of capitalism is the increase in productive capacity: the ability to produce vast quantities of goods and services. As noted in Chapter 5, it would be simplistic to assume a necessary connection between this achievement and the increase of human happiness. Some of the things produced are of dubious merit. Some are destructive. And the distribution of the goods and services has commonly been so inequitable that more than two centuries of economic growth has not eradicated poverty, even within affluent nations. Still, notwithstanding these reservations, the overall expansion of production and consumption under capitalism has been spectacular in comparison with anything that came before it. The process continues, as new production technologies and new products are developed, and consumerism becomes an ever more deeply entrenched culture.

The driving force of growth in a capitalist economy is the accumulation of capital. Business enterprises seek profit and, if successful, they usually invest at least some of it in expanding their output and market share. It is by increasing the amount of capital under their control that individual businesses grow. So it is for the economy as a whole: the overall rate of economic growth depends on the rapidity of the capital accumulation process.

What conditions are conducive to the accumulation of capital? The classical political economists pondered this question, as noted in Chapter 10. Marxist political economy develops a rather different two-pronged response. One involves the use of a formal analysis of the process of reproduction and growth, based on a two-sector model of the economy.[1] The other involves an examination of the capital accumulation process, emphasising how the system changes as it grows over time. We emphasise the latter here.

The capital accumulation process involves quantitative change, increasing in the volume of productive capacity and the size of the economic surplus. It also involves qualitative change, processes of institutional adaptation that make further economic growth possible. From a Marxian perspective, three aspects of qualitative change are particularly significant:

- the changing form of labour's reserve army
- the concentration and centralisation of capital
- the process of imperialism.

Labour and its reserve army

Capital accumulation typically generates an increase in the demand for labour. Larger outputs of goods and services usually require more workers to make them. Whether the rate of increase in the demand for labour is equivalent to the increase in output, or proportionately less, depends on whether production is labour intensive or capital intensive. Either way, any increase in the demand for labour may cause rising wage rates. From a capitalist perspective, any such wage rise creates the unwelcome possibility that it will cut into surplus value and thereby reduce profits.

What can prevent this from happening? Malthus famously claimed that population growth would do so. The growth in the supply of labour, he thought, would continually outstrip the demand for labour, forcing the prevailing wage rate back to a mere subsistence level. The 'insatiable lusts of the masses' would thereby prevent wages encroaching on the economic surplus. Marx called this a libel on the human race.[2] What keeps wages in check, he argued, is something internal to capitalism itself: the continual recreation of a reserve army of labour.

In general terms, this reserve army of labour comprises those members of the working class who are unemployed or intermittently employed.[3] The existence of this relative surplus population, Marx claimed, keeps wages at subsistence level. If the members of the reserve army are willing to work for rock-bottom wages, employed workers cannot easily gain significant wage rises because capitalist employers can always draw from the reserve army to replace their existing employees. So, the existence of the reserve army keeps wages down and profits up.

Herein lies a paradox. Leaving people unemployed is not an altogether rational state of affairs for capitalists: unlike people at work, unemployed people are not creating surplus value for their employers. The Marxist argument is that the unemployed may make an equally important contribution to capitalist interests—by keeping the brake on other workers' wage rises. No permanent balance exists. A rapid burst of capital accumulation may result from a new technological innovation or from the opening up of a new market. On those occasions, the reserve army is diminished, and wages may indeed rise at the expense of surplus value. However, as Marx pointed out, 'As soon as this diminution touches the point at which the surplus labour that nourishes capital is no longer supplied in normal quantity, a reaction sets in: a smaller part of the revenue is capitalised, accumulation lags and the movement of rise in wages receives a check.'[4] Capitalists in general would prefer this not to happen, because it means that the reserve army is replenished at the expense of economic growth. They would prefer the reduction in the number of unemployed people because of economic growth to be offset by new sources of potential workers replenishing the reserve army.

In Marx's own time, the principal sources of the reserve army were peasants displaced from their traditional livelihood on the land and artisans displaced by mechanisation. These people—victims of what we would now rather politely call structural economic change—swelled the growing ranks of the potential working class. Desperate for employment, they usually moved from rural areas to the growing industrial towns.

Such social upheavals continue in the poorer developing nations today, as people move from rural areas to the burgeoning cities in quest of whatever work they can find. However, in the more advanced capitalist nations, the potential sources of a reserve army have changed over the last half century. Women, previously excluded from many areas of employment and told that their 'proper place' was in the home, have increasingly participated in paid work. Indeed, paid work has become the norm, although women's employment remains disproportionately concentrated in casual and part-time jobs, often without employment security. These are distinctive reserve army characteristics.

The spectacular growth in the numbers of immigrant workers can be interpreted in similar terms. In Europe, millions of 'guest workers' have swelled the workforce, while in the USA, millions of illegal immigrants from Central America work for much lower wages than those paid to American citizens. The internationalisation of capital has been accompanied by a significant internationalisation of labour supply, notwithstanding the border controls that individual nation states seek to enforce. As a consequence, the reserve army function has been displaced significantly to immigrants.[5]

The employment experiences of many young people today also have significant 'reserve army' characteristics. Working on casual contracts—or sometimes directly for cash-in-hand payments—in businesses like fast-food outlets, cafes, and bars gives little continuity nor security of tenure. The boss calls you in, sometimes at quite short notice, when your labour is needed but provides no guarantee of regular work in the longer term. It is a flexible employment arrangement, with flexibility usually on the employer's terms. Young people, seldom backed by membership of a trade union and with little bargaining power, are offered this work on a 'take it or leave it' basis by employers who know that there are often plenty of alternative candidates. For students expecting eventually to move on to more secure employment situations, this may well be a tolerable, if sometimes stressful, phase in their working lives; but for those who have no other long-term options, it is a consignment to an ongoing reserve army of labour.

So, while its character and composition have changed over time, the reserve army of labour has enduring relevance in modern capitalism. The emphasis on workforce flexibility in modern capitalist businesses accentuates economic insecurity for many workers. In order to maintain continued employment in an increasingly insecure economic environment, they are effectively forced into competition. The resulting downward pressure on wages helps businesses keep their production costs down.

Concentration and centralisation of capital

The accumulation of capital is also accompanied by changes in the organisation of capital. Individual capitalist businesses generally grow larger and seek to increase their scale of production, a process that Marx called the concentration of capital. Concurrently, firms often combine through mergers and takeovers, a process that Marx termed the centralisation of capital. These are important qualitative changes that accompany the quantitative growth process. They have significant consequences for the nature of work, the rate of technological change, and the growth of monopoly power.

The consequential changes in the nature of work are partly a matter of scale. Being employed in big factories rather than small workshops, or in big rather than small offices, often significantly changes working conditions. Big business does not necessarily mean big workforces in big workplaces: many capitalist enterprises divide their operations between multiple sites and some continue to have only a handful of employees. The fundamental point is the rationalisation of the labour process itself. This is not simply a matter of having a more complex division of labour, as in Adam Smith's famous example of the pin factory. It is, in Marx's own words, 'the progressive transformation of isolated processes of production carried on in accustomed ways into socially combined and scientifically managed processes of production'.[6] The adoption of scientific management and of systems of technical and bureaucratic control (as noted in Box 14.1) are twentieth-century examples. These practices have tended to change the nature of employment experiences and to enhance the capacity of employers to extract surplus value.

The concentration and centralisation of capital also tends to accelerate technological change. To quote Marx again, 'Centralisation, by thus accelerating and intensifying the effects of accumulation, extends at the same time the revolution in the technical composition of capital which increases its constant part at the expense of its variable part and thereby reduces the relative demand for labour.'[7] This process is not inexorable; experience shows that smaller firms are sometimes more technologically progressive than larger ones. However, the centralisation of capital does generate the resources that make major investments in innovation possible. Historically, the trends towards rapid technological change and the concentration and centralisation of capital have run in tandem.

The growth of monopoly power has been a predictable accompaniment. The larger firms usually have more control over the prices of their products because the size of their market share makes them less vulnerable to competitive pressures. Sometimes the larger firms collude with one another for these purposes. Their economic power can also be used politically to pressure governments to change business regulations or tax rates in order to give an advantage to particular corporate interests. Thus, the concentration and centralisation of capital has enormous political economic significance. It tends to change the balance of power between capitalist business enterprises answerable to their financial backers and the institutions of government supposedly embodying democratic principles.

Some Marxists use the term 'monopoly capitalism' to draw attention to these trends.[8] They contend that the process of capital accumulation has fundamentally transformed capitalism from an economic system based on competition to one in which the use and abuse of monopoly power is its most pervasive and distinctive characteristic. Others argue the contrary, that global expansion has been associated with the breakdown of local monopolies, leading to greater competition between capitalist enterprises on a world scale.[9] It is a fascinating debate in which Marxist scholars enjoin with other contemporary analysts arguing from different political economic positions. All agree that the capital accumulation process has wrought qualitative change in the institutional character of the capitalist economy.

Imperialism

The process of capital accumulation significantly shapes the nature of the international economy too. Capital accumulation can take place within a locality or within a nation, but in practice it tends to break down those spatial constraints on economic activity. In that sense it is a globalising process. Capitalist businesses now search the world for the cheapest available labour or raw materials. They look for new markets in other regions or nations to provide outlets for their growing production of goods and services. They may also seek to minimise the taxes on their profits by finding the countries with the lowest tax rates so that they can locate their activities there—or at least make it appear that their profits are generated there. Shopping around for the locations with the least restrictive environmental regulations has a similar corporate logic. Having a global reach thereby increases the range of business options. Not surprisingly, a tendency towards geographical expansion is one of the inherent features of the capitalist economy.

Historically, this process of international expansion has been associated with imperialism. Relationships of domination and dependency have been imposed by the ruling classes in the stronger nations on the poorer people of the periphery. Territorial conquest and colonial exploitation have been the historical hallmarks of imperialism. Interestingly, the empire builders themselves were sometimes not at all coy about this. Cecil Rhodes, for example, a pioneer of British imperialism in Africa during the nineteenth century, stated the goals of imperialism as clearly as any Marxist might. In his own words:

> We must find new lands from which we can easily obtain raw materials and at the same time exploit the cheap slave labour that is available from the natives in the colonies; the colonies would also

provide a dumping ground for the surplus goods produced in our factories; the Empire, as I have always said, is a bread and butter question. If we want to avoid class struggle in the UK, we must become imperialists.[10]

Lenin, the father of the Russian revolution, wrote of imperialism as 'the highest stage of capitalism'.[11] He saw it as a process shaped by a number of interconnected features:

- several advanced capitalist nations competing for world markets
- monopoly capital being the dominant organisational form of capital
- considerable exporting of capital, not just trading in goods and services
- severe rivalry occurring in world markets, leading alternately to cut-throat competition and the development of international monopoly combines
- the world economy being territorially divided.

This last feature was particularly pronounced at the time Lenin was writing. By the start of the twentieth century, the British, French, Dutch, Spaniards, Portuguese, and Belgians had carved up much of the world among themselves. Africa, less than 10 per cent of which had been under external domination in 1875, was almost completely partitioned by the European nations over the next quarter of a century. Such imperialist processes were accompanied by ruthless forms of oppression and militarism. It was this situation about which Lenin wrote.

There are continuities and discontinuities between the situation then and now. The USA effectively took over from the European states as the leading imperialist power in the second half of the twentieth century, but the USA has usually based its dominance, particularly in Latin America, on having compliant satellite states rather than on colonies.[12] There are also significant differences between the classical form of imperialism described by Lenin and its characteristic modern forms. Instead of the poorer nations being dominated by individual advanced capitalist nations, the contemporary face of imperialism is of transnationalised domination by global institutions. Transnational corporations, supported by international agencies such as the IMF and the World Bank, play a dominant role in the economies of the poorer nations in particular, strongly influencing their possibilities of economic development. So, here too we can see that the accumulation of capital has given rise to qualitative change—from classical imperialism to its modern form as 'imperialism without colonies'.[13]

Conclusion

Marxist economic analysis emphasises that growth is integral to capitalism. It is not simply a matter of the economy becoming quantitatively larger: the capital accumulation process also drives qualitative change. Some of the most important of these historical changes have been in the reserve army of labour, the concentration and centralisation of capital, and the character of imperialism.

The growth process opens up more and more opportunities for profit. As Australian historian Humphrey McQueen puts it, 'The essence of capitalism is capital's need to expand'.[14]

However, capital accumulation is not unproblematic for capitalist businesses. The necessary conditions for the achievement of coordinated expansion can be quite elusive. There is a permanent tension between capitalists' desire for immediate enjoyment and the drive for long-term self-enrichment—manifest in the choice that they have to make between luxury consumption and productive investment.[15] Whether the economic system rides out such problems depends substantially on its capacity to meet the requirements for the continued circulation of capital. It is with these matters that the next chapter is concerned.

KEY POINTS

- Capital accumulation, the driver of growth in capitalist economies, depends on particular structural conditions.

- Historically, capital accumulation has gone hand in hand with the reproduction of a reserve army of labour, the concentration and centralisation of capital, and the process of imperialism.

- The continuing expansion of capitalism, nationally and internationally, generates new sources of labour for the reserve army, new patterns of monopoly capitalism, and imperialism without colonies.

16 Reproduction, Growth, Change

What is the circuit of capital?

What political economic conditions underpin this circuit of capital?

How has capitalism adapted in practice to meet these conditions?

The task of understanding the economy requires looking beyond surface appearances in order to discern the broader forces shaping its development. We need to see how the various parts of the capitalist economic system fit together and how they relate to the social and political institutions. A Marxian theory of the circuit of capital can be adapted for this purpose. This chapter presents a simple version of this model to show how capitalism works in its entirety as an integrated system.

The circuit of capital

Think of a young person setting up a small firm (to make surfboards, glove puppets, or jewellery, for example). This person would normally begin with capital in money form (perhaps the result of past savings, or a loan from family or a bank). That money can be used to rent business premises, buy raw materials, and hire labour. Production can then be undertaken, at which stage the capital takes the form of some as yet unsold commodities. If all goes well, those commodities are then sold, thereby transforming the capital back into a monetary form as sales revenue. If that final amount of capital is greater than the initial capital, the business has made a profit.

Successfully completing this sequence makes it possible for the business to undertake another round of production. Indeed, the next round of production can be on a larger scale, if the person is able to hire the necessary additional means of production and labour power, manage the expanded production process, and find markets for the increased number of commodities produced. That being so, the business has reproduced itself and created the potential for further growth. The circuit of capital has been completed and capital accumulation can proceed.

Looking at the capitalist economy as a whole, as if it were a single firm writ large, we can observe a similar process. The steps involved in the circuit of capital are formally represented in Box 16.1 below. This way of setting up the issue enables us to see how the necessary conditions for capital accumulation are met in practice.[1] It is a means of drawing together various themes from preceding chapters in order to illuminate the working of the economy as an integrated system.

BOX 16.1   THE CIRCUIT OF CAPITAL

Capitalist business activity can be represented as a sequence, as follows:

$$M - C^{LP}_{MP} ...(P)...C^1 - M^1$$

M denotes the initial capital in a monetary form.
C denotes capital in the form of commodities used for producing commodities.
LP is labour power.
MP is the means of production.
P is production.
C^1 denotes capital in the form of the produced commodities.
M^1 denotes capital in a monetary form after the sale of the produced commodities.
The dashes represent the movement of capital: they are not minus signs.

The point of this model is to show how capital expands as a result of the successful completion of the various stages in the production process. The amount of expansion ($M^1 > M$) is equivalent to the surplus value generated during production, as described in the preceding chapter. The process becomes a 'circuit' when the expanded capital (M^1) feeds back into a new sequence, on a bigger scale: more capital, more output, more sales, more profits.

This model can be used to identify the five necessary conditions for capital accumulation, as follows:

- minimising costs (in the M–C stage of the sequence above)
- producing surplus value (in the M...[P]...C^1 stage)
- realising surplus value (in the C^1–M^1 stage)
- rapid circulation of capital (the dashes between M, C, C^1, and M^1 above)
- economic and social reproduction (underpinning the whole process of capital accumulation).

We consider each in turn.

Minimising production costs

As every business manager knows, it is important to keep costs of production down. This is best done by finding the cheapest labour, raw materials, and equipment appropriate for the particular task at hand. The last phrase here is an important reminder that minimising costs is always relative to a given quality and quantity of output. So, it is not necessarily a matter of buying cheap at the expense of product quality (although this is common) but of avoiding unnecessary costs and waste. How is this to be done?

Extending the geographical area from which resources are drawn is one means. If firms can shop around the globe for labour, machinery, and raw materials, this can help them to minimise their costs (although it may simultaneously impose other costs on the community). Their capacity to shop around may also intensify the competitive character of the economic environment, causing suppliers to drive their prices downward. The cost of transportation limits this process to some extent, as there may be a trade-off between lower resource costs and higher transport costs. However, in general, internationalisation of production is conducive to minimising the overall costs of production for capitalist businesses.

Firms may also reduce the costs of labour through hiring people from particular social groups at lower wage rates. If women can be employed more cheaply than men to do similar work, if black people can be employed more cheaply than white, or if young workers can be hired at lower wages than adults, it is in the immediate interest of the firms to exploit those inequalities. Historically, racial and sexual discrimination in labour markets has been a significant means of keeping wage costs down, although, in more recent decades, governments have increasingly implemented regulations to limit such practices.

The presence of unemployment is also conducive to keeping costs to a minimum. In the absence of strong trade unions or government regulations, competition among workers for jobs tends to drive wage levels downwards. Where there are significant levels of unemployment, this tendency may be accentuated. In this respect, as noted in the preceding chapter, the interests of capitalist employers are served by having a reserve army of labour. Therein lies a significant social and economic waste.

Generating surplus value

Firms need to organise their production processes to create propitious conditions for extracting surplus value. Surplus value is the source of profit. How are firms to ensure it is kept at a high level? Pushing production costs down helps. Businesses are, understandably, concerned to ensure that not all the value created by producing goods and services is returned to their workers as wages. It is equally important for capitalist firms to ensure a high volume and value of goods and services produced. The rate of surplus value—the total surplus value divided by total wages—is the indicator of their success in this aspect of the capital accumulation process.

Raising the productivity of labour is one means by which capitalist businesses can ensure a high rate of surplus value, so long as the labour productivity gains are not matched by corresponding wage rises. Employers have a collective interest in training workers with this goal in mind. However, because there is always the possibility of workers moving to other employers, this collective interest is not always perceived and acted on by individual employers. They may prefer to poach skilled workers from elsewhere rather than undertake the long-term commitment of training. As a result, governments often act on behalf of the collective interests of capitalist employers, providing the education and training facilities from which capitalists as well as workers collectively benefit.

Policies to raise the intensity of labour have an even more direct effect on the rate of surplus value. Prevailing upon workers to work harder, faster, or smarter is a key concern for capitalist employers. It may be achieved through various types of management strategies, as summarised in Box 14.1.

Mechanisation of the production process may also contribute to a higher surplus value. Equipping workers with more technologically advanced means of production usually raises the volume and/or value of output. Whether it actually raises the rate of surplus value depends on the cost of the machinery and on whether higher wage rates have to be paid to ease the acceptance of the more mechanised production. Mechanisation tends to reduce the relative importance of direct labour in the production process. Therein lies a potential contradiction because, from a Marxian perspective, labour is the source of value from which surplus value derives. So what is rational for one capitalist enterprise may not be in the interests of capital as a whole.

Realising surplus value

Capitalist businesses also have to sell the goods and services they produce. Surplus value is not realised in a monetary form as profit unless the products are actually sold. Not surprisingly, then, much individual capitalist business activity goes into marketing products as well as making them. The capitalist economy as a whole works best when economic conditions are conducive to the effectiveness of such marketing efforts. This means that there must be a high overall demand for goods and services to match the growing volume of the goods and services produced. How is this requirement met?

Fundamentally, markets must be created. Capitalism as an economic system has, historically, done this through the commercialisation of social life. Education and health services, for instance, have been made into salable items. Music and sport have become focal points for commercial enterprise, not purely means of personal fulfilment. New avenues for profit making and capital accumulation are thereby created.

Meanwhile, the sales effort by capitalist businesses seeks to ensure that consumers' demand grows in both new and existing markets. For the individual firm, this is usually a matter of trying to maintain or expand its market share. When all firms are simultaneously engaged in such practices, the effect is to intensify the culture of consumerism, in which commodity consumption is glamorised and represented as the means to personal satisfaction. The sales effort by individual firms generates, in effect, a want-creation industry. Advertising becomes increasingly sophisticated, sometimes playing on fears (of lack of personal freshness, of social rejection, of sexual failure, for example) and then showing the product that will remove that anxiety. Luxury consumption, often involving products that have built-in obsolescence or are based on consciously engineered, short-term waves of fashion, is vigorously promoted as markets for basic necessities become saturated. The process is extended internationally. Tobacco companies, for example, have sought new territories as their principal existing markets have come to be constrained by health regulations, while companies producing baby foods have, for decades, sought to persuade women in the poorer nations to switch from breastfeeding to the more 'modern' formula feeding. The quest to realise surplus value evidently has enormous social implications.

So does the extension of credit facilities that has occurred alongside these marketing efforts. The capacity to consume, as well as the willingness to consume, determines the level of demand. That is why credit is so important: it enables people to consume in excess, or at least in advance, of their income. The market for houses, for example, depends overwhelmingly on such credit facilities, without which few people would ever have the savings to buy such an expensive item outright. Demand for a wide range of consumer durables is also based on ready access to loan finance. Commercial institutions relentlessly seek further avenues for the proliferation of credit facilities. Importantly, while this facilitates the realisation of surplus value, it also adds to the potential instability of the economy.

The rapid circulation of capital

The annual rate of return on capital is higher if investments quickly generate profits that can then be reinvested. The rapid circulation of capital is therefore in the interests of those who own and control productive capitalist businesses. What this means, in terms of Box 16.1, is that the movements of capital between its successive stages (M, C, C^1, and M^1) should be, as far as possible, unimpeded. Blockages on the road to capital accumulation must be removed.

The image of the road is particularly apt in this context because improvements in transport technologies have made a major contribution to the rapid circulation of capital in its physical forms—as raw materials, machinery, labour power, and outputs of finished products. It is not simply a matter of more and better roads to permit faster movement of goods and people. Historically, the construction of canals and railways was crucial to capitalist development; more recently, larger freighters, container ships, and air cargo have also made significant contributions. The common element is the role of transport technology in extending the terrain of capital. Improvements in information technology are currently further overcoming the constraints of distance.

Urbanisation can also speed the circulation of capital. As such, urbanisation is functional for capitalism. It brings different elements in the production and consumption process into greater spatial proximity. On the other hand, as cities grow and become more congested, impediments to rapid circulation may reassert themselves. So, there are potential contradictions here: overcoming some impediments to the circulation of capital can create new ones.

Banks and other financial institutions also provide means whereby the rapid circulation of capital is achieved. Their activities facilitate the movement of capital between its physical and monetary forms. Think, for example, of a small manufacturer of, say, bicycles. A protracted period of bad weather may temporarily undermine the demand for her product. This will cause a crisis because the cash flow is inadequate to meet the ongoing costs of rent, wages, and so forth. So, she requests a loan from a bank to tide her over. The bank manager, noting that the manufacturer has a warehouse full of bicycles that can be expected to sell again when the weather improves, accedes to the request. The manufacturer stays in business, pays the interest on the loan, and eventually repays it in full when the stock of bicycles is sold. The bank has helped the firm bypass a bottleneck that might otherwise have caused business failure.

Not all relationships between productive and financial institutions are as harmonious as this. Indeed, as noted in Chapter 4, some political economists regard financial capital as partly undermining productive capital, channelling funds into speculative activities and adding to the instability of the system. However, for better or worse, finance is a key element in the capital accumulation process. According to Marxist analysis, financial institutions do not themselves create value, but are crucial for the capacity of modern capitalism to reproduce the conditions for capital accumulation.

Economic and social reproduction

Yet more fundamental are those social institutions that underpin and legitimise the capitalist system. Like any economic system, capitalism depends on the capacity and willingness of people to make it work. In other words, it has systemic requirements for its own reproduction. The workforce must be continually regenerated, the underlying class relationships between capital and labour must be seen as acceptable (or there must be mechanisms for their enforcement), and the people as a whole must regard the economic arrangements as tolerable, if not the best of all possible worlds. Herein lie complex interconnections between the capitalist economy and the institutions of modern capitalist society.

Consider the family, for example. The simple biological reproduction of the workforce does not require any particular family structure but, as Marxist feminists have frequently pointed out, the gendered division of labour within households tends to serve the needs of capital. Children are reproduced, nursed, and educated mainly by women, usually at no direct cost to the capitalist employers. Yet the employers eventually benefit from those domestic processes by having a healthy and appropriately disciplined workforce. The structure of the household, ostensibly standing outside the marketed production processes of the capitalist economy, may be crucial for the economy's reproduction.

Similar considerations apply to the state. Do the institutions of the modern state constitute a non-capitalist sphere of society? At first, it might seem so. Their presence is commonly justified by the need to have institutions concerned with social goals broader than the ones capitalist businesses normally address. Their organisation need not be directly geared to the accumulation of capital. However, as Marxists have often emphasised, the state in a capitalist society operates within the constraints of that economic system and may be interpreted as directly serving it. The 'ideological state apparatus' is a term sometimes used in this context. This term draws attention to the role of the state in the dissemination of ideologies that reinforce the existing economic and social order—ideologies about the importance of private property rights, for example. The ideological state apparatus may be defined very widely to include not only the institutions of government but also the churches, the media, and the education system. Within such institutions, there are sometimes dissident, even anti-capitalist, voices, but the actions of such institutions are usually supportive of the prevailing economic and social order; were they not, political destabilisation would be recurrent.

If the ideological state apparatus does not work effectively, the repressive state apparatus may be mobilised. Every society, other than an anarchist society based on voluntary cooperation, has some sort of backup system of a coercive nature. The legal system, the police, the armed forces, the prison system, and the intelligence agencies are its usual key elements. According to Marxist reasoning, what is distinctive about capitalism is the way in which these institutions serve the dominant class interests. The legal system may help in the settlement of interpersonal disputes, while the police may facilitate traffic flows, but their broader socioeconomic function is the enforcement of property rights. Is this repressive? This role of the state apparatus is usually relatively uncontentious in liberal capitalist societies, except at times when coercion is used for particular class purposes, such as when police or defence force personnel are used as strike breakers. However, many capitalist nations have more authoritarian traditions and structures; imprisoning political dissidents and deploying the military against civilians have been commonplace in many nations in the Americas, Asia, and Africa. Therein lies an obvious tension: insofar as the political economic system manifestly depends on its forced imposition, its legitimacy is undermined.

Conclusion

Capitalism is an adaptable economic system. It has its own systemic needs, which can be understood in terms of a Marxist model of the circuit of capital. These needs are fivefold: minimising costs, managing production, marketing products, rapidly circulating capital, and reproducing the economic and social order. Capitalism has been remarkably successful in meeting these systemic requirements. It has adapted diverse institutions for these purposes, wreaking massive transformations in technology and the organisation of work, social structure, and ideology.

These adaptations have not generally been the product of a master plan. No assertions about conspiracy are necessary either. The adaptations have largely been the product of decisions by the owners and managers of capitalist enterprises pursuing their own self-interest. Politicians and bureaucrats have played supportive roles, but generally fallen short of providing coherent, long-term economic planning. The adaptations of the capitalist system, as described in this chapter, have occurred in response to changed historical circumstances and been driven mainly by the imperative of profit seeking. It is somewhat ironic that we can use a Marxist model to understand the success of capitalism in making these adaptations.

It is not a success story in all respects. As noted throughout, the systemic requirements and the adaptations involve numerous tensions. Generating unemployment to restrict the power of labour constitutes a significant economic waste. Reducing wages to lower production costs tends to undermine the demand for the commodities produced. Developing financial institutions to facilitate the circulation of capital may lead to speculation that steers capital away from productive uses. And heavyhanded measures by the state to ensure social control can undermine the perceived legitimacy of the system. These tensions inhibit the achievement of any comfortable equilibrium outcome. Indeed, the picture painted here is one of an economy beset with internal contradictions. The resulting stresses are manifest in uneven development—both spatially and temporally. Some areas prosper while others decay, and periods of rapid capital accumulation and economic expansion are interrupted by periods of economic crisis.

KEY POINTS

- The circuit of capital functions most effectively when there are propitious conditions for businesses to minimise costs, produce a high rate of surplus value, and expand the markets for their products. There must also be no major impediments to a rapid circulation of capital and to economic and social reproduction.

- Much effort goes into ensuring that these conditions are met: businesses shop around for cheap resources, use technology that raises productivity, market an increasingly diverse array of goods and services, speed the movement of capital, and reproduce the workforce with the required skills and attitudes.

- Notwithstanding these efforts, fundamental contradictions arise in the capital accumulation process.

17 Economic Crises

Why is economic growth periodically interrupted by economic crises?

What contradictions are embedded in the system of production for profit?

Do these problems imply the eventual breakdown of the system?

Why should there ever be problems in an economic system in which capitalists put so much effort into pursuing profits, capital accumulation, and economic growth? Adam Smith expected that such commercially motivated behaviour would produce generally positive economic outcomes. Marx disagreed, emphasising the flaws in the system that would lead to deepening crises and, eventually, capitalism's demise. Marx thought capitalism was progressive in comparison to what had preceded it, in that it helped to eradicate 'the idiocy of rural life'[1] and facilitated the development of the forces of production. So why might it be only a transient phase in human history, eventually yielding to a yet more progressive socioeconomic system?

The most remarkable of all Marxist claims is that capitalism will eventually be replaced by socialism. The claim rests on distinctive views about the combination of structural forces and purposeful political activity capable of effecting that transformation. Elements of both structure and agency are integral to the process.

The structural aspect concerns economic crises. These are periods during which capital accumulation slows, the production of goods and services falls, and unemployment rises. 'Economic crisis', 'slump', 'depression', and 'recession' all describe essentially the same objective phenomenon: economic downturn. Marx thought that capitalism would be afflicted with such periodic downturns and, indeed, that the crises would likely deepen over time. Why? His reasoning rests on three distinct theories: the theory of disproportionalities, the theory of the tendency of the rate of profit to fall, and the theory of underconsumption.[2] It is useful to look at each of these explanations of economic crisis first, before asking how they interrelate, whether they do indeed explain economic crises in practice, and, if they do, what political responses might follow.

The anarchy of capitalist production

There is a recurrent possibility in a capitalist economy that the production decisions of firms in different industries will not be synchronised. Steel producers usually have to decide how much steel to produce before they know how much steel will be bought from them by car manufacturers, engineering firms, and their other customers. Car manufacturers, in turn, have to decide how many vehicles to produce without knowing (unless they engage in illegal industrial espionage) how many vehicles their competitors are planning to make. They cannot know for sure what their market share will be. Even the total market demand is uncertain. An unexpected event, such as a sharp rise in petrol prices, may cause consumer demand for cars to deviate from projections based on past trends. So, firms' production decisions, in the absence of industry-wide planning, do not necessarily produce a balance between supply and demand.

Why describe this situation as the 'anarchy of capitalist production'? Anarchy in this context denotes an unplanned, quite likely chaotic, situation (not to be confused with anarchism, which is a coherent political philosophy emphasising the desirability of basing society on voluntary cooperation rather than state-sponsored coercion). The absence of a centralised planning mechanism in a capitalist economy is the source of the uncertainty, if not chaos. Such central planning mechanisms have their own problems, if only because of the sheer size and complexity of the task of coordination. Further, markets are not altogether chaotic, because the price mechanism plays a coordinating role. If a steel producer makes too much steel, for example, the market price will fall, which will help sell the surplus steel and also signal the need to scale back production. The price system thereby restores some balance between output and demand. The problem is that it operates after the decisions about steel production for the coming period have been made. In the interim, the imbalance may spiral into a generalised economic crisis.

Why might this occur? Consider the steel industry example further. If the steel producer makes too much steel, workers at the steel plant are likely to be laid off. Without income, these workers will not be likely to buy cars or washing machines, for instance. This will mean that the producers of such consumer goods will demand less steel from the steel producers. The laid-off workers will also have less income to spend on food or clothing, which will create economic downturn and unemployment in the food and clothing industries. Thus, a localised structural imbalance becomes a generalised recession. The original disproportionality between the outputs of the different industry sectors triggers an economic crisis.

The value of this strand of Marxist crisis theory is its insight into the transmission process: it shows how a localised problem can trigger an economy-wide downturn and how the price mechanism performs a corrective function when such a downturn does occur. As already noted, discounting unsold stock may help it to be sold. Fundamentally, the cheapening of capital will tend to restore the potential for future profitability. This is what Marxists call the 'devalorisation of capital'. The reduction in the value of capital helps raise the rate of profit, because less capital now has to be outlaid to achieve those profits. Recessions are painful for capitalists as well as workers: usually, some capitalist enterprises are forced out of business altogether. Marxists regard the weeding out of the more inefficient capitals as 'cleansing' the economy as a whole, thereby creating the conditions for renewed capital accumulation process. No pain, no gain, it seems. The swelling of the ranks of the reserve army of unemployed labour is also conducive to the enforcement of more discipline on the workforce. For all these reasons, a capitalist economy is likely to bounce back from a recession brought on by structural imbalance or disproportionality. Yet, according to a second strand of Marxist crisis theory, more fundamental problems remain.

The tendency of the rate of profit to fall

Is the problem of recession deeply embedded in the capital accumulation process itself? This second strand of Marxist crisis theory posits that the more successfully capitalists accumulate capital, the greater the downward pressure on the rate of profit. Seeing their profit rates falling, capitalists will be less inclined to expand the productive capacity of their enterprises. Investment and output fall. An economic crisis occurs. Individual success causes systemic failure.

This paradox can be explained in various ways. Box 17.1 (on p. 145) sets out the formal explanation, using some simple algebraic notation. The basic proposition is that the capital accumulation process tends to raise the organic composition of capital, which is the ratio of constant capital to variable capital. Broadly speaking, this means that capitalists install more machinery and equipment in the process of expanding their businesses. If the rate of surplus value remains unchanged, the rate of profits would then tend to decline. This is definitional, but what is the underlying economic logic? Recall that, according to the labour theory of value, labour produces value. So, if the process of capital accumulation causes less labour to be used in production (relative to capital goods such as plant, machinery, and equipment), the rate of profit will fall. The total amount of surplus value generated may well continue to rise but, expressed as a ratio of total capital outlaid (constant capital and variable capital), the rate of profit will decline.

One might wonder why capitalists would continue to accumulate capital and expand their businesses if the effect is to undermine their own rate of profit. It seems self-defeating. The best explanation of this paradox hinges on the tension between individual and collective rationality. It is indeed rational for individual capitalists to invest, perhaps by installing the latest equipment in order to gain an advantage relative to their rivals. If their rivals follow suit, however, the advantage is eradicated. All the firms then face the general tendency for the rate of profit to fall. The source of capitalism's vitality—individual initiative in search of higher profits—becomes its Achilles heel as falling profit rates periodically herald recession.

Explained in this way, one might think that recession would not be merely an intermittent problem. The tendency for the rate of profit to fall could be expected to be even more persistent than the problem of sectoral disproportionality, perhaps destined to sound the death knell of the whole system. Indeed, Marx did expect this tendency of the rate of profit to fall to be manifest in intensifying economic crises over time, but he also conceded that there would be offsetting forces. The rate of surplus value could rise. That would offset the effect of increases in the organic composition of capital. Of course, capitalists are always concerned to raise the rate of surplus value. If installing new machinery enables capitalist firms to increase the pace of work performed by their workforce, they thereby increase the intensity of labour. If the resulting increase in the rate of surplus value is proportionately larger than the increase in the organic composition of capital, the overall profit rate will actually rise. The crisis tendency is averted.

Other offsetting forces noted by Marx included the effect of foreign trade in cheapening raw materials, the depression of wages below the value of labour power, and the cheapening of constant capital. The first of these—foreign trade—may provide a short-run counter to a falling profit rate. However, by drawing distant lands into the capitalist production process (what we would now call globalisation), it ultimately reproduces the same systemic contradictions, but on a larger scale.

The second offsetting force—depression of wages—looks the most obvious counter to the falling rate of profit. Marx actually placed little stress on it because of the general assumption that all wages and prices are market determined. Wages in general, therefore, reflect the value of labour power. However, where employers have particular monopoly power, and where the replenishment of the reserve army of labour weakens the bargaining position of labour, wage cutting is always an option. That, too, may offset the tendency of the rate of profit to fall.

As for the third factor—cheapening of constant capital—it is important to understand that, in Marxist theory, the organic composition of capital is defined in terms of labour values, not market prices. If machinery and other capital goods are becoming relatively cheap in the market, increased mechanisation is possible without raising the organic composition of capital. In such circumstances, the overall rate of profit may be constant, or even rising, and there need be no general tendency towards economic crisis.

An apparently weak conclusion beckons. The rate of profit may go up or down according to the relative strength of a rising organic composition of capital and these various offsetting forces. In other words, what starts out as a strong proposition about the inexorable tendency towards economic downturn ends up saying that the outcome is contingent. Capital accumulation can create the conditions for recession, but, equally, it may create the conditions for yet more accumulation. Is this a weak conclusion? Perhaps not. Capitalism does, indeed, alternate between periods of growth and recession. The Marxist theory suggests this pattern is explicable in terms of the relative movements in the rate of surplus value and the organic composition of capital.[3] The wave-like motion of capitalist development is thereby explained.

| BOX 17.1 | THE MECHANICS OF THE FALLING RATE OF PROFIT |

The total value of commodities produced = $c + v + s$

> where c is constant capital
>
> v is variable capital
>
> s is surplus value

Three important ratios using these terms can be defined as follows:

> s/v is the rate of surplus value (sometimes called the rate of exploitation)
>
> c/v is the organic composition of capital
>
> $s/(c + v)$ is the rate of profit.

This rate of profit can be expressed in terms of the rate of surplus value and the organic composition of capital by dividing each term in the numerator and denominator by v; that is:

$$\frac{s/v}{c/v + 1}$$

This is an alternative expression for the rate of profit, showing its positive relationship with the rate of surplus value (s/v) and its inverse relationship with the organic composition of capital (c/v).

Why does this rate of profit tend to fall as capital accumulation occurs? Consider the effect of a rise in c/v, caused by businesses installing more plant and machinery in their production processes. If s/v remains constant, any such rise in c/v depresses the rate of profit.

The assumption of a constant s/v is crucial to this reasoning; however, the assumption may be relaxed. Then the rate of profit may rise or fall depending on the relative size of changes in c/v and s/v. In other words, the rate of profit may fall (heralding a recession) or rise (heralding a period of expansion) according to the relative movements in the rate of surplus value and the organic composition of capital.

Underconsumption

What about consumers? Is the inadequacy of their spending, relative to the vast growth in output of goods and services, an alternative explanation of recurrent economic crises? Here is a third strand of reasoning about the cause of recurrent economic crises. As Marx put it:

> the epochs in which capitalist production exerts all its forces are always periods of overproduction, because the forces of production can never be utilised beyond the point at which surplus value can be not only produced but also realised; but the sale of commodities, the realisation of the commodity capital and hence also of the surplus value, is limited not only by the consumption requirements of society in general, but by the consumption requirements of a society in which the great majority are poor and must always remain poor.[4]

Monopoly Capital: An Essay on the American Economic and Social Order, an influential book by American Marxist economists Paul Baran and Paul Sweezy, develops this reasoning. According to Baran and Sweezy, modern capitalism is monopoly capitalism.[5] The large companies that now dominate the economy have the power to raise the prices of their products simultaneously, and sometimes collude to do so. They also have the ability to lower their costs through technical innovation. A widening gap between prices and costs results, making possible an even greater economic surplus. The problem is who is to buy the goods. Capitalists try to keep workers' wages down, but thereby undermine the major source of potential consumer spending. Capitalists' own consumption can partly fill the gap, but the scope for this is limited because capitalists must channel a proportion of their funds into business investment if capital accumulation is to continue. Commercial advertising helps to promote sales and, more generally, to foster a consumerist culture. The extension of credit facilities enables consumers' spending to exceed their incomes, at least in the short run. Governments also do their bit to pump up the aggregate demand through various forms of civilian and military expenditure, thereby helping to absorb the economic surplus. However, to the extent that these expenditures are financed by general taxation, they only divert expenditures from private to public sectors; the general problem of underconsumption remains. The root problem is the restricted purchasing power of the mass of the people, which prevents the growth of productive capacity being easily matched by a corresponding growth of demand.

Setting this underconsumptionist reasoning in the context of Marxist theory illustrates the inherent tension between the conditions for the production and realisation of surplus value. The production of surplus value requires low wages, whereas the realisation of surplus value is facilitated by high wages. Low wages keep production costs down, but high wages help capitalists sell their products. From the viewpoint of an individual capitalist, the ideal solution is obvious enough: keep the wages of your own workers down but encourage other capitalists to pay high wages to their workers in order to generate a buoyant market demand for your products. However, if all capitalists seek that outcome, it just cannot add up. The tension is systemic. From the viewpoint of capitalists as a whole, wages are always simultaneously too high and too low. This is because wages have a dual role—as a cost of production and as a source of demand for goods and services. Oscillations in the level of economic activity are the result of capitalist firms, and governments acting on their behalf, wrestling with this contradiction.

Economic crises and social change

These three strands of Marxist crisis theory—emphasising disproportionalities, the tendency of the rate of profit to fall, and the problem of underconsumption—can all be applied to understanding downturns in the level of economic activity in the real world. Explanations for particular economic crises at specific times and in specific places cannot simply be read off from these theories, but they direct attention to key variables for analysis. A fuller understanding of particular crises, such as the global financial crisis that began in 2007–08 and created deep recessions in many nations, requires consideration of the historical context. Such consideration includes the monetary factors associated with financial institutions, the role played by governments, the problems of inflation and deflation, the impact of international trade, and so forth. The Marxist analysis focuses on basic underlying conditions, rooted in the nature of capitalist production, but recognises that other factors may play a part.[6]

An economic crisis does not necessarily herald the demise of capitalism. If it precipitates structural economic changes that are conducive to renewed capital accumulation, slump turns into boom. It is rather like a crisis in your personal life: if you make the necessary adjustments to cope with it, life goes on and may even be better than before. In the case of economic crises, the adjustments are often painful, usually involving the closure of businesses and the loss of jobs. However, if that weeding out of inefficient elements results in a more dynamic economy, then capitalism moves again into an expansionary phase. Looked at from this perspective, a theory of periodic economic crises is not a theory of breakdown. It is an explanation of alternating booms and slumps, what orthodox economists more politely call 'the business cycle'.

Whether it is sensible to retain an economic system whose structural contradictions cause recurrent recessions—not to mention alienation and class inequality—remains the big question. If enough people think not, and decide to do something about it, alternative political economic arrangements can be fashioned. This is where the Marxian view turns towards the workers, not as victims of capitalist exploitation, but as the active agents of progressive political economic change. Marx anticipated that the working class, enlightened by radical intellectuals like himself, would bring about the revolutionary transformation from capitalism to socialism.

More moderate reformers have advocated incremental changes to the economic system to reduce its tendency to periodic crises. Keynesian and institutional economists have done so, as we will see in later chapters. Marxists are usually sceptical of such attempts to put 'band-aids' on the structural problems of capitalism. The fundamental flaw in the system that they identify is that economic crises are a feature of an economic system based on production for profit. Crises arise whenever the conditions for profit are not present, whether because of structural imbalances, insufficient demand, or any other factor. At such times, unemployment and unfilled social needs coexist. Any genuinely rational economic system would mobilise the unemployed resources to make the goods and services to satisfy those needs. Capitalism does not do this, because it is based on production for profit rather than production to directly satisfy human needs.

Therein lies the general Marxist case for moving from capitalism, with its inherent class conflicts and crisis-prone character, to a socialist alternative. Marx anticipated that the problems of recurrent economic crisis would fuel this revolutionary sentiment and bring more converts to the socialist cause. The penultimate chapter in this book returns to the question of why this has not come to pass—or at least not yet—in the advanced capitalist nations.

Conclusion

Marxism provides insight into how cooperation and conflict coexist within the capitalist economy. It emphasises the economy's inherently contradictory character. Workers and capitalists have to cooperate to win their daily bread (and cake), but there is a fundamental conflict of interest, manifest in distributional struggles and crisis tendencies. In seeking to develop an analysis of these conditions, Marxist political economy presents us with some particularly distinctive propositions:

- profits come from the exploitation of labour
- growth comes from the accumulation of capital
- crises come from contradictions in the system of production for profits
- conflict comes from the class structure
- change comes from class struggle.

This interpretation of capitalism is as contentious today as it was when it was first developed. Marx just will not lie down. Although his ideas were formulated in an early phase of capitalist development, they continue to have striking resonance today. Indeed, as long as capitalism exists, Marxism is bound to be a major reference point for the analysis of its contradictions. Equally predictably, the Marxist interpretation of capitalism is hotly contested by those with a stake in maintaining the existing economic system.

KEY POINTS

- Disproportionalities may develop into recessions because of the lack of planned industry coordination in a market economy.
- The tendency of the rate of profit to fall may lead to economic crises as the capital accumulation process raises the organic composition of capital.
- A tendency to underconsumption may be endemic if productive capacity expands more rapidly than workers' incomes.
- These economic crises, although hurtful to both workers and many businesses, can create conditions conducive to the transition from capitalism to socialism.

PART V

The Ideology of the Market

Neoclassical Economics

18 Free-market Economics

Why study neoclassical economics?

What were the origins of this influential school of economic thought?

What support does this type of economic theory give to neoliberalism today?

There is much more to capitalism than markets. There are underlying property rights and class relationships, economic activities undertaken by the state, and distinctive ideologies—as emphasised by the definition of the capitalist economy in Chapter 6. However, a dominant, if not exclusive, focus on markets is characteristic of orthodox economics. The core of that orthodoxy for more than a century has been neoclassical theory. Its exponents seldom use the term 'capitalism'. They represent the economy as a set of interconnected and self-regulating markets in which buyers and sellers freely interact without the need for substantial government regulation.

Neoclassical economic theory has been particularly influential in the past three decades as a means of reshaping the economy and the economic functions of government. It has also influenced other social sciences, as a form of economic imperialism, reshaping how political and social processes are understood as responses to individual economic incentives. It needs to be understood both as economic analysis and as ideology.

The market rules

Why are markets held in such high regard by mainstream economists? The short answer is because they are thought to permit mutually advantageous exchanges and ensure the efficient allocation of economic resources. Markets allow consumers to shop around for what suits them best, at a price they can afford. Producers seek to satisfy those consumer demands: those whose goods are not favoured by consumers will go out of business. There is no coercion and no intervention by third parties to disrupt or impede the transactions between self-interested buyers and sellers. From this perspective, in the words of one textbook author, 'Markets are the most effective as well as the most democratic mode of economic organisation that has yet been developed.'[1]

Underlying this faith in markets are two related assumptions: the desirability of private property and the undesirability of a substantial role for the state in economic affairs. These are the hallmarks of free-market ideology. Private property is favoured because it is the basis of the individual interests and incentives that drive a market economy. Collectively owned and managed property is held to be less conducive to the development of markets. Similarly, a substantial role for government in the economy is held to constitute an unwarranted intervention, likely to 'distort' patterns of resource allocation. The institutions of the state generally cannot know what serves individuals' interests as well as the individuals do themselves. Because the collective well-being of society is no more than the sum of individual well-being, it is best to leave individuals to organise their own transactions in the economic marketplace.

A variation on this theme emphasises the dynamic character of the market as its principal virtue. According to this view, markets encourage innovation and risk taking, while penalising failure. A world of rugged individualism provides the necessary incentives for economic progress. Thus, the strength of the market economy is not that it necessarily produces an efficient allocation of resources at any time, but that it is conducive to change and growth. This view of the market, significantly different from the view of the market as an equilibrium mechanism, derives from the Austrian school of economic thought, most notably the work of Frederik von Hayek (1899–1992), one of the most controversial winners of the Nobel Prize in Economic Sciences.[2] What it shares with neoclassical theory is a strong belief in the market economy as the best of all possible worlds.

These pro-market economic theories have significant echoes of social Darwinism, emphasising as they do the struggle for existence and survival of the fittest in producing a healthy society. Modern economists generally eschew any explicit connection with these social principles, which were popular a century ago and most clearly expounded by Herbert Spencer (1820–1903).[3] The implicit connection is still there, though. Because markets—in theory, at least—reward enterprise and weed out inefficiency, mainstream economists continue to hold them in high regard. By emphasising those features, neoclassical theory links up with what Daniel Fusfeld calls 'the folklore of individualism'.[4] It links up with neoliberal beliefs favouring free enterprise and freedom of choice, and opposing 'politically motivated' interventions in economic affairs. As such, neoclassical economics is an intriguing blend of technical analysis and ideology.

The origins of neoclassical economics

Neoclassical theory originated in the 1870s when scholars, working independently in different countries, laid the foundations for a new paradigm of economic analysis. The most prominent among them were the English economist William Stanley Jevons (1835–82), the Austrian economist Carl Menger (1840–1921), and the Swiss economist Leon Walras (1834–1910). Earlier in the nineteenth century, David Ricardo had steered economic analysis towards more abstract reasoning, paving the way for the theoretical model building of orthodox economics.

The neoclassical economists took this model building further, narrowing the broad-ranging concerns of classical political economy to a formal analysis of individual economic behaviour and the functioning of markets.

Menger and Jevons simultaneously developed the basic principles of marginal analysis, still the core of the neoclassical method today. Marginalism emphasises small adjustments, such as the adjustments a consumer might make in deciding which combinations of commodities might yield most pleasure. 'A little more of this and a little less of that', or 'a little more of that and a little less of this'. This incrementalism in individual choices is presented as the essence of economic decision-making. Rational consumers, one may surmise, will shift their spending between commodities until the utility, or satisfaction, given by each is equalised at the margin.

Jevons also posited that the utility gained from consuming extra units of each commodity would diminish as more of it were consumed. This is the basic principle of diminishing marginal utility: the more you have of something, it is implied, the less extra satisfaction results from having a little more of it. So, commodities that are abundant in supply generally command lower prices; consumers, experiencing diminishing marginal utility, are reluctant to pay much for additional units. Scarce commodities, on the other hand, are expensive, not necessarily because of the amount of labour that has gone into their production, but because they yield higher utility at the margin. Hence, diamonds are more highly priced than water, notwithstanding the fact that the latter is of greater importance to life.

Walras developed a view of the economy as a whole that showed how consumers' decisions interlock with producers' decisions. Changes in consumers' purchasing patterns, it was argued, would change the prices of the goods and thereby change the amount of each that would be supplied in the market. Thus a web of intricate relationships would ensure that the pattern of production would continuously adjust to the pattern of demand. Walras represented this interdependence in a mathematical model of the equilibrium conditions for an economy with numerous producers and consumers. It forms the basis of what is known as general equilibrium theory.[5]

These were powerful theoretical innovations. Classical explanations of value, emphasising the role of labour, were challenged and, according to the neoclassical economists, refuted. Utility replaced labour values. As Menger put it, 'The value of goods arises from their relationship to our needs, and is not inherent in the goods themselves. With changes in this relationship, value arises and disappears.'[6] Concern with analysing the total economic surplus was also jettisoned, along with the labour theory of value. Only individuals are considered to have surpluses, and these are of a psychological kind, arising when the utility derived from a commodity is over and above what the consumer had to pay for that commodity. The social perspective changes accordingly. The previous political economic concerns about classes, their competing interests, and the conditions for social progress—characteristic of both Marx's and the classical political economists' analyses—have no place in these new theories. Instead, the spotlight shifts to the behaviour of individuals and competitive markets, and to how consumers' demand influences prices and the allocation of resources.

A synthesis of these ideas, and further extensions and practical applications, was provided by Alfred Marshall (1842–1924). His *Principles of Economics*, first published in 1890, was the standard economics textbook in the first few decades of the twentieth century. Even today, it is possible to come across economists who claim that pretty much all worthwhile economic reasoning can be found in Marshall's text. Marshall's work was certainly a significant achievement. It blended the central concepts of marginal analysis with enduring ideas from classical political economy, and added some more practical concerns about industry and trade, and introduced (mainly in footnotes) a distinctive form of diagrammatic representation that has been widely used in orthodox economic analysis ever since. Marshall was not blind to the social problems that accompanied capitalist economic development in his time. However, his interest in social reform was secondary to the development of an economic theory that was, in essence, a sophisticated exposition of the self-adjusting mechanisms operating in a competitive market economy.

BOX 18.1   ALFRED MARSHALL (1842-1924)

Alfred Marshall was Professor of Economics at the University of Cambridge in the United Kingdom during a period when that university was renowned for its Victorian piety and temperance. In his inaugural lecture in 1885, Marshall set himself three tasks: to strengthen the scientific authority of economics, to align it with the Victorian moral and political mood, and to draw the best Cambridge men to the subject. During the 23 years he occupied the chair, he energetically pursued these goals, and did so with considerable success.

As a mathematician, Marshall thought that economics would have greater potential for scientific development if it were detached from moral philosophy. But he believed that mathematics should only be an adjunct to the expression of economic ideas in clear writing.[7] Subsequent neoclassical theorists have tended to invert these priorities, defining the concerns of the subject in terms of analytical technique. In Marshall's work the mathematics and diagrams are usually in the footnotes, not in the body of the text.

Marshall's alignment with Victorian sentiments was evident in the way he sought to reconstruct economics to mirror the ethical aspirations of the enlightened middle class of his time. His political inclination was to favour incrementally raising the living standards of ordinary people, but only as part of a process of raising the moral tone of society, 'as capitalists and workers learnt to behave more honourably towards each other'.[8] He had some interest in socialism, but came to strongly oppose it. He was cautious about trade unionism and evidently feared the exercise of union power. Of the 1887 engineers' strike, he said, 'I want these people beaten at all costs: the complete destruction of Unionism would be … not too high a price'.[9]

His lectures did indeed attract able students. Marshall initially supported women's rights to study at the university—a contentious issue in the late nineteenth century—but later opposed the granting of degrees to women.

One of Marshall's biographers describes him as 'the Soaring Eagle',[10] but others regard him as a rather pedestrian figure. He exemplified the Victorian concern to blend practical concerns with a more scientific method of analysis. His synthesis of economic analysis in the *Principles of Economics* had original elements. However, in trying to make economics more rigorous in its methods, he imposed a particular analytical orientation that excluded radical and challenging lines of enquiry. The price of respectability was, and is, a narrowing of vision.

Why neoclassical theory?

It is interesting to reflect on why neoclassical theory, pioneered by Menger, Jevons, and Walras, and synthesised by Marshall, developed at this particular time and came to be readily accepted as orthodox. At first sight it seems incongruous. Capitalism in practice was experiencing turbulent times, contrasting vividly with the picture painted by equilibrium theory. A deep, prolonged, economic depression had occurred in the 1880s, imperialist adventures were proceeding apace in the late nineteenth and early twentieth centuries, and corporate capitalism was on the rise. As another economist describes the situation:

> Just as competitive capitalism seemed to be achieving its greatest successes, the forces that Marx had predicted would lead to the concentration of capital began to show themselves. Improvements in technology were such that larger-sized plants were necessary to take advantage of the more efficient methods of production. Competition became so aggressive and destructive that small competitors were eliminated. Large competitors, facing mutual destruction, often combined in cartels, trusts, or mergers in order to assure their mutual survival.[11]

For neoclassical economists to be theorising at such a time about free markets, consumer choice, and the stability of equilibrium seems to indicate the existence of an enormous gulf between economic theory and actual economic conditions.

How can this be explained? A number of possibilities may be considered. One view emphasises the extension of markets. By the end of the nineteenth century, the spread of market relationships was much in evidence. The proponents of this process needed it to be seen as legitimate and advantageous, particularly because of its links in practice with imperialism: it was more reassuring to the dominant social classes to emphasise the invisible hand of the market than the iron fist of imperial domination. Theoretical developments focusing on the pervasive and generally beneficial character of market relationships fitted well with these developments and attitudes.

Second, an antidote was needed to the 'dangerous doctrines' of Karl Marx.[12] It is not that the leading neoclassical scholars of the time had read Marx, or were consciously attempting refutations—usually, that was not the case—but the economic and social elite of the time, fearing the possibility of popular uprisings that might threaten the existing political economic order, were naturally attracted to a theory that showed capitalism in its most favourable light as a market economy in which freedom of exchange would ensure socially beneficial outcomes.

The theorists themselves were more concerned with finding solutions for puzzles carried over from classical political economy. Therein lies a third explanation, of a purely intellectual character, for the ascendancy of neoclassical economics. The classical theory of value was rejected because it seemed to pay insufficient attention to demand-side considerations. Shifting the focus from how labour creates value to how consumers shape the demand for products seemed to fill a gap in the prevailing economic theory. According to this view, the rise of neoclassicism was partly the consequence of novel solutions to some unresolved conceptual issues in classical political economy.

Last, it is pertinent to note that the neoclassical economic ideas reflected the state of thinking in other fields of intellectual activity. The growing influence of utilitarian philosophy, associated with the ideas of Jeremy Bentham (1748–1832), is particularly noteworthy.[13] The neoclassical economic terminology shows some obvious links with utilitarianism; utility and disutility, for example. Here are particular economic instances of the pleasures and pains that shape all human conduct, according to utilitarian philosophy. From this perspective, neoclassical theory can be regarded as the application to economics of a prevailing intellectual fashion of the nineteenth century.

All this took place in the context of a general reverence for science in social enquiry. No doubt the pioneering neoclassical economists thought they were applying unprecedented scientific rigour to the study of economic phenomena. The delineation of economics as separate from other social studies reflected this. The label 'political economy' was beginning to be regarded as value laden; 'economics' was preferred because it sounded more like 'physics'. This attempt to emulate the scientific method so successfully used in Newton's physics was not altogether novel—it had been evident in classical political economy, too—but it reached its peak in neoclassical theory. One critic has called it 'physics envy'.[14] Hence the emphasis in neoclassical theory on the behaviour of atomistic units (treating firms and consumers as the molecules in the economic system) and on equilibrium conditions (determined by the interaction of those molecules according to the laws of economic motion). In neoclassical economics, the principal law of motion is not gravity, as in Newtonian physics, but economic self-interest. Markets are posited as the natural state in which the equilibrating mechanisms work best.

Some continuity between classical political economy and neoclassical economics can be discerned in all this. A pro-capitalist ideology is the common element. Economic liberalism lives on in neoclassical economics, as it does to the present day in extensions of this mainstream current of economic thinking. A preference for the market and a general aversion to state intervention are manifestations of what has now come to be known as neoliberalism. Adam Smith's ethical concerns and subtle reservations about market behaviour are shorn away in the transition.

Analytically, however, there is a fundamental discontinuity between neoclassical economics and classical political economy. Gone is the classical political economists' quest to understand the complexity of economic, social, and political institutions and the conditions for social progress. In its place is the more limited neoclassical concern to model the price system under conditions of market competition. Concern with which social classes get the economic surplus is replaced by concern to explain market equilibria. The focus narrows from production, distribution, growth, accumulation, and crises to only exchange relations. We enter a theoretical world of buyers and sellers interacting on a level playing field.

Demand and supply, prices and equilibrium

How are the interactions between buyers and sellers to be understood? Box 18.2 shows the most fundamental of all orthodox economic propositions: the theory of the determination of price by demand and supply, represented by the Marshallian cross.

Neoclassical economic analysis, as depicted in Box 18.2, represents demand and supply as being of equal importance in determining prices. According to Alfred Marshall, 'We might as reasonably dispute whether it is the upper or under blade of a pair of scissors that cuts a piece of paper, as whether value is determined by utility or cost of production.'[15]

BOX 18.2	THE DETERMINATION OF PRICE BY SUPPLY AND DEMAND

If sellers supply more of a commodity when its price rises, and buyers demand more of a commodity when its price falls, supply and demand curves can be constructed with the following characteristics:

FIGURE 18.1 MODELLING SUPPLY AND DEMAND

In Figure 18.1, price *OA* ensures that supply equals demand. Quantity *OX* is bought and sold at that price. The market clears.

The market price will then respond to any change in consumer demand. For example, if a product suddenly becomes more fashionable, its demand curve will shift to the right—from Demand 1 to Demand 2 in the following diagram. The equilibrium price rises to *OB* and the amount bought and sold rises to *OY*.

FIGURE 18.2 MODELLING A SHIFT IN DEMAND

The market price also responds to a change in supply conditions. For example, lowering of the costs of production following the implementation of new technology may shift the supply curve, as shown by the shift from Supply 1 to Supply 2 in the following diagram. The equilibrium price falls to *OC* and the amount bought and sold rises to *OZ*.

FIGURE 18.3 MODELLING A SHIFT IN SUPPLY

Marshall's dual emphasis on demand and supply was not novel, having been evident in Adam Smith's work, for example. But Marshall formalised it—as in the diagrammatic 'Marshallian cross' shown in Figure 18.1 opposite. The effect was to balance the early neoclassical theorists' emphasis on utility and demand with some consideration of supply conditions. The role of labour in production, which had been the principal focus of value theory hitherto, was to be regarded subsequently as only one of many factors shaping prices.

Three other points about neoclassical theory are notable. One is its posited generality. The theory of demand and supply is held to apply to all goods and services, whether they be agricultural products or minerals, manufactured goods or services. It is also held to apply to factors of production, whether they be different types of labour, or land or capital. For each factor there is a demand that normally varies inversely to its price, and a supply that responds positively to price changes. For each product or factor of production (except in perverse cases where demand or supply curves bend backwards) there is just one market clearing price at which demand equals supply.

Second, following from this last observation, there is the claim that markets tend towards equilibrium. A rise in price will cause supply to exceed demand, so sellers will bid against one another for customers, causing the price to go down again. A fall in price will cause demand to exceed supply, so buyers will bid against one another, causing the price to climb again. An analogy can be drawn with the equilibrium of a ball in a saucer. The ball will be disturbed if the saucer shakes, but it will tend to revert to its central position. So it is, according to this model, with market prices. The prevailing prices respond to changes in the conditions of demand (resulting from changes in consumers' tastes, for example) or the conditions of supply (resulting from the development of new production technologies or the entry of new firms into the market, for instance). Each response involves a shift to a new equilibrium position. A systemic stability prevails.

Third, the way in which neoclassical economics accounts for these posited features of the market economy is distinctive. Everything is modelled according to marginal analysis. The focus is on incremental adjustments: on how small changes in the conditions of demand and supply bring about the small changes in prices necessary to restore equilibrium. The door is opened to the use of differential calculus. Neoclassical theory becomes, in effect, a means of applying that particular mathematical tool to the study of individual choice and market behaviour.

For this purpose, a number of simplifying assumptions are made. Consumers' tastes are taken as given. So too is the distribution of income and the state of technology. The analysis is thereby made tractable, but at the expense of assuming away an array of important political economic considerations. Alongside this distinctive methodology is a distinctive ideology: the belief that only small adjustments are necessary in order to achieve optimal economic outcomes. The big concerns of Marxist economics—class struggle, economic crises, and revolution (or even evolution)—have no place in such an idealised world.

Normative implications

Neoclassical economists claim to be concerned with positive economics—with understanding what is, rather than what ought to be. Characteristic questions are, 'Why do peaches cost more than potatoes?', 'Why are carpenters' wages higher than those of clerks?', and 'Why is the value of the national currency rising or falling relative to the currencies of other nations?'

These relative prices are held to be the key to understanding how economic resources are allocated. Their explanation requires analysis of the demand and supply conditions relating to each of the products, factors of production, or assets in question.

Neoclassical economics also has a normative dimension in practice. Notwithstanding the professed emphasis on 'positive economics', value judgments intrude in various ways. The underlying assumptions are based on judgments of what matters. The market economy is shown in its most favourable light, as a mechanism responsive to changes in the conditions of demand and supply, continually reconciling competing interests. Buyers cannot always obtain what they want at the price they want. Sellers cannot charge whatever price they like for their products. But the interaction of buyers and sellers establishes the conditions for mutually acceptable exchanges. The price system mediates, even resolves, conflict. Moreover, it allocates resources efficiently, responding instantly to changes in the prevailing technologies of production and revealed consumer preferences. Showing the market economy in this favourable light is the ideological role of neoclassical theory.

BOX 18.3	COMPARING NEOCLASSICAL AND MARXIST VIEWS

Neoclassical economics	Marxist economics
Deductive methodology	Study of historical processes
Focus on the individual	Focus on classes
Analysis of exchange based on the theory of utility	Analysis of production based on the labour theory of value
Marginal analysis, substitution, and equilibrium	Analysis of major structural political economic changes
Assumption of competition	Concentration and centralisation of capital
Markets leading to harmony	Capitalism characterised by conflict

Conclusion

To illustrate the most distinctive features of neoclassical economics, Box 18.3 above shows its contrasts with Marxism. There are significant differences of methodology, significantly different assumptions, and striking contrasts of political interpretation. The neoclassical approach to economic analysis focuses on an abstract world comprising individuals and markets, not classes and power relationships. A connection between that abstract world of pure markets and the real world of capitalism is often implied, though. If the principles of demand and supply can show competitive markets to be efficient allocative mechanisms, one may infer that capitalism, notwithstanding the market imperfections it features in practice, has similar tendencies. But how close is the connection? Political economic critics of neoclassical theory commonly argue that there is a wide gulf between the theory and actually existing capitalism. So the foundations of this influential theory warrant careful consideration. This is the linking theme in the next five chapters.

KEY POINTS

- Neoclassical economic theory has been the dominant economic orthodoxy for over a century.

- It presents an analysis of the market economy that is methodologically distinctive, emphasising individual utility-maximising behaviour in competitive markets, marginal analysis, and equilibrium conditions.

- It also conveys a distinctive ideology, representing the market as the necessary underpinning for freedom of choice and for the efficient allocation of economic resources.

19 Consumers

What is consumer rationality?

How do neoclassical theorists analyse consumer behaviour?

Does this give us a useful guide to the behaviour of consumers in practice?

The orthodox economic theory of markets pays considerable attention to consumer behaviour. This should come as little surprise. Markets are focal points for the interaction between buyers and sellers. The sellers normally make the first move, bringing to the market what they have for sale. But they will have wasted their time and effort if consumers do not buy. Those sellers would then disappear from the market, to be replaced by others whose goods have characteristics and prices more to the consumers' liking. The story becomes a little more complicated when retail stores act as intermediate institutions between the buyers and the producers of the goods. It becomes more complicated still when the preferences and behaviour of the consumers are shaped by processes of commercial advertising and other forms of demand management.

Neoclassical economists adopt a very distinctive approach to the analysis of consumer behaviour. They build particular models based on assumptions about utility maximisation, consumer rationality, and consumer sovereignty. This chapter explores this modelling process and these assumptions, raising questions about the relationship between the theory and the practical processes of consumer choice. In what sense, if any, are consumers rational? Is it sensible to regard consumers as the most powerful actors in the economic drama? If they are not the most powerful actors, who is?

Consumer rationality

Let's start with some introspection. If you ask yourself whether your decisions are rational, can you feel confident about giving a clear answer? Few of us would willingly admit to recurrent irrationality, even if we concede that we sometimes make ill-informed or unwise choices that we subsequently regret. Our consumption decisions are a case in point. They may vary from the impulsive to the habitual, but both extremes may be justified as suiting our personal circumstances, needs, and desires. We do not usually like to admit to being manipulated by sales promotion. Of course, we see and hear the commercials, but we generally prefer to feel ourselves sufficiently selective, critical, and maybe just downright cynical about them.

The claim to consumer rationality implies a clear yardstick by which we can measure the effectiveness of our actions. Does rationality imply something about the process by which we make choices; collecting information about all the available products, for example? How much of this information is it rational to collect, given that the information-gathering process itself may be costly or time-consuming? Or does rationality only imply something about the outcome of choice—the absence of regret, or a perceptible increase in personal happiness, for example? These are not easy questions to answer.

Neoclassical economists often seek to cut through this complexity, saying that only 'revealed preferences' matter. Thus, when a consumer is faced with a choice between alternative products with different prices, we can observe her or his behaviour and infer the relevant preference ordering. However, if this process of choosing is to be regarded as rational, then some general goal-achievement process must be involved. For this purpose, neoclassical economists have posited the goal of utility maximisation. While it is conceded that consumers have varying personalities and preferences, they are assumed to pursue a uniform objective: the greatest utility (or satisfaction) that is attainable with their disposable income. Rationality implies seeking and achieving that goal. At first sight, it seems a reasonable, if rather general, proposition. It implies that considerations of self-interest dominate all other influences in the consumption process. It implies that consumers have sufficient self-awareness to know which goods and services best suit their own needs and desires. It implies purposive action.

The problem is that this assumption of utility maximisation may involve circular reasoning. Anything that consumers do maximises their utility: otherwise they wouldn't do it. Consuming addictive drugs, for instance, may be deemed to satisfy one person's particular needs. Making impulsive consumer decisions rather than carefully considered ones may be interpreted as utility-maximising behaviour for someone who places a high premium on the time spent making choices or on the thrill of a spontaneous and risky decision. Each of us has different preferences. So, it is difficult to establish that any particular patterns of choice are not self-interested and rational for the people concerned. Utility maximisation starts to look like a tautology: a proposition that cannot be refuted, and which therefore has no place in any enquiry purporting to be scientific.

Notwithstanding these concerns, the utility maximisation postulate has a central place in neoclassical theory. It offers a theory of the consumer to represent the behaviour of all consumers. In this way, *Homo economicus*, the universal rational economic person, is born.[1]

Modelling consumer choice

Box 19.1 shows the formal process of modelling the consumption decisions of a utility-maximising individual. It considers the simplest case of a choice between two commodities. The consumer is deemed to be in an imaginary situation where there are just two commodities;

in our example, bread and wine. It is the sort of situation depicted in the following stanza from *The Rubaiyat* by Persian astronomer–poet Omar Khayyam:

> *A book of verses underneath the bough*
>
> *A loaf of bread, a jug of wine and thou*
>
> *Beside me singing in the wilderness*
>
> *Oh wilderness were paradise enough.*[2]

BOX 19.1

THE NEOCLASSICAL THEORY OF CONSUMER CHOICE

The essential features of neoclassical consumer theory, in the simplest case of a consumer facing a choice between two commodities (say, bread and wine), can be summarised as follows.

Assumed objective

The consumer seeks to maximise his or her utility.

Given knowledge of

- the consumer's income
- the prices of the commodities
- the consumer's utility function, which shows how his or her utility depends on the quantities of bread and wine consumed.

Deduce

The consumer selects the optimal commodity combination such that

$$\frac{\text{marginal utility of bread}}{\text{marginal utility of wine}} = \frac{\text{price of bread}}{\text{price of wine}}$$

The marginal utility of a commodity is the additional utility the consumer derives from consuming one more unit of it. By consuming products so that their relative marginal utilities are equal to their relative prices, the consumer maximises utility.

What balance between the two commodities—bread and wine—will the consumer select? If the consumer's income is limited, her or his choice will depend on each product's relative prices and their expected contribution to the consumer's satisfaction. This latter aspect can be represented in terms of a utility function, showing the extent to which different quantities of the two commodities contribute to the consumer's total satisfaction. Utility is a function of (or depends upon) consumption. Thus, the utility function denotes the functional relationship between the consumer's utility and the quantity of bread and wine consumed.

If the consumer has all the relevant information (that is, income, commodity prices, and the characteristics of his or her own utility function), the best selection may be deduced. This optimal combination of the two commodities is that at which the ratio of marginal utilities for bread and wine equals the ratio of their prices, as shown in Box 19.1.

FIGURE 19.1 THE NEOCLASSICAL ANALYSIS OF CONSUMER DEMAND:
THE CASE WHERE ONE CONSUMER IS CONFRONTED WITH A CHOICE BETWEEN TWO COMMODITIES

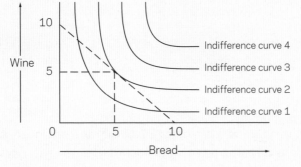

Marginal utility is the additional amount of utility or satisfaction generated by the last unit of the product consumed; that is, by consuming one more loaf of bread or one more bottle of wine. Where the ratio of marginal utilities between any pair of commodities (known as the marginal rate of substitution) equals the ratio of their prices, the consumer cannot do any better. One can think of the consumer juggling the pros and cons of having a little more wine and a little less bread, or a little more bread and a little less wine, until the balance is just right. Formally, the conclusion can be established using some diagrams, as shown in Figure 19.1.

The budget line in the first diagram of Figure 19.1 shows how much bread and/or wine the consumer can afford with his or her existing income. If the consumer has $10 to spend and units of bread and wine both cost $1 each, then the consumer can have 10 units of wine and none of bread, 10 units of bread and none of wine, or any intermediate combination. The slope of the budget line depends on the relative prices of the two commodities; the line's distance from the point of origin depends on the consumer's income.

The indifference curves in the second diagram depict the consumer's utility function. An indifference curve connects the combinations of the two commodities that give equal utility (or satisfaction) to the consumer. The shape of each indifference curve depends on the willingness with which the consumer would substitute one product for the other (which will depend on the characteristics of the products and on the consumer's personal tastes). Higher indifference curves indicate higher levels of utility (or satisfaction). Assuming that more of each commodity is preferred to less, the indifference curves will normally be roughly parallel to each other and will not intersect. They are like the contour lines on a topographic map of a hill, each connecting points of the same height (or, in this case, satisfaction). In effect, they represent contour lines on a hill of pleasure.

Superimposing the budget line (Diagram 1) on the indifference curves (Diagram 2) enables us to identify the consumer equilibrium (Diagram 3). In this case, given the consumer's income, indifference curve 2 is revealed as the highest level of utility attainable. The consumer will spend his or her income on five units of wine and five units of bread. This is better than buying eight units of wine and two of bread, or two of wine and eight of bread, both of which would result in the lower level of utility associated with being on indifference curve 1. On the other hand, the higher utility levels represented by indifference curves 3 and 4 are unattainable: the consumer's income and the prevailing prices of bread and wine put those levels of happiness beyond reach.

The equilibrium point is where the budget line is at a tangent to the highest attainable indifference curve. At that point, the ratio of the prices of the two commodities is equal to the ratio of their marginal utilities to the consumer. It should not be too difficult to see why. The ratio of the prices is given by the slope of the budget line, while the ratio of the marginal utilities is given by the slope of the indifference curve. At that point where the two ratios are equal is the equilibrium outcome. This is the point of tangency between the budget line and the indifference curve, as shown in Diagram 3. It conforms with—indeed, purports to prove—the consumer's decision rule posited earlier in Box 19.1.

Consumer demand

The neoclassical economic theorising about the processes involved in consumers' decisions sounds rather complicated. It actually involves a simple linear process, almost ludicrously simple by the standards of modern psychology.[3] Consumers, knowing their own utility functions, weigh up the price of each product against the pleasure they will derive from consuming incremental units of it and select an optimal combination within their budget.

You may wonder if consumers actually do this, but neoclassical economists make no such claim. To them, it does not matter whether consumers actually go through this systematic thought sequence before they buy bread and wine, or bars of chocolate, suits of clothes, cars, or houses. What does matter is that consumers act *as if* they do.

All that we can observe in practice are the outcomes of the consumers' decision-making processes. One commonly observable outcome is described by the so-called 'law of demand': this is the proposition that the demand for a commodity tends to fall when its price rises, if other influences on demand remain unchanged. It is a generally accepted proposition, although there are exceptions, such as when goods are purchased mainly for their status or snob appeal.[4] It underpins the depiction of the demand curve introduced in the preceding chapter.

The simplest explanation of the law of demand builds on the *principle of diminishing marginal utility*. This holds that the more units of a commodity a person consumes, the less additional satisfaction is derived from each successive unit. The standard example is that of a man who, having been lost in the desert and dying of thirst, is offered successive glasses of water. The first glass gives enormous satisfaction; it saves his life. The second is delicious, the third very enjoyable, the fourth less so, and so on. Eventually, more water adds nothing to his well-being. By implication, the amount a consumer would be willing to pay for successive units of the commodity declines, until a point is reached at which she or he is not willing to pay anything at all for one more unit.

Further reflection suggests two supplementary reasons for a generally inverse relationship between the price of a product and the demand for it. One is the *substitution effect*. In a market economy a consumer is likely to substitute another commodity for one whose price has risen. If wine is rising in price, a consumer may buy beer or whisky instead. The other influence is the *income effect*. A rise in price of any commodity, particularly if it is one on which the consumer spends a substantial proportion of his or her income, effectively reduces that person's real disposable income. As a result, the consumer will be likely to buy less of the commodity—and less of other commodities, too. The two effects together explain the generally inverse form of the relationship between demand and price.

These kinds of consumer responses to price changes are observable in market behaviour. They enable the empirical estimation of demand curves. The grander ambition of neoclassical theory is to 'go behind the demand curve' to explain the underlying utility-maximising processes. Based on the analytical devices introduced in Figure 19.1, the effects of a change in the price of a commodity on an individual's demand for it can be interpreted as a series of consumer equilibria, each equilibrium relating to a different budget line. A fall in the price of bread (causing the budget line to hinge outward to the right), for example, enables the consumer to do one of the following: buy much more bread, and less wine, which is now relatively more expensive; buy rather more of both bread and wine; or buy the same amount of bread and use the benefits of lower bread prices to buy more wine. Which of these responses actually occurs depends on the consumer's preferences. In the aggregate, though, one would normally expect that the higher the price of a product, the lower the demand for it will be—so the demand curve will slope down to the right.

Voila! The connection between the general law of demand and the theory of individual consumer choice is demonstrated.[5]

This is the grand claim of neoclassical consumer theory: that it links observable empirical phenomena, such as demand curves, with theorising about the nature of consumer behaviour. Thus, it claims to reveal the fundamental features of rational choice. If individual consumer choices can be understood in this way, the argument runs, we can infer something about the processes underpinning the swings in the behaviour of consumers as a whole. We can also introduce the concept of *elasticity* to measure the strength of the relationship between changes in prices and changes in demand.

BOX 19.2   ELASTICITY OF DEMAND

Orthodox economics provides a tool for measuring the responsiveness of consumer demand to changes in price, income, or other relevant variables. This is the elasticity of demand.

The responsiveness of demand for a commodity to changes in its own price can be quite readily assessed. If the proportionate change in demand is less than the proportionate change in price, the demand is said to be inelastic. This is typically the case where a product has no readily available substitute, especially if that product accounts for a small proportion of total consumer expenditure. Salt is a classic example. On the other hand, if a change in the price of a commodity brings about a more than proportionate change in the demand for it, the demand is said to be elastic. This is the usual case where substitutes are readily available. Whether this is so depends, in part, on the breadth of definition of a commodity. Thus, the overall demand for food or for clothing may be relatively inelastic, but the demand for particular types of food or for particular items of clothing is normally much more elastic.

This notion of elasticity is useful as an antidote to the popular view that sellers always make more revenue by raising the price of their products. They will do so only when the demand for their products is inelastic. When the demand is elastic, the higher price will cause potential customers to stop buying, so the total sales revenue will fall. So, if you are running a dance party, you do not necessarily make more income by raising the admission price. Similarly, a bookseller does not necessarily make more profits by raising the prices of the books. Evidently, knowing about elasticity is useful for sellers who have the ability to make independent decisions about their pricing policies.

Different measures of elasticity can show the responsiveness to other variables, too. The income elasticity of demand, for example, measures the responsiveness of demand to changes in consumer incomes. The cross-price elasticity of demand measures the responsiveness of the demand for one commodity to changes in the price of others (how much the demand for wine responds to changes in the price of bread, for instance). Elasticity can be applied to supply, too: elasticity of supply shows the responsiveness of the supply of a commodity to changes in its price.

Measures of elasticity are useful tools for empirical research. However, their use for such practical purposes is quite independent of any connections with neoclassical economic theory.

Consumer sovereignty?

There is a normative dimension to consumer demand theory. This is because its primacy in neoclassical economics embodies a distinctive assumption about consumer sovereignty.

What does consumer sovereignty mean? To quote Paul Samuelson, the Nobel Prize-winning economist who set the standard for all textbooks of orthodox economics in the last half century, it implies that 'the consumer is, so to speak, the king ... each is a voter who uses his money as votes to get the things done he wants done'.[6] (The gender bias in Samuelson's language is, presumably, not meant to deny a similar role for women as queens of the marketplace.) All consumers, by their purchasing decisions, send signals to the producers as to which goods and services to continue supplying. Thus, the pattern of consumer preferences determines the pattern of production. Shoppers rule.

Were this consumer sovereignty assumption to hold true in practice, it would be a very attractive feature. It could be inferred that a market economy is conducive to maximum consumer well-being. Indeed, the opponents of government regulation of markets commonly base their arguments on this very presumption.[7] However, the claim has also been subjected to regular criticism.

The most obvious challenge is to the underlying assumption of consumer rationality. A particular difficulty in this respect concerns the origin of consumer preferences. For the purposes of constructing neoclassical theory, consumers' tastes are taken as a given. This may be described as the 'immaculate conception of the indifference curve'. The failure to address the formation of preferences means that the theory is inherently incomplete. We need to ask how tastes are formed and how rational those processes are.

In practice, consumers' tastes depend on a number of interconnected social influences; such as custom, habit, and social emulation.[8] Does this undermine the assumption of the cool, calm, calculating consumer considering the consequences of alternative courses of action? Unless we are willing to accept utility maximisation as a tautology (that is, whatever consumers do maximises their utility), then we are bound to question whether the outcomes of socially conditioned consumer choices are rational in any objective sense. If they are not rational, then the presumption that their free expression will lead to optimal outcomes looks correspondingly dubious.

A second strand of criticism links these concerns to the effort by firms to shape consumers' demand. If consumers base their decisions on incomplete information, we cannot automatically assume that the outcome of their choices is utility maximising. If they base their decisions on biased information, the problem is significantly worse. In practice, of course, much of the information that consumers have comes in the form of commercial advertising messages disseminated by the firms trying to sell their products to them. One might try to differentiate the informational from the persuasive elements in those messages, but this is very difficult in practice. The common aim of the messages is to adjust demand to supply, rather than vice versa.

Of course, consumers are not always responsive to the advertising messages: sometimes new products are commercial failures. There are also occasions when the advertising messages of rival producers cancel one another out. Market research may also play a part in product design and modification, providing a feedback loop between supply and demand. However, the general assumption of consumer sovereignty looks significantly less tenable in conditions where 'sales and production efforts interpenetrate to such an extent as to become virtually indistinguishable'.[9]

A third, rather different, reservation about the conventional neoclassical reasoning accepts the assumption of consumer rationality but emphasises the problems arising from consumers' constrained array of choices. In other words, consumers are regarded as doing their best with their restricted incomes and with less-than-perfect information. However, they only get to choose from a limited range of possibilities that serves the interests of capitalist businesses, not the interests of society more generally. Under capitalism, the only choices offered to consumers are those from which profits can be generated, unless governments or other non-profit agencies intervene to supply public goods serving collective social needs, such as a cleaner environment. So, consumers buy flashier cars, for example, seeking to enhance their personal pleasure (by increasing their social status, or compensating for their sexual inadequacies, for instance), or four-wheel drive SUVs, which are prodigiously wasteful of fuel. As a consequence, the cities become more congested, the atmosphere becomes more polluted, and our energy resources become more depleted. The aggregation of individually rational choices does not necessarily produce socially rational outcomes.[10]

A variation on this last theme is the problem posed by the presence of 'positional goods'.[11] Some goods that consumers seek are inherently limited in their accessibility. Not everyone can live in a house by the beach or in the most prestigious suburb. Not everyone can own an original Monet or Picasso painting. With rising incomes, the competition to attain these goods intensifies. This raises their price. Or, if some other types of positional goods do become more widely consumed, their value tends to be eroded. Thus, the personal enjoyment of visiting a mountain wilderness area diminishes as more visitors come; those seeking tranquillity and communion with nature now need to spend more time and money going further afield.

There is an even more fundamental tension. This concerns the interdependence between consumers' aspirations and achievements. If, having attained a particular standard of living, consumers aspire to yet higher consumption levels, the utility they derive from current consumption tends to diminish. Of course, it is in the interest of capitalist businesses to fuel those consumer aspirations, because it helps to sell their products, but the effect is to perpetuate dissatisfaction. If consumer well-being reflects the relationship between aspirations and achievements (the wish to buy and the capacity to buy), then it is continually frustrated in these circumstances.

Conclusion

Neoclassical theory presents us with an elegant theory of consumer demand. In an age when consumerism is pervasive, the emphasis on consumers may be regarded as appropriate, but whether neoclassical theory helps to illuminate consumer behaviour in the real world is contentious.[12] The reflections in this chapter suggest that a fuller consideration of consumer behaviour needs to consider the social context within which consumers' tastes are formed.

The study of consumer behaviour must also be linked with a study of business behaviour. The consumer sovereignty assumption—that consumers have the ultimate power over firms—is challenged where the firms are giant corporations equipped to promote brand loyalty for their products. From a political economic perspective, it may be inferred that the relative power of consumers and firms depends on the resources available to them and the extent to which each is organised to pursue their collective interests. Even from the more narrow, neoclassical perspective, it is important to bring firms into the picture. Just as it takes two to tango, interactions in markets always involve at least two parties.

KEY POINTS

- The assumption that consumers act rationally is central to neoclassical theory because it provides a basis for building a model of systematic consumer choice.
- Similarly, the assumption of consumer sovereignty is central in neoclassical theory because it represents consumer preferences as the driver of economic activity, and thereby shows the market to be a want-satisfying mechanism.
- Both of these assumptions are questionable.

20 › Firms

What are firms? What do they seek? How do they get it?

How do neoclassical economists analyse firms?

Does this provide a useful guide to business behaviour in practice?

Firms are key players in the capitalist drama. Their behaviour shapes the overall character of the economic system. Whether firms are the drivers of exploitation and class inequality, as Marxists contend, or instruments for serving consumers' interests, as the neoclassical consumer sovereignty model implies, is a crucial question in any assessment of the capitalist economy. This chapter examines how firms are viewed within neoclassical theory, and seeks to emphasise the distinctive underlying assumptions and the inferences drawn about business efficiency.

Diverse businesses, single theory

What are firms? Business organisations come in many shapes and sizes. Some are engaged in agricultural production, some in mining, some in manufacturing, some in finance, and some in the provision of services. Some are big, some small. Some are companies, some partnerships, and some sole traders. Some are transnational corporations, some are local corner stores. Neoclassical economics attempts to build a single theory that applies to them all. Alfred Marshall paved the way for this with his notion of the 'representative firm'.[1] Contemporary neoclassical economics textbooks develop this theme by presenting models purporting to show the universal features of business behaviour. This is not to claim that all firms are identical; rather, it is to assert that common principles apply, notwithstanding the differences in scale, organisation, and type of activity. It is a bold claim.[2]

Firms are not markets. Firms may raise capital in financial markets, they may hire their workers from labour markets, and they may sell their products in markets for goods and services; however, they are not markets themselves. Their internal characteristics are based on non-market principles: hierarchy and command. The allocation of resources is determined by managerial fiat. As Italian economist Stefano Zamagni puts it, 'In general, economic activity can be organised according to two modes, the market and the system of firms: the latter is the antithesis of the former.'[3] Following this reasoning, one might expect the theory of the firm to be based on the study of organisational form and power relationships. While there have been some interesting developments along this line,[4] the dominant tradition within neoclassical theory has been to treat firms as single decision-making units operating in a market context, as atomistic units in an economic environment characterised by equilibrating processes.

What do firms seek? An obvious answer is profits. Indeed, if firms do not make an excess of revenue over costs they are likely to have difficulty continuing in business. But do they always seek to maximise profits? In practice, some small family businesses may be concerned with attaining only that level of profit necessary for a comfortable material standard of living, especially if making more profit would require greater personal effort or risk taking. On the other hand, big businesses are commonly concerned with security and long-term growth, the pursuit of which may not be consistent with relentless profit maximisation.[5] Some observers of business behaviour contend that 'satisficing' (attaining a satisfactory, rather than necessarily maximum, rate of return on capital) is more common.[6] Indeed, the notion of a firm consistently seeking a single objective is itself highly contentious; decisions in large businesses are usually outcomes of group decision-making processes that are not amenable to such simple interpretation. Neoclassical theory attempts to cut through these real-world complexities, indeed, to assume them away. Profit maximisation is taken as the universal goal.

BOX 20.1

THE NEOCLASSICAL THEORY OF A FIRM'S CHOICE OF OUTPUT

The essential features of the neoclassical theory of the firm can be summarised as follows:

Assumed objective:
The firm seeks to maximise its profit.

Given knowledge of:
- the firm's production function, showing the relationship between the physical quantities of inputs (land, labour, and capital) used and the output of the finished product
- the prices of the factors of production (land, labour, and capital)
- the demand curve, showing the feasible combinations of output and price.

Deduce:
The firm produces the level of output such that:

$$\text{marginal cost} = \text{marginal revenue.}$$

Marginal cost is the additional cost of producing an extra unit of output, and marginal revenue is the additional income that results from selling that extra unit of output. Where marginal revenue equals marginal costs, the firm maximises its profit.

How do firms attain the goal of profit maximisation? All kinds of strategic behaviour may be envisaged. Producing goods and services at minimum cost and selling them for the greatest attainable revenue are two obvious dimensions of profit-maximising behaviour.

Profit maximising may involve quite different patterns of behaviour in practice. On the one hand, firms may simply take the existing production technologies, labour wage rates, raw material prices, and market demand conditions as given and seek to optimise their production and sales levels accordingly. That is the behaviour implied by the neoclassical model set out in Box 20.1 (opposite). On the other hand, firms may pursue more active strategies to shape their economic environment. They may do so by developing (or suppressing) new technologies, by colluding to drive down the wages of workers or the prices of other inputs, or by fostering new markets for their products, for example. Again, neoclassical theory takes a distinctive stance. Its core model represents the firm as a fundamentally passive respondent to existing market conditions. This is not to deny the possibility that, in practice, firms may indeed seek to shape their economic environments. Nor does it deny the possibility of 'learning by doing', drawing on past experience to acquire information that helps firms gain or maintain a competitive advantage in their industry.[7] It simply reflects the particular methodological stance of neoclassical theory, which emphasises the construction of a theory of the firm based on a given state of technology, factor prices, and market demand.

Modelling the profit-maximising firm

The key steps in constructing the basic neoclassical theory of the firm, set out in Box 20.1, parallel the model of consumer choice set out in Box 19.1. This analytical symmetry is one of the most striking features of neoclassical theory, the source of much of its appeal to theoreticians. Having posited the universal goal of profit maximisation and taken three sets of data (about technology, factor prices, and product demand) as given, the quantity of each product the firm should make can be deduced. The firm is assumed to know the production function; that is, how much output of each product is attainable from different combinations of the factors of production: land, labour, and capital. It is assumed to know the prices of the factors of production, and can obtain as much of each as it wishes at the prevailing market prices. It is also assumed to know the market demand for each of its products; that is, how much output it can sell at different prices. Given that information, the firm's decision focuses on the optimal level of output and sales, this being the quantity for which marginal cost equals marginal revenue for each type of product being made.

This conclusion can be understood intuitively by considering how a profit-maximising firm will decide when to stop expanding. It is a decision made incrementally; that is, by reference to marginal adjustments in the volume of output produced. Thus, the firm can be expected to continue making more output if the extra costs of producing it are less than the extra revenues derived from selling it. It makes a profit on each such additional unit in those circumstances. However, when the extra cost of the last item produced (the marginal cost) just equals the extra revenue obtained from selling it (the marginal revenue), the firm can be expected to

FIGURE 20.1 THE NEOCLASSICAL THEORY OF THE FIRM: DIAGRAMMATIC ANALYSIS

Diagram 1   Relationship between output of finished product and quantity of the variable factor of production (e.g. labour)

Diagram 2   Relationship between output of finished product and costs of production

Diagram 3   Determining the equilibrium output for the profit-maximising firm in a perfectly competitive market stop making more output. Indeed, it should be indifferent about whether to produce the last item, because it just breaks even at that point, making neither a profit nor loss on that last unit produced and sold. If further units of output then cost more to make than they generate in extra revenues, it is not sensible for the firm to produce them. In other words, the firm should not expand beyond the point at which marginal cost equals marginal revenue. That is where the profit-maximising output is attained.

Figure 20.1 elaborates this model by introducing some diagrams (characteristic of neoclassical reasoning). They relate to the simplest case: a single-product firm in a competitive market. It is a short-run model, in the sense that the firm can vary the quantity of only some of its factors of production (labour, in this case), while others (such as land and capital) are assumed to be fixed in quantity. The short run is defined, not as a particular time period, such as a week or a year, but as the circumstances in which not all factors of production are variable. In the long run, all quantities of land, labour, and capital could be adjusted by the individual firm, but in the short run depicted here, all the firm can do is vary the amount of labour added to the temporarily fixed factors of production.[8]

Imagine the firm is a wheat farm. In the short run, 100 hectares of land, one tractor, one combine harvester, and one storage barn are available to the farmer. How many workers should the owner of the farm employ? If only one is hired, that worker will probably produce only a small output of wheat. It is possible that two workers could produce more than twice as much, if there are some benefits arising from cooperation between them in the production process. Perhaps a third worker would also substantially increase the total output of wheat. Eventually, however, extra workers are likely to add smaller and smaller increments to production. This is because of the *principle of diminishing returns*. Formally, this states that, if additional units of a variable factor of production are combined with a fixed factor of production, after a certain point the additional quantity of output will decline (as shown in the diagram at the top left of Figure 20.1). The principle of diminishing returns explains why the total product (measured on the vertical axis) rises at a slower rate as more labour is employed (measured along the horizontal axis). In the top right diagram, the same processes are shown in terms of average and marginal product curves. The average product is the total product divided by the amount of the variable factor of production used. The marginal product is the addition to total product resulting from the last unit of the variable factor of production used. Both rise and then fall as the initial benefits of cooperation are outweighed by the principle of diminishing returns.[9]

One might infer that this principle of diminishing returns favours small-scale production over large-scale production. This is not so. When all factors of production are variable (in the long run), bigger firms may be able to produce at lower average costs because of economies of scale. The point being emphasised here is that, in the restricted, short-run situation, if a firm tries to expand output by adding more of the variable factor of production to the fixed factor of production, it usually raises its average costs of production per unit of output made. In the example of the wheat farmer, 501 workers on the 100 hectares (with only one tractor, one combine harvester, and one storage barn among them) are unlikely to produce more wheat than 500 workers. By that stage, extra workers would simply be getting in the way of one another. In the extreme case, hiring extra workers would actually cause total production to fall, so the marginal product would be negative.

Another point to note about this analysis is of a technical character. It concerns the relationship between average and marginal product. In the top right diagram in Figure 20.1 (on p. 174), the marginal product curve cuts the average product curve at its highest point. Why? It is a matter of simple arithmetic, which any cricketer or baseball player will readily understand. Where a marginal score (in the last innings, for instance) is above the player's average score (for the season so far), the player's average rises; where the marginal score is below the average, the player's average falls. The same reasoning applies to marginal and average products for a firm. So, is the optimal output where the average product is at its highest? One might initially think so, but the identification of the optimum output actually depends on costs and market demand too. The information about the production function needs to be supplemented with information about factor prices and sales revenues for this purpose.

Having information about the prices of factors of production enables us to shift from analysing the quantity of product to the costs of producing it. In Figure 20.1, this is shown in the second pair of diagrams. Note that in those diagrams the horizontal axis now represents the output of the finished product (for example, wheat), and the vertical axis the costs of making that product. If we assume that the price of the variable factor of production does not vary with the number of people employed (the farmer can, for example, hire as many workers as she wants at $200 each per day), then there is a mirror relationship between the total product curve and total variable cost curve. The early benefits of cooperation, which cause the total product curve to rise more steeply, cause the total cost curve to rise more slowly. As the principle of diminishing returns then sets in, the total product curve rises more slowly and the total variable cost curve climbs more sharply. In other words, larger outputs generate more than proportionately greater costs of the variable factor of production. Finally, adding the fixed costs for the land and capital (OA in the diagram) to the total variable costs for each level of output enables us to calculate the total cost curve. We can see the total costs incurred in producing different quantities of wheat on the farm.

The second diagram in the middle row in Figure 20.1 shows the same relationships in terms of average and marginal costs. Marginal cost is the additional cost of producing an extra unit of output (for example, one bushel of wheat). Average cost is the total cost of production (including fixed costs) divided by the number of units of output. As output expands, the marginal cost starts to rise as the process of diminishing returns (increasing costs per extra unit of output) sets in. Eventually, the marginal cost curve rises above the average variable cost curve, thereby pulling it upwards (the cricket or baseball scores analogy applies again here). The average total cost curve is also pulled upwards, but, as the fixed costs are spread over a larger and larger volume of output, this curve does not rise as steeply.

The analysis moves towards an interim conclusion when information about revenues (in this case, from the sale of the wheat) is introduced. Here, too, the simplest possible assumption is made: that the price of the product is unaffected by the quantity the individual firm offers for sale. The firm's output is assumed to be so small, relative to the total supply of this product, that it has no effect on the prevailing market price. This is characteristic of the extreme situation of perfect competition, which we look at more thoroughly in the next chapter. Suffice it to note here that, under these particular market conditions, the individual firm is a price-taker. It cannot affect the price of its own product, which is set in the market according to the balance between total consumer demand and the supply of all the firms making that product. The firm's only decision is how much of the product to supply at the prevailing market price.

The third row of diagrams shows the firm's choices. On the left we see the total revenue curve sloping up to the right. The greater the amount of the product that is produced and sold, the greater the firm's income in direct proportion. Total revenue equals price per unit multiplied by the quantity of units produced. In perfect competition, the total revenue curve is a straight line because the price is fixed, irrespective of the amount that the individual firm produces and sells in the market. So, what level of output should the firm aim for? Superimposing the total cost curve (the same curve shown in the diagram above) enables us to discern at which level of output the total revenues exceed total costs by the greatest amount. In the case illustrated, it is at output *OB* on the horizontal axis. At that point the profit made is shown by the distance *DC*, measured in dollars on the vertical axis. This is the profit-maximising situation.

The bottom-right diagram in Figure 20.1 shows the same reasoning in terms of marginal cost and marginal revenue. Marginal cost, remember, is the additional cost of producing an extra unit of output; the marginal cost curve shown here simply reproduces the curve in the diagram above. The marginal revenue, on the other hand, is the extra revenue derived from selling an extra unit of output; the marginal revenue line shown here is horizontal because the price of the product does not vary with the output for a firm operating in a perfectly competitive market. Optimal output is the point where marginal cost equals marginal revenue (output *OB* in the diagram). Up to that level, a marginal profit is made on each unit of output produced (that is, marginal revenue exceeds marginal cost). For higher levels of output, a marginal loss would be made (that is, marginal costs exceed marginal revenue). An efficient profit maximiser will not expand beyond the optimal output *OB*.

What would happen if the prevailing market price were to increase suddenly (that is, if the horizontal marginal revenue line in the bottom diagram were to shift upwards)? The profit-maximising firm would now expand output to the point at which the existing marginal cost curve would cut the new marginal revenue curve. In other words, the rising part of the marginal cost curve is the firm's supply curve, because it shows how much output the firm will supply at different prevailing market prices. Elasticity of supply is a measure of this responsiveness of output to price changes—an obvious parallel to demand elasticity in consumer theory.

Note the analytical symmetry between this theory of the firm and the theory of consumer demand in the preceding chapter. Here again is a posited link between an empirically observable phenomenon (the amount a firm supplies at different prevailing market prices) and a model of the behaviour of a representative agent (based on assumptions about the firm's motivation and its information requirements for making optimal decisions). As with the consumer theory, the claim is not necessarily that firms actually go through the analytical procedures described here before making their decisions (although this may be intuitively more plausible than in the case of consumers); rather, that they are presumed to act *as if* they do.[10]

Economic efficiency

As in the theory of consumer sovereignty, there is also a normative dimension to the neoclassical theory of the firm. The point is not purely to model the behaviour of an individual firm in highly restrictive economic conditions (perfect information, perfect competition, continuous small changes in production levels, and so on). It is also to show the economic efficiency of the market economy in which 'free enterprise prevails'.

Why is economic efficiency implied? The neoclassical reasoning posits this as a structural imperative, effectively imposed on firms by the competitive economic environment in which they operate. An efficient allocation of economic resources is the product of four forces.

- Firms must combine the factors of production efficiently, given the existing state of technology and the prices of those factors of production. They must be producing at a point *on* the total cost curve rather than producing at a higher cost for the same level of output. Failure to do so can be expected to result in the firm being driven from the industry by firms who do use efficient production methods.

- Each firm must produce the most efficient level of output. 'Marginal cost equals marginal revenue' is the optimising rule. As in the story of Goldilocks, it is a matter of not too little, not too much, but just the right amount. All profit opportunities are taken, but respect for the principle of diminishing returns ensures that firms do not seek to expand output by using inefficiently large amounts of the variable factors of production.

- The total number of firms in each industry also tends to be just right in the long run. If existing firms are making substantial profits, new entrants will be attracted to the industry. The extra output supplied by those new firms would then add to total supply and thereby drive prices down until the excess profits were eliminated. If this process were to overshoot and firms started to make losses, those firms would leave the industry, thereby reducing supply. This would cause the market price to rise and normal profitability levels to be restored. 'Normal' in this context means a rate of return on capital that is just sufficient to keep the firms in the industry.

- Consumers obtain the product at the lowest possible cost, given the prevailing state of technology and factor prices. Because firms must combine factors of production efficiently and produce optimal output levels, the prevailing market price is kept at the minimum. Thus the consumer sovereignty assumption reappears in a yet more attractive guise: not only do consumers' choices signal what is to be produced, but consumers also acquire their goods and services at the lowest prices consistent with sustaining the necessary levels of production.

This seems a thoroughly admirable state of affairs. Whether these attractive features are manifest in reality, however, depends on whether conditions in the real world approximate those assumed in the theory. There are pervasive reasons for doubt. In practice, capitalist businesses may use their power over economic resources to suppress socially beneficial technical innovations, to limit the freedom of entry of new firms, to reduce or otherwise eliminate market competition, or to influence government policy to serve their interest at the expense of other community concerns. Such conduct implies a quite different normative assessment of the attractiveness of the free enterprise system. Exploring its significance requires going beyond the view of the firm as an atomistic unit operating in a competitive economic environment to a more realistic view of firms in practice.

Herein lies a troublesome feature of neoclassical theory. The theory of the firm is presented by economics textbooks as a means of modelling the behaviour of capitalist businesses. Yet it largely ignores the concern by capitalist businesses in practice to reshape their economic environment in order to loosen the constraints that competitive markets would impose on their activities. Ironically, the neoclassical theory's greater value may be for the organisation of a planned non-capitalist economy. In other words, the decision rules for determination of price and output (and the criteria for assessing allocative efficiency) may be more appropriate as socialist planning tools than as means of understanding actual capitalist businesses.

Conclusion

The neoclassical theory of the firm—typically taking up many chapters in neoclassical economics textbooks and presented only in brief outline here—is an elegant edifice. As the core of orthodox economic thinking about business behaviour, it warrants careful consideration. Like the theory of the consumer, it is based on some distinctive assumptions about rationality and the nature of the environment within which economic decisions are made. It presents a general view of firms as instruments for making choices conducive to clearly defined goals. Also like consumer theory, it seeks to link behavioural postulates, such as the quest for profit maximisation, with empirically measurable constructs, such as supply curves showing how much output firms will produce at different market prices.

The theory of the firm is more than an exercise in geometry though; it also conveys a powerful message about the nature of a free enterprise capitalist economy. It emphasises the relentless pressures for efficiency and the essential subservience of business interests to those of consumers. As such, it is the basis for a powerful economic ideology. The question is: how much of it starts to unravel as the simplifying assumptions of the theory are relaxed? The assumption of perfect competition is particularly crucial in this respect, as the following chapter reveals.

KEY POINTS

- Neoclassical economics interprets business behaviour in terms of a theory of the firm seeking maximum profits in a competitive environment.
- According to this theory, the profit-maximising firm selects the optimum output where marginal cost equals marginal revenue.
- This representation of firms as engines of efficiency is a focal point for critics of neoclassical economics.

21 Market Structures

What types of market structure are identified by neoclassical theory?

Are competitive markets ideal?

What policies are necessary for imperfectly competitive markets?

Consumer behaviour and business behaviour cannot be understood independently of each other. Consumers buy from businesses, and firms must have customers for their products. How best to understand those interactions? The neoclassical economic stance is distinctive, using models of different market structures to analyse the interconnections of demand and supply. Particular emphasis is placed on how competitive markets differ from less competitive ones.

Four categories of market structure are distinguished: perfect competition, monopolistic competition, oligopoly, and monopoly. Almost without exception, neoclassical economics textbooks contain a chapter on each, describing their characteristics in detail and adapting the analysis introduced in the preceding chapter of this book to examine the different equilibrium conditions. We can do that more summarily here, revealing the distinctive character of these neoclassical concerns, examining the implications for public policy, and teasing out the underlying assumptions about the nature of competition and economic power. In this way, a political economic perspective on the neoclassical theory of market structures can be developed.

Perfect competition

Table 21.1 shows the three bases on which the four types of market structure are defined: the number of sellers, the nature of the products supplied, and the entry conditions.

Perfect competition is the usual starting point. This theoretical model is at the heart of neoclassical economics. It is the extreme case, where the number of firms is so large and the product each makes so uniform that no single firm can affect the price of its products. Consumers cannot distinguish between the products made by the different producers. As a result, each firm has to accept the prevailing market price and simply decide how much to produce and sell at that price. Since there are no barriers to the entry of new firms, the existing firms cannot make profits over and above the bare minimum needed to maintain the existence of the industry in the long run.

TABLE 21.1 A GENERAL CLASSIFICATION OF MARKET STRUCTURES

Type of market situation	Number of sellers and importance of each	Nature of products supplied	Entry conditions
Perfect competition	A large number of sellers, each accounting for a very small proportion of the total output of the industry	Homogeneous (i.e., perfectly substitutable products supplied by each firm)	No restriction on entry of new firms
Monopolistic competition	Normally fewer sellers than under perfect competition, but the proportion of output supplied by each is still relatively small	Although broadly substitutable, the products are differentiated from one another	Usually no restriction on entry
Oligopoly	A few important sellers accounting for a large proportion of the total output	The products are normally differentiated (e.g., according to brand names)	Usually some restriction on entry
Perfect monopoly	One seller	No directly competitive product	Some restriction (otherwise the monopoly will only be temporary)

Is perfect competition an ideal market structure? It is certainly not ideal from the viewpoint of the firms themselves. They must strive continuously to minimise their costs for fear of being driven out of business by more efficient rivals. They have no customers on whose loyalty they can rely. Even if they do stay in business, in the long run their profits will be minimal. This is a business nightmare. On the other hand, from the consumers' point of view it seems to be a very attractive scenario. Consumers are well served by a multitude of firms who compete with one another for market share and keep product prices at the lowest possible level, given the current state of technology and the costs of the factors of production.

How is that market price for the product determined? The neoclassical answer is simple: by the principle of demand and supply. As noted in Chapter 18, this is the ubiquitous principle said to be continuously reconciling the interests of buyers and sellers in the marketplace. The aggregate (industry) demand curve is derived as the sum of all individual consumer demand curves for the product in question. It shows how much the consumers as a whole are willing to buy at different market prices for the product. The aggregate supply curve is derived, by similar reasoning, from the sum of individual producers' marginal cost curves. It shows how much will be on the market at various market prices. Putting the aggregate demand and supply curves together enables us to identify the market-clearing price. This price continually adjusts to changes in demand and supply, restoring equilibrium.

Perfect competition is seldom found in the real world, however. Some markets for agricultural products, where a large number of small farmers produce an identical crop and where there are low barriers to entry (for example, just the initial cost of acquiring the necessary land and tools), may approximate it. Some financial markets, where numerous buyers and sellers are each too small to influence market prices, may have some of these competitive characteristics, too. But these are exceptional instances.

The centrality of perfect competition theory in neoclassical economics has less to do with its practical relevance than with its analytical elegance and its posited ideal normative properties. Perfectly competitive markets are held to be ideal because they ensure maximum efficiency in the use of factors of production, continuous adjustment of market prices to changes in the conditions of demand and supply, and the elimination of any excess profits that would result from the exercise of monopoly power. Perfect competition is not a common market structure in practice because it is normally in the interest of firms to try to deviate from this ideal. They differentiate their products, seek to establish customer loyalty, and erect barriers to the entry of potential competitors. Such business behaviour tends to result in monopolistic competition, oligopoly, or monopoly.

Monopolistic competition

The smallest deviation from the perfectly competitive extreme takes us into the realm of monopolistic competition. In this market situation there is still a large number of firms, but there is some degree of product differentiation. In monopolistic competition, the consumers can tell the difference between the products of the various firms in the industry, although they are usually broadly substitutable in practice. All petrol stations sell essentially the same fuel, but they may be differentiated in the eyes of consumers according to the convenience of their location or the friendliness of their staff. Similarly, all chemist shops sell essentially the same pharmaceutical products, but may differ in the perceived attractiveness of their premises, the helpfulness of the resident pharmacist, or—again—their location.

Location is perhaps the most pervasive form of product differentiation leading to monopolistic competition. If convenience of access is relevant to consumer choice (as it usually is), a situation that might otherwise tend towards perfect competition almost invariably becomes monopolistic competition in practice. Indeed, one may reasonably conclude that, because a spatial dimension exists in virtually all economic behaviour in the real world, perfect competition is a logical impossibility. Even the development of modern information technologies and increasingly rapid means of transport does not wholly eradicate the tyranny of distance. Goods purchased on the internet still have to be physically transported to the consumer. In practice, monopolistic competition is about as competitive as markets usually get.

The possibility of persistent economic inefficiency exists in such a market structure, for product differentiation may cause duplication and waste of resources. Do we need petrol stations on each corner at major road intersections? Do we want chemist shops clustered in the high street, while outlying areas are less well served? Are economic resources wasted on product differentiation that is sometimes of a spurious nature? Such deviations from the norm of perfect competition are commonly regarded as drawbacks of monopolistic competition, although neoclassical economists usually regard them as relatively unimportant so long as the barriers to entry of new firms are low. It is the latter aspect—competition from potential new entrants to the industry—that is said to keep existing firms on their toes and to inhibit the tendency to excessive waste.

Oligopoly

Oligopoly involves a more major departure from the perfectly competitive norm. This is a market structure in which there are relatively few firms in an industry, and each usually produces differentiated (brand-named) goods or services, the prices of which are directly under the control of the firms themselves. New firms have difficulty coming into the industry, either because of the inherent difficulties of establishing sufficiently large productive capacity or because the collusive practices of existing firms (sometimes involving government cooperation) impose substantial barriers to entry. This is the world of big business, as perceived by neoclassical economists.

Commonly cited examples of industries with these general oligopolistic characteristics are oil production and distribution, steel and aluminium production, car production, the manufacture of computers, food processing, the manufacture of laundry detergents, aircraft production, and airline travel. Oligopoly can also exist in service industries. Some would say that universities—large institutions vigorously competing for students, research funds, and sponsors—now have the characteristics of oligopolistic industries, too. A cynic would add political parties, the biggest of which compete with one another for market share, differentiating their offerings to the extent necessary to secure a strategic competitive advantage. In all these cases, the dominant feature is competition among the few. There may be a number of smaller players alongside the bigger ones, but it is the behaviour of the latter that determines how the industry functions.

Such behaviour is shaped by the perceived interdependence of the major players. Each seller in an oligopolistic industry recognises that any change in its policies (regarding production technologies, production locations, the range of product lines, prices, and commercial advertising strategies, for instance) is likely to precipitate changes in its rivals' policies.

This perceived interdependence gives rise to distinctive patterns of behaviour. Price rigidity is a predictable outcome. It is a common consequence of interdependent behaviour under conditions of oligopoly, even without explicit collusion. Prices tend to be sticky, remaining fixed for quite long periods of time, despite fluctuations in demand and supply conditions that would cause price fluctuations in more competitive markets.[1] Periodic bouts of vigorous price competition may occur, especially when a new entrant threatens to invade the market territories of existing firms.[2] Typically though, non-price competition prevails. Rivalry over market shares, focusing on commercial advertising, may be intense, but it is a very long way from the business behaviour required in the realm of perfect competition.

Collusion is a strong tendency under conditions of oligopoly. It can take many forms. Firms in an oligopoly may, for example, agree to a territorial division of the market. A mutual interest in the avoidance of beggar-thy-neighbour competition may also lead firms to collude in pricing their products. They recognise that one firm seeking to increase its market share by lowering its prices is likely to trigger a price war, which would eventually cause each firm to suffer reduced profits. Better not let the process start. So, a system of tacit price leadership, whereby one firm in the industry (not necessarily the biggest) sets the general industry standard and the others follow suit, is commonly adopted. In effect, collusive oligopoly converges on monopoly.

BOX 21.1   GAME THEORY

Many economic decisions involve strategic choices. When setting the prices of their products, for example, individual firms, particularly in oligopolistic market situations, have to try to anticipate the impact of their decision on the pricing policy of their rivals. They weigh up the anticipated advantages and disadvantages of competitive and cooperative strategies, taking into account the likelihood of any cooperative agreement being maintained in practice and the possible consequences of its being dishonoured.

The term 'game theory' implies a sporting analogy. Indeed, the complex and shifting relationship between cooperation and competition is one of the more intriguing aspects of sporting endeavours. Warfare is the yet more obvious arena in which strategic choices are important. The development of mathematical models to help decision-making processes was, in fact, stimulated by the Second World War and the subsequent Cold War. Its application to economics followed quickly. John Nash, the mathematics professor on whose remarkable life the Hollywood movie *A Beautiful Mind* was based, was a particularly significant contributor to its development. The Nash equilibrium is a central concept in game theory. Essentially, this is the situation created when the set of strategies that individuals willingly choose as the best response to the predicted strategies of other players produces strategically stable or self-enforcing outcomes in which no single player wants to deviate from his or her predicted strategy.

Applying game theory to the study of economic behaviour has been a focal point in the further development of mathematical economic theory. It has also produced some more down-to-earth experimental studies that involve putting real people in simulated strategic-choice situations and monitoring their behaviour. Is this merely fun and games? On the one hand, game theory has demonstrated that the mainstream microeconomic theory of individually rational decision-makers is internally inconsistent and descriptively inaccurate. As such, it has strengthened the critique of conventional neoclassical theory. On the other hand, it has difficulty producing alternative, well-defined predictions of economic behaviour and therefore remains constrained by a choice-theoretic methodology, even while trying to push against the boundaries of orthodox economics.

Perfect monopoly

As global media magnate Rupert Murdoch once said, 'Monopoly is a terrible thing until you have it.'[3] Strictly defined, perfect monopoly is the polar extreme of perfect competition. This is where there is only one firm supplying the product in question: the firm is the industry. It usually maintains its monopoly position by imposing barriers to the entry of new firms. It also takes advantage of its monopoly position by restricting output and raising prices in order to generate maximum profits. So, the prevailing market price will be higher than that under perfect competition—assuming that production costs are the same in either case. That is the basis for neoclassical economists' antipathy towards monopoly. It fits with the popular presumption that monopolists tend to exploit their economic power by charging higher prices for their products.

Whether markets that are more competitive do actually generate lower prices depends crucially on the level of production costs. The foregoing case against monopoly rests on the assumption that an industry's production costs would be the same irrespective of whether it is organised as a monopoly or as perfect competition. This is not necessarily the case. A monopolist lacks the imperative to minimise costs that firms have in perfectly competitive market situations. However, a monopolist usually has more resources at its disposal to invest in new technologies, and product innovations, if it so wishes. Because the costs of production may be either higher or lower for the monopoly in practice, we cannot know for certain how the prevailing price level compares with the perfectly competitive norm. All we can say with confidence is that, whatever the costs of production may be, monopolists have the capacity, unless constrained by government regulations or faced with a highly elastic demand for their products, to seek higher profits by raising prices.

This illustrates a general feature of the neoclassical theory of market structures. Only in the perfectly competitive case does the market structure actually determine the conduct and performance of the firms. The further one deviates from this norm, the greater the scope for firms to engage in strategic action, which, by its very nature, is harder to model and predict. This is particularly so for oligopoly, where the uncertainties associated with the perceived interdependence of firms are most striking. Neoclassical economists have sought to apply game theory in this context in order to graft on some models of strategic behaviour.[4] This helps to inject some realism into the analysis of business behaviour, but at the price of producing more uncertainty about the predicted outcomes. The general problem remains: the greater the departure from the perfectly competitive ideal and the closer the approximation to real-world market situations, the less effective is neoclassical theory as a means of explaining and predicting market behaviour.

In discussing the features of different market structures, the term 'monopoly' is often used interchangeably with 'imperfect competition'.[5] In other words, it is used to refer to any market situation in which firms have the capacity to differentiate their products, command some degree of brand loyalty among their customers, impede the entry of new firms, or otherwise mould the operations of the market to their own interests. This is a much broader use of the term than that of 'pure' or 'perfect' monopoly, where only one seller exists. It is a use of the term associated with the concern to understand business behaviour in all contexts—other than the idealised perfect competition—and to decide what to do about it.

Structure, conduct, performance

The mainstream economic approach assumes that the structure of a market shapes the conduct and performance of firms operating within it. In a perfectly competitive structure, firms' conduct is necessarily that of the price taker; therefore, their performance depends on efficient cost minimisation, and their capacity to make profits is always constrained by the actual or potential entry of new firms into the industry. The structure of monopolistic competition, on the other hand, allows for more competitive conduct through price and product differentiation—although firms' ability to generate high levels of profit is still constrained by the relative ease of entry. In oligopoly, the structure makes strategic conduct a business imperative, and successful performance in these strategic games is usually rewarded with substantial profits. In conditions of pure monopoly, the structure imposes no requirement on the firm to act efficiently, other than in securing its own monopoly position, and its profit performance can be enhanced by monopoly pricing (subject to the constraint imposed by the elasticity of demand).

This structure–conduct–performance approach to understanding business behaviour embodies a distinctive interpretation of what competition means.[6] It treats competition as an end state, as a consequence of market structure rather than a process. A contrast may be made with Adam Smith's conception of competition as a process of rivalry, such as that between producers in different locations. This alternative, more dynamic view of competition has strong echoes in Marx, Marshall, and the Austrian tradition of economic analysis, from Menger through to Schumpeter and Hayek. It puts more emphasis on entrepreneurship as an active element in business behaviour. Entrepreneurship is the process by which firms create business opportunities. It is a means by which firms pursue rivalrous business behaviour. It has no equivalent place in the standard neoclassical approach, notwithstanding the common (and confusing) reference to the firm as the 'entrepreneur'. Rather, in neoclassical theory, the extent of competition is understood to be determined by the industry structure, particularly the number of firms in the industry in question.

The concept of efficiency in neoclassical theory is largely restricted to considerations of resource allocation. The typical concern is with how resources are being allocated between industries, given the prevailing state of technology and pattern of consumer demand. Questions about resource *creation* are paid significantly less attention. Yet the issue of whether competitive or oligopolistic industries are more likely to generate technological progress over time (or to improve the quality of human capital) may be much more important than the question of which market structure is more conducive to allocative efficiency at any given point in time.

A restricted view of economic power is also evident in the neoclassical theory. Economic power is only market power. The power of oligopolists or monopolists is their ability to charge higher prices than would prevail under perfectly competitive conditions (assuming similar production costs). Firms may also have power to reduce the costs of factors of production—because of their monopolistic position as buyers of labour, for example. However, their power to shape the broader economic environment is not usually considered. Yet therein may lie the major consequences of the transition from competitive to monopoly capitalism. Insofar as giant businesses in the modern economy can influence government policies (on taxes, tariffs, industry subsidies, and other forms of 'corporate welfare'), or play off national governments against one another through the international movement of capital, they have far greater power than these models of imperfect competition imply. To the extent that their activities foster consumerist behaviour and/or deplete natural resources, the social and environmental consequences of their activities are far-reaching.

Taming the tigers?

The neoclassical theory of market structures, based on these distinctive views of competition, efficiency, and market power, could be expected to generate clear guidelines for public policy. It categorises types of market structure according to their presumed deviation from the competitive ideal.[7] Its process of formal modelling emphasises key economic variables, setting aside other complexities. It should have something to say about policies towards markets in practice. Indeed, this is a significant focus of the theory as it is presented in the mainstream economics textbooks. In line with the structure–conduct–performance continuum, three policy approaches may be discerned.

First is the emphasis on policies to influence market *structure*. If perfect competition is an ideal in the normative sense, then, presumably, public policy should seek to achieve it in practice, or at least to approximate it. A case is thereby made for breaking up large firms into smaller ones, or preventing smaller ones from combining into larger ones through mergers and takeovers. This is the characteristic anti-monopoly stance of neoclassical economics. Historically, it has been influential in a number of countries, including the USA. It was the rationale for the decision by the US Supreme Court in 1911 to break up Standard Oil into 34 smaller companies. It implicitly underlay the US District Court ruling in 2000 that giant software company Microsoft be divided in two (still giant) companies.[8] It is an approach to economic policy that seems to prioritise consumers' interests relative to those of business (although it should be noted that, in practice, many of the consumers of big businesses are other businesses, big and small). As a general policy approach, it is bedevilled by the tension between the concern to prevent monopoly pricing and the desire to reap the economies of large-scale production. Moreover, especially for governments of smaller nations, it now sits uncomfortably with the strategy of promoting big firms as 'national champions' capable of competing effectively in world markets.

A second approach, focusing on firms' *conduct*, emphasises the case for the regulation of business behaviour. Restrictions on monopoly pricing, collusive activities, and other restrictive trade practices are implied. Box 21.2 gives some examples of what has come to be generally known as competition policy. It has been a major feature of public policy in practice in many countries, such as the USA, the UK, and Australia, and is supported by neoclassical economic reasoning emphasising the perfectly competitive ideal. It requires a regulatory role for government that sits uncomfortably with the more purist strain of economic liberalism that harbours deep distrust of government intervention of any sort.

BOX 21.2   COMPETITION POLICY

How much competition among firms supplying goods and services is necessary, desirable, or possible? How concerned should governments be about enforcing competition? Herein lie major dilemmas. The case for a capitalist market economy relies on the posited link between competition, efficient resource allocation, and consumer welfare. Yet, ever since Adam Smith, it has been recognised that the forces of competition are continually confronted, even thwarted, by the forces of monopolisation. Governments have sought to deal with these tensions by having national competition policies.

Legislative restrictions and regulations have generally sought to preclude business practices such as:

- anti-competitive agreements and exclusionary provisions, including primary and secondary boycotts
- misuse of market power, such as charging excessively high prices
- exclusive dealing, such as when a large firm insists that its suppliers do not deal with other firms
- resale price maintenance, whereby manufacturers insist on the price at which retailers sell their products
- mergers that have the likely effect of substantially lessening market competition.

In the last two decades, governments have extended national competition policies to previously exempt areas such as public utilities. In effect, competition policy thereby becomes linked to the push for privatisation, either directly transferring public enterprises into private hands through the sale of their assets, or requiring public enterprises to act more like private-sector enterprises. Insisting on 'contestable markets' for the provision of all services is a recurrent theme, with the declared aim of enforcing efficiency on the providers of public services. In practice, it usually results in services previously provided by public enterprises (such as electricity and gas suppliers) being contracted out to private-sector firms, and the relinquishment of community service obligations that previously guided the behaviour of the public enterprises.

The Organization for Economic Cooperation and Development (OECD) has been trying to promote convergence of national competition policies in different nations. It stresses the need for competition laws to be applied uniformly with a minimum of exceptions. This has the appeal of creating a so-called level playing field for business, but in practice it can mean a level playing field on which transnational corporations can extend their domination.

A third type of policy dealing with market structures focuses on *performance*. 'Let the structures of imperfect competition remain; let firms decide what strategic business behaviour and pricing policies are best for them; just focus on dealing with the outcomes', this argument runs. Profit outcomes are a particular focus. If oligopoly or monopoly generate excessive levels of profit (however that be defined), then business taxation can cream off whatever portion is necessary in order to finance government expenditures. This deals with the consequences rather than the causes of monopoly power. However, it offers a potentially appealing way of dealing with the lack of adequate competition in industry—appealing to citizens, not to big business, of course.

Note, though, that the victims of monopoly pricing, for example, are not necessarily the same people as the beneficiaries of the government spending financed by taxes on monopoly profits. So complex redistributions between losers and winners may ensue. Yet more troubling is the evident aversion by most governments nowadays to imposing substantial business taxation. In a world of increasingly mobile capital, there is the frequent fear that such taxes may precipitate 'capital flight' to other nations where tax rates are lower. Faced with this threat, real or imagined, the prevailing tendency is to shy away from tackling the power of big business.

So, governments, faced with practical decisions about coping with big business and restrictive trade practices, tend to take a more pragmatic approach, seeking 'workable competition' rather than perfect competition. It seems that the closer one gets to matters of practical judgment, the cloudier the issues become and the less relevant the principles derived from the neoclassical theory appear. 'Workable competition', in one wry opinion, is 'a vague term meaning simply the degree of competition considered acceptable by the economist calling it workable'.[9]

Conclusion

The neoclassical theory of market structures is superficially attractive: it recognises a spectrum from perfect competition to perfect monopoly. However, closer investigation indicates some fundamental problems with this body of analysis.

It quickly becomes open-ended in what it says about expected business behaviour as soon as the perfect competition model is set aside. The result is that the precision sought by neoclassical theorists cannot be achieved, except by making some truly heroic assumptions (such as costs of production being independent of market structure).

These difficulties also limit the use of the theory of market structures in the formulation of public policies. How best to promote business competition and limit monopoly power? No clear policy prescriptions emerge, despite the strong commitment to the perfectly competitive ideal. Competition policies in practice oscillate between attempts to influence structure, conduct, and performance. The tension between the principle of competition and the practice of capitalism remains.

In the end, one has to wonder what the point of the theory is. Is its purpose to describe (or at least approximate) real-world market structures? Is it meant to provide a normative ideal that can be used as a basis for policy formulation? Or is there a yet more contentious purpose: to provide an ideology that diverts attention from the actual structures of economic power, thereby serving as a legitimising device for capitalist interests? These three possibilities apply not only to the theory of market structures, but also to neoclassical economics as a whole, including what it has to say about the distribution of income between land, labour, and capital.

KEY POINTS

- Neoclassical economists distinguish between perfect competition, monopolistic competition, oligopoly, and monopoly as the principal market structures.

- Because perfect competition is held to be the normative ideal, more common market structures in modern capitalism may be targets for government policies intended to affect industry structure, business conduct, and performance.

- Critics of neoclassical theory emphasise that this idealised view of market structures neglects many aspects of actual business behaviour that involve the use of economic power.

22 ▸ Distribution

What shapes the distribution of income?

Does it reflect the productivity of the various factors of production?

Does neoclassical theory explain economic inequalities in practice?

Political economists have always been concerned to analyse economic inequalities. David Ricardo's assertion that understanding the distribution of income among the social classes is the principal problem in political economy is a pertinent reminder of that. In popular discussions of economic matters today, the question 'Who gets what?' is no less dominant—although many people feel uncomfortable about explicit reference to class.

Explaining economic inequalities has a more shadowy role in neoclassical economics. Early writers in the development of this analytical tradition—notably, the American economist J. B. Clark (1847–1938)—explicitly linked explanations of income distribution with propositions about the role of markets in creating social equity. According to Clark, 'The distribution of the income of society is controlled by a natural law ... which assigns to everyone what he has specifically created.'[1] In a similar vein, the Italian economist and social theorist Vilfredo Pareto (1848–1923) claimed that the 'constancy of inequality in the distribution of income reflects inequality of human ability, which is a natural and universal category'.[2] These days, neoclassical economists usually restrict their analysis to attempted explanations of the prices of the different factors of production.

Even that narrower agenda raises some interesting issues. Why are some occupational groups paid more than others? What determines the relative share of income going to labour as a whole, compared with the share going to the owners of capital and land? Can those patterns of reward be changed without impairing economic efficiency?

Demand and supply—again

Box 22.1, on the next page, shows the interconnecting influences in an orthodox economic explanation of income distribution. It emphasises the connections between the distribution of income, the distribution of economic resources, and the price that each commands in the market. In other words, 'who gets what' depends on 'who owns what' and on what prices prevail for those factors of production.

BOX 22.1 EXPLAINING THE DISTRIBUTION OF INCOME

FIGURE 22.1 THE INTERCONNECTING INFLUENCES ON INCOME DISTRIBUTION

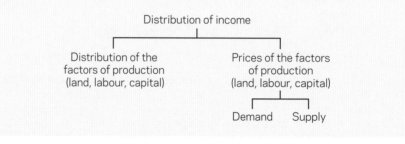

Neoclassical economic theory focuses on the right-hand side of this tree by looking at the roots of income distribution in the demand and supply for capital, labour, and land. For each of these factors of production (and their constituent parts), determination of the market price is represented by the now familiar 'Marshallian cross'.

FIGURE 22.2 THE 'MARSHALLIAN CROSS' APPLIED TO FACTORS OF PRODUCTION

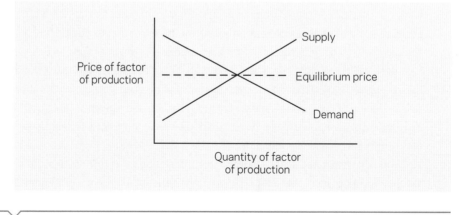

Conventionally, three factors of production are identified: land, labour, and capital. Reference to these as the defining features of three rival social classes—landowners, workers, and capitalists—is muted, if not altogether absent, in neoclassical theory. Taking the distribution of economic resources as given (in much the same way the theory of the consumer takes preferences as given, and the theory of the firm takes the state of technology as given), the analytical task narrows to identifying what shapes the pattern of factor prices. The standard neoclassical position is that the supply and demand for each factor of production determines its price. Note that the roles of buyers and sellers are reversed in factor markets: firms are the buyers and households the sellers of factors of production.

Looking first at the demand side, a formal statement of the relevant variables is presented below in Box 22.2. The business objective of cost minimisation is the assumed starting point; this is a necessary but insufficient condition for the general goal of profit maximisation (as discussed in Chapter 20). To minimise costs, each firm needs to know what volume of output it is aiming to produce, the ways in which it is technically possible to combine the various factors of production, and the prevailing prices of those factors of production.

BOX 22.2

THE NEOCLASSICAL THEORY OF THE DEMAND FOR FACTORS OF PRODUCTION

The essential features of a firm's demand for factors of production can be set out as follows.

Assumed objective
The firm seeks to minimise costs.

Given knowledge of:
- the volume of output produced by the firm
- the production function, showing what combinations of factors of production (labour, capital, and land) can be used to produce the required output
- the prices of the factors of production.

Deduce
The firm employs factors of production such that the ratio of their price to their marginal productivity is equal. So, considering just two factors, labour and capital:

$$\frac{\text{marginal product of labour}}{\text{marginal product of capital}} = \frac{\text{price of labour}}{\text{price of capital}}$$

The marginal product of a factor of production is the extra amount of output generated by employing one more unit of that factor in conjunction with the other fixed factors of production. According to this theory, where the ratio of the marginal products is equal to the ratio of prices of those factors of production, the firm has an optimal use of capital and labour.

The first of the information requirements listed in Box 22.2 is particularly important. Firms do not employ factors of production other than as a means to an end, and the end is producing goods and services for profit. The significance of this is that the demand for a factor of production is a derived demand: it derives from the demand for the product that it contributes to making. To illustrate the point, consider a firm that has already decided on the level of output to produce, following the procedure described in Chapter 20 (or acting *as if* it followed those steps). If, according to the reasoning in Chapter 21, the firm enjoys a monopoly position, its demand for factors of production would be less than that of an equivalent firm in an industry organised on the principle of perfect competition. Because a monopolist can be expected to restrict output and raise the price of its product, its derived demand for factors of production is correspondingly reduced—other things being equal. So, the primary influence on the demand for factors of production is the output of the firms employing them.

The second influence is the state of technology, as shown by the production function. There are usually alternative ways of producing a particular output, whether by capital-intensive or labour-intensive methods of production, for example. Selecting from among these options requires a firm to have information on the relative factor prices. At first sight, this is a strange data requirement, since the point of the analysis is to explain how the demand for the factors of production influences their prices. It seems that we need to take as given what we are seeking to explain. The conundrum is resolved by recognising that, according to neoclassical theory, the aggregate demand by all the firms for each factor of production influences its market price, but that, once established, that market price must then be taken as given by individual firms. Essentially the same model-building methodology that was applied to the study of consumer demand (in Chapter 19) and the theory of the firm (in Chapter 20) is now applied to the study of factors of production.

Finally, given all this data, the coolly calculating, cost-minimising firm selects the particular production method that satisfies the decision rule shown in Box 22.2: it employs factors of production in such proportions that the ratio of the marginal products of any pair of them equals the ratio of their market prices. Marginal product is the extra quantity of output generated by hiring one more unit of a factor of production. So if, say, labour costs twice as much per unit as does a unit of capital (setting aside for the moment how those units are measured), then it makes sense to employ labour and capital in the proportion that ensures the product of the last person employed is twice that of the last unit of capital. Thus is cost minimisation achieved.

It is pertinent to note in passing that this analysis regards cost minimisation by firms as essentially a matter of making wise choices about optimal combinations of land, labour, and capital. There is no concern here with the actual processes of managing the factors of production—labour in particular—that are such a concern in Marxist analysis, for example (see Chapter 14). Rather, the efficient management of resources is simply assumed (and class conflict in the workplace is assumed away) for the purpose of building a model to explain how much land, labour, or capital will be employed. The focus here, as elsewhere in neoclassical theory, is on choice rather than on conflict or coercion.

If each firm decides on the quantity of each factor of production it would employ at each price, the totals can be added to determine the aggregate demand for each factor of production. Thus, the demand curve, as shown in Box 22.1, can be constructed. A downward slope to the right indicates that the higher the price of the factor of production, the less of it will be demanded. The nature of this relationship is shaped by both substitution and output effects (analogous to the substitution and income effects in the analysis of consumers' demand considered in Chapter 19). A high price for a factor of production will encourage firms to adopt production technologies that use little of that factor—so they substitute cheaper factors of production for the high-priced one. This is the substitution effect. A high price of a factor of production also increases firms' overall cost levels (assuming that they cannot avoid using that factor of production altogether). Because that reduces the optimum level of output (where marginal cost of production equals marginal revenue), it also reduces the demand for all factors of production. This is the output effect. Both substitution and output effects work in the same direction, producing an inverse relationship between price and demand.

What about supply? Neoclassical economists generally assume, as shown in Box 22.1, that the supply of a factor of production and its market price will have a positive connection. In other words, a higher market price for a particular factor of production will draw forth a greater supply of it. Generally, this sounds plausible, particularly for subcategories of factors of production (for example, different types of labour, such as professors, electricians, or garbage collectors). In the case of labour, there are possibilities of occupational substitution (professors becoming garbage collectors, for instance), if the relative market rewards change sufficiently. Existing workers in any one occupation may also work for longer hours if the rewards are higher. Other workers, attracted by the higher wages, may migrate from other geographic regions.

None of these supply-side responses is inevitable. In practice, there are often substantial constraints on occupational and geographical mobility. The number of hours of work may be institutionally fixed. Even when working hours are variable, perverse outcomes may occur; workers may actually work fewer hours when their wage rates are raised, for example, because they need to commit less time to work in order to achieve their target incomes. In this case, the income effect of the wage rise dominates the substitution of work for leisure. For all these reasons, the supply curves for factors of production may be quite inelastic, even backward bending (indicating a negative association between rewards and the amount of the factor of production supplied). However, as long as there is a unique point of intersection between the aggregate demand and supply curves, a market-clearing equilibrium price can be established. Thus, neoclassical theory seeks to indicate how factor prices reflect the conditions of demand and supply.

Rewarding productivity?

This explanation of income distribution—or what should more properly be called a theory of factor prices—has, at first sight, a pleasing symmetry with other elements of neoclassical theory. It is very similar to the theory of how prices for goods and services are determined. It also implies a symmetry between the rewards for capital, land, and labour. In this latter respect it stands in striking contrast to Marx's theory of exploitation of labour by capital, and to Henry George's claim that the revenues obtained by landowners are 'always ultimately at the expense of the value of labour'.[3] There is no economic surplus. Rather, everything is rewarded in proportion to its productivity at the margin.

Orthodox economists today seldom make the sort of explicitly normative claims about the distribution of market incomes that were made by J. B. Clark and Vilfredo Pareto (quoted at the start of this chapter). However, the general inference remains: that reward according to marginal productivity is both efficient and fair. Therein also lies a reason why orthodox economists are commonly reluctant to prescribe substantial income redistributions in order to satisfy broader, social objectives. Meddling with the distribution of income, it is implied, is likely to have economically damaging consequences. Milton Friedman, for example, has argued strongly against 'the attempt to separate this function of the price system—distributing income—from its other functions—transmitting information and providing incentives', claiming that 'If prices are prevented from affecting the distribution of income, they cannot be used for other purposes'.[4] This sort of reasoning suggests that we must accept substantial economic disparities as a necessary feature of a capitalist market economy. It is an argument that requires critical reexamination, focusing on the connections between rewards, productivity, and power in a market economy.

Rewarding power?

One gap in the orthodox reasoning is resource ownership. As noted in Box 22.1, the overall extent of income inequality depends on both the distribution of resource ownership and the pattern of factor prices. To adapt Marshall's famous phrase in this different context, these two aspects of income distribution interact like the two blades of a pair of scissors. To neglect 'who owns what' impedes an understanding of 'who gets what'. Formally, any given pattern of factor prices is consistent with an infinite array of income distributions, depending on the inequality of resource ownership. If land, labour, and capital resources are widely dispersed among the population, the distribution of income is likely to be more egalitarian than if they are concentrated in the hands of a few—whatever the pattern of factor prices. On a practical level, policies to secure more dispersed patterns of resource ownership can be expected to produce more equitable distributional outcomes. However, on this issue the neoclassical theory is silent; it takes the distribution of resource ownership as given, in the same way that consumers' tastes and technology are taken as given in other aspects of the theory.

A second problem with the orthodox neoclassical theory is that it ignores the role of economic power in shaping the pattern of factor prices. In practice, professional groups, such as lawyers and doctors, use their representative institutions to restrict entry (usually in the name of maintaining quality) and thereby ensure high rewards for themselves. Trade unions seek to push the wage rates of their members above those that would prevail in more perfectly competitive market conditions. Employer organisations concurrently pursue the reverse goal. The actual wage outcomes—and, generally, the relative income shares of labour and capital—depend on the relative power of these organised groups and on the institutional context within which the contest between them occurs. The non-symmetrical nature of the power relationship between capital and labour in a capitalist economy underpins all such processes. Neoclassical theory is sometimes modified to take account of institutional rigidities, but it remains fundamentally ill suited to considering the nature and consequences of the resulting power plays.

The role of the state also needs to be considered. The state is not external to the political economic conditions shaping the distribution of income. Indeed, insofar as it enforces the underlying property rights and implements industrial relations policies, it is a key participant in the power plays. Its effects on income distribution are not only the result of explicit intervention in redistributing market incomes through taxation and public expenditure. The power relationships of capital, labour, and the state also intertwine in shaping all aspects of the distribution of pre-tax incomes and wealth in a capitalist society.

Other fundamental conceptual problems bedevil the attempt to theorise income distribution in terms of the productivity of labour, land, and capital. What the neoclassical theory must do, if it is to be consistent, is relate the income of each factor of production to an empirical measure of its productivity. Rent must be shown to reflect the measured productivity of land, wages must be shown to reflect the measured productivity of labour, and profits must be shown to reflect the measured productivity of capital. Unfortunately for neoclassical theory, this cannot be done.

Part of the problem is that of disentangling the relative productive contributions of land, labour, and capital when all (or even just two) of the factors must be combined in order to produce goods or services. This difficulty can be addressed (in theory) by holding one factor constant and observing the impact on output of variations in other factor(s) at the margin. In practice, the empirical measurement of marginal products is usually difficult, if not impossible, to achieve.

Yet more fundamental is the conceptual problem of finding consistent units of measurement for each of the factors of production. This is not a major difficulty in relation to labour: inputs of labour can be measured in terms of person hours of work, so the reward to labour can be expressed as a wage rate per hour and related to the productivity of that hour's labour. It is also possible for land: inputs of land can be measured in terms of hectares, so the reward to land can be expressed as a rental per hectare and related to the productivity of that land. No such physical measure exists for capital. Capital goods comprise diverse items—machinery, equipment, tools, plant, and buildings—for which the only common measure is their market value. But that market value depends on the profitability of the firms using those capital goods. There is the rub. Because the productivity of capital goods affects their valuation, measuring a rate of return on capital involves circularity. When business is profitable, capital has a higher market value; when it is unprofitable, capital has a lower market value. So, the estimated rate of return on capital is not independent of the valuation of the capital input.

This last point may seem somewhat esoteric, but its economic significance is substantial.[5] It means that the neoclassical attempt to establish a theory of distribution that treats land, labour, and capital in a symmetrical fashion is, ultimately, unsuccessful. Profit cannot be treated as a payment for the productivity of capital in the same way that wages reflect the productivity of labour, or rent reflects the productivity of land. The root problem here is the attempt to eradicate the notion of an economic surplus from economic theory. In the classical and Marxist economic traditions profit is treated as a surplus, arising after wages, rent, and other costs have been deducted from revenue. It is the neoclassical economists' attempt to explain profits in terms of the marginal product of capital rather than the class power of capital that is so deeply problematic.

Entrepreneurship may be posited as a fourth factor of production. Perhaps this can help neoclassical economics to escape the conceptual problem of defining and measuring a return to capital. Profits can then be regarded as a reward for entrepreneurship, reflecting the skills of capitalist managers in organising the other factors of production, innovating, and taking risks in the process of running their businesses. In effect, this means distinguishing between entrepreneurial incomes and the more routinely market-determined interest payments that are the reward for capital (in its monetary form). This usefully acknowledges the dynamic element in business management. However, the analytical difficulty remains. There is no general measure of the quantity or quality of entrepreneurship other than the profitability of the firm. Good entrepreneurship is presumably that which earns high profits; poor entrepreneurship is that which results in low profits or causes losses. The problem of circular reasoning recurs: the link between entrepreneurial quality and profits is either tautological or untestable. Faced with these kinds of problems, some neoclassical theorists have resorted to declaring their 'faith' in the neoclassical analysis,[6] but that is a less than satisfactory stance for a school of economic thought claiming scientific status for its approach to economic enquiry.

BOX 22.3   JOAN ROBINSON (1903-83)

The economics profession has been dominated by males, but not exclusively. Joan Robinson is probably the most distinguished female economist, certainly from the political economy perspective. A student and, subsequently, a colleague of John Maynard Keynes at Cambridge University, she made substantial contributions to neoclassical economics, Keynesian economics, Marxist economics, and post-Keynesian economics at various stages of her career.

Robinson's early work adapted neoclassical theory in the light of the growth of big business, providing the foundation for a theory of imperfect competition. Her analysis remained constrained by neoclassical assumptions, but showed that exploitation could result from firms with market power depressing wage rates below the level that would prevail under perfectly competitive conditions. This gave a slightly radical twist to the distributional implications of mainstream economic theory.

Robinson went on to become a significant figure in the formulation and teaching of Keynesian ideas. Her *Theory of Employment* (1937) was a point of access for many students. Her subsequent books, particularly *An Essay on Marxian Economics* (1942), took a more anti-capitalist turn, although her embrace of Marxism was only partial. The labour theory of value had no place in her political economy, because she thought it unnecessary as a basis for understanding profits and the exploitation of labour. Indeed, she held that any theory of value was metaphysical and not helpful in understanding capitalism in practice.

Joan Robinson drew on the ideas of the Polish political economist Michal Kalecki, as well as those of Marx, in developing the analysis of economic growth in *The Accumulation of Capital* (1956). Turning her attention to the critique of neoclassical theory, she also wrote important journal articles that demonstrated the incoherence of the orthodox theory of income distribution. She showed that the marginal productivity theory rested on a concept of capital that was theoretically unsound and not amenable to measurement, arguing that this was a reflection of a deeper problem—the ahistorical character of neoclassical economics. She launched many other assaults on orthodoxy, repeatedly stressing the need to tackle the neoclassical theorists on their own terrain by showing the logical flaws in the reasoning.

Joan Robinson took the view that economics should be considered as a tool kit. In her judgment, the best introduction for students would be to combine the study of economic history, the history of economic thought, and economic statistics.[7]

Conclusion

The analysis of income distribution is of fundamental importance in political economy. Neoclassical theory draws attention to the role of productivity in shaping the financial rewards going to different factors of production. However, there are substantial difficulties in measuring productivity and in applying the analysis of productivity to land, labour, and capital in a symmetrical manner. Neoclassical theory also omits consideration of the distribution of ownership of economic resources and the power that owners may exercise, individually and collectively, in the pursuit of their sectional interests.

Introducing these considerations into the study of distribution also raises practical questions about the scope for governments to pursue policies of income redistribution. If policies were to target the ownership of economic resources explicitly and/or the power that the owners of economic resources exercise in pursuit of their interests, they could presumably produce more equitable distributional outcomes. Whether that pursuit of greater equity would adversely affect economic efficiency is debatable. Whether such forms of government intervention are compatible with the pursuit of enhanced social wellbeing is also contentious. Further exploration of these issues requires more explicit analysis of economic welfare.

KEY POINTS

- Neoclassical theorists seek to explain the distribution of income in terms of the productivity of labour, capital, and land.
- Critics of neoclassical theory contend that distribution is more fundamentally shaped by the power relationships between the owners of labour, capital, and land.
- 'Who gets what' depends on 'Who owns what', as well as on the relative magnitude of wage payments, profits, and rents.

23 Economic Welfare and Neoliberalism

> Does equilibrium in the economy necessarily imply socially desirable outcomes?
>
> Can neoclassical economics provide a basis for judging the desirability of economic changes?
>
> How does neoclassical theory link to neoliberal policy prescriptions in practice?

Orthodox economists often claim to be concerned with positive economics. This implies an analysis free of value judgments. As earlier chapters have argued, a value-free economics is difficult, if not impossible, to attain in practice. The values—customarily associated in neoclassical theory with the tradition of economic liberalism—are implicit. If economic analysis is to be applied to the great tasks of public policy formulation and social betterment, it is necessary to make them explicit. We need clear guidelines for making judgments about what would improve the well-being of the community and how economic policy might contribute to serving that goal.

Some neoclassical economists have responded to these concerns by developing an explicitly normative analysis, generally known as welfare economics. Its limited achievements are reviewed here. Attention is also given to contemporary arguments about the relative importance of market failure and government failure, drawing on the theory of public choice. The uncomfortable connection between interventionist and free market currents of thought in mainstream economics today is thereby revealed.

General equilibrium

If we are to evaluate the working of the economy as a whole, there must be some basis for seeing how all the parts fit together. General equilibrium theory performs this function in neoclassical economics. General equilibrium is said to exist when a set of prices for goods and factors of production equates supply and demand in all markets simultaneously. It is a purely theoretical situation. No neoclassical theorist would claim that the real world ever achieves this state. There are always some forces bound to cause disequilibrium in particular markets; a change in consumer preferences or in the state of technology affecting the production process in one or more industries, for example. Once one market has been disturbed by such changes, there are bound to be knock-on effects in other markets. An increase in demand for ice cream because of a long spell of hot weather, for example, will tend to increase the demand for milk (if that is what ice cream is made from), which will increase the demand for workers in the dairy industry, which may affect the prevailing wage rates, which may then affect the demand for the various products that the dairy industry workers consume. These changes may then lead to changes in commodity prices, consequent changes in the demand for the factors of production used in making them, and so on. A change in one market can cause changes in many others.

The notion of general equilibrium draws attention to this interdependence of markets in the economy as a whole. It may readily be conceded that, at any particular time, general *dis*equilibrium is the normal state. However, according to neoclassical theory, market adjustments operate relentlessly in the direction of restoring general equilibrium, even though the system is unlikely to ever reach equilibrium before it is disturbed by other 'shocks'.[1] The analogy of the ball on a saucer, introduced in Chapter 18, is pertinent here, too: if the saucer is frequently knocked or shaken, the ball will keep moving, but it will always tend towards the middle of the saucer. A general equilibrium that is unique and stable has a similar character: it may be seldom, if ever, attained, but it is a condition to which the economy continuously tends.

This notion of general equilibrium, though abstract, is an influential way of envisaging the economy as a whole: as a network of interdependent markets producing overall stability. In the hands of neoclassical theorists, working in the tradition pioneered by Leon Walras, general equilibrium theory has been developed into a sophisticated mathematical model. It is a model that, typically, takes as given some key socioeconomic conditions: consumers' tastes, the state of technology, the ownership of economic resources, and workers' preferences between income and leisure. These affect, respectively, the demand and supply for goods and services, the distribution of income, and the supply of labour. Critics argue that the model takes as given the key variables that really ought to be explained. Mathematical precision evidently comes at a high price in terms of practical relevance.

From a political economic perspective, what is more important than the technical specifications of general equilibrium theory is the vision it presents of a self-regulating market economy. This is its normative application: supporting the belief that markets are the best means of economic organisation. As such, it has a powerful ideological function supporting laissez-faire principles.

Welfare and optimum

Whether an equilibrium situation constitutes an optimum condition requires more systematic consideration. A market economy may or may not have an underlying tendency towards general equilibrium in practice, but, even if it does, this does not necessarily refute the case for economic planning or other forms of state policies. A world of general equilibrium, should it ever exist, would not necessarily be desirable in all respects. The continual flux in the process of adjustment to new equilibria may have undesirable social consequences; instability in employment, for example. The general equilibrium situation itself may have some socially undesirable features, such as a highly unequal distribution of income, or excessively high prices for particular goods that society considers necessary or meritorious. An equilibrium situation is not necessarily an optimum situation.

Explicit normative standards are required if economists are to pronounce systematically on what is optimal. Yardsticks are needed, against which progress towards more desirable outcomes can be measured, particularly if economists are concerned to be relevant to public policy discussions. It is for these reasons that neoclassical economists developed welfare economics, as a bridge between the analysis of what is and the discussion of what ought to be.

In his book *The Economics of Welfare*, A. C. Pigou, who succeeded Alfred Marshall as Professor of Economics at Cambridge, laid some important foundations.[2] Pigou recognised that economic welfare (or well-being) is only one aspect of broader societal goals. Economic welfare is not synonymous with social welfare. Nor is it independent of the distribution of income. If, for example, the principle of diminishing marginal utility applies to income in general, a strong case for egalitarian redistribution can be made. The last dollar received by a rich person is likely to add little to his or her economic well-being, whereas an extra dollar received by a poor person is likely to add significantly. The rich person may not even notice that marginal dollar, whereas for the poor person it may be the difference between eating and starving. The obvious policy prescription is to redistribute income from the rich to the poor in order to increase total economic welfare. Logically, that process of progressive redistribution until the marginal utility of income is equal for all citizens.

This seems to be a rather radical policy prescription, argued from an impeccably orthodox economic stance. Not surprisingly, it is not the sort of economic reasoning universally acceptable to the wealthy. Nor to other neoclassical theorists, who attacked Pigou's underlying logic. Interpersonal comparisons of utility are illegitimate, they asserted. We cannot know for sure how much the dollar taken from the rich person will reduce that person's welfare. It may do so substantially if, for example, the rich person is a miser who is deeply distressed at having that dollar taken away. On the other hand, the poor person may be an individual with no economic aspirations, who is quite content with a meagre income and will derive little, if any, pleasure from the extra dollar. So we cannot be absolutely certain that the posited income redistribution adds to total economic welfare. Perhaps there is no systematic way of comparing people's subjective well-being. However, this leaves no obvious basis for making judgments about appropriate public policies.

If interpersonal comparisons of utility cannot be made, orthodox economists conclude, we can only say that a redistribution of income (or any other change) constitutes an improvement if it makes some person (or people) better off without making anyone worse off. This is the Pareto Principle, named after the Italian economist Vilfredo Pareto. It is much weaker than the principle underlying Pigou's reasoning. Is it a useful guideline? On the one hand, it is unobjectionable in the sense that it seems to have no significant exceptions; if you are better off and no one is worse off as a consequence (or even feels worse off), then it seems reasonable to conclude that we are collectively better off. On the other hand, it only rarely applies in the real world: almost every economic change generates winners and losers, and in such circumstances the Pareto Principle cannot tell us if the change constitutes a general improvement. We are left with an agnostic position.

Responding to these difficulties, other welfare economists in the twentieth century developed supplementary principles based on compensation payments. If, for example, a person or people who benefit from an economic change can financially compensate the losers such that the latter feel no net disadvantage as a result, then that change may be deemed socially desirable. Or, to be yet more restrictive, if that compensation principle is met, the compensation is actually paid, and the income distribution is no more unequal at the end of the process than it was at the start, then the change is deemed desirable. Here are some interesting thought experiments.[3] The problem with their practical application is that there is no general mechanism for those compensation payments to be enforced in a pure market economy. In effect, the chain of reasoning leads towards the advocacy of a much more substantial economic role for the state than economic liberals would normally allow. There would need to be detailed government regulations or legal procedures to enforce income redistributions associated with a vast array of otherwise private market transactions.

In practice, the problems of identifying consistent welfare criteria and compensation principles usually lead to a laissez-faire response. Since it is very difficult to justify any economic policy intervention by reference to the Pareto test, so the argument runs, it is best to leave resource allocation processes to the market. This is not a matter of logic: the market is no more 'natural' than government and therefore has no innate claim to priority. Rather, the stance reflects the general ideological orientation of neoclassical economists towards a preference for the market.

There is yet one more big fly in the ointment: the *theory of second best*. This theorem shows that, if not all the conditions for an optimal economic outcome are attainable, then a move towards that optimum may not constitute an improvement.[4] In other words, if the first best outcome is not possible for some reason, then the second best may be quite a different situation from the one that approximates the optimum. Take the example of market structures. We might agree in principle, if we were persuaded by neoclassical reasoning, that it would be best for all markets to be perfectly competitive. If that were not possible (perhaps because of the economies of large-scale production or the existence of natural monopoly in one or more markets), then it might not be desirable to try to move closer to perfect competition in the other markets. The second-best outcome might involve balancing the power of some big businesses or strengthening the market power of consumer groups or trade unions. We cannot know for sure. So, public policies that make incremental changes—and that is all that normally can be done—have inherently uncertain effects on overall economic welfare. According to the neoclassical economists' own reasoning, it starts to look silly to talk about universal optimum conditions at all.[5]

Market failure

In practice, a more pragmatic approach to considering economic policy is commonly adopted. Neoclassical economists seek to reconcile their general laissez-faire inclinations with selective public policy proposals by emphasising, or at least acknowledging, the problems of market failure. The market is taken as the norm, but some imperfections are recognised, and remedial public policies recommended in specific circumstances. So, what are these circumstances in which markets are not likely to produce an optimal allocation of resources?

The first is where markets fail to provide public goods. Where people cannot readily be excluded from enjoying the benefits of particular goods or services that are inherently collective in character, they cannot be charged individually for consuming them. Such is the case with the provision of defence services for a nation. Fire services, public parks, and libraries also have public good characteristics. Public provision of these goods or services is necessary, or they will usually not be provided at all.

The second type of market failure concerns externalities. Some goods are overprovided in a market economy, while others are underprovided because the costs and benefits they confer on society are not adequately taken into account by the market mechanism. If environmental goods, such as clean air, rivers, and oceans, are free to the individual consumer and producer, they are used without restraint and are correspondingly degraded. Education, on the other hand, is generally underprovided and underconsumed because its positive externalities are not reflected in a market price. So, the free market produces a lopsided pattern of economic activity. The rationale for government intervention in these circumstances is to correct the market prices and to compensate for the resource misallocation.

The next issue concerns equity in distribution. As Amartya Sen has noted, an economic situation can be both 'Pareto optimal and … sickeningly iniquitous'.[6] The neoclassical economists' advocacy of the market economy is based more on considerations of allocative efficiency than on claims to fairness. An economic system, on this reasoning, may be efficient, even though the distribution of incomes—and, hence, access to the consumption of goods and services—is manifestly inequitable. Indeed, there is a presumption of inequality in a market economy because material incentives drive the system. However, distributional equity may be a precondition for the cooperation needed for superior economic performance. It may be necessary for social cohesion. So some redistributive role for government may be warranted, even from an economic liberal perspective.

The fourth source of market failure is imperfect competition. Neoclassical economists are generally uncomfortable about any deviations from the perfectly competitive ideal. Only under conditions of perfect competition are markets held to produce economic efficiency and to ensure the provision of goods and services to consumers at the lowest possible prices. Yet in the real world, monopolistic competition, oligopoly, and monopoly are more common market structures. While the orthodox economists have no agreed prescriptions for dealing with these circumstances, as noted in Chapter 21, they do concede some role for government in redressing the market distortions resulting from imperfect competition.

Finally, there is the problem of instability. As noted earlier, proponents of general equilibrium theory usually represent a free-market economy as basically stable, though they sometimes concede that the processes of adjustment to changing equilibria are not instantaneous and may impose social costs. Critics of the theory emphasise more substantial flaws in the adjustment mechanisms of capitalism in practice, such as the tendencies to alternating boom and slump and to recurrent unemployment. These tendencies violate the orthodox economists' own criterion of efficiency, for it is blatantly inefficient for resources to be left idle while social needs for goods and services are simultaneously unfulfilled.

This all adds up to a quite considerable indictment of free-market capitalism within a body of analysis predisposed to favour the market. The acknowledgment of the various sources of market failure provides a strong rationale for trying to rectify the recurrent problems of markets by developing appropriate government policies. This is the liberal-interventionist position. It has usually been embraced by economists seeking a compromise between their professional adherence to neoclassical theory and their personal commitment to economic reform and social progress. The liberal-interventionist position is associated with the use of techniques such as cost–benefit analysis (see Box 23.1 below) to decide about public policies.

There is no consensus though. The liberal-interventionist position has always had its critics among other neoclassical economists concerned to maintain the faith in the free-enterprise system. In the last three decades, this purist position has been the dominant orthodoxy, variously labelled neoliberalism, economic rationalism, and economic fundamentalism.[7] Its conceptual basis is the notion of government failure.

BOX 23.1 COST-BENEFIT ANALYSIS

Most economic decisions generate social costs and social benefits. Cost-benefit analysis is a means of comparing these beneficial and adverse consequences in order to determine whether the expected outcomes are, on balance, in the public interest. It has become a widely used method for evaluation of public investment projects.

The procedure involves five steps:

- identify all the relevant consequences of a particular public policy decision
- evaluate all these consequences in monetary terms, so as to derive values for the costs and benefits expected to accrue to society as a whole
- estimate the net present value of the future costs and benefits
- compare the net present value of the costs and the net present value of the benefits, that is, the overall benefit:cost ratio
- select all the policy alternatives where the benefit:cost ratio is higher than 1; or, in the case of mutually exclusive alternatives, select the policy alternative with the highest benefit:cost ratio.

Consider, for example, the construction of a new urban freeway. The first step would require the analyst to list all the likely effects, such as how travel times for freeway users and for users of existing roads would be affected, the likely incidence and severity of traffic accidents, the expected impact on atmospheric pollution, noise pollution, the effect on residents along the path of the freeway, and the expected loss of flora and fauna resulting from this change in land use. The second step would require putting a dollar value on each item; that is, the value of travel time saved, the value of lives lost or saved, the health cost of air pollution, and the value of the threatened species. The third step would involve expressing these various streams of costs and benefits in terms of their current value equivalent, on the assumption that future costs and benefits should have less weight than immediate costs and benefits. How much less weight depends on the choice of a discount rate. The fourth step would involve comparing the costs of the freeway construction with its estimated benefits, all expressed in terms of these monetary net present values. The freeway is then deemed to be socially desirable only if the benefits exceed the costs. If two or more freeway routes were under consideration, the preferred route would be the one with the highest benefit:cost ratio.

Proponents of cost-benefit analysis emphasise the advantages of having a method of project evaluation that increases the consistency of decision-making. Its critics challenge the legitimacy of trying to place monetary values on intangibles such as environmental quality, even on life itself. Cost-benefit analysis shares with neoclassical welfare economics a distinctive set of assumptions about the nature of the economy and society. It is, for better or worse, a monetary calculus of the determinants of community well-being.

Government failure

Scepticism about government is a long tradition that has various manifestations, both popular and academic. Politically, it has a base in anarchist thought as well as right-wing libertarianism. The latter viewpoint derives in part from social Darwinism; it sees the struggle for existence and the survival of the fittest as elements in a natural order, which governments should not spoil by attempting to redress economic inequality and other social problems. The aversion to government also has roots in popular folklore, particularly in the USA, about the advantages of a society that promotes individualism rather than seeking the redress of its problems through collective action. According to this view, anyone can make it from rags to riches by individual initiative. Governments, however well intentioned, stand in the way of such drives for personal advancement in a free society. Worse, they may be parasitic and/or corrupt.

Developments in economic theory during the last two decades have given some academic legitimacy to these popular beliefs. *Public choice theory* is particularly significant in this respect. It has been an increasingly influential current of thought running between neoclassical economics and political science.[8] It represents politicians and bureaucrats as subspecies of *Homo economicus*, self-interested individuals whose actions are calculated responses to vote-maximising processes. They tend to implement policies to satisfy the demands (and secure the votes) of sectional interest groups, systematically violating any broader national interest. Manufacturers win the tariff protection they seek, unions secure minimum wage legislation, housing tenants get rent control, and so forth. The overall effect is a series of incoherent regulations and policy interventions that impede the capacity of the market to ensure an efficient allocation of resources.

Variations on this theme are developed with varying degrees of analytical sophistication. In the words of one of the leading proponents of this theory, 'In a very real sense, public choice theory offers a theory of government-political failure that is on all fours with the theory of market failure that emerged from the theoretical welfare economics of the 1950s.'[9] Indeed, it has become more powerful since then, as right-wing politicians have argued that government failure is more deeply problematic than market failure.

Critics of public choice theory have countered by emphasising its neglect of the institutional and sociological factors that cause political processes to work quite differently from economic markets.[10] It is quite bizarre, one might infer, to apply market economic reasoning to the sphere of politics, the very existence of which reflects the inadequacies of the market as a means of providing for all our societal needs. The proponents of public choice theory have evidently been little perturbed by such criticisms. Their work has been influential as a supporting ideology for systematic assaults on the welfare state and government regulations on business. Its practical consequence is neoliberal politics.

Neoliberalism

Neoliberalism is to politics what neoclassicism is to economics. In both cases there is a strong emphasis on beliefs about freedom of choice and the ideal properties of markets. The rhetoric of neoliberalism is all about 'slimming the state' and reducing government 'red tape' in order to provide more scope for individual initiative and enterprise. The neoclassical economic underpinnings indicate the desired goal of an efficient market economy.

The importance of the economic dimension in neoliberal politics is also reflected in the use of the related terms 'economic rationalism' and 'economic fundamentalism'. The former has been widely used in Australia, for example, and the latter in New Zealand. Economic rationalism involves the extension of neoclassical economic reasoning to the realm of public policy. The terminology conveys a strong inference that subjecting policy issues to a rigorous economic analysis is conducive to rationality. However, economic rationalism is not necessarily rational. The term 'rationalism' is better understood as 'deriving from theory'; in this case, neoclassical economic theory and its variant, public choice theory. It is the opposite of empiricism, which is the gaining of knowledge from experience. In practice, economic rationalism has the characteristics of a creed, emphasising faith in the free market to deliver superior outcomes to government intervention.

'Economic fundamentalism'—sometimes called market fundamentalism—implies a similar commitment to a neoclassical perspective, prioritising market principles over other social and political judgments. The most obvious manifestations of economic rationalism and market fundamentalism in practice are policies of privatisation, deregulation, trade liberalisation, reductions in the level and progressivity of income taxation, contracting out of public services, and the withdrawal of governments from their previous commitment to universal social security. The provision and maintenance of public highways is increasingly being contracted to private companies, who construct and manage what then become private tollways. Even health and education services are increasingly financed and provided along market principles. The array of public goods is being scaled back. Defence remains a public commitment (although mercenary armies are available for hire), but many other aspects of public provision are being corporatised and marketised. Privately owned prisons, for example, would have been considered laughable a couple of decades ago, but are now common. The speed and comprehensiveness with which this neoliberal program has been pursued varies from country to country: generally, it has been less pronounced in continental Europe than in the UK, North America, Australia, and New Zealand, but it has been pervasive.

Whether this all adds up to 'slimming the state', as its proponents commonly claim, is debatable. The implementation of neoliberal policies has involved a change in the functions of the state: a shift from direct service provision to regulation of private providers, for example. However, there has not been a consistently marked diminution in the public sector's proportion of gross domestic product. 'Actually existing neoliberalism' involves a strong state serving capitalist interests, not a withdrawal of the state from the economy.[11]

The onset of the global financial crisis in 2007–08 provided a significant jolt to neoliberal principles and practices. Some prominent politicians, such as Nicolas Sarkozy in France and Kevin Rudd in Australia, proclaimed the end of the neoliberal project. Yet the ideas and policy practices are still influential post GFC. It is a time of contestation between radically different views about markets and states and of major experiments in the application of those competing views. The neoliberal ideologies and politics are a distinct element in this process. They are a practical extension of neoclassical reasoning, stripped of its caveats about market failure and problems of second best. They are a vulgarised form of neoclassical economics in action in the political arena.

Conclusion

There is a paradox to confront. It concerns the relationship between economic theory and the practice of economic policy. On the one hand, neoclassical economic theory, particularly its general equilibrium variant, largely ignores the messy complexities of the real world. The centrality of the perfect competition model in the teaching of economics is a symbol of this. As a consequence, neoclassical theory faces the repeated charge of failing to engage with capitalism in practice. The attempts by the neoclassical economists to erect a bridge between their theories and practical concerns about economic policy—through the development of welfare economics—have also been largely unsuccessful. Welfare economics has turned out to be a cul de sac.[12] Yet many of the major political economic changes in the real world in recent decades have reflected the influence of neoclassical economic theory.

There are contrary trends, too. The neoliberal drive is not all one-way traffic. It has strong political opponents, whose opposition connects with other popular beliefs (about egalitarianism, social solidarity, community, and collective action, for example). Some neoclassical economists themselves are less than enthusiastic about 'actually existing neoliberalism' because it strips away the qualifications they attach to their theories about markets. Those of a more liberal-interventionist bent continue to subscribe to the view that market failures require systematic redress through government policies. This division among the neoclassical economists themselves gives the appearance of internal diversity, thereby providing some defence against charges that mainstream economics is monolithic or dogmatic. Yet stronger opposition to neoliberalism comes from other currents of political economic thought—from Marxist economics, of course, but also from Keynesian economics and institutional economics. It is to a consideration of these latter alternatives that we now turn.

KEY POINTS

- Neoclassical economists use general equilibrium theory to show the interdependence of markets and the possibility of stability in a pure market economy.

- An economic equilibrium is not necessarily a social optimum. Judging what is desirable requires explicit welfare criteria, but the attempts by neoclassical theorists to develop such criteria have proved deeply problematic.

- Neoclassical theorists' views on economic policy tend to reflect the relative importance they place on problems of market failure and government failure.

PART VI

Evolution and Reform

Institutional Economics

24 Economy and Society

Why focus on economic institutions?

What does an evolutionary approach to economics entail?

What were the main ideas of Thorstein Veblen, the leading light in the development of institutional economics?

Institutional economists have mounted a strong challenge to the dominance of neoclassical economics. They argue that the pure market economy is little more than a fiction. Market arrangements in practice are socially embedded, dependent on supportive structures for their effective operation. They depend on legal institutions to establish and enforce property rights and contractual principles; on financial institutions, which underpin the legitimacy and value of the means of exchange; and on social institutions, which reinforce ideologies underlying the existing economic order. As William Lazonick puts it, 'History shows that the driving force of successful capitalist development is not the perfection of the market mechanism but the building of organisational capacities.'[1]

According to institutional economists, these are the real political economic phenomena that need to be studied—not the unrealistic abstractions about perfectly competitive markets. In effect, institutional economists are making a plea for the reintegration of economic enquiry into the social sciences: sociology, politics, history, geography, industrial relations, and anthropology. Institutional economics, reflecting this orientation, has sometimes been called economic sociology.[2] This is sometimes taken to imply that it is not real economics; however, its proponents argue that it studies economic issues in their real-world context, where they are inexorably linked with social and political matters, and nothing could be more real than that.

Institutions and evolution

Institutional economics takes an evolutionary rather than mechanistic view of the economy.[3] Its focus is on history rather than equilibrium. It is concerned with studying the interactions between social values, technology, and economic institutions. In this respect, it can be seen as exploring the very things that neoclassical economists take as given in their models; for example, consumers' tastes, the state of technology, and the ownership of economic resources. According to institutional economists, it is through the study of these socially moulded phenomena that a better understanding of the evolution of economic society can be constructed.

This orientation also leads to a focus on the diverse patterns of capitalist development. The economic institutions of countries such as the USA, the UK, Australia, Japan, Germany, Sweden, and Singapore are quite different. We need to understand why. Such understanding can only come from the detailed study of each country in its historical context. Taken to the extreme, this denies the possibility of a general explanation of the structure and functioning of capitalism. The quest, common to Marxist and neoclassical economics, for a unified theory to explain the economic system, may be regarded as misplaced in this respect. Perhaps it is more important to look at the variety of economic experience in American capitalism, Australian capitalism, Japanese capitalism, and so on. The result may be less tidy, but, according to its proponents, it is likely to be markedly more realistic.[4]

Still, some structural guidelines are imperative for any political economic enquiry. The capital–labour–state framework is useful in this regard. As noted in preceding chapters, these three conceptual categories are used in other currents of economic thought. What is distinctive about the institutional approach is the treatment of them as institutional clusters having internal diversity, particularly in respect of their relative economic power. Capital is not an amorphous factor of production; rather, it is something that comes in many institutional forms, ranging from large multinational corporations to smaller businesses whose behaviour is moulded by local conditions. The institutional forms of labour also vary significantly, according to whether workers are organised into trade unions and whether they are fragmented by locality, gender, or race. The institutions of the state are yet more varied, ranging from public enterprises, concerned with the direct provision of goods and services, to agencies responsible for the provision of infrastructure, central banking, regulation of markets, and arbitration of wages and industrial disputes.

How these institutions of capital, labour, and state interact is not an equilibrium process; it is a power play. It follows that the study of economic power—its sources, its uses and abuses—is a necessary part of institutional analysis. Of course, power is also part of the Marxist and neoclassical stories: class power in the former, and market power in the latter. The conception of power in institutional economics is more broad ranging, as we shall see in the next two chapters. As a bridge between economics and sociology, it is not surprising to see in institutionalism the influence of seminal social theorists such as Max Weber and Emile Durkheim.[5] The influence on the institutional economics tradition of the German historical school of the nineteenth century is also significant.[6]

As a distinctive tradition of economic analysis, institutionalism's peak was in the USA in the first half of the twentieth century. Indeed, it is no exaggeration to claim that it then rivalled the neoclassical school as the most influential type of economics. It was more evidently in tune with changes taking place in the real world in the late nineteenth and early twentieth centuries: increasingly powerful economic institutions were coming to dominate the economy, corporate power was growing, trade unions were forming, and states were assuming a yet more extensive role in the management of economic affairs, including the orchestration of imperialism on a world scale. The incapacity of neoclassical economics to illuminate these changes was a particular focus of criticism by institutional economists. The most notable of the critics was the dissident American economist, Thorstein Veblen (1857–1929). As we shall see, his concerns have continuing resonance today.

BOX 24.1   THORSTEIN VEBLEN (1857-1929)

Thorstein Veblen is widely acknowledged as the pioneer and principal inspiration of institutional economics. An American of Norwegian descent, he had an outsider's view of the society in which he lived. He saw its excesses, its inefficiencies, and its wastes, and he wrote about them with insight and wit. Among his books, *The Theory of the Leisure Class* (1899), *The Theory of Business Enterprise* (1904), and *Absentee Ownership and Business Enterprise in Recent Times* (1923) are notable.

Veblen held a series of academic appointments, but he did not enjoy the secure tenured status accorded to many lesser scholars. It is difficult to escape the inference that he was discriminated against because of his dissident views, although his reputation for having affairs with the wives of faculty members may also have contributed to his difficulties in securing continuous academic employment.

By all accounts he was an eccentric character, in his appearance and his personal habits. He had an unkempt moustache and a short, straggly beard. His socks were sometimes held up by safety pins attached to his trousers. He is said to have not washed his dishes after meals, preferring to hose down stacks of them periodically. He was taciturn in manner and a notoriously dull teacher, mumbling into his beard and setting long reading lists designed to discourage all but the most conscientious students.

Notwithstanding these personal eccentricities and foibles, Veblen was undoubtedly one of the most perceptive social scientists of his era. He was eventually invited to be president of the American Economics Association, but turned down the invitation, saying that the position should have been offered to him earlier in his academic career when it could have been of some professional value. He died in 1929 in relative poverty and obscurity. His legacy to society was his published work. His books and articles are still frequently referred to, whereas those of his more 'respectable' colleagues have long since been forgotten.

The social nature of consumption

Veblen sought to develop a more subtle view of the relationship between the individual and society than in the orthodox conception of *Homo economicus*. An analysis of the social character of consumption is central to this endeavour. People's preferences, which shape their consumption of goods and services, cannot sensibly be taken as given, Veblen thought, because they are socially determined. Our tastes are learnt as we grow up, and that learning process can produce quite different patterns of demand within and between different localities and different social groups. Moreover, those demands themselves commonly have as much to do with the expected social consequences of consumption (such as social status) as with its purely physical consequences (such as eating to stop hunger and wearing clothes to keep warm). This is particularly so for those who have the greatest disposable income.

Veblen called the trendsetting affluent social stratum 'the leisure class', emphasising its tendency to engage in conspicuous consumption and conspicuous leisure. (These terms, it may be noted, have since acquired common usage.) In Veblen's day, the leisure class was itself notably conspicuous. The late nineteenth century in the USA is sometimes known as the era of the robber barons. Families such as the Vanderbilts, Astors, Whitneys, and Rockefellers became prodigiously rich, often through activities involving the unscrupulous exercise of economic power.[7] Karl Marx would not have been surprised by this, of course, since he foresaw that the concentration and centralisation of capital would make for growing class inequality. Henry George argued that the roots of the prodigious wealth lay in the alienation of land and the unearned increment of incomes deriving from its ownership. Veblen's concern was more with the social consequences of such concentrations of wealth.

Conspicuous consumption means buying things for the purpose of display. The ideal house is not merely one in which it is comfortable to live, but also one whose palatial characteristics impress the neighbours, friends, and passers-by. A motor car has to be not simply a reliable means of transport, but also a status symbol: it must be expensive, and widely perceived as such. Likewise a yacht. Clothing has to be more than functional; it must indicate to all who care to observe that the wearer is a person of economic wealth and social position, if not refinement. If the apparel signals that the wearer does not have to toil for a living, so much the better, for that is the hallmark of the leisure class. White shoes and white gloves are ideal accoutrements for all who want to show their social distance from the world of manual labour. Wives are particularly useful in this process, as objects of display for wealthy men, to be dressed in whatever finery most clearly signals that they have no need to work.

Such social pretension is all too familiar to us in an era of McMansions, designer clothes, SUVs, and luxury sports cars. Veblen wrote of its development a century ago in a way that was witty and insightful. His observations in *The Theory of the Leisure Class* are like those of an anthropologist observing a strange tribe, or of an ecologist observing an exotic species of bird. One can almost imagine a nineteenth-century David Attenborough crouching in the shrubbery at a garden party thrown by a member of the leisure class, saying, 'See how the male of the species is inclined to predatory behaviour, but always finds time to display his acquisitions. And look at how the apparel of the women indicates their social position. See how they strut and preen themselves at every occasion. And note how the whole process is reproduced in succeeding generations through careful attention to encouraging the offspring to adopt similar modes of behaviour.' The human ape is under observation and looks risible.

There is a more serious point here, however. Because the leisure class devotes prodigious economic resources to this conspicuous consumption and conspicuous leisure, there is social waste. Can throwing extravagant parties, where champagne flows like water and people light cigars with twenty-dollar bills, be held, by any standard, to be an efficient allocation of resources? The neoclassical economists duck the issue, protesting their reluctance to make value judgments about consumers' preferences. Veblen was more concerned to describe than to judge; but drawing attention to the social excesses invites normative reflection. In effect, Veblen was observing the tendency, not towards efficiency, but towards waste as the central feature of capitalist society. His analysis was a forerunner of modern concerns about consumerism, its excesses and its dubious connection with enhanced community wellbeing.

The problems of ultimately unsatisfying consumption are magnified by the process of 'social emulation' (another piece of Veblen's terminology that has since gained widespread currency). It is, of course, difficult for poor people to copy the living standards of the wealthy. They may seek to do the best they can, consuming scaled-down and cheaper versions according to the limits of their incomes (and sometimes beyond), but it is a process fraught with inherent frustration. If our perceived well-being depends on what we have relative to what others have, mass consumerism is a recipe for permanent dissatisfaction. The neoclassical assumption of a direct correlation between increased consumption and higher utility cannot be sustained.

The social nature of production

Veblen also made major contributions to understanding business activities. As with the analysis of consumption, his analysis of the processes of production draws attention to the sources of tension, waste, and inefficiency. The production of goods and services is not treated, as in neoclassical theory, as a technical puzzle involving the selection of the least-cost combination of factors of production and a profit-maximising output. It is treated as a social process. As such, it reflects a fundamental disjuncture between the instinct of workmanship and the predatory instinct. Veblen posited these two instincts as universal features of human behaviour.

The tension between the instinct of workmanship and the predatory instinct is particularly problematic in capitalist businesses. Workmanship is the productive aspect, involving the use of land, labour, and capital to make useful goods and services. Predatory behaviour, on the other hand, includes activities that enhance profit without adding to productive capacity. The former is socially beneficial (setting aside the issue of environmental exploitation and decay);

the latter is counterproductive, although it may be an attractive strategic option in the short term. Both aspects coexist in the real economy.

Somewhat schematically, this dualism can be described as a tension between industry and business. These two terms are often used interchangeably in popular discourse (and elsewhere in this book), but the suggestion here is that they represent contrary tendencies. Industry is productive activity focused on the use of the physical means of production, and on technological possibilities for the development of new products or better ways of making existing products. This is the realm of the engineers. Business, on the other hand, is concerned with monetary values and financial flows, with the so-called bottom line. This, and this alone, is the interest of the owners of the businesses, particularly where they are what Veblen called absentee owners; that is, shareholders having no direct involvement in the management of the enterprises. This is the realm of the financiers.

The tension between the engineers and the financiers is manifest in the management of technological change. Engineers are concerned with the development of new technologies, but this may undermine the value of existing capital equipment, even make it obsolete. Technological change may, therefore, be perceived as working against the interests of the absentee owners of businesses.

One way of handling this dilemma, Veblen noted, is for business managers to try to eliminate competition between firms, or at least to reduce it to a level that enables them to exercise some control over the rate and form of technological process. Innovations may be suppressed, contrary to the interests of both the engineers and consumers.

This incompatibility of modern technology with competition was Veblen's explanation for the great wave of mergers and cartel formation taking place in his time. In the present age, the desire to control technology continues to be a major factor influencing business strategy and industrial concentration. It is a two-way process, though; being in the forefront of new technological developments can be a key factor in the growth of businesses, while big businesses are better able to control the form that technological change takes.

Veblen also sought to explain the tendency to economic recession. He considered that, even if mergers and the formation of cartels produced coordination on the supply side of the economy, the problem of ensuring sufficient demand for the growing volume of goods and services would likely remain. Prodigious productive capacity was being developed, but the distribution of income set a limit to what could be sold at the prices monopolists require in order to get an acceptable rate of return on their capital. Echoes of the overproduction and underconsumption problems discussed by Marx are clearly audible here. Veblen's analysis of the wasteful expenditures of the leisure class drew attention, in effect, to a partial solution to those problems. Wasteful public expenditures—on grandiose public edifices, diplomatic and ecclesiastical establishments, military service, and armaments—could also play a significant part.

However, Veblen doubted that these wasteful expenditures would be capable of growing indefinitely at the same rate as the productive power of industry. Hence, he forecast a great depression. His analysis of it was loose and imprecise, but the conclusion that tendencies towards depression were endemic in the economic system preceded Keynes's more thorough analysis by almost three decades.

Veblen further noted that the most successful form of wasteful expenditure is war. War is hell, of course, but it can give temporary stimulus to an economy with an inbuilt tendency to depression. His analysis proved prescient; the First World War broke out in 1914, leading to devastating loss of life but providing no ongoing basis for economic prosperity.

Veblen also predicted the rise of fascism and the emergence of the corporate state, a scenario in which military authoritarianism and the interests of capitalist big business would prevail over nominally democratic institutions. This too subsequently became a feature of European nations, such as Germany, Italy, and Spain, in the years leading up to the Second World War. Veblen's engagement with these broad political economic issues foreshadowed one of the major themes raised by institutional economists today: the awkward, even incompatible, relationship between capitalism and democracy.[8]

Conclusion

Thorstein Veblen's work provided a substantial foundation for the development of institutional economics. It may be regarded as everything that the neoclassical economists' theories were not—and still are not. It was interdisciplinary in character, with strong historical and anthropological emphases. It examined the evolution of the economy rather than the properties of posited equilibrium conditions. It explored the origins of the things that orthodox theorists normally take as given: tastes, technology, social structure and economic inequality. The focus on these matters, particularly tastes and technology, enabled Veblen to illuminate the discordant aspects of the economy. He showed an economy rife with waste and internal contradictions, not an economy producing harmonious outcomes. This is the reasoning of an uninhibited social scientist developing a trenchant critique of the economic basis of the society of his day.

Was Veblen the American equivalent of Karl Marx? In a society with a deep attachment to capitalism as the expression of economic individualism, Veblen was about as radical as someone seeking a significant audience for their views can be in the USA. However, a balanced assessment of his contribution must also acknowledge two contrary features. First, there is not the same analytical rigour as is found in Marx's political economy. Veblen's rejection of neoclassical theory led him to a looser style of reasoning, featuring social observation and witty criticism. Second, Veblen had no political program comparable to that proposed by Marx. His analysis of the contradictions and wastes of the American economy did not lead to substantial proposals for different economic arrangements that would offer more favourable prospects for progress. There is the hope, even the expectation, that the engineers would take over from the financiers as the economic managers of society, but no analysis of any such transition and no manifesto for an alternative political economic order. This is not to belittle the importance of his work. Veblen paved the way for a significant dissident tradition in economic thought: the tradition of institutional economics.

KEY POINTS

- Institutional economics focuses on evolution rather than on equilibrium, showing how the institutions of capital, labour, and the state acquire and use economic power.

- Thorstein Veblen analysed the social character of consumption and production in order to highlight key characteristics of the American economy in practice.

- This analysis paved the way for the development of an institutional economic tradition challenging the unrealistic nature of neoclassical theory.

25 A Dissident Tradition in Economics

> *What are the characteristics of institutional economics?*
>
> *What contributions has this tradition made to economic thought?*
>
> *What impact have institutionalists had on economic policy in practice?*

Many dissident economists, following in the footsteps of Veblen, have been concerned to understand economic issues in their social context. These economists do not form so clearly a defined school of thought as Marxist and neoclassical economists. They have no clear analytic framework equivalent to Marxist value theory or neoclassical marginal analysis. Indeed, institutionalists normally reject both value theory and utility theory as abstractions that are not empirically operational. Their preference is for less explicitly theoretical and more open-ended lines of enquiry. This attracts little academic prestige. Nevertheless, institutional economists can claim to have had a major influence on government policies, tempering the instability and inequality generated in a capitalist economy.

The loosely bounded character of the institutional economics tradition is both its strength and its weakness. It makes for illuminating analyses of the connections between economic, social, and political issues. It has also opened up new lines of enquiry, helping to spawn academic disciplines such as economic statistics and industrial relations. However, critics of institutionalism claim that its loosely bounded character shows a lack of analytical rigour.

Some stocktaking of the contributions of, and the competing claims about, institutional economics is warranted. Six general characteristics of institutional economics, while not applying equally to all its practitioners, indicate the broader orientation of this tradition in political economy. These are as follows:

- Institutionalists have generally been critical, indeed, often downright disrespectful, of economic orthodoxy. Their iconoclasm has challenged the 'conventional wisdom' in economics, thereby clearing the decks for more down-to-earth institutional investigations.

- Institutional economists have been concerned with the empirical study of the real world. They emphasise its complexity, but also try to discern recurrent patterns. This empirical approach is the antithesis of the 'armchair theorising' that has tended to dominate mainstream economics.

- Institutionalists have been concerned with reintegrating economics with sociology, politics, and the other social sciences. The world does not come in neat analytical compartments, they argue, so the analysis of it must have a correspondingly interdisciplinary character.

- Institutionalists also emphasise the pervasive influence of ideology in shaping economic behaviour, and the inevitability of normative judgments shaping economic analysis. From this perspective, the notion of 'positive economics' is a fiction. Values influence all aspects of economic and social enquiry.

- Economic systems are also constantly changing. Institutionalists argue that the methodology of economic enquiry must, therefore, be evolutionary, emphasising the forces that shape the institutions of capital, labour, and the state, and the corresponding processes of social change.

- A common theme in institutional economics is that the development of the economic system can be—indeed, invariably is—steered by the state. Economic knowledge thereby becomes a key element in the process of taking control of our own destinies. This reformist view of the state tends to situate institutional economists, politically, in a broad middle ground between neoclassicals and Marxists.

American institutionalism

Significant numbers of economists, seeking to apply the foregoing principles in building an alternative to orthodox neoclassical economics, have contributed to institutional analysis. Politically, institutionalism has tended to become more conservative as Veblen's breadth of vision has given way to more detailed contributions to empirical research. However, in the twentieth century, as the work of institutional economists came to be more acceptable to the political establishment, some of the reformist prescriptions had significant influence on public policy. In the USA especially, institutional economics was a serious rival to orthodox economics during the first half of the century. It continues to be a source of constructive dissent.

In listing the major contributors to this political economic tradition, it is appropriate to begin with John Commons (1862–1945). His publications included the ten-volume *Documentary History of American Industrial Society* (1910–11). He also wrote *The Legal Foundations of Capitalism* (1924), which examined the relationship between the economic and legal systems: an important connection because, to this day, these continue to be the twin foundations of social order. Commons emphasised the need to study the economy as 'a going concern', evolving in response to real pressures, rather than abstract principles. His writings were packed with the results of his painstakingly detailed and descriptive institutional enquiry: the sort of work that everyone says is useful but few ever read. Even so, he had some practical influence in his own day, particularly in the development of the policies of the New Deal introduced by President Franklin D. Roosevelt to combat the chronic economic and social problems of the Great Depression.[1]

Wesley Mitchell (1874–1948) was another prominent American institutional economist. A friend and former student of Veblen, Mitchell is renowned for his investigations of trends in capitalist development, especially the cyclical character of economic growth. He compiled enormous volumes of statistical data to describe and analyse these trends. 'Measurement without theory' his critics called it. One can discern in this work the origins of the discipline of economic statistics, later to become econometrics. At first sight this does not fit comfortably with the general character of institutional economics as a dissident current in the economics discipline.[2] However, there is actually a common theme: the emphasis in institutional economics on empirical observations of the real world rather than abstract theorising. Mitchell emphasised the quantitative aspects of this empirical enquiry. Computers, of course, have made the analysis of large-scale data sets of economic variables much easier today than it was in Mitchell's time.

Gardiner Means (1896–1988) made equally important contributions to understanding the qualitative changes in twentieth-century capitalist development. Together with Adolph Berle (1895–1971), he is best known for the book *The Modern Corporation and Private Property* (1932), which explored the significance of the separation of ownership from control in the modern corporation. Treating the firm as a single decision-making unit, as mainstream economists usually do, was shown to be out of kilter with real firms. The growth of absentee ownership (shareholders who have no direct managerial role) had opened up major potential conflicts of interest in the running of the corporations. The detailed study by Berle and Means of these changes and tensions was a significant contribution to understanding the origins and consequences of the managerial revolution. Their work continues to resonate, as corporate power becomes more concentrated and more globalised.[3]

A final example of the major figures in the tradition of American institutionalism is Robert Heilbroner (1919–2005), who comes close to rivalling John Kenneth Galbraith as its most outstanding representative since the Second World War. A big thinker and prolific writer, Heilbroner, perhaps more than any other modern political economist, was willing to speculate on the future prospects for capitalism. His focus was not on the short-term trends in economic indicators beloved of the financial market pundits, but on the broad trajectory of economy and society over the decades ahead. His *An Inquiry into the Human Prospect*, for example, reflects on the pressures resulting from population growth, environmental stress, and military conflict. It looks at the difficulties of our political institutions in making the necessary adaptations. It also looks at the limits of human nature, boldly stepping beyond the usual limits of political economy into the realm of social psychology. Heilbroner's evolutionary perspective is blended with an emphasis on the limits of industrial society, or what he elsewhere calls 'business civilisation'. Writing before the current wave of concerns with terrorism and environmental crisis, Heilbroner anticipated convulsive change; that is, 'change forced on us by external events rather than by conscious choice, by catastrophe rather than by calculation'.[4]

Circular and cumulative causation

How economic and social change occurs is a central theme in institutional economics. Perhaps the most significant interpretation is the principle of circular and cumulative causation. The notion has its roots in Veblen's writing, and has since been developed by other institutional economists, most notably the distinguished Swedish political economist Gunnar Myrdal.[5] Its key proposition is that economic inequalities, once established, tend to self-perpetuate and grow. In one respect, this theory is an uncomfortable product of institutionalism, because its practitioners are usually suspicious about claims regarding universal economic principles. Circular and cumulative causation looks like a general theory proposed by critics of general theory. Perhaps the best way of interpreting it is as a notion that can be applied in numerous specific contexts, ranging from the analysis of sexual and racial discrimination, to regional and national underdevelopment, and the formulation of industry policies. It is not so much a general theory as a 'way of seeing' that opens up new directions in analysis and policy.

The contrast with the equilibrium tendencies posited in neoclassical theory is certainly striking. Recall the analogy of the ball on a saucer, in which the ball invariably tends to a middle position in spite of external disturbances: this is the essence of the neoclassical view of the economy in equilibrium. In circular and cumulative causation theory, if there is any equilibrium at all, it is the equilibrium of a pencil standing on its end. Once disturbed, the pencil will fall further and further away from its initial vertical position. This analogy illustrates the contrast with neoclassical theory, or equilibrium economics, as Nicholas Kaldor, another of the proponents of the principle of circular and cumulative causation, labels it.[6] But this does not adequately convey the key feature of the institutional economic reasoning, which is more about processes than end states. Circular and cumulative causation processes arise because relationships in the real world between economic and social variables are seldom linear. Economic changes interact with social changes in ways that open up opportunities for economic growth and social progress. Meanwhile, problems beget problems.

Consider some examples. One is racial discrimination, the focus of one of Myrdal's early books.[7] If ethnic minority groups—such as people of African descent in the USA or the Aboriginal peoples of Australia—are subject to discrimination, they are consigned to generally inferior economic and social circumstances, usually manifest in lower incomes and higher unemployment. These circumstances cause the victims of discrimination to cluster in areas where housing is cheaper, to wear clothing of inferior quality, and perhaps also to adopt self-destructive or antisocial patterns of personal behaviour. That provides a basis and apparent justification for further discrimination against them. A vicious cycle of disadvantage and more entrenched prejudice develops.

A similar story can be told about unemployment. People who lose their jobs (or have difficulty finding a first job) usually experience a predictable sequence of responses. The longer they remain out of work, the more likely it is that their optimism about employment prospects will turn to pessimism. Their personal characteristics, such as regular timekeeping, that employers usually look for in job applicants, atrophy. Potential employers are also often suspicious of people who have significant gaps in their employment record. Eventually, the unemployed people may rationalise their own situation by saying they do not want to work anyway; then, it seems, they are not failures in their own eyes. The 'dole bludger' or 'work-shy' welfare recipient is thereby created. Conservative political campaigns then turn these undeserving individuals into scapegoats for the unemployment problem, a process generally supported by the tabloid press and other capitalist-owned media. The victims become the problem.

This sort of sequence, writ large, is also central to the problem of economic underdevelopment. To quote the economic historian Ragnar Nurske:

> a poor man may not have enough to eat; being undernourished his health may be weak; being physically weak, his working capacity may be low, which means that he is poor, which in turn means that he will not have enough to eat; and so on. A situation of this sort, applying to a country as a whole, can be summed up in the trite proposition 'a country is poor because it is poor.[8]

This is a simple but powerful insight into the general nature of international economic inequalities. Although it does not address the origin of the inequalities, it stands as a powerful antidote to the conventional economic claim, from Ricardo onwards, that more openness to trade is necessarily to mutual advantage. The creation of a level playing field for market exchange may tend to give the already big players even more competitive advantage, accentuating the international economic inequalities.

Within nations there are also observable tendencies towards cumulative regional inequality. Particular cities and regions usually lead the way in economic growth. Those with the head start, for whatever historical or geographical reasons, forge further ahead. Their better-developed infrastructure makes them attractive to both capital and labour, with the result that migratory flows accentuate their growth. Meanwhile, emigration from the peripheral regions depletes the 'human capital', particularly their younger and more entrepreneurial people. These are what Myrdal calls the 'backwash effects' in regional economies.[9] Then the firms in the core regions, having best access to consumer markets and factors of production, develop economies of scale, and external economies arise as firms cluster in those localities. 'Spread effects' from this growth, may benefit firms in neighbouring regions who serve the core regions with foodstuffs or ancillary services. However, the 'backwash effects' normally dominate, increasing regional economic inequalities. The 'urban bias' in poorer nations tends to have a similarly circular and cumulative character.[10]

These illustrations of the processes of circular and cumulative causation present a rather depressing picture. The possibilities for more balanced economic and social progress recede. Greater inequalities—racial, international, and regional—seem inevitable as a result of the operation of normal socioeconomic processes. That is the bad news. However, once understood, circular and cumulative causation analysis opens up more positive possibilities. It enables us to envisage what is needed to generate better outcomes. This is the good news. With strong policy commitments (and a little bit of luck), vicious cycles can be turned into virtuous cycles. Affirmative action policies can help to reverse the disadvantages suffered by 'minority' groups subject to discrimination. More balanced regional development can be fostered by policies that locate growth centres in underdeveloped regions, giving them the opportunity to become 'counter-magnets' to the otherwise cumulatively dominant metropolitan centres. More effective industry policies can also be constructed, recognising the technical interdependencies of industries and developing institutions to foster the cooperation of firms within those industries.[11]

No general panacea is implied. Problems of social exclusion, stigmatisation, and racial discrimination are seldom easy to turn around, because of their socially embedded character. Regional and industrial inequalities are difficult to redress, and always entail opportunity costs if the policy measures divert public expenditures from elsewhere. The problems of international economic inequality are particularly hard to resolve, because of the need for international cooperation in the pursuit of solutions. Long-term commitments, emphasising a necessary role for the state as a manager of the process of reform, are required. This means more than the augmentation of the market economy with selective government intervention: it entails a holistic approach to economic and social policy.

BOX 25.1   ## JOSEPH SCHUMPETER (1883-1950)

Joseph Schumpeter is not usually considered an institutional economist, but his work has many of the characteristics of institutionalism. He was certainly a big thinker, seeking, as he did, to understand the trajectory of the economic system as a whole.

He grew up in an aristocratic household in Vienna before the First World War. At that time, Vienna was a thriving centre of learning in the social sciences, and Schumpeter became interested in both neoclassical and Marxist economics, although his own work did not fall clearly into either category. He fled Europe as fascism spread, and he then spent most of his professional career in the USA. While a professor at the Massachusetts Institute of Technology (where his penchant for wearing riding boots, even to faculty meetings, was notorious), he wrote the most comprehensive survey of the history of economic thought published to that date.

Schumpeter's best known political economic contribution is the book *Capitalism, Socialism and Democracy* (1943). In it, he poses the question 'Can capitalism survive?', and answers, 'No, I do not think it can'. He saw the most attractive feature of capitalism as the dynamism generated by entrepreneurship and innovation, which created a 'perennial gale of creative destruction'. This would be eroded, he anticipated, by the development of large corporations. A managerial class would emerge, more concerned with sheltering from the perennial gale of creative destruction than in fostering it. The dynamism of the system would be throttled. This, he predicted, would pave the way for change to socialism. It was a change that he saw as regrettable but inevitable. Politically, this was 'Marx upside down'.

Schumpeter viewed competition as crucial to the dynamism of capitalism, but it was competition among entrepreneurs seeking monopoly profits, not competition in perfectly competitive markets à la neoclassical theory. From this perspective, oligopoly is actually preferable to perfect competition because it enables firms to make sufficient profits to invest in research and development. The inherent danger, though, is that rationalising innovation eventually leads to managerial capitalism being prone to stagnation.

There has been a recent revival of interest in Schumpeter's economic analysis, sometimes labelled neo-Schumpeterian. The modern variant is less concerned with the broad political economic trajectory of capitalism than with pragmatic aspects of industry policy. It sets aside Schumpeter's personal conservatism in favour of a more interventionist approach to fostering innovation in industry. This focus on innovation as the key to economic dynamism underlies public policies of expenditure on education and training, and research and development. It is hoped that these will promote a 'high road' for economic development, providing interesting and secure careers. If so, it is a more attractive alternative than the 'low road', which emphasises cost reduction, particularly wage cutting, as the means of securing national competitive advantage.[12]

A new institutionalism?

A survey of the major institutional economists and their practical contributions would be incomplete without considering what, in recent years, has been described as 'new institutionalism'. Its leading practitioners include the American economists Richard North, Oliver Williamson, and Richard Langlois. New institutionalists are concerned with analysis of the relationship between individual and institutional behaviour.[13] Corporate hierarchies and non-market institutions are studied in relation to the rational choices of self-interested individuals within them. The underlying view is of society as a market in which individuals have continual opportunities to make mutually beneficial exchanges. Contracts may be made (explicitly or implicitly) between the parties in order to specify future rights and obligations. What bedevils the process is the pervasive problem of transactions costs. The costs of gathering information and specifying and enforcing contracts, for example, must be taken into account. The resulting institutional arrangements are, therefore, an outcome of more complex negotiations than normally assumed in mainstream economic theory.

This way of interpreting business behaviour, and social behaviour generally, is helpful in drawing attention to the effect of transactions costs on economic choices. However, putting the individual at the centre of attention gives a distinctly neoclassical orientation to this 'new' institutional economics. Much of transactions cost theory makes assumptions about individuals with given preferences. This tends to give primacy to the market, as in neoclassical theory. 'In the beginning there were markets,' says Williamson in one of his books.[14] From that beginning some individuals go on to create firms and hierarchies, which endure if they can keep transactions costs down. Williamson claims a close connection between this focus on transactions costs and John Commons's idea of a transaction, but there is a fundamental difference of emphasis. As institutional economist Geoff Hodgson puts it, 'For Williamson the unit of analysis is the given, abstract, atomistic and "opportunistic" individual, whereas Commons presupposes and stresses the organic and collective quality of institutions.'[15] What fades from view in the 'new' institutionalism are the characteristic concerns of 'old' institutionalism, such as how preferences, aspirations, and behaviour are moulded by circumstances and become embedded in the habits and customs of the people. Here, it seems, is a case where the new is *not* an advance on the old.

In a similar vein, it is pertinent to note the awkward relationship between 'new growth theories' and the old institutionalist principle of circular and cumulative causation. New growth theories study the path-dependent character of economic growth.[16] The central proposition is that what happens tomorrow depends crucially on what happened yesterday and on what exists today. That means that the economic growth that a region or nation can achieve is constrained by its past experience. To give an example: implementing a particular government economic policy (such as tighter monetary policy) tends to change the overall level of national economic activity, which in turn affects future growth prospects and limits future policy options. This path dependency has long been recognised by the proponents of circular and cumulative causation. However, the formal models of the new growth theorists purge the circular and cumulative causation theory of its qualitative insights into economic and social processes. As with the tension between the new institutional theories of the firm and the older institutionalist tradition, the key difference is one of methodology—whether to make the simplifying assumptions necessary for the construction of formal models or to emphasise the complex, qualitative changes associated with evolutionary processes.

Conclusion

Institutional economists have had diverse concerns. They form a motley crew, some would say. However, the contributions of institutionalism to political economy are important in at least three respects. They are a consistent source of critique within the economics profession, challenging the dominance of neoclassical theorising and the unrealism of its underlying assumptions. They contribute useful concepts, such as the principle of circular and cumulative causation, for understanding and shaping the evolution of economic society. They have also had a significant practical influence on policies to ameliorate the extremes of a capitalist market economy, particularly through the development of institutions to steer processes of socioeconomic development.

A common element in all those contributions is the concern of institutional economics with economic power: its sources, uses, and abuses. This theme is further developed in the next chapter, which looks in particular at one of the most interesting figures of the economics profession, the American political economist John Kenneth Galbraith.

KEY POINTS

- The longstanding tradition of institutional economics provides a more interdisciplinary approach than the dominant neoclassical economic theory.

- Processes of circular and cumulative causation accentuate socioeconomic inequalities unless they are actively countered by interventionist policies.

- 'New' institutionalism tends to have more in common with the methodology of neoclassical economic theory.

26 Economic Power

What are the principal sources of economic power?

How have power structures changed in modern capitalism?

Can the power of capital be matched by the power of a reforming state?

The analysis of economic power is central to political economy. Indeed, this is its most obvious point of departure from the neoclassical orthodoxy. Power in neoclassical economics is limited to the study of power in the marketplace. This is the power exercised by consumers over firms as they make their purchasing decisions, or the power of monopolists to raise their prices above the level that would prevail under mere competitive conditions. Looking at only these forms of power gives a myopic view, focusing on only part of a bigger picture. As Marx emphasised, there are more systemic dimensions of power, such as the power that capital as a class exercises over labour.

Institutional economists have emphasised other types of power, too: the power that business corporations may exercise over governments, for example, and the power that they can exercise over consumers through processes of commercial advertising. Collective organisations, such as workers in trade unions or environmentalists in active pressure groups such as Greenpeace, can exercise power to offset the power of corporate capital. The relative strength of these different kinds of power, and their sources and uses, warrants attention.

| BOX 26.1 | JOHN KENNETH GALBRAITH (1908-2006) |

Galbraith has been a towering figure in institutional economics, literally (being more than two metres tall) and figuratively. He made an enormous contribution to enhancing popular understanding of the modern economy. His numerous books on political economy have probably been more widely read than those of any other twentieth-century economist.

Galbraith was born in 1908 into a Canadian farming family of Scottish descent. He studied agriculture at the University of Toronto and subsequently completed his PhD in economics at the University of California, Berkeley. During the Second World War he was appointed Deputy Director for Price Administration for the US government, a post that gave him practical experience in the exercise of regulatory processes to control the inflationary pressures that invariably occur in wartime.

Galbraith became Professor of Economics at Harvard University, lectured at many other universities, and was elected President of the American Economics Association in 1972. He had a longstanding association with the Democratic Party, giving advice to presidents, including John F. Kennedy, who appointed him US Ambassador to India in the period 1961–63. He also wrote two novels and a book on Indian painting.

However, it is for his writing and public speaking on political economic issues that he is best known. Books such as *American Capitalism* (1952), *The Affluent Society* (1958), *The New Industrial State* (1967), *Economics and the Public Purpose* (1974), *Money* (1975), and *The Culture of Contentment* (1992) have been bestsellers. He also made a television series called *The Age of Uncertainty*, which critically and wittily assessed the relationship between economic history and the development of economic ideas. For over half a century his was an outstanding voice against conservative economists' 'conventional wisdom' (Galbraith's notable phrase for that which is conventional but not actually wise). Echoes of Thorstein Veblen's concerns are to be found in his writing: the shallowness and waste of consumer society, the shifts in power over key economic decisions, and the evolutionary character of the economy. Like Veblen, Galbraith also enjoyed ambiguous status in the economics profession: he has been widely praised for his elegant writing and engagement with the major practical concerns of the day, but also been derided for his dissident views and preference for verbal argument rather than formal economic modelling.

His son, James K. Galbraith, has followed in his footsteps as a prominent critic of mainstream economic theory and of what passes for orthodoxy today in the realm of economic policy.

This chapter puts particular focus on the contributions of the distinguished political economist J. K. Galbraith to the study of economic power. His numerous books have ranged over almost every conceivable aspect of political economy, but the study of power has been a central theme.

The anatomy of power

Galbraith wrote a book devoted to this topic, appropriately titled *The Anatomy of Power*.[1] It distinguishes three forms of power: condign, compensatory, and conditioned. *Condign* power is associated with coercion and punishment. It is the type of power exercised by a slave owner over his slaves. More mildly, it is evident in all social behaviour constrained by the fear of rebuke. The common element in condign power is that submission occurs as the result of threatened or actual adverse consequences. *Compensatory* power, by contrast, works by offering rewards. If the fear of rebuke is a mild form of condign power, the pursuit of praise is its equivalent in terms of compensatory power. More specifically in the modern economy, compensatory power usually takes the form of pecuniary reward. Submission to the economic purposes of others finds its compensation in a monetary payment. This is central to the functioning of capitalism. So, too, is the third type of power, *conditioned* power, which is exercised by influencing people's beliefs. As Galbraith puts it, 'Persuasion, education, or the social commitment to what seems natural, proper or right causes the individual to submit to the will of another or of others.'[2] Submission may not be—indeed, normally is not—conscious. The essence of conditioned power is willing, even enthusiastic, compliance. Social conformity is its hallmark.

So, what differentiates those who wield power from those who submit to it? Galbraith continues his analysis of power by identifying its three sources: personality, property, and organisation. Personality in this context is broadly interpreted as the *personal* qualities of leadership, ranging from physique to persuasiveness. Charisma is one commonly cited manifestation, albeit one that is notoriously difficult to define. Property is the more obviously *economic* source of power. This is the power that derives from wealth, including command over resources, and the capacity to hire and dismiss employees. However, according to Galbraith, it is *organisation* that is the most important source of power in modern societies. The power of corporate executives or of senior state bureaucrats derives from their organisational positions, not primarily from their personalities or personal property. Power attaches to their office, not their person. On their retirement, their power disappears overnight. Similarly, in the political arena, the power of a politician derives from having a senior position in government or having the capacity to influence colleagues in such positions. Again, on losing office, the personal power usually disappears; the retired politician may command an interested audience—and sometimes a handsome appearance fee—but he or she usually wields little or no power.

Rather more contentiously, Galbraith asserts a general correlation between the three types of power and the three sources of power. According to this reasoning, the exercise of condign power is most directly associated with personality or leadership; compensatory power has its strongest linkage with power structures deriving from property; while conditioned power is characteristic of organisational sources of power. These he calls 'primary but not exclusive associations', conceding that there are also 'numerous combinations of the sources of power and the related instruments'.[3] The taxonomy starts to look less tidy.

Galbraith's *Anatomy of Power* is a starting point for thinking about the avenues through which power is exercised, but deeper insights come from his other books, particularly those he identified as his principal political economic quartet: *American Capitalism*, *The Affluent Society*, *The New Industrial State*, and *Economics and the Public Purpose*. Figure 26.1 later in this chapter shows some of the major themes developed in these books, and provides a summary of his important contributions to the understanding of power in modern capitalism.

Technology, planning, the corporation

Technology is Galbraith's distinctive starting point in understanding the modern economy. He regards capitalism as being, in substantial measure, the offspring of technology.[4] He emphasises the incessant pressures for economic change due to 'the systematic application of scientific or other organised knowledge to practical tasks'.[5] These tasks involve the provision of services as well as the production of goods, particularly during the present era, when the spread of information technologies has been so rapid. Relentless technological change has always been a prominent feature of capitalist development. Building up vast productive capacity based on increasingly sophisticated production and transportation technologies is perhaps its greatest achievement. Indeed, what Marx called the 'forces of production' have been revolutionised.

Does this constitute a technological imperative? Galbraith's critics accuse him of technological determinism, of implying that technological change has a life of its own rather than being a product of capitalist interests.[6] Indeed, technology may have its own partially independent momentum, driven by the findings of scientists researching new materials, processes, and applications, for example. This independence is lessened, of course, as research becomes more dependent on corporate funding. Much of the research leading to innovation is now done by the companies themselves, particularly when associated with new product development. So, the form and direction of technological change is directly linked to capitalist interests. This has major implications for the organisation of the companies, their relationship with one another, and the broader society.

Galbraith's analysis emphasises that an economy based on increasingly sophisticated technology must necessarily be a planned economy. In a capitalist system, it is the big firms that are the planners. They need to make long-term, large-scale commitments of capital because the capital goods embodying the complex technologies are so expensive; the commitment of funds to research and development adds further to the cost. Therein lies a paradox: the capitalist system, whose supporting ideology emphasises free markets, has become characterised, in practice, by institutions engaged in economic planning. A world of rapidly changing technologies is always one of uncertainty. Committing capital to the purchase of equipment based on a particular technology is a risky business, for those capital goods can be quickly superseded by further innovations. It is for this reason that planning is inescapable. The competitive marketplace is too unstable, too focused on the short term, for a technologically sophisticated economic system requiring long-term, large-scale commitment of capital.

Does this comprise a 'new socialism'?[7] As the corporate sector of capitalism becomes a planned economy, does the system take on a characteristic more commonly associated with the socialist alternative? This possibility, sometimes labelled the convergence thesis, was a controversial interpretation of the long-term trajectories of capitalism and socialism in the twentieth century. In essence, the claim is that the rival systems, notwithstanding their competing ideologies, must necessarily come to look alike, because all economic activity is shaped by common technological and organisational imperatives. But the term 'new socialism' does not necessarily connote a complete convergence; it certainly does not mean that capitalism fades away. What Galbraith is talking about is a system run by corporations for corporations. The planning is for private interests rather than for broader social goals. It only takes on any sort of socialist character if the corporations are forced—by the countervailing power of governments or trade unions, for example—to assume wider social responsibilities. In Galbraith's analysis, 'new socialism' would imply a more substantial role for the state in managing and steering the economy, notwithstanding the rhetoric equating capitalism with free markets.

Overall, the picture presented by Galbraith is one in which several hundred giant corporations, able to control technology and plan for their own corporate interests rather than simply responding to market forces, dominate the economy. This corporate sector of the modern economy controls key parts of contemporary industry. Its enormous economic power reshapes economic relationships—within the corporations, between firms, and with consumers, workers, and governments.

Power within corporations

Those who control the information necessary for the day-to-day running of the corporate economy are, according to Galbraith, the focal point for the exercise of corporate power. These people he labels collectively as the 'technostructure', comprising 'all who bring specialised knowledge, talent or experience to group decision-making'.[8] Technicians, scientists, engineers, financial controllers, market researchers, and human resource managers are among the technostructure's members. University qualifications are the norm—which may be reassuring to some readers of this book, knowing that they are on the road to joining the most powerful group in modern capitalism.

It is important to distinguish the technostructure from the owners of the big corporations. The crucial feature of the former is not ownership, nor even an elevated position in the organisational hierarchy: it is control of information. The technostructure has the detailed knowledge about running the business, whereas the owners have only a pecuniary interest in the outcomes. This aspect of Galbraith's analysis builds on the earlier work of institutional economists Berle and Means (discussed in the preceding chapter), which explored the significance of the separation of ownership from control in the modern corporation. Galbraith goes one step further, however, distinguishing between the formal power of the capitalist owners and the practical power of the technostructure, which derives from its control over the sources and uses of information. The latter has more day-to-day opportunity to shape how capitalist businesses operate in practice.

Galbraith justifies his emphasis on the power of the technostructure with a character-istically neat argument. Under feudalism, he notes, land was the key factor of production, so the owners of land were the dominant class. With the development of industrial capitalism, capital became the key factor of production, and power switched to its owners and controllers. With the advent of the information age, he says, those who generate and control information become the key group. Here is a strong contrast, both with the neoclassical assumption of the firm as a single decision-maker and with the Marxian view of the continuing dominance of the capitalist class. Galbraith emphasises the latter contrast as follows:

> Once, all economic and social thought turned on a bilateral economic and social structure. There were capital and labour, the capitalist and the worker. There were also, to be sure, farmers. And intellectuals and others. But capital and labour, capital versus labour, that was the basic dialectic. Marx had an authority here that would have surprised even him. This is no longer the case in the advanced industrial countries. The great political dichotomy—the capitalist and the working masses—have retreated into the shadows. It survives not as a reality but as mental commitment. In place of the capitalist there is now the modern great corporate bureaucracy. Not capitalists but managers.[9]

Whether or not the managers serve the capitalists is, of course, the crucial question. In general, one may expect them to do so.[10] However, according to Galbraith, there is some evidence of a different, self-serving tendency. Managers, he notes, are commonly concerned with corporate growth, even at the expense of profit maximisation, since therein lies the strongest basis for their own employment security, income, and prestige. This reinforces the growth orientation of the modern capitalist system as a whole, what Galbraith had earlier called 'the paramount position of production'.[11] Evidence of yet more directly self-serving tendencies today are the increasingly generous managerial remuneration packages and the perquisites of office. But these prodigious incomes are mainly enjoyed by chief executive officers (CEOs) and other top managers; the members of the technostructure generally receive rather more modest rewards, notwithstanding their key role in actually running the corporations.

Power relations between corporations

The scope for the discretionary exercise of managerial power depends crucially on the relationships between the corporations themselves. These relationships are both cooperative and competitive. Large firms in the corporate sector must continually make strategic decisions about the use of power. Theirs is a world that neoclassical economists describe as oligopolistic (see Chapter 21), using this term to describe the structural relationship between firms in a particular industry. Actually, in modern capitalism, large corporations often straddle different industries, making a range of products that defy categorisation into a single industry sector. This is the essence of the corporate economy: what Galbraith calls the planning system.[12] This system comprises large corporations that are individually powerful in shaping their own market shares, corporate culture, and organisational practices, and that are collectively powerful in reshaping the world in their own image and interests.

Alongside this planning system is a market system comprising smaller businesses, where more traditionally competitive practices operate. Galbraith concedes that the sort of market principles discussed by neoclassical theorists under the rubric of imperfect competition may have some role to play here, thereby reinterpreting the neoclassical theory of oligopoly as relevant to the realm of relatively small, rather than big, business. But the situation is complicated by the dependence of these firms in the market system on the giants in the planning system. The former usually supply the latter with intermediate products, services, and subcontracted elements in the production process. This dependent, or subordinate, character of the market system is its most general characteristic. The dualism of the planning and market systems involves a dramatic asymmetry in the distribution of economic power.

Corporations and consumers

What about the consumers? Their purchases are essential for the corporations to achieve their goals and for the relentlessly growth-orientated capitalist system to continue functioning. According to the neoclassical theory of consumer sovereignty, it is the consumers' preferences that call forth the products: the pattern of consumption thereby determines the pattern of production. Galbraith posits that the reverse situation is more typical. This is what he calls 'the revised sequence', perhaps the most controversial of Galbraith's claims about the use of corporate power in modern capitalism.[13] According to his reasoning, it is imperative that large firms seek, as far as possible, to control the demand for their products. Integral to long-term corporate strategy, this is made necessary by the major commitments of capital necessary for the large-scale production of their goods. Hence the channelling of prodigious resources into commercial advertising and other sales promotion activities designed to create product acceptance and ensure brand loyalty. The preferred pattern of production shapes the pattern of consumption. Producer sovereignty replaces consumer sovereignty.

Stated so baldly, the argument is not compelling. It is not as if firms can simply mould and exploit gullible consumers—at least not all the time. Galbraith himself acknowledges important exceptions to producer sovereignty and the importance of the context within which product choices are made.[14] New products, even extensively advertised ones, sometimes fail. And brand loyalty can wane when rival firms are simultaneously pursuing extensive sales promotion activities for their own products. Market research also provides something of a feedback loop, ensuring that the want-creation process has some basis in consumers' potential preferences, founded on aspirations or psychological fears that can be exploited for commercial advantage. Most significantly, it all takes place in a broad social context that glamorises consumption. A widespread acceptance of the consumerist ethos—'I consume, therefore I am'—is the necessary condition for the effectiveness of producer sovereignty.

The inclusion of these contextual considerations gives Galbraith's argument much greater force and generality. It also raises some profound questions about the purposes of economic activity in an affluent society. Is there a reliable connection between consumption and happiness? Does the production of ever more goods and services contribute to a good society?

Galbraith's analysis has an explicitly normative dimension. It is not simply a matter of countering the neoclassical theory of the consumer with a more realistic view of the power relationships involved in consumption processes in practice. It is also a matter of drawing attention to the roots of pervasive social problems. Perhaps most fundamental is the tendency towards ever higher levels of goods and services being consumed. Consumption has its purposes, but they are increasingly social in character, once basic needs for food, clothing, and shelter have been met. Even these basic goods come to be consumed increasingly as means of social display. On the subject of clothing, for example, Galbraith says 'to a marked extent, attire remains to this day ... a prime badge of social position and distinction'.[15] An echo of Thorstein Veblen is clearly audible there. If we can distinguish between needs and wants—Galbraith differs from the neoclassicals in arguing that we should do so—and if the wants are becoming increasingly frivolous, then there is no necessary connection between increased consumption and social well-being.

The tendency towards the dichotomy of 'private wealth and public squalor' makes the situation yet worse.[16] According to Galbraith, private sector consumption tends to expand at the expense of the quality of the public sector. So, we have fabulously expensive private cars, but inadequately maintained public roads on which to drive them. Our poorly funded public education and public health systems struggle to maintain quality alongside vastly more affluent private schools and elaborate private medical services. These are striking examples of social imbalance in modern capitalism.

Corporations and the state

Can we look to the state to rectify problems of social imbalance and, generally, to manage capitalism in the public interest? Indeed, we must, says Galbraith. However, we also need to recognise the major tensions arising from the power relationships between corporations and the state. The focus on the balance of power between the corporations and the state is the crux of Galbraith's political analysis and, as we shall see in Chapter 38, is crucial in the construction of modern political economy.

In his early writing, Galbraith was relatively optimistic that the growing power of corporations would be checked by other sources of countervailing power, particularly the power of government and unions.[17] His later work emphasised the problems of growing power imbalance as the corporate sector has become ever more dominant. But this imbalance can be corrected by strengthening the capacity of the state: hence, the need for a theory, and program, of economic reform to curtail corporate power and pursue 'the public purpose'.[18]

At one level, this reformist position echoes the liberal interventionism of some orthodox economists, giving primacy to the market but acknowledging a supplementary role for the state. The 'market failure' perspective is evident in Galbraith's proposition that: 'There are some things the market system does not do well or sometimes even badly. These must be the responsibility of the state.'[19] However, for Galbraith, the range of such intervention is atypically broad. Ensuring that all citizens have access to a basic source of income, to a decent educational system that may facilitate upward social mobility, to low-cost housing, and to good health services, and ensuring that there is funding for the sciences and the arts, that peace is maintained, and that recession is avoided—these are the characteristic policies that he regards as necessary if we are to live in a good society. 'This requires positive government intervention', says Galbraith, adding, with his characteristic humour, that 'prediction and prayer, the instruments of policy in past years, will not serve'.[20]

Support for systematically reformist policy measures, he had earlier argued, might be expected to be forthcoming from the educational and scientific estate, comprising the better educated and more economically advantaged social strata.[21] Galbraith's writing over many decades became more pessimistic about this potential source of support for economic and social reform. His observations suggest that the political will to effect the reforms has slipped away (at least in the USA, which is his principal focus), particularly among the members of the middle class who might be expected to have the most enlightened reformist views.

FIGURE 26.1 ELEMENTS IN GALBRAITH'S ANALYSIS OF ECONOMIC POWER: A SUMMARY

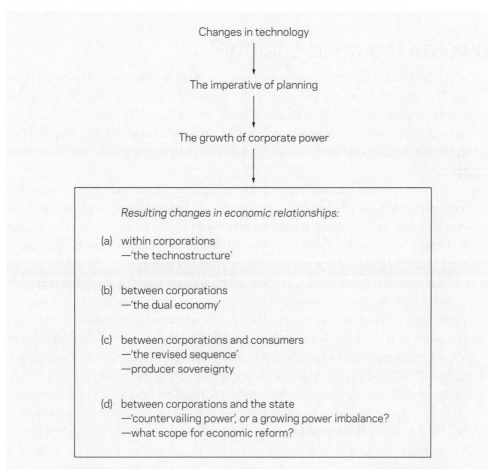

Changes in technology

↓

The imperative of planning

↓

The growth of corporate power

↓

Resulting changes in economic relationships:

(a) within corporations
—'the technostructure'

(b) between corporations
—'the dual economy'

(c) between corporations and consumers
—'the revised sequence'
—producer sovereignty

(d) between corporations and the state
—'countervailing power', or a growing power imbalance?
—what scope for economic reform?

Galbraith wryly refers to 'the culture of contentment' in the USA.[22] An electoral majority, enjoying the fruits of a consumer society, has become defensive, conservative, and fearful of change. Its members no longer look to government as an instrument for social betterment. Instead, their concerns have turned inwards, away from political processes and the collective provision for social needs, to market processes and individual provision. They aspire to, and often inhabit, a demi-world of private schooling, private health insurance plans, and private houses in private security-patrolled gated communities, insulated from the social underclass. They are extremely reluctant to pay the taxes that would be necessary to fund higher levels of government expenditure on the provision of public goods. The 'Tea Party' movement in the USA, which developed in 2009–10 in the aftermath of the global financial crisis is an extreme case, financed by big wealth but also drawing in some lower-income people enthused by anti-government rhetoric. Galbraith did not live long enough to see this far-right populist campaign to 'get government out of the economy'. Had he done so he would surely have said 'I told you so', ruing its attempt to remove the economic system from control by the political process and thereby frustrate the possibility of achieving the 'good society' to which he aspired.

Towards the good society?

Galbraith's political economy exhibits the pessimism of the intellect and the optimism of the will. The latter aspect usually prevails. The last section of *Economics and the Public Purpose* explores the possibilities of significant political economic reform—notwithstanding the powerful reasoning in the preceding chapters about the concentration of economic power that stands in its way. *The Good Society* presents a significant reformist agenda for capitalism in the years ahead.

First and foremost, Galbraith argues, public policy must address the fate of the underclass: the social stratum comprising people excluded from the 'culture of contentment'. Some are unemployed or have only marginal attachment to the workforce, effectively forming a modern industrial reserve army. Some do heavy repetitive industrial work; others are engaged in doing the jobs that make life pleasant for the corporate bureaucrats, the diverse smaller entrepreneurs, the lawyers, doctors, teachers, and other professionals—'the cultural elite, as it has been called, and the large pensioned and rentier community'.[23] Members of the underclass harvest their fruit and vegetables, clean their streets, and collect their garbage. A very broad interpretation of underclass is evident here, straddling traditional views of the working class, economically marginalised segments of society, and minorities subject to discrimination. It serves Galbraith's purpose in drawing attention to the continuing need for public policy to be concerned with economic inequality. Ultimately, it is a concern for social order, a concern that 'those who have no other outlet for political expression may well take to the streets in protest or ... escape civilised reality into drugs and crime'.[24]

Generally, the case for public policy to assist the underclass reflects an egalitarian political sentiment, as much as can be tolerated in modern American society: hence, the case for policies to expand employment opportunities, to improve opportunities for upward social mobility, and, as a last resort, for the state to provide basic income. As Galbraith says, 'There can be no claim to civilised existence when such a safety net is not available.'[25] It is symptomatic of the welfare state being in retreat that such a case even needs to be restated.

The rationale for direct government provision of public goods also has an egalitarian dimension to the extent 'that many of these services—public works, parks, and recreational facilities, police, libraries, and many others—are more important for, more needed by, the poor than the affluent'.[26] On the other hand, the case for extending public provision in the arts and the sciences, including medical research, reflects their general neglect in a market economy with a short-term orientation. Galbraith notes that: 'Some of our most important American achievements of recent generations—the great improvements in agricultural productivity, modern air transport, advanced electronics—have depended heavily on public investment.'[27]

Public investment is also necessary because, according to Galbraith, 'the tendency of the market system to periods of despondency and depression' is a basic feature of the economy.[28] The echoes of Marx in this view of capitalism are muted by the Keynesian commitment to, and confidence in, the possibilities of remedial policies being implemented by governments. Indeed, this is the characteristic political stance throughout the Galbraithian analysis: the continued reassertion of the need for our political institutions to effect the necessary remedies for pervasive socioeconomic problems. It is an exemplary social democratic stance.

Galbraith's writing is not blind to the obstacles to reform. His calls for the emancipation of the state, freeing government from domination by corporate interests, and for the emancipation of belief—challenging the dominance of orthodox economic beliefs in particular—illustrate the immensity of the task.[29] And therein lies a tension between Galbraith's analysis and his prescriptions. The penetrating analysis of the power structures shows the obstacles to the reforms that are advocated. It is a tension that cannot be resolved purely in the realm of political economic analysis. As Galbraith repeatedly emphasised, it is the 'march of circumstances', not the theories or wishful thinking of economists, that is ultimately decisive.[30]

Conclusion

Galbraith's political economy provides useful insights into the analysis of modern economic institutions and their power. It also draws attention to the forces driving political economic change and the possibilities for steering change by the exercise of political power. It regards orthodox economics as being fundamentally misleading, because it emphasises equilibrium conditions, implicitly treating the economy as a stable, immutable structure. Galbraith's alternative is evolutionary economics *par excellence*. The capitalist economy is understood in terms of changes driven by technology—moulded by powerful institutions—and reshaping economic structures, social behaviour, and political possibilities.

Galbraith's analysis of this world of powerful economic institutions is wide-ranging. It lacks the precision—certainly, it lacks the formal model construction—of neoclassical theory (and, to some extent, of Marxist economics, too). It is on these grounds that Galbraith's work has often been criticised by more conservative economists, and even some on the political Left. This reflects a general tension in political economic analysis between elegance and relevance. In Galbraith's work, elegance comes through the careful crafting of arguments and through his mastery of the English language, not through the use of formal theory, diagrams, and mathematics. Indeed, the study of economic power—its sources, uses, and abuses—is not conductive to facile formalisation. Galbraith's analysis is directly relevant to contemporary economic, social, and public trends. It poses a particularly fundamental challenge for people of a social democratic inclination looking to the state as an instrument for economic reform and social progress.

KEY POINTS

- According to J. K. Galbraith, economic power has three forms: condign, compensatory, and conditioned.
- Galbraith's analysis of how economic power is exercised considers the sources of power within corporations, and relations between corporations, their customers, and the state.
- This analysis indicates a growing imbalance of economic power, posing a major challenge for proponents of the political economic reforms necessary for a good society.

27 Economic and Social Reform

Can the state reform the economy?

What tensions are associated with the welfare state?

Can the state subordinate economic interests to political priorities?

Is progressive economic reform possible? Can the power of the state be harnessed for the purpose of making the economy more responsive to the needs of the people than to corporate power? This is an intriguing possibility that many social scientists have explored. Institutional economists are particularly significant contributors to this topic because they pay particular attention to the role of the state in the economy. Their concerns are both analytical and political: to understand how the state has shaped the patterns of economic development in different countries and to explore what more can be done.

This emphasis on the state as manager of the process of reform contrasts with the more restrictive neoclassical economic view of limited government 'intervention' in an otherwise self-regulating market economy. The institutional economists do not speak with a single voice on the issue; indeed, their political perspectives are many and varied. The common element is the recognition that the state is at least as important as markets in shaping our economic experiences and opportunities, and that therein lies the possibility of further political control over economic outcomes.

The state: democratic, capitalist, and bureaucratic

To analyse the possibilities for economic reform requires, first and foremost, a definition of the character and scope of the state. Most simply, we can depict it as a set of interrelated institutions concerned with public policy and public administration. At its core is the government. Indeed, the government is so obviously central to the state that one may be forgiven for using the two terms interchangeably. Therein, too, lies the source of some confusion, because the state also includes other institutions. Alongside governments—and acting as a partial check to their activities in formally democratic states—are parliamentary assemblies. Political parties not in government oppose, and may use whatever channels are formally open to them to impede, particular government policies. Where there are bicameral parliamentary arrangements, for example, an opposition that has a majority in the upper house may constitute a major constraint on a government's power. So, too, may tensions with subnational governments, where federal arrangements exist within a nation's polity, as in Australia, Canada, Germany, and the USA, for example. Other checks and balances arise from the relationship between government and other institutions within the state apparatus, such as the public service, the central bank, the judiciary, and the armed forces.

Generalising about the state as if it were a unified entity is fraught with difficulty. Yet, the other extreme, of restricting analysis of the state to the individual institutions within it, is problematic for different reasons. Rich descriptive detail is generated—the stuff of political science—but there is a loss of perspective on broader political economic aspects. This is indicative of a universal tension in social enquiry, of course, between the focus on the specific and the general. An intermediate construction recognises the need to keep the focus on the whole, but to emphasise tensions between the parts. In the case of the state, this involves looking at its democratic, capitalistic, and bureaucratic aspects.[1] We can thereby develop insights into the character, complexity, and contradictions of the state.

Is the state *democratic*? Yes, insofar as it is accountable to the public at large and subject to control through electoral processes. In the advanced industrial nations with long democratic traditions, we tend to take that for granted, while grumbling about imperfections of the democratic arrangements in practice. Therein lies the root of the belief in the state as an instrument of economic reform, and of social progress more generally. The expectation is that the state, subjected to the influence of democratic processes, will implement policies that serve the national interest—beyond any individual or class interests.

However, not all parts of the state are democratic, even in principle. Public servants, judges, and military personnel are typically recruited, promoted, and dismissed according to institutional procedures in which the public has no direct voice.[2] Direct elections are focused primarily on the periodic contest for seats in parliamentary and local government assemblies. Under the Westminster system, government is then formed by the party that has won the majority of seats, or whatever workable coalition of minorities can achieve an effective majority. To the extent that the elected government then has power over other elements within the state—through the appointment of senior public servants and policy advisers, for example—it may be said that the democratic impulse radiates outwards to other parts of the state (although, in practice, the processes are often soured by the influence of political patronage).

Not all countries have even this imperfect democratic element at the core of their states. Dictatorships have been common, particularly in many of the former colonial nations of Africa, some parts of Asia, and South and Central America. In those cases, it is the political inclinations of the senior military personnel and control over the armed forces that are decisive. Such interludes of democratic government as may occur depend heavily for their stability on the elected political leaders commanding the loyalty of the military. In countries that pride themselves on democratic traditions and have had no recourse to recent military intervention, there is often evidence of economic forces producing rather different forms of political closure. In the USA, for example, it is inconceivable that any presidential contender who did not have, or could not raise, millions of dollars to finance his or her electoral campaign would be successful. Generally, economic inequality can effectively subvert the egalitarian principles formally underpinning democracy. As Galbraith reminds us, 'Forthright purchase of votes was commonplace in various parts of the USA until comparatively recent times.'[3] Rather more circumspectly, American economist Arthur Okun notes: 'Money is used by some big winners of market rewards in an effort to acquire extra helpings of those rights that are supposed to be equally distributed.'[4]

The influence of these economic factors brings us to a second theme: the extent to which the state is a *capitalist* state. The relationship of capitalism to the state is a concern that may be seen as a specific example of the base–superstructure relationship discussed in Chapter 13. The focus is on how the functioning of political institutions is constrained and shaped by the structure of the economic system, and the interests of capital in particular. Phrases in the political economic literature such as 'the capitalist state' and 'the state in capitalist society' directly draw attention this connection.[5] It is not simply a matter of economic wealth buying political influence. What is at issue here is a more systemic relationship. At root, it is structural. If the state is concerned with managing or steering the economy, it must have due regard to the dominant interests whose cooperation is essential for the achievement of successful outcomes. To put the point negatively, if an economic crisis occurs because the state fails to ensure the conditions for capital accumulation, this is likely to precipitate political crisis and change of government. Not surprisingly, it is a scenario that state leaders would normally wish to avoid. In these circumstances, working in tandem with the interests of capital has a political logic.

The third aspect of the state is its *bureaucratic* character. This shifts our gaze to the structures within the state and how they shape its functioning. Instead of looking at how the state responds to external pressures—whether from the citizenry via democratic processes or from capitalist economic interests—the internal bureaucracy itself now comes under scrutiny. The term 'bureaucracy' is not used here in a derogatory sense. Indeed, as the sociologist Max Weber emphasised, bureaucratic procedures are generally necessary in large organisations to ensure that there is consistency in the processes of public administration. However, once a large state apparatus is created, its members tend to develop their own interests, which may be different from, even contrary to, those of their 'political masters' in government. An old BBC television series *Yes, Minister* wittily illustrated this theme. Anyone with experience of working in large institutions, whether in the public or private sectors, will have firsthand experience of familiar bureaucratic tendencies. Its normal manifestations are seeking continuity in public administration and security for public administrators. Policy paralysis is a predictable outcome when these concerns are at odds with the reforms sought by governments. In the extreme case when corporate corruption of state officials occurs, the bureaucratic character of the state tends to closely align to its capitalist character.

A schematic representation of these three influences on the state, together with quotations emphasising each aspect, appears in Figure 27.1 (overleaf). The resulting tensions ensure that the state, in practice, is always contested terrain. This is nowhere more evident than in looking at the development of, and attacks on, the welfare state.

FIGURE 27.1 UNDERSTANDING THE STATE: LINKING DEMOCRACY, CAPITALISM, AND BUREAUCRACY

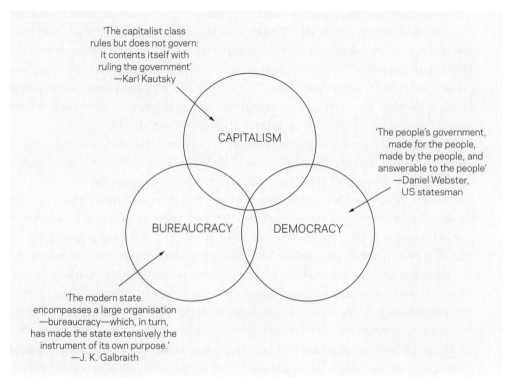

'The capitalist class rules but does not govern: it contents itself with ruling the government'
—Karl Kautsky

CAPITALISM

'The people's government, made for the people, made by the people, and answerable to the people'
—Daniel Webster, US statesman

BUREAUCRACY   DEMOCRACY

'The modern state encompasses a large organisation —bureaucracy—which, in turn, has made the state extensively the instrument of its own purpose.'
—J. K. Galbraith

The welfare state

One reason why analysis of the state features more prominently in institutional economics than in the other traditions of economics already considered in this book is the generally reformist inclination of institutional economists. They are usually looking for ways in which institutions can be developed and adapted to resolve socioeconomic problems and to manage the evolution of economic society. Probably the most important expression of this reformist inclination, linking the concerns of institutional economics with the practical politics of social democracy, is the development of the welfare state. This was one of the great practical political economic achievements of the twentieth century, tempering the capitalist economy with institutions to enhance economic security and reduce economic inequality. Since, as the target of neoliberal austerity measures, it is a development in danger of being rolled back in many countries in the twenty-first century, it is important to consider this legacy of economic and social reform.

It is usual to think of the welfare state as having experienced its most spectacular development in the years after the Second World War. Yet its foundations were laid earlier, during the late nineteenth century in Germany and the UK. Many intellectuals, as well as practical politicians, contributed to its development, supporting social reform based on legislative change and the extension of government's role to foster social institutions with humanistic goals.

One such important intellectual was John Hobson (1858–1940), a British economist who wrote prolifically on economic and social issues in the early twentieth century. He has been described as 'the Godfather of the newly formed British Labour Party'.[6] His wide-ranging concerns included the analysis of the causes of economic depression, imperialism, monopolies, and economic inequality. Denied a university post because of his unorthodox views, he may be seen in retrospect as a visionary of the welfare state. As the American institutional economist Daniel Fusfeld puts it: 'Hobson believed that government action could end poverty, unemployment, and insecurity, and could establish a society in which human happiness prevailed. Utopian, yes—but this was the vision that lay behind English social legislation. Hobson did not originate it, but he was one of its best spokesmen.'[7] Here was a foundation on which practical reformers such as Britain's Lord Beveridge would later build, establishing the welfare state in practice by extending the provision of social security, pensions, unemployment insurance, public education, and public health facilities.

The welfare state has found its most fully developed form in the Scandinavian nations: Denmark, Norway, Sweden, and Finland. Swedish political economist Gunnar Myrdal was a significant contributor to this process (see Box 27.1). The Scandinavian experience suggests that having social democratic parties in government is crucial for the full realisation of welfare state ambitions. However, even some conservative political parties have, in the past, accepted its logic. Both in the UK and Australia, for example, conservative governments during the 1950s and 1960s consolidated and, in some respects, extended welfare state provisions. Political economists were wont to infer that the welfare state served capitalist interests in the long term, by ensuring a healthy workforce with the requisite skills, ensuring the high levels of consumer spending on which the economy depends, and contributing to the legitimation process that prevents fundamental challenge to the prevailing socioeconomic system.[8]

BOX 27.1

GUNNAR MYRDAL (1898-1987)

Swedish political economist Gunnar Myrdal is the most distinguished non-American in the institutional economics tradition. As well as being an academic economist, he was a member of the Social Democratic Party in the Swedish parliament, serving for a couple of years as Minister for Trade and Commerce and contributing significantly to developing the institutions that made Sweden one of the most economically secure and egalitarian nations of the world.

His numerous books include *An American Dilemma* (1944), which examines the problem of racial discrimination; *Economic Theory and Underdeveloped Regions* (1957), which analyses how processes of circular and cumulative causation accentuate regional economic inequality; *The Political Element in the Development of Economic Thought* (1954), which shows that economic analysis has never been value free; and *Asian Drama* (1968), a three-volume work on the problems of economic underdevelopment.

Gunnar Myrdal was awarded the Nobel Prize in Economic Sciences in 1974, although he reportedly said afterwards that he regretted accepting it because his whole professional career had been spent arguing that economics cannot be a science. In *The Political Element in the Development of Economic Thought*, he wrote: 'Every economist is painfully aware that there exists widespread doubt about the supposed "scientific" character of economics. The distrust is, indeed, well founded.'[9] He further argued that there were three main focal points for the 'political speculation which has permeated economics from the very beginning': the idea of value, the idea of freedom, and the idea of social economy or collective housekeeping. The last of these is particularly interesting, touching as it does on different views about the link between the household and the national economy, and the role of the state in national economic management.

The Swedish economy is a striking example of the concept of social economy being given its broadest interpretation in practice. In effect, it constitutes a major experiment in seeking to blend capitalism and socialism. Instead of social liberalism, wherein problems such as poverty and unemployment are seen as frictions in an otherwise harmonious system, the Social Democrats in Sweden, in conjunction with the Labor Organisation, developed policies to challenge capitalist principles on a more programmatic basis. These policies have included reduced wage differentials, a high progressive income tax, the pursuit of full employment through a permanent labour-market policy, industrial democracy, and the use of superannuation funds to finance nationally targeted investment priorities. Sweden's welfare state, although recently under challenge, has been the envy of the world.[10] Even the self-proclaimed right-wing 'Republican Party reptile', P. J. O'Rourke, conceded that it constitutes 'good socialism'.[11]

So, was the welfare state won or given? Its uneven realisation was the product of social and political struggle in various countries. However, its development was also increasingly accepted by capitalist interests, who could see the economic benefits it generated. The Achilles heel, it seems, has been the issue of how to finance it. There is no problem in principle. Taxes can generate the revenue needed to finance welfare state expenditures: it is just a matter of allocating some of our national income, via taxes, to finance our collective social needs. In practice, though, this process is beset with tensions. In the early 1970s, the economist James O'Connor, drawing on Marxist reasoning, argued that a fiscal crisis of the state would frustrate further development of the welfare state.[12] The reluctance of upper-income groups and businesses to contribute the tax revenues necessary to finance a comprehensive welfare state has since been the major source of tension in practice.

The ascendancy of neoliberal ideologies has undermined the perceived legitimacy of this substantial role for the state. Indeed, some see this as the primary political target of neoliberalism. Governments influenced by neoliberal ideology have sought to cut back welfare state provisions, typically replacing citizens' universal entitlements to benefits with more selective targeting of government expenditures (and a corresponding tightening of eligibility criteria). Because such a policy shift has an adverse impact on particular social groups, it is almost invariably controversial. So attempted welfare state cuts continue to be a focal point for contemporary political economic debate and struggle. This is a powerful reminder that the evolution of economic institutions is seldom free from contradictions.

Politics in command?

Some modern institutional economists, as well as other political scientists with a social democratic inclination, continue to argue that the dominant historical tendency is towards greater governmental influence on the economy, notwithstanding the assaults on the welfare state mounted by neoliberals. 'Putting politics in command of the economy' is the theme. In other words, progress comes through making more and more issues of resource allocation and wealth distribution subject to collective societal processes rather than leaving them to the marketplace. Individual choice and market processes have their appeal, particularly from an economic liberal perspective, but they need to be constrained, if not altogether replaced, by government policies reflecting societal concerns. Such policies range from occupational health and safety, health care more generally, public educational standards, security and pensions, to regulation of monopolies, provision of infrastructure, determination of minimum wages and employment conditions, protection of consumers' interests, and environmental conservation.

Australian political economist Geoff Dow, for example, contends that addressing these concerns is part of the historic mission of the state—past, present, and future—in the pursuit of social progress. He argues that diverse currents of political economic and social, even religious, thought have fostered such an expectation.[13] The Papal encyclical *Rerum Novarum* (1891) is one example, in which Pope Leo XIII denounced the effects of labour markets, enthused about experiments in industrial democracy, and emphasised the need for social rather than economic imperatives to be dominant.[14] At around the same time, the emerging tradition of economic sociology, springing from the work of French sociologist and philosopher Emile Durkheim, stressed that economies are necessarily embedded in social conditions. The later work of Max Weber posited the need for deliberative processes to be exercised by the modern state to impose a political rather than market logic on economic outcomes. Karl Polanyi, another interesting social scientist, emphasised that the market economy could not sensibly be regarded as a natural state of affairs, since it had been nurtured by social institutions and therefore there should be no political presumption towards laissez-faire rather than towards institutions protecting the interests of the people.[15]

All these currents of thought, flowing into the critique of economic liberalism, put emphasis on the need for institutional arrangements designed to produce social and economic progress. Merely relying on 'the market' won't suffice. The German historical school of the nineteenth century had also laid foundations for this statist orientation within the institutional economic tradition. Friedrich List, author of *The National System* of *Political Economy*, published in 1841, is notable for his emphasis on the importance of national strength for economic survival.[16] The liberal case for freedom of trade might suit British interests, he argued, but would likely result in greater British domination over less economically developed nations. German national interest required a different, state-centred, approach. German intellectual culture was also of less liberal inclination than its British counterpart, in that it emphasised a more corporative sense of community. The German historical school of economic enquiry reflected this orientation, stressing the social and historical context of economic activity, rather than the abstract theorising, which became the hallmark of the British approach to economic analysis. As noted in Chapter 24, this historical school was to have a major influence on the development of institutional economics.

Modern institutional economists also commonly note that, in recent international experience, some of the best economic performance—according to quite conventional GDP measures—has been in nations where the state has played a major role in steering economic development. Japan's spectacular economic progress after that nation's devastation at the end of the Second World War, for example, was attributable in no small measure to the steering role of state institutions such as the Ministry of International Trade and Industry (MITI). Similarly, the role of the 'developmental state' in nations such as Singapore, Taiwan, Malaysia, South Korea, and Thailand has been crucial to these nations' industrialisation and economic advance.[17] In more recent years, the People's Republic of China, with its peculiar blend of an authoritarian state and economic liberalisation, has emerged as an economic superpower. As Dow concludes, 'Actual economic development, in rich and poor countries alike, does not follow the script imagined in abstract economic inquiry.'[18] Nor should it, economic reformers contend, if economic interests are to be tempered by broader social concerns.

So what policies for economic and social reform are now appropriate for the advanced capitalist nations of Australasia, North America, and Europe? Table 27.1 shows what could form a viable social democratic alternative to the neoliberal policies of the last three decades. Corresponding with each of five social goals (prosperity, equity, security, participation, and civility) are focal points for policy (investment, income distribution, the labour market, economic democracy, and social capital) and institutions for the administration of those policies. To achieve greater prosperity, the volatile patterns of investment that characterise the capitalist economy could be stabilised and coordinated through tripartite bodies, including government, industry, and union representatives responsible for industry policy. A national investment scheme could expand the role of public investment by steering an agreed portion of workers' savings now held in superannuation funds into targeted national priorities. Corresponding focal points for policy and institutional development are indicated for the other four social goals in Table 27.1. This does not provide a fully comprehensive reformist agenda: it does not include policies relating to urban planning, regional development, childcare, and pension arrangements, for example. However, it is indicative of how social democratic goals could be pursued through systematic economic and social reform. Whether there is state capacity for this sort of radical reformism is an issue to which we return in Chapter 38.

TABLE 27.1 DIRECTIONS FOR ECONOMIC AND SOCIAL REFORM

Goal	Focus of policy intervention	Type of policy institution
Prosperity	Investment	▪ Tripartite bodies (government, business, unions) for developing industry policies ▪ National investment scheme, drawing on superannuation funds
Equity	Income distribution	▪ Compulsory arbitration of wages (through a court system) ▪ Taxation authority to implement progressive tax reform
Security	The labour market	▪ Managed labour market (including training/retraining) ▪ Government as employer of last resort
Participation	Economic democracy	▪ Industrial democracy (for example, worker representatives on company boards) ▪ Cooperatives

Source: adapted from G. Dow, 'Neoliberal Corporate Governance of the Australian Economy', in S. Bell (ed.), Economic Governance and Institutional Dynamics, *Oxford University Press, Melbourne, 2002.*

Conclusion

Institutional economists emphasise the evolution of economic society. In that respect the state is evidently significant, if not paramount. Historically, it has been a key driver and manager of capitalist development. Its taxation and expenditure has shaped the balance between private and public sectors in the economy and the changing distribution of income. The development of the welfare state in the twentieth century was a particularly important transformation. International variation in the form of government economic activity today gives capitalism a qualitatively different character in different nations.

Questions about the possibility of economic and social reform and the role of the state in this process are of crucial importance. 'Reform' in this context has quite a different meaning from its recent usage by neoliberals as a term to describe rolling back the state through policies to cut taxation and remove tariff protection, deregulate labour and capital markets, and privatise public enterprise. Reform should mean change for the better through making the economy serve a broader array of social goals, such as economic and social security, and distributional equity. As this chapter has emphasised, important analytical currents emphasise the need for the state to serve this reforming mission. The challenge in practice is to mobilise the necessary political support. It is a challenge that, in the modern world, also needs to take account of the constraints imposed on the capacity of the nation state by corporate globalisation.

KEY POINTS

- The prospect of using the state as a means of subordinating economic interests to broader societal purposes is a significant theme in institutional economics, linking with other currents in the social sciences.

- The modern state is shaped by the influences of democracy, capitalism, and bureaucracy, so the possibilities for progressive economic and social reform are seldom straightforward.

- The development of the welfare state, one of the great institutional achievements of the twentieth century, is subject to challenge and change.

28 Corporate Globalisation

What are the main dimensions of the process of globalisation?

What are the implications for political economic analysis and policy?

How does globalisation change the balance of economic power?

Globalisation is one of the most frequently mentioned trends of the present era. It is also one of the most hotly debated concepts in political economy. At one extreme are those who consider globalisation to be a relentless process, driven by technological and commercial imperatives and rapidly undermining the sovereignty of nation states, perhaps even destroying the political economic significance of national boundaries.[1] At the other extreme are the globalisation sceptics, who argue that there is nothing new about international commerce, and that the task for nation states, as ever, is to determine how to reconcile it with the pursuit of national and local economic interests.[2] Analytically, many questions arise in such debates. How is globalisation to be defined? How does the globalisation of capital relate to the globalisation of labour, the state, and nongovernmental organisations? Is globalisation orchestrated by a transnational capitalist class? Are nation states independent of such interests? What are the implications for democratic processes? Who wins from globalisation? Who loses?

Institutional economists have a head start in contributing answers to these questions because of their longstanding concern to understand the evolving characteristics of economic society. Their focus, as set out in the preceding four chapters, is on what is distinctive about the institutions of capital, labour, and the state, how they are changing over time, and how the economic, social, and political aspects of that institutional behaviour interact. The work of Australian political economist Ted Wheelwright exemplifies these concerns. The subsequent analysis draws on his pioneering contributions to the analysis of globalisation.[3]

TED WHEELWRIGHT (1921–2007)

Ted Wheelwright was an inspiring figure in the development of Australian political economy. He taught at the University of Sydney for more than three decades, retiring in 1986. As a teacher, he was much respected by his students for his emphasis on up-to-date developments in the real world rather than the repetition of outdated theories. Like Galbraith, Wheelwright was always inclined to poke fun at the conventional wisdom in economics—but with serious intent.

Ted Wheelwright's research and writing focused on the analysis of globalisation long before that term became popular. He pointed to the dangers of overreliance on foreign investment. He emphasised that transnational corporations have created a new corporate world economic order. He predicted that governments seeking to attract investment by transnational corporations would tend to become 'client states', effectively at the service of the corporations.

These developments, Wheelwright argued, would accentuate the tendency for the economic interests of capital to work against the interests of ordinary working people. A two-volume history of Australia, *False Paradise: Australian Capitalism Revisited, 1915–1955*, written in conjunction with economic historian Ken Buckley, extended this working class perspective to a broader description and critique of capitalist development down under. Other themes in Wheelwright's political economy include the ascendancy of Asian capitalism and the influence of Japanese investment on other nations, particularly Australia. His writing was consistently critical of the concentration of corporate power and of the complicity of orthodox economics in this process. He established the Transnational Corporations Research Project at the University of Sydney as a means of encouraging research on global big business.

Together with other dissident political economists, Wheelwright also participated in the long struggle to establish political economy courses at the University of Sydney, a focal point in Australia for the challenge to conservative economic orthodoxy. The struggle bore fruit in 1975 with the introduction of the first of a sequence of undergraduate units of study in political economy. Other course developments, both undergraduate and postgraduate, followed. The *Journal of Australian Political Economy* was introduced as a means of disseminating political economic analyses and ideas within academe and in the community at large. Four decades later, these initiatives continue to flourish. They make the University of Sydney one of the key centres, internationally as well as nationally, of teaching and research in political economy.

Transnational corporations

It makes sense to begin the study of globalisation by looking at the major institutional actors. These are, first and foremost, the transnational corporations (TNCs), companies that have subsidiaries or associate companies in more than one country, often in many. Their distinctive feature is not that they engage in international trade—lots of businesses do that—but that they have financial sources, manufacturing operations, administrative offices, and marketing operations in different countries.

There are many such companies. In the 1970s there were about 7000 TNCs.[4] A recent report by the United Nations estimates that in 2009 there were 82 000 TNCs, with over 810 000 foreign affiliates.[5] Many are now bigger than nations in terms of the total wealth at their disposal.

TNCs have their headquarters in various countries. Among the best known TNCs with headquarters in the USA are General Electric, Ford, General Motors, Microsoft, Exxon Mobil, IBM, and Coca-Cola Amatil. TNCs based in Europe include Vodafone, Nestlé, GlaxoSmithKline, and Royal Dutch Shell. The biggest TNCs based in Japan are Toyota, Honda, Mitsubishi, Sony, and Nissan. North America, Europe, and Japan together account for the overwhelming bulk of TNC headquarters. The products of these corporations cover the gamut of consumer goods, from processed foods and cigarettes to pharmaceuticals, cars, televisions, and other electronic consumer durables, as well as the full range of producer goods, such as steel, aluminium, chemicals, and plastics.

Alongside the giant firms producing those tangible products are other institutions carrying out financial functions. Most prominent among these are the banks, many of which have themselves become TNCs. Until the 1980s, most banking institutions were national, having overseas operations only as an adjunct to their major domestic activities. Since the 1980s, however, there has been a dramatic, although less than complete, globalisation of financial services. The major banks, whether originally based in New York, Tokyo, London, Paris, or any other city, now carry out their banking operations in numerous countries worldwide. This growth of the transnational banks—and of global finance generally—is in the interests of TNCs producing goods and services. The transnational banks help them arrange their global financial requirements, and thereby play a key role in the globalisation of capital. The banks themselves are also in a position to be global profit maximisers, arranging their activities on a world scale in order to minimise the constraints imposed by nationally based regulatory agencies, which gives them tremendous economic power.

Industrial concentration, world industries, conglomerates

The growth of TNCs has generated significantly different patterns of industrial concentration. One conventional national measure of concentration is the proportion of the total output in a particular industry that is produced by the largest, say, six firms in that industry. Where TNCs dominate, such measures of concentration are, typically, increased. The process has now broken the bounds of national economies and has led to the development of world industries, in which a handful of TNCs are the dominant players.

Manufacturing industries that are particularly highly concentrated on a global scale include aluminium production, oil refining and the distribution of petrol, the production of tobacco products, the manufacture of computers, and the production of cars. TNCs also dominate the world's trade in agricultural products. Seven firms control 85 per cent of the global trade in grain, eight firms control 60 per cent of the trade in coffee, seven firms control 90 per cent of the global tea trade, three firms control 83 per cent of the trade in cocoa, and three firms control 80 per cent of the banana trade.[6] The largest 500 TNCs in the world today control an estimated 70 per cent of the global trade.[7] Industrial concentration has also affected service industries, although these have traditionally been more localised than manufacturing industries. Twenty years ago, for example, people referred to the big eight accounting firms who provided financial services internationally, mainly to other businesses; now, as a result of mergers in the industry, it is the big four.

Having only a relatively small number of players does not mean that competition disappears. On the contrary, competition among TNCs for market share is often vigorous. However, it is usually non-price competition, focusing instead on product differentiation and corporate image, for example. It is not the competition of the perfectly competitive markets analysed by neoclassical economists. Even the stylised neoclassical theories of imperfect market structures, such as monopolistic competition and oligopoly, have dubious relevance in relation to industries characterised by such striking concentrations of economic power.

The situation is further complicated because many of the TNCs are conglomerates, giant organisations with diverse productive activities straddling different industries. A modern example of a conglomerate is Virgin: it is involved in airlines, mobile phones, radio, music, books, hotels and resorts, fitness and leisure, soft drinks and wines, bridal wear and accessories, cars, cosmetics, superannuation, credit cards, online gaming, hot air balloon flights, and even sending paying passengers into space through its Virgin Galactic division. Because companies such as this are engaged in many industries, it is hard to analyse them using the conventional economic notions of 'industries' and 'firms'. The image of an industry as comprising firms that make broadly similar products does not apply to conglomerates. The proliferation of conglomerates in recent decades therefore challenges the basic categories of orthodox economics. It also challenges political economists considering the significance of this further concentration of economic power.

Negation of the market?

A market system imposes some discipline on economic life. According to neoclassical economists, it ensures that what goods and services are produced corresponds to the pattern of consumers' preferences. To the extent that the economic prosperity of TNCs, including conglomerates, depends ultimately on them selling their products, the market continues to exert that ultimate discipline. However, many of the activities of TNCs are concerned with bypassing, even undermining, the market system. Many of their transactions do not occur through markets. Over one-third of global merchandise trade is between TNCs and their subsidiaries: in other words, it is intra-corporate trade.[8] This opens up possibilities for business reciprocity: the practice of making sales to, and purchases from, corporations that are customers of conglomerates. As Crough and Wheelwright noted: 'This new kind of "market" responds much more to the procedures developed to maximise global profits by head office than to traditional market signals or the administrative fiats of national governments. Hence a new form of "international" capitalism is born, very much less susceptible to traditional market forces, beyond the control of any national government; and no international government exists.'[9]

There are some apparent advantages for consumers arising from this global character of production and distribution. The companies may reduce costs by taking advantage of economies of scale and of global sourcing of their production and financial requirements; consumers may benefit if competition leads to part of those savings being passed on in the form of lower product prices. Consumers gain easier access to products from distant lands; they can, effectively, shop in a global bazaar. For those consumers who travel internationally, there may be some advantages in the standardisation of product quality: a can of Coke, a packet of Dunhill cigarettes, or a night in a Holiday Inn, each has a predictable standard, almost irrespective of the place where it is purchased. Other, less mobile, consumers may derive psychological pleasure from buying products commonly identified through commercial advertising with international celebrities or global brand imagery.

Some profound concerns also arise from the concentration of economic power in the TNCs. The promotion of consumerism, accentuated by the quest for maximum penetration of global markets, is the most obvious. Whether it is sustainable in the longer term is a moot point. Whether it even leads to greater consumer satisfaction is also dubious, since the process of sales promotion increases aspirations at the same time as promising to satisfy those aspirations. The greater uniformity of products is also a mixed blessing, as some say it tends to undermine cultural diversity. This process is particularly evident in the media and entertainment industries. Any benefits consumers derive from having access to a range of global products also have to be set against the environmental impacts of using so many resources for long-distance transportation. The spectre of climate change hangs over the whole scene. Global trade also has impacts on local economies. Local industries may be destroyed or taken over by TNCs, and regional economies may become increasingly dependent on decisions taken by businesses with no roots in the locality. It has been said that the ideal factory would be one that is built on a floating platform that could be towed around the world to where wages and other cost considerations would make it most advantageous to produce at the time.[10] It is a fantasy, but one that accords with the processes actually shaping the global distribution of production and jobs.

A changing international division of labour

Whether globalisation gives rise to a new international division of labour, and what form it takes, has been one of the more controversial issues in modern political economic analysis.[11]

Division of labour, as emphasised by Adam Smith, involves different people working on different stages in a production process. It has long been a feature of international economic specialisation, but there has been a significant reorientation of its geographical form in recent years. On a world scale it has become increasingly differentiated, because TNCs can divide their activities between operations in different regions and nations.

Some manufacturing jobs have been relocated to countries of the developing Third World. From the 1970s onwards, free-trade zones and export-processing zones were focal points for industrialisation in former colonial nations. Host governments offered cheap premises, tax holidays, and low-wage and often union-free labour to attract TNCs to operate there. Rapid, but unbalanced and dependent, patterns of economic growth have been the typical outcome. There is always the fear that the TNCs may pull out if they are not given yet more generous incentives to stay.

The other side of the coin is the partial deindustrialisation of the formerly more economically developed nations. Job losses in particular manufacturing industries have been significant. The loss of jobs in clothing manufacture in Australia that followed the reorientation of the industry towards offshore production and sources of garments (for example, in Fiji and the People's Republic of China) is one case in point. However, it is important to put this trend in perspective. The changing international division of labour cannot wholly account for the relative decline in manufacturing employment in the advanced industrial nations. As a number of economic commentators have pointed out, the total figures do not tally.[12] Shifts of manufacturing plants to lower-wage nations account for only a part of the total manufacturing job loss, much of which has more to do with the effects of technological change and higher labour productivity that has raised the ratio of output to labour employed.

The international division of labour is itself rapidly evolving, so it is not as if there is a clear divide between the old and new arrangements. Indeed, there are interesting contemporary trends towards greater global mobility of the workers themselves, both among the professional and managerial elite and among unskilled and semiskilled workers at the bottom of the workforce hierarchy. Networks of international contracting and subcontracting are also developing as a major feature of contemporary transnational business activity. These pressures for more international mobility of labour sit uneasily with the traditional concerns of the richer nations to regulate immigration processes. 'Border protection' and the interests of global capital are uncomfortable bedfellows.

Synchronisation and disarticulation

Synchronisation results from international interdependence. The buoyancy—or otherwise—of the economy is more rapidly transmitted between nations, synchronising their economic conditions. It is summed up in the phrase 'When the United States sneezes, the rest of the world catches a cold'. That was clearly evident in 2007–09, when problems arising in US housing and mortgage markets quickly developed into a global financial crisis. But even changes in the economic conditions of smaller nations can have major international repercussions. In 1997, the sudden deterioration of the Thai economy had triggered an economic crisis throughout the countries of South-East Asia. Global interdependence makes it increasingly difficult for any one nation to insulate itself against external shocks of this kind.

The transmission mechanisms are many and varied: direct flows of investment, the demand for goods and services produced for international markets, interest rates for borrowed funds, and the credit ratings applying to those international borrowings, for example. Even the general state of business optimism or pessimism may have a significant bearing on the decisions of TNCs about whether to expand or contract their activities. For better or worse, these factors tend to synchronise economic conditions across nations.

This international interdependence also goes hand in hand with *disarticulation* within national economies. Where strong linkages exist between industries in a nation, expansion in one industry tends to pull others along behind, leading to generalised economic growth. Disarticulation occurs when these links are weak or broken. Open-cut mining in Queensland, Australia, for example, produces coal that is taken directly to the coast for export, particularly to Japan. There is a strong link between coal mining in Queensland and Japanese manufacturing, but only a weak link with the rest of the Australian economy. Such regional disarticulation is common in an increasingly globalised economy.

Two consequences are increasingly uneven patterns of regional development and greater regional economic vulnerability. Articulated regions, sometimes transcending national boundaries, as in the case of the Singapore–Johor Bahru (Malaysia)–Bintan Island (Indonesia) triangle, may experience rapid surges of economic growth. Meanwhile, other regions become marginalised, effectively bypassed by the dynamic processes of technological and structural economic change. 'Billabong regional economies' is a possible characterisation, drawing on the Australian word for an area of water cut off from the main flow of a river. The spectacular economic growth of some areas and the stagnation of others are related phenomena. But even those regions experiencing rapid growth become dependent on economic conditions elsewhere, over which the local businesses and governments can exert no significant economic control.

A changing balance of economic power

The institutions that have become the most spatially mobile have gained power relative to those that remain localised. The former are most obviously the institutions of capital, including the TNCs producing goods and services and the transnational financial institutions that serve their needs. They can rearrange their activities strategically in the pursuit of their corporate goals, or minimise their taxation, for example, by the use of tax havens or transfer pricing.[13] Corporations commonly reduce costs by relocating their activities to where wages are lowest or environmental standards most lax.

By contrast, the institutions representing workers, consumers, and environmentalists and citizens in general are generally less mobile, and are correspondingly limited in their strategic options. Labour is organised mainly on local and national scales through trade unions, and the proportion of workers in unions has been declining in most of the advanced nations over the past couple of decades.[14] Consumers, to the extent that they have any collective voice at all, have organisations that are mostly national. Environmental organisations have a characteristically local focus too. Governments relate to nation states, or components thereof (in federal systems, such as the USA, Germany, Canada, and Australia). These institutions are all more spatially bounded than TNCs. Each has elements of international coordination—the International Labor Organization, the International Consumers' Association, Greenpeace, and the United Nations, for example—but these do not have economic power comparable to the transnational institutions of capital.

Some social scientists argue that a transnational capitalist class has developed, effectively coordinating the collective interests of capital on a global scale.[15] The class, broadly defined, comprises not simply the senior corporate executives, but also bureaucrats, politicians, and some academics whose activities are increasingly connected with global corporate interests. The extent of coordination is debatable, of course, but few would doubt the prodigious economic power of capital on a global scale relative to more localised interests.

The power shift is towards essentially undemocratic institutions. The corporations are ultimately accountable to their own shareholders (an accountability based on the principle of 'one share, one vote'). In reality, the fragmented nature of shareholdings leaves effective power in the hands of the major institutional investors and the managers of the corporations. Governments, on the other hand, are the formally democratic institutions, normally elected on the principle of 'one person, one vote'. But their policies need to accommodate the interests of the TNCs on whose decisions the prosperity, or otherwise, of national economies depends. Crough and Wheelwright called this the development of a 'client state'.[16]

Governments are tending to become puppets of international business, according to this view. They give priority to corporate interests, defining success largely in terms of economic goals, and determining foreign policy mainly according to commercial criteria. As Associate Director for the Centre for International Business at the University of Cambridge, Noreena Herz, puts it, 'Instead of creating a better world for people, governments work to create a better environment for business.'[17] This does not mean that governments only ever act in the interests of big business. The attempt by the Australian government in 2010 to impose a new tax on the 'super profits' of mining companies was an interesting case in point. However, faced with a barrage of political advertising funded by the companies, the government backed off to a more modest tax reform. The much celebrated connection between capitalism and democracy is increasingly questionable in circumstances like these. Indeed, the broad historical correlation between the development of market freedoms and political freedoms now looks much more tenuous. The growth of power of the TNCs makes private economic interest increasingly dominant relative to the formally democratic institutions to whom we have entrusted the protection and advancement of a broader public interest. As Marxist political economists have long emphasised, one should not idealise national governments, for their activities have always been intertwined with the interests of the capitalist class. The point is rather that the scope for independent governmental action has been further reduced by the globalisation of capital. In the extreme, political authoritarianism becomes the precondition for maintaining an essentially undemocratic economic system.

Change and challenge

These observations about institutional change on a global scale pose big challenges. Analytically, they pose a fundamental challenge to conventional economic theory. They indicate the need to come to terms with a very different world from that depicted in the conventional textbooks. Politically, they pose a major challenge to workers, consumers, environmentalists, and indeed, to all citizens who are uncomfortable about allowing corporations to restructure the world economy in their own interests and image.

Economic discourse has conventionally rested on two major assumptions: the existence of national economies and the operation of a market system. These underpin the standard division in the economics discipline between macroeconomics and microeconomics. Macroeconomics is about national economies; microeconomics is about how markets function (or, in neoclassical theory, about how stylised models of markets function). The institutional economic analysis of globalisation casts significant doubts on the value of this disciplinary structure. Instead of a world economy comprising an aggregation of national economies, we now have a world economy in which the main components are corporate institutions. That being so, the conventional construction of macroeconomics, even so-called 'open-economy macroeconomics', looks inappropriate. Similarly, the microeconomic assumption that markets shape economic outcomes looks increasingly untenable in a world shaped by the exercise of corporate power. So the twin pillars of conventional economics—the assumption of national economies and free markets—seem to stand on ever more shaky ground.

Some institutional economists contend that we need a *mesoeconomics*—intermediate between micro and macro—to supplement microeconomic and macroeconomic analysis, if not to replace them altogether. Mesoeconomics focuses primarily on the institutions wielding the corporate power. As British political economist Stuart Holland, the leading proponent of this view, has argued, 'Modifying conventional models of international trade and payments to account for the rise of multinational capital is imperative if we are to understand how the world has changed both since Keynes and since Ricardo ... Analysis of the modern meso economy and the role of multinational capital is integral to such qualifications of conventional macroeconomic theory.'[18]

Not all political economists agree with this argument for a new institutional meso-economics. Some say that the application of the theory of capital accumulation to the study of globalisation is all that is needed. Marxist political economists point out that Marx anticipated the tendency for the relentless capital accumulation process to transcend national boundaries, emphasising that globalisation is an extension of longstanding processes of imperialism. They sometimes also argue that, far from eradicating competitive processes, the contemporary globalisation of capital extends them on a world scale. From this perspective, it is inter-corporate competition that drives the TNCs to behave in ways that systematically violate the interests of labour.[19] Whether the processes are predominantly competitive or collusive remains a matter for rival political economic interpretations. What is less in dispute is that the outcome is a world order in which the collective interests of capital dominate.

Marx and Engels ended their *Manifesto* with the famous rallying cry, 'Workers of the world unite: you have nothing to lose but your chains.' As Ted Wheelwright wryly noted, it is the capitalists, not the workers, who seem to have taken that advice, integrating their activities on a global scale, while workers remain more poorly organised at the local or national scale.[20] But the situation is not altogether clear-cut, and certainly not static. Campaigns involving international solidarity between trade unions frequently occur. Groups concerned with consumers' interests and environmental protection have also developed international linkages. The activist organisational principle 'Think global, act local' has obvious resonance in these circumstances.

BOX 28.2   GLOBAL INSTITUTIONS

Much of international trade and finance is mediated by three multinational institutions: the International Monetary Fund (IMF), the World Bank, and the World Trade Organization (WTO).

The genesis of the IMF was the international Bretton Woods conference in 1944. The IMF now comprises 187 member countries. Its role is to oversee the stability of the global financial system, including exchange rate adjustment and convertibility. When countries join the IMF, they agree to subject their economic policies to IMF scrutiny, with IMF standards and codes used to assess the potential consequences of domestic policies and to provide macroeconomic policy advice. The IMF also provides technical and financial assistance to implement these policies.

The World Bank also grew out of the Bretton Woods deliberations. It is a group of financial institutions that are jointly owned by the 187 countries. It has the stated aim of assisting poorer nations with economic development through loans (often with low or no interest rates) to fund investment and reduce poverty. World Bank-funded projects include industrial and agricultural development, education, health care, and anticorruption programs.

Formed in 1995, the WTO is the newest of the three institutions. It is an intergovernmental body with representatives from 153 member countries. The WTO determines the rules governing international trade and is committed, in practice, to trade liberalisation and removing impediments to the global mobility of capital. It administers the General Agreement on Tariffs and Trade (GATT), which originated in the late 1940s, as well as subsequent international trade agreements.

The operations of these three institutions have been strongly criticised in recent years. Critics argue that the IMF has far outgrown the original intentions of its creators. Under the Bretton Woods agreement, receiving an IMF loan required member countries to implement programs to keep their currencies relatively stable. Over time, this loan conditionality has been interpreted more broadly, leading to a situation in which the IMF can have a major influence on a country's economic policies. Its assistance to individual countries is almost invariably conditional upon governments implementing a range of neoliberal policies. Indeed, Joseph Stiglitz, formerly chief economist and senior vice president at the World Bank, has recurrently criticised the IMF for not giving countries the right to an informed choice in economic policy.[21]

Similarly, the World Bank has been subject to strong criticism for its structural adjustment programs and other neoliberal macroeconomic policy prescriptions for countries in receipt of World Bank loans. Critics argue that these policies have harmed local industries, undermined the viability of small farms, been insensitive to environmental concerns, undermined the position of workers, particularly women and the poor, and increased current account deficits and external debt problems for developing nations. Critics have also argued that the policies create a debt trap for developing countries. This is a problem that the IMF and World Bank have, in effect, conceded in responding to these arguments by providing some debt relief to the most heavily indebted nations.

Criticisms of the WTO stem from its approach to trade policy. While it represents itself as a neutral forum in which governments debate the rules of international trade, many argue that the WTO's strong free trade commitment is, in effect, an ideological mission. Alternatives to neoliberal trade policies have received scant attention. In this way, the WTO is seen as serving the interests of large multinational corporations at the expense of poorer nations, workers, and the environment. Indeed, this perception, particularly among the representatives of developing countries, has resulted in many WTO initiatives for multilateral trade liberalisation being unsuccessful. Attention has switched to more limited bilateral and regional trade deals.[22]

Two other global institutions—the United Nations (UN) and the International Labor Organization (ILO)—also have important roles. They operate quite differently. The UN was established in 1945, with the stated aim of building international cooperation in the pursuit of economic and social development, peace, and human rights. It has since developed a substantial body of international law and political practice in pursuit of these broad but often elusive goals. The ILO was founded in 1919, and since 1946 has been an agency of the UN. Its specialised role is to set international standards on labour rights, which have some bearing, albeit a much weaker one, on the global economy, tending to constrain the excesses of corporate globalisation and the neoliberal economic policies pursued by the World Bank, the IMF, and the WTO.

Conclusion

Corporate globalisation is a process driven by the profit motive, facilitated by technological advances, encouraged by neoliberal policies, and compounded by consumerism. The consequent growth of international trade, investment, and financial flows accentuates economic interdependence and tends to cause disarticulation of national economies. These are significant contemporary trends to which institutional economists and other political economists have sought to draw attention. It is the interpretation of these trends that is crucial in shaping social and political responses. An interpretation of globalisation as unavoidable, necessary, and desirable generates a quite different politics from one that sees it as contingent and malleable.[23] Seeing globalisation as a contested process and a contestable discourse directs attention to political processes and choices.

What political responses to corporate globalisation are appropriate? Some make the case for a defensive nationalism, trying to use the power of the nation state to regulate some of the stresses. Others argue for a progressive internationalism that emphasises the globalisation of human rights, environmental consciousness, and the interests of labour as a counter to corporate globalisation. Localist responses at the urban or regional level also have the potential to build alternative community structures and spawn grassroots movements to challenge the hegemony of multinational capital.[24] All three levels—local, national, and international—are important. The main issue is how to integrate them. Of course, there are strategic choices to be made, but it is inevitable that political groups responding to globalisation will continue to operate at all three levels. The key practical challenge is to enhance their effectiveness by sharing information and forging cooperative relationships.[25] By addressing these issues, modern institutional economics links with contemporary political activism.

KEY POINTS

- The growth of transnational corporations has produced world industries in which markets are constrained and shaped by the exercise of corporate power.

- Corporate globalisation changes the international division of labour, creates regional and national disarticulation, and reduces the capacity of nation states to insulate themselves from global political economic trends.

- There has been a corresponding change in the balance of private and public power, bringing into question the historical association between capitalism and democracy and generating diverse political responses.

PART VII

Stabilising the Economy

Keynesian Economics

29 The Disillusioned Defence of Capitalism

Why worry about unemployment?

What was distinctive about the economics of John Maynard Keynes?

What are the principal implications of Keynesian economics?

John Maynard Keynes (1883–1946) once said that it would be good for economists to be like dentists. Most of us require the services of a dentist from time to time, but we do not let dentists dominate our lives; the less we need their services, the better. Is it possible that the economic system could operate in such a way that only occasional minor repairs would be needed?

To try to perfect, or at least improve, the economic system is a worthy goal. Marxist political economists, you will recall, have always claimed that radical change is needed. They contend that capitalism is inherently conflict ridden and crisis prone, and so the quest to perfect it is ill-conceived. The only adequate solution is its replacement by socialism (although that still leaves some big questions unanswered about what form socialism should take in practice and how to bring the change about). On the other hand, the neoclassical economists see a competitive market system as basically self-regulating, producing optimal (or, at least, relatively efficient) outcomes. According to the more extreme variations on this neoclassical theme, since most economic problems are caused by governments interfering with the 'natural' operations of the market mechanism, achieving perfection requires less, not more, government intervention. An intermediate, reformist inclination is evident in the tradition of institutional economics, as noted in the preceding four chapters. It is also the characteristic policy stance of Keynesian economists.

BOX 29.1

JOHN MAYNARD KEYNES (1883-1946)

Often described as the greatest economist of the twentieth century, Keynes continues to occupy a central place in modern debates about economic analysis and policy.

The son of a Cambridge University academic administrator, Keynes was educated at Eton, England's most elite boys' school, where he excelled at everything: the classics, mathematics, history, debating, rowing, even the peculiar sport known as the Eton Wall Game. At university, he studied mathematics and became president of the Union and the Liberal Club. He became interested in economics, too, and attended Alfred Marshall's lectures. When he fared disappointingly in an economics test for entry to the UK public service, he is reputed to have said that this indicated he knew more about economics than his examiners. It was probably true.

After leaving university, Keynes did work in the civil service. As a Treasury official he attended the peace conference at Versailles at the end of the First World War. Incensed by the Allies' policy of seeking punitive reparations from a vanquished Germany, he wrote a controversial book called *Economic Consequences of the Peace* (1920), which warned of the damaging consequences of that policy.

He returned to Cambridge as an academic economist and established an enviable reputation for combining economic theory with an understanding of how the world actually works—a rare combination indeed. His most important books were *A Treatise on Money* (1930) and *The General Theory of Employment, Interest and Money* (1936). His influence on the economics profession was through his writing, but he also had direct influence on the formulation of public policy in his role as economic adviser to successive British governments.

On a personal level, Keynes is renowned for his connection with the Bloomsbury set, an avant-garde artistic and literary circle whose members also included Lytton Strachey and Virginia Woolf. In 1925, Keynes married Lydia Lopokova, a Russian ballerina, although his sexual preference was well known to lie in a rather different direction. These aspects of his life, although not directly relevant to his economics, are relevant to an understanding of his distinctive status, as simultaneously an influential figure within the British Establishment and an intellectual and social nonconformist.

Keynes worked hard to inject sense, as he would have seen it, into practical economic policy during the turbulent years of the Great Depression and the Second World War. He represented the British Government at the Bretton Woods conference in 1944, concerned with setting up institutions to provide for a more prosperous postwar period, but was not wholly successful in winning acceptance for his proposals. Worn out by relentless overwork, he died in 1946.

Keynesian economists emphasise the positive role governments can play in stabilising an otherwise unstable capitalist system. The eradication of involuntary unemployment is perhaps its most distinctive target.

Unemployment, depression, social turmoil

The need for economic analysis and policy to focus on the causes of, and cures for, unemployment is obvious. Unemployment is economically irrational. It involves underutilisation of economic resources and failure to satisfy social needs. For the involuntarily unemployed people themselves—whether they are unable to find a first job or have been made redundant by their last employer—there are considerable personal costs, which include not only the absence of a regular wage income, but also severance from the social contacts usually associated with the workplace. Moreover, in a society where people's status is defined primarily by their work, unemployment frequently leads to social marginalisation and stigmatisation. Employment may be alienating, but unemployment is usually more so. Being out of work for a significant period of time also usually causes skills to atrophy and may lead to attitudinal changes that make it harder to reenter the workforce.[1]

There are other social costs of unemployment that have to be borne by society at large. Government expenditure rises if those out of work receive regular unemployment benefits. Simultaneously, government income is reduced because unemployed people generally pay no taxes, while tax revenues from business profits also decline. So, there is a strong tendency towards government budget deficits. This is not altogether a bad thing, according to Keynesians, but something that may create political pressures to prune other areas of government expenditure, such as health, education, public transport, and social services. Therein lie further contradictions because, insofar as unemployment causes ill-health (and there is considerable evidence of statistical and causal connections), the need for medical services tends to rise. Similarly, to the extent that unemployment is associated with a higher incidence of crime, the costs of policing, incarceration, and other forms of social control also tend to increase.[2]

Fundamentally, though, the problem of unemployment is one of *opportunity cost*. The society has to forgo the goods and services that the unemployed people would have produced were they in useful employment. That is the opportunity cost of unemployment: its cost in terms of opportunities (for production and consumption) forgone. It shows the irrationality of an economic system simultaneously having unused resources and unfulfilled social needs. Reducing unemployment therefore raises the tantalising possibility of a win–win situation, because the unemployed people benefit by getting jobs while society benefits from the extra goods and services they produce and the extra tax revenues they pay. Policies to reduce unemployment make a valuable social contribution.

Keynes certainly thought so. He was analysing the situation before and during the Great Depression. It was a time of terrible economic difficulties, causing major social stresses and threatening political turmoil. Here were circumstances crying out for careful analysis and remedial policies. It is pertinent to look back at that time, partly because it had such impact on political economic attitudes, and also because of its interesting parallels with the global financial crisis that began nearly 80 years later in 2007–08, indicating that the crisis-prone tendency of capitalism remains.

It is conventional to associate the start of the Great Depression with a single day: 'Black Thursday', 24 October 1929, when there was a major financial crash on the Wall Street Stock Exchange in New York. The sharp fall in share values triggered a stampede of panic selling that led to further falls in the following days and weeks. Fortunes were lost. According to popular accounts of the time, people checking into high-rise New York hotels were being asked if they wanted a room for sleeping in or a room for jumping out of the window.

Along with the financial crisis came a crisis in the real economy: rapid decline in the levels of output, income, and employment. Here the parallel with the more recent global financial crisis (GFC) is all too obvious. In both cases, the financial crash exposed more long-term structural problems. As Galbraith indicated in his magnificent book *The Great Crash*, the crisis that heralded the Great Depression resulted from problems with the corporate structure, the banking system, the distribution of income, international economic imbalances and the 'bad state of economic intelligence'. These economic problems had been developing even before the stock market crash. They set in with a vengeance thereafter. Over the next two years, the volume of farm produce fell by more than half and industrial production fell by almost a half. Nearly one-third of all workers suffered unemployment. The adverse economic conditions spread quickly to other capitalist national economies, including Canada (always immediately vulnerable to changes in US economic conditions), the UK and continental Europe, Australia, and New Zealand. Charitable soup kitchens provided some assistance to the unemployed, but there was little institutionalised state support for the unemployed in those days, unlike when the more recent GFC hit the advanced capitalist nations. People who had no jobs during the Great Depression commonly suffered eviction from their homes, destitution, and even starvation.[3]

What had gone wrong? The farms and factories were still there. There was no shortage of people willing to work in them. The problem was that the capitalist economy could not be relied upon to mobilise unemployed people for socially useful production.

Of course, the problem of economic depression was not new; a deep and prolonged depression had occurred in the 1880s, for example. Earlier still, Marx had pointed out this flaw in the capitalist system, emphasising its innate tendency to generate a reserve army of labour and periodic economic crises. Marx's reasoning, developed many decades before the Great Depression, evidently tallied with the observable conditions of the time, and an increasing number of people came to believe that only socialism could provide a solution. Indeed, while the capitalist countries were suffering the Great Depression in the 1930s, the Soviet Union, then the major experiment in constructing a socialist alternative, was experiencing full employment and continuing economic growth. Meanwhile, in Germany and Italy fascist governments were offering another solution, mobilising unemployed people to build highways and public housing—and manufacture tanks and bombs. Notwithstanding its authoritarian and racist aspects, the fascist alternative attracted growing numbers of followers. So the future of liberal capitalism, flanked on the left by socialism and on the right by fascism, was starting to look very insecure. Both alternatives seemed to be doing so much better economically; support for revolutionary change was widespread. Marx's famous prediction, 'socialism or barbarism', seemed to be materialising.

This was the economic, social, and political context in which Keynes made his analytical and practical contributions. Although he described capitalism as 'morally objectionable', he judged its reform and survival the best of the available options. Solving the unemployment crisis was the top priority. Keynes did marvellously well in this respect. Not only did he find an explanation for unemployment, but he also showed how appropriate government policies could substantially reduce, if not eliminate, it. The market did not have to be left to find its own equilibrium, Keynes argued; rather, a managed equilibrium of full employment could be engineered. While that would not resolve all economic difficulties, it would create the more stable macroeconomic environment within which other economic and social problems could be more readily addressed. This, in the words of his student Joan Robinson, was Keynes's 'disillusioned defence of capitalism'.[4]

Challenging classical prescriptions

Keynes faced a major task in turning around the dominant explanations of unemployment and the preferred policy prescriptions. They were deeply entrenched in the prevailing economic orthodoxy. This is what Keynes called the classical explanation of how the economy functions. The word 'classical' here refers to the ideas of classical political economists such as Jean-Baptiste Say and the ideas of neoclassical economists. From Keynes's vantage point, these were all classical ideas, because they predated his reconstruction of economic analysis.[5] His first task was to refute these pre-Keynesian orthodoxies.

Say's Law is at the root of the problem. It has numerous variations, but, as summarised in Chapter 8, its key proposition is that supply creates its own demand. This implies that prolonged economic depressions cannot be the result of insufficient demand for goods and services. The possibility of unemployment arising for other reasons is not denied: it could be structural (unemployed workers having the wrong skills relative to the available jobs) or it could be frictional (unemployed workers having difficulty making quick transitions to new jobs), but demand-deficient unemployment should not arise. The process of producing goods and services generates the income that is necessary in order for those goods to be purchased and consumed. As Cambridge professor A. C. Pigou put it during the depths of the Great Depression, 'With perfectly free competition … there will always be at work a strong tendency for wage rates to be so related to demand that everyone is employed.'[6] How, then, to account for the observable unemployment in practice? Why had it quite suddenly assumed such massive proportions?

The real world was obviously not behaving like the textbooks said it should. So the textbooks were wrong. They did not recognise that the tendency to recurrent recession is a systemic feature of the capitalist economy. One explanation for the unemployment problem was couched in terms of external shocks to which the economic system was vulnerable. It is a view that remains common to this day. It had originally been a feature of the 'sunspots' theory developed by William Stanley Jevons in the late nineteenth century to explain fluctuations in the level of economic activity. Indeed, if periodic sunspots do change weather patterns, they can impact on agricultural harvests, which may then affect the economy as a whole. However, to base a general explanation of the cyclical behaviour of the capitalist economy on external forces of this kind is quite bizarre. It diverts attention from capitalism's own internally generated contradictions.

Neoclassical theory is equally oblivious to the structural problems. The labour market is regarded as operating pretty much like any other market. The changing conditions of demand and supply are held to be mediated by adjustments to market prices. The wage rate, being the price of labour, is the adjustment mechanism. If supply exceeds demand, rather than there being prolonged unemployment, the wage rate falls. That increases the demand for labour, as employers become willing to employ more of the now cheaper workers. The market clears. Unemployment is eradicated. If, in the real world, unemployment persists, it therefore must be because of some impediment preventing the price mechanism from working properly. The solution is obvious: governments must seek to remove these impediments. If trade unions, for example, are preventing wages from falling, their power to do so must be broken (for the workers' own collective good, of course).

The Keynesian viewpoint

Keynes provided a critique of the prevailing orthodoxy and a fundamentally different interpretation of unemployment. Demand and supply still figure in his story, but the labour market is not treated as if it operates like other markets. A distinctive analysis of money markets is also introduced. The analysis is reorientated to the determinants of the aggregate demand and supply for goods and services, for labour, and for money. This emphasis on the analysis of the economy as a whole is the essence of a distinctively *macroeconomic* approach.[7] The macroeconomy is seen to be functioning according to principles that cannot be derived simply by adding up all its microeconomic elements.

Consider the effect of wage cuts, for example. They were favoured by neoclassical economists in Keynes's day (and are still frequently advocated by neoliberals today). Wage cutting has a seemingly obvious rationale whenever there is widespread unemployment. If workers were cheaper to employ, individual employers might, indeed, be willing to hire more of them—but only if they are confident of selling the extra products. According to Keynes, wage reductions in practice generally make the unemployment problem worse. If workers have lower incomes, they have less to spend on goods and services, so firms will sell fewer products and consequently reduce their demand for labour and unemployment will rise. Wage cutting has perverse effects, because it decreases the aggregate demand for goods and services. Indeed, the problem of depressed demand tends to become even more entrenched because businesses usually respond to reduced sales of their products by cutting their investment spending, which then reduces the productive capacity of the economy. A vicious cycle of economic contraction occurs.

A better strategy, Keynes argued, would be to implement policies to expand the aggregate demand for goods and services, which would lead to increased levels of employment. How best to do this? Governments do not usually have direct control over the wage rates that employers pay to their employees (although they do have direct control over the wages they pay to their own public sector employees, and they may also be able to exert some indirect influence on wages in the private sector, especially in countries where arbitration institutions oversee wage outcomes). However, a government can always adjust the level and pattern of its own expenditure in order to pursue the goal of full employment. If it spends more on building schools, hospitals, bridges, or railways, for example, that creates jobs for construction workers. Those workers are then able to spend more on food, cars, and clothing, which creates jobs for farmers and car and clothing manufacturers. The extra incomes lead to extra spending, which then stimulates higher outputs and creates more jobs. A virtuous cycle of economic expansion occurs.

Whether this process is virtuous in all respects is a matter of judgment. Producing more goods and services to create more jobs may concurrently entail environmental damage or foster an ultimately unfulfilling consumerism. However, for directly tackling the social evil of widespread unemployment—the principal problem when Keynes was writing—the justification for the policy is abundantly clear. Keynes himself felt so strongly about this that he made the memorably puckish statement that:

> If the Treasury were to fill old bottles with banknotes, bury them at suitable depths in disused coal-mines which are than filled up to the surface with town rubbish, and leave it to private enterprise on well-tried principles of *laissez-faire* to dig the notes up again ... there need be no more unemployment and, with the help of its repercussions, the real income of the community, and its capital wealth would probably become a good deal greater than it actually is. It would, indeed, be more sensible to build houses and the like; but if there are political and practical difficulties in the way of this, the above would be better than nothing![8]

Students tend to remember this as Keynes advocating filling mine shafts with banknotes, or digging holes and filling them in again. He meant nothing of the sort. He favoured mobilising the unemployed for socially useful production, for 'building houses and the like'. His point is that, from a purely job-creating viewpoint, these other bizarre forms of activity would serve the purpose almost equally well. They would certainly be better than policies of wage reduction and fiscal austerity.

Increasing government expenditure as a means of resolving economic difficulties was heresy in Keynes's day, and has become so again since. For Keynes it was not only a matter of economic logic; but it was also a moral imperative. Unemployment was a social scourge. The policies that he advocated for its eradication were based on the presumption that government could, and should, serve broad social purposes. This entails the pragmatic application of economic knowledge to the improvement of existing conditions.

Job creation had top priority in Keynes's own time because unemployment was so obviously the main economic problem requiring resolution. Some contend that this is still the case, particularly in the aftermath of the GFC. However, Keynesian analysis is equally applicable to the analysis and control of *inflation*. Broadly speaking, the reverse policy measures apply. If inflation is the product of an excess of aggregate demand for goods and services, its reduction requires curtailment of that demand. The reduction of government spending is the most obvious prescription. These are circumstances in which Keynesians might well regard fiscal restraint as appropriate. Cuts in government spending may be supplemented by policies restricting the supply of money and/or raising the rate of interest, if there is a need to discourage spending further in the private sector. Such policies of macroeconomic 'fine tuning' can steer the economy along the sensible path between unemployment on one side and inflation on the other.

Keynes's own analysis of the economy and economic policy was much more sophisticated than this summary implies. His best known book, *The General Theory of Employment, Interest and Money*, is a particularly complex work, and most students prefer their Keynes in a more clearly organised and digestible form. Nevertheless, his *General Theory* (as it is almost universally abbreviated) can rightly be said to 'stand as one of the three key books in the development of economics … together with Adam Smith's *Wealth of Nations* and Marx's *Capital*'.[9] The parallels are significant. All three works can be criticised for their lack of organisational clarity and their sometimes convoluted reasoning, but all three created significant paradigm shifts in the understanding of political economic matters. They contributed to radical changes in economic thought and political practice.

Conclusion

Keynes's ideas have left an enduring legacy. First, and most fundamental, is the inference that understanding the nature of economic problems requires rigorous analysis. This is the rationale behind the model building described in the next two chapters. Intellectual effort is needed to understand and shape the world in which we live. Prejudice will not do. Blaming unemployment on too many immigrants, on women taking men's jobs, or on work-shy welfare recipients may be effective populist rhetoric for conservative politicians, but it is counterproductive for those who really want to understand the systemic problems of the modern economy.

Second, there is the imperative to act. Explaining the roots of unemployment in terms of a deficiency of aggregate demand, or explaining inflation in terms of excess demand, is not an end in itself. It is a means towards the formulation of effective practical policies, such as policies of demand management. Keynes took the view that 'the ultimate end of rational human action was the generation of as much intrinsic goodness as possible, and in which the means embraced all the sciences, politics and economics included'.[10] Economics, from this perspective, has an ethical purpose. It is the means by which we come to understand the world in order to manage it better in the service of broader social goals.

Third, there is an optimistic view of the capacity of government to pursue those social goals. In particular, government is seen as an effective vehicle for improved economic management. Here is a point of contrast with both the revolutionary Marxist and free-market neoclassical stances. The characteristically Keynesian belief is that government can, and should, contribute to social progress, working within the general context of a capitalist economy to eradicate its most antisocial features. It is not that governments always get it right. Governments may exacerbate economic problems—but Keynes would have thought this most likely to be the result of muddled thinking. Soundly advised (by people like him), Keynes believed that governments should play a significant role in securing the 'possibility of civilisation'.

KEY POINTS

- Unemployment is economically irrational, generating personal and social costs as well as having opportunity costs in terms of the goods and services forgone.

- Unemployment is a recurrent feature in capitalist economies, but Keynes showed that, once its causes are known, appropriate remedial policies can be implemented. Policies of demand management can also be used to control inflation.

- In developing his analysis of the problems of contemporary capitalism, Keynes pointed to the necessity—indeed, the moral imperative—of economic reform.

30 Constructing a Keynesian Model

> *What determines the overall volume of economic activity?*
>
> *How can we understand the aggregate demand for goods and services?*
>
> *What are the causes of periodic recessions?*

Keynesian analysis focuses on understanding the economy as a whole and the appropriate means of managing it. In principle, the economy could be that of a particular locality or region, a nation, or even the world. Normally, it is taken to be the national economy, since the nation is the most clearly bounded space, and national governments are the most obvious institutions for the implementation of economic policy. This primary focus on the nation contrasts with the Marxist emphasis on class and the neoclassical emphasis on the individual, although the practitioners of all schools of economic thought would ultimately assert a concern to understand the economy in its entirety. What Keynesian economics does is provide a basis for a coherent macroeconomics. It emphasises key variables, the interaction of which determines the overall levels of income, output, and employment.

The circular flow of income

The most common way of illustrating the Keynesian macroeconomic viewpoint is through models of the circular flow of income. Figure 30.1 (on p. 275) shows two variations.[1] The top diagram shows the simpler case. Here, there are just two sets of participants in the economy: households and firms. Households supply the factors of production and are rewarded with corresponding income flows: wages (paid to workers), rent (paid to landowners), and profits (such as dividends paid to shareholders). Firms supply the goods and services that households purchase with their incomes. The higher the incomes, the higher the outputs, and, presumably therefore, the greater the number of jobs. In other words, both firms and households benefit from a larger circular flow.

The bottom diagram in Figure 30.1 shows a rather more complex, and more realistic, situation. Here, it is recognised that the circular flow may be reduced by three *leakages*:

▪ households may put part of their incomes aside as saving, which detracts from the demand for goods and services

▪ households may spend part of their incomes on imported products rather than locally produced goods and services

▪ households may have to pay part of their incomes to governments in the form of taxes, so that this portion of their income does not add directly to the aggregate demand for goods and services.

The larger these leakages are from the circular flow, the greater is the tendency towards economic contraction. On the other hand, there are three *injections* into the circular flow that have the reverse effect, of stimulating the overall level of economic activity:

▪ firms may invest by buying plant and equipment to modernise or expand their businesses, which adds to the circular flow of income

▪ firms may export some of their products, the payments for which also add to the flow of income in the national economy

▪ government expenditures—on social service payments, public education, infrastructure provision, and so on—further add to the circulating incomes.

There is no reason why the three injections should balance the three leakages. This important point is not obvious from the bottom diagram in Figure 30.1. It may seem that, if household savings are deposited in financial institutions, and firms borrow funds from those institutions to finance their investment, this pair of leakages and flows is likely to balance. It is not necessarily so. Savings and investment are undertaken by different people—by households and firms, respectively—and so it is quite possible for one to exceed the other. Similarly, there is no reason why the payments received for exports should balance the expenditure on imported goods. Indeed, international trade imbalances of that kind are common. Finally, there is no necessary equality between taxation and government expenditure, unless the government has a commitment to balanced budgets and is capable of realising that goal in practice. Keynes himself thought such a commitment unwise, since budgetary deficits and surpluses can be used as policy instruments to adjust the level of national economic activity.

An understanding of these injections and leakages in the circular flow of income can help to explain the ups and downs of the economy. If savings exceed investment, for example, national income tends to decline. At first sight, this seems strange. Isn't a high rate of household saving desirable? Indeed, saving is usually good for individual households; thrift, if not inherently virtuous, is a means of personal insurance against future poverty. However, thrift can do more harm than good for the economy as a whole. When people save, they buy fewer goods and services, so the aggregate demand falls, reducing the output of goods and services and the national income. People's plans to save may not then be realised because, having reduced incomes, they cannot readily achieve their original savings intentions.

It is investment, not saving, that drives economic expansion. From a national economic viewpoint, saving is only economically beneficial if it is matched by investment. But businesses will only engage in investment spending when they anticipate a growing demand for their products. That, in turn, is likely to depend on whether national income is growing or contracting. Evidently, striking the right balance between saving and investment is difficult. Striking the right balance between all the leakages and injections is yet more so.

FIGURE 30.1 THE CIRCULAR FLOW OF INCOME

(a) Simplest model

(b) More complex model

The model of the circular flow of income is a useful starting point for interpreting complex behavioural relationships and economic interdependencies. It can be developed in various ways. Some economists at the London School of Economics and Political Science once built a hydraulic contraption made of pipes and valves, physically simulating the structure of an economy seen from a Keynesian perspective. Extra water poured into the export revenue tube, for example, would flow through the apparatus, leading to higher levels of consumption and saving (depending on the relative diameters of those tubes) and higher levels of national income and tax revenues (depending on the amount of water diverted from the main flow into the government tank). The consequences of a surge in exports could thereby be predicted. Similarly, one could monitor how injections of higher government expenditure or business investment, for example, would affect the overall level of incomes and expenditures. The model was an interesting combination of Keynesian economics and some simple hydraulic engineering. Gumboots, to be worn at times of excessive leakages, were presumably an advisable accessory.

Macroeconomic models are now constructed in statistical form, using computer technology. Such econometric analysis is more sophisticated than the hydraulic contraption (and less prone to flooding the floor), but not fundamentally different in character. Its results depend, like the hydraulic model's, on the assumptions made about each of the variables in the model and their interrelationships. What determines the value of each of the variables? How do they interconnect? A macroeconomic view focuses on the factors shaping the overall supply and demand for goods and services.

Aggregate supply and demand

It is often said that the Keynesian emphasis on the importance of aggregate demand results in the relative neglect of aggregate supply. This is misleading. Keynes was well aware that the relationship between aggregate demand and supply determines the prosperity of the economy in the long term. In other words, the crucial relationship is that between the overall demand for goods and services and the productive capacity to supply them. Building up productive capacity is necessary for increasing national income and employment in the long term. Investment has a crucial role in this process, since it is both a source of demand for goods and services and the means by which the extra capacity to supply them is created.

However, at any particular point of time, the productive capacity of the economy can be taken as given. It depends on the number and size of factories, offices, trucks, tools, and so on. The question is how fully they will be utilised. It is understandable that Keynes focused on this more short-term question in the 1930s, for the underutilisation of existing productive capacity caused the chronic unemployment of the Great Depression. In our time, too, understanding the causes of periodic economic downturns can be usefully based on the analysis of capacity utilisation. We need to know under what conditions aggregate demand will be insufficient to ensure that the existing productive capacity is fully utilised. Focusing on this key concern puts the spotlight directly on the five determinants of aggregate demand.

The standard exposition of the Keynesian analysis of aggregate demand identifies five components that together determine the level of national income (Y). These are consumption (C), investment (I), government expenditure (G), exports (X), and imports (M). Thus:

$$Y = C + I + G + X - M$$

If these components are growing (shrinking, in the case of M), then national income will tend to grow. Any spare productive capacity in the economy will then be utilised. If they are declining (increasing, in the case of M), then national income will fall and the economy will tend to slide into recession. In the latter case, surplus capacity will become an economic problem. It is therefore important to understand what determines the size of each of the components of aggregate demand.

Consumption

Consumer spending (C) is invariably the biggest item in the national income (Y). It also tends to be fairly stable over time (other than seasonal fluctuations, such as the annual surge in consumer spending in Western societies at Christmas).

What determines the total volume of consumer expenditure on goods and services? First and foremost, it depends on income. This is true for individual consumers and for the economy as a whole. Therein lies a significant analytical problem, though. In trying to explain the level of national income, consumption is identified as its largest component; but we then say that consumption spending depends on national income. It seems to be circular reasoning. The getout is that not all income is usually spent on consumption; some is saved. If we can explain what proportion is saved, a coherent theory of consumption is possible.

As noted in Box 30.1 (overleaf), numerous social and institutional factors can be expected to have a bearing on the nature of the relationship between income, consumption, and saving. According to Keynesian economics, the rate of interest is not particularly important in this respect. In this, Keynes differs significantly from pre-Keynesian economists, who thought that the level of savings would respond positively to a higher interest rate. The pre-Keynesian view sounds logical enough: higher interest rates would mean a higher financial reward for saving, so people would be inclined to save more, would they not? Indeed, people certainly might want to save more if the rate of interest were higher, but because high interest rates deter investment, they also tend to reduce national income, which then reduces people's capacity to save. On the whole, Keynesians doubt the capacity of changes in interest rates to produce equilibrium between the levels of investment and savings in the economy. Keynesians typically take the view that interest rates shape *how* people save—whether they stuff their savings under the mattress, or put them in bank savings accounts or fixed term deposits, for example—rather than *how much* they save.

WHAT SHAPES CONSUMER SPENDING?

FIGURE 30.2 THE CONSUMPTION FUNCTION

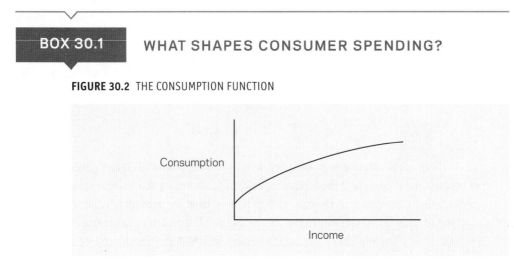

The slope of the above relationship between consumption and income depends on what proportion of each extra dollar received is spent rather than saved. Keynesian economists call this proportion the marginal propensity to consume. Increases in consumption are normally associated with increases in income, so the marginal propensity to consume will be somewhere between zero and unity. At a hypothetical level of zero income, some consumption would have to occur if the individual (or society) were to subsist; this would presumably require dis-saving from funds accumulated in a previous period or increasing debts to be repaid in a future period. As income rises, consumption rises, but usually at a decreasing rate. Rich individuals can usually afford to save a higher proportion of their income than can poor individuals; whole societies can be expected to exhibit a similar tendency.

The marginal propensity to consume for a whole society normally also depends on the distribution of income. Because poor people tend to spend all their income and rich people tend to save more, the distribution of income between them affects the overall consumption–saving ratio. The propensity to consume also depends on the availability of credit facilities. Some societies have institutional arrangements that impose forced savings requirements, such as the compulsory occupational superannuation schemes in Australia. Numerous social and cultural considerations further affect the propensity to consume: the influence of consumerism and commercial advertising, the prevalence of social emulation, and the extent to which consumers feel confident about their future incomes, their personal job prospects, and the state of the economy as a whole.

Investment

Investment (*I*) is the second component in aggregate demand. While not usually as large as consumption, it is usually more volatile. That is why it is so important as a determinant of the overall volume of economic activity. The volatility of investment can cause major fluctuations in the level of national income, output, and employment. It warrants careful analysis.

Investment is undertaken primarily by capitalist businesses. They invest in new plant, equipment, premises, and capital goods in general. Since the profit motive is the driving force in a capitalist economy, investment will be undertaken when it is expected to be profitable. This, according to Keynesian economics, will be when the expected rate of return on investment exceeds the rate of interest on funds borrowed to undertake the investment. Box 30.2 explains the reasoning.

BOX 30.2   WHAT SHAPES BUSINESS INVESTMENT?

Investment is expenditure by firms on capital goods. Its aim is to expand firms' productive capacity. The overall amount of investment undertaken by firms depends on the relationship between the marginal efficiency of capital and the prevailing rate of interest, as shown in the following diagram.

FIGURE 30.3 THE INVESTMENT FUNCTION

The marginal efficiency of capital indicates the expected rate of return on an additional unit of investment expenditure. Imagine a businessperson considering the various possible investments that could be made: that person ranks them in order of expected rates of return, with the most profitable being undertaken first, the second most profitable being undertaken next, and so on. In other words, the marginal efficiency of capital declines as the amount of investment increases. Similar reasoning applies to the economy as a whole. Hence, the downward sloping m.e.c. schedule in the above diagram.

The rate of interest, on the other hand, must usually be taken by firms as given. It is the rate that banks or other financial institutions charge for money borrowed from them. A profit-seeking businessperson will normally weigh up that cost of borrowing against the income expected to be generated by using the borrowed funds for investment (that is, the marginal efficiency of capital). All projects for which the expected rate of return is greater than the rate of interest are profitable to undertake; they would be given the go-ahead. Projects in which the expected rate of return is less than the prevailing rate of interest would be unprofitable to undertake. Thus, investment ceases at the point where the marginal efficiency of capital equals the rate of interest (that is, at *OA* in Figure 30.3). The higher the rate of interest, the less the amount of investment undertaken.

It does not matter in principle whether firms are borrowing money to undertake investment or financing it out of profits. In the former case, the rate of interest is the actual cost of obtaining capital; in the latter, it is the opportunity cost, since it indicates the rate of return a firm could have earned by lending its money rather than using it for its own investment. (For simplicity here, we assume that borrowing and lending rates, if not identical, move in tandem.) Either way, the rate of interest is a negative influence on investment.

The positive influence is the expected rate of return. 'Expected' is the key word here. Keynesians stress the importance of business expectations in determining the level of investment undertaken.[2] The marginal efficiency of capital is the anticipated return on the last unit of investment spending undertaken. If business decision-makers are optimistic about the future, this marginal efficiency of capital will be high; if pessimistic, it will be low. The level of optimism is not simply a matter of whether they get out of bed in the morning feeling cheerful or not; it depends on their judgments about the prospects for profitability of their business, based on assessments of market demand, and on broader perceptions of the state of the national and international economies, as shaped by media interpretations, political pronouncements, and so on. For this reason, governments regularly try to talk up business confidence by presenting rosy assessments of the economy.

Herd behaviour by business investors is common, as is usually the case where there is interdependence of information and strategic decisions. Keynes said that investment, that most crucial influence on a nation's income, output, and employment, is dependent on the 'animal spirits' of business people.[3] Some might think an analysis that has such a crucial variable depending on psychological factors is incomplete. Marxist political economy explains the interruptions to the capital accumulation process in terms of the internal systemic contradictions of capitalism. But animal spirits are not like sunspots: they are shaped by material economic conditions. Marxist and Keynesian economists agree that, as far as the real economy is concerned, dependence on animal spirits is a less than robust basis for economic prosperity.

When things are going well in the economy, they tend to go very well. An increase in investment creates extra jobs and extra incomes; those incomes are then spent on other goods and services, which creates more demand, more output, more incomes, and more jobs. The total impact on national income can be many times greater than the initial investment that began the process. This is the *multiplier effect*, a key element of Keynesian economic analysis. The size of the multiplier depends on the extent of the leakages from the circular flow of income. It is highest when these leakages are smallest; that is, when there is a low marginal propensity to save, a low marginal tax rate, and a low propensity to import. Then, the bulk of any extra incomes flows through the economy in a cumulative process of expansion. If, on the other hand, consumers save a high proportion of their extra incomes, spend a great deal on imported goods, or pay high marginal rates of tax (without corresponding increases in government expenditure), the multiplier effects are bound to be more modest and economic expansion peters out more quickly.

The multiplier effect also operates in reverse. So when things are going badly in the economy, they tend to go very badly. Falls in investment, occurring when those animal spirits take a pessimistic turn, have a multiplied impact on the decline of national income. Therein lies the principal source of recession. Therein also lies the need for government expenditure as an antidote to these socially damaging outcomes.

Government expenditure

This third component in the aggregate demand for goods and services is directly under the control of the government. Government spending is partly on items of consumption (for example, the direct provision by government of services, such as public education and health, or social security transfers that enable poorer people to consume more goods and services than they otherwise could). Another part usually takes the form of public investment (such as building bridges, electricity supply systems, railways, roads, hospitals, schools, libraries, or art galleries). Its macroeconomic effects, including its multiplier effects, can be expected, as a first approximation, to be similar to private sector consumption and investment.

The principal difference is that government expenditure is a policy variable. In other words, it can be determined consciously by the government in order to achieve national economic and social goals. It can, for example, be adjusted to compensate for variations over time in the volume of private sector consumption and investment, and used as an instrument for economic stabilisation and the pursuit of full employment, which is why it is of such significance from a Keynesian perspective.

Exports and imports

These final two components of aggregate demand are much harder to control. They depend significantly on what is happening in the rest of the world, over which local economic institutions, public or private, usually have no substantial influence. The volume of export sales (X) from any nation may be enhanced by the strategic efforts of local producers, and may be encouraged in various ways by the government, but it depends ultimately on the incomes and consumption preferences of the citizens of other nations. An international economic recession or switch in consumers' tastes can make sudden and substantial dents in a nation's export earnings.

Meanwhile, the volume of expenditure on imports (M) depends on the preferences of local consumers for those imported goods relative to local products. It also depends on the strategic behaviour of firms both inside and outside the country (such as when TNCs have a policy of importing from their subsidiaries or affiliate companies rather than buying from local producers). Governments commonly seek to exert some control over imports, directly through the imposition of tariffs and quotas on imported goods, and indirectly through campaigns to encourage the purchase of local products. Exchange rate policy may also be adjusted as a means of trying to improve the trade balance ($X-M$), although its effectiveness depends on the elasticity of demand for the exported and imported products. Overall, balancing imports and exports does not happen naturally, and constitutes a major challenge for public policy.

A diabolical adjustment mechanism

The foregoing considerations about the components of aggregate demand draw attention to numerous interdependent relationships, some of which may be responsive to government policy, while others seem to have their own momentum. The savings habits of consumers, the animal spirits of business investors, and the external conditions affecting imports and exports are the elements most difficult to control.

The next step in developing a Keynesian interpretation of the economy is to ask how the economy adjusts to changes in these components of aggregate demand. What, for example, happens when the level of aggregate demand is rising? In the short term (when aggregate supply or productive capacity is fixed), it depends on whether the economy is operating at full capacity or has surplus capacity. If there is surplus capacity, the previously underutilised resources will be put to productive use and unemployment can be expected to fall. On the other hand, if the economy is already operating at full capacity, the expansionary pressures are likely to cause shortages of goods and services. In the latter circumstances, inflation is a probable outcome.

The reverse chain of reasoning applies to a reduction in aggregate demand. Inflationary pressures may be eased if the economy were previously operating at full capacity. Increased unemployment of resources (labour, capital, and land) is the more likely outcome, as capacity utilisation falls. This is the recession scenario.

These considerations illustrate a Keynesian insight of great social significance: the mechanism that balances aggregate demand and supply is change in the levels of national income, output, and employment. This can be a painful adjustment process that entails major social damage when aggregate demand declines: people lose their jobs and face falling incomes. Equilibrium in the economy may be reestablished, but it is not necessarily—indeed, not typically—an equilibrium of full employment.

Pre-Keynesian economists had generally been more complacent. If, as they argued, the rate of interest serves as the adjustment mechanism between savings and investment, there need be no major volatility in the economic system. Equilibrium in the economy would be continually restored without any major social costs (other than fluctuating incomes from interest payments for those with surplus funds to lend). Similarly, if exchange rate adjustments automatically restore balance between national exports and imports, then temporary trade imbalances need cause no concern. It is for those reasons that the pre-Keynesian view (which still has numerous adherents) produces a more laissez-faire inclination. It is this political complacency that Keynes and Keynesians have continually challenged.

The Keynesian view does not deny the existence of adjustment mechanisms. In that sense, Keynesian economics still has some of the features of an equilibrium theory. However, the Keynesian emphasis on changes in income, output, and employment as the principal adjustment mechanism leads to a quite distinctive interpretation of the problems of a capitalist economy. If the amount consumers plan to save exceeds the amount firms plan to invest, for example, the national income falls and the consumers are not able in practice to save as much as they originally intended. A recession restores the equilibrium of savings and investment. Similarly, if imports exceed exports, there will be a downward pressure on the national income, tending to reduce people's capacity to spend on imports, or on locally produced goods for that matter. Reduced material living standards occur. The adjustment mechanism in both cases is the overall level of economic activity. Therein lies the source of systemic instability, the cause of alternating booms and slumps, and the Keynesian rationale for significant government intervention in order to stabilise an otherwise unstable capitalist economic system.

Conclusion

The Keynesian analysis, focusing on the factors affecting the aggregate demand and supply for goods and services, provides a coherent explanation for some of the recurrent problems of capitalism. The explanation of the problems of unemployment and inflation is particularly powerful. The confidence in the capacity of economic policy to correct these flaws is an equally distinctive feature of Keynesian reasoning, contrasting with both Marxian and neoclassical perspectives. In this last respect, Keynesian economics has more in common with some of the more politically optimistic currents within institutional economics. The story becomes rather more complicated when the role of money in the economy is considered. Further sources of economic instability then arise, but also further opportunities for management of the economy as a whole.

KEY POINTS

- The volume of economic activity depends on the relationship between the aggregate demand for goods and services and the aggregate supply, or productive capacity of the economy as a whole.

- Aggregate demand is driven by consumer spending, business investment, government expenditure, and export sales. It is retarded by savings, taxes, and spending on imports.

- Fluctuations in these variables cause recurrent instability in the overall level of income, output, and employment, amplified by multiplier effects.

31 Instability in a Monetary Economy

Does money matter?

How do money markets, goods markets, and labour markets interact?

Is the economy naturally stable? Can it be more effectively stabilised?

Keynesian analysis interprets capitalism as a monetary economy. To understand it requires study of the aggregate demand for, and supply of, goods and services, as set out in the preceding chapter. More than that, it requires study of the significance of money itself in the economy.

An immediate difficulty must be confronted. People usually talk about money and income as if they were the same thing. This is understandable because we usually receive our income in the form of money, but an important analytical distinction between money and income must be made. Money comprises cash, most obviously, the notes and coins that are used to facilitate exchange. As normally defined by economists, it also includes other liquid assets, such as bank deposits, which can be readily converted into cash (by withdrawing funds from the bank or from an ATM).[1] Income, on the other hand, comprises payments that people receive as rewards for their work, as interest on their savings, as profits on their investments, or perhaps because of an inheritance or a lucky win while gambling. Income may be received in the form of money or in the form of goods and services.

Distinguishing between money and income is easy, but discerning their relationship is harder. Does the role of money in the economy facilitate or hinder the achievement of higher levels of national income? And does the use of money and the behaviour of financial institutions affect how the economy works, for better or worse? Does including such monetary considerations lead to a different view about the stability or instability of the economy? Does it lead to different prescriptions for economic management? Exploring these questions takes us into some of the more complex dimensions of Keynesian economics. We can start simply, by asking what is the significance of money in the general functioning of the economy. This draws attention to the role of money as a store of wealth as well as a means of exchange.

Does money matter?

Economists have sometimes said that money is a veil, a shroud that conceals the underlying economic fundamentals. It is certainly prominent on the surface of economic life: wages are usually paid in the form of cash, cheques, or deposits into a bank account, while prices of commodities are set in terms of the amount of money that must be paid for them. However, behind the appearances are real economic variables: the quantity of goods and services that a money wage can buy, and the quantity of one commodity that will exchange in the market for another. The use of money should not obscure these fundamental features.

This view of money as a veil applies to each of the principal currents of economic thought preceding Keynes, subject to relatively minor qualifications. Each sought to lay bare the economic foundations underpinning a monetary economy. Recall classical political economist Adam Smith's famous statement about the relative value of deer and beavers being determined by how much time must be spent catching them: the price of beavers can be specified in terms of deer without any direct mention of money. In Marxist economics, the ability of employers to appropriate some part of the value produced by labour shapes the relative income shares of capitalists and workers; money enters the story only as a means of facilitating the (unequal) exchanges. In neoclassical theory, the relative prices of different goods and services, and of factors of production, are determined by the forces of demand and supply; only when the focus shifts to the absolute level of prices does money enter the story.

In the real world, too, economic activities could continue without the use of money. We could rely instead on *barter*, which is the process of direct commodity exchanges. Life would not be easy, though. If you were paid your weekly wages in commodities—say, 10 loaves of bread, 6 litres of milk, one bicycle, and one pair of shoes—it would be most inconvenient. You might already have enough shoes, but might need a new pair of jeans, in which case you would need to find someone willing to exchange a pair of jeans that are surplus to that person's requirements for a pair of shoes that he or she wants. Similarly, if you already have a bicycle you might want to swap the new one for, say, a laptop computer; but it may be difficult and time consuming to find someone able and willing to do that deal. Life in a pure barter economy is complex.[2] It is easier if there is some common *medium of exchange*. Money usefully serves that function.

If that is all that money did, however, it would not be of fundamental economic importance. It would not significantly affect the overall level of economic activity, the sectoral composition of production and consumption, or the distribution of income and wealth. It could rightly be regarded as a veil shrouding the real economy. In building economic analysis, we might properly seek to strip it away in order to reveal the underlying forces at work.

Keynes took a quite different view, arguing that money does affect the functioning of the real economy, particularly the overall level of economic activity. This is because money is more than a means of exchange; it is also a *store of value*. It may be held in order to purchase assets when they are cheap in the hope of selling them subsequently for higher prices, thereby making speculative gain. Such speculation imparts a greater degree of uncertainty and instability to the economic system. The functioning of financial institutions also becomes important in determining the likelihood of prosperity or recession. That became particularly evident during the global financial crisis: many commentators argued that speculative elements in financial markets created the vulnerability to the crash, while failing financial institutions were one of its clearest manifestations. Money matters; an understanding of its influence is essential for managing the economy.

The demand and supply of money

Why hold money? At first sight, doing so seems illogical. Holding substantial amounts of cash, for example, incurs an obvious opportunity cost. The opportunity cost in this case is the income forgone by not putting that cash into some interest-earning form. If, instead of holding cash, you put your money into an interest-earning deposit account at a bank or other financial institution, you would be making your money work for you. As George Argyrous, from the University of New South Wales, puts it: 'Surely a rational person would either consume their income, and thereby gain immediate satisfaction, or else lend their income to a capitalist and thereby receive an interest payment which will increase their ability to consume in the future. Why give up present gratification for no reward when a reward is available? Money is barren—only a miser can get satisfaction from the holding of cash as such.'[3]

Keynes identified three reasons why rational people—not just misers—might, indeed, want to hold their wealth in a liquid form as cash or an 'at call' bank deposit. These constitute the three types of demand for money.

- *Transactions demand*
  We usually need to keep some money handy for our normal day-to-day shopping and other expenditures. If workers are paid weekly, for example, they need this pocketful of money to see them through to the next pay day. Less frequent, say monthly, payments could be expected to result in higher average amounts of money being held.

- *Precautionary demand*
  Some additional money may be kept handy as a safeguard against unforeseeable personal problems, such as ill-health or personal accidents, or to take advantage of opportunities that are difficult to foresee.

- *Speculative demand*
  Financial speculators may choose to hold money rather than interest-bearing assets so that they can quickly buy financial assets at a later date if the prospect of making capital gains is greater.

The first two of these three sources of demand for money can be expected to be pretty stable and predictable, rising and falling broadly in proportion to national income. The third is, potentially, much more volatile. Keynes, a successful financial speculator himself, thought that the speculative demand of money was particularly significant in determining how the economy functions—for better or worse.

Consider, for example, a speculator choosing between holding two types of asset: cash and government securities. These securities, sometimes called bonds, command a fixed rate of interest. If the current interest rate is 5 per cent, a bond costing $100 will yield a guaranteed

$5 annual income to its holder. That sounds more attractive than simply holding cash, does it not? There is no risk associated with government bonds, unlike with shares in corporations and other financial assets whose market prices are volatile. But what if the rate of interest applying to bonds were to rise to 8 per cent in the next year? The holder of this year's bond, earning only $5 per annum, would want out. The holder would want to sell the old bond in order to buy a new one that would give a higher yield. However, no one would buy that old bond at its face value of $100, because a new bond yielding 8 per cent interest would be a better deal. The old bond will sell in the market for only $100 $\times \frac{5}{8}$. So, selling it would entail a substantial capital loss. With the benefit of hindsight, it was a mistake to buy the bond in the first place. The speculator would have done better to hold cash and wait for the interest rate to rise before buying a bond. Of course, the problem is that one can never know for sure how interest rates will move in the future. So, whether speculators hold cash or interest-bearing assets depends crucially on their expectations about interest rate changes.

Why does any of this matter? If speculation were simply part of an economic sideshow in which people gambled against future price movements, sometimes making capital gains and sometimes making losses, it would be of no great significance (other than the diversion of human energies into what is essentially a zero-sum game of no public benefit). Keynes recognised that it is more than this. The activities of the speculators have real economic impacts that affect society as a whole.[4] This is partly because their speculative activities tend to have self-fulfilling effects.

Consider, for example, a situation in which speculators are anticipating a rise in interest rates. A surge in inflation or the nation's trade deficit often leads the financial media pundits to make such a prediction. Speculators will then want to hold cash rather than interest-bearing assets. They exhibit what Keynes called a strong *liquidity preference*. But if the supply of money is fixed, the speculators can only hold more cash if ordinary household savers hold less cash. That means a higher market rate of interest is necessary in order to induce household savers to put the cash that they would have otherwise held into buying interest-bearing financial assets. The effect of the speculators' actions has been to push the interest rate up. Their expectations have become self-fulfilling.

It sounds like a complicated process that produces a strange outcome. The role of the rate of interest is at the heart of the matter. Herein is a striking contrast between the neoclassical and Keynesian views about how the economy works. The neoclassicals expect interest rate changes continually to restore a balance between savings and investment, the market interest rate rising when investment exceeds saving (thus discouraging investment and encouraging saving) and falling when savings exceed investment (thus discouraging saving and encouraging investment). By contrast, Keynesians emphasise that market interest rates do not depend on the overall level of savings, but on whether people want to hold their savings as cash or as interest-bearing assets. But their liquidity preference itself depends on the prevailing rate of interest and predictions about its likely future movements. The overall effect is a tendency to economic instability, accentuated by self-fulfilling expectations.

Whether the monetary authorities can, or should, do anything to stabilise this otherwise unstable economy is an interesting question. The analysis so far has assumed that the supply of money is fixed; however, the supply of money in practice is variable. The key question is: who or what determines it? The standard Keynesian view is that it is a policy variable (similar, in this respect, to government expenditure, as analysed in the preceding chapter).[5] The supply of money may be varied by the central monetary authority (for example, the Reserve Bank), usually working in tandem with government for social goals, such as employment and the elimination of inflation. So, if speculative activities are causing interest rates to rise, thereby threatening to cause a recession, it is possible for the monetary authority to intervene in order to offset that tendency. It can, for instance, increase the money supply, which will normally cause interest rates to fall and thus encourage investment and economic growth.[6] From a Keynesian perspective, control of the money supply is, in principle at least, integral to stabilising an economy otherwise afflicted by undesirable fluctuations in the levels of income, output, and employment. It has to be done judiciously in order to avoid creating inflation, but it is an important policy instrument.

A rather different post-Keynesian view emphasises the supply of money being determined directly by the banks in the private sector. The banks can lend money to borrowers, including business investors, over and above what they have in deposits. Thus they create credit money directly in the act of bank lending. In effect, the supply of money continually adjusts to demand. The central bank can try to influence this process, but its influence is quite secondary to the pressure of demand for loans from the banks. As James K. Galbraith argues: 'The central bank ... does not control the money supply, only the excess reserves in the system. Banks may or may not lend all the excess reserves and the public may or may not demand loans sufficient to absorb them ... Money is therefore always and everywhere non-neutral. The dynamic consequence is business cycle instability.'[7]

An integrated Keynesian model

The analysis of money markets needs to be integrated with the macroeconomic analysis of the markets for goods and services in order to arrive at a total picture of how the economy works. Box 31.1 presents one analytical device conventionally used for this purpose. It is introduced here—with some reservations—mainly because it has been so influential in the teaching of a rather mechanistic, textbook interpretation of Keynesian economics.

One economic reviewer has argued that it was the embrace of this model by younger economists, rather than Keynes's own ideas as set out in *The General Theory*, that marked the start of what came to be known as the Keynesian revolution.[8] Perhaps its most useful feature is that it draws attention to the role of the rate of interest as a mechanism linking the markets for goods and money. If, for example, a high liquidity preference prevails among those with loanable funds, a high rate of interest is necessary in order to induce them to buy interest-bearing assets and thereby produce money market equilibrium. That high rate of interest will then affect the level of productive output and incomes via its negative impact on investment.

BOX 31.1	**A MECHANISTIC INTERPRETATION OF KEYNESIAN ECONOMICS**

One neat—perhaps too neat—representation of an integrated Keynesian model is the *IS/LM* diagram. It shows how the market for total goods and services interacts with the market for money. '*IS*' stands for investment and savings, '*LM*' for liquidity and money.

The *IS* curve indicates the various combinations of the rate of interest and national income that bring savings and investment into equality, thereby producing overall equilibrium in the market for goods and services. It is downward sloping to the right because the higher the rate of interest, the less the investment and, hence, the lower the national income.

The *LM* curve indicates the combinations of the rate of interest and national income that produce equilibrium in the money market. The higher the national income, the greater the transactions and precautionary demands for money, and the less money available for speculation (given a fixed supply of money at any time). Higher rates of interest are then needed to induce savers to purchase interest-bearing financial assets. So, higher national income is associated with higher interest rates. The curve slopes up to the right, indicating this generally positive relationship.

FIGURE 31.1 THE IS/LM ANALYSIS OF MACROECONOMIC EQUILIBRIUM

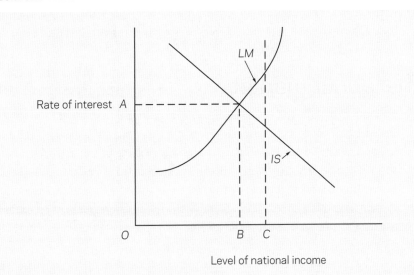

In the situation shown here, the goods and money markets are in simultaneous equilibrium when the rate of interest is at level *OA* and the level of national income is at *OB*. Keynesian economists using this model emphasise that there is no necessary connection between this equilibrium and the condition of full employment. The level of national income necessary to bring about full employment might, for example, be *OC*. It would be pure chance if *OB* and *OC* were to coincide. In other words, there is no market mechanism that ensures full employment.

This particular analysis also draws attention to how the money markets and markets for goods and services are linked through the level of national income. This is what was termed 'the diabolical adjustment mechanism' in the preceding chapter. This phrase is a reminder that such equilibrium processes that do exist in the economic system take effect through their impact on people's livelihoods.

However, the *IS/LM* analysis shown in Box 31.1 has limited application (and is somewhat out of tune with the general tenor of Keynes's own views) because it abstracts from the important role of *expectations* in the capitalist economy. Each *IS/LM* diagram is drawn for a given state of expectations that determine the marginal efficiency of capital and the liquidity preference and, therefore, the *IS* and *LM* curves respectively. A different set of expectations among investors and speculators would mean different positions for the *IS* and/or *LM* curves. Moreover, any change in expectations that causes a shift in one curve would tend to cause a shift in the other. So there may be no unique equilibrium at all.[9]

The *IS/LM* analysis is also limited in that it does not—indeed, cannot in this two-dimensional diagrammatic form—show how these variables are linked to labour market conditions. All one can say is that there is no necessary convergence between the equilibrium level of national income and the level that would be necessary to establish full employment. It would be quite accidental if the equilibrium level were also the full employment level. Further consideration of the labour market, including analysis of how technological change may affect the ratio of output to employment, is needed in order to assess the prospects for full employment in practice.

The labour market

Do income, output, and employment move together? So far, this has been assumed. When the output of goods and services is rising, more incomes are generated, and more employees will presumably be hired to produce the growing volume of products. Conversely, if output is shrinking, total income falls and jobs can be expected to become scarcer. It seems a reasonable assumption to make about the behaviour of the economy in the short term, when its productive capacity is relatively fixed. It is integral to the Keynesian reasoning as it explains changes in the number of people employed by reference to changes in the level of output and national income.

What view about the labour market is implied? Keynesians do not regard it as a market in which changes in wage rates ensure equilibrium. In this respect, Keynesian economics differs in both analytical construction and policy implications from neoclassical economics. Neoclassical economists tend to advocate wage reductions to deal with unemployment, since they see it as resulting from the excess supply of labour relative to the demand for labour. Where supply exceeds demand, the price (in this case, the wage rate) should fall. Any market imperfections that impede that outcome should be removed. Keynesians, on the other hand, usually point out that wages are generally not flexible downwards. Of course, wage cuts for particular groups of workers may, and do, occur; but workers, certainly those who are organised in trade unions, can be expected to use their collective organisational strength to resist such cuts. What does often happen, though, is that the real value of wages is eroded by inflation. That is one reason why trade unions advocate wage rises to protect the real purchasing power of their members. The apparent gains from a rising money wage may be eroded by further rises in the price of goods and services, so that there is no increase in the real wage (the quantity of goods and services that can be purchased with the money wage).

In any case, from a Keynesian perspective, a general policy of wage reduction is not a sensible economic strategy for dealing with unemployment because of its negative effects on the demand for goods and services and, therefore, on the demand for labour. Keynesians, while not necessarily aligned with working class interests, at least recognise the importance of wages as a source of aggregate demand. They emphasise the positive role of wage incomes in the realisation of surplus value (to use the Marxian terminology), rather than the more negative role (from a capitalistic viewpoint) of wage costs in the production of surplus value.

Over a longer period of time, another type of threat to full employment has to be considered. When the nature of technology is variable, labour displacement may occur, even though output is increasing. Most goods and services can be produced in various ways, and the type of technology a business chooses to use can be influenced by the prevailing level of wages relative to the cost of capital goods. So, if wage rates are rising relative to the cost of capital goods, labour displacement is likely. Generally, the effect of technological change is to open up possibilities for increasingly sophisticated methods of production, including automation. Under these circumstances, the conventional Keynesian assumption that income, output, and employment move together is less reasonable.

In the extreme case, increases in output may occur without any corresponding increases in employment. This is the controversial phenomenon of 'jobless growth'. In Keynes's time it could safely be ignored: the immediate task was to get the masses of unemployed people back to work by creating conditions conducive to economic expansion. During the more recent global financial crisis, a comparable immediacy was needed in economic policy to prevent a deepening recession. In the longer term, though, policies concerned with the redistribution of work—its more equitable sharing throughout the society—are likely to be of comparable importance in resolving the persistence of the unemployment problem.[10]

Conclusion

'Money', according to the old adage, 'makes the world go round'. Keynes showed that it also makes it go up and down. Monetary factors, especially those associated with speculation, impart particular sources of instability to the economy. Where speculators have a high liquidity preference, for example, the savings that would otherwise be available for productive investment may be diverted into speculative activities. Upward pressure is exerted on the market rate of interest, with potentially damaging consequences for investment, employment stability, and economic growth.

Keynes said that 'If the capital requirements of the economy are determined as a side-effect of a casino then the job is likely to be ill-done'.[11] He also expressed a broader concern about the adverse economic consequences of the persistence of the rentier class—those who derive incomes from the ownership of assets without contributing directly to productive activity. Keynes welcomed the prospect of the 'euthanasia of the rentier'.[12] In this respect, the Keynesian view is akin to Veblen's, at least in distinguishing between the contribution of those who use capital productively and those who pursue more predatory purposes. It contrasts with the Marxian view about the need to challenge the dominance of the capitalist class as a whole. What all these viewpoints—deriving from Marx, Veblen, and Keynes—have in common is the recognition of systemic structural flaws in the capitalist system. Politically, what distinguishes the Keynesian view is its emphasis on the role that governments can play in redressing these adverse aspects of the capitalist economy by seeking goals such as full employment without inflation.

KEY POINTS

- The analysis of capitalism as a monetary economy is a distinctive feature of Keynesian economics.

- People may hold assets in the form of money for transactions, precautionary, and speculative purposes. Their inclination to do so determines the overall liquidity preference in the economy, which influences the prevailing rate of interest and therefore affects the levels of investment and income.

- Additional sources of uncertainty arise because the response of the demand for labour to changes in national income also depends on technological change.

32 Macroeconomic Policy

Why is economic policy necessary?

What are the principal policy instruments advocated by Keynesian economists?

Do they work?

It is one thing to analyse capitalism; it is another to manage it. Most of the key decisions affecting the overall level of economic activity are taken by self-interested actors in the economic drama: employers, consumers, investors, and speculators. Yet we generally hold the elected governments of nation states responsible for the prevailing economic conditions. In certain respects it is a distinctively Keynesian legacy to hold governments, rather than capitalist businesses or the capitalist system in general, accountable for problems such as unemployment or inflation. It is based on a view of the state as the guardian of national economic performance.[1]

What should governments do? What follows from Keynesian economic analysis about the appropriate form of economic policy? How effective are such policies, and why have they not been more systematically implemented? This chapter explores these policy aspects of Keynesian economics.

The economic policy imperative

The argument that governments are responsible for national economic performance essentially rests on three pillars. First is the observation, stressed in the preceding three chapters, that the capitalist market economy is not adequately self-regulating. Keynes swept complacent laissez-faire views aside. In Galbraith's words:

> It was the historic achievement of John Maynard (later Lord) Keynes in the mid thirties, in the wake of numerous less reputable voices (who lacked Keynes' prestige and the savage reinforcement of the circumstances of the Great Depression), to destroy Say's Law virtually without trace and

therewith the illusion of a self-righting economy. After Keynes it was accepted that there could be a shortage (or surplus) of purchasing power in the economy and that neither wages nor interest rates reacted usefully to correct it. A reduction in wages might merely reduce purchasing power—aggregate demand, as it came to be called—yet more and make things worse. In the absence of sufficient demand even the lowest interest rates, as the Depression experience showed, would not encourage the needed investment and thus enhance demand. Stagnation would continue. The only answer was for the state to intervene.[2]

The recent global financial crisis has been a potent reminder of the enduring relevance of this Keynesian viewpoint.

The second pillar in the case for government economic policy has more to do with political philosophy than economic analysis. It is the view of the state as an instrument for the pursuit of social goals and, generally, as the embodiment of the public interest. Individuals may act on the basis of self-interest and greed, but the state can pursue nobler goals. This is an essentially liberal democratic stance, but also quite compatible with an evolutionary socialist perspective. As Rod O'Donnell, a scholar of Keynes's economics and philosophy, puts it, 'While rejecting laissez-faire capitalism and state socialism as global frameworks, Keynes sought a fusion or "amalgam" in which the best features of each could be retained and the worst discarded.'[3]

The third pillar is confidence in the capacity of the state to act systematically in the pursuit of the goal of social betterment. This does not deny the possibility that mistakes may be made; however, it does presume some coherence in the organisation of the state and its ability to apply economic policy in a deliberate manner. It requires, as a bare minimum, that the government should have good information about the national economy and an effective array of policy instruments with which to manage it.

BOX 32.1   NATIONAL ECONOMIC ACCOUNTING

Any management system depends on the existence of a good information base. For national economic management that means a comprehensive system of national economic accounting. Governments need to know the trends in national income, expenditure, output, and employment in order to judge whether particular forms of economic steering are appropriate. Historically, the development of Keynesian economics, together with the work of economists such as the Australian Colin Clark and the American institutionalist Wesley Mitchell, helped to establish consistent annual national economic accounts. Those national accounts use neither neoclassical concepts, such as marginal product and marginal cost, nor Marxist value categories, such as the rate of surplus value or the organic composition of capital. They use Keynesian economic concepts, such as aggregate consumption and investment expenditures, as discussed in the preceding three chapters.

There are normally three sections of the national income accounts, relating to national expenditure, income, and output. The expenditure tables show what is happening to consumer spending, investment spending, government spending, imports, and exports. The national income tables show the values of wages and salaries, profits, interest, and rents received. The output tables show the value added by different industries: agriculture, forestry and fishing, mining, manufacturing, and services, such as health, education, recreation, and entertainment. These three sets of statistical tables represent three ways of looking at the same national economy, and the three sets of statistical tables should, therefore, have consistent totals.

Ensuring the accuracy of these accounts is a problem. In practice, the estimation of the annual economic aggregates is rather rough and ready. Sometimes quite major revisions to each year's data occur, often over many subsequent years, as errors are located and new information comes to light. Quarterly national income accounts are worse still because the trends they show are commonly revealed by subsequent revisions to have actually been moving in the opposite direction. Such elements of unreliability in the data base make the process of managing the economy more difficult. If the government doesn't know for sure whether the economy is expanding or contracting, it cannot reliably determine the appropriate economic policy stance. However, the deficiencies of national income accounting are not an absolute impediment. Interpreted cautiously, and supplemented by other data sources, such as surveys of consumer confidence and business investment intentions, national income accounts provide a useful foundation for policy formulation.

Policy instruments

In addition to a good information base, economic management requires a range of effective policy instruments. It is useful in this regard to distinguish between policies for short-term macroeconomic stabilisation and policies to steer economic growth and development in the longer term. These may be seen as the two faces of Keynesian economic policy, reflecting liberal and radical interpretations of the contribution by Keynes. Fiscal and monetary policies are the basic stock-in-trade of the liberal interpretation, while the more radical view also embraces policies to shape the distribution of incomes, as well as the patterns of investment, industry development, and trade. Each policy requires careful consideration of its potentials and pitfalls.

Fiscal policy

Fiscal policy is the most direct means of managing the overall level of income, output, and employment in a national economy. It entails adjustments to government expenditure and taxation. Of course, governments usually do an annual stocktake of their spending and income anyway, and vary expenditure patterns and tax rates to accord with their political priorities. From a liberal Keynesian perspective, the key issue is the overall fiscal stance. This may be either expansionary or contractionary. The standard prescription is for a budgetary deficit (an excess of expenditure over taxation) to deal with recession and unemployment, and for a budgetary surplus (an excess of taxation over expenditure) to deal with excess demand and inflation.

This emphasis on judgments about deficits and surpluses stands in striking contrast to the pre-Keynesian view (subsequently revived as a new orthodoxy) that governments should seek a balanced budget. A balanced budget—not spending more than you earn—sounds like a prudent basis for household management, but, as Keynes emphasised, it is usually not good macroeconomics. Indeed, it is a fetish, standing in the way of more responsible judgments. In recent years, neoliberals have gone further, arguing for persistently surplus budgets, implying that anything less is symptomatic of inefficient or irresponsible government policy. Keynes would be turning in his grave. He thought that, over the whole of an economic cycle, perhaps spanning a decade or more, it would be sensible to balance expenditures and taxation levels roughly, but that, in any one year, it would be better to use fiscal policy in a counter-cyclical manner.

Deficits and surpluses tend to happen anyway, as the economy moves between periods of recession and growth. During a recession, social security expenditures rise because there are more claimants for unemployment benefits, for example. Meanwhile, tax revenues tend to fall because average incomes are lower and there are fewer people working. Income taxes and consumption taxes generate less revenue in those circumstances, so a natural tendency towards budgetary deficit exists during a recession. This is good, Keynesians argue, because that injection of government expenditure into the circular flow of income helps to raise the overall level of economic activity and bring the recession to an end. The reverse reasoning applies in a boom: government social security expenditures tend to fall and tax revenues tend to rise, causing a budget surplus that damps down the rate of economic growth and reduces potential inflationary pressures.

There is a strong case for supplementing these automatic stabilisers with discretionary fiscal policy to smooth out the ups and downs in the level of economic activity even more. On this reasoning, governments should run even larger deficits in times of recession in order to kickstart economic recovery, either by cutting tax rates or increasing expenditures. That is the best time to spend on infrastructure construction projects that will create jobs. In boom times, on the other hand, bigger surpluses can be engineered by increasing tax rates or cutting back on government spending.

There are significant pitfalls in the application of these discretionary fiscal policies. The timing has to be good, otherwise there is the danger that the policies may accentuate rather than dampen the amplitude of the economic cycle. The effect of fluctuations in government expenditure on investment expenditure in the private sector also needs to be considered. How changes in a government's fiscal stance affect volatile business expectations will have a major bearing on the macroeconomic outcomes. The distributional consequences of changing patterns of taxes and expenditures also warrants further attention, because there are always winners and losers in such policy changes. And, as a matter of political expediency, the relationship between the economic cycle and the political electoral cycle can be expected to have an influence on a government's fiscal policy stance. Increasing spending before elections in order to woo voters and increasing taxes after being elected may be effective, albeit cynical, politics;[4] however, it makes no positive contribution to, and may significantly undermine, macroeconomic stability.

These features notwithstanding, discretionary fiscal policy has the obvious appeal of providing a direct means of levelling out the ups and downs to which the capitalist economy is otherwise prone. It simultaneously extends political decision-making over the allocation of economic resources in order to achieve broader social goals.

Monetary policy

Governments may also influence the general state of the economy through their influence over the supply of money and the cost of borrowing it. The instruments of monetary policy can be used either as supplements or as alternatives to fiscal policy in a counter-cyclical economic strategy. Few would claim that monetary policy can contribute, like fiscal policy, to broader social goals in the long term, but it can have a significant effect on economic conditions in the short term.[5]

The relevant policy instruments, in principle, are clear. Governments directly control the issue of notes and coin; they may indirectly influence the extent to which banks and other financial institutions extend credit facilities; and they may determine the general direction of change in interest rates. Through these measures they can influence the levels of consumption and investment in the private sector of the economy and thereby seek to steer the economy towards a more stable growth path consistent with full employment without inflation.

In practice, things are much more complicated. Indeed, developments since Keynes's time bear heavily on how monetary policy can actually be applied. First, governments often do not have the policy instruments directly at their disposal. Monetary policy is commonly in the hands of central banks that have a considerable degree of independence from governments. The extent of such independence in policy varies: the German Bundesbank has had more than the Bank of England, and the Reserve Bank of New Zealand has more than the Reserve Bank of Australia, for example. The goals that the central banks should pursue (whether full employment or the control of inflation, for example) are also matters of intense political controversy in many countries. The dominant tendency seems to be towards the central banks being given more independence and asserting the control of inflation as their main, if not sole, concern. This makes monetary policy less directly amenable to a Keynesian policy agenda and undermines its coherence in relation to other aspects of government policy. So, when economic commentators talk about the policy mix between fiscal and monetary policies, it is important to remember that the responsible authorities are not necessarily the same. Sometimes they are not even working comfortably in tandem, notwithstanding the frequent exchange of information between them.

A second consideration is how monetary policy has been constrained by the process of financial deregulation that has taken place in many nations in the last three decades. Deregulation has meant that some of the direct controls over financial institutions that were previously exercised by governments and/or central banks have been relinquished. Its vigour has varied from country to country. Direct controls over how banks hold their assets (how much should be held as government securities, for example) and of how they allocate their lending (what proportion should go to house purchasers rather than businesses, for example) have been common casualties. The proponents of financial deregulation have consistently claimed that the result would be a more competitive and efficient banking sector but, in practice, the outcomes have often been rather different.[6]

The main effect of deregulation, as far as monetary policy is concerned, has been to leave the central monetary authority with indirect control over the general level of interest rates as its main, if not sole, remaining policy instrument. It can be a potent policy. Changes in the interest rate at which a country's central bank lends to other banks—known locally as the 'cash rate'—usually flow through into corresponding changes in the rates that banks charge, and pay, their customers. It tends to be a process of 'follow the leader', although individual financial institutions make their own judgments about how quickly and how closely to follow. The changes in prevailing interest rates then affect consumption and investment behaviour. Higher rates (a tight monetary policy) make debt more expensive and therefore tend to discourage both consumer spending and business investment, while low rates ('cheap money') can be expected to have a stimulatory effect. So interest rate policy can be a powerful means of influencing the overall level of economic activity.

As with fiscal policy, there are potential pitfalls. Indeed, the issue of timing is more crucial in the case of monetary policy. There are usually long and uncertain time lags between the policy process and its economic effects. It may be some time before the monetary authority sees the need for a policy adjustment (the recognition lag), and more time may elapse before it decides which particular adjustment to monetary policy is appropriate (the implementation lag). There may then be a significant period during which consumers and business people decide how to modify their plans for consumption and investment spending (the decision lag) and yet more time before those decisions affect the output of goods and services produced (the impact lag). By that time, the prevailing national economic conditions may be markedly different. In the worst-case scenario, a supposedly counter-cyclical policy can turn out to accentuate the amplitude of the cycle.

Monetary policy also tends to have a non-symmetrical impact. It is most powerful as a contractionary measure. Higher interest rates can be relied on to depress the level of economic activity. Raising the cost of borrowing money has a particularly strong impact on investment by small businesses and on home loans (and, therefore, on the construction industry). Monetary policy usually works less well in the opposite direction. Interest rate cuts will not necessarily stimulate business investment, for example, because businesspeople also have an eye on the market for their products. If they are experiencing stagnant demand and are pessimistic about future prospects, investment may stay low despite falling interest rates. At the time of the global financial crisis, official interest rates fell almost to zero in many countries, but the stimulatory effects were weak. Some countries had recourse to 'quantitative easing', whereby central banks were allowed to create 'money from nothing' by increasing their nominated assets with the specific purchase of buying government securities. Desperate measures indeed …

Finally, the impact of monetary policy is not selective. An increase in interest rates usually has depressing effects on investment levels throughout the economy. This can be problematic because different regions or industries in a nation may be experiencing quite different economic conditions; some may be buoyant, while others are economically stagnant. An interest rate rise designed to choke off inflationary pressures in booming regions may send other regions into recession. The same may occur with fiscal policy, but in that case there is the possibility of targeting public expenditures at particular regions or industry sectors according to the prevailing economic conditions in those regions or sectors. In the case of monetary policy, no such possibility exists. That is why it is sometimes called 'a heavy, blunt instrument'.

None of this means that monetary policy is redundant or unimportant. On the contrary, the monetary policy stance adopted by a government and/or the central bank normally has a significant bearing on the state of the economy. Its relationship to the government's fiscal policy stance—whether expansionary or contractionary—determines the policy mix (about which conventional economic policy commentators argue incessantly). However, if that were the be-all and end-all of government economic policy, it would be a very limited agenda. In practice, other policies may be more important in fostering the conditions for economic prosperity in the longer term. Such measures include incomes policy, investment and industry policies, and international economic policy.

Incomes policy

Incomes policies require a more extensive role for government in economic affairs. Managing the relative shares of wages, profits, rent, interest, and other incomes is no easy matter, but a number of policy instruments are available if governments choose to use them. The share of labour in the national income can be influenced by setting minimum wage standards or, where centralised arbitration systems exist, intervening generally in the processes of wage fixation. Direct controls over professional fees and rents may also be implemented in seeking to control non-wage incomes. Setting limits on executive remuneration has been widely advocated in recent years, because those managerial incomes have escalated so dramatically, notwithstanding the managerial practices that contributed to the global financial crisis. Disallowing such company payments as a legitimate expense to be set against the company's income in calculating its tax liabilities would be one mechanism for exercising that influence. Direct control over profits in general is harder in a capitalist economy, but, insofar as profit is a surplus payment, policies to control the other income sources that are costs to business can have some indirect effect.

Why would a government make these more extensive policy interventions? It may do so because of a concern with social equity, although that need not involve policies to influence income shares at source; it could equally be the focus of redistributive policies through taxation. A second, more macroeconomic, rationale for incomes policy is that income shares have a bearing on the overall level of economic activity. Consider, for example, a situation in which workers spend all their incomes but capitalists save a significant proportion of theirs. Under these conditions, a redistribution of income from capital to labour would increase the total level of consumption, fuelling aggregate demand and thus, ironically, adding to the income stream of capitalists, too, in the longer term. Capitalists, acting individually, would never seek to initiate such redistributions, although they would ultimately benefit from the resulting boost to the level of economic activity. Incomes policy requires government intervention because none of the other players in the economy has the capacity to implement it.

Of course, all government economic activity has distributional consequences. In practice, the issue is only whether incomes policy should be implicit and passive, or explicit and purposeful. If the latter, then it can be linked more directly to goals such as the pursuit of a more equitable society. Keynes himself thought that a less unequal income distribution would be economically and socially desirable. In his own words: 'I believe that there is social and psychological justification for significant inequalities of income and wealth, but not for such large disparities as exist today ... Much lower stakes will serve the purpose equally well, as soon as the players are accustomed to them.'[7]

Incomes policy in practice does not necessarily produce egalitarian outcomes. The Labour government in the United Kingdom in the 1970s, for example, adopted a 'social contract' with the trade union movement that emphasised control over wage increases to combat inflationary pressures, but the absence of any corresponding regulation of the incomes of capital led to the policy becoming widely regarded as a 'social con trick'. The Labor government in Australia between 1983 and 1996 also used an incomes policy, rather more successfully, as part of its Accord with the trade union movement, but it also eventually suffered loss of support because, among other reasons, the wage restraint was unmatched by any control over the sources and disposition of non-wage incomes.[8]

Investment and industry policies

From a Keynesian perspective, expenditure on investment in the economy is crucial for two reasons. In the short run, it boosts the level of effective demand, raising incomes, output, and employment. In the long run, it adds to productive capacity. Because it has an impact on both aggregate demand and aggregate supply, it is a key determinant of economic prosperity. Yet, as previously noted, when left purely in private hands, investment tends to be volatile, fluctuating according to changes in the 'animal spirits' of businesspeople. Is there a role for government here, too, in the regulation or direct control of investment expenditures?

Keynes used the memorably enigmatic phrase 'a somewhat comprehensive socialisation of investment' to indicate what he thought might be needed. To quote him in full:

> It seems unlikely that the influence of banking policy on the rate of interest will be sufficient by itself to determine an optimum rate of investment. I conceive therefore that a somewhat comprehensive socialisation of investment will prove to be the only means of securing an approximation to full employment; though this need not exclude all manner of compromises and of devices by which public authority will cooperate with private initiative.[9]

Not surprisingly, debate continues about what is implied by such an open-ended policy prescription. Possibilities include joint ventures between government and private sector enterprises, and interventionist industry policies designed to create the conditions for more stable and/or buoyant patterns of private-sector investment. Although Keynes did not personally favour the extension of government ownership of key industry sectors (nationalisation), a similar logic could apply. Because investment is so important to the state of the economy, it cannot sensibly be left to businesspeople alone.

One particularly interesting possibility arises from the expansion of superannuation schemes in recent decades. Workers' savings in those superannuation funds could be systematically steered into investment projects of national economic benefit. This would build a direct bridge between savings and investment. The savings in the superannuation funds—'pension funds', as they are sometimes called—are normally invested in shares, government bonds, real estate, and other financial assets in order to maximise private rates of return. Capitalist investment criteria currently prevail. If, instead, the process were coordinated through a national investment fund, the savings could be channelled into the development of particular industries that the government wishes to promote: technologically advanced sectors requiring substantial research and development expenditures, for example, or industries conducive to more ecologically sustainable development. 'Picking winners' this is sometimes called, especially by critics who are worried by the possibility of governments picking losers. Some nations, such as Sweden, have used national investment schemes as instruments for successful industry development.[10] Some level of public sector investment is integral to the financing of infrastructure and public goods, anyway—a fact acknowledged as necessary by economists ever since Adam Smith. The issue in practice is deciding on the most appropriate public–private balance and how best to achieve it.

The international context

The assumption of a national economy, and of the possibility of managing it systematically, pervades most discussion of Keynesian economics. However, policies that treat the national economy as if it were a closed economy are of limited effectiveness. This was so in Keynes's time; it is even more so in the current age of globalisation. A modest response to this challenge involves using policy instruments that impinge on the relationship between the national economy and the rest of the world. Exchange rate policy and tariff policies, for example, can be used. A more ambitious response is to seek to influence the broader international economic conditions themselves, through international agreements on trade, debt, and taxation.

It is axiomatic that a nation's external sector has a significant bearing on its level of income, output, and employment. The standard Keynesian macroeconomic analysis shows that a trade deficit will have an economically depressing effect, unless offset by a government budgetary deficit (and the latter may not be a sustainable option if the trade deficit persists across all stages of the economic cycle). Putting *tariffs* on imported goods is a direct means of addressing the problem, for a tariff operates as a tax, the effect of which is to make imports relatively more expensive for domestic consumers. Whether the effect is to reduce expenditure on imports depends on their elasticity of demand, which in turn depends on the availability, price, and quality of locally produced alternatives. There are also some strategic considerations, such as whether the imposition of tariff protection is likely to cause other national governments to retaliate by increasing tariffs to give more protection to their own industries. They do not necessarily do so, but, if they do, export sales may decline along with import expenditures.

Some similar considerations apply in respect of *exchange rate* policy. If the relativities between currencies are not fixed, governments may seek to manipulate the exchange rates in order to achieve better trade outcomes. Central banks sometimes intervene as buyers and sellers in foreign exchange markets, usually in the attempt to stabilise otherwise volatile currency prices. They may even make a profit if they buy their own country's currency when its price is falling and if that purchase turns out to be effective in reversing the trend. In the longer term, the key question is: what exchange rate will have the most beneficial effect on the trade balance? It is often said that a lowered value of the local currency helps in this regard, since it makes locally produced goods cheaper, and therefore more competitive, in international markets, while making imports dearer in the local currency. Whether this does actually improve the trade balance depends, again, on the elasticity of demand for those exports and imports. It seems that there are few certainties in managing the external sector.

Keynes thought that these nationally based policy instruments needed to be complemented by more proactive interventions in the international arena. The key question in Keynes's day was what international monetary arrangements would be conducive to prosperity in the world economy following the devastating effects of the Great Depression and the Second World War. At the Bretton Woods conference, Keynes was opposed to the adoption of floating exchange rates; he wanted a scheme for expanding international finance, including an expanded international currency unit (Bancor) that would not need to be fully backed by gold or international currencies. The outcome of the Bretton Woods negotiations was closer to the proposal advocated by Harry White, the American representative, which gave a more central role to the US dollar as an international reserve currency. But Keynes's energetic participation was not in vain; it contributed to an agreement that did create more stable conditions for the settlement of international debts and which helped foster growth—in the more advanced economies at least. The subsequent quarter-century long boom rested, in part, on these international political economic arrangements.

In our own time, there is a quite different proposal for international economic cooperation, the *Tobin tax*, first proposed by US Keynesian economist James Tobin, winner of the 1981 Nobel Prize in Economic Sciences. The Tobin tax is advocated as a means of discouraging international currency speculation. It would be a tax on all international transactions, probably set somewhere in the range of 10 to 25 cents per $100 value of currency transacted. Its effect would hit hardest at currency transactions of a short-term, speculative nature, rather than at those directly concerned with the financing of international trade and investment. Whether it would, indeed, discourage speculation would depend on the rate at which the tax was set, but if it did not do so it would generate considerable revenues that might be used to help the development of poorer nations in the world economy. That would depend, of course, on there being effective monitoring and compliance, based on intergovernment agreements to enforce a uniform system. At present, it remains a pipe dream, but today's pipe dream can be tomorrow's policy.[11] The global financial crisis has given considerable momentum to this policy proposal as a potential means of reducing the vulnerability of the world economy to volatile movements of speculative capital.

Conclusion

Managing a capitalist economy is never easy. Many of the key decisions are in private rather than public hands. Governments can seek to play a steering role. Keynesian political economy indicates how to do so, showing the data requirements, the necessary policy instruments, and the principles and pitfalls that determine their use. A key ingredient in this policy process is political will. Keynes argued that governments could and should strive towards important social goals through the pursuit of policies to expand job opportunities and create the conditions for long-term prosperity.

Given that political will, there are numerous weapons in the armoury of government economic policy. There is potentially much more to a comprehensive Keynesian policy approach than merely fine-tuning the level of aggregate demand in a national economy. However, assumptions about the adequacy of economic analysis and of economic information, such as national income accounting, underpin these policy prescriptions. So do political economic judgments about the nature of the state, its capacity to use the policy instruments effectively, and the ethical basis of public policy. Not surprisingly, these are matters of disagreement. They were in Keynes's time, and they are today. This helps to explain why the political economy of Keynes is such a contested legacy.

KEY POINTS

- Fiscal and monetary policy instruments are those most commonly associated with a Keynesian policy approach to macroeconomic fine tuning.

- A broader interpretation of Keynesian economics also emphasises that incomes policy, investment policy, industry policy, exchange rate policy, and trade policy are important means of producing a more buoyant economy in the long term.

- The capacity of the state to implement these policies systematically depends on macroeconomic analysis, national income accounting, and political will.

33 The Keynesian Legacy

> *Was there a Keynesian revolution?*
>
> *Why did Keynesian policy prescriptions fall from favour—and then return?*
>
> *How useful is post-Keynesian economics?*

'In the long run we are all dead' is the one quotation from Keynes that students invariably get right (while usually missing his point). 'Yes, but not all at once,' added Joan Robinson later. A focus on resolving short-run economic problems is necessary, socially and politically, but it is not enough. Dealing with unemployment was the immediate priority in Keynes's time and, although that problem is currently less acute, it has become reestablished as a seemingly permanent feature of modern capitalist economies. Achieving full employment is still an important issue. Keynes was also concerned, more generally, with the conditions conducive to economic and social progress. Joan Robinson's quip is a reminder that society, as an ongoing entity, has to be concerned with those long-term goals.

How have Keynes's ideas fared in this context? We conclude our consideration of Keynesian economics by looking at its influence and the subsequent backlash against it. How could it have once commanded widespread respect but become vulnerable to the resurgence of pre-Keynesian views? Why has it experienced a recent revival and what are its prospects now?

Foundations for a partial revolution

Keynes expected his *General Theory* to 'largely revolutionise ... the way the world thinks about economic problems'.[1] Indeed, his ideas had a dramatic impact on economic analysis and policy between the 1930s, when his *General Theory* was published, and the 1970s, when his ideas proved vulnerable to the attack mounted by the monetarist economists.

The initial resistance to Keynesianism was strong among academic economists and among businesspeople and politicians who were uncomfortable with the interventionist approach to the management of capitalism that his ideas implied.[2] However, the force of actual political economic circumstances was decisive. Economic conditions had been improving slowly during the middle to late 1930s, but sharply deteriorated again in 1937–38. The Second World War restored full employment to the capitalist nations. War preparations had already reduced unemployment in Nazi Germany, prompting Galbraith's subsequent ironical remark that Adolf Hitler was 'the true protagonist of the Keynesian ideas'.[3] Keynes would not have approved, of course, favouring employment for socially useful, peacetime production, but, in purely macroeconomic terms, the effect was similar. Many people who might otherwise have been unemployed were enlisted in the armed forces by both sides in the military conflict; others were employed in industries producing munitions, uniforms, and so on. In nations partly cut off from international trade by naval blockades, more land was brought under cultivation to feed the citizenry. The whole process—the war effort—was coordinated by the respective national governments.

The war itself inflicted widespread economic devastation on the countries at the centre of the action. In the victorious and the defeated nations, the bombing destroyed houses, factories, bridges, roads, railways, ports, and electricity supply systems. After the war, this infrastructure had to be rebuilt. Even in nations geographically distant from the principal theatres of war (such as Australia and mainland USA), a major backlog in the building of houses and social infrastructure had developed because resources had been diverted to the war effort. When the war ended there was much work to be done, which ensured the continuation of full employment, although the transition from military to peacetime production was not always smooth.

Politically, too, this economic reconstruction and expansion was imperative. People make enormous personal sacrifices during times of war, forgoing much of the consumption they normally enjoy. Their homes may be bombed and sometimes family members killed or maimed. Such sacrifices need to be justified as the price to be paid in the struggle for a better society, or at least compensated for by a significant social dividend. After the Second World War, it was inconceivable that the people who had made such sacrifices would tolerate a return to the conditions of the Great Depression. A more prosperous and secure society had to be engineered in the victorious nations. Having won the war, it was now necessary to win the peace.

Meanwhile, the countries that lost the war would have to be reconstructed under international supervision—a process dominated in practice by the USA. The shortsightedness of impoverishing the defeated nations through punitive war reparations had been realised in the years following the end of the First World War. Keynes had warned at the time about the likely adverse consequences of pursuing that strategy and, in practice, the rise of fascism had proved his point. For all the capitalist nations, victors and vanquished alike, policies to promote economic prosperity were the priority after the Second World War.

These political economic conditions were fertile ground for the acceptance and implementation of Keynesian economics. Governments in the major capitalist nations committed themselves to the pursuit of full employment as the primary economic objective. The British government, for example, formally committed itself to full employment in 1945, and the Australian government issued a White Paper on full employment in the same year. In the USA, the *Employment Act* of 1946 proclaimed 'the continuing policy and responsibility of the Federal government to use all practical means ... to promote maximum employment, production and purchasing power'.

Concurrently, the foundations for a more extensive welfare state were being laid, with governments in the leading capitalist nations introducing legislation to extend social security provisions, provide more public housing, provide better public education, and (with the notable exceptions of the USA and Australia) establish publicly funded national health services.[4] Public sector employment expanded. Firms in the private sector also received a boost from the stimulus to the demand for their products and, as a result, took on more employees in order to expand output and make more profit. The marriage of Keynesian economics and welfare state commitments proved remarkably fruitful. Some say it was the saviour of capitalism in those turbulent times.

Whether, and to what extent, the subsequent long boom in the major capitalist economies was a product of Keynesian economic policies continues to be a matter of controversy. Sometimes the causal connection is simply assumed. The period from the late 1940s to the early 1970s was one of sustained economic growth in the major capitalist nations, with full or near-full employment and generally low rates of inflation (with the significant exception of the Korean War period in the early 1950s, when inflation surged). Keynesianism was the official basis of policy, right up to the early 1970s when US President Richard Nixon made the famous statement, 'We are all Keynesians now' (just when it was ceasing to be true). *Ergo*, Keynesianism caused the long boom. One may equally posit the reverse causation: the prosperity of capitalism made some degree of Keynesian policy interventionism tolerable to the corporate interests who would otherwise have vigorously opposed it. One thoughtful analyst of the period suggests that, to the extent that government policies underpinned the long boom, they were more to do with policies for industry development and the building of appropriate regulatory institutions than Keynesian macroeconomic demand management.[5]

One of the problems of making grand claims about Keynesian policies underpinning the long boom is that Keynesianism then takes the blame for its eventual collapse. And collapse it did. In most of the advanced capitalist nations in the 1970s, economic growth stalled, unemployment rose, and inflation surged. Was this indicative of a failure of Keynesianism? Left-wing critics, drawing on Marxist analysis, say that it showed Keynesianism to be incapable of resolving the inherent structural contradictions of capitalism.[6] The contradiction between the necessary conditions for the production and realisation of surplus value remains. Keynesian policies, boosting aggregate demand, facilitate the realisation of surplus value. If those same policies cause wage levels to rise (and if labour gains more bargaining power when full employment prevails), the conditions for the production of surplus value are eventually undermined. So, the tendency towards economic crisis reasserts itself.

Echoing some of these concerns, but couching them in more acceptably conservative language, was the right-wing critique of Keynesianism. Milton Friedman argued that Keynesianism in practice caused more problems than it solved. As he saw it, the extension of state intervention during the years of the long boom caused inflation and, more generally, throttled the dynamism of the free-enterprise system. Friedman's view is that Keynesian attempts to fine tune the economy should be abandoned. According to Friedman, economic policy should simply ensure the steady expansion of the money supply at a rate matching the long-term growth of economic output. This is the essence of the monetarist position that was embraced—but not consistently implemented—by right-wing politicians in the 1970s and 1980s.[7]

BOX 33.1

MILTON FRIEDMAN (1912–2006)

Milton Friedman is the best known of the right-wing economists responsible for the ascendancy of neoliberalism in economic analysis and policy. In the 1950s and 1960s, while teaching at the University of Chicago, Friedman was a persistent exponent of free-market economics. His stridently free-enterprise views and antipathy to Keynesianism made him a somewhat marginal figure. He was at odds with the economics profession's general acceptance of the pragmatic marriage of Keynesian macroeconomics and microeconomics (what the more liberal-interventionist economist Paul Samuelson proclaimed as the 'neoclassical synthesis'). Friedman's methodological view, that the test of an economic theory is not the reasonableness of its assumptions but only the accuracy of its predictions, was also widely regarded as extremist.

From early in his career, Friedman showed a willingness to combine economics with politics. His book *Capitalism and Freedom*, published in 1962, made an explicitly political case against any semblance of economic collectivism. It was in tune with Cold War ideology, emphasising the virtues—political and economic—of the free-enterprise system.

When, in the 1970s, there was a sudden intensification of economic problems in the capitalist nations, it seemed as if Friedman's time had come. He had a political platform for his critique of Keynesianism and his advocacy of a neoliberal alternative. His monetarist views, based on the pre-Keynesian quantity theory of money, were supported by empirical economic analysis founded on the extreme methodological proposition that he had earlier enunciated. Inflation, he sought to demonstrate, was the product of too much expansion of the money supply fuelled by excessive government intervention in the economy. Politicians such as then British prime minister Margaret Thatcher seized on his laissez-faire prescriptions. Milton Friedman became a household name, synonymous with monetarism and the broader political program of 'slimming the state'. In Chile, after the 1973 US-backed overthrow of the government of Salvadore Allende, US-trained economic advisers (known as 'the Chicago boys') recommended a yet more audacious experiment in free-market economics. Policies of privatising public enterprises, and removing government regulation of business, led to glaring disparities in the distribution of income and wealth.[8]

Friedman can claim to have rivalled J. K. Galbraith as the most popular interpreter of contemporary economic affairs in the late twentieth century—although consistently arguing from an opposite political position. He made a television series of his best-selling book, *Free to Choose*. His combination of neoclassical economics and right-wing libertarian politics was distinctive and highly influential.

Monetarism and the new classical revival

Monetarism has its roots in pre-Keynesian economics, specifically, in the quantity theory of money. This is most simply expressed as the equation of exchange:

$$MV \equiv PQ$$

In this formulation, M is the money supply, V is the velocity of circulation (the rate at which money moves around the economy), P is the general price level for goods and services (a measure of inflation), and Q is the output of goods and services produced in the economy. This equation of exchange is written as an identity ($\equiv$) because its proponents say it is true by definition; thus, for any given level of output (Q), changes in the money supply (M), and the price level (P) will always move together, assuming the velocity of circulation (V) is fixed. In other words, the effect of increases in the money supply, over and above increases in the volume of goods and services produced, is always to raise the general price level. Expansionary monetary policy causes inflation. So, too, will expansionary fiscal policy, if the government finances the budgetary deficits by money supply increases.

According to monetarists, inflation is a scourge: it erodes the value of savings, creates greater economic uncertainty among consumers and investors, and becomes self-perpetuating because it comes to be built into consumers' and investors' expectations and the behaviour resulting from those expectations. However, since its cause is clear—excessive growth in the money supply—its remedy is equally obvious. Governments must manage a slower and steadier expansion in the supply of money that is just sufficient to match the growth in the output of goods and services.

Monetarists acknowledge that there are some safety valves. If workers are willing to work harder at the current wage rate, for example, total output can be raised and the inflationary pressures alleviated. Alternatively, inflationary pressures are reduced if households are willing to save more of their income at the current rate of interest; the problem of 'too much money chasing too few goods' then becomes less severe. In both cases, sacrifices must be made—harder work and deferral of the gratification from consumption. Austerity, targeted particularly at the working class and those benefiting from an expansion of state support, is the implied antidote to the forces that otherwise fuel inflation. As former Australian prime minister Malcolm Fraser (himself only a half-hearted convert to monetarism) said at the time when monetarism was coming into vogue, 'Life wasn't meant to be easy.' It certainly is not easy when monetarists are in charge.

On closer examination, the monetarist interpretation of the equation of exchange can be seen to rest on some dubious assumptions. The economy is taken to be operating at full capacity, for example. If it were not, it is possible that an increase in the money supply could flow through into increased output. The monetarist assumption of a fixed velocity of circulation (V) is also questionable. In practice, the speed with which money circulates may vary according to institutional factors, such as how frequently people are paid and how much cash they choose to hold for transactionary and precautionary purposes. If changes in the money supply interact with changes in the velocity of circulation, the direct relationship between M and P (the posited inflationary effect of expanding the money supply) ceases to be inexorable. But questioning assumptions in this way is not a characteristically Friedmanite methodology. Look at the evidence, Friedman would say, not at the reasonableness of the underlying assumptions.[9] And the evidence, during the 1970s in particular, revealed the emergence of a dual problem of unemployment and inflation, or 'stagflation' as it came to be known. This heralded a new era of troubled economic times. Its interpretation in terms of the Phillips curve is set out in Box 33.2.

BOX 33.2   A TRADE-OFF BETWEEN UNEMPLOYMENT AND INFLATION?

The Phillips curve is a popular means of interpreting the relationship between unemployment and inflation. It takes its name from a diagram constructed by A. W. Phillips, a New Zealand economist working in London during the 1950s (also the inventor of the hydraulic Keynesian model mentioned in Chapter 30). He studied the levels of unemployment and inflation in the British economy over a number of years and found a generally inverse relationship. The years when unemployment was high generally had low inflation, while the years when unemployment was low typically featured a higher rate of inflation.

FIGURE 33.1 THE PHILLIPS CURVE

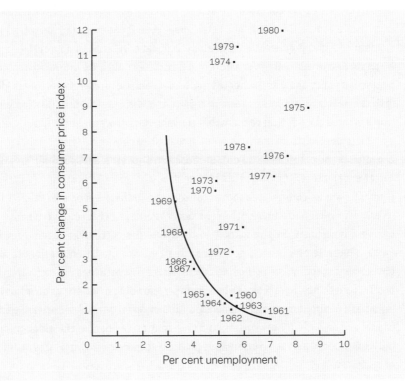

The nature of this unemployment–inflation relationship evidently changed throughout the major capitalist nations in the 1970s. Figure 33.1 (on the previous page) plots conditions in the USA. Join the dots. The scatter of observations for the 1960s suggests a pretty standard Phillips curve relationship (as represented by the line drawn through the lower part of the scatter). Then, starting in 1970, things seem to go haywire. Some years (1970-71, 1972-73, 1974-75, 1977-78) exhibit the normal inverse relationship, but others (1969-70, 1973-74, 1979-80) show unemployment and inflation rising together; while others (1971-72, 1975-76, 1976-77) show unemployment and inflation falling together. It seems pretty chaotic.

What had gone wrong? An empirical description cannot indicate the causal factors underlying this change in the patterns of unemployment and inflation. Posited explanations were plentiful at the time: some blamed trade unions (for seeking wage increases in excess of labour productivity growth); others blamed governments (for the failures of macroeconomic fine-tuning). Reviewing the state of professional opinion, one orthodox economist concludes that the 'inflation-unemployment trade-off has a secure place in economics … [but] the bad news is that the dynamic relationship between inflation and unemployment remains a mystery'.[10]

Keynesian economics, at least in its mechanistic interpretations, had difficulty in coming to terms with stagflation. In the simple Keynesian model, there is either unemployment (in which case an expansionary approach to demand management is warranted) or inflation (requiring a contractionary demand management policy stance). Coping with the two problems simultaneously is problematic, both analytically and in terms of appropriate policy response. No doubt Keynes himself—ever astute and flexible—would have proffered a solution. The more pedestrian policy analysts—schooled in the mechanistic interpretation of his ideas associated with the neoclassical synthesis—were thrown into disarray when stagflation hit in the 1970s, which created the political vacuum that the monetarists were able to fill.

The monetarists at the time argued against expansionary fiscal policies (as right-wing economists and politicians still do). Because extra government spending 'crowds out' private-sector expenditure, they say, it is impotent as a means of boosting the national economy. It might even be counterproductive, causing the national income to fall. So it is important to ask why such 'crowding out' might occur. Perhaps because governments compete with business investment in the market for loanable funds, thereby driving up interest rates. Perhaps because of a general political antipathy by capitalist enterprises to any increase in government spending, bringing on a capital strike. The evidence for such effects is sketchy, at best.[11] If anything, there seems to be a stronger 'crowding in' effect, as government spending—on infrastructure, for example—opens up further opportunities for private sector profits and capital accumulation. Notwithstanding this contrary evidence, the assumption of 'crowding out' continues to pervade conservative political economic discourse. It is an influential legacy of monetarism.

The case against running budget deficits as a conscious macroeconomic policy measure has also been buttressed by the so-called 'twin deficits' thesis, which posits a link between government budgetary deficits and external current account deficits. Like the evidence for crowding out, the evidence supporting a twin deficits connection is flimsy, at best. Some government spending may directly increase imports (such as the purchase of foreign-made fighter aircraft), but other government spending may help to increase exports (such as research and development subsidies or industry development policies to assist local firms). There is no reliable general connection between the size of budgetary deficits and current account deficits in practice.[12]

The monetarists' critique of fiscal policy did not, contrary to widespread popular belief, lead to an advocacy of stronger reliance on monetary policy. Monetarists emphasise the pitfalls in using *both* monetary and fiscal policies as instruments of fine tuning (as discussed in the preceding chapter). What they favour is for a slower and steadier expansion of the money supply that is just sufficient to match the growth of output. They reject the use of discretionary monetary policy aimed at smoothing the economic cycle. This is the essence of the pursuit of a simple monetary rule as the principal instrument of economic policy. More extreme monetarists—to the political right of Milton Friedman, if that is possible—have argued even against that, saying that government should have no role at all, and should leave the creation and control of money to the private sector.

Perhaps the most distinctive feature of monetarism, as it came to be adopted in practice, was the emphasis on the need to 'fight inflation first'. The case for so doing is usually argued in terms of the need, as monetarists see it, to restore the economic system to its natural equilibrium state, before excessive government intervention and excessive wage demands had triggered the inflationary process. The effect of so doing is to jettison the commitment to full employment. Instead, monetarists argue that, in place of full employment, a natural rate of unemployment should be allowed to prevail. This is commonly defined as a non-accelerating inflation rate of unemployment (NAIRU). Formally, this is the rate of unemployment below which the tendency towards inflation in the economy becomes pronounced. In practice, supporters of this concept use it to justify, more or less, whatever rate of unemployment currently prevails.[13]

Why bother with monetarism? It was a fad that petered out in the 1980s, as successive governments abandoned their official commitment to the sort of monetary targeting that Friedman advocated. Few economists would call themselves monetarists now, preferring the labels 'new classical' and 'new Keynesian'. Some have asserted the existence of a 'new consensus' on monetary theory and policy. This rejects the simple monetary rule of a targeted steady expansion of the money supply, preferring the use of interest rate policy to keep inflation low. In practice, there is considerable continuity with monetarist reasoning. The NAIRU continues to feature prominently in government policy documents. The preference for monetary policy over fiscal policy seems to have become institutionalised. One reviewer of the state of play in macroeconomic theory and policy concludes that 'The influence of monetarism on how we all think about macroeconomics today has been deep, pervasive and subtle', indeed, so pervasive as to constitute 'intellectual hegemony'.[14] Early in the twenty-first century, governments and central bankers continued to prioritise the control of inflation over policies for full employment, even though the inflationary tendencies of the 1970s had not recurred. Most capitalist countries were back at the low inflation–high unemployment end of the Phillips curve (see Box 33.2, on p. 309).

The onset of the global financial crisis in 2007–08 was a major challenge to this complacency, of course. Most governments responded in a time-honoured Keynesian manner. They increased their own expenditures in order to generate an offsetting fiscal stimulus and, in conjunction with central banks, lowered official interest rates to encourage renewed investment. The conception of an economic system that could be left to self-regulate was revealed as laughable. Yet the Keynesian policy revival soon had its critics, warning that the medicine might be more dangerous than the disease. The budgetary deficits, and associated public debt, became a target for particular criticism, and strong political pressures developed in support of austerity measures. In the UK in 2010, the newly elected Conservative–Liberal Democrat government introduced draconian cuts to public expenditure in its first budget. Other countries' attempts to pass the costs of the capitalist crisis on to working people—in the form of reduced government-funded services and higher ages to qualify for pensions, for example—provoked substantial backlash. The conservative antipathy to government deficit budgeting has evidently not been displaced by Keynesian reasoning. The simple analogy with prudent household budgeting—an analogy that Keynes argued was quite misleading—remains deeply entrenched.

Meanwhile, despite the increased focus on fiscal policy during the global financial crisis, monetary policy continues as the principal policy tool to control the economic cycle. This is ironic in that the pervasive problems associated with monetary policies (also described in Chapter 32) featured prominently among the reasons earlier put forward by monetarists for the adoption of a simpler, long-term monetary rule. It is doubly ironic that, in the meantime, financial deregulation has effectively left pressure on interest rates as the only available policy instrument—and that is usually in the hands of central bankers rather than elected governments. Indeed, proponents of the so-called 'new consensus' are emphatic that central bank independence from government is the precondition for effective monetary policy.[15] This means that the control of the economy slips away and passes from democratic institutions to bodies that are appointed rather than elected.

Perhaps the most extreme form of anti-Keynesian economics comes in the form of the 'policy ineffectiveness' proposition. Here is the claim that, because people have rational expectations about the future, economic policy is generally impotent. People anticipate the consequences of any change in policy and, by modifying their behaviour appropriately, negate its effects. According to this reasoning, as people come to know more about the economy and anticipate government policy changes, the policies become ineffective. If rational people know that economic policies have no effect, the policies in practice work only if people make systematic errors. This sort of reasoning is typical of what has come to be known as *new classical* economics.[16] Its emphasis on individual choice and equilibrium outcomes gives new classical economics more in common, analytically and politically, with neoclassical economics than with classical political economy. Like the posited 'natural rate of unemployment', the effect of the policy ineffectiveness proposition is to buttress neoliberal free-market ideology. Notwithstanding some analytical novelty, the practical upshot looks more like a revival of an old-time religion.

Post-Keynesian economics

Where does all this leave Keynesian economics today? Rather schematically, two types of Keynesian economics can be identified. One is what has earlier been called the mechanistic interpretation of Keynes, illustrated by the analysis in Box 31.1. Analytically, it stresses the equilibrium tendencies in the macroeconomic system, albeit not guaranteeing full employment. Politically, it accepts the case for a limited set of discretionary fiscal and monetary policies to fine tune the economy, reconciling equilibrium with full employment, but otherwise leaving the economy to function largely according to the principles of private enterprise. In the economics textbooks, this is the interpretation of Keynes that Paul Samuelson proudly proclaimed as the 'neoclassical synthesis', combining neoclassical microeconomics with a mechanistic interpretation of Keynesian macroeconomics. It is what Joan Robinson later called, rather less flatteringly, 'bastard Keynesianism': the illegitimate product of marrying Keynes to neoclassical theory. 'Neo-Keynesianism' is a less pejorative term. It always suffered from a problem of incoherence because it spliced together a microeconomics emphasising the general desirability of free markets and a macroeconomics stressing the need for recurrent government intervention.

This mainstream (mis)interpretation of Keynesian economics was the obvious casualty of the stagflation era and the monetarist assault. Many of the orthodox economics textbooks have since been purged of their residual neo-Keynesianism, a process that their authors have sometimes sought to justify by claiming the need for better developed 'micro foundations of macroeconomics'.[17] Such a quest for greater analytical coherence is reasonable. The problem is that coherence is (re)established on the neoclassical terrain. In effect, it constitutes a return to pre-Keynesian economic theory, but under the name of new classical economics. Concurrently, in the policy arena, the primary emphasis of government policies switched from macroeconomic management to 'microeconomic reform'.[18] This is no coincidence. This policy push, which has focused on labour-market deregulation, privatisation, and trade liberalisation, has been part of the reassertion of free-market economics. It constitutes a return to pre-Keynesian economics in the realm of public policy.

A second, quite different, interpretation of Keynes is possible, which provides the basis for a more progressive post-Keynesian economics. This places more emphasis on Keynes's view of the economy as an inherently unstable system; indeed, one might argue, not really a system at all. The crucial but volatile character of investment—responding to the 'animal spirits' of businesspeople and needing 'somewhat comprehensive socialisation'—is a focal point.

So, too, is income distribution, since that has a major influence on the size of the multiplier and the determination of the overall state of the economy, as well as being a social issue in its own right. These original concerns of Keynes were marginalised, if not lost altogether, in neo-Keynesianism. From a policy perspective, they are incompatible with a laissez-faire stance, perhaps even with a liberal-interventionist stance. Their re-emphasis by post-Keynesians puts more extensive policy reforms on the agenda. Incomes and industry policy are particular focal points. Recently, there has also been a strong revival of interest among post-Keynesians in policies to combat unemployment, by extending the role of the government as 'employer of the last resort'.[19]

BOX 33.3   POST-KEYNESIAN ECONOMISTS

Post-Keynesian economic theory, drawing on a more radical interpretation of Keynes, has been influenced by the work of Keynes's colleague at Cambridge, the Italian economist Piero Sraffa. Sraffa's contribution is based primarily on a mathematical model of 'the production of commodities by means of commodities' that shows how the structure of the economy as a whole can be analysed without recourse to the market theories of the neoclassical school.[20] The technical interdependencies of the different sectors in the economy determine the conditions for efficient production, leaving questions of income distribution to other processes of a social and political character. Echoes of David Ricardo and John Stuart Mill can be heard in the (implicit) politics of this analysis.[21] The implication is that a more equitable distribution of income is compatible with an efficient system of production.

The contribution of Michal Kalecki (1899–1970) to post-Keynesian economics is of more explicit political economic significance. Kalecki, a Polish economist working within the Marxist tradition, developed a penetrating analysis of capitalism at about the same time as Keynes was working on his *General Theory*. Like Keynes, Kalecki emphasised the inherent tendencies of capitalism to recession and unemployment, but he went further by emphasising the significance of income distribution and the degree of monopoly enjoyed by capitalist firms. Moreover, he showed the political obstacles facing the implementation of Keynesian-type policies. Measures to produce full employment, he argued, would have the effect of increasing the power of labour relative to capital, and would be resisted by employers for that reason.[22] How right he eventually proved to be.

Other contributions to the development of post-Keynesian economics have been many and varied. Joan Robinson (1908–1983), the Cambridge political economist, was important in giving coherence to this school of thought through her work on capital theory, capital accumulation, and employment. Alfred Eichner (1937–88) also put the pricing and investment behaviour of big businesses ('megacorps') in the spotlight, showing how prices are set in order to generate required rates of return rather than according to market principles of demand and supply.[23] This links up with the more general post-Keynesian concern with the process of 'mark-up pricing', whereby firms with market power administer the prices of their products to reduce risk and increase corporate growth.[24]

The work of Hyman Minsky (1919–97) added significantly to the understanding of how financial institutions affect the vulnerability of the economy to economic crises. According to Minsky, the complexity of the financial arrangements underpinning modern capitalism produces a layering of debts and financial assets that has the potential to collapse like a house of cards.[25] Many post-Keynesians have argued that the onset of the global financial crisis in 2007–08 was an extreme 'Minsky moment'. A build-up of debt had, in effect, operated like a speculative 'Ponzi scheme',[26] based on the assumption of perpetually rising asset prices. It was a bubble that eventually had to burst.

A common element in all these contributions to post-Keynesian analysis is a rejection of the neoclassical conception of the market as a self-regulating system that ensures economic stability and efficient resource allocation.[27]

Whether post-Keynesian economics constitutes a coherent school of thought, comparable to Marxist or neoclassical economics, is debatable. Perhaps a better parallel is with institutional economics. In both cases there is a group of economists opposed to the prevailing economic orthodoxy, but who have diverse views about what alternative analysis would facilitate understanding, and changing, modern capitalism. Some concepts, such as the theory of circular and cumulative causation (discussed in Chapter 25), are applied by scholars from both institutional and post-Keynesian schools of thought. Some policy reforms, such as incomes policies, industry policies, and extensions of public-sector employment, also command widespread support from both camps. The difference between them is more to do with matters of methodology—whether to emphasise institutional description or more theoretical economic modelling. The common concerns flow through into the broader issues explored in Part VIII of this book, which deals with the main themes in modern political economy.

Conclusion

Like Marx, Keynes just will not lie down. He created a revolution in economic theory and in economic policy. However, it was an incomplete revolution. In the realm of theory, Keynes's ideas were steered into an uncomfortable marriage with neoclassical economics. In the realm of policy, they were interpreted as requiring governments to undertake selective demand management only as an adjunct to the functioning of an otherwise sound capitalist market economy. For about a quarter of a century, this neo-Keynesianism seemed to work quite well in the realms of theory and of policy, but it proved vulnerable to the monetarist assault when economic conditions changed at the end of the long boom. Now the monetarist alternative, and its new classical variations, seems to have run its course. The global financial crisis triggered a substantial revival of Keynesian economic policy as a pragmatic and effective response to a sudden economic downturn.

Deep challenges remain. The periodic incidence of recession continues to be a source of instability in the capitalist economy. Globalisation, by increasing the economic interdependence of nations, makes them more vulnerable to the forces generating volatile investment patterns. The capacity of the state to act as 'demand manager, spender, social guardian and umpire of the competitive process'[28] is continually in question. Drawing on post-Keynesian economics for more radical understadings of the state and the economy makes sense in these circumstances. So, too, does further exploration of the Marxian and institutional economics traditions. The fusion of these schools of thought can provide a strong basis for the construction of a modern political economy.

KEY POINTS

- The Keynesian revolution involved fundamental challenges to orthodox economic theory and new approaches to macroeconomic policy.

- The monetarist and new classical assaults on Keynesian theory and policies subsequently caused a return to pre-Keynesian orthodoxies; but the global financial crisis produced a resurgence of Keynesian economic policy.

- Post-Keynesianism, like institutional economics, puts emphasis on a broader array of interventionist policies for economic planning, industry development, and income redistribution.

PART VIII

Contemporary Concerns

Modern Political Economy

34 A Radical Reconstruction

On what currents of economic thought does modern political economy draw?

What contemporary political economic problems does it address?

What analytic framework can facilitate progress in political economy?

The challenge for modern political economy is threefold: to develop the critique of orthodox economics, to combine the currents flowing against the mainstream into a more coherent alternative, and to use that analysis to contribute to progressive social change. These three elements are interdependent. Critique is a springboard for the development of alternatives that explain the real world and contribute to effective political strategies for dealing with current economic problems. The elements have an iterative character, too. The changing character of the real world, itself partly shaped by the application of orthodox economic ideas, requires alternative political economic ideas to take us in a different direction. This is the essence of praxis—the integration of theory and practice—in the development of modern political economy.

The preceding chapters in this book have surveyed the evolving nature of economic enquiry, emphasising not only the principal analytical tools of each of the main schools of thought, but also their distinctive political economic worldviews. Each school emphasises different aspects of the same economic system. In that sense, they are complementary, but rival, discourses. Each embodies different assumptions and beliefs about the relationship of the economy to society. It is now time to explore how a more coherent modern political economy can be developed by drawing on these schools of thought to provide a means of understanding—and changing—contemporary capitalism.[1]

Multiple currents against the mainstream

Look back at Figure 7.1 (p. 61) to remind yourself of the principal currents of economic analysis. Historically, classical political economy provides a common basis. The mainstream flows through neoclassical economics, merging (temporarily) with Keynesianism in the neoclassical synthesis, and reemerging in a more explicitly right-wing political form in monetarism and neoliberalism. The dissident currents challenging this mainstream are Marxist economics, institutional economics, and the more radical interpretation of Keynes represented by post-Keynesian economics.

A first approximation of a definition of modern political economy is that it is a fusion of the last three bodies of analysis. This suggests some common features of modern political economy:

- analysis of how an economic surplus is generated, who gets the surplus, and for what purposes it is used

- emphasis on capital, labour, and the state: their relationships, relative power, and institutional forms

- study of the evolving character of the economy, looking at change in actual historical time rather than studying static equilibrium

- identification of processes of circular and cumulative causation that shape economic and social developments

- analysis of how resources are created and destroyed—not simply how they are allocated—focusing on the role of politics as well as markets in those processes.

The first of these concerns has its source in classical political economy, and then flows through into Marxist and neo-Marxist economics.[2] Arguably, it is the most fundamental and longstanding analytical feature of the political economy tradition, contrasting sharply with the turn taken by neoclassical economics to an equilibrium analysis, in which the notion of economic surplus has no place. But the other four features also distinguish the dissident traditions of political economy from the economic mainstream. Studying the interaction of capital, labour, and the state in real historical time, and focusing on processes that create cumulative changes and shape the creation and destruction of economic resources: these are the hallmarks of political economy.

To define modern political economy in terms of this fusion of the concerns of Marxism, institutionalism, and Keynes and post-Keynesianism is both too grand and too modest. It is too grand, in that it implies synthesis is simple. In practice, the characteristic concerns of the three schools of thought are quite different. Marxist value theory, for example, sits uncomfortably with Keynesian concepts and with the more descriptive institutional approach to understanding the evolution of economic society. Important differences of emphasis and interpretation allow no easy reconciliation.

The claim that modern political economy synthesises these three main dissident currents of economic thought is simultaneously too modest, in that it neglects other potential contributory elements. Environmentalism and feminism are obvious cases in point. Both have developed as important channels of enquiry and as significant social movements. Environmental analysis and politics focuses on perhaps the most fundamental tension in the modern economy: capitalism's rapacious relationship with nature and its consequent unsustainability. Feminist analysis and politics emphasises gender as a significant source of contemporary social inequality and tension, alongside class differences. Both environmentalism and feminism warrant serious attention in the construction of modern political economy. This is not simply a matter of broadening the range of topics discussed. It also imparts a distinctively normative element to modern political economy. Feminists and environmentalists have in common a recognition of the importance of ethical questions in economic reasoning.

Modern political economy also needs to engage with the concerns and contributions of other contemporary social scientists whose work does not fit neatly into the major schools of economic thought. There are important debates about the significance of technological change, the future of work, and work–life balance.[3] Analyses of how ethnicity relates to class and gender also have the potential to enrich our understanding of economy and society.[4] Some mainstream economists have embraced behavioural and experimental economics in the attempt to ground the analysis of choices on a more realistic basis. Ideas about innovation originating in the writing of Joseph Schumpeter have been given a modern policy-orientated twist. And the land question, raised earlier by Henry George, warrants renewed consideration in the light of contemporary social and environmental concerns. There is no shortage of interesting themes. The question is how to structure and integrate their exploration in the most useful way.

BOX 34.1   **BEHAVIOURAL ECONOMICS**

One body of economic analysis that has become quite controversial in recent years is behavioural economics. It draws ideas from social psychology as well as mainstream economics, and seeks to inject more 'realism' into the analysis of economic behaviour. For example, instead of simply assuming that consumers maximise utility through making repeatedly rational choices, behavioural economists argue that consideration must be paid to a broader array of social issues that impinge on consumers' choices.

The quest for a more realistic basis for the study of economic choices leads to a more 'grounded' analysis, drawing on evidence from experimental methods. Observations of actual behaviour tend to replace generalisation based on models of 'ideal' behaviour. Behavioural economics recognises that emotions, prejudices, and biases influence how we behave in practice. So too does the social context in which choices are made.

The range of choice is relevant, for example. Neoclassical economists tend to assume that the more choice the better. Behavioural economists disagree, noting that an 'overload' of choices can lead people to either 'walk away' from the market without making a selection or just to plump for 'whatever' before escaping the bewildering situation. How a choice is presented matters too. If people are asked to tick a box saying they are willing to donate their organs for medical purposes, many fewer do so than in a situation where they have to tick a box saying they are *not* willing to do so. In other words, 'contracting in' and 'contracting out' produce markedly different outcomes. So too do repeated choice situations. 'Let bygones be bygones' is one of the famous strictures arising from mainstream economics, strongly urged by Paul Samuelson in his best-selling *Economics* textbooks. Yet in practice, we observe behaviours that recurrently violate it. When a spun coin has come up tails five times in a row most people will say that 'it must be time for tails' even though the formal probability is unchanged at 50:50. Such behaviour has a major bearing on how people respond to repeated risks, as in buying insurance. If businesses and public policy-makers need to deal with how people actually behave rather than how they 'should' behave, it is pertinent to draw on these behavioural insights.

There is nothing fundamentally new in these observations, notwithstanding claims to novelty by modern behavioural economists. Before Adam Smith wrote *The Wealth of Nations* he penned *The Theory of Moral Sentiments*, in which he discussed the social bonds, including interpersonal trust, that are necessary for social cohesion and economic exchange. Thorstein Veblen was a major forerunner too, emphasising processes of social emulation and conspicuous consumption as key elements in economic behaviour. As noted in Chapter 26, J. K. Galbraith stressed consumerism as a social process with deeply contradictory features in terms of want satisfaction. Karl Polanyi also emphasised the social foundations of the market economy, emphasising 'embeddedness' as a condition for making the system work. All these political economists rejected the simple assumption of rational *Homo economicus* and sought to understand how social processes shape economic behaviour.

So is the recent surge of enthusiasm for 'behavioural economics' progressive? Certainly it is a welcome antidote to some of the more simplistic features of conventional neoclassical theory. It imparts a more empirical orientation to the discipline. However, for the most part it remains confined within a 'choice-theoretic' framework. As such, it shares with neoclassical economics an orientation to methodological individualism, rather than the broader concerns with inequalities of economic power, class relations, and economic evolution that are characteristic of modern political economy.[5]

Rethinking political economy

Table 34.1 suggests one framework for organising the various concerns of political economy. It focuses on four themes around which modern political economic analysis can be structured. As with any simple taxonomy, it purports to demonstrate neither how its components should be analysed, nor what concepts are likely to be most useful for that purpose. It merely lists the four themes, and hints at some potential interdisciplinary links.

TABLE 34.1 FOUR THEMES IN MODERN POLITICAL ECONOMY

Themes	Interdisciplinary links
Economy—nature	Biological sciences, geography
Economy—technology	Industrial relations, engineering
Economy—society	Sociology, history, cultural studies, anthropology
Economy—state	Political science, government

The most fundamental of these four themes is the relationship of the economy to nature. Starting here is an acknowledgment that an economy must necessarily be embedded in the physical world. The spotlight immediately turns to the problems associated with existing forms of economic growth that deplete natural resources and pollute the environment. From a strategic policy perspective, the central issue is whether the economy can be restructured so that it is ecologically sustainable. Some economists contend that piecemeal policy changes, such as better pricing of scarce environmental resources, can make a major contribution to this reform process. But capitalism has a particularly problematic relationship with the environment because of its systemic association with exploitation and accumulation, individualism, and consumerism. Whether it can be made to meet the prerequisites for ecological sustainability, or, if it cannot, finding out the sort of economic system that could, are matters deserving careful consideration. In such investigations it is useful to place particular emphasis on the role of land and other natural resources in the production and disposition of the economic surplus.

The second theme turns the spotlight on to the relationship of technology to the economy. It requires analysis of how the process of economic production shapes, and is shaped by, scientific knowledge and its embodiment in capital goods. More than that, it requires study of the institutions shaping how technology is harnessed for the purpose of enhancing the economic surplus. Veblen's distinction between industry and business is relevant here. It is manifest today in the tension between productive and speculative uses of the surplus. We are living in an era of rapid technological change, sometimes said to be creating a 'new economy' based in information technologies and more knowledge-intensive production. If so, what are the implications for education and training, for the nature of work, and for social structure? Who acquires the fruits of higher productivity? Why is there a gulf between winners and losers; between the workers in primary and secondary labour markets, and between the overworked and the unemployed, for example? Is there a means of reconciling technological and structural economic change with broader social goals? This broad sweep of concerns with how production is organised and how an economic surplus is generated is central to modern political economic analysis.

The third theme concerns the relationship of the economy to society. Class, gender, and ethnicity are key considerations here. As Marxists have always emphasised, the capital–labour relationship is the key to understanding the functioning of the economy, its contradictions, conflicts, and distributional outcomes. From this economic fountainhead of class differences, many other dimensions of social inequality can then be seen to flow. Embracing other currents of contemporary social science, such as feminism and studies of racial inequality, necessarily broadens the focus to include gender and ethnicity. This is not simply a matter of describing how economic inequalities are structured according to sex and race, but also of understanding their articulation with class and the changing characteristics of capitalism. Political economic and sociological enquiries merge in the analysis of these contemporary phenomena. The issue of how the disposition of the economic surplus effects the distribution of income, wealth, and life chances is a central concern.

The fourth theme is the relationship of the state to the economy. This turns attention to the capacity of governments to deal with the concerns raised by the first three themes: managing the relationship of the economy with the natural world, shaping technology and productivity, and managing the economic outcomes associated with class, gender, and ethnicity. Analysis of the state has always been a major theme in political economy. It has been, implicitly or explicitly, an issue on which the major dissident traditions have taken quite different positions. Whereas Keynesians have had a basically optimistic view of the capacity of the state to redress specific problems such as inflation and unemployment, institutional economists have advocated broader economic and social reforms, while Marxist political economists have generally been sceptical of these reformist perspectives. Seeking some common ground among these competing currents of analysis is bound to be problematic. It is more so in the circumstances of modern capitalism, where concerns about ecological sustainability and social justice exist alongside the continuing concerns about economic prosperity. Is using the state as a vehicle for 'radical reformism'—emphasising immediate benefits but prefiguring more radical, long-term transformations—a viable strategy? If not, then what other vehicle can facilitate social progress? Such issues necessarily feature prominently on any modern political economic agenda.

Is this cluster of themes for the organisation and development of modern political economy logical and coherent? Modestly, it may be regarded as just four convenient headings under which we can explore contemporary problems and policy issues. More ambitiously, it may be regarded as an organisational basis for the integration of different streams of political economic analysis. Thus, it successively explores the layered relationships of capital to nature, technology, socioeconomic structure, and politics. The shift, schematically, is from the fundamental concern with the nature–economy relationship, to the economy–technology relationship, then the economy–society relationship, and, last, to the question of the state (including its role in managing the tensions arising from the three preceding relationships). Here is a nested and sequential set of analytical concerns.

Conclusion

In studying political economy today, we are confronted with a formidable legacy, comprising various currents of analysis. First and foremost, we need to understand that legacy. However, we also need to transcend it; the evolving form of the political economic system in the real world demands nothing less. How best to do this is, inevitably, a matter about which reasonable people can reasonably disagree.

What is presented here is a suggested way forward. It draws on ideas from classical political economy and Marxist economics, from the tradition of institutional economics, and from Keynes and the post-Keynesians. It incorporates concerns raised by environmentalists, feminists, and other contemporary social scientists. It purports to give some coherence to modern political economy by emphasising four themes concerned with the interrelationships between the economy and nature, technology, society, and politics. Whether it constitutes a useful way forward can only be demonstrated by putting the plan into action. This requires bringing political economic analysis to bear on the questions of crucial importance in the twenty-first century.

KEY POINTS

- Modern political economy draws on dissident currents in economic thought, such as Marxism, institutionalism, and post-Keynesianism.

- It is also influenced by environmentalism, feminism, and studies of ethnicity.

- Synthesising these elements leaves considerable scope for different political economic approaches, but there are common analytical concerns with the relationship of the economy to nature, technology, society, and the state.

35 Economy and Environment

How does the economy interact with the physical environment?

Can capitalism be made compatible with ecologically sustainable development?

How does a political economy of the environment differ from free-market 'environmental fine-tuning'?

Analysis of the relationship between the natural world and the economic system is of central importance in modern political economy. Indeed, it is of central importance to the future of humankind, not to mention the future of other species threatened by the effects of further environmental degradation. Political economists have to take seriously the growing concerns about the impact of economic activity on environmental quality and the prospects for ecologically sustainable development. They have a responsibility to contribute to an understanding of the economic causes of environmental decay and of what changes in political economic structures and policies might contribute to effective solutions.

This chapter considers how to cope with these challenges. Attention is given to proposals for extending neoclassical economic reasoning to the study of environmental issues, since this has been a major element in the drive towards 'environmental fine-tuning'. This is contrasted with the view that the embrace of market principles is part of the problem, rather than part of the solution. Henry George's ideas about land are revived and integrated with broader environmental concerns. All this is intended to contribute to a better understanding of economy–environment interactions and the requirements for sustainability.

The nature of environmental problems

Environmental stresses take various forms and are manifest on various spatial scales. Some affect the planet in its entirety while others are more localised in their immediate impacts. What are the common elements? One useful classification has been suggested by David Attenborough, whose television documentaries have consistently emphasised the need to care for the natural environment more effectively. Attenborough distinguishes between the effects of

- *overharvesting*, which takes resources from forests, seas, and nature in general at a rate faster than that at which they are replenished

- *introduction of alien species*, which relocates plants and animals, deliberately or accidentally, thereby upsetting the local ecological balance and causing the loss of other species of flora and/or fauna

- *destruction of habitat*, which converts wilderness into agricultural or urban land, thereby reducing biodiversity and also often causing species loss

- *islandisation*, the process whereby patches of natural habitat become cut off from one another by degraded environments, such as those converted from natural to agricultural or urban land uses

- *pollution*, which uses the physical environment as a receptacle for waste products, with damaging consequences for the quality of the environment and its capacity for renewal.[1]

All five processes are currently happening at an unprecedented rate. They are not all of recent origin, but there is a strong general correlation, in the last half-century in particular, between their intensification and the relentless growth of population and economic activity.

There are echoes here of the warning about the unsustainability of demographic and economic trends issued four decades ago by the team of scientists sponsored by the Club of Rome.[2] There has been incessant debate about the nature of the causal connections in the intervening years.[3] The role of population growth has been the subject of particularly intense controversy.[4] It has a direct connection with the severity of the pressures on finite environmental resources. However, distributional elements have to be considered too. An extra body in one of the affluent nations, for instance, adds many times more to demands on natural resources than an extra body in one of the poorer nations—although there, too, the increased pressure on the physical environment may be intense. Economic growth has yet more fundamental consequences for environmental quality. It is directly implicated in at least the first and last of Attenborough's five factors. However, the extent of environmental damage depends on the form the economic growth takes, the technology on which it is based, the spatial distribution of the growth, whether it uses renewable or non-renewable resources, and the extent to which materials are recycled. All these factors have a major bearing on how economic activities affect environmental quality. A principal task for modern political economy is to contribute to analysing these connections.

Ecologically sustainable development

Figure 35.1 presents a simple schematic representation of the principal economy–environment interactions. It contrasts a throughput economy with a spaceship economy. In the former, the economy has a rapacious relationship with the environment, treating natural resources as inputs, and using the physical environment as a receptacle for outputs, including waste products. In the latter, the nature of economic activity, the type of resources used, and the emphasis on their reuse reduces, if not eliminates, the damaging consequences for the physical environment. The inference is that the latter economic arrangement would be more conducive to ecologically sustainable development.[5]

FIGURE 35.1 ECONOMY–ENVIRONMENT INTERACTIONS

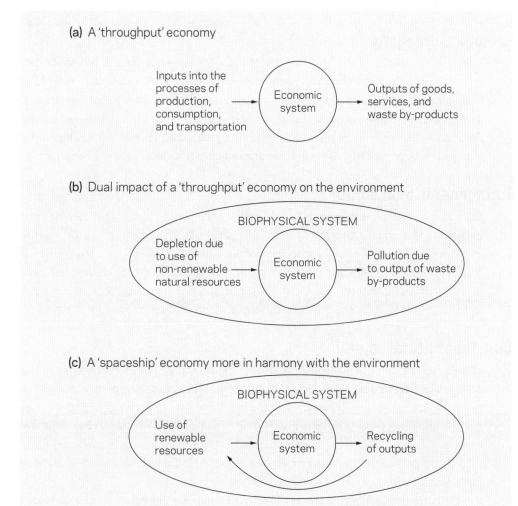

(a) A 'throughput' economy

Inputs into the processes of production, consumption, and transportation → Economic system → Outputs of goods, services, and waste by-products

(b) Dual impact of a 'throughput' economy on the environment

BIOPHYSICAL SYSTEM

Depletion due to use of non-renewable natural resources → Economic system → Pollution due to output of waste by-products

(c) A 'spaceship' economy more in harmony with the environment

BIOPHYSICAL SYSTEM

Use of renewable resources → Economic system → Recycling of outputs

Ecologically sustainable development—ESD for short—has been one of the buzz phrases of the last two decades (perhaps surpassed in popular political economic discourse only by 'globalisation'). Its meaning is not always clear. One way of defining it is in terms of its four essential principles, two of which are fundamentally biophysical and two of which are more socioeconomic in character.[6] These are set out on the following page.

Biodiversity

ESD requires, first and foremost, that destruction of species be avoided and biodiversity thereby maintained. This requirement has a moral dimension that emphasises the responsibility of humans to ensure that their domination over nature is not at the expense of the survival of other species: fauna and flora. A supplementary economic rationale exists, too, because any reduction in the gene pool associated with loss of species destroys an asset with significant economic value: in medical applications, for example.

Ecological integrity

ESD requires that the health and resilience of natural life-support systems be maintained. This does not rule out all temporary environmental damage, for ecological systems have natural mechanisms for self-repair. Winds, waves, and water currents are effective dispersal mechanisms; and waste materials that are organic eventually biodegrade. However, beyond threshold levels of pollution or resource depletion ('tipping points'), irreversible environmental changes may be precipitated. Ecological integrity requires that these levels not be surpassed.

Intergenerational equity

ESD also requires that each generation bequeaths to the next a physical environment in no worse state than when it was inherited. In other words, we should not live at the expense of future generations. This is a key socioeconomic principle, although its interpretation is somewhat ambiguous. Whether improvements in the quantity or quality of some resources constitute adequate compensation for the damage to others is a debatable point. How we deal with this issue is linked to the fourth ESD principle, which emphasises how we value nature.

Constant natural capital

ESD requires that there be no depletion of the total stock of productive soils, fresh water, and other available natural resources. It is a tall order, since current patterns of economic growth commonly use non-renewable resources, or use renewable resources more rapidly than nature can replenish them. A commitment to maintaining constant natural capital requires a means of regulating the use of resources (whether through the price mechanism or through more direct control over the exploitation of resources) and a mechanism for natural resource accounting (a stocktaking of assets).

The latter requirement, natural resource accounting, has immediate political economic implications. Our current framework for national economic accounting—based on Keynesian concepts—has no place for such measurement. This contrasts with normal business accounting practices. Businesses annually calculate (normally, as a legal requirement) a profit and loss statement and a balance sheet (now officially called the 'statement of financial performance' and 'statement of financial position').[7] The former shows incomes and expenditures over the year; the latter shows assets and liabilities at the end of each year. No business would consider a profit (shown in the profit and loss account) that has been generated solely by running down its assets (shown in the balance sheet) to be sustainable in the longer term. However, because there is currently no equivalent to the balance sheet in our national income accounting, we cannot tell whether our income, as a nation, has a sustainable character. Some economic activities may generate income without depleting the stock of natural capital, but others clearly do not. The proceeds from the export of minerals, for example, are matched by the reduction in the value of the nation's natural capital.

Here is an obvious gap in current national accounting practices. To fill it, a system of stock accounting (including natural resource stocks) needs to be developed to supplement the existing flow measures of national income. If this were done, we would be in a position to see whether we are indeed living at the expense of nature and of future generations. However, seeing is one thing; acting is another. The key issue is to consider what policy measures could actually achieve a transition to ESD.

Environmental fine-tuning

The usual response of orthodox economists to the problem of environmental decay is to interpret it in terms of markets and to propose environmental pricing.[8] The key underlying concepts are 'market failure' and 'externalities', which derive from neoclassical theory, discussed in Chapter 23. Market failure is said to exist because no price normally applies to the use of environmental goods such as clean air and rivers, so consequently they are overused; for example, as receptacles for the waste products of economic activity. Even where prices do apply, as in the case of fossil fuels used for energy, the prices do not reflect the full social costs, because the consumption of these items has negative spillover effects, such as atmospheric and water pollution. These negative spillovers are said to be the externalities of an imperfect market economy.

The policy implication is to make adjustments to the price system so that these environmentally damaging effects do not occur. In effect, the environmental improvement comes through changing the economic incentives. Putting prices on environmental goods— by imposing taxes on their use, for example—provides an incentive to limit the demand for them. It also creates an incentive to develop alternative technologies that do not require the (now more expensive) resources. Internalising the externalities brings the prices consumers must pay for environmental goods into line with the social costs arising from their use. The consumers can still exercise their freedom of choice, but the changed price structure applying to environmental goods aligns the equilibrium market outcome more closely with the optimum environmental outcome.

This is impeccable neoclassical economic reasoning. It can be extended with greater theoretical sophistication and more practical examples. The basic message is that the resolution of environmental problems requires more, and more effective, markets. It is a message with obvious appeal to those who are attracted by the prospect of having both individual market freedoms and better environmental outcomes. Politically, it has become increasingly influential within individual nation states and in international forums where responses to the global challenge of climate change are discussed.

The necessary policy instruments are readily at hand. Tradable pollution permits, for instance, giving the right to pollute up to a specified level, are issued by governments.[9] Bought and sold in the market, these permits go to the highest bidders. Those who cannot afford to buy them have to cease their polluting activities. Carbon taxes can also be used. Levied on commodities according to the quantity of fossil fuels that go, directly and indirectly, into their making, a carbon tax could be expected to discourage the consumption of those commodities.[10] Aluminium products, notoriously energy-intensive to make, would become much more expensive, for example, thereby providing an economic incentive to switch to the production and consumption of substitute products that are less environmentally damaging. Raising existing petrol taxes should, in principle, also provide an incentive to switch from cars to other modes of transport that make fewer demands on the depleting stock of fossil fuels. In practice, switching of this sort is impeded by the lack of good quality public transport in many suburban and rural areas, which causes demand for car travel to be quite price inelastic. However, the incentive to switch to more fuel-efficient vehicles is potentially a significant contributor to reducing environmental stress.

Pragmatically, such ecological taxes appeal to governments because they also generate revenues. Therein lies a conundrum: the more inelastic the demand for the product causing the environmental damage, the greater the revenues from environmental taxes, but the smaller the reduction in environmentally damaging activities. Of course, even where demand is inelastic there may be indirect environmental benefits if the extra revenues generated by the taxes are spent by the governments on repair of environmental damage. There are political constraints on this, though. Governments usually feel it necessary to compensate motorists for having to pay higher petrol prices, for example, by promising to allocate the additional tax revenues to expenditure on roads. A process of circular and cumulative causation results.

Perverse effects can also result from raising the prices of scarce environmental goods. As the populations of 'big cats' and rhinos dwindle in Africa, the market prices for skins and rhino horns rises, which, in turn, provides an extra incentive for hunters, acting illegally, to capture and slaughter more animals. Without extreme vigilance by regulatory authorities, the rate of depletion increases. In such a case, the process of circular and cumulative causation, working through the price mechanism, produces an equilibrium of ecological catastrophe.

The distributional consequences of environmental policies are also a fundamental problem. All market-based approaches to environmental concerns tend to have adverse impacts on equity. Because environmental taxes add to the prices of scarce environmental goods, they push them increasingly beyond the reach of the poor. Access to the environmental requirements for a healthy life—in the extreme, for life itself—becomes increasingly restricted to the wealthy.

Structural constraints also recur. The neoclassical case for environmental fine-tuning assumes ease of substitution in the patterns of production and consumption. In practice, this is not necessarily the case. Inertia commonly arises from the spatial forms of urban and regional development, the distribution of employment opportunities, and the existing state of technology. These constraints limit the capacity of production and consumption patterns to adjust in response to price changes. In the longer term, all these factors become variable, one might reasonably argue, but resistance from existing political economic interests still has to be countered. Opposition from the powerful institutions of corporate capital to policies that undermine consumerism may be anticipated, for example. Such considerations suggest the need for an analysis of the causes of environmental decay that has a more political economic character.

BOX 35.1   ## PUTTING A PRICE ON CARBON

A principal cause of human-created climate change is the burning of fossil fuels (oil, coal, and gas) and the resulting emissions of carbon into the atmosphere. Recognising this, it is not surprising that the major focus of debates about remedial policies responses has been on how to reduce this ecologically unsustainable process. Of course, there are many possibilities: reducing the production of goods, changing energy technologies to less damaging forms, trying to find other places to dispose of carbon deposits, and so forth. Not surprisingly, during a period when neoclassical economics and neoliberal politics have been dominant in policy-making circles, the primary government focus has been on using the price mechanism to drive change.

In practice, the choice of pricing policy mechanisms comes down to two options: carbon trading and carbon taxation. The former is usually called an emissions trading system (ETS) or a 'cap and trade' system. The government decides on the 'cap' on carbon emissions that will be allowed and sells the corresponding number of permits to pollute. Those permits can then be traded, on normal market principles, among businesses seeking to continue their polluting activities. If the cost of those permits is significantly above zero, the cost of production is raised. That higher cost is normally passed on as a higher price charged to consumers. For the other alternative, the carbon tax, the additional cost is more directly imposed; for example, through the tax levied on the use of coal or gas used for energy production. In both cases, the market is the mechanism for transmitting the signal to producers and consumers to switch production and consumption. They have an incentive to switch to other products and processes that are now relatively cheaper since they are less carbon emitting.

Which policy is preferable? According to neoclassical economics, both operate similarly according to the principles of supply and demand. With an ETS, the government controls the output—by setting an upper limit on permits to pollute—and allows the price to be set in the market. With a carbon tax, the price is directly set—by the amount of the tax above the price that would otherwise prevail—and the market determines the output. It all seems symmetrical; either policy can produce the same result. On balance, a preference for the ETS may be inferred, purely because that policy option produces the more directly assured reduction in output of pollutants. With a carbon tax, the rate of tax might need quite a few adjustments before that targeted change in output could be achieved.

This neoclassical reasoning ignores some issues that, once taken into account, make the carbon tax the better option. Consider just two such concerns. One relates to property rights and ethics. An ETS effectively confers rights to pollute: once a permit has been purchased its owner has a complete right—and the economic incentive—to continue with the environmentally degrading activity. With a carbon tax, by contrast, the economics and ethics are better aligned from an ecological perspective. The tax is both an economic incentive to desist from the environmentally degrading activity and a signal that the society deems the activity to be antisocial. Like a tax on cigarettes or other activities that the society wishes to discourage, a carbon tax may not eradicate the antisocial activity altogether, but there is no ambiguity about the signal or intent.

A second advantage of a carbon tax is that it is less prone than an ETS to generate speculative markets. With an ETS, new markets are created for the buying and selling of pollution permits, but secondary markets—trading in futures and other derivatives— also inevitably develop. Much activity predictably goes into market creation and manipulation, with a view to financial gain through trading in the market. For those who regard environmental decay as the product of overreliance on a market economy, this consequence would be a great irony indeed. For those fearful that more speculative markets add to the instability of modern capitalism, there is a double whammy. The goal of environmental protection becomes interlinked with the development of volatile markets based on the further extension of private property rights to nature.

Green critics of both approaches to putting a price on carbon usually conclude that, while a carbon tax is preferable to an emissions trading system, neither is sufficient to stop the economy having adverse climate change effects. Prohibition, regulation, and public investment are also part of the more comprehensive policy package that is necessary.

The political economy of environmental decay

Corporate power may systematically limit the range of technologies and consumer choices, effectively ruling out more ecologically sustainable options. An obvious example is transport, which is central to the problem of environmental damage, both as an energy user and as a pollution generator. The major automobile manufacturers, oil companies, highway construction companies, and suppliers of motor vehicle components and accessories collectively comprise a 'roads lobby', which has a well-documented track record of suppressing innovations that might threaten its economic interests and of pressuring governments to pursue policies consistent with those interests.[11]

The wielding of this corporate power was significant in the effective destruction of the public transport system in many American cities, for example. The classic case is Los Angeles. In the late 1930s, National City Lines, a holding company formed by General Motors in conjunction with the Firestone Tyre and Rubber company and Standard Oil of California, bought the light rail systems that served the scattered communities of the southern California region. It ripped up the tracks and replaced the rail service with buses (built by General Motors, running on Firestone tyres, and fuelled by Standard Oil). The deteriorating quality of service effectively forced most citizens to turn to private cars in order to move around the area. This, of course, was a transport option immensely more lucrative for General Motors, Firestone, and Standard Oil. The state responded by building more and more freeways to accommodate the cumulative growth in vehicle use. A region of fragrant orange groves and clean air was thereby converted into a sprawling metropolis with chronic problems of traffic congestion and atmospheric pollution levels regularly exceeding safe health limits. No doubt, rising incomes would have led to growth in private car ownership, anyway; however, the process was accelerated by the corporations restructuring the transport options to serve their own purposes, irrespective of the environmental damage this caused. National City Lines was responsible for the removal of light rail operations in more than a hundred other cities around the USA. A conspiracy against the public interest? Under antitrust legislation a federal grand jury ruled it to be so. The corporations involved were fined $5000, a sum that, even allowing for the higher value of the dollar then, was almost laughably small in relation to the damage caused.[12]

A sad endnote to the story is that the city of Los Angeles, recognising the need to restore better public transport, has since rebuilt some of the light rail system at enormous public expense. However, it is having difficulty making it economically viable because, as residential and commercial activities have developed the sprawling, low-density suburban patterns characteristic of car-orientated cities, fixed-route public transport systems have become a less effective means of serving people's transport needs.[13]

This example of corporate power is by no means exceptional. In Australia, for example, the influence of mining companies is a significant obstacle to more sustainable energy policies. Given the nation's reliance on exporting coal, iron ore, and other minerals, it is not surprising that these mining businesses have relentlessly sought to frustrate any climate change abatement policies that would work against their corporate interests.[14]

Expanding corporate power and profits through consciously violating ecological sustainability is common in many industries throughout capitalist economies.[15] Producing goods with built-in obsolescence is a case in point. This involves making products with working lives that are shorter than necessary, or making frequent style changes to products to render earlier lines unfashionable or redundant. It enhances producers' profitability, but at the expense of two forms of environmental damage: the greater use of resources to make the larger outputs of products, and the disposal of the discarded products. These are the familiar features of a junk economy based on the production of disposable products. The profligate use of packaging, an integral part of many firms' marketing strategies today, accentuates the problem.

Consumers come to be complicit—sometimes reluctantly, sometimes enthusiastically—in these processes. Indeed, this is the essence of consumerism. Fostered by relentless sales promotion, the high levels of consumption on which the modern capitalist economy depend come to be regarded as normal, desirable, even laudable. Consumerist ideology is central to the process of environmental decay, while the related ideology of individualism has the concurrent effect of eschewing collective responsibility for finding solutions. As the economist Ken Boulding put it, 'The presence of pollution is a symptom of the absence of community.'[16] *Homo economicus*, it seems, is not the ideal candidate for the job of securing a harmonious relationship with nature.

These various considerations lead to the conclusion, contrary to the claims of free-market environmentalism, that the capitalist market economy is the problem, not the solution. In its modern form, shaped by corporate power, consumerist practices, and the prevailing ethos of individualism, it stands as the antithesis of ecological sustainability.

What is to be done? Change the ownership and/or control of economic activities in order to sever the nexus between corporate interests and environmental damage? Instigate a values revolution to shift consumer behaviour to more environmentally conscious practices? Lower consumption levels, at least in the more affluent nations, in order to live within the ecological limits set by spaceship earth? These are revolutionary prospects indeed. Perhaps a useful pragmatic start can be made through the promotion of 'green jobs'.

BOX 35.2   GREEN JOBS

It is commonly argued that there is an inherent tension between the economy and nature. An inescapable trade-off is implied: jobs versus the environment. Certainly, there are circumstances where environmental protection threatens existing jobs; in logging old-growth forests and coal mining, for example. However, environmentalism can be job creating too, generating jobs in renewable energy production, energy efficiency, waste management, recycling, and many other industries. Identifying ways in which progress can be made towards a more sustainable economy while simultaneously creating more employment opportunities is an attractive 'win–win' strategy. This is the 'green jobs' approach to the environmental challenge.

Green jobs may emerge through market mechanisms when a price is put on carbon emissions, because—depending on the price—it may then become more profitable to use solar or wind power, for example, rather than coal-fired power stations. However, a more comprehensive green jobs strategy requires economic planning. It requires identification of the industries whose expansion is to be encouraged because of their relatively attractive environmental impacts, such as energy efficiency, public transport, retro-fitting buildings with co-generation heating and cooling systems, and other 'green buildings' features.[17]

A green jobs development strategy also requires complex economic–environmental modelling, including applications of input-output analysis, to work out what will be the secondary changes having an impact on output and employment in other industries. To put the plans into practice requires the cooperation of businesses and trade unions to manage the employment changes. It requires the educational institutions—technical and further educational colleges in particular—to be geared up for providing the necessary workforce skilling and retraining programs. Such processes are often best managed at the urban and regional scale, where there is a directly perceived local commonality of interests.

A green jobs strategy is not unproblematic, however. Even defining a green job is not easy. If a steelworks switches from producing steel for cars to producing steel for bicycles or wind turbines, for example, does that change the foundry workers' jobs from 'brown' to 'green'? Just as much coking coal and iron ore may be mined, and the production process may be equally polluting in either case, even though the products that are made may be more compatible with environmentally responsible consumption behaviours. Similarly, a recycling plant, designed to reduce wastage of materials, may be carbon emitting. Indeed, it is rare for any job to have a zero carbon footprint. Evidently, there is a spectrum of possibilities, such that, while we may say one job is 'greener' than another, taking account of all aspects of both inputs and outputs, there is not a sharp division between jobs that are green and those that are not.

A further complication arises where labour organisations require that green jobs be well paid and secure as well as environmentally responsible.[18] Such concerns about the nature of work are appropriate, of course, but setting them as a necessary condition for defining green jobs predictably reduces business enthusiasm for green jobs projects. In other words, class interests are not eradicated, and can frustrate transitions. So too can regional interests: where new green jobs are located in areas distant from disappearing jobs in existing industries (as in mining regions), problems of labour migration and resettlement may be daunting. Evidently, making a transition to a sustainable economy is a huge challenge.

While a 'green jobs' strategy provides no panacea for dealing with environmental stress, it does raise fundamental issues that need to be addressed in meeting that challenge. It signals the need to consider economic and environmental goals simultaneously. It signals the need for economic planning to be linked to a policy process in which all sections of the community are represented. It can drive change to a more ecologically sustainable economic future.

Land, natural capital, ecological balance

Radical reforms may not be sufficient to achieve sustainability on a global scale, unless they embrace the spiritual and moral issues at the heart of the environmental crisis. Our relationship with land, to nature generally, has an inherently spiritual dimension. Consider the Aboriginal peoples of Australia, who lived in harmony with nature for more than 40 000 years before the European invasion of the continent. Their relationship with the land was integral to their culture, to their very being. Of course, it is difficult to reconcile that sort of relationship with nature with a modern, affluent, urbanised, industrial society. However, policy changes can render nature less vulnerable to exploitation for personal economic gain.

Henry George's ideas warrant revisiting in this context. George was concerned (as described in Chapter 11) with the effects of private land ownership and the potential for land taxation to redress economic inefficiencies and socioeconomic inequities. The type of analysis he developed can be extended from land to nature in general. Such an analysis recognises that the privatisation of natural assets allows a rent to be appropriated, and that therein lies the root of a range of economic, social, and environmental problems.

Incomes from rent derive from the economic surplus generated by the application of capital and labour to nature. The owners of privatised environmental assets derive that income not through productive effort but solely as a result of their ownership of the resources. As economic growth proceeds, they usually capture an increasingly large share of the fruits of growth. If urban development, for example, raises the price of urban land—as it usually does—that increases the rental income of existing landowners. Landowners also stand to make unearned income from capital gains on the sale of their property. Not surprisingly in these circumstances, land is commonly held for speculative purposes. Henry George argued that the site rents (based on the unimproved capital value of the land) should be taken as tax, and used to finance social expenditures by government. *Resource rent taxation* constitutes a broader application of the same principle, capturing for public purposes the economic surplus that would otherwise go to the owners of scarce environmental resources.

A case can be made for extending a similar policy to all environmental assets. These include land, minerals, and other natural resources, and 'common heritage capital'.[19] The latter includes human-made as well as natural assets whose value derives from their uniqueness or social significance. The use of bandwidth for radio, television, mobile phone, and other communications purposes is also relevant in this connection. Media and telecommunications companies currently derive enormous rents from their use. More extensive application of resource rental taxation can be of great value as a means of constraining the use of, and generating public revenues from, all these resources. No problem of trade-off between revenue-raising and environmental effectiveness need arise, as it does with taxes on the consumption of goods with environmentally damaging consequences, because the tax is on rent. Therein lies the advantage of a policy designed to capture an economic surplus.

There is a moral, as well as an economic, element in this analysis and policy. The key principle is that nature is not to be exploited for financial gain. More extensive land and resource rent taxation stops short of the comprehensive socialisation of natural assets, and it is no panacea for environmental problems that are deeply embedded in existing institutional practices, power structures, and prevailing ideologies. However, it could effectively capture for public purposes the economic surplus arising from the use of environmental assets. These public revenues can then be used in ways that enhance environmental quality; for example, investment in renewable energy technologies. Whether, in the longer term, any such reformist measures can trigger the broader values revolution required for the achievement of ecological sustainability remains an open question.

Conclusion

Political economic analysis is enriched by recognising the embeddedness of the economy in nature. All economic activity occurs in a biophysical context, using land and other natural resources, and generating products, including waste products, that have an impact on the environment. To neglect such connections is not only to limit the potential contribution of political economic analysis to environmental concerns, but also to impoverish the study of the economy.

Consideration of environmental problems and policies paves the way for the construction of an alternative ecological economics.[20] It indicates, albeit tentatively, how the general principles of modern political economy outlined in the preceding chapter can be applied to environmental analysis and policies. The focus on an economic surplus draws attention to land, and nature generally, as a source of unearned income. It signals the potential role of resource-based taxation, as well as environmental regulation and public investment, as potentially effective means of limiting environmental damage from the exploitation of the environment. A focus on capital, labour, and the state also puts the significance of corporate power into the spotlight, including its impact on transport options and the production of goods with built-in obsolescence. The concern with evolution is manifest in the analysis of how the economic system can be restructured to satisfy the requirements for ecologically sustainable development. The process of circular and cumulative causation is illustrated by the vicious cycle of environmental decay that occurs in the absence of such remedial measures. Finally, the political economic emphasis on long-term processes of resource creation and destruction contrasts with the typical neoclassical economic focus on how markets allocate a given set of resources goods.

In a world experiencing accelerating resource depletion and environmental stresses, escape from the straitjacket of conventional market economic principles and the development of an ecological political economy may be necessary conditions for survival.

KEY POINTS

- Analysing the socioeconomic roots of environmental problems and contributing to policies for ecologically sustainable development is a major challenge for modern political economy.

- Neoclassical economists interpret environmental problems as caused by externalities and capable of being resolved by policies of 'environmental fine-tuning'.

- An alternative political economic perspective shows the need for a more holistic view of the environment, the influence of prevailing ideologies and power structures, and the need for more radical policy responses.

36 Technology, Industry, Work

> Is capitalism changing to a new economy?
>
> Is there a shift towards post-Fordism?
>
> Does speculation impede the quest for a more productive economy?

Any analysis of the modern economy must pay due regard to questions about how the technical and social organisation of production affects the prospects for material progress. Do new technologies necessarily contribute to higher productivity and/or open up possibilities of liberation from toil? Or is the potential for progress being sidetracked because our economic institutions are unsuited to realise that potential? These big issues have always been central to political economic enquiry. Recall Adam Smith's focus on the division of labour as the driving force of economic progress (but causing the workers to become 'stupid and ignorant'). Recall Karl Marx's analysis of the connection between the development of the forces and relations of production, showing therein the sources of workers' alienation and exploitation. Recall Veblen's worry that the instinct of workmanship in industry would be negated by the predatory instinct of businesspeople. Recall Schumpeter's pessimistic prediction that the progressive role of innovation in industry would be throttled by the development of large corporations.

In our own time similar concerns come in many guises. Some political economists argue that we have experienced a transition from a Fordist to a post-Fordist organisation of production, with major implications for the nature of work and the distribution of power. Some point to the technological changes, particularly information technologies, that are ushering in a new economy—although what is new about it and who benefits from the novelty remain matters of controversy. The diminution of work is posited as one possible outcome, as the technological changes displacing workers from their previous occupations fail to create a comparable number of new employment opportunities. For social scientists emphasising the liberating effects of technology, this is not necessarily an unwelcome scenario; it shifts attention from the Keynesian concern with job creation to the design of institutional arrangements for a more equitable distribution of working time and incomes.

It would be an exaggeration to say that there is a comprehensive analysis of these issues in modern political economy. Rather, what exists is a rapidly expanding literature that is exploratory in method and diverse in political perspectives. This chapter seeks to identify some of the significant themes.

Towards a new economy

How is capitalism changing? Sectoral shifts, affecting the balance of output and employment between agricultural, manufacturing, and service industries, are ongoing. Concurrently, firms and markets, as they channel investments into new and diffusing technologies, are undergoing transformations. This is the essence of what political economist Edward J. Nell has called 'transformational growth', involving qualitative as well as quantitative change.[1] How to understand it and judge the significance of the effects of the technological changes are the key issues.

Popular interpretations centre on the role of technology in the development of a new economy. Indeed, few doubt that new technologies are affecting many, if not most, aspects of economic and social life. The microelectronic revolution has led to computer technologies affecting an ever wider range of industries and economic activities. Information and communications technologies have transformed many aspects of people's working and social lives. Developments in biotechnology are having dramatic economic and social effects. The application of robotics is also starting to have significant consequences for production processes. Some contend that the magnitude of the economic changes wrought by these innovations is comparable to the effects of earlier technological transformations, such as the development of railways in the mid nineteenth century and motor cars in the early twentieth century.

Does the ever wider application of technological change constitute a basis for the development of a new economy, partly displacing the old economy based on mining, heavy engineering, and other traditional manufacturing and transport industries? What is implied is not simply a change of production technologies, but also fundamental changes in economic and social structures. Social theorists such as Manuel Castells have heralded the arrival of an 'informational economy', while terms such as 'network society' and 'knowledge economy' have gained currency.[2] Economist Lester Thurow contends that a third industrial revolution has been occurring, with impacts similar to those of the steam engine and the development of electricity.[3] Discussion of this posited revolution is often couched in exhortatory terms, advocating greater priority in public policy to developing the knowledge base and skills to ensure that companies—and whole nations—are at the forefront of the processes of change.

On closer inspection, the evidence of the impact of new technologies on productive activity remains ambiguous. The development of e-commerce, for example, may be threatening to profitability, and thus to the economic surplus available for investment in innovation, because it enables customers to shop around more readily for the cheapest priced products by browsing the web.[4] Even the basic issue of what constitutes the knowledge economy is ambiguous. According to one writer, it is much broader than information technology, and may also include 'the development of aerospace, artificial intelligence, bio-technology, eco-tourism, gene technology (including genetically modified food, gene shears and cloning), medical technology, miniaturisation, multimedia, nanotechnology, new materials, pharmaceuticals, solar and other renewable energies, telecommunications, waste use and re-use'.[5] This broader view suggests that the development of the knowledge economy depends essentially on fostering the necessary human capital. The political economic focus shifts from technology per se to the role of labour, albeit primarily intellectual rather than manual labour. Therein lie big difficulties, such as the tension between privatisation of knowledge as a means of generating greater profits and the assertion of a public interest in how the knowledge is used (for instance, the potentially hazardous consequences of genetically modifying food).

Overall, it is not clear that the posited new economy changes anything fundamental about capitalism. It does not change the relationship between capital and labour, the process of surplus generation, or the tensions over the use and distribution of the economic surplus. Yet something new seems to be afoot.

From Fordism to post-Fordism

One view of political economic transformation rests on the theory of post-Fordism. It is a theory influenced by a modern school of political economic thought, originating in France, known as Regulation Theory. The shift from Fordist to post-Fordist arrangements is said to have constituted a significant economic transformation in the current era. Whether this is a useful way of conceptualising contemporary change in the capitalist economy has been one of the most controversial issues in modern political economy.

Fordism is the label applied to the phase of capitalist economic development based on mass production for mass markets. Henry Ford, the American car maker, is generally regarded as its pioneer. He introduced the use of the endless-chain conveyor belt into car production, facilitating a detailed division of labour and an enormous increase in labour productivity. He paid his workers $5 per day to accept the new working arrangements, a wage rate much higher than that then prevailing in American industry (a decision he later described as 'the best cost-cutting move I ever made'). Nearly 17 million of Ford's standard black Model T cars rolled off the production line between 1908 and 1927, revolutionising the vehicle industry and the transportation system. Other car makers followed suit. The basic principle of standardised mass production spread to an ever wider range of industries. By the 1950s and 1960s, Fordism had become the norm for industrial production, not only in the USA, but also in other industrialised countries. According to the theorists of post-Fordism, this period of the long boom was the zenith of the Fordist system, the years when it reached its most well-developed form.

What are the essential features of Fordism as a regime of accumulation? As shown in Table 36.1, the characteristic Fordist production units are large factories. Interfirm relationships are competitive, at least as far as market shares are concerned, with oligopoly—competition among the few—being the usual market structure. The products are standardised, made by methods of mass production, for sale in mass consumer markets. Work is organised in terms of a detailed division of labour and is, typically, monitored and regulated by hierarchical modes of control. 'Scientific management', pioneered by F. W. Taylor as a means of asserting that control, is applied more or less explicitly. So are other techniques, such as time-and-motion study, that seek to minimise the discretion exercised by workers in deciding how the work is done.[6]

What about the features of Fordism as a mode of social regulation? Rather more contentiously, Table 36.1 suggests that the application of Fordism in industry tended to go hand in hand with a broader set of macroeconomic and social arrangements: the regulation of the capital–labour relationship (through the use of arbitration and other regulatory institutions, for instance), the implementation of Keynesian policies, and the development of the welfare state.[7] Looking at the extension of Fordist arrangements during the long boom years of the 1950s and 1960s in particular, the inference is that these macroarrangements were part of a political deal. An implicit social contract compensated workers for their acceptance of alienating work by giving them greater economic security and the social benefits arising from the welfare state. This can be regarded as part of a broader capital–labour settlement.

This characterisation of Fordism, as both a set of business practices and a socioeconomic system, looks neat but may be deceptively neat. The causal connections between the micro aspects and the macro characteristics of the long boom period are unclear. What drove what? Or did the changes in business organisation and regulation just happen simultaneously? These are concerns of historical interpretation. All we can confidently say is that the combination of the macroeconomic, social, and political conditions with Fordist workplace practices did look like a winning formula at the time. The economic crisis caused by the collapse of the long boom in the 1970s changed all that. This is what is said to have ushered in the post-Fordist alternative, driven by the quest to restructure industries in order to establish renewed conditions for capital accumulation.[8]

TABLE 36.1 CONTRASTS BETWEEN FORDISM AND POST-FORDISM

	Fordism	Post-Fordism
Regime of accumulation		
Structure of industry	Large factories	Networks of small production units
Interfirm relationships	Competitive	Competitive and cooperative
Outputs	Standardised products for mass markets	Diverse products for niche markets
Capital	Machinery for mass production	Reprogrammable machinery; for example, CAD/CAM
Labour	Detailed division of labour	Multiskilled workers
Workplace relations	Hierarchical, scientific management	Partial autonomy, flexibility
Mode of social regulation		
Broader socioeconomic system	Macroregulation, Keynesian policies, welfare state	Deregulation, privatisation, neoliberalism
Political disposition	Centralised	Decentralised
Cultural character	Modernist	Postmodernist

What is different about post-Fordism? As shown in Table 36.1, business production units are typically smaller, and they are linked by networks of cooperative interfirm relationships. Competition for market share continues, but the competing firms simultaneously cooperate by pooling information about technologies and market trends, perhaps setting up industry service organisations for this purpose. As for the types of products being made, these are diverse, and may be individually customised for small niche markets. Technologies often involve computer-assisted design (CAD) and computer-assisted manufacturing (CAM). The reprogrammable nature of the machinery imparts more flexibility to production. So does the use of multiskilled labour, often organised in work teams with partial autonomy in determining how the tasks are organised and executed. Just in time (JIT) systems of managing the production flows may also obviate the need for substantial stocks of raw materials and spare parts to be kept on hand, just in case they are needed.[9]

Post-Fordist theorists often contrast Fordism and post-Fordism in a rhetorical manner, as a challenge for firms to adopt the new practices. The implicit alternative is for a firm to stick with the old ways, incorporating new technologies and management practices only insofar as they preserve the organisational patterns and social relations of Fordism. This conservative response, said to result in neo-Fordism, offers little future. So the challenge to embrace post-Fordism sounds rather like being made 'an offer you can't refuse': embrace the new system or go under. In practice, both systems coexist in different industries and sometimes side by side in the same sector.

The association between post-Fordism in industry and the changes in the broader socioeconomic system—between the regime of accumulation and the mode of social regulation—is also less clear than Table 36.1 might seem to suggest. As noted in earlier chapters of this book, the neoliberal political program—scaling back Keynesian policy measures, deregulating capital and labour markets, privatising public enterprises, and squeezing the welfare state—has been dominant in the last three decades. This is the period during which post-Fordism is said to have been challenging Fordism as the principal form of capitalist production. As with the correlation between Fordism and the capital–labour settlement of the long boom years, the causal connection is contentious. The rhetoric of flexibility has certainly been characteristic of both the micro (industry) and macro (state) spheres in this more recent era, but that does not prove that neoliberalism necessarily accompanies post-Fordist production arrangements. Indeed, many proponents of post-Fordism see any association with neoliberalism as negating its potentially progressive political possibilities.

Table 36.1 (on p. 341) also posits a link between the economic shift to post-Fordism and a broader social and cultural shift to postmodernity. This may be regarded as a flight of fancy. It is mentioned mainly to indicate an aspect of modern political economy that has some connections with contemporary cultural studies. Postmodernity as a social phenomenon is associated with a shift from the primacy of class relationships to more complex dimensions of social identity that exhibit diversity and difference. Postmodernism as a form of social enquiry emphasises competing discourses and the impact of language and media on how we see and relate to the world around us (if, indeed, any such world exists independently of how we see it!). Post-Fordism, like any 'ism' or totalising discourse, does not sit altogether comfortably among such concerns. However, there have been some interesting explorations of how economic arrangements emphasising flexible specialisation relate to the cultural context of postmodernity.[10]

How significant is post-Fordism in practice? Its proponents have pointed to particular regions that have achieved economic prosperity through the adoption of at least some of its characteristics. These 'new industrial spaces' include Silicon Valley in California, the central-northeast region of Italy (the city of Bologna in particular), Baden-Württemberg in Germany, and the M4 motorway corridor in England, regions that are geographically distinct from the former heartlands of Fordist production, such as the midwest and northeast regions of the USA, the Milan–Turin–Genoa triangle in northwestern Italy, the Ruhr in Germany, and the Midlands in England. They differ in many respects. Some see them as modern expressions of the industrial districts discussed a century ago by Alfred Marshall. Others posit a connection with a neo-Schumpeterian view of innovation and technological change as the key ingredients in industrial success.[11]

From a modern political economic perspective, perhaps the most interesting question is whether these regional enclaves of so-called hi-tech cottage industries are forerunners of a system that can be expected to spread, or whether their existence is made possible by the continued prevalence of Fordist arrangements elsewhere.[12] The issue is of considerable policy significance. Proponents of post-Fordism commonly posit the model as desirable, if not inevitable. The policy implication is that communities and governments should be trying to foster the development of industry clusters with post-Fordist characteristics. From this perspective, post-Fordism is a formula for being a winner, regionally or nationally, in circumstances of increasingly vigorous global competition. Post-Fordism is also held to open up possibilities for more interesting work, the extension of industrial democracy, and the decentralisation of political economic power.[13]

Critics, on the other hand, argue that the flexibility post-Fordism offers is generally used as a means to divide the workforce and extend the power of capital over labour. They also point to the implicit technological determinism, arguing that the assumption that new production technologies lead to new work opportunities and more progressive social outcomes neglects the capitalist power relations that shape how the technologies are used in practice.[14]

The debate is ongoing, notwithstanding some waning of interest in the concept of post-Fordism in recent years. The spectacular success of the People's Republic of China in becoming a powerhouse of manufacturing industry seems to have had many characteristics of a more traditional Fordism. Yet that observation, for some, makes even more important the questioning of what will be the future of work in the already developed industrial—or post-industrial—economies.

Redistributing work in a technologically advanced society

Recent structural economic changes certainly pose major challenges for the future of work. Some fundamental questions about the distribution of jobs arise. How, for example, will work be shared between those with educational attributes and skills in high demand and those who are less able to command roles as 'symbolic analysts', to use Robert Reich's term?[15] A decade ago two German writers, H.-P. Martin and H. Schumann, posited a striking 20:80 ratio as the most likely outcome, a situation in which only a minority of the population (perhaps 20 per cent) will benefit from the hi-tech advanced human capital growth path, while the majority (perhaps 80 per cent) will be struggling or marginalised.[16] Policies for distributing the required skills more broadly are necessary in these circumstances. A shorter standard working week for all is another possible policy response. European nations, France in particular, have taken the lead in reducing working hours in order to spread the work (and leisure) more broadly across the population. Companies such as Volkswagen, Hewlett-Packard, and Digital Equipment Corporation (now merged with Hewlett-Packard) have successfully implemented shorter working hours policies to prevent dramatic numbers of job losses.[17]

Of course, there is a problem with shorter hours if the corollary is lower wages. Whether this is part of the deal depends, *inter alia*, on how productivity per hour is affected by the changes in hours worked. If productivity per hour rises when hours are cut, there need be no fall in incomes. In any case, workers' willingness to accept wage–leisure trade-offs may be greater than generally believed; surveys indicate that as many as 50–60 per cent of workers would prefer shorter hours to higher wages.[18] Some employers and workers will inevitably resist change, but there are relatively modest measures that could be widely implemented in order to facilitate shorter hours for those who are enthusiastic. Possibilities include:

- taking the benefits of productivity improvements as shorter hours rather than higher wages

- changing working-time arrangements, to a four-day week, for example

- allowing workers to take long periods of leave without pay, with income spread over working and non-working periods.[19]

Some ideas of the controversial social scientist, Andre Gorz, are worth noting in this context. Books by Gorz posit a more radical response to the challenge of combining new technologies with an equitable sharing of work, also emphasising how we can enjoy more leisure time.[20] One suggests that a lifetime commitment of, say, 20 000 hours from each person would be sufficient to generate the goods and services needed for a reasonably affluent society. Ideally, individuals should have choice about how they organise this, whether in full-time work leading to early retirement, in more continuous part-time work, or in blocks of work interspersed with periods of education or recreation, or both. Ideally, too, the income stream should be reasonably consistent over time, irrespective of the pattern of work. This throws up a major challenge for capitalist institutions, for which the direct nexus between work and wages has always been a central feature.

Gorz's analysis presents us with a vision of a postcapitalist society—even a postindustrial society—in which the relationships between work and leisure, economy and social structure are transformed. Its achievement is inconceivable without a fundamental shift in prevailing economic structures and ideologies. There would need to be significant changes in the role of women and men in families, in communities, and in social arrangements generally. The conventional notion of breadwinner is already breaking down, as men and women juggle increasingly complex patterns of paid and unpaid work. Whether reducing the dominance of work—for those who have too much of it and those who have too little—would reduce the stress associated with these imbalances and social shifts depends on the social valuation of leisure, of people's contributions to community organisations, and of citizenship in general. Taking advantage of technological change to liberate *Homo economicus* remains an enormous political economic challenge.

Productive investment or speculation?

A growing economic surplus is made possible by technological changes and increases in labour productivity. What determines its disposition? Is the surplus used for wealth-enhancing or wealth-redistributing purposes? Generally, productive investment has the former characteristic, speculation the latter. Productive investment, as Keynes emphasised, adds to the aggregate demand for goods and services in the short run and to the capacity of the economy to supply more in the long run. Speculation, on the other hand, adds nothing to the wealth of society: it is a zero-sum game in which the winners make gains at the expense of the losers. Worse, to the extent that speculation diverts resources from more directly productive purposes, it can be a negative-sum game for society as a whole.

The distinction between productive investment and speculation is not always clear in practice.[21] Some markets characterised by speculative activities seem to be necessary adjuncts to productive economic activity in a capitalist economy. If people are to be willing to advance their savings to businesses by buying shares, for example, there must be secondhand markets where they can resell those shares if they need cash or if they judge their original purchases to have been unwise. As soon as those markets are established, though, they become arenas for speculative buying and selling. Similarly, foreign exchange markets are needed to facilitate foreign trade and foreign travel, but the overwhelming bulk of transactions in those markets have little to do with those real activities; currencies are bought and sold according to their expected future price movements in the hope of securing capital gains.[22]

Futures markets are a yet more striking example. Farmers may need to insure against big fluctuations in their incomes (for example, when caused by the unforeseeable impact of weather on harvests) by entering into futures contracts that effectively give them a guaranteed price for their produce. But those futures markets, whatever their original economic rationale, then become magnets for speculative funds. In practice, this has been one of the most striking contemporary trends. The estimated daily average global turnover in derivatives markets tripled between 2001 and 2007, reaching a figure of more than 4 trillion US dollars every day.[23] When the global financial crisis developed in 2007–08, the existence of these tremendous volumes of speculative capital became particularly problematic, accentuating the systemic instability of the global economy.

The term 'casino capitalism' (introduced in Chapter 4) draws attention to these speculative tendencies. Seymour Melman, an American economics writer with an engineering background, previously identified its origins in the quest for 'profits without production', attributing the low productivity growth in the USA to 'the looting of the productive capital of the system on behalf of short-term money making (and military-political power)'.[24] There is an obvious parallel with Veblen's criticisms of the ascendancy of the financial managers over the production engineers. According to Melman, the influence of the financiers increased dramatically in the twentieth century. The production managers—the 'organisers of industrial work'—were once the key personnel, then the marketing executives, but now the 'financier–strategists' are in control, focusing on 'combining disparate firms into conglomerates … [and] maximising the short-term profit-making opportunities afforded by tax laws, securities transfers, the milking of production assets and other financial legerdemain'.[25]

In the language of Marxist political economy, this would imply a systemic shift from the production of surplus value to the realisation of surplus value, and thence to the circulation of capital and the subdivision of surplus value. Of course, all these aspects are continually relevant to capital accumulation. Indeed, for capital as a whole, the notion of profits without production is nonsensical. Melman's point can be reinterpreted as a claim that the circulation of capital has come to be a disproportionate concern in modern capitalism, involving financial pursuits that redistribute income without contributing directly to the generation of value.

To develop this analysis rather more fully, it is useful to distinguish between the sphere of production and the sphere of circulation. In the former, money capital is used for the purchase of labour power and the means of production, and the power of the owners of capital is used to appropriate surplus value from the value of commodities produced by labour. In the sphere of circulation, the money capital obtained through the sale of the commodities is channelled into the financing of further economic activities in order to facilitate the accumulation of capital as a whole. These activities include further rounds of commodity production, of course, but may also involve adjuncts to the production process, such as those activities performed by capital and the state to ensure economic and social reproduction. Exchange of financial assets (whether shares, titles to real estate, futures, insurance policies, or whatever) have their place here in the sphere of circulation.

Setting up the analysis in this way suggests that, because surplus value is generated only in the sphere of production, the profits of enterprises engaged in the sphere of circulation—including banks and other financial institutions—must derive ultimately from that source.

In effect, the financial institutions rely on capturing a subdivision of the surplus value generated elsewhere in the economy. They get interest payments from loans advanced to productive business enterprises which reduce the profits of those businesses. They also get interest payments from households with housing loans, while credit charges and insurance premiums further swell the incomes of financial institutions. Little wonder that, in the aftermath of the global financial crisis, financial institutions came under such critical scrutiny. In Australia, for example, the big four banks—ANZ, NAB, CBA, and Westpac—made historically unprecedented profits, provoking strong public demands for more control over the charges and interest rate margins from which their profits derive.

US political economist Michael Hudson contends that 'the global financial system has decoupled from trade and investment, taking a life of its own'. He argues that:

> Financial conquest is seeking today what military conquest did in times past: control of land and basic infrastructure, industry and mining, banking systems and even government finances to extract the economic surplus as interest and tollbooth-type economic rent charges.[26]

This is a strong expression of the effect of 'financialisation' in extending financial operations across an even broader landscape of economic activities.

BOX 36.1   FINANCIALISATION

Financialisation is a fairly recently coined term to describe the process whereby an increasing array of economic activities are made exchangeable according to financial criteria. Most directly, this means turning everything into either a financial instrument or a derivative of a financial instrument. More generally, what is implied is a vastly expanded influence of financial motives, financial markets, and financial institutions in determining how the economy works. To the extent that this shifts the locus of profit-making from commodity production and trade to capital accumulation processes centred on financial markets, it significantly changes the nature of modern capitalism. Thus, in the context of the discussion in this chapter, financialisation may be regarded as further enhancing the orientation of the economy towards wealth-redistributing rather than wealth-creating activities, although its advocates contend that it concurrently breaks down non-market barriers to capital accumulation.

How does the process relate to the broader theme of this chapter: technology, industry and work? Financialisation is facilitated by new technologies in the field of information and communications that permit ready access to financial markets and instantaneous worldwide financial transactions. It gives rise to substantial change in industrial structure as finance takes centre stage in the economy; in the USA the share of the financial industry in total GDP has risen fourfold since the end of the Second World War.[27]

Financialisation has produced corresponding changes in the structure of work, with the financial services sector employing a steadily increasing proportion of the workforce in the last three decades.

Financialisation involves more profound changes too. It also entails 'the growing infusion of financial calculation and criteria into a wide range of spheres of economic and political life'.[28] The implications of this are considerable, both economically and socially. The distinctive discipline that financial markets exercise on investment behaviour prioritises a short-term focus on maximising shareholder value. As Australian political economist Geoff Dow notes, this 'finance-led capitalism disadvantages firms that need long-run rather than short-run criteria in the provision of finance (that is, most manufacturing operations), but also the economy as a whole, by increasing the volatility of "hot money" flows and investment generally'.[29]

Another effect of financialisation is to constrain government initiatives, favouring those consistent with a short-term market-orientated agenda over other policies with a more long-term developmental nation-building and egalitarian intentions. The international credit-rating agencies are effectively working off a neoliberal scorecard in determining what risk premium will be added to the interest rate applicable to federal and state government borrowings. And, socially, the more general effect of financialisation is to further emphasise financial gain over other criteria of what matters in life. By implication, if the value of an activity cannot be measured in dollar terms, it is of less economic worth than one that can. One is reminded of Oscar Wilde's famous comment about 'knowing the price of everything but the value of nothing'.

Conclusion

Technology does not directly determine the way in which economic production is organised, still less how its fruits are distributed. Its effects are mediated by the exercise of economic power. The interaction of these technological and political economic forces can be regarded as shaping the *social structure of accumulation*. This is 'the specific institutional environment within which the capitalist accumulation process is organised'.[30] It reflects the nature of business organisations, the financial institutions and credit system, the character of class relationships, and the pattern of state involvement in the economy.

The concerns of this chapter can be interpreted as exploring whether a different social structure of accumulation is now emerging. Arguments about the new economy, a posited transition to post-Fordism, and the speculative uses of capital are aspects of this political economic exploration. At this stage, it is premature to announce the arrival of a new social structure of accumulation. However, insofar as there is a central theme in the political economic changes in the current period, it seems to be flexibility: flexibility in the flow of funds between alternative uses (facilitated by 'financialisation'), flexibility in labour markets (resulting in less economic security for labour), and flexibility in the organisational forms of capital (the structure of firms, subcontracting and other inter-firm relationships). Political choices are not thereby eradicated. Workers—and citizens in general—are not necessarily compliant when faced with a new social structure of accumulation. That depends, among other things, on whether there is sufficient unity of interests to pursue progressive alternatives, or whether this possibility is impeded by social divisions based on class, gender, and ethnicity.

KEY POINTS

- New technologies, adapted to serve the interests of capital, drive political economic change.
- Important changes in the nature of work have occurred, but whether the technological, economic, and social changes over the last half century are usefully characterised as a shift from Fordism to post-Fordism is contentious.
- Important shifts have also taken place in the organisation and mobility of capital, changing the balance between its productive and speculative uses.

37 Class, Gender, Ethnicity

Is class relevant in modern capitalism?

What shapes the gender dimension of economic inequalities?

Does capitalism eradicate or foster racism?

Analysis of socioeconomic inequalities has always been a central concern of political economy. Recall Ricardo's description of the study of distribution between classes as 'the principal problem of political economy'.[1] For Marx, the study of the capital–labour relationship was the key to understanding the capitalist system, linking distribution with production, growth, and economic crises. Keynes, whose primary concern was with macroeconomic aggregates, recognised the importance of income distribution as an influence on the state of the economy and a legitimate focus for public policy. Prominent figures in the institutional and post-Keynesian traditions, including Galbraith, Myrdal, Kalecki, and Robinson, have also made the study of economic inequality part of their political economic analyses. Other modern scholars concerned with the problems of economic development and underdevelopment, such as Amartya Sen, place the issue of inequality at the forefront of their studies.[2]

Neoclassical economics is the exception. As noted in Chapter 22, some pioneers, such as J. B. Clark, sought to use marginal productivity theory as an explicit justification of the economic inequalities generated in free-market economies. In the last century, systematic concern with economic inequality has usually dropped out of the picture, the existing distribution of income and wealth being taken as given for the purposes of constructing models of resource allocation. Thus, the neoclassical focus on efficiency has virtually eclipsed the concern with equity, which is often labelled 'political' and hence not properly a matter for economic enquiry. To the extent that equity issues enter the analysis at all, it is usually with reference to a trade-off between efficiency and equity, implying that the pursuit of distributive justice necessarily comes at an economic cost.[3]

The marginalisation of concern about economic inequality in mainstream economics is an imbalance that warrants redress. Economic inequalities, their causes, consequences, and possible reduction, are among the key issues of the present time. Understanding the causes of economic inequalities and formulating possible remedies is a major challenge requiring reconsideration of some key concepts in political economic analysis. Whether the longstanding concern with class is still relevant, and how class relates to inequalities associated with gender and ethnicity, are issues requiring particular attention.

Reconsidering class

The obvious starting point for a reconsideration of class in political economy—its definition, its interpretation, and its usefulness—is Marx. It was with Marx's analysis that the concept of class took on its radical character. Marx and Engels began the *Manifesto of the Communist Party* with the words: 'The history of all hitherto existing societies is the history of class struggles.' Class was also an important concept in Marx's theoretical works, such as *Capital*, and historical works, where it is employed as a means of explaining economic, social, and political change. Of course, class has always been central to the characteristic Marxist political prescription that workers should recognise their collective interest in transforming capitalism into socialism.

How relevant are these ideas today? At first, they sound somewhat archaic. Many people are uncomfortable about even using the word 'class', perhaps because of its association with the political program of Marxism and its exhortation to class struggle. Even talking about class is regarded by some as a source of unnecessary social division. It is a perspective that reflects the absence of a prevailing class consciousness. It does not necessarily refute the relevance of class as an analytical tool.

How is the concept of class actually used in Marxist political economy? It is not a matter of social pigeonholing, of putting people into categories according to their personal characteristics, or their perceptions of their own social status. The characteristic Marxist concern is with class *relationships* rather than class positions. It is the posited asymmetry of these class relationships that is distinctive. Not that there is anything particularly novel about that. As Marx and Engels emphasised, in every form of society a dominant class has been able to organise systematically the extraction of surplus labour from another class. This was quite blatant under slavery and feudalism. Under capitalism, it continues—albeit in a less immediately visible form—in the relationship between capital and wage labour. As argued in Chapter 14, because workers in general are not paid wages equivalent to the full value of the commodities that their labour creates, there is an economic surplus that takes its most immediately obvious form in the profits of business enterprises. Despite all the changes to capitalism that have occurred since Marx's time, as long as profits continue to be generated in this way, the economic basis for class division remains.

From this perspective, it is largely immaterial whether capitalist employers are nice or nasty people, whether they have extravagant or frugal lifestyles, or whether they exhibit snobbish personal manners. Class derives from the structural relationship of capital to labour as the basis on which a capitalist economy functions.

According to Marxist political economy, this capital–labour relationship is essentially contradictory: it requires cooperation between classes who have fundamental conflicts of interest. Cooperation is necessary to keep the wheels of industry turning, whether in transnational corporations or small businesses, whether in extractive, manufacturing, or service industries, and whether unionised or not. Without this cooperation, both the owners of capital and the workers lose income. However, there is a simultaneous conflict of interest under capitalism, manifest in the continual contest over the distribution of the total income generated, managerial prerogatives, and other aspects of industrial and workplace relations. This uncomfortable nexus between cooperation and conflict is the essence of the capital–labour class relationship.

Certain things follow from this way of conceptualising class. The focus on relationships to the means of production gives the definition of class a distinct economic character, which contrasts with sociological views of class. The Marxian approach does not define class according to income: capitalists can be rich or poor. It is the source of their income that differentiates them from workers. By the same reasoning, people's different consumption patterns do not define their class position: capitalists may ride bicycles rather than drive expensive cars; workers may go to work in overalls or suits. Of course, people's income levels and patterns of consumption, insofar as they correlate with their ownership of the means of production, may be useful secondary indicators of class position, but they are not themselves primary, defining features.

Nor need class consciousness be a defining feature. Individual workers sometimes perceive themselves to have common interests with other workers in the same firm, in other firms, or in distant lands, but they often do not. Indeed, they may perceive themselves to have more interests in common with their employers. That will have a significant bearing on their behaviour, including their political inclinations, but it does not refute their class position as workers. The definition of class is based on objective rather than subjective characteristics.

These are bold assertions. For those who feel uncomfortable about using the term 'class' at all, such reasoning may reinforce the discomfort. So be it. The point is an *analytical* one, to establish a clear starting point for class analysis, quite different from popular perceptions of what class might mean. We then have a basis for considering how class analysis may be adapted to deal with an array of contemporary concerns: the significance of the middle class, the effect of spreading share ownership, the general lack of class consciousness, the effect of intra-class inequalities, and how class interacts with other dimensions of economic and social inequality. These concerns impart more subtlety to the consideration of class and reflect the complexities of class in the real world.

The question of the middle class is particularly important in considering the contemporary relevance and meaning of class. The Marxist analysis begins with what is essentially a two-class model: bourgeoisie and proletariat, or capitalist class and working class. Marx conceded that reality was more complex—that self-employed artisans and a petit bourgeoisie existed alongside these two major classes, for example—but the expectation, forcefully argued in the *Communist Manifesto*, was that capitalist development would tend increasingly to polarise society.[4] Has it done so? The prominence of a middle class in modern capitalist societies would suggest not. People commonly talk nowadays about this middle class as the largest social group, and, in surveys of personal class identification, the majority of people almost invariably describe themselves as 'middle class'. The traditional Marxist response is to describe this as evidence of their false consciousness, of a subjective misreading of the objective reality of their class position. According to this reasoning, while self-identification as middle class may serve people's social and psychological needs, the majority of them derive their income principally from the sale of their labour power and, in so doing, they are working class.

On this reasoning, class is not determined by whether you work in white-collar or blue-collar jobs, whether you are employed in mental or manual labour, in hi-tech or smokestack industries, or whether your remuneration is called a wage or salary. It is a matter of whether you own the means of production. This is not to say that the false consciousness of people describing themselves as middle class is irrelevant. On the contrary, it is a powerful explanation for their failure to act in the unified manner that Marx advocated and predicted: to form a class *for* itself rather than be merely a class *in* itself. The political inference is clear: these workers need to be persuaded to abandon their false consciousness. Much of the political activity of far-left political groups continues to be based, explicitly or implicitly, on this presumption.

A rather different response to the question of the middle class recognises that changing economic conditions have indeed changed the class structure. One aspect is the spread of share ownership. In countries where there has been substantial privatisation of public enterprises and where there has been a vigorous political promotion of 'people's capitalism', many workers have bought shares in private sector businesses. The overall distribution of share ownership usually remains sharply concentrated, and the dividend payments for 'mum-and-dad' shareholders are usually small relative to their wage incomes.[5] However, the recipients feel themselves to have some stake in both capital and labour—as indeed they have. Many other workers with savings in superannuation funds, which are partly invested in capitalist businesses, may also feel themselves to have a similar dual interest. Ascription to the middle class looks a more reasonable response in these conditions.

The effect of economic inequalities *within* classes also needs to be considered. Those who derive their income principally from the sale of their labour power have income differentials that have been accentuated by recent technological and structural economic changes. Workers with key specialist knowhow often command quite impressive wage incomes. Others in more traditional 'blue-collar' occupations have been fighting a rearguard action, many being forced into casual and part-time work in the secondary labour market or into the reserve army of labour. Some have been permanently excluded from the waged workforce. This range of economic circumstances sits uncomfortably with a notion of common working-class interests.

Meanwhile, there is blurring of the boundaries of the capitalist class. Senior executives in large corporations often receive massive remuneration packages, sometimes including shares in the companies that employ them. They are employees, but their incomes are many times bigger than those who own and control their own small- or medium-sized business, even though the class position of the latter, formally, is more unambiguously capitalistic.[6]

The tension between ownership and control in the modern corporation, a central concern of institutional economists, underpins this difficulty of imposing a clear definition on the capitalist class. The resulting fuzziness in class delineation is problematic.

Three principal types of response are possible. One is to take the traditional position that the capital–labour relationship is a functional relationship independent of the identity of the capitalists and the workers, of the degree of inequality in the distribution of income, and of people's perceptions of how they relate to the socioeconomic system. It is a position that separates economic analysis (of the distributional shares of capital and labour) from social analysis (of the extent of personal inequalities) and from political analysis (of how people respond to economic and social inequalities). This disciplinary fragmentation of class analysis sits awkwardly with a holistic political economy perspective.

A second response is to recognise that contemporary capitalist economic and social developments call for a more flexible approach to the interpretation of class. This means modifying, if not scrapping altogether, the traditional Marxist dual-class thesis and the concept of false consciousness. The model from some of the early work by sociologist Erik Olin Wright, reproduced in Box 37.1, illustrates one step in this direction. Six categories, rather than two, are identified. This recognises that supervisors, managers, semi-autonomous wage earners, and self-employed businesspeople may, indeed, have distinct class characteristics that are not reducible to the working-class–capitalist-class dichotomy.

| BOX 37.1 | CLASS IN CONTEMPORARY CAPITALISM |

The following model, developed by Erik Olin Wright, shows a simple way of reconciling class analysis in the Marxist tradition with a recognition that the economic conditions of modern capitalism do not produce a simple dichotomy of capital versus labour.

FIGURE 37.1 A MODEL OF CLASS RELATIONSHIPS[7]

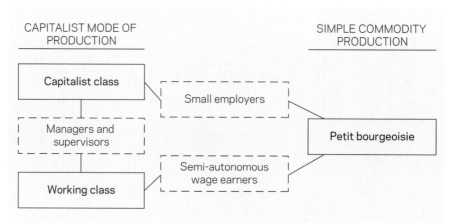

Wright's model shows the capitalist class and the working class as key groups within the capitalist mode of production. Neither is homogeneous, however. Workers differ in terms of how much control they have over their work. Capitalists differ in economic power according to the size of the businesses they control. And between these classes are managers and supervisors in contradictory class locations. Meanwhile, a sector of simple commodity production, not eradicated by the forward march of capitalism, ensures the continued significance of a self-employed class, or petit bourgeoisie. Small employers and semi-autonomous wage earners are represented as intermediate groups between the main categories, having hybrid characteristics in terms of

- their ownership and control of property and investment
- their control over the physical means of production
- their control over the labour power of others and over the sale of their own labour.

The model illustrates how class analysis can be developed. It provides a basis for empirical measurement (such as the relative size of each of the groups in different nations) and for political analysis (of class consciousness or electoral behaviour, for instance). Wright's more recent work shows other ways in which sociological analysis can be blended with the concerns of political economy, but the basic model here remains useful as a means of illustrating the complexity of class structures.[7]

How the members of the intermediate socioeconomic categories (or contradictory class locations) align politically is crucial to the functioning and stability of capitalism. If they see themselves as having common cause with the working class, their combination produces a powerful force that is potentially challenging to the prevailing political economic order. The late twentieth century experience of people's power toppling tyrannical and corrupt governments in, for example, the Philippines and Indonesia comes to mind in this context; these broad, cross-class coalitions successfully challenged the prevailing political order. If, as is more usually the case, those in contradictory class locations see their interests aligned with the capitalist class in maintaining the present political economic arrangements, a more conservative scenario prevails. If some of the working class share that perception too, as is also often the case, the conservatism is yet more pervasive.

Italian writer and politician Antonio Gramsci's notion of *hegemony* warrants consideration in this context. Hegemony entails the widespread acceptance of beliefs supportive of a particular political economic system.[8] The hegemony of bourgeois values is partly a product of people's conditioning (through institutions such as the media, the churches, and the education system) and partly a product of their practical need to fit in with the existing socioeconomic arrangements.[9] The dominant ideologies are commonly accepted by those whose objective class position might otherwise lead to a more dissident political stance. Therein lies an explanation for the coexistence of class inequality and widespread political conservatism. Its political implications are far-reaching. Instead of trying to exhort workers to see the error of their ways by exposing the true nature of capitalist class relations, the emphasis switches to challenging the institutional arrangements whereby capitalist ideology is perpetuated. It is a theme to which we return in the penultimate chapter.

A third approach to the interpretation of class imparts yet more fluidity by emphasising distributional struggles rather than structural class relationships. This is what its proponents call 'postmodern Marxism'.[10] The emphasis is on replacing an essentially dualistic conception of class with a more complex and nuanced analysis of class relationships that emphasises the processes of class formation operating at specific times in particular places. The analysis retains a Marxist character, in that it stresses the existence of an economic surplus. However, there is no presumption that the surplus goes directly as income to the capitalist class. Rather, the surplus is regarded as the focus of numerous distributional struggles. Environmental movements, for example, can be effective in acquiring some of the surplus for cleaning up hazardous wastes or restoring environments degraded by capitalist enterprises. These struggles over the surplus are treated as being of comparable importance to the struggles between capital and labour within the capitalist mode of production—the traditional Marxian focus. The relationship of class with gender and ethnicity also comes into the spotlight, since gender and ethnicity can be significant seams of socioeconomic inequality and conflict.

Recognising gender

Gender divisions in society are more visible than class divisions because there is less ambiguity about the basis of classification; with very few exceptions, people are either female or male. The term 'gender', however, refers specifically to the socially constructed roles for men and women. Gender inequalities are not necessarily based on biological differences. Often, the fact that men and women do different jobs is not attributable to their different physical capabilities. Women and men may face a different array of economic opportunities, and their average income levels are characteristically uneven. Any analysis of the political economy of inequality needs to take account of this gender dimension of the way in which the economy functions, as well as the class dimension. Then, we are in a better position to consider strategies for change.[11]

Gender and class dimensions of inequality are not synonymous, of course. One way of conceptualising them is in terms of the relationship between patriarchy and capitalism.[12] Put simply, patriarchy is the power structure in which men dominate women, and capitalism is the power structure in which capital dominates labour. Analytically, the task is to examine the relationship between these two structures. One way of doing so is in terms of the Marxist model of the circuit of capital, introduced in Chapter 16, which situates gender within the sequential conditions for accumulation. The three conditions that are directly relevant in this context are the reproduction of labour power, the production of surplus value, and the realisation of surplus value. In each case, gender inequalities can be seen as functional for capital in the sense of helping to ensure that the requirements necessary for its expansion are met.

The *reproduction of labour power* is the fundamental precondition for the continued functioning of the economic system. First and foremost, it means producing and raising children. This is characteristically women's work. Men play only a small part in biological reproduction, often a very small part indeed. Notwithstanding the fact that more men are involved in childrearing today than in the past, women remain the principal carers for children. In the advanced capitalist nations at least, it is also common for mothers to combine their role as childrearers with participation in waged work.[13] Yet domestic labour still tends to be done disproportionately by women. Sustaining the existing workforce—by maintaining health, providing adequate nutrition, and creating leisure activities conducive to physical and emotional well-being—is an important aspect of economic and social reproduction that is based in the household.

Not surprisingly, the study of domestic labour and the associated gender inequalities has been a primary focus of feminist political economic analyses. The household is commonly said to constitute a private sphere, subordinate to the public sphere of paid employment and the political and economic institutions usually dominated by men.[14] It is typically excluded from the gaze of orthodox economics because the economy, from a neoclassical perspective, is defined in terms of production for market exchange. Yet, according to various estimates, the value of domestic economic production carried out in the household—disproportionately by women—amounts to about half of the gross national product.[15] The neglect of this crucial economic contribution of domestic production constitutes a significant gender bias in orthodox economics.[16]

How to situate the household sector in a reconstructed modern political economy is a contentious matter. At first sight, much, if not all, household production seems to have a non-capitalist character. Useful goods and services are produced, but usually for direct consumption rather than for market exchange, and intra-household income transfers are more typical than direct wage labour. Some families, in which both men and women have paid jobs, purchase domestic services (such as cleaning, ironing, cooking, even dog walking) rather than do all their own domestic labour, but most is still done by members of the household. The provision of these services in the household is crucial to the functioning of capitalism. Capitalist employers need new generations of workers who are fed and reasonably well educated—job ready, so to speak. Schools and hospitals also have a role to play in the functions of social reproduction, but the nurturing capacity of the household is fundamental to the requirements of the economy.

The labour expended on these tasks within the household is also provided typically at no direct cost to capital. There may be an indirect contribution, to the extent that firms pay taxes that go partly to family support payments, child allowances, and other transfer payments to households. However, unpaid domestic labour is an effective means whereby the cost of reproduction of labour power is shifted from firms onto the state and onto households themselves. Looked at from this viewpoint, it suits the class interests of capital to retain the household—and its typically gendered division of labour—as a subordinate, non-capitalist sector of the economy and society. One might draw a parallel with the advantages the advanced capitalist nations derive from poorer developing nations that serve as sources of cheap labour.

The *production of surplus value* is the second requirement for capital accumulation. The gendered character of *waged* work is the central feature here. Marxists have sought to apply the concept of the reserve army of labour in this context, because many women have had a more marginal attachment to the waged workforce than have men. A striking historical example of this reserve army characteristic was the sudden entry of women into paid jobs during the Second World War (to support the war effort) and their subsequent return to unpaid domestic duties after the war (resuming 'their proper place in the home').[17] However, the growing proportion of women who have become permanent members of the waged workforce in recent decades sits uncomfortably with the view of women as a reserve army. Far from being marginal to wage labour, more and more women have become direct and regular contributors to the production of surplus value.

The more persistent problem is the gendered division of labour in waged work. Labour-market segmentation entails distinctive concentrations of men and women in different industries and occupations; that is, in different labour-market segments. Women have been disproportionately represented in occupations that are perceived to be extensions of their traditional household work: nursing, cleaning, primary education, the preparation of food, clothing manufacture, and clerical work, for example.[18] The patterns are not static; in the nineteenth century, for example, secretaries were usually male, the occupation becoming characteristically female only in the early twentieth century. Later in the twentieth century, the gender composition of bank tellers underwent a similar shift. In other fields, such as nursing and clothing manufacture, the gendered character of work remains striking. In the modern economy, the services sector has a range of occupations in which face-to-face interactions are crucial and client emotions have to be managed; these are occupations where women are concentrated, too.[19]

Labour-market segmentation has a strong association with gender-biased wage inequalities. Insofar as average wages tend to be lower for characteristically female jobs, it is not surprising that a gendered inequality in the overall distribution of wage incomes persists. The higher incidence of part-time work among women also biases the distributional outcomes. Even after accounting for that factor, women's average full-time wage incomes tend to average only about 80 per cent of men's.[20] Recognising the importance of redressing such systemic economic discrimination according to gender, governments have sought to prevent employers paying different wages to men and women doing similar jobs. Where men and women are doing different jobs, however, a requirement of equal pay for equal work does not eliminate gendered wage inequalities. The principle of equal pay for work of *comparable worth* needs to be applied to wage-setting in those circumstances.[21] But in unregulated labour markets no such principle applies, and wage relativities are shaped by market power.

The problem of differential promotion prospects is a further source of gender bias. Ensuring wage parity for people in different occupations, even breaking down the labour-market segmentation process, does not ensure equality of gender outcomes if there is gender bias in promotion processes. The problem is sometimes ascribed to women interrupting their career for childbirth. Claims about a 'glass ceiling' setting a definite but invisible limit on women's career progress, including the progress of women who do not have children, suggest a more profoundly discriminatory process. This glass ceiling may work against business interests in the long term, for failure to take full advantage of the potential leadership roles of women constitutes a waste of talent. Its persistence implies that, in this respect, patriarchal influences dominate over the interests of capital.

A gendered division of labour is seldom absolute. Glass ceilings may have cracks. Women may become chief executive officers of large corporations, high court judges, even prime ministers. Some do. Their statistical underrepresentation at those levels is well documented, however, and shows little sign of dramatic change, notwithstanding conspicuously successful individuals.[22] And, to the extent that women remain disproportionately concentrated in more lowly paid occupations, the gendered division of labour in waged work serves capitalist interests. It facilitates the production of surplus value by keeping down wage costs. This is the result, directly, of women's wages being lower than men's, on average. It is the result, indirectly, of gendered divisions among workers undermining their collective bargaining power: this is the divide-and-rule process at work.

What about the *realisation of surplus value*? This third requirement for capital accumulation has a less obvious link with gender divisions in the economy and society. For the capitalist system as a whole, the realisation of surplus value in a monetary form as profit depends primarily on the maintenance of a high level of demand for goods and services. Both women and men are consumers and, as such, both contribute to meeting this particular systemic requirement. However, women have usually managed a larger share of the consumption process, especially in the purchasing of clothing and day-to-day food and household items, rather than big-ticket items such as cars. The advertisers certainly seem to think women are the key consumer group, judging from the way they target commercials at them. These commercials commonly play on presumed fears and aspirations; to be the perfect mother who feeds her children the right breakfast cereal and washes their clothes in the most effective laundry detergent, for example. The role of women in the management of consumption is thereby linked with the perpetuation of sexist stereotypes. This reasoning suggests that women as shoppers, as well as housewives and workers, are crucial to the functioning of the capitalist economy. This is the sense in which Galbraith wryly described women as comprising 'a crypto-servant class'.[23]

The distinctive economic positions of women and men can be analysed in various ways. The political economic perspective presented here has a distinctly Marxist feminist angle, emphasising how the gender division of labour helps capitalism meet its own systemic requirements for reproduction and growth.[24] This is not to deny some fluidity in patterns of gender inequality, or that government policies to limit discrimination and promote affirmative action can make a difference. Certainly, it does not imply passivity in the face of structural disadvantage. Indeed, it is a chain of reasoning with a politically powerful punchline. It indicates that the movement for gender equality, if it is to be fully successful, also involves a struggle against the prevailing structures and interests of capital.

Emphasising ethnicity

Economic inequalities based on ethnicity parallel gender inequalities in some respects. People of different ethnic origin are often clustered in different types of occupations. They may face an unequal array of economic opportunities. Their average income levels are sometimes markedly uneven.

The nature and extent of those inequalities varies from country to country. In the USA, for example, the relative economic disadvantage of African-Americans is notorious; even after a century and a half of freedom from slavery, and even after having elected Barack Obama as the first African-American president of the USA, economic disadvantage remains entrenched. The relative economic disadvantage of people from Central and South America and the Caribbean islands is equally striking. In England, immigrants from India, Pakistan, and, again, the Caribbean have been the major groups to experience economic and social disadvantage. In Australia, the most disadvantaged groups are the Aboriginal peoples; but recently arrived immigrants from non-English-speaking backgrounds commonly face particular problems in establishing socioeconomic equality. Immigrants to any nation usually do it tough before they establish themselves; in societies where racism is pervasive, a further impediment exists to achieving parity in economic opportunities.[25]

Is there a connection between racially discriminatory practices and the operations of capitalism? Since racism predated capitalism, it would be facile to suggest a simple or direct causal connection. One view is that it is quite independent of the economic system. From this perspective, racism, and the associated processes of discrimination and socioeconomic disadvantage, are not attributable to capitalism, and are equally likely to characterise any other socioeconomic system that might succeed it. Its roots are not economic—or, at least, not systemically so. The solution, accordingly, is independent of the economic arrangements of society. It is a matter of changing personal attitudes through public education or of developing institutions that foster greater mutual understanding among different ethnic groups.

Yet the economic dimension of racism cannot reasonably be ignored. How does it operate? Among social scientists, there are sharply divided views about whether capitalism ameliorates or accentuates the problem. In the former camp are neoclassical theorists, such as Gary Becker, who received the 1992 Nobel Prize in Economic Sciences for his application of orthodox economic reasoning to social phenomena. Becker's analysis emphasises the exercise of individual choice in competitive markets. It generally takes the tastes informing those choices as given. So, in respect of racial discrimination, it assumes that some employers have a preference for white employees over black employees; that is, that they have some sort of racist inclination. That being so, white workers will be in greater demand. In a market economy, that will cause the prevailing wage rates for white workers to be above those of black workers. So, racially discriminating employers must pay bigger wage bills than non-discriminating employers. The former will have higher costs of production and therefore lower profits. In a competitive market economy, they will eventually be driven out of business. Only the non-discriminating employers will remain.[26]

Milton Friedman, taking a similar view, has argued: 'A businessman or entrepreneur who expresses preferences in his business activities that are not related to productive efficiency is in effect imposing higher costs on himself than are other individuals who do not have such preferences. Hence, in a free market they will tend to drive him out.'[27] Thus, capitalism eliminates racism. Indeed, on neoclassical reasoning, it would be best for the government to refrain from trying to prohibit discrimination. The neoclassical analysis predicts that such regulations would cause higher rates of unemployment among the less-favoured ethnic groups: in other words, enforced wage parity would benefit those fortunate to be employed, but at the expense of those who now find it harder to get work at all.

Like neoclassical economics in general, the preceding arguments rest on some distinctive assumptions. The origin of the original preference for white over black (or whatever is the relevant racist inclination) is unquestioned. The analysis is ahistorical. Both labour and commodity markets are assumed to operate in a competitive manner. Rejecting these assumptions, political economists regard the problem of racial discrimination quite differently. Racism is seen not as a matter of individual preference but as a feature of the normal functioning of institutions. It is a systemic rather than personal phenomenon. The origins of the discriminatory preferences and the institutional mechanisms by which they are reproduced come under more critical scrutiny. So do the economic interests with a stake in their perpetuation.

This political economic analysis of racism imparts an historical dimension to the analysis. It also puts capitalism back in the dock. If, for example, the perpetuation of racism results in divisions among workers that undermine their ability to achieve higher wages through collective action, then one may judge that to be in the general interests of capital, irrespective of individual employers' racist or non-racist preferences. The divide-and-rule strategy, while not necessarily causing the racism, may perpetuate it to the advantage of employers.[28] The political implications of this view are strikingly different from those of the neoclassical analysis. The inference is that, like the movement for gender inequality, the movement against racism must challenge the prevailing power structures of capitalism as a necessary, albeit not sufficient, precondition for eradicating economic disadvantage.

The principle of circular and cumulative causation—introduced in Chapter 25 in the context of the study of institutional economics—has particular relevance to the explanation of racism and its perpetuation. It helps to explain why a disadvantaged minority group, identifiable by its skin colour, for example, may face a vicious cycle of discrimination and material disadvantage. Being relatively poor, its members are likely to be poorly educated, poorly dressed, and more inclined to antisocial behaviour, such as crimes against property. That fuels the belief that the minority group is inherently different, unworthy of a helping hand, and probably best avoided, if not actively suppressed. In effect, the legacy of past discrimination becomes a justification for further discrimination.

The *spatial* dimension of racial inequality compounds the problem. This is most obviously the case in ghettoes, where disadvantaged minority groups are geographically concentrated. The possibility of an individual achieving upward economic and social mobility is thereby made more remote. However, spatially targeted policies can play a significant role in the redress of economic inequalities in these circumstances. The same applies to inequality between classes; spatial segregation accentuates the differences of access to economic opportunities, but also provides a basis for targeting policies to ameliorate, if not eradicate, the inequalities. In both cases, however, the precondition for the redress of inequalities is a government with a strong commitment to using vigorous policies for social reform.

If the market will not eradicate discrimination—if, indeed, the most powerful participants in the market profit from it—then it necessarily becomes a concern for the state. Proponents of purposive intervention, sometimes drawing on the principle of circular and cumulative causation, contend that policies of affirmative action are needed. The victims of discrimination must be given explicit preference (in education and employment, for example) for a period of time before equality of opportunity can eventually be established. Not surprisingly, opponents of such a policy call it 'reverse discrimination', and emphasise its apparent incompatibility with efficiency in the use of human resources during the period of transition.[29] A level playing field is an admirable goal, but the path towards it is fraught with conflicting economic interests and difficult political judgments.

Conclusion

The analysis of economic inequalities according to class, gender, and ethnicity is central to modern political economy. This chapter has merely touched on some of the major concerns, and indicated some lines of fruitful enquiry. Further analysis would emphasise the interconnections between these three dimensions of socioeconomic inequality, recognising that the socioeconomic conditions of disadvantaged groups are multidimensional. The different economic positions of black, female employees, and white, male employers, for example, are attributable to differences of race, gender, and class that are multiplicative rather than additive. Integrating considerations of class, gender, and ethnicity also illuminates the dynamics of capital accumulation as well as the distribution of income, wealth, and economic opportunities. In other words, it is of fundamental economic, as well as social, significance.

Equally important are the politics. The complexity of class, gender, and ethnicity as dimensions of 'who gets what' in the modern economy is matched by the complexity of struggles to make a difference. The drive to eradicate exploitation, discrimination, and oppression takes many forms, generating more diverse social movements than a traditional focus on the binary opposition of capital and labour would suggest. Focusing on the study of these inequalities and the social movements to which they give rise is the source of much dynamism in modern politics.

What are the appropriate policy responses to inequalities associated with class, gender, and ethnicity? This too is a contentious matter. The traditional focus of those committed to the eradication of unjustifiable inequalities has been the *politics of redistribution*, seeking to create greater equality through the redistribution of income and social expenditures.

A different approach is the *politics of recognition*, which emphasises the distinctiveness of minority groups and the desirability of maintaining the cultural differences, while at the same time reducing economic inequalities.[30] This entails an official commitment to multiculturalism and the recognition of the special rights of indigenous peoples in respect of land, for example. The two approaches do not always sit comfortably together. Can public policy move on both fronts simultaneously? It is a big challenge for the institutions of the state.

Thus, concerns about economic inequality, as with other contemporary concerns about environmental decay, technology, industry, and work, lead us to reflect on the potential for political control over market processes in the pursuit of broader social goals. It seems that all roads lead to the state.

KEY POINTS

- Class analysis is central to modern political economy. It raises complex issues about the nature of the capital–labour relationship, the middle class, class consciousness, and class struggles.

- Gender inequalities associated with patriarchal power structures are pervasive and persistent, interacting with class inequalities under capitalism.

- Racism, as a pervasive social phenomenon, adds a further dimension to economic inequalities. Its eradication calls for policies that recognise the sources of discriminatory practices as well as redistributing economic opportunities.

38 ▶ The Political Economy of the State

Can the state be an instrument for economic and social progress?

How is it constrained by the interests of capital?

What is implied by regarding the state as an arena for struggle?

Analysis of the state is central to political economy. It makes no sense to treat it as external to the economy, as a *deus ex machina* that intervenes intermittently in an otherwise self-regulating economic system. The state has been integral to the history of capitalist development. It has been involved in providing infrastructure and services, regulating business behaviour and markets, establishing and enforcing property rights, managing trade relationships, imposing taxation, and spending public revenues (making governments, without exception, the largest consumers of economic resources within individual nations). The precise form of these activities has varied from country to country, according to particular historical conditions. A comprehensive political economic analysis needs to identify both the general patterns and the more nation-specific aspects. Understanding how the state is shaped by competing political economic interests and ideas is the core analytical concern.

For those who would wish to engineer new directions of economic development, capitalist or otherwise, the question of the state also raises explicitly normative political concerns. Judging what role the state can play is the key issue in formulating political strategy, whether the intent is to expand or contract the range of hands-on functions the state performs. Social democrats contend that the long-term trend is, and should be, towards expanding the sphere of politics. This renders more of our economic and social choices inherently political.[1] How best to steer the state and use public policy to mediate between the interests of capital and labour—and between differences of class, gender, and ethnicity—then becomes the focus. For those of a more libertarian disposition, the question is how best to roll back the state and thereby extend the realm of individual (market) freedoms.[2] Either way, a prescriptive view of the state is implied.

Perhaps it is because these analytical and prescriptive elements inexorably intertwine in discussions of the state that the topic is notoriously complex, if not confusing. Analysis of what the state does tends to be mixed up with prescriptions about why it should do those things or do different things. This chapter seeks to impose some order by examining each of the three principal prescriptive positions: radical, reformist, and conservative. It builds on the analysis of the state at the intersection of democracy, capitalism, and bureaucracy that was introduced in Chapter 27. Starting from that basis, it explores whether the modern state is an instrument for social progress, or so constrained by the interests of capital and/or bureaucracy that it obstructs progressive social change.

An instrument for social progress

One does not necessarily have to be of a democratic temper to see the state in a positive political economic light. As noted in Chapter 9, the tradition of mercantilist thought and practice, prevalent in the seventeenth and eighteenth centuries, saw a strong state and a strong economy as the twin necessities for national power. This was in an age before democratic rights were extended to the people as a whole. Emphasising the need for state-directed policies to ensure national strength and stability was a pragmatic response to conditions of growing international economic rivalry.

It was against this mercantilist emphasis on the necessary regulatory role of the state that Adam Smith reacted, arguing that it tended to stifle enterprise. But even Smith was cautious about the consequences of market freedoms. He supported British colonialism and the naval power that the state provided to support it, seeing this as securing the big market necessary for the detailed division of labour and for greater economic liberties in Great Britain. Smith also thought that a significant role for government, supplemented by the moral influence of the church, would continue to be necessary to ensure the social bond that the pursuit of commercial gain might otherwise threaten. Thus, a conservative concern for social stability continued to put the state in the spotlight, despite the growing influence of economic liberalism. The awkward blend of these two currents, observable in Smith, continues today in the positions to the right of centre in economic policy debates.

These differences of analytic orientation are manifest in different views about the appropriate role of the state in economic management. The modern neoliberal view, which emphasises the virtues of free trade and individual enterprise, contrasts with the corporatist view of the state, which emphasises the need to consciously engineer and secure cooperation between the major interest groups in the economy. The latter inclination is reflected in conservative political thought as well as in reformist ideas stemming from the works of Veblen, Galbraith, and contemporary post-Keynesian advocates of incomes policies (as discussed in Chapters 24, 26, and 32, for example). Institutional economics, perhaps more than any of the other major schools of thought, is generally inclined towards this positive view of the state as a vehicle for economic reform, as noted in Chapter 27.[3]

A positive position on the state is even to be found within the neoclassical economic tradition. As noted in Chapter 23, the economic problems arising from the inadequate supply of public goods in free-market economies, as well as the problems of imperfect competition and of externalities, are held by many neoclassical economists to justify a substantial ameliorative role for the state. Neoclassical economics thereby concedes that there is a case for government in correcting the anomalous tendencies in free-market economies. The assumed primacy of the market remains distinctive, though. The state intervenes only to apply bandaids to an otherwise healthy economic body. The implicit presumption is that, while enlightened state policies can help to reconcile capitalism with broader social concerns about efficiency, equity, and environment, only the lightest touch is needed. Here, in effect, is a view of the state as an instrument of reform by default, stepping in only when the market fails to ensure an optimal allocation of resources.

The view of the state in Keynesian economics, at least in its mainstream 'neo-Keynesian' interpretation, has a similar character, although it recognises the need for a more substantial range of policy measures. Government intervention is warranted, according to this perspective, because of the basic flaws of a free-market economy. In this case, the principal difficulty is that of ensuring continuous full employment and, as a secondary concern, controlling inflationary tendencies. That provides a rationale for government policies to manage and stabilise an otherwise unstable economy. It may even extend to a 'somewhat comprehensive socialisation of investment'. Again, there is no significant political economic analysis of the state; instead, the implicit assumption is that it can be an instrument for effective reform, just so long as it is informed and guided by people of intelligence and sound values.

Fabianism shares this latter presumption, but marries prescriptions about reform to goals of a more explicitly socialist character. Early Fabians, such as Sidney (1859–1947) and Beatrice Webb (1858–1943) and George Bernard Shaw (1856–1950), considered that greater knowledge about economic and social conditions would be the key to forging incremental improvements in public policies. Finding out about the conditions in which people work, their occupational health hazards, patterns of remuneration, and attendant social problems, for example, would lead to legislative and regulatory changes producing more socially beneficial economic outcomes. The state would be the vehicle for that process of reform.[4] The enfranchisement of all citizens would ensure that the state would no longer represent the interests of only the dominant class. Not surprisingly, when these sentiments were becoming widespread in the early twentieth century, Fabians saw the then newly established Labour parties as instruments of reform. Subsequent disillusionment with the ability, or even the inclination, of Labour parties to engineer evolutionary socialism in practice has weakened the Fabian tradition over the last half-century. Yet it remains a significant intellectual current in the analysis and advocacy of progressive economic reforms.

The underlying tension in any reformist political economic agenda is between strong reformism and weak reformism. The former runs the risk of provoking a destabilising backlash from those who own and control the bulk of the capital, if the policies go against their interests. The latter runs the risk of loss of support among the citizenry if the slow pace of reform leaves expectations and aspirations for change frustrated. There is no easy solution to this dilemma. As the British socialist intellectual R. H. Tawney said, you can peel an onion layer by layer but you can't skin a tiger paw by paw (and capitalism, by this reasoning, is surely one big pussy cat).[5]

The notion of 'radical reform' may be considered a practical response to this dilemma. The British political economist Stuart Holland has talked about this as a means of bridging the longstanding divide between reformist and revolutionary currents in leftist politics; in effect, it is the assertion of the strong reformist case.[6] André Gorz, the French social scientist whose prescriptions for radical change in the distribution of work and incomes were considered in Chapter 36, has also promoted this view. In his words, 'The task of politics here is to define intermediate strategic objectives, the pursuit of which meets the urgent needs of the present while prefiguring the alternative society that is asking to be born.'[7] This sounds like a remarkable blend of pragmatism and idealism. However, it is not difficult to cite positive examples. One is the redistribution of working time, dealing with the immediate problems of unemployment and overwork, while simultaneously prefiguring more fundamental long-term challenges to the capitalist wages–work nexus. Another is the introduction of a carbon tax as a practical policy measure to deal with environmental decay, and as a step towards producing the attitudinal and structural economic changes necessary for the transition to ecological sustainability (see Box 35.1). As with Fabian socialism, the advocacy of all such reforms is based on the underlying presumption that the state can be a vehicle for addressing fundamental social needs currently violated by the interests of capital.

Serving the interests of capital

Other currents in political economy—Marxism, most obviously—are less sanguine about the possibilities of progressive reform. Marxists argue that claims about the state serving the national interest typically mask a class interest. The key question that they pose is: how does the state actually relate to the conflicting class interests in a capitalist society? The characteristic answer emphasises the dominant tendency to serve the interests of capital. The simplest and most often cited expression of this view is the statement in the *Manifesto of the Communist Party* by Marx and Engels: 'The executive of the modern state is a committee for managing the common affairs of the capitalist class.'[8]

The supplementary questions are *why* and *how* this role is played by the state. It is in answering these questions that a distinction between structuralist and instrumentalist theories of the capitalist state has often been drawn.[9] The *structuralist* approach emphasises the pressure on the state to act in this way because of the necessity to secure the conditions for capital accumulation; it must prioritise the pursuit of economic growth. The state is also necessarily concerned with legitimisation; it must ensure that the existing socioeconomic structure is regarded as legitimate in the eyes of the citizens. The former requires that the government, and the state in general, be continually mindful of the need to ensure profitability, not necessarily for all firms, but for capital in general. The latter may require some ameliorative policy measures, such as income redistribution or welfare state provisions to help the poor. The task is to find an effective combination of policies for capital accumulation and legitimisation; for example, by devising a tax system that is effective in producing the necessary revenues without violating capitalist class interests.[10] Maintaining the structure of the capitalist economy and society requires nothing less.

The *instrumentalist* variant on the Marxist theory of the state puts more emphasis on the personnel within the state apparatus. Insofar as politicians, judges, and senior members of the armed forces and public service have backgrounds and values in common with members of the capitalist class, they can be expected to have common interests, too. The old school tie and club memberships play a part in this story. So, too, may freemasonry, at least in certain sections of the public service and the police force.[11] This starts to make the process linking economic and political interests and ensuring coherence within the state apparatus sound conspiratorial. Perhaps, but it is not necessarily so. All one need posit is that the confluence of interests and values between the dominant economic class and the political elite leads to a generally harmonious relationship. The use of the state as an instrument by the capitalist class then becomes relatively uncontroversial, notwithstanding the veneer of accountability to a broader citizenry.

The globalisation of capital is often said to compound this tendency for the state to serve the general interests of capital. As argued in Chapter 28, corporate globalisation tends to constrain the policies of states further, to the extent that there is a fear of capital flight in response to unsympathetic government policies. Trying to create the conditions conducive to investment by multinational businesses tends to force states into beggar-thy-neighbour competition. Reducing wages, trade union rights, business tax rates, and environmental protection are the characteristic policy responses. Faced with these dominant pressures, Marxist political economists argue that the prospects of progressive reform have become yet more remote.[12]

This implies a greater degree of unanimity than is actually the case. Marx himself did not develop a comprehensive analysis of the state, and there are numerous places in his writing where one may discern support for particular measures of reform. Notwithstanding the polemical, revolutionary tone of the *Manifesto*, one can find in it a shopping list of reformist demands, on which he and Engels thought the movement for socialism could focus. The socialist tradition has been replete with controversy about the possibility of progress through the state ever since the debates between Marx and revisionist Eduard Bernstein in the late nineteenth century. Bernstein argued that an evolutionary transition from capitalism to socialism was possible, a view that Marx denounced as incompatible with a revolutionary perspective. The controversy continues in today's debates over the scope for radical reform.

Almost without exception, states have played a greater role in capitalist economies over the last century. While many of these state functions have directly served the interests of capital, this has not been the case all the time. The extensions of protection against racial and sexual discrimination in the workplace, occupational health and safety provisions, environmental protection, and urban zoning to prevent incompatible land uses are just a few examples.

Of course, one may take the view that any policies serving to defuse potential social discontent are, by definition, in the interests of capital, but that would be a very uncompromising stance. On that reading, just about anything the state does fulfils its pro-capitalist functions of facilitating accumulation and/or ensuring legitimisation. The role of the state in serving the interests of capital becomes a tautology so long as capitalism remains the dominant economic system.

An impediment to social progress

A quite different critique of the state comes from the anarchist position. Anarchists have had a bad press, but they have a positive political philosophy. One recurrent theme is the preference for voluntary cooperation rather than the exercise of state power. The state is seen as an instrument of oppression—perhaps an even more fundamental obstacle to social progress than the class exploitation on which Marxist political economy focuses. It is a chain of reasoning that derives, in part, from the aversion to coercion. As anarchist writer Giovanni Baldelli puts it, 'Coercion, whether by society or individuals, runs counter to the needs and purposes of the individual and is therefore evil. It forces a human being to behave according to the needs, feelings, thoughts and will of another, as if he had none himself.'[13] The state, as the source of officially sanctioned coercive power, is necessarily a principal target of this ethically based anarchist critique. In a capitalist society, this position converges with the Marxian view of the state; but anarchists go further in arguing that the oppressive character of the state applies to other social formations too, not only the capitalist state. The state, from this perspective, is deeply problematic.

Coming from a different political perspective, but arriving at a similar conclusion, are the exponents of *public choice theory* within orthodox economics. These are strange bedfellows indeed. Public choice theory shares the same assumptions about individualism and the rationality of market exchange that pervade neoclassical economic theory. As orthodox economist D. C. Mueller puts it, 'The assumption that the electorate is ignorant and greedy underlies much of the public choice literature.'[14] According to the public choice theorists, such an electorate gets the politicians it deserves. Favours are bestowed on interest groups in order to gain their political support, thereby creating inefficiencies, distortions, and overload in public policies, as the number of government promises and policies extends beyond the capacity to deliver. The public service bureaucracy, not being subject to the 'market for votes', has a yet stronger propensity to inefficiency, according to this reasoning. The resulting problems of government failure far outweigh the problems of market failure. Slimming the state by reducing the range of functions that government performs then becomes the characteristic prescription.

Public choice theory has been subjected to trenchant critique.[15] Essentially, the theory extends neoclassical reasoning from the economic into the political arena. As such, it carries all the general limitations of that economic theory, as discussed in Chapters 18–23, while also having the disadvantage of being applied in an arena where market logic is of more dubious status. The presumption that political actors behave like *Homo economicus* is particularly contentious. There is an essentially collective element in political choice that requires explicit consideration of the processes by which collective goals are formulated and implemented. The assumed purity of the market system with which the corrupted political process is contrasted is deeply problematic. In the words of Peter Self:

> Those thinkers such as Friedman and Hayek who laud the market system, and want it to operate largely free from control, seem to be living in a vanished world. Theirs is a world of individuals bettering themselves and their society through hard work, enterprise and saving in some useful trade or occupation. Such individual efforts are still highly valuable to society and still continue to be made, yet they seem rather far removed from modern economic realities. The virtues of hard work and saving lose much of their moral appeal in a society where economic growth is directed more towards titillating individuals into consuming luxuries than meeting more basic needs; and the virtues of private enterprise seem less obvious when it takes the form of financial speculation, monopolistic profits or tendentious advertising.[16]

The free-market alternative has a less clear rationale in these circumstances. So, notwithstanding the scepticism about the state expressed by libertarians on both the political Left and Right, we come back to where we started, wondering about the way in which collective control over our economic destinies may be implemented.

An arena of struggle

What are we to make of these competing views of the state? The most evenhanded approach is to acknowledge at least a partial truth in each of the three principal viewpoints.

From the proponents of the state as an instrument for social progress comes the simple, but fundamentally important, observation that the presence of the state is not at issue. As Australian political economist Evan Jones puts it, 'Reformers see policies for stabilisation and regulation not merely as desirable but as inevitable. Societies (including the business community itself) will not tolerate the anarchy of unregulated commercial activity. When one set of stabilisation measures breaks down, a new set will ultimately have to be formulated and constructed. Measures of economic and social stabilisation have to be on the policy agenda, whether one likes it or not.'[17] The key issue from a political economic perspective is not *whether* to have public policies but what *type* of public policies to have. Will they be consciously developed and systematically coordinated or *ad hoc*? Will they be coherent or incoherent?

From the Marxist political economists comes a similarly basic, but also fundamentally important, observation: the importance of power inequalities in shaping public policy. The power of capital in general is a central consideration, but it continually vies with the power of labour. The latter depends on the effectiveness of its industrial and political organisation and its links to other social movements, such as those concerned with social justice, human rights, and environmental quality. Political coalitions that bring together the interests of labour with social movements can potentially be a significant challenge to the interests of capital and a powerful force for political economic change.[18] Moreover, the interests of capital are not always unified; different fractions of capital are common. Multinational capital versus local small business, manufacturing against mining, rural interests versus urban capitalist interests: the types of intra-class conflict are many and varied. Proponents of progressive reforms can take advantage of that by making alliances with supportive fractions of capital in the process of lobbying state personnel.

From the more libertarian perspective comes the reminder that the possibility of abuse of state power is ever present. Analytically, this suggests the need for investigation of governmental and administrative processes to be part of political economic enquiry, not leaving this matter exclusively to the separate discipline of political science. Politically, it suggests the need for emphasis in policy processes to be placed on measures of public accountability, constraining the self-serving practices of corrupted political elites, and fostering a genuine commitment to public service. A bottom-up politics, featuring community development and political mobilisation, challenges the top-down statist tendency.

Putting these three themes together produces a view of the state as an arena of struggle. The competing views about the state can be interpreted in this context as ideologies marshalled for political economic purposes. This draws attention to the articulation of the state's democratic, capitalist, and bureaucratic aspects. This chapter has considered the three aspects separately, but in practice they are interwoven. On any specific policy issue—whether it be tax reform, tariff policy, or superannuation policy—the interests of the general public (and segments thereof), the capitalist class (and factions thereof), and the bureaucracy (and different departments therein) vie for influence.

Conclusion

The analysis of the state is not a matter of purely academic concern. It is crucial for all who are concerned with contributing to progressive political economic change. Each of us has limited personal time and energy, so the strategic question of how to use that time and energy is crucial. Seeking change by working within the apparatus of the state, as a public servant, or by becoming a politician, is one option. Working against the state, through participation in protest movements of various kinds, is another. Building alternative communities, perhaps in conjunction with strategies focused on local government, is a third strategy. On a quite different spatial scale, seeking to influence supranational institutions such as the United Nations, the International Monetary Fund, the World Bank, and the World Trade Organization, is a fourth possibility. It may be asking too much of political economic analysis to resolve the personal dilemma of how best to channel your energies for socioeconomic change—choosing from among these options for working in and/or against the state—but it helps to clarify the broad strategic options.

There is a strong contrast here with conventional economics, most of which has little to say about the nature of the state. Neoclassical economics is essentially a theory of markets. It offers few significant insights into improving the effectiveness of public policies and public-sector management. Its major contemporary application, public choice theory, is largely a supporting ideology for a right-wing libertarianism. Rather than being an analysis of what the state does, it is an argument for why it should stop doing it.

While modern political economy offers no ready-made alternative to fill this vacuum, it does situate the question of the state in a broader analysis of modern capitalism. It identifies the state as an arena of struggle. It emphasises the state in relation to conflicts arising from the capital–labour relationship in the sphere of production, conflicts over distribution, and a wide range of other tensions in modern capitalist society. It is a reminder that the economic is not separable from the political. This is the crux of political economy.

KEY POINTS

- The state is not external to the economy, as the conventional term 'government intervention' may imply, so study of the state is integral to political economy.

- The democratic aspects of the state give it the potential to be an instrument for social progress, tempering the market economy with policies emphasising goals related to efficiency, equity, environmental quality, and national development.

- Because the modern state is simultaneously constrained by existing capitalist economic structures and its own bureaucratic characteristics, it is an arena for struggle in which competing interests and ideologies vie for dominance.

PART IX

Whither Political Economy?

Conflict and Progress

39 Why Do Economists Disagree?

What theories of knowledge underpin competing economic viewpoints?

What ideologies underpin the competing viewpoints?

Is reconciliation and/or synthesis possible?

The contest of economic ideas is ongoing. Controversies, discord, even bitter confrontations, pervade economic debate. This makes the subject interesting, albeit difficult, to study. However, it is frequently perplexing to members of the general public who, not unreasonably, expect economists to get their act together and speak with a more unified voice. The reasons for the lack of harmony warrant consideration. Is it a matter of personal caprice, the product of the cantankerous disposition of economists? Such a possibility cannot be wholly discounted. However, we have already seen enough of the contest of economic ideas to indicate some more fundamental reasons for the disharmony. Underlying the competing schools of thought are different methodological and philosophical positions. It is time to make them explicit.

Economists disagree about what they consider the appropriate methods of enquiry, and this is reflected in their different constructions of economic analysis. Their disagreements also derive from distinctive value judgments, based in rival traditions of political philosophy. These differences underpin the endless professional disputes over the relative merits of theoretical modelling, applied research, and historical/institutional investigations, of big-picture assessments versus more detailed case studies, even of what constitutes useful facts. They further underpin the sharply divergent views about what would make the economy serve social needs better, about what those social needs are, and how such changes might best be effected.

How do we know what (we think) we know?

Economic disagreements are rooted in different views about the nature of knowledge itself. It is interesting to see how this fundamental issue—formally, epistemology—shapes economic enquiry. It is related to the general question of how we understand the world in which we live.

Think back to being a child. It was a very small world, was it not? Initially, a baby's personal range of vision is very limited. Even as eyesight improves, mobility remains restricted. For the first few months, the relevant world is the cot, the mother (or whoever else does the feeding), and little else. Then, little by little, the world expands as the child grows. Spatially, it expands from the bedroom to the whole house, then to the neighbourhood, later a school, and then perhaps to a university and the broader world of work and recreation, maybe eventually involving nationwide or international (even interplanetary?) travel. Socially, a similar cycle is typical—beginning with parents and siblings, and widening to include neighbours, schoolmates, teachers, work colleagues, and others.

What has this to do with the nature of knowledge? As the relevant social and spatial scales widen, we are confronted with a correspondingly expanding array of experiences and information. It sometimes threatens bewilderment. Modern information technologies accentuate this: the web contains masses of information, but is it all useful? Or true? We have to develop sorting and selection processes. We have to have some basis for deciding what, among all the information to which we are exposed, we accept.

The initial basis is *authority*. In the early stages of our lives, particularly before we start using modern information technologies, our parent(s) effectively define for us what is true. We look to them as the source of authority. Eventually, though, the statement 'Because mummy says so' starts to have a hollow ring. Then comes the perplexing, but delicious, moment when you discover your parent(s) have got something wrong, or at least seem to be at odds with other authority figures. Who are those rival authorities? Other parents, or older children, school teachers most obviously, and perhaps a religious figure. As they arrive on the scene, parental fallibility becomes evident. But the new authorities may eventually prove fallible too, and lose our respect as repositories of useful knowledge. At university you may find courses of study purposely constructed to emphasise the disagreements within and between various disciplines. And books like this. If the experts cannot agree, authority based on expertise collapses as an effective basis for sifting information and deciding what is true, rather than what is merely expedient.

What alternatives exist? *Faith* is a possibility. In an uncertain world, faith may serve valuable purposes. It may be a source of personal love, strength of commitment, and direction in life. However, it cannot reasonably serve as a basis for making judgments about the truth of competing claims about knowledge. It is, in effect, an extreme version of the authority approach. It also entails an element of arbitrariness: in whose teaching or doctrine does one have faith? In Jesus or Mohammed, in Karl Marx or Milton Friedman? In practice, many academic disciplines comprise practitioners sharing more or less unquestioned beliefs. Economists adhering to a particular school of thought usually exhibit faith, perhaps most strikingly in the cases of Marxism and neoclassicism. Sharing that sort of faith gives focus and personal reassurance, but it tends to shelter the practitioners from other viewpoints. As a basis for making judgments that have legitimacy beyond a circle of fellow disciples, faith simply will not do.

A pragmatic alternative focuses on the organic character of the acquisition of knowledge. Think again of that expanding universe we confront as we grow up. The bases on which information is accepted or rejected as we start to make up our own minds may be quite varied. Sometimes it is a matter of 'seeing is believing': we observe the characteristics of things and the connections between them. Sometimes it is a matter of logic: we accept propositions because they are based on sensible reasoning. Sometimes it is a mixture: we do not see the light in the refrigerator go out when we close the door, but we accept that it (probably) does because we observe that other switches in the house turn lights on and off, and we accept (usually implicitly) some theory about electricity that enables us to extend that generalisation. Little by little, our prior experiences interact with information generated in new situations, which is accepted or rejected according to its consistency with those prior understandings. In effect, whether or not something is accepted as true depends on whether it fits in with what we already believe.

This organic view of how we sift and acquire knowledge emphasises that knowledge does not accrue in a random way. Rather, it accrues through the use of an 'image' that helps us to sift through the array of information with which we are presented in our daily lives.[1] That image gives us a relatively coherent framework for interpreting the world in which we live. It is resilient in the face of new information that does not fit—but not indefinitely so. Repeatedly challenged by information that is fundamentally incompatible with it, the image itself may eventually be radically, and perhaps quite suddenly, transformed.

A parallel may be drawn with Kuhn's notion of paradigms in scientific enquiry and how these may periodically be transformed (as discussed in Chapter 7). The issue here is more about how individuals respond to information that conforms to, or challenges, their existing understanding and beliefs. It is an issue that goes to the heart of both our personal learning experiences, and the very nature of knowledge itself.

Epistemology and economics

The different theories of knowledge, and how they influence the nature of economic enquiries, can be formally classified in the following manner.[2]

Empiricism

Empiricists regard *experience* as the source of all knowledge. In other words, it comes through direct engagement with the real world: through seeing, touching, hearing, smelling, tasting.

In respect of knowledge in the social sciences, sight is the most important of these sensory processes. 'Seeing is believing' is the popular expression of this view.

The research method that this approach to knowledge implies is observation and induction. Question: how to find out? Answer: go and look. A process of sifting through the observations can then be undertaken in order to find patterns that can form the basis for generalisations. This is the essence of the *inductive* method.

This research method is characteristic of substantial parts of the work of institutional economists. As illustrated in Chapters 24–28, institutional economists have eschewed the construction of abstract economic theory in favour of an empirical approach to the study of the economy. This is perhaps most strikingly the case in the 'measurement without theory' undertaken by Wesley Mitchell in his studies of economic growth and fluctuations. It is also characteristic of those institutional economists who have emphasised the close observation of corporate behaviour. Others, such as Veblen and Galbraith, more concerned with broad generalisations, claim to derive their insights from observations (of the behaviour of the leisure class or the technostructure, for instance). Even the notion of the economy as a coherent system sometimes sits uncomfortably with the institutional economists' down-to-earth study of distinct economic events, actual economic institutions, and their changing character over time.

Rationalism

Rationalists regard *reason* as the primary means by which we come to understand anything. Knowledge, from this viewpoint, is the set of logical implications of innate ideas. In social enquiry, for example, propositions such as the primacy of the individual in society or the self-interested character of individual motivation are innate ideas. It is on the basis of those axioms that more complex theories can be constructed.

The associated methodology is one of *deduction* and model building. Propositions are deduced logically from the presumed self-evident axioms. No direct observation of the real world is required, hence the common representation of this process as 'armchair theorising'.

This method is characteristic of neoclassical economics. One of the founders of the neoclassical tradition, W. S. Jevons, made this explicit when claiming that 'the science of Economics, however, is in some degree peculiar, owing to the fact that its ultimate laws are *known to us immediately by intuition* or at any rate are furnished to us ready made by other mental or physical sciences' (emphasis added).[3] In other words, economic theory can simply build on axioms that do not need to be questioned. Chapters 18–23 illustrated this deductive method in the model-building process of neoclassical theory. Starting with the innate idea (or assumption) that consumers maximise utility, for example, neoclassicists construct a model of their optimising behaviour that requires no observation of actual consumers. Similarly, basing a model of the firm on the assumption of profit maximisation leads to the deduction of the marginal cost equals marginal revenue decision rule without any need to study real firms.

Critical rationalism

Critical rationalists seek to combine empiricism and rationalism in a particular way. They regard experience as the source of knowledge, but recognise that experience is usually dependent on theory. Knowledge is usually selected, organised, and interpreted according to existing theoretical concepts. However, the soundness of those theoretical concepts needs to be reconsidered in the light of experience. A continuous iterative process, combining empiricism and rationalism through the confrontation of experience and reason, is implied.

The research method of critical rationalists typically involves the juxtaposition of model building and observation. The models are tested against observations of the real world and rejected if they prove unsatisfactory. Falsifiability is the essential characteristic of competing hypotheses, and continually attempting their refutation is the required scientific practice.

Most mainstream economists would claim to proceed in this way. Indeed, this is the most 'respectable' economic methodology. Macroeconomics developed from the basis of Keynesian economics has perhaps the strongest claim to be doing it. Macroeconomists love model building, and use their models to interpret and predict measurable macroeconomic trends. However, in practice, some of the models seem to have had a longevity warranted by neither their explanatory power nor their predictive accuracy.[4] So, while many economists would wish to claim that they adopt a critical-rationalist stance, there is a tendency not to practise what is preached.

Moreover, there is also ambiguity about what constitutes satisfactory or unsatisfactory performance of these models: should it be their explanatory power or their capability to yield accurate predictions?

Critical realism

Picking up on this last concern, the proponents of critical realism challenge the emphasis critical rationalists usually place on statistical modelling and predictive capacity. They argue that more attention needs to be focused on the structures, powers and processes that explain observed economic and social phenomena.[5] This emphasis on causal structures is a distinctive feature of the critical realist alternative, and is more characteristic of research in modern political economy, drawing on institutionalist and Marxist traditions.

The opening paragraph of this book asserted that the purpose of studying economics is to understand the world so that we may act in it intelligently and effectively. This emphasis on 'understanding' means that we rely wholly on neither theoretical models nor predictive devices. Contrary to the notorious claim of Milton Friedman,[6] the validity of assumptions does matter in economic analysis. Understanding economic processes requires a 'down-to-earth' engagement in which observation, reason, and judgment all play a part.

Praxis

It is also important to consider the *social* construction and use of knowledge.[7] Social scientists emphasising this feature often take the view that passive, detached observation is not fruitful, producing only 'unreal' abstractions. Useful knowledge comes through direct interaction between the investigator and the world being investigated.

The associated research method is direct *participation* in the process being studied. Such direct engagement is the antithesis of scholarly detachment. In the case of social enquiry, it means becoming involved in processes of social change. It means coming to know more about the world through participating in changing it.

In political economy, this method is most obviously characteristic of Marxism. Again, significant qualification of these generalisations is warranted. In Marxism, for example, there are both rationalist and empiricist elements. The Marxist theory of value is essentially rationalist in construction. It takes as axiomatic the proposition that labour is the source of value and develops the critique of capitalism (as a system of class exploitation) by logical extension of that reasoning. Meanwhile, an empiricist element comes through the detailed study of the historical development of capital–labour relations. Modern Marxists differ markedly in the extent to which they adopt these different epistemological stances in their research.

The element that distinguishes Marxists in practice from those who are merely scholars of Marxism is *praxis*. Praxis is not simply a matter of applying economic analysis to the real world; rather, it is a matter of developing the analysis through the process of active political engagement. Feminism and environmentalism also have this essential element of praxis. These are simultaneously bodies of analysis and political commitments. Understanding patriarchy is inseparable from the political process of trying to eradicate it. Understanding environmental decay is part and parcel of the process of promoting change to a more ecologically sustainable system. Rationalist, empiricist, and critical-realist elements may be identified within all these traditions, but this emphasis on praxis is the most distinctive element.

Economic discourse as conversation

These categories of theories of knowledge and research methodologies are not, in practice, clearly separated. The third obviously overlaps with the first two, while the fourth and fifth cut across the first three. A further category can also be added: the view of economic discourse as *conversation*. This is different because of its emphasis on the contingent and subjective characteristics of knowledge.

Quotations from two economic geographers help to show this alternative view in a positive light. Alan Scott talks of 'a conception of knowledge as an assortment of relatively disconnected (but internally reasoned) fragments, partially formed constellations of ideas and attitudes that are picked up, worked on for a time, then pushed aside again as the tide of social change sweeps along'.[8] Trevor Barnes says: 'Knowledge is acquired in many different ways; there is no single epistemology that reveals "the truth". To see how knowledge is acquired, we must examine the local context; that is we must see how knowledge is obtained, used and verified in a particular time and place.'[9] These are relativist viewpoints, denying the existence of absolutes in knowledge.

Support for this relativist approach may be derived from philosopher Richard Rorty's view that metaphors, rather than statements, determine most of our philosophical convictions. Rather than seeking to hold a mirror up to nature, Rorty prefers the metaphor of 'conversation'. Acquiring knowledge is not a matter of 'getting reality right', but rather a process of open-ended engagement: 'a matter of acquiring habits of action for coping with reality'.[10]

This sceptical stance is also consistent with Deirdre (formerly Donald) McCloskey's observation that the rhetoric of economists employs a wider array of persuasive techniques than any formal methodology would allow.[11] It is how most economists actually work. What distinguishes the *political* economists is that they are more frank about this. Whereas the orthodox economists see applied work emanating from their deductive core theory, modern political economists tend to be more eclectic in practice, as illustrated in the preceding four chapters.

Extreme relativism is a feature of postmodernism, which not only denies the possibility of objective knowledge, but also the existence of any reality beyond, or independent of, the various discourses of the investigators. Therein lies a methodological vacuum, putting into question the possibility of progress in political economy, or social science generally. The postmodernist stance is capable of yielding valuable insights into how people in different walks of life interpret their own situations and experiences. However, from a political economic perspective, the problem is that such epistemological agnosticism provides no basis for assessing the relative effectiveness of different explanations of economic phenomena: your truth is simply what you see.[12] Whatever its relevance as a basis for cultural studies (where it has been particularly in vogue), this methodology seems incapable of providing a basis for a coherent analysis of material economic conditions.

Is synthesis possible?

The interim conclusion to this chapter is obvious enough. It is that, because different views of knowledge underpin the various schools of economic thought, synthesis is difficult. One might wish to bring together the useful contributions of each school, but doing so butts up against the existence of irreconcilable methodological differences. The descriptive work typical of institutional economics cannot be simply pooled with the abstract theories of neoclassical economics. Macroeconomic modelling is bedevilled by disagreements over the relevant evidence and testing procedures to apply. The praxis of the Marxists is anathema to the neoclassical theorists, while the armchair theorising of the neoclassicals is equally unacceptable to the Marxists. The institutional economists join the Marxists in rejecting neoclassical methodology as a legitimate basis for trying to understand a complex and changing world, but shy away from the value theory on which much of Marxist analysis has been based.

To make matters yet more complex, these methodological obstacles to a synthesis of the competing schools of economics are accentuated by fundamental differences of an *ideological* nature.

Ideology in economics

An ideology is a system of belief. It may provide support for an existing social, economic, or political order, or be the basis for a critique of it. Pro-capitalist ideology continually vies with anti-capitalist ideology, for example. There is nothing unusual about that; all societies have dominant ideologies, but critical, even subversive, alternatives are common, too.

Ideologies pervade society. All of us are influenced by them, knowingly or unknowingly—usually the latter. Indeed, the hallmark of an effective ideology is its broad acceptance, such that the views it embodies come to be regarded as natural or self-evident. Where the dominant ideology legitimises the existing socioeconomic arrangements, the status quo is likely to face no major challenge from within. More volatility can be expected if more critical, or subversive, ideologies becomes widespread. In the extreme, those dissident ideologies may fuel revolutionary challenges.

Economics has always had an ideological character. This is hardly surprising, given the central importance of economic interests in shaping social order and political processes. It is not necessarily the case that economists consciously set out to serve this ideological function. They do so sometimes, but, even if they do not, interest groups in society will filter out and select the particular economic ideas that suit their purpose.

Because economic discourse has this inherently ideological character, it is futile to debate whether the subject is, could be, or should be value free. Economists have wasted much ink on such claims, sometimes even titling their textbooks 'positive economics' in order to advertise their purportedly value-free character.[13] In practice, different currents of economic analysis have always been intertwined with value judgments and have served political functions.[14] That is not to denigrate the subject; rather, it is to acknowledge its practical importance in the real world. The presence of ideology only becomes a problem when it takes the form of mystification. If, for example, the centrality of the perfect competition model in neoclassical theory leads to the belief that capitalism is actually like that model, therein lies mystification.

On the other hand, the ideological character of economics can be a positive attribute. If perfect competition is indeed an ideal state, one may infer that making real-world market structures perfectly competitive would be a desirable aim of economic policy. Looked at in this light, the ideological element in economics can be integral to its policy-orientated or strategic purposes. The key question then becomes: which purposes? One has to ask what vision of society informs the construction of economic ideas. This, not surprisingly, is another area where economists disagree.

Political philosophies

Some of the differences in political stance adopted by classical political economists, neoclassical economists, Marxists, institutionalists, and Keynesians should be clear from preceding chapters. However, it is useful to step back to see from where they spring. Their common basis in *humanism* is a key starting point. Humanist views about our relationship to the world in which we live became prevalent in the seventeenth and eighteenth centuries. They provided the philosophical foundation for modern approaches to the arts and sciences, social enquiry in general, and political economy in particular. Three key features of these humanist principles can be identified:

- as the terminology implies, humanism is a human-centred, rather than a God-centred, outlook
- humankind is regarded as the embodiment of reason, capable of controlling the social environment and thereby influencing its own destiny
- social progress is possible.[15]

These propositions, so seemingly normal now, were deeply challenging to beliefs about human destiny and the will of God. The challenge to the expectation that life for one generation would be pretty much as it had been for preceding ones was particularly fundamental. Having opened up the possibility of progress, all sorts of technological, social, economic, and political innovations could then operate. The gate was opened for scientists and engineers to reshape nature for that social purpose.

The gate was also opened for people with political ambitions to create a better future for the masses of people previously consigned to lives of drudgery. Liberation through political economic transformation beckoned. Examples of this quest to free humankind from servitude and to assert the dignity of all people were the Declaration of Independence of the United States of America in 1776 (the same year that Adam Smith's *Wealth of Nations* was published), abolitionists' speaking out against slavery, the French Revolution of 1789, and the French Constituent Assembly's passing of the Declaration of the Rights of Man and the Citizen. The French revolutionaries' famous rallying cry of 'Liberty, Equality, Fraternity' is an enduring symbol of this belief in the possibility of social progress.

From this common basis in humanism came two great traditions of political thought: *liberalism* and *socialism*. These two rival political philosophies may be differentiated according to their key beliefs:

- the liberal focus on individual initiative contrasts with the socialist focus on collective action
- the liberal emphasis on reward according to merit contrasts with the socialist preference for distribution according to need
- the liberal inclination towards equality of opportunity contrasts with the socialist emphasis on equality of outcome
- the liberal ideal of individual freedom of choice and free enterprise contrasts with the socialist preference for community values and social ownership or control of the means of production.

In terms of their political economic implications, the attitudes to private property and the state constitute the crucial differences. The liberal philosophy is favourably inclined to the institution of private property, of course. This has its clearest expression in Adam Smith's claim that the invisible hand of the market would, subject to certain qualifications, reconcile self-interest with socially beneficial economic outcomes. This positive attitude to the market has as its corollary a more cautious, often negative, view of the state. Herein lies a significant tension between the general tradition of liberal political philosophy and economic liberalism in particular. The latter's antipathy to the state, flowing through into modern neoliberalism, is not characteristic of liberalism in general. However, a general wariness of the state is understandable in historical context. In the eighteenth century, when the state was enmeshed in mercantilist practices, it was, understandably, seen as an obstacle (in Great Britain particularly) to the individualistic, free-enterprise principles that the classical political economists espoused. The direct link between the state and the interests of landowners was further reason to presume that the state would pursue the sectional interests of landed capital ahead of merchant and industrial capital. The economic liberal view opened up more economic opportunities for the ascendant capitalist class as a whole.

Socialism, by contrast, has always been more hostile to private property, at least in regard to ownership of the means of production. Socialists have no antipathy to private property per se; they oppose it only when it conveys the power to exploit others. Socialism thus shares with liberalism an emphasis on the desirability of personal freedom, but freedom of the individual is held to be an illusory notion because people only become free (or unfree) in a social context. The class character of capitalism prevents freedom being enjoyed by all. The state provides no solution to this problem because, under capitalism, it operates generally to support the interests of the capitalist class, as discussed in the preceding chapter. Freedom, this reasoning suggests, requires a simultaneous assault on private property in the means of production and on the class-biased character of the state.

During the last century, these two great traditions of political philosophy—liberalism and socialism—had to come to terms with major changes in the nature of private property and the state. Therein lies the explanation of further significant ideological divisions between competing schools of economic thought.

What were those major changes influencing economic beliefs? For liberalism, the major challenges have arisen from the growth of corporate power and the more extensive functions carried out by the capitalist state. Responses to these trends, which sit so uncomfortably with the tenets of classical liberalism, have been basically of two forms. Some liberals have maintained the faith, arguing that the trends are fundamentally undesirable, and that the task of liberalism is to stem, if not reverse, the tide. Hence the rhetoric, if not the policies, emphasising the need for more competitive business enterprises and to slim the state. This is the position of the right-wing libertarians, or neoliberals. Other liberals have taken a more pragmatic stance, welcoming (albeit with reservations) the expansion of the state as a balancing force against corporate power and as a vehicle for the extension of market-augmenting policies in pursuit of goals like equality of opportunity. This is the general position of modern liberal democrats.

Somewhat similar tensions have shaped the evolution of socialist ideologies over the last century. The most obvious dilemma for socialists has been how to respond to the changes,

FIGURE 39.1 COMPETING POLITICAL PHILOSOPHIES AND CURRENTS OF ECONOMIC THOUGHT

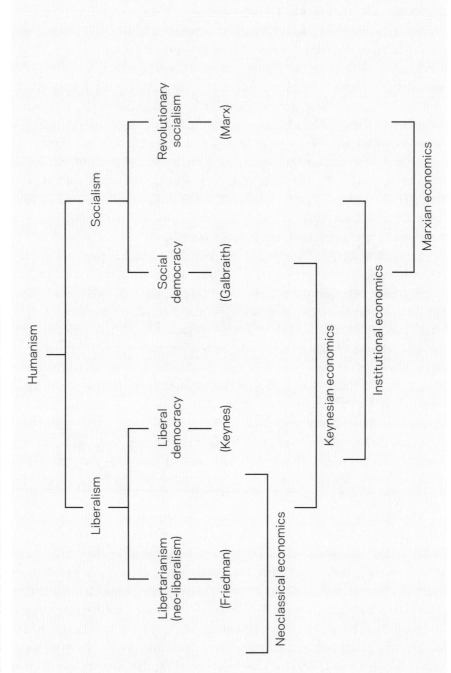

actual and potential, in the character of the state. The extension of democracy has made the capitalist state less obviously an instrument of class domination. With universal suffrage and the development of labour and social democratic political parties, there arose the tantalising prospect of pursuing socialist goals, not through revolution, but through incremental changes to public policies. Chapter 38 considered the different responses to these new political opportunities.

Mirroring the split in the liberal tradition, the split between the evolutionary and revolutionary wings within the socialist tradition is explicable in these terms. The revolutionaries in the Marxist camp assert the need to overturn the capitalist state as a precondition for the achievement of socialist goals. Their scepticism about the possibility of incremental reform is reinforced by corporate globalisation. Radical reformists, on the other hand, advocate seeking whatever progressive reforms are possible, working within the state in the attempt to transform its character in a more socialist direction. From this perspective, the globalisation of corporate capital adds to the difficulties of reformism, but does not fundamentally negate the possibilities of using democratic institutions—local, national, and international—in the pursuit of socialist-orientated goals.[16]

Thus, four principal strands of political philosophy and practice can be seen to have evolved from a common basis in humanism. These are libertarianism, liberal democracy, social democracy, and revolutionary socialism. They form a spectrum of possibilities rather than four distinct categories. Figure 39.1 illustrates this, listing selected economists whose political stance illustrates the different positions on this spectrum. Rather more contentiously, the major schools of economic thought are represented in terms of the same spectrum: in each case there is a range, but it is a subset of the full set of political positions.

A more fully comprehensive stocktaking would also need to consider other political positions.[17] However, this analysis suffices to illustrate the connections between the major schools of economic thought and the most influential political philosophies. It brings into sharp relief the political obstacles to the synthesis of economic analyses. Keynesians, Marxists, and neoclassical and institutional economists cannot be expected to find points of agreement easily, given the fundamentally different political philosophies that infuse their economic analyses. Just as differences in the underlying theories of knowledge and research methodologies impede an easy synthesis of economic ideas, so too do these fundamental differences of political judgment and political purpose.

Conclusion

Economic prescriptions are rooted in different frameworks of analysis and competing political ideologies. As a guiding first principle, it is essential to scrutinise critically the nature of economic propositions. We must examine their sources, underlying assumptions, and political purposes. A second principle is to try, periodically if not continually, to subvert the dominant paradigm, for progress in understanding and changing the world is likely to come from the clash of ideas. Third, it is good to remember that diversity is preferable to uniformity. As the anarchist philosopher Paul Feyerabend has argued, the semblance of absolute truth is nothing but absolute conformism.[18] A range of political economic perspectives, though sometimes perplexing, is the hallmark of an open society.

These principles recognise the impossibility, perhaps even the undesirability, of a complete synthesis of the competing economic analyses. By recognising the differences between the schools of economic thought, which derive from their views on the nature of economic knowledge and their preferred political philosophies, we can see what each has to offer. We can draw from the various analytical tool kits the tool that is appropriate for the task at hand. We can reconstruct a modern political economy to come to terms with the complex and changing character of the world around us.

The obstacle to progress, looked at from this viewpoint, is not the diversity of economic views but spurious notions such as 'economic science' and 'positive economics'. Their denial of legitimate diversity constitutes dogma. It is better to live with the diversity, sorting out facts, judgments, and ideals with as much cool objectivity as possible. This conclusion is deliberately couched in a pluralist manner to draw attention to the obstacles to its realisation in practice. It is the absence of a level playing field for economic ideas that gives the challenge to orthodoxy mounted by political economy its distinctively radical edge.

KEY POINTS

- The competing schools of economic thought are underpinned by different views about the nature of knowledge.
- The competing schools of economic thought are also associated with rival political philosophies.
- We have to understand and work with these methodological and ideological differences in order to make progress in political economy.

A Level Playing Field for Economic Ideas?

40

What institutions shape the influence of economic ideas?

What biases are thereby imparted in economic prescriptions and beliefs?

How can progressive political economic ideas be fostered?

Economics, like many fields of social enquiry, is a controversial discipline with competing currents of analysis. What is distinctive about economics is the direct link between the competing ideas and competing material interests. Some economic ideas provide legitimacy for the existing economic and social order, and therefore have ready appeal to those with a large stake in its maintenance. Others provide a critique of the *status quo*, giving inspiration to those who see themselves likely to benefit from its root-and-branch transformation. Yet other economic ideas, with reformist implications, appeal to specific groups whose circumstances could be improved as a result of particular economic policies; these groups may include consumer groups, small-business people, or farmers, for example.

This is not to imply that self-interest alone determines the acceptability of competing economic ideas. The association between economic ideas and broader social values—different views about what constitutes a good society—is also important, especially for a broad stratum of intellectuals. Nor is it to imply that the relationship between the contest of ideas and the contest of interests is always simple. Neoclassical economics, for example, does not directly justify the dominant position of those who own and control the means of production. Indeed, it does not mention such class interests at all. Rather, its critics contend that it serves the interests of capital by presenting the market economy in its most favourable light, thereby making capitalism appear a more efficient and equitable arrangement than it actually is. Hence the view of orthodox economics as bourgeois ideology.

How is an economic ideology like this perpetuated? How does it retain its dominance in the face of competing views that draw attention to the conflicts, contradictions, and abuses of economic power that capitalism fosters? How, indeed, does it come to be accepted even by many people whose interests it would seem to violate? These questions are explored in this chapter, with reference to the key institutions involved in the transmission of economic ideas. The contest of ideas takes place not on purely intellectual terrain—a level playing field of economic ideas—but within institutions that favour some viewpoints and marginalise others. Most prominent among these institutions are schools and universities, the public service, the media, think tanks, and the institutions of corporate capital itself.

Schools and universities

The teaching of economics (to millions of students worldwide annually) is constrained by the prevailing orthodoxy within the curriculum. What is in the textbooks shapes what is taught in the classroom. Some students subsequently become academic economists, going on to produce further rounds of basically similar textbooks. But it is not a totally closed loop. Some teachers take advantage of whatever academic freedom they enjoy to explore more dissident ideas, pursuing the principles of liberal education that educational institutions usually formally espouse.[1] Books that suggest a less conventional approach to the teaching and study of economics occasionally appear. These are exceptions to the general rule, however. What has to be explained is why and how the orthodoxy retains its dominance.

The simplest explanation is inertia. This is the tendency of teachers to simply reproduce, with minor embellishments, what they themselves were taught. It is evident in the structure of the leading international bestselling textbooks over the last half century. Ever since Paul Samuelson's introductory *Economics* effectively defined the field over half a century ago, there has been broad consistency in the basic structure of the standard textbooks, and even in the details of the models they present. The influence of Keynesian analysis has waned somewhat during that period, as a consequence of the push by neoclassical and 'new classical' economists to rebuild macroeconomics on microeconomic foundations. However, the basic division of the subject into microeconomics and macroeconomics remains well nigh universal, while chapters with the headings 'Demand and Supply', 'Perfect Competition', 'Factor Markets', and so on appear with monotonous regularity. Total uniformity is only impeded, it seems, by such minor product differentiation as is required for textbook marketing in conditions of monopolistic competition. Teachers of orthodox economics—dominated by this neoclassical approach—will often frankly admit that they teach it because 'this is what economics is', even though they may have personal doubts about its usefulness in illuminating the real world. This is the effect of systemic disciplinary reproduction.

How the orthodoxy maintains its dominance reflects the pervasive influence of authority structures within educational institutions. Recall the discussion in the preceding chapter of how people are influenced by authority figures, such as parents and teachers, in the process of finding out about the world in which they live. Although authority is a fundamentally flawed basis for the definition of useful knowledge, its use seldom, if ever, disappears. It is certainly pervasive in educational institutions. Think of university students writing essays; they support their arguments with quotations from, or references to, the leading authorities in the field. The students who most effectively craft their essays from those sources are awarded the best marks and go on to honours, and sometimes postgraduate, degrees. If they become academics, they enter at the base of hierarchical employment structures within faculties where the senior professors are the dominant authority. It is compatibility with the judgments of these senior academics that is commonly crucial in career success. Dissidents have a harder time—if they manage to survive at all. The senior academics also act as editorial gatekeepers for the leading professional journals, deciding what will be published and what will not. Their status gives them the effective authority to decide what will see the light of day.

This is a process of professional socialisation, which has a self-reinforcing character. Of course, there is often lively debate among academic economists, but it is mainly within parameters set by the prevailing orthodoxy. At times, the exclusion of dissident views is conscious, such as when the key decision-makers in the less prestigious educational institutions seek to emulate the more prestigious universities, which are the citadels of orthodoxy. At other times, it is the result of wilful negligence or lack of interest—as in the case of the orthodox economics professor who said of a junior lecturer (with a strong post-Keynesian orientation) that he had decided not to renew his contract because he could not see the point of his work.[2] In the more extreme case, dissident views are simply purged from a faculty because they directly challenge the prevailing orthodoxy in the profession.[3]

If these processes of professional reproduction—and occasional blatant discrimination—were purely internal to the educational institutions, one might think them of minor significance. The tendency towards conformity is regrettable, to be sure. Inculcating students in a particular analytic framework rather than exciting them with more profound intellectual challenges is a missed educational opportunity. Discrimination against dissidents also results in a depletion of the talent. But the bigger problem is that these processes within educational institutions have wider social consequences. The conformity produced by educational process is not conducive to economic innovation and progress. The students themselves tend to change as a result of studying economics, becoming less inclined to altruism and cooperation, and more imbued with individual materialistic values.[4] This is, in effect, the cloning of *Homo economicus*. The teaching of economics also affects—it is tempting to say infects—the functioning of other institutions in the wider society. The biases flow through into the world of practical economic policy.

The public service

Many of the best economics graduates—usually those who have most thoroughly absorbed the orthodoxies at the core of the syllabus—are employed in the public service, particularly in key policy departments such as Treasury, and in other important institutions such as the Reserve Bank. Although their initial responsibilities may be quite minor, some eventually attain senior positions where they can exert a substantial influence over the administration of economic policy and the advice given to government ministers about desirable policy changes. What sort of influence and advice do they provide? There is significant evidence that its tenor derives from their earlier economic studies. It does not necessarily come directly from particular textbook models, rather from the general orientation imparted by their schooling in mainstream economics.

One controversial study by academic sociologist Michael Pusey, for example, showed that the values held by senior Australian public servants had strong connections with whether they specialised in economics during their university studies.[5] Pusey conducted extensive interviews with these bureaucrats, revealing a pervasive adherence to 'economic rationalist' values. Important differences were revealed between the attitudes of those who had studied economics at university and those with a more liberal education. The former were twice as likely to say that the distribution of income is biased to wage and salary earners, and to say that trade unions have more power than business interests. They were significantly more likely to approve of deregulation of the labour market, and to deny the existence of any exploitative character in the relationships between capital and labour in a market economy.

Pusey's study, although now rather dated, showed that the character of a university education can have a lasting effect on attitudes to public policy. Indeed, it can be 'an even more powerful predictor of orientations to policy and management than such other variables as age, socioeconomic status, school, years of service in the Public Service, seniority in the SES [Senior Executive Service] and perhaps even gender'.[6] A university education in mainstream economics is not the sole influence undermining a broader view of the state as an instrument for nation building, however. The aversion to policies for industry development, for example, is also the product of the agencies responsible for industry policy being marginalised in the decision-making processes relative to the central agencies, such as Treasury, where the economists dominate. The general problem is the hollowing out of state capacity for effective economic management. The result of the influence of neoliberalism has been a dramatic set of interventions (using the term in its proper sense, to denote acts that radically change the character of the state) in which free-market economics has played a significant role. Therein lies a great irony because, to be consistent, one might think that the first act of a free-market economist in the public service should be to resign.

The media

There is also a direct link between economics education and the media. Some of the best economics graduates go directly into journalism, including financial journalism, as well as more general current affairs reporting. Their usually limited exposure to competing frameworks of economic analysis may constrain how they report and interpret economic developments in the real world. Whether this effect operates as strongly as it does for public policy bureaucrats is doubtful, though. Any such bias is likely to be tempered by the broadening effect of previous studies in other social sciences or in communications. Journalism also seems to attract rather less conformist individuals; giving a new angle on the issues being reported is a distinctive aspect of the journalistic ethos.

In practice, the constraining influence within the media is the nature of the organisations within which journalists work. Most are themselves capitalist organisations. In the print media, in radio, and in television, the principal businesses are run for profit, and therefore have a collective interest in reproducing the conditions of capital accumulation. Writing of the print media in particular, British media analyst Wayne Parsons sums up the situation as follows:

> Newspapers in many senses could be said to lie at the very core of the capitalist process and the 'free market' idea and consequently have a key role to play in the way in which 'economic culture' is communicated and its myths and discourse sustained and propagated ... They not only sell the information which keeps the wheels of the economy turning but in so doing they also purvey and reinforce the values and ideas, language and culture, which underpin the existence of the market economy ... [They] serve as crucial mediators between the price system and the political system, and enable politicians, businessmen and men of ideas to set the parameters of ruling opinion.[7]

How does this translate into particular journalistic limits? Media proprietors, most notoriously Rupert Murdoch, have not been averse to direct interference in determining editorial content. Usually, however, they rely on appointing editors whose general line will make such interventions unnecessary. An implicitly accepted set of beliefs about what constitutes acceptable limits on sensible opinion prevails. American author Daniel Hallin talks about this in terms of three regions: the 'sphere of consensus', the 'sphere of legitimate controversy', and the 'sphere of deviance'.[8] The first constitutes accepted wisdom that requires no debate, not even a disinterested journalistic stance, so the journalist's role is as 'advocate or celebrant of accepted values'. The second allows for controversy in political and economic debate, but within the parameters set by the two-party system, the associated electoral contests, and legislative and administrative processes. It is lively, but limited. The third is simply off limits. It is 'the realm of those political actors and views which journalists and the political mainstream of the society reject as unworthy of being heard'. If journalists do venture into this last territory, it is usually to expose or condemn, thereby reinforcing the consensus.[9]

This analysis has proved to be particularly prescient for the era during which neoliberal values have been dominant, if not hegemonic, in the discussion of economic policy. Tariffs on imported goods are bad because they create economic distortions, so all that need legitimately be discussed is the timing and the rate at which they should be reduced for different industries. Public enterprises, lacking the drive of the profit motive and the disciplining effect of competitive markets, are inherently inefficient, so the principal questions are only about the selection of priorities for privatisation and the appropriate extent and prices of asset sales. Dissident voices on these issues have occasionally received a hearing, but the dominant feature is continuous reinforcement of the limits of acceptable political economic discourse.

Individual journalists also rely extensively on information about economic issues that is provided by institutions who are themselves interested parties. Facing the pressure to produce articles and features on a regular, sometimes daily, basis, journalists have recourse to the most accessible information sources. These include the research departments of major banks, who feed regular bulletins on contemporary economic affairs to the journalists. Some of the most assertive of the information providers are corporate-funded think tanks.

Think tanks

It should come as little surprise that the large, powerful institutions of corporate capital fund organisations to produce information and promote values conducive to their interests. Often nominally established as research centres, these think tanks are usually concerned with propaganda; not much thinking necessarily occurs. The typical *modus operandum* is dissemination of pro-business information and ideology through schools and the media, and the direct lobbying of decision-makers in government and other public institutions. The think tanks make common cause in this endeavour with right-wing economists, including some of quite senior professional standing, who they often invite to speak at their public events.

An illuminating analysis of think tanks and their impact is provided in Richard Cockett's book *Thinking the Unthinkable: Think-tanks and the Economic Counter-revolution.*[10] The counter-revolution to which Cockett refers was an organised reaction—from the 1950s onward—against the influence of Keynesian economics, which its critics claimed was paving the way for collectivism and welfarism in public policy. Right-wing libertarian intellectuals and capitalist businesspeople, not necessarily having much in common in other respects, found unity in their opposition to what they regarded as a pernicious assault on free-market capitalism. Think tanks such as the Mont Pelerin Society (composed of conservative economists from all over the world), the Institute of Economic Affairs (in the UK), and the Centre for Policy Studies (also in the UK) provided the vehicle for their cooperation. Financed by individual businesspeople, most notoriously the wealthy chicken farmer Anthony Fisher, these think tanks provided means by which the views of economists such as Milton Friedman and Frederik von Hayek would have a wider influence in society. Their impact on politicians in the 1980s is now legendary, former British prime minister Margaret Thatcher, in particular, being greatly influenced by their work. It is little exaggeration to say that therein lay much of the momentum for the neoliberal ascendancy that has dominated economic and social policy for the last three decades.

The work of these think tanks is ongoing. In the USA, the best known among literally hundreds of conservative and neoliberal think tanks are the Heritage Foundation and the Hoover Institute. In Australia, the list includes the Institute for Public Affairs, the H. R. Nicholls Society, the Centre for Independent Studies, the Tasman Institute, and the Sydney Institute. The occasional critical, even left-of-centre, research centre is set up by progressive activists in the attempt to provide some balance.[11] However, for research centres of genuinely independent inclination, the difficulty of obtaining financial support is a perpetual problem. Corporate funding causes a seemingly inevitable right-wing bias in the overall character of think tanks.

Extending the interests of corporate capital

Figure 40.1 illustrates some of the important links between these various institutions, which, individually and collectively, tilt the playing field on which economic ideas compete. Underpinning the processes are the interests of corporate capital. The corporations are not always the most visible elements. Senior corporate executives themselves are usually too preoccupied with their own immediate interests and managerial concerns. Working to ensure a healthy bottom line for their businesses (or to maximise their own personal remuneration packages) usually leaves little time for taking an explicitly ideological line. Employer associations exist to give clearer focus to those common or collective interests.[12]

The funding of right-wing think tanks results in a greater number of ostensibly independent voices representing business interests. The development of global corporate capitalist organisations, such as the World Economic Forum, also provides institutional focal points for the reinforcement of common interests and values.[13] These are important adjuncts to the direct influence of corporate interests through the media and their sponsorship of think tanks. There is also direct corporate lobbying of politicians, ranging from the provision of selective information favouring business interests to the outright corruption of the political process.

Does this all add up to a conspiracy? At the very least, it constitutes a set of interacting influences that operates to support capitalist corporate goals. At the other extreme, it amounts to the hijacking of the educational, informational, and political institutions that should be the guardians of a free and open society. Either way, it strengthens the nexus between economic ideas, economic interests, and their political expression.

FIGURE 40.1 INSTITUTIONS SHAPING THE INFLUENCE OF ECONOMIC IDEAS

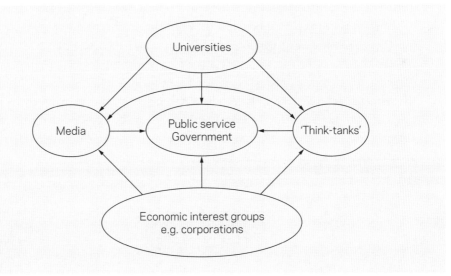

Conclusion

This book is about political economy as the contest of economic ideas. It is simultaneously concerned with the contest of economic interests. The history of economic thought is replete with examples of how these ideas and interests intertwine. Not surprisingly, the competing interest groups now actively seek to promote the economic ideas that suit them best. Predictably, the most economically powerful interest groups are best able to fund and influence the outcomes of this contest. Therein lies systemic bias. The continued dominance of neoclassical theory as the core of economic orthodoxy may be interpreted in these terms, as expressing the interests of those with the biggest stake in maintaining the existing political economic order.

It is a conclusion that requires qualification. Neoclassical economics seems rather ill suited to being a legitimising ideology for capitalism in practice. It may be a perfect supporting ideology for a competitive free-market system.[14] However, its focus on an abstract realm of pure competitive markets sits uncomfortably with the real world of corporate power in the twenty-first century. Some might reasonably conclude that a better ideology for capitalism would be an economic analysis that studied capitalism as it actually is, providing an explicit justification for the concentration of corporate power. Earlier attempts to develop a theory of the 'soulful corporation' may be interpreted in this light, but, lacking the conceptual elegance of neoclassical theory, they never seemed to develop a significant foothold in mainstream economics.[15] Neoclassical economists, with their preference for perfectly competitive markets, should be quite critical of the corporate character of actually existing capitalism. The followers of Milton Friedman may argue that competition between giant corporations is an acceptable substitute for perfect competition, but this blending of neoclassical reasoning with political pragmatism lacks coherence. And whenever there is incoherence in the dominant economic ideology, there are opportunities for alternative views to have critical impact.

Whether modern political economy, as articulated in Chapters 34–8, has any chance of trouncing, or even severely denting, orthodox economics remains a matter of opinion. Over 30 years ago, when there was a particularly strong movement of young political economists challenging the economic orthodoxy, J. K. Galbraith said, 'I would judge as well as hope that the present attack will prove decisive.'[16] He was wrong, or at least substantially premature, in this judgment. However, the challenge continues. It can be expected that modern political economy will exert increasing influence as it is more thoroughly developed, and as the disjuncture between economic theory and observable features of the real world becomes yet more glaring.

KEY POINTS

- The influence of economic ideas in the broader society is shaped by institutions that propagate particular ideas and suppress others.
- The key institutions involved are schools and universities, the public service, the media, think tanks, and the institutions of corporate capital.
- The contest of economic ideas is thereby shaped by the contest of economic interests.

41 W(h)ither Capitalism?

> *What structural contradictions drive political economic change?*
> *Who are the agents of practical political economic change?*
> *What sort of political economic arrangements could replace capitalism?*

Has capitalism a future? It has an impressive past, proving to be more durable than political economists such as Karl Marx or Joseph Schumpeter anticipated. The dynamism of the system has been its most obvious strength. However, the global financial crisis that began in 2007–08 has raised fundamental questions about its stability and prospects. The difficulty of adjusting the economy to deal with the problem of climate change is perhaps even more profound. Can capitalism continue to survive the stresses generated by its own disrespect for existing social structures, technologies, and states of nature? And what could replace it? It is appropriate in this penultimate chapter to look at how the economy is evolving and what sort of alternative political economic arrangements might develop in the future.

One way of addressing these themes is by drawing on the contributions to the development of political economic analysis reviewed in the preceding chapters. Marx, for example, emphasised features of the capitalist economy that endure: how the pursuit of profits through capital accumulation continues to drive economic growth and social change. Marx was equally prescient in pointing to the *contradictions* generated by the capital accumulation process, manifest as problems of alienation, exploitation, and recurrent economic crises. Where the Marxist analysis is less persuasive is in positing a direct connection between those structural contradictions and the agents of social transformation. The *Manifesto of the Communist Party* said: 'What the bourgeoisie produces, above all, is its own gravediggers. Its fall and the victory of the proletariat are equally inevitable.'[1] But the gravediggers have evidently not been able to complete the job. The call for the victory of the proletariat and the claim that any particular political economic future is inevitable have less resonance for people living in a more sceptical age, even after making allowances for the rhetorical flourishes of the *Manifesto*.

Revisiting Keynes also provides a springboard for useful reflections about the possibilities for reforming capitalism. Keynes thought that a more rigorous understanding of economic processes, married to an enlightened view of the state as an instrument for progress, could result in the eradication of unemployment, the amelioration of economic insecurity, and perhaps the diminution of rentiers' capacity to reward themselves without making any productive economic contribution. Here, too, things seem to have turned out rather differently in practice; the reformist road has proved to be littered with obstacles, and those socioeconomic problems persist and proliferate. Yet the underlying belief that economic knowledge should be used in the formulation of interventionist public policies for social betterment remains, despite the contrary influence of neoliberalism.

A reconsideration of the institutional tradition in economics, from Veblen to Galbraith, can also help in assessing the future for capitalism and the potential for political economic reform. More than the other major economic traditions, institutionalism has stressed the interconnections between technological change, the evolving character of the economy, and its social implications. In his reflections on the future of industrial society, the American big-picture institutionalist Robert Heilbroner blamed the sundry disappointments of capitalism and socialism in the twentieth century on the common reliance on 'the presence of scientific technology and the industrial civilisation that is built on it'.[2] The troubled relationship between advances in economic productivity and human happiness continues to require attention, even more so in the current century. If, as Galbraith also frequently emphasised, no reliable connection exists, then a sustainable and satisfying common future requires a major reorientation of the economy away from money making towards broader social and environmental goals.[3] Whether capitalism has the adaptability to meet this challenge then appears as the key question. Can it match its proven effectiveness as a machine for expanding capital—by grinding out more and more commodities and persuading us to consume them— with its effectiveness in serving broader social and environmental goals?

Here are fundamentally important issues to puzzle over. Revisiting the claims of Marx, Keynes, Galbraith, and other great figures in the development of political economic thought can be a means of considering how best to cope with the contradictions of contemporary capitalism. Both nationally and internationally, the system exhibits profoundly unsettling characteristics: glaring socioeconomic inequality, recurrent instability, and persistent insecurity. The capital accumulation process seems incapable of delivering indefinitely on the promises of a relentlessly consumerist society. The very possibility of continuing with such a growth-orientated economic system looks increasingly doubtful because of the environmental constraints of a finite planet. Capitalism, even when successful, is in deep trouble.

Exploring this conundrum requires critical examination of some interrelated issues. What drives political economic change? What structural contradictions are embedded in the capitalist economy? Do those contradictions generate agents capable of producing fundamental social change? What alternative vision might inspire that change?

Drivers of political economic change

Technological progress is one force that might cause the complex structure of modern capitalism to change fundamentally. In the extreme, it could cause labour to be eradicated from the processes of production. Then capitalism could not survive. Wage labour and the expenditure of wage incomes on the products of capitalist businesses are essential to capitalism. In a fully automated economy, a distributional mechanism other than a wages system would have to be developed in order to circulate the fruits of productive activity throughout the society. That would indeed be an ironic means of fulfilling the prophecy of Marx and Engels that 'the development of modern industry ... [would] cut from under its feet the very foundations' on which the capitalist economy is based.[4]

Alienation is a second tension with the potential to drive political economic change. The problem, stressed in Marx's early writings, such as the *Economic and Philosophical Manuscripts* of 1844, continues to pervade industrial society. Some say alienation is a general problem of the human condition, because we are castaways on this planet, trying to cope with the unknowableness of the reason for our existence. From a more political economic perspective, it is a problem arising from how our particular economic system is organised, with workers divorced from control over their own labour process and from the products of their work. In Marx's time, the transformation of peasant and artisan patterns of working and living brought the origins of this economic alienation into sharp focus. Numerous studies of working conditions over the last century have shown the ongoing links between alienation in the workplace and an array of industrial and health disorders. It is equally evident that alienation has not been a stimulus for radical challenge to the existing economic order. For most workers, it seems, growth in material living standards has been adequate compensation for the acceptance of the alienation of labour under capitalism. And many capitalist businesses are now using increasingly sophisticated managerial practices to give at least the veneer of job satisfaction to workers, individually and in small work teams. Yet it would be facile to dismiss alienation as a driver of political economic change. It now takes more diverse forms, as social, environmental, and political alienation.[5] As market criteria increasingly dominate our lives, their clash with a holistic view of ourselves in relation to nature, society, and polity becomes an ever more profound source of discontent.

What about *exploitation*? Political economists ever since Marx have recognised that the capture by capitalist employers of part of the value created in production by workers is at the core of class conflict. This structural exploitation is the most striking source of the economic inequality between wage earners and those who derive their income from the ownership and control of the means of production. Profits depend on its continuation. But other incomes, such as those of landowners, also ultimately derive from the exploitation of labour, as do the incomes of supervisors and other workers who do not directly generate value in the production of goods and services. This is one among many reasons why the continuing process of exploitation has not led to a greater class consciousness among workers and to the overthrow of the capitalist system, as Marx predicted. The complexity of the channels of exploitation also operates against solidarity. Some workers in industrialised countries benefit from the higher rate of exploitation of workers in poorer countries, while some administrative, technical, and supervisory workers regard themselves as an 'aristocracy of labour', not having interests in common with other workers. The popular use of the term 'exploitation' to describe only extreme cases of unusually low wages or particularly adverse working conditions indicates the general acceptance that some part of the income generated through work is due to the employer. Income shares, not the nature of the economic system itself, have become the battleground. On that battleground, those who own and control the bulk of the capital have won most of the battles.

Structural contradictions

So, has capitalism triumphed? Political economists have long considered the recurrence of economic crises to be capitalism's Achilles' heel. Marx thought this tendency to crises would create the material conditions in which radical change of the system would be both possible and necessary. Keynes agreed that, left to its own devices, capitalism could not ensure continuous full employment, although he envisaged the possibility of significant repair. Institutionalists have also emphasised the need for economic regulation to deal with systemic instability. The problem evidently persists. An economic system that cannot consistently reproduce itself and expand—lapsing into periodic recessions with large-scale unemployment and financial turmoil—necessarily has an uncertain future. So it is worth reflecting on the nature of the structural contradictions underpinning this systemic instability.

What about the problem of disproportionality? Does the increased complexity of industry make more likely the possibility of structural imbalances, as Marx anticipated? Without central planning, incompatibility between the production decisions of firms in the different sectors of the economy producing capital and consumer goods is always likely. The resulting gluts and shortages have the potential to trigger generalised recessions. As noted in Chapter 17, this is a specific manifestation of a general problem arising from the anarchy of capitalist production. The complex planning processes now undertaken by the giant corporations themselves— and the collusion between them—can provide a source of some stability. However, sectoral coordination remains an ongoing problem of modern capitalism, made worse to the extent that governments, under the influence of neoliberal ideology, have withdrawn from the regulatory measures and processes of indicative planning that imparted some degree of stability in the past. No wonder that the global financial crisis provoked some reconsideration of whether governments should undertake more regulation and planning in order to avoid similar crises in future.

Whether economic crises associated with the tendency of the rate of profit to fall are likely to recur is yet more contentious. To the extent that industrial expansion leads to a higher organic composition of capital, as mechanisation continues and the ratio of capital to labour rises, then one may infer that there will be a long-term tendency for the rate of profit for capitalist industry as a whole to be squeezed. However, offsetting tendencies, such as increased productivity and increased intensity of labour, pull in the opposite direction. Aggregate profit rates are apt, for this reason, to exhibit cyclical tendencies rather than a downward secular trend. Politically, it is buoyant profits (and their distribution to corporate executives via inflated remuneration packages) that fuel anti-capitalist sentiments—not a tendency to falling profits. But any plunge in the overall rate of profit, leading to a recession, reveals the inherent insecurity of a capitalist economy. Unemployment continues to be an obvious manifestation of the structural contradictions of the capitalist economy. Neither Marxist nor Keynesian economists find anything surprising about that. Marxists have always argued that the existence of a reserve army of labour is integral to the accumulation process. Keynesians have consistently emphasised that there is no inherent tendency towards a full-employment equilibrium.

The global financial crisis necessarily brought such political economic perspectives back into vogue—with many countries adopting Keynesian stimulus measures to keep unemployment lower than would otherwise have been the case. However, the subsequent rejection of Keynesian policy by governments more concerned with restoring surplus budgets has added further to the problem of persistent unemployment in many countries, particularly the USA, the UK, and across Europe. Shifting the costs of the crisis to those with least market power has been quite blatant in same cases. There is a more long-term issue too. Can the economic system be adapted in such a way that work is more secure and evenly distributed? The alternative is a society increasingly polarised between those who benefit directly from the capital accumulation process and those who get only trickle-down benefits, at best, from the economy.

The problem of underconsumption is a related issue. Insofar as wage incomes are pushed down and/or made more unequal, then the issue of who will buy the outputs of the production process becomes more problematic. Of course, luxury consumption by capitalists and workers in well-paid positions provides one avenue for the absorption of the economic surplus, as does consumption and investment expenditure by the state. Veblen drew attention to these aspects of consumption spending a century ago, and they have grown spectacularly since then. However, the capacity of the system to continue matching the growth of productive capacity with a corresponding growth of effective demand for goods and services is more troubling at a time when global competition increases the downward pressure on wage rates.

Of course, the counter-tendencies are many. Waves of new product developments, based on new technologies, have made electronic equipment, personal computers, mobile phones, iPhones, iPods, and so forth, the focal points for growth of production and consumption. Consumerism, promoted by commercial advertising, underpinned by credit, and fostering the global expansion of markets for consumer goods, continues to spread. Political economists such as Sweezy and Galbraith recurrently pointed to the vast resources used to prop up the economy in this way. Yet therein lie further tensions and sources of potential crises. Catering to the contrived wants of a consumerist society becomes ever more patently unsatisfying. As Esterlin puts it, the 'triumph of economic growth is not a triumph of humanity over material wants: rather, it is the triumph of material wants over humanity'.[6]

Consumerism also generates enormous social waste, partly in the sales promotion process itself and partly in the built-in obsolescence of the products. To the extent that the accumulation of capital depends on the proliferation of credit, it also means that the system becomes ever more vulnerable to crises emerging from financial institutions: 'casino capitalism' is an inherently unstable system.[7] Modern capitalism also makes rapacious use of the physical environment: as such, it is an inherently unsustainable system. Of course, if economic policies could switch the focus from aggregate production and consumption to redistribution and restructuring for sustainability, one could be more optimistic about the prospects for dealing with these tensions but, as we have seen in previous chapters, the current structures of political economic power are ill suited to the management of such progressive transformations. An economic system based on production for profit has its own internal dynamic, but it is not conducive to social equity, economic security, or ecological sustainability.

Agents of change

If Marx, Keynes, Veblen, and other significant figures in political economy were fundamentally right in their depiction of capitalism as a system based on fundamental contradictions, why has it not been subjected to more radical challenge? And who now could precipitate major systemic change? Such considerations switch attention from structure to agency.

Marx thought that an increasingly politicised and cohesive working class would be the driving force of social transformation. Certainly, workers, collectively organised through trade unions, are frequently engaged in struggles against capitalist employers. The organisation of labour sometimes transcends national boundaries, with unions in different countries working together to inhibit further reductions in working conditions, as in the case of waterside and maritime workers. Even so, the collective struggles of working people are, for the most part, redistributive rather than transformative in their goals.[8] The waged workforce has been largely incorporated into the existing political economic system.

There are many reasons for this incorporation. As we have seen, the capitalist system generates pressures for both cooperation and conflict. An emphasis on only the conflicting interests—on recurrent or prolonged strikes, for example—impoverishes workers as well as their employers in the short term, while providing no guarantee of material improvement further down the road. It is an option to which workers resort only when they are in desperate circumstances. In any case, potential solidarity is frequently impaired by nationalist, racist, and sexist ideologies and practices that set worker against worker. Other pervasive ideologies—regularly voiced by conservative politicians and in the mainstream media—set workers against 'undeserving' welfare recipients, particularly the unemployed. Add the hegemonic effects of capitalist ideology, educational institutions, and a repressive state apparatus, and the reasons for the waged workforce's tendency to work within rather than against the system become increasingly evident.

It follows that whatever can be done within those institutions—the state, the media, and the educational institutions—to develop progressive ideas and practices contributes to building a viable alternative. Indeed, that alternative can—and must—be fostered within the institutions of the existing political economic order. The sharp distinction that radical activists have sometimes drawn between reform and revolution is not helpful in this respect. The denigration of the former because it does not directly achieve the latter deflects attention from the important work to be done now. Working within the state to develop programs of progressive reform takes advantage of avenues for change made available by the existence of political institutions capable of controlling the economy. That is why the challenge to the prevailing neoliberal ideologies and practices—and the underlying economic theories—is so important. Not only politicians, but also reform-minded public servants, teachers encouraging critical enquiry, and investigative journalists have important roles to play in this process.

There are other potential agents of change. The unemployed and the otherwise economically dispossessed have the least direct stake in the existing economic structures. They may lack the direct capacity of an organised working class to impair the functioning of the economic system, but they have the indirect capacity to challenge its legitimacy and capacity for reproduction. They have less to lose. With the development of the welfare state, a social safety net has been provided for many of the economically marginalised (although its form is subject to continual contestation). Yet economic marginalisation continues to be associated with social challenges of various forms. The resort to crime on the part of a social underclass is perhaps the least consciously political, but the most widely feared, consequence throughout contemporary capitalist society, particularly in the USA. The wealthy are taking refuge in residential and commercial enclaves patrolled by private security guards. The jails fill. As modern capitalism takes this economically polarising and socially repressive form, Marx's prediction of socialism or barbarism looks increasingly relevant.[9]

Environmentalists and other social movements activists are also challenging the existing structures of political economic power. By comparison with the economically dispossessed, they also have more coherent strategies for change. The focus on the tensions between environment and economy is of particular importance. If the crisis of contemporary capitalism is increasingly an environmental crisis—an incapacity to live within the sustainable limits of nature—then it is not surprising that the agents of change reflect this contradiction. 'Environmentalists of the world unite' may be the relevant rallying cry today, and we are all environmentalists insofar as our capacity to live in some degree of harmony with nature is essential to our well-being and, ultimately, our continued existence. As capitalism marches onwards, its contradictions evolve; a modern 'green politics' is a key element in dealing with the distinctive contradictions of modern capitalism and the practices through which we seek more progressive outcomes.[10]

Towards an alternative economy?

How an alternative economic system could look in the future warrants careful consideration. Some form of socialism has usually been seen by political economists as the principal alternative to capitalism. Notwithstanding the disappointing twentieth-century experience of the command-administrative model used in the former Soviet Union, the sources of appeal of some other kind of socialist alternative are enduring. There is the appeal of *rationality*: the replacement of the so-called anarchy of capitalist production with a planned economy geared to the satisfaction of social needs. There is the appeal of *equity*: the replacement of a class society with a society that, if not classless, delivers more equal living standards than capitalism ever could. There is the appeal of *democracy*: the extension of democratic principles to all aspects of our lives, including our working lives. There is the appeal of *liberty*: the freedom from exploitation and oppression, which is a precondition for voluntary cooperation in the construction of social order. There is the appeal of social *solidarity*: the process of working together in pursuit of these interconnected goals.

To this list it is important now to add the appeal of *sustainability*: living in harmony with nature, not simply because it is ultimately necessary for economic reproduction, but also because it is an essential element in a full and balanced life. Capitalism, whatever its capacity to generate material affluence—and to commodify more and more aspects of our lives— cannot readily deliver on this aspiration. Indeed, the more it moulds us in the image of *Homo economicus*, the more unsatisfying and unsustainable it becomes.

How to translate these principles into practice is the big question. It requires the development of an alternative to both capitalism and the command-administrative model of socialism. The latter, based on the distinctive trilogy of state ownership of the means of production, central planning, and a one-party state, has shown itself in practice to have politically authoritarian, economically inefficient, and environmentally degrading tendencies. But it is not the only possible form of socialism. Exploring viable alternatives requires consideration of what a good economy and society for the rest of the twenty-first century could look like, and of the transitional process for getting from here to there.[11]

First, there is a need to consider technology and its implications for work. Modern technology opens up tantalising possibilities of liberation from toil. Work may be part of the human condition, but it need not be alienated labour, and it can be more equitably shared. Evidently, modern capitalism has great difficulty adapting to these technological possibilities, although the system has played a major role in precipitating them. The possibility of an economy that allows greater personal flexibility in working lives (involving continuous part-time work or periods of full-time work interspersed with periods of leisure, education, or other creative pursuits) has considerable appeal. How to balance the progressive liberation from alienated work against the concern to extend social employment, build the infrastructure, and provide the services to satisfy social needs remain open questions.

Second, there is the question of how to combine markets and planning. A capitalist market economy has an inbuilt tendency to produce inequitable outcomes. But the alternative of economic planning, particularly of a centralised kind, is also problematic. Being sensitive to the complex patterns of consumer preferences, industrial production possibilities, and new technologies is a major, some would say impossibly difficult, task. So, the key question is how planning—shaping the broad directions of economic development to serve social purposes— can be combined with some role for markets in fine-tuning the system. There are some interesting possibilities. With the aid of modern computer technology, regional and sectoral planning can be used to set the broad parameters for economic development without negating the freedom of consumer choice that markets permit.[12] Importantly, that planning framework must embody goals of ecological sustainability by regulating the use of environmental assets and by responsibly husbanding non-renewable resources.

How to control investment is the third issue. The private appropriation of an economic surplus and its disposition to serve particular class interests is the essence of the capitalist system. Arguably, in any modern industrial economy there must be some such surplus. Not all the value created by labour can be returned to the workers as wages, or there would be no funds available to replace wornout plant and machinery or for investment in collectively needed infrastructure. The essence of a viable twenty-first century socialism is not the eradication of the economic surplus, but the control of that surplus for social purposes. How much surplus and how it is used then become essentially political decisions. Here are some echoes of Keynes's enigmatic reference to a 'somewhat comprehensive socialisation of investment'. The use of superannuation or pension funds for investment projects serving broad social interests is one modern means of pursuing this goal.[13]

The appropriate form of ownership in industry is also a contentious matter. It is conventional to associate capitalism with the private ownership of the means of production and socialism with collective ownership. But various forms of collective ownership are possible. Collective ownership by the state of all productive enterprises is neither necessary nor desirable. One can conceive of a three-tier system in which the commanding heights of industry are either publicly owned or regulated by planning agreements to ensure corporate commitment to community service obligations, while medium-sized firms are organised as worker cooperatives, leaving small businesses to be operated as private enterprises.[14]

As a means of diffusing control to the populace, industrial democracy is also important. Indeed, the spread of democratic processes may be ultimately more important than the spread of ownership of the means of production. Democracy under capitalism is restricted to the political sphere, focusing mainly on periodic parliamentary elections. A progressive alternative needs to take democracy more seriously, particularly with regard to democracy in the workplace. At a minimum, it is a matter of designing mechanisms so that multiple social interests—stakeholders, to use the modern jargon—are represented in decision-making processes in all economic institutions, rather than only the interests of a managerial or capitalist class.

Does this mean the creation of a classless society? How much inequality could be permitted in practice in a modern society organised on more socialist principles? What, for example, would be the tolerable limit of the ratio of the highest income to the lowest? Would, say, 3:1 be appropriate as a means of allowing for material incentives, while still emphasising social cohesion? The policy instruments by which more egalitarian outcomes are to be achieved also need consideration. The possibilities include policies on inheritance and other sources of cumulative wealth, policies to balance wages against other income sources, and more progressive income taxation.

What about the basis for economic motivation? The collective pursuit of social needs is a worthy principle, highlighting the need to redress the perpetual imbalance between the private wealth and public squalor that Galbraith stressed. However, it is a tall order to appeal to collective rationality alone. Altruism and social responsibility seem unlikely to provide a sufficiently robust basis for a productive economy in the foreseeable future. Yet, the situation changes if the emphasis on the pursuit of economic growth is tempered with greater concern for ecological sustainability. The motivation to maximise profits, outputs, and market shares then becomes less important than inculcating the desire to attain more socially and ecologically balanced outcomes.

Underpinning all these concerns are difficult issues about the functions of the state. The eventual 'withering away of the state' has long been a cherished ideal of libertarian socialists. It is a useful antidote to the general, but misleading, perception of socialism as requiring an all-powerful regulatory state. However, some coordinating role for government is indispensable if collective social goals are to be achieved. Liberty is not inversely proportional to the size of the state, since states may ensure freedom *from* oppression and exploitation, as well as ensuring freedom *to* undertake individual pursuits that are consistent with the public interest. There is no simple formula for balancing these competing concerns. The extension of political control over economic issues is the essence of democratic socialism—and the state is necessarily part of this process. Other constraints arising from the global economy would remain. The institutions of multinational capital make it difficult for an individual country to take an independent policy direction. Capital strike is an ever-present threat. However, a nation's vulnerability to this problem can be reduced by the development of institutional mechanisms to channel local savings directly into the required investments. Threats of withdrawal by multinational capital would not then be such a damaging prospect. Autarky—complete self-sufficiency—is not implied. Indeed, the globalisation of human rights, labour organisations, and environmental consciousness can be progressive antidotes to the globalisation of capital. They have the potential to give strength and support to new forms of socialism.

Is there is a real possibility of any such alternative political economic path coming into being? The prevailing characteristics of global capitalism at present are not encouraging. However, the future is inherently uncertain. Flux, contradiction, and dialectical processes of change are constant features on the political economic landscape. Change is inevitable. The key questions are: in which direction? and driven by whom? The preceding list of concerns is an elaboration of those themes. It illustrates Joan Robinson's renowned claim that the answers to most economic problems are political questions.[15]

Conclusion

The ultimate purpose of political economy is to contribute to changing our world for the better. Understanding the world better is a good first step. As we have seen, this concern has been common to all the currents of analysis within political economy. Those currents of analysis have themselves been closely linked to competing political philosophies, embodying different value judgments about the economy and society and how progress might be achieved.

In these circumstances, it would be facile to expect consensus on what comprises an ideal economic system or on how to attain it. Whether the economic system is sufficiently adaptable to resolve its internal contradictions and external stresses also remains an open question. Only one thing is certain: that the economy in 50, even 20, years' time could not possibly be the same as it is today. Imagining how it might change is not a matter of crystal gazing or dreaming of Utopia. The future will be shaped by how we address the practical problems that dominate our concerns in the twenty-first century. From this perspective, the ultimate test of our study of political economy is whether it contributes positively to understanding and resolving contemporary economic, social, and environmental problems. If it contributes further to human well being and happiness, that is a bonus.

KEY POINTS

- We can draw on the principal currents of thought in political economy to analyse the contradictions of contemporary capitalism and the prospects for developing different economic arrangements.

- Economic transformation involves both changes to economic structures and actively interventionist agents for change.

- The answers to most economic problems are political questions.

42 A Happy Ending?

> *What is the purpose of economic activity?*
>
> *Does economic growth produce happier societies?*
>
> *Can better indicators of socioeconomic progress be developed?*

What is the purpose of economic activity? 'Getting rich', you might quickly reply. Indeed, much economic activity, both by individuals and whole nations, is directed to that goal. However, a number of recent social surveys reveal that increasing economic growth, incomes, and wealth have not produced significantly happier societies. Summarising the evidence, Richard Layard, a leading economist in the field of happiness research, states that 'People in the West have got no happier in the last 50 years. They have become richer ... they have longer holidays, they travel more, they live longer, and they are healthier. But they are no happier'.[1] 'Why not?' is an important question to pose and explore.

This final chapter begins by considering what it means to seek happiness as a goal, then examines the correlation between income and happiness, taking account of how personal happiness relates to material economic circumstances, as well as some international comparisons of well-being. It digs deeper by looking at the evidence that, in general, the happier societies are the more equal societies. Finally, the chapter looks at whether new indicators of 'genuine progress' can replace conventional indicators like GDP. Overall, the purpose is to cast light on the weak connections between economic growth and well-being that have brought us, as a society, to this troublesome impasse.[2]

Happiness as a goal

Is it possible to establish a clear meaning of happiness as a measure of individual and societal well-being? Some clarity about the goal is needed. This is easier said than done, because the concept of happiness is inherently subjective, having different meanings for different people. Neoclassical economists cut boldly through this complexity with their assertion of utility as the primary—indeed, exclusive—indicator of each individual's well-being. Utility is the satisfaction derived by individuals from their different patterns of consumption or from different courses of action. It may be regarded as synonymous with happiness, subject to the mainstream economists' usual *ceteris paribus* assumption; that is, that other influences on happiness are not affected. Herein lies a paradox because, notwithstanding its claim to be creating positive economics, neoclassical theory itself is centred on an inherently subjective concept. As Hirata argues:

> economics has adopted a conception of behavior that is largely identical with the Hobbesian doctrine of psychological hedonism that states that nature endowed the human mind with but a single motivation which is the attainment of pleasure.[3]

This theory takes the individual's concern to maximise utility and society's concern to maximise economic growth as axiomatic. It ignores more sophisticated influences on both individual and social well-being. A more comprehensive and critical basis for exploring happiness as a goal is needed.

It seems reasonable to posit that the ingredients of happiness have a hierarchical form, starting from the basic needs in life and ascending to higher elements of subjectivity and spirituality. The well-established pyramid of needs identified by behavioural psychologist Abraham Maslow can be used to support this interpretation. At the bottom of the pyramid are the basics of life, such as food, housing, and material comfort. Next are safety and security, followed by love and belongingness, including the desire to feel accepted by the family and community. After that comes the need for esteem and other people's respect and admiration. At the top comes what Maslow calls 'self-actualisation', where people start enjoying what they have and finding happiness in their own attainments without being influenced by those who are materially better off.[4] Each level of need has to be broadly satisfied before progressing to the next, moving from mere survival to self-fulfilment. This reasoning would tend to imply a positive correlation between economic circumstances and happiness, but a correlation that diminishes in strength after basic material needs are met.

A further consideration relates to time. Are we concerned with short-term gratification or more sustainable long-term improvement in our well-being? This question is fundamentally important because two components of happiness may be distinguished: the hedonic level of affect (the degree to which a pleasant feeling dominates) and contentment (perceived realisation of wants).[5] The former produces transient effects, while the latter has enduring effects. It is an important distinction that directs our attention toward what will *sustain* our feeling good. It is in this context that the goal of happiness can be most usefully situated in political economic analysis. If happiness is to be a measure of economic success, then it must be associated with sustained improvements in personal and social well-being.

Income and happiness

Can more money buy more happiness? In practice, the most direct way of finding out whether higher incomes make people happier is to put the question directly to them. Individuals' assessments of their own happiness can then be compared with their personal incomes. For whole societies, patterns of reported happiness can be compared with changes in national income.

Many such studies have been done in recent years. The bulk of evidence generated by them indicates that, over time, growing affluence is not delivering corresponding increases in happiness. It seems that, no matter how wealthy people are, they usually believe they need more income to be happy. Australian researcher Clive Hamilton infers that:

> most people act as if more money means more happiness. But when people reach the financial goals they aspire to, they do not feel any happier. They therefore raise their threshold of sufficiency even higher, and thus begin an endless cycle.[6]

According to Hamilton, this is a process of 'serial disappointment' that has given rise to the phenomenon of the 'suffering rich'. The prevalence of some such process is confirmed by the results of a survey of Australian households, in which nearly two-thirds of the respondents said that they could not afford to buy everything they really needed. Significantly, more than a quarter of the wealthiest households surveyed (that is, those with incomes over $70 000 a year), said that they spent 'nearly all of their money on the basic necessities of life'. Nearly half of respondents with annual incomes of $50 000–$69 000 shared this belief. On the other hand, it is interesting to note that over 20 per cent of survey respondents in the lowest-income group (with incomes below $20 000 a year) reported that they had no difficulties in affording everything they really needed. As Hamilton argues, these data suggest that 'above some fairly low threshold, feelings of deprivation are conditioned by expectations and attitudes rather than real material circumstances'.[7]

Similar studies have been conducted for other wealthy countries and regions, including the USA, Japan, and Europe. Layard notes that in the USA, although GDP per head had risen by around 50 per cent since 1975, the proportion of people who claim that they are happy has remained virtually unchanged over the following quarter-century.[8] Similarly in Japan, the sixfold increase in income per head since 1950 has been accompanied by no significant change in reported levels of happiness. In Europe, the *Eurobarometer* series has found no increase in happiness since the early 1970s. Layard concludes that, once a country's average level of income reaches about $15 000 per head, the happiness of its citizens becomes, over time, independent of the average income, although the richer people within those countries still tend, on average, to be happier than the poorest. So if a given individual in a given country becomes richer, that person is likely to become happier, but 'if the whole society becomes richer, nobody seems to be any happier'.[9]

Why does affluence have this frustrating effect? Robert Frank, author of a book called *Luxury Fever*,[10] suggests one explanation: that, as people's standard of living increases, they quickly begin to take those new standards for granted. Improvements in material well-being may make them happier for a while, but the effect gradually fades away. Several empirical studies have confirmed the existence of this process of adaptation,[11] which is sometimes called 'habituation'. It applies particularly to modern consumer goods, for which expectations are increasingly ratcheted up. Thirty years ago central heating, for instance, was considered a luxury, as was the mobile phone a decade ago, but today these are viewed as normal requirements, if not essentials, by most people. In affluent societies, if people get used to every new acquisition, as the theory of habituation would suggest, then relentlessly pursuing such material possessions becomes futile. However, the same tendency may not apply to other aspects of life, including time spent with family and friends and the level of autonomy one has at work. These qualitative experiences are quite different to processes of commodity acquisition, which are more quantitative in character. Hence, to the extent that rising incomes are associated with a decrease in personal leisure time or job satisfaction, the finding that people's level of happiness is not rising should come as little surprise.

Frank also argues that increasing income tends to skew people's spending patterns towards conspicuous consumption, such as expensive clothes, cars, or housing, for example, which are taken as a signal of their competency at work or their social status.[12] As most people can afford these items, other yet more expensive goods become the sought-after status items. It is a never-ending spiral. Meanwhile, because conspicuous consumption also increases the material aspirations among many less wealthy people, it makes them increasingly dissatisfied with what they have. Empirical studies support this argument. In a Gallup Poll conducted in the USA, for example, respondents were asked, 'What is the smallest amount of money a family of four needs to get along in this community?' Over time, the reported amounts rose in line with the increase in actual incomes.[13]

As Layard argues, this relational aspect belies the maxim of conventional economics that since 'private actions and exchanges get us to a Pareto optimum where no one could be happier without someone else being less happy ... the higher the real wage the happier the population'.[14] Not only does this orthodox economic theory assume that individual actors have perfect information about the choices available to them, it assumes that people's tastes are constant. Hence, 'it fails to realise that our wants (once we are above subsistence level) are largely derived from society ... To a large extent we want things and experiences because other people have them'.[15] The implication is clear: some people getting higher incomes can have adverse consequences for other members of society, making them feel relatively worse off even if their incomes have not actually fallen. Continued striving to match the material affluence of the most wealthy members of society tends to be self-defeating. It appears as an endless treadmill without progress.

Inequality and unhappiness

Is economic inequality at the root of the weak correlation between income and happiness? Is it the persistence of substantial economic inequalities that accounts for the evident dissatisfaction with material economic progress? Posing such questions shifts attention away from aggregate measures of income and happiness to more explicitly distributional concerns.

An important book called *The Spirit Level*, written by epidemiologists Richard Wilkinson and Kate Pickett, parades some relevant evidence.[16] It shows that, for a range of countries and for the various states in the USA, there is a strong statistical association between the extent of income inequality and an array of social problems, including physical and mental health, obesity and family breakdown, violence and prison incarceration. The correlations between inequality and the incidence of these social problems are consistently higher than the correlations between average incomes and the social problems. In other words, if the goal is to reduce the incidence of social problems that impede the achievement of a secure, healthy, contented society, it would be better to give priority to income redistribution rather than further income growth.

Why might inequality undermine well-being and happiness in society? One explanation is to be found in neoclassical economic theory. As noted in Chapter 19, one of the core propositions of neoclassical economics is the principle of diminishing marginal utility. Applied to income, this principle states that, as a person's income rises, that person normally gets less additional utility from each extra increment. Thus, the first $10 received by a poor person gives great pleasure: it may mean the difference between starving and eating. But an extra $10 received by someone who already has $1 million would hardly be noticed. Increases in income produce little extra happiness among those who are already materially well off. If this is the case, the failure of increased wealth to generate proportionate increases in well-being is not surprising. Indeed, it seems likely that taking from the rich and giving to the poor can be expected to reduce the utility of the former less than it increases the utility of the latter.[17] So, if the principle of marginal utility applies to income, and if interpersonal comparisons of utility are deemed to be legitimate, progressive income redistribution has a strong rationale. By this reasoning, more egalitarian economic arrangements are likely to produce a society in which people are, on average, happier. There is a delicious irony in developing such a conclusion from mainstream economic theory.

Other traditions of political economic thought emphasise the societal context within which individual preferences and aspirations are shaped. A rather different reason why more income and wealth do not automatically make everybody happier then comes into view: because people tend to compare their situation with that of others. As Karl Marx put it, 'A house may be large or small; as long as the surrounding houses are equally small, it satisfies all of our social demands for a dwelling. But if a palace rises beside the little house, the little house shrinks into a hut.'[18]

Indeed, there is considerable evidence that people's aspirations, and therefore their satisfaction with their current circumstances, are strongly determined by the reference group to which they compare themselves. Job satisfaction, for example, is lower where there is a higher incidence of promotion among peers.[19] Similarly, several studies of happiness indicate that, beyond a fairly low level of material affluence, income differences relative to reference groups have stronger effects than absolute income. This observation has become known as the 'relative income hypothesis'.[20] It undermines the conventional neoclassical economic view, based on the assumption that people's preferences are independently determined and stable, and that increases in income and consumption will increase utility.[21] On the contrary, if people's preferences are influenced by what others have, increases in income or wealth, beyond a certain point, will generate no necessary increase in satisfaction if the unequal distribution of income and wealth persists.

To illustrate this relative income hypothesis, researchers Clark and Oswald calculated 'comparison incomes' for British workers, these being the average incomes of people with the same jobs, education, and socioeconomic position.[22] They found that, while absolute incomes had small effects on satisfaction, comparison incomes had a much greater effect. The smaller the difference between their own incomes and those of people performing comparable jobs, the more satisfied the employees were. The study also found that satisfaction with pay was lower if spouses or other household members earned more. A similar study of graduate students in the USA asked whether they would prefer (a) $50 000 a year while others received half of that or (b) $100 000 a year while others received double that. A majority chose option (a). They evidently thought they would be happy with less than the maximum attainable income as long as they were better off than others.[23]

Robert Frank contends that such findings explain why people in the wealthy nations are increasingly locked into a competitive race for the trappings of status and success.[24] It is an argument that echoes institutional economist Thorstein Veblen's late nineteenth-century writing on the subject of 'pecuniary emulation'.[25] As we noted in Chapter 24, Veblen argued that the consumption of the wealthy 'leisure class' was fuelled by the quest to display its wealth as a means of attaining social esteem. The profligate consumption patterns of this elite thereby set the aspirational standard for other social groups, notwithstanding the latter's lack of comparable economic means. So social dissatisfaction became endemic—along with the wasteful consumption behaviour of the leisure class. In our era, emulating the lifestyles of the rich and famous is yet more pronounced. Television and other media bring the pictures of those lifestyles into the homes of people in diverse economic and social circumstances, while commercial advertising relentlessly promotes the products necessary for their pursuit.

Another current of political economic analysis that is useful for understanding this connection between inequality and happiness derives from Fred Hirsch, author of *Social Limits to Growth*.[26] This emphasises that it is relative, rather than absolute, income that increases a person's access to the scarce items that are available to those who can most afford them. Hirsch called these items 'positional goods'. A house in a prestigious residential area is a classic example. The more people who want to buy a house in that locality, the more demand exceeds supply and the higher the prices of the houses will be. This causes the area to become even more exclusive and highly sought after. So the aspiration of the less wealthy to live in the area is continuously thwarted. By their very nature, positional goods are those goods that we cannot all have. To continue to pursue them in an unequal society is, inevitably, frustrating.

A necessary change in our attitudes to wealth and its distribution is indicated. We cannot be happy if we continue to compare ourselves to those who own or earn more than us or if we fail to appreciate what we already have. First and foremost, we need to redress the glaring inequalities that condemn some to poverty while fuelling a pervasive sense of economic insecurity even among those with all the available material comforts. In this way we can create the economic preconditions for a more contented society. Other socioeconomic, environmental, and political problems would still confront us, but we would then have a more cohesive basis for addressing those challenges.

BOX 42.1   **AFFLUENZA**

Researchers at the Australia Institute have used the term 'affluenza' to describe the pervasive 'sickness of affluence', which they define as:

- the bloated, sluggish, and unfulfilled feeling that results from efforts to keep up with the Joneses
- an epidemic of stress, overwork, waste, and indebtedness caused by dogged pursuit of higher consumption levels
- an unsustainable addiction to economic growth.[27]

Consumerism has become a social treadmill. As the society becomes richer, rather than becoming more contented, it becomes yet more focused on higher levels of production and consumption. The appetite grows on that with which it is fed. The emphasis on relentless commodity acquisition creates greater stresses on finite natural resources and leads to prodigious levels of waste. It also leaves the public sector with less economic capacity to deal with these stresses.

Economic inequalities compound the problem. Several studies of happiness indicate that, beyond a fairly modest level of material affluence, relative income differences have stronger effects on happiness than absolute incomes. People's preferences are influenced by what others have. So general increases in income or wealth, beyond a certain point, do not necessarily create satisfaction if the unequal distribution of income and wealth persists.

Moreover, the dogged pursuit of wealth in an unequal society can adversely affect happiness by simultaneously undermining factors that more reliably increase personal well-being, such as leisure time and close personal relationships with family and friends. As people make material success their first priority, it crowds out the time and energy needed to develop those relationships.

This affluenza thesis is highly controversial. It cannot gainsay the need for the poorest members of our society, nationally and internationally, to escape from conditions of absolute poverty. These people have a reasonable expectation that higher incomes will contribute to their happiness. However, it is equally clear that the efforts of a broader social stratum to improve their situation through a dominant, even exclusive, focus on getting a higher income may be self-defeating.[28] Our current focus on economic growth and ever-increasing incomes is not providing the widespread contentment and social well-being that had been predicted and expected. If the purpose of the economy is to serve the needs of society, rather than vice versa, evidently something has gone wrong.

Towards genuine progress?

As this chapter has shown, despite significant growth in GDP and average incomes, people in wealthy nations are not getting generally happier. This finding comes as a major shock to the conventional economic theories that have been based on the general assumption of a positive correlation between material progress and human well-being. Some political economists conclude that economic analysis has to be reorientated towards different principles: of sufficiency and sustainability. Others argue for new measures of progress, replacing the conventional indicator of GDP.

Attempts have been made, for example, to construct a genuine progress indicator (GPI).[29] This takes the GDP as a starting point, but modifies it by adding estimates for the value of non-marketed production, subtracting the costs of environmental decay, adding the value of leisure, and weighting the index according to the degree of inequality in the income distribution. Such GPI estimates may be rough and ready, but the results often provide a striking contrast to the conventional GDP indicators. They tend to show that increases in 'genuine progress' have been very much slower than increases in GDP as conventionally measured. In other words, economic growth has tended to undermine other social and environmental requirements for genuine progress.[30]

An alternative approach to measuring economic performance and social progress involves the development of multiple indicators. Instead of a single measure of GDP, an array of indicators is used, relating to standards of health and life expectancy, education and literacy, housing conditions, gender equity, economic security, and other influences on the quality of life. The United Nations has been doing this for decades in its monitoring of development in different nations. Compiling the results into a composite index, such as the Human Development Index (HDI), for the purpose of overall crossnational comparisons, is more contentious, because that exercise requires somewhat arbitrary decisions to be made about the relative weights given to the various components. Without such a composite index, however, the array of data on different variables makes generalisation about economic performance and social progress difficult.

These concerns have been widely discussed in recent years. One weighty report was produced by prominent economists Joseph Stiglitz, Amartya Sen, and Jean Paul Fitoussi, at the invitation of the French president in 2008. It argued the case for assessing sustainability as well as current well-being. It advocated giving more prominence to the distribution of income, consumption, and wealth, rather than focusing on the volume of production. It stressed the need to broaden income measures to include non-market activities, and to emphasise that quality of life depends on people's capabilities as well as their current material conditions. That emphasis on capabilities builds on a longstanding argument of Sen's that what really matters to people's well-being is the extent of their opportunity set and their freedom to choose the life they value from among that set of options.[31] Subjective data, deriving from enquiries into how people assess their own well-being, are necessary accompaniments to objective data if we are to adopt this judgmental basis for assessing well-being.

The final question is whether adopting new measures of economic and social progress would change behaviour. Would replacing GDP by GPI, for example, lead capitalist businesses or national governments to pursue different goals or embrace different policies? Not necessarily. To the extent that capitalist businesses are driven by the imperative of profit seeking, one may anticipate continuation of 'business as usual'. Governments would be more likely to change their political economic priorities, but only if electorates actually embrace the wider set of concerns with 'genuine progress' in their voting behaviours. Governments that pursue policies emphasising income growth rather than equity-enhanced capabilities and quality of life would need to be punished at the ballot box. Ultimately, new measures of economic and social progress only matter if they contribute to systemic change. The debate about economic growth, happiness, and alternative measures of progress needs to contribute actively to material political economic transformation.

Conclusion

Shifting out of absolute poverty fairly reliably increases personal contentment. However, beyond that, there is little evidence of any positive association between increased wealth, personal happiness, and social progress. This is a sobering realisation. Evidently, many people get at least transient pleasure from shopping for non-essential items, but an existence centred on consumerism is ultimately unsatisfying. A similarly sobering realisation is that the production of an ever more complex array of goods and services to satisfy consumerist aspirations is unsustainable anyway. The environmental constraints cannot accommodate endless economic growth. For both social and environmental reasons, we evidently need to rethink the basic assumption about the nature of unlimited economic advance that is embedded in mainstream thinking about economic issues. Arguably, this is the most fundamental challenge for modern civilisation. It must be confronted by a new generation of active citizens, well versed in political economic analysis. The future for a secure, satisfying, and sustainable society depends upon it.

KEY POINTS

- Material economic progress and human happiness are not strongly correlated, other than at low income levels.
- There is a clearer correlation between societal well-being and the reduction of economic inequalities.
- A strong case therefore exists for reorienting economic analysis and policies towards principles of equity, sustainability, and work-life balance, rather than further economic growth.

Endnotes and Suggestions for Further Reading

1   What is Political Economy?

1   The quoted sentence could equally apply to any aspect of studying social sciences. It comes originally from P. Baran and P. Sweezy, *Monopoly Capital: An Essay on the American Economic and Social Order*, Monthly Review Press, New York, 1966, pp. 27–8. A more recent book that admirably applies this principle of 'illuminating the world ... so that we may act in it intelligently and effectively' is J. Stanford, *Economics For Everyone: A Short Guide to the Economics of Capitalism*, Pluto Press, London, 2008. For a collection of articles that illustrates how different currents of political economy seek to apply this principle, see G. Argyrous and F. Stilwell (eds), *Readings in Political Economy: Economics as a Social Science*, Tilde University Press, 3rd edn, 2011. In effect, these works are companion volumes to this book.

2   For discussion of problems in conventional economics, see S. Keen, *Debunking Economics: The Naked Emperor of the Social Sciences*, Zed Books, Sydney, 2004; E. Fullbrook (ed.), *The Crisis in Economics*, Routledge, London, 2003; and J. Quiggin, *Zombie Economics: How Dead Ideas Still Walk Among Us*, Princeton University Press, Princeton, 2010.

3   See H. Sherman, *The Roller Coaster Economy: Financial Crisis, Great Recession and the Public Option*, M. E. Sharpe, New York, 2010; M. Konings (ed.), *The Great Credit Crash*, Verso, London, 2010; and the articles in the special issue of the *Journal of Australian Political Economy* on the global financial crisis (GFC), no. 64, Summer 2010.

4   For discussion of how to 'do' political economy (for example, in research-orientated long essays and theses), see T. Anderson, 'Some Thoughts on Method in Political Economy', *Journal of Australian Political Economy*, vol. 54, December 2004.

5   See, for example, R. Bryan and M. Rafferty, *The Global Economy in Australia: Global Integration and National Economic Policy*, Allen & Unwin, Sydney, 1999.

6   This interpretation of Keynes was pushed strongly by the distinguished US economist Paul Samuelson, along with his emphasis on a more mathematical emphasis in the construction of economic analysis.

7   See P. Kriesler, 'Post-Keynesian Economics', in G. Argyrous and F. Stilwell (eds), *Readings in Political Economy: Economics as a Social Science*, Tilde University Press, Melbourne, 2011, pp. 186–90.

8   This issue is the theme of Chapter 34; see also J. Paton, 'Sustainable Development', in Argyrous and Stilwell, op. cit., pp. 206–12, and articles in the journal *Capitalism, Nature, Socialism*.

9   For further discussion of teaching and learning in political economy, see F. Stilwell, 'Teaching Political Economy: Curriculum and Pedagogy', *Australasian Journal of Economics Education*, vol. 2, no. 1, 2005, pp. 66–82; and 'Teaching a Pluralist Course in Economics: The Sydney Experience', *International Journal of Pluralist Economics Education*, vol. 2, no. 1, 2011, pp. 39–56.

2   The Personal is Political Economic

1   This analysis was set out more fully in F. Stilwell, *Changing Track: A New Political Economic Direction for Australia*, Pluto Press, Sydney, 2000, ch. 9.

2   The distinction between markets, state, and community as three types of economic organisation has become pretty standard fare in the social science literature. It is traceable *inter alia* to the sociologist Talcott Parsons, who identified the 'two principal competitors' to the market as 'requisitioning through the direct application of political power' and 'non-political solidarities and communities'; see T. Parsons (ed.), *Sociological Theory and Modern Society*, Free Press, New York, 1967.

3   Structural Economic Changes

1   Other aspects of this problem of jobless growth are explored in Chapter 36.

2   For further discussion of these social and cultural aspects of globalisation, see M. Rupert, 'Reflections on Some Lessons from a Decade of Globalisation Studies', in A. Payne (ed.), *Key Debates in New Political Economy*, Routledge, London and New York, 2006; B. Millward, *Globalisation: Internationalisation and Monopoly Capitalism*, Edward Elgar, Cheltenham, 2003; G. Buckman, *Globalisation: Tame It or Scrap It?*, Zed Books, London, 2004; W. Bello, *Deglobalisation: Ideas For a New World Economy*, Zed Press, London, 2004; and B. Dunn, *Global Political Economy: A Marxist Critique*, Pluto Press, 2009.

3   See J. Kelsey (ed.), *No Ordinary Deal: Unmasking the Trans-Pacific Partnership Agreement*, Allen & Unwin, Sydney, 2010.

4   The analysis of post-Fordism is a concern of Chapter 36.

5   'Economic fundamentalism' is commonly used in New Zealand, while 'economic rationalism' has been a common term used in Australia. For discussion of neoliberalism more generally, see D. Harvey, *A Brief History of Neoliberalism*, Oxford University Press, Oxford, 2007; and D. Cahill, L. Edwards, and F. Stilwell (eds), *Neoliberalism: Beyond the Free Market*, Edward Elgar, Cheltenham, 2012.

6   '... and there are families', she added, thereby opening a Pandora's box of conceptual confusion. If families may be held to constitute something more than the aggregations of individuals, then so may classes or whole societies.

7   See C. Freedman, *Chicago Fundamentalism: Ideology and Methodology in Economics*, World Scientific Publishing, Singapore and Hackensack, NJ, 2008; P. Mirowski and D. Plewhe (ed.), *The Road from Mont Pelerin: The Making of the Neoliberal Thought Collective*, Harvard University Press, Cambridge, MA, 2009; R. Cockett, *Thinking the Unthinkable: Think-tanks and the Economic Counter-revolution, 1931–83*, HarperCollins, London, 1995; and S. Beder, *Free Market Missionaries: the Corporate Manipulation of Community Values*, Earthscan, London, 2006. Chapter 40 returns to this issue of how think tanks influence economic beliefs and policies.

8   J. Robinson, *History Versus Equilibrium*, Thames Economic Papers, Middlesex Polytechnic, London, reprinted in *Collected Economic Papers*, vol. 5, Blackwell, Oxford, 1979, pp. 48–58.

4   Political Economic Challenges

1   The classic study of this problem of international economic inequality, urging remedial action, is the report of the commission headed by former West German chancellor Willi Brandt, *Common Crisis: North–South Cooperation for World Recovery*, Pan Books, New York, 1983. For a more hard-hitting assessment of the political economic forces impeding balanced economic development, see M. Chossudovsky, *The Globalisation of Poverty*, Pluto Press, Sydney, 1998. Books discussing the political economy of development include H.-J. Chang and I. Grabel, *Reclaiming Development: An Alternative Economic Policy Manual*, Zed Books, London, 2004; and P. McMichael, *Development and Social Change: A Global Perspective*, Sage Publications, Los Angeles, 4th edn, 2008.

2   For more on terrorism, see T. Bjorgo (ed.), *Root Causes of Terrorism*, Routledge, London, 2004; and on the failure of US policy, see R. Burbach, *Imperial Overstretch*, Zed Books, London, 2004, and J. Langmore, *Dealing with America: the UN, the US and Australia*, UNSW Press, Sydney, 2005, chs 2 and 3.

3   W. Ellwood, *The No-Nonsense Guide to Globalisation*, New Internationalist Publications, Oxford, 2001, p. 47.

4   The former phrase comes from Susan Strange, *Casino Capitalism*, Basil Blackwell, Oxford, 1986, and the latter from S. Melman, *Profits Without Production*, Knopf, New York, 1983. We return to a fuller consideration of these issues in Chapter 36.

5   International Labour Organization (ILO), *Global Employment Trends 2011*, International Labour Office, Geneva, 2011.

6   W. Hutton, *The State We're In*, Vintage, London, 1995, pp. 105–9.

7   P. Roberts, *The End of Oil*, Bloomsbury, London, 2004; J. Leggett, *Oil, Gas, Hot Air and the Global Energy Crisis*, Portobello, London, 2005; and B. Fleay, *Decline of the Age of Oil*, Pluto Press, Sydney, 1995. On the 'wicked' character of energy policy in a nation-specific context, also see L. Chester, 'An Inevitable or Avertable Energy Crisis?', in G. Argyrous and F. Stilwell (eds), *Readings in Political Economy: Economics as a Social Science*, Tilde University Press, Melbourne, 2011, pp. 299–306.

8   See, for example, C. Hamilton, *Running from the Storm: The Development of Climate Change Policy in Australia*, UNSW Press, Sydney, 2001; and *Scorcher: The Dirty Politics of Climate Change*, Black Inc., Melbourne, 2007.

9   The latter view is forcefully argued in J. Kovel, *The Enemy of Nature: The End of Capitalism or the End of the World*, Zed Books, London, 2002. We return to a fuller consideration of these competing views in Chapter 35.

10   See T. Trainer, *The Transition: Getting to a Sustainable and Just World*, Envirobook, Sydney, 2010.

11   The literature on the interacting global energy and climate change crises is now enormous. One book looking at regional and geopolitical aspects is J. M. Chevalier (ed.), *The New Energy Crisis: Climate, Economics and Geopolitics*, Palgrave Macmillan, Basingstoke, 2009.

5   Economic Systems

1   On the economics of provisioning, see P. Elkins and M. Max-Neef, *Real-life Economics: Understanding Wealth Creation*, Routledge, London, 1992; and J. Nelson, 'The Study of Choice or the Study of Provisioning', in M. A. Ferber and J. Nelson (eds), *Beyond Economic Man: Feminist Theory and Economics*, University of Chicago Press, Chicago, 1993.

2   See the seven articles appearing in G. Argyrous and F. Stilwell (eds), *Readings in Political Economy: Economics as a Social Science*, Tilde University Press, Melbourne, 3rd edn, 2011, pp. 22–51.

3   See B. Spies Butcher, 'Social Capital', in Argyrous and Stilwell, op. cit., pp. 43–7; and B. Fine, *Theories of Social Capital: Researchers Behaving Badly*, Pluto Press, London, 2010.

4   See G. Hardin, 'The Tragedy of the Commons', *Science*, vol. 162, no. 3859, December 1968, pp. 1243–8.

5   See, for example, R. Eckersley (ed.), *Measuring Progress*, CSIRO, Melbourne, 1999.

6   See R. Lekachman, *Economists at Bay: Why the Experts Will Never Solve Your Problems*, McGraw-Hill, New York, 1976, p. 122.

6   Capitalism

1   In the words of Karl Marx and Friedrich Engels: 'The bourgeoisie has left no other nexus between man and man than naked self-interest, than callous "cash payment". It has drowned the most heavenly ecstasies of religious fervour, of chivalrous enthusiasm, of philistine sentimentalism, in the icy water of egotistical calculation. It has resolved personal worth into exchange value'. *Manifesto of the Communist Party*, Foreign Languages Publishing House, Moscow, 1960 (1848), p. 50.

2   We return to this issue in Chapter 41.

3   The rules of the game in industrial relations are not fixed. In Australia, for example, new legislation in 2005 put much more emphasis on individual contracts and reduced the role of trade unions in wage bargaining. Public dismay at this policy played a major role in the following general election, leading to a change of government and some subsequent amelioration of the industrial relations policy. See K. Muir, *Worth Fighting For: Inside the 'Your Rights at Work' Campaign*, UNSW Press, Sydney, 2008.

4   On the study of consumerism, see B. Fine, *The World of Consumption: The Material and Cultural Revisited*, Routledge, London and New York, rev. edn, 2002.

5   For a critique of the generalised use of the term 'interventionist', see E. Jones, 'Government Intervention', in G. Argyrous and F. Stilwell (eds), *Readings in Political Economy: Economics as a Social Science*, Tilde University Press, Melbourne, 3rd edn, 2011, pp. 26–9.

7   Economic Theories

1   K. Boulding, *Economics as a Science*, McGraw-Hill, New York, 1970, p. 2.

2   J. Duesenbury, *Business Cycles and Economic Growth*, McGraw-Hill, New York, 1958, pp. 14–15.

3   T. Kuhn, *The Structure of Scientific Revolutions*, Chicago University Press, Chicago, 1970.

4   This is sometimes known as the 'Hawthorne effect', named after the factory where studies of the workforce produced this notorious result.

5   E. J. Hobsbawm, *Industry and Empire*, Pelican Economic History of Britain, vol. 3, Pelican Books, Harmondsworth, 1979, p. 245.

6   J. M. Keynes used this phrase in concluding an address to the Royal Economic Society in the UK in 1945.

7   My teaching philosophy, which informs this approach, includes a belief in an iterative method, whereby one begins with first approximations that can be subsequently developed in more sophisticated ways through further study and reading. It is particularly necessary in introducing the history of economic thought, a topic for which few students have a prior disposition. Thankfully, there are some excellent books on the topic. R. Heilbroner, *The Worldly Philosophers*, Simon & Schuster, New York, 1968, is a classic exposition of the ideas of the key figures in the development of economic thought and is still the liveliest introduction to the history of the subject. E. Ray Canterbery, *A Brief History of Economics*, World Scientific, New Jersey, 2nd edn, 2010, is a modern equivalent. Other succinct introductions that show the political element in the development of economic ideas are D. Fusfeld, *The Age of the Economist*, Addison-Wesley, Boston, 9th edn, 2002; and E. K. Hunt, *Property and Prophets*, M. E. Sharpe, New York, updated 7th edn, 2003.

8   Capitalism Emerging

1   See P. Ehrlich and A. Ehrlich, *The Population Explosion*, Simon & Schuster, New York, 1990; and P. Dasgupta, 'The Population Problem: Theory and Evidence', *Journal of Economic Literature*, vol. 23, no. 4, December 1995, pp. 1879–1902.

2   A. K. Sen, *Development as Freedom*, Knopf, New York, 1999, p. 23.

3   For detailed description of how the market participants and corporate players dealt with the emerging crisis, see A. R. Sorkin, *Too Big to Fail*, Penguin, New York, 2010.

4   D. Fusfeld, *The Age of the Economist*, 9th edn, Addison-Wesley, Reading, 2002, p. 23.

5   The phrase comes from the title of the book by Karl Polanyi, *The Great Transformation*, Beacon Press, New York, 1944.

6   See, for example, M. Dobb, *Studies in the Development of Capitalism*, Routledge & Kegan Paul, London, 1963; E. P. Thompson, *The Making of the English Working Class*, Vintage Books, New York, 1966; and. E. Meiskens Wood, *The Origin of Capitalism*, Monthly Review Press, New York, 1999.

7   Great Britain was not ahead of the pack before the eighteenth century. Arguably, the Dutch economy exhibited the most modernising, dynamic economic growth in the preceding two centuries; see J. der Vries and A. van der Woude, *The First Modern Economy: Success, Failure and Perseverance of the Dutch Economy, 1500-1815*, Cambridge University Press, Cambridge, 1997.

8   The classic works on this topic are R. Tawney, *Religion and the Rise of Capitalism*, Harcourt, New York, 1947; and M. Weber, *The Protestant Ethic and the Spirit of Capitalism*, George Allen & Unwin, London, 1930.

9   These were the Tolpuddle Martyrs; see H. V. Evatt, *The Tolpuddle Martyrs: Injustice Within the Law*, Sydney University Press, Sydney, 2009.

9   Private Vices, Public Virtues

1   E. K. Hunt, *Property and Prophets: The Evolution of Economic Institutions and Ideologies*, Harper & Row, New York, 6th edn, 1990, p. 25.

2   ibid., p. 11.

3   ibid., p. 10.

4   A. Smith, *An Inquiry into the Nature and Causes of the Wealth of Nations*, Modern Library, New York, 1937 (1776), p. 421.

5   ibid., p. 423.

6   The original work is B. Mandeville, *The Fable of the Bees: Or Private Vices, Publick Benefits*. For a brief discussion of its interpretation, see J. Robinson, *Economic Philosophy*, Penguin, Harmondsworth, 1964, pp. 19–24.

7   The quotation comes from C. Hill, *Protestantism and the Rise of Capitalism*, cited in Hunt, op. cit., p. 33.

8   Hunt, op. cit., pp. 44–5. These assumptions of economic liberalism were, in effect, imported into classical political economy from the philosophy developed by Jeremy Bentham and other philosophical radicals of the early nineteenth century.

9   A. O. Hirschman, *The Passions and the Interests: Political Arguments for Capitalism Before its Triumph*, Princeton University Press, Princeton, 1977, cited in K. Tribe, 'Adam Smith: Critical Theorist', *Journal of Economic Literature*, vol. 37, no. 2, June 1999, p. 611. Tribe's article provides a useful discussion of the conservative and radical interpretations of Smith; see also J. T. Young, *Economics as a Moral Science: The Political Economy of Adam Smith*, Edward Elgar, Cheltenham, 1997.

10 A. Smith, cited in D. Fusfeld, *The Age of the Economist*, Addison-Wesley, Boston, 2002, p. 30.

11 Fusfeld, op. cit., ch. 3.

12 A. Smith, cited in Fusfeld, op. cit., p. 35. The gender-biased terminology 'man' was the norm in those days.

13 R. Heilbroner, *The Nature and Logic of Capitalism*, W. W. Norton, New York, 1985, p. 113.

14 ibid., p. 114; see also R. Heilbroner, *The Essential Adam Smith*, Oxford University Press, Oxford, 1986.

15 C. Woodham-Smith, *The Great Famine: Ireland 1845–9*, Penguin, Harmondsworth, 1962, pp. 54–5.

16 R. Bronk, *Progress and the Invisible Hand*, Warner Books, London, 1999, p. 239.

10   Value, Distribution, Growth

1   A. Smith, *An Inquiry into the Nature and Causes of the Wealth of Nations*, Modern Library, New York, 1937 (1776), p. 20.

2   A. Smith, cited in T. Riddell, J. Shackleford, and S. Samos, *Economics: A Tool for Understanding Society*, Addison-Wesley, Reading, 1987, p. 82.

3   T. R. Malthus, *Essay on the Principle of Population*, Dutton, New York, 1961 (1798), cited in D. Fusfeld, *The Age of the Economist*, Addison-Wesley, Boston, 2002, p. 40.

4   E. R. Canterbery, *The Literate Economist: A Brief History of Economics*, HarperCollins, New York, 1995, p. 68.

5   According to Smith, 10 men making pins and dividing the sequential tasks between them might make 48 000 pins a day (averaging 4800 each), whereas one man doing all the steps would make between one and 20 per day. The principle is sound although these actual figures are somewhat difficult to accept.

6   Smith, op. cit., p. 340.

7   For a critique, see R. Gollan, *The Myth of the Level Playing Field*, Catalyst Press, Sydney, 1995; see also T. Lang and C. Hines, *The New Protectionism: Protecting the Future Against Free Trade*, New Press, New York, 1993; and C. Hamilton, 'The Case for Fair Trade', *Journal of Australian Political Economy*, no. 48, December 2001, pp. 60–72. For a social justice perspective, see K. Macdonald and S. Marshall, *Fair Trade, Corporate Accountability and Beyond: Experiments in Globalizing Justice*, Farnham, Ashgate, 2010.

8   J. K. Galbraith, *Economics and the Public Purpose*, Houghton Mifflin, New York, 1973, p. 21.

9   T. Carlyle, cited in Canterbery, op. cit., p. 74. It may also be noted that economics was 'dismal' to Carlyle because classical political economists such as J. S. Mill advocated the abolition of the slave trade and thereby put the interests of 'subhuman' Africans above the interests of English workers; see L. S. Moss, review of M. A. Lutz, *Economics for the Common Good*, in *Economic Journal*, vol. 111, no. 469, February 2001, pp. 129–36.

10   R. Heilbroner, *The Worldly Philosophers*, Simon & Schuster, New York, 1967, p. 117.

11   ibid.

12   Quoted in Heilbroner, op. cit., p. 119.

13   ibid., p. 121.

11   Land and Economic Surplus

1   For a brief introduction to the physiocrats, see R. Lekachman, *A History of Economic Ideas*, McGraw-Hill, New York, 1976, pp. 80–6.

2   D. Ricardo, *On the Principles of Political Economy and Taxation*, Dent, London, 1962 (1817), quoted in M. Dobb, *Theories of Value and Distribution*, Cambridge University Press, Cambridge, 1973, p. 72; see also R. Heilbroner, *The Worldly Philosophers*, Simon & Schuster, New York, 1967, pp. 87–90.

3   See F. Stilwell, 'Land, Inequality and Regional Policy', *Urban Policy and Research*, vol. 17, no. 1, March 1999, pp. 17–24.

4   H. George, *Progress and Poverty*, Robert Schalkenback, New York, 1966 (1879), p. 224.

5   For an argument, and some supporting calculations, to suggest that land tax could indeed be a sufficient source of tax revenues, see P. Day, *Land: The Elusive Quest for Social Justice, Taxation Reform and a Sustainable Planetary Environment*, Australian Academic Press, Brisbane, 1995. A subsequent book by the same author, also addressing the land question (with particular focus on Australia), is *Hijacked Inheritance: The Triumph of Dollar Darwinism?*, Copyright Publishing, Brisbane, 2005.

6   For further discussion of Georgist ideas, see C. Collier, 'Henry George's System of Political Economy', *History of Political Economy*, vol. 11, no. 1, Spring 1979, pp. 64–93; M. Gaffney and F. Harrison, *The Corruption of Economics*, Shepheard-Walwyn, London, 1994; F. Stilwell and K. Jordan, 'The Political Economy of Land: Putting Henry George in His Place', *Journal of Australian Political Economy*, no. 54, December 2004, pp. 119–34; and J. Laurent (ed.), *Henry George's Legacy in Economic Thought*, Edward Elgar, Cheltenham, 2005.

7   George, op. cit., p. 224.

8   D. Harvey, *The Urban Experience*, Basil Blackwell, Oxford, 1989, pp. 265–6.

12   Contesting Capitalism

1   For discussion of the remarkable survival of Cuba during a period when other socialist experiments in the twentieth century were in deep trouble, see T. Anderson, 'Island Socialism', *Journal of Australian Political Economy*, no. 49, June 2002, pp. 56–86.

2   Samuelson later expressed regret for this slur, admitting that the neglect of Marx in the teaching of orthodox economics had been 'a scandal'. His best-selling textbook continued to perpetuate the neglect, however.

3   See, for example, the various contributions to G. Dow and G. Lafferty (eds), *Everlasting Uncertainty: Interrogating the Communist Manifesto*, Pluto Press, Sydney, 1998.

4   J. K. Galbraith, *The Age of Uncertainty*, BBC, London, 1977.

5   For a fuller discussion of these non-Marxist socialists and their influence, see D. Fusfeld, *The Age of the Economist*, 9th edn, Addison-Wesley, Reading, 2002, pp. 56–9, or E. K. Hunt, *Property and Prophets: The Evolution of Economic Institutions and Ideologies*, HarperCollins, New York, 7th edn, 1995, ch. 5.

6   The classic description of the living conditions is in F. Engels, *The Condition of the Working Class in England in 1844*, Macmillan, New York, 1958 (1845); see also F. Engels, *The Housing Question*, Progress Publishers, Moscow, 1975 (1873).

7 See, for example, F. Stilwell, *Changing Track: A New Political Economic Direction for Australia*, Pluto Press, Sydney, 2000, ch. 8.

8 K. Marx, *Critique of Political Economy*, New World Paperbacks, New York, 1970 (1859), p. 20.

9 Friedrich Engels, quoted in D. McLellan, *Karl Marx: His Life and Thought*, Harper & Row, New York, 1973, p. 14.

10 K. Marx, *The German Ideology*, cited in R. Freedman (ed.), *Marx on Economics*, Penguin, Harmondsworth, 1961, p. 5.

11 K. Marx and F. Engels, *Manifesto of the Communist Party*, Foreign Languages Publishing House, Moscow, 1960 (1848), p. 45.

13   The Mode of Production

1 K. Marx, *The Critique of Political Economy*, reprinted in part in H. Selsam and H. Martels (eds), *Reader in Marxist Philosophy*, International Publishers, New York, 1963, p. 186.

2 V. I. Lenin, *Marx-Engels-Marxism*, Progress Publishers, Moscow, 1968. 'Determine' is the contentious word here. As E. K. Hunt notes: 'To argue that Marx believed that the economic base determined, completely and rigidly, every aspect of the superstructure is grossly inaccurate (although it is often done). He did assert, however, that the mode of production was the most important single aspect in determining not only the present social superstructure but also the direction of social change.' See *Property and Prophets: The Evolution of Economic Institutions and Ideologies*, Harper & Row, New York, 1990, p. 75.

3 For discussion of these concerns in the political economy of education, see S. Slaughter and L. L. Leslie, *Academic Capitalism: Politics, Policies and the Entrepreneurial University*, Johns Hopkins University Press, Baltimore, 1997; and S. Marginson and M. Considine, *The Enterprise University: Power, Governance and Reinvention in Australia*, Cambridge University Press, Cambridge, 2000.

4 K. Marx, *A Critique of the Gotha Programme*, cited in R. Freedman (ed.), *Marx on Economics*, Penguin, Harmondsworth, 1962, p. 241. Note that the gendered terminology is in the original, as was normal for all writing at that time. In the modern context, the principle embraces both women and men.

5 For an excellent discussion of the cooperative movement and the alternative it offers to capitalism, see R. Mathews, *Jobs of Our Own: Building a Stakeholder Society*, Pluto Press, Sydney, 1999.

6 M. Dobb, *Studies in the Development of Capitalism*, Routledge & Kegan Paul, London, 1963, ch. 1.

14   Labour, Value, Exploitation

1 E. Mandel, *An Introduction to Marxist Economic Theory*, Resistance Books, Sydney, 2002.

2 K. Marx, *Wage Labour and Capital*, Progress Publishers, Moscow, 1976 (1849), p. 26.

3 The significance of this problem for the coherence and applicability of Marxian theory has been hotly debated. See, for example, A. Shaikh, 'Marx's theory of Value and the Transformation Problem', in J. Schwartz (ed.), *The Subtle Anatomy of Capitalism*, Goodyear, Santa Monica, 1977. For a brief summary of the issues see B. Fine and A. Saad-Filho, *Marx's Capital*, 5th edn, Pluto Press, London 2010, pp. 108–15.

4 K. Marx, *Capital*, vol. 1, Progress Publishers, Moscow, 1974 (1867), p. 164. For further discussion of the concept of labour power, see K. Marx, *Wages, Price and Profit*, Foreign Languages Press, Peking, 1970 (1865), pp. 43–6.

5 This is partly why Marxian class analysis, in its modern forms, emphasises complexity rather than a simple binary opposition; see J. K. Gibson-Graham, S. Resnick, and R. Wolff, 'Towards a Poststructuralist Political Economy', in J. K. Gibson-Graham, S. Resnick, and R. Wolff (eds), *Re/Presenting Class: Essays in Postmodern Marxism*, Duke University Press, Durham, 2001. We return to this issue in Chapter 37.

6 For further discussion of shorter working time initiatives, see A. Hayden, *Sharing the Work, Sparing the Planet*, Pluto Press, Sydney, 1999; for discussion of work–life balance, see B. Pocock, *The Work/ Life Collision*, Federation Press, Sydney, 2003.

7 Joan Robinson, for example, took this view. In an article titled 'The Labour Theory of Value', she wrote: 'We are told that it is impossible to account for exploitation except in terms of value, but why

do we need value to show that profits can be made in industry by selling commodities for more than they cost to produce, or to explain the power of those who command finance to push around those who do not?' *Monthly Review*, no. 29, 1977, p. 51.

8   H. Braverman, *Labor and Monopoly Capital: The Degradation of Work in the Twentieth Century*, Monthly Review Press, New York, 1975.

9   R. Edwards, *Contested Terrain: The Transformation of Work in the Twentieth Century*, Basic Books, New York, 1979. See also P. Thompson and C. Warhurst (eds), *Workplaces of the Future*, Macmillan, Basingstoke, 1998, for a compilation of articles on trends in work organisation and capital–labour relations.

10   E. Applebaum and R. Batt, *The New American Workplace: Transforming Work Systems in the United States*, ILR Press, Ithaca, 1994.

15   Capital Accumulation

1   See K. Marx, *Capital*, vol. 2, Progress Publishers, Moscow, 1974 (1867), pp. 493–527.

2   See K. Marx, *Capital*, vol. 1, Progress Publishers, Moscow, 1974 (1867), p. 579, n. 2.

3   For discussion of this concept of the reserve army of labour and its relevance, see J. Collins, 'Marx's Reserve Army of Labour: Still Relevant One Hundred Years On', *Journal of Australian Political Economy*, no. 16, March 1984, pp. 51–65.

4   See K. Marx, *Capital*, vol. 1, Progress Publishers, Moscow, 1974 (1867), p. 582.

5   For an example of this reasoning, see Collins, op. cit.

6   Marx, op. cit., p. 588.

7   ibid.

8   See, for example, P. Baran and P. Sweezy, *Monopoly Capital: An Essay on the American Economic and Social Order*, Monthly Review Press, New York, 1966.

9   For Marxian analyses of globalisation as a process that extends its competitive features worldwide, see B. Dunn, *Global Political Economy*, Pluto Press, London, 2009; and R. Bryan and M. Rafferty, *The Global Economy in Australia: Global Integration and National Economic Policy*, Allen & Unwin, Sydney, 1999.

10   C. Rhodes, reported in the *Spectator* on 26 January 1885 and cited in D. Bhattacharya, *Economic Development and Underdevelopment*, Australian Professional Publications, Sydney, 1987, p. 157.

11   V. I. Lenin, *Imperialism: The Highest State of Capitalism*, Foreign Languages Press, Peking, 1970 (1917).

12   See E. Hobsbawm, *The New Century*, Little, Brown & Co., London, 1999, pp. 52–3.

13   H. Magdoff, *Imperialism: From the Colonial Age to the Present*, Monthly Review Press, New York, 1978, p. 117.

14   H. McQueen, *The Essence of Capitalism*, Sceptre, Sydney, 2001, p. x.

15   See B. Norton, 'Reading Marx for class', in J. K. Gibson-Graham, S. Resnick and R. Wolff (eds), *Re/Presenting Class: Essays in Postmodern Marxism*, Duke University Press, Durham, 2001, pp. 45–8.

16   Reproduction, Growth, Change

1   For a non-technical discussion of this analysis of the circuit of capital, see R. Heilbroner, *Beyond Boom and Crash*, W. W. Norton, New York, 1978; an extract from this book appears in G. Argyrous and F. Stilwell (eds), *Readings in Political Economy: Economics as a Social Science*, Tilde University Press, Melbourne, 3rd edn, 2011, pp. 99–104.

17   Economic Crises

1   K. Marx and F. Engels, *Manifesto of the Communist Party*, Foreign Languages Publishing House, Moscow, 1960 (1848), p. 53.

2   A fuller exposition of these three theoretical strands is in the classic work by P. Sweezy, *The Theory of Capitalist Development*, Monthly Review Press, New York, 1968.

3   One Australian study, for example, sought to apply this reasoning to explain the booms and slumps experienced in the twentieth century, showing that a rising organic composition of capital in the

1920s and early 1930s led to the Great Depression. Then, a rising rate of surplus value facilitated economic expansion through the 1950s and 1960s, then into the 1970s, when the rate of surplus value stopped rising and boom turned again to recession. See R. Kuhn and T. O'Lincoln, 'Profitability and Economic Crises', *Journal of Australian Political Economy*, no. 25, October 1989, pp. 44–69. For a rather different attempt to adapt these Marxian analytical concepts to studying the forces underpinning boom and slump, see S. Mohun, 'The Australian Rate of Profit 1965–2001', *Journal of Australian Political Economy*, no. 52, December 2003.

4   Marx, quoted in P. Sweezy, *Theory of Capitalist Development*, p. 177.

5   P. Baran and P. Sweezy, *Monopoly Capital: An Essay on the American Economic and Social Order*, Monthly Review Press, New York, 1966. The term 'monopoly' here embraces oligopoly as well as single-firm industries, so it is a general description of big business. J. B. Foster, *The Theory of Monopoly Capitalism*, Monthly Review Press, New York, 1986, provides an assessment of Baran and Sweezy's influential political economic contribution.

6   For an exposition of Marxist principles that is sensitive to this concern, see B. Fine and A. Saad-Filho, *Marx's Capital*, 5th edn, Pluto Press, London 2010. For examples of this approach applied to current economic problems see A. Glyn, *Capitalism Unleashed: Finance, Globalisation and Welfare*, Oxford University Press, Oxford, 2006; H. Sherman, *The Roller Coaster Economy: Financial Crisis, Great Recession and the Public Option*, M. E. Sharpe, New York, 2010; and D. McNally, *Global Slump: The Economics and Politics of Crisis and Resistance*, PM Press, Oakland, 2011.

18   Free-market Economics

1   R. Dorfman, *Prices and Markets*, Prentice Hall, Englewood Cliffs, 1967, p. 146. This laudatory view of the market in neoclassical economics may be compared with the critical perspective in R. Hill and T. Myatt, *The Economics Anti-Textbook: A Critical Thinker's Guide to Microeconomics*, Zed Press, London, 2010.

2   Hayek was joint winner (ironically, with Gunnar Myrdal) of the Nobel Prize in Economic Sciences in 1974. Hayek's best known political tract is *The Road to Serfdom*, Routledge, London, 1944. For an evaluation of Hayek's work, which is sympathetic to his methodology but critical of the political inferences, see J. Mulberg, *Social Limits to Economic Theory*, Routledge, London, 1995. For a shorter sketch of Hayek's approach, see Y. Varoufakis, *Foundations of Economics: A Beginner's Companion*, Routledge, London, 1998, pp. 187–90.

3   For a brief discussion of Spencer and social Darwinism, see D. Fusfeld, *The Age of the Economist*, 9th edn, Addison-Wesley, Reading, 2002, pp. 76–8; see also R. Hofstadter, *Social Darwinism in American Thought*, Beacon Press, Boston, 1959.

4   Fusfeld, op. cit., pp. 80–1; see also T. Arnold, *The Folklore of Capitalism*, Yale University Press, New Haven, 1937.

5   On a personal level, Walras was a reformer favouring a good deal of state intervention. The incoherence of his theoretical and practical positions is not unique among economists. In a similar vein it is pertinent to note that Vilfredo Pareto, originator of the liberal economic principle discussed in Chapter 23, became a supporter of fascism in Italy.

6   C. Menger, *Principles of Economics*, trans. J. Dingwall and B. Hoselitz, Free Press, London, 1950, p. 120.

7   In a letter to another economist, Marshall set out his views on maths in economics: '(1) Use mathematics as a shorthand language, rather than an engine of inquiry. (2) Keep to them till you have done. (3) Translate into English. (4) Then illustrate by examples that are important in real life. (5) Burn the mathematics. (6) If you can't succeed in 4, burn 3'; see J. K. Whitaker (ed.), *The Correspondence of Alfred Marshall*, Cambridge University Press, Cambridge, 1996.

8   R. Lekachman, *A History of Economic Ideas*, McGraw-Hill, New York, 1976, p. 274.

9   R. Skidelsky, *John Maynard Keynes*, vol. 1, 1883–1920, Macmillan, London, 1983, p. 48.

10   P. D. Groenewegen, *A Soaring Eagle: Alfred Marshall, 1842–1924*, Edward Elgar, Cheltenham, 1995.

11   See E. K. Hunt, *Property and Prophets: The Evolution of Economic Institutions and Ideologies*, Harper & Row, New York, 1990, p. 90.

12 Even John Stuart Mill's political economy could be considered 'dangerous' from a particular class perspective, because it opened the door for income redistribution from rich to poor.

13 See Fusfeld, op. cit., pp. 49–52.

14 B. Toohey, *Tumbling Dice: The Story of Modern Economic Policy*, Heinemann, Melbourne, 1994, ch. 4.

15 A. Marshall, *Principles of Economics*, 8th edn, Macmillan, London, 1959, bk 5, ch. 3, s. 7, p. 290.

19   Consumers

1 The term *Homo economicus* commonly has a somewhat tongue-in-cheek ring. For an example of its more serious usage, see J. Friedman, Introduction, in J. Friedman (ed.), *The Rational Choice Controversy: Economic Models of Politics Reconsidered*, Yale University Press, New Haven, 1995, pp. 1–24. On the origin of the concept, with particular reference to J. S. Mill, see J. Persky, 'The Ethology of *Homo economicus*', *Journal of Economic Perspectives*, vol. 9, no. 2, Spring 1995, pp. 221–31.

2 *The Rubaiyat of Omar Khayyam, The Astronomer-Poet of Persia*, Edward Fitzgerald (ed. and trans.), Bernard Quaritch, London, 1859.

3 For discussion of what economics could learn from psychology, see M. Rabin, 'Psychology and Economics', *Journal of Economic Literature*, vol. 36, no. 1, March 1998, pp. 11–46, and R. H. Thaler, 'Doing Economics without Homo Economicus', in S. Medema and W.J. Samuels (eds), *Foundations of Research in Economics: How Do Economists Do Economics?*, Edward Elgar, Cheltenham, 1996.

4 See the classic article by H. Leibenstein, 'Bandwagon, Snob and Veblen Effects in the Theory of Consumers' Demand', reprinted in E. Mansfield (ed.), *Micro-Economics: Selected Readings*, W. W. Norton, New York, 1971, pp. 12–30.

5 For a geometrical demonstration of this link between indifference curve analysis and demand curves, see D. McTaggert, C. Findlay, and M. Parkin, *Microeconomics*, Addison-Wesley, Reading, 1996, p. 176.

6 P. Samuelson, *Economics: An Introductory Analysis*, 6th edn, McGraw-Hill, New York, 1964, p. 56.

7 See, for example, G. Stigler, 'Can Regulatory Agencies Protect the Consumer?', in G. Argyrous and F. Stilwell (eds), *Readings in Political Economy: Economics as a Social Science*, Tilde University Press, Melbourne, 3rd edn, 2011, pp. 124–7.

8 This observation that preferences are shaped by social experience tends to lead to a more institutionally focused economic analysis; see S. Bowles, 'Endogenous Preferences: The Cultural Consequences of Markets and Other Institutions', *Journal of Economic Literature*, vol. 36, no. 1, March 1998, pp. 75–111.

9 P. Baran and P. Sweezy, *Monopoly Capital: An Essay on the American Economic and Social Order*, Monthly Review Press, New York, 1966, p. 126.

10 This type of critique is developed by H. Gintis in 'Consumer Behaviour and the Concept of Sovereignty: Explanations of Social Decay', in E. L. Wheelwright and F. Stilwell (eds), *Readings in Political Economy*, vol. 2, ANZ Book Co., Sydney, 1976, pp. 15–28; see also S. Himmelweit, R. Simonetti, and A. Trigg, *Microeconomics: Neoclassical and Institutionalist Perspectives on Economic Behaviour*, Open University/Thomson Learning, London, 2001, pp. 47–56.

11 This reasoning derives from F. Hirsch, *Social Limits to Growth*, Routledge, London, rev. edn, 1995.

12 There have been attempts to reconstruct consumer theory on different lines. See, for example, Kelvin Lancaster's attempt to focus on how consumers might seek to attain particular characteristics (for example, transport) rather than commodities as such (for example, cars or bicycles); K. Lancaster, 'A New Approach to Consumer Theory', *Journal of Political Economy*, vol. 74, 1966, pp. 132–57. The theory of revealed preference, pioneered by Paul Samuelson, had earlier sought to do away with the indifference curve apparatus. However, within the neoclassical approach (as represented in the undergraduate textbooks), the emphasis on an individualistic, rational, maximising decision process remains hegemonic.

20   Firms

1 Marshall used this concept as a means of talking about the dynamic equilibrium of an industry, rather than as a deductive tool for a general theory of economic agents.

2 Critics have argued that it is fundamentally misleading. In the words of A. G. Papandreou (before he became prime minister of Greece): 'To extend, unwittingly or not, the analytical conclusions of a model best fitted for the study of shopkeeper society to present-day capitalism is probably the supreme form of ideological bias.' *Paternalistic Capitalism*, University of Minnesota Press, Minneapolis, 1972, p. 40.

3 S. Zamagni, *Microeconomic Theory: An Introduction*, Basil Blackwell, Oxford, 1987, p. 442.

4 This tradition of analysis derives from the pioneering article by R. H. Coase, 'The Nature of the Firm', *Economica*, vol. 4, 1937, pp. 386–405. Coase said, 'The distinctive characteristic of the firm is in its overcoming of the price mechanism.'

5 The view is expounded by J. K. Galbraith, *The New Industrial State*, Penguin, Harmondsworth, 1969, ch. 15.

6 This view is associated with the behavioural theory of the firm developed by R. M. Cyert and J. G. March, *A Behavioral Theory of the Firm*, Prentice Hall, Englewood Cliffs, 1963.

7 See N. Lamoreaux, D. Raff, and P. Temin (eds), *Learning by Doing in Markets, Firms and Countries*, National Bureau of Economic Research Conference Report Series, University of Chicago Press, Chicago, 1999.

8 This distinction between the short run and the long run is a distinctive legacy of Marshall's *Principles of Economics*. It seems to introduce a time dimension into the analysis, but does not treat time as a continuous variable. As such, it is part of the problem rather than part of the solution in dealing with the temporal dimension of economic activity.

9 The principle of diminishing returns, it should be emphasised, was not a neoclassical innovation. It was a well-established principle in classical political economy. The diagrammatic exposition and its incorporation into a general theory of supply and demand are the distinctively neoclassical elements here.

10 As with the theory of the consumer, there are many variations on this core theory of the firm. Neoclassical economists have experimented, for example, by changing the assumed objective of short-run profit maximisation to sales revenue maximisation, by considering the effect of joint production, and by incorporating 'learning by doing' as a means by which firms acquire information to gain or maintain their competitive advantage in industry.

21 Market Structures

1 A standard model of this tendency to price rigidity under conditions of oligopoly is the kinked demand curve model developed by, among others, Paul Sweezy, who was later to become renowned as a Marxist economist; see P. M. Sweezy, 'Demand under Conditions of Oligopoly', *Journal of Political Economy*, vol. 47, no. 4, August 1939, pp. 568–73. For more recent contributions to oligopoly theory, see R. E. Keunne, *Price and Nonprice Rivalry in Oligopoly*, Macmillan, Basingstoke, 1998; and S. Himmelweit, R. Simonetti, and A. Trigg, *Microeconomics: Neoclassical and Institutional Perspectives on Economic Behaviour*, Open University/Thomson Learning, London, 2001, ch. 11.

2 The Australian passenger airline industry in the 1990s provided a striking example. Every time a new airline challenged the market shares of existing airlines, vigorous price cutting occurred. At the start of the 2000s, Virgin Blue established a firm foothold, but Ansett, hitherto one of the two major airlines, then folded.

3 Rupert Murdoch, quoted in the *Sydney Morning Herald* (a newspaper he does not own), 25 January 2001, p. 13.

4 On game theory, see S. P. Hargreaves Heap and Y. Varoufakis, *Game Theory: A Critical Text*, Routledge, New York, 2nd edn, 2004.

5 The terminology 'monopoly capitalism' is particularly associated with P. Baran and P. Sweezy, *Monopoly Capital: An Essay on the American Economic and Social Order*, Monthly Review Press, New York, 1966. The foundations for theories of imperfect competition were earlier laid by Joan Robinson, later renowned as a leading post-Keynesian economist, and by E. H. Chamberlin. Robinson's book is *The Economics of Imperfect Competition*, Macmillan, London, 1933; Chamberlin's is *The Theory of Monopolistic Competition*, Harvard University Press, Cambridge, MA, 1933.

6   A classic exposition of the structure–conduct–performance approach is R. Caves, *American Industry: Structure, Conduct, Performance*, Prentice Hall, Englewood Cliffs, 4th edn, 1977; see also F. M. Scherer and D. Ross, *Industrial Market Structure and Economic Performance*, Houghton Mifflin, Boston, 3rd edn, 1990. The influence of this approach can be discerned in D. W. Carlton and J. M. Perloff, *Modern Industrial Organisation*, 3rd edn, Pearson Education Australia, Sydney, 2000.

7   It is pertinent to note that there is a conservative critique of the view that perfect competition is ideal. This points out that, because many firms have high fixed costs, marginal cost pricing could generally cause losses, bankruptcies, and recession. To the extent that this view has any policy implications, it stresses the desirability of business self-regulation; see M. Perelman, *The End of Economics*, Routledge, London, 1996.

8   In the US Department of Justice's battle against Microsoft, the reasoning underlying the government's case also drew on game theory, involving strategic entry, deterrence, and raising the costs of business rivals; see W. A. Kovacic and C. Shapiro, 'Antitrust Policy: A Century of Economic and Legal Thinking', *Journal of Economic Perspectives*, vol. 14, no. 1, Winter 2000, pp. 43–60.

9   J. Quiggin, 'Dilemmas of Competition Policy', in G. Argyrous and F. Stilwell (eds), *Economics as a Social Science: Readings in Political Economy*, Pluto Press, Sydney, 2003, pp. 286–9.

22   Distribution

1   J. B. Clark, *The Distribution of Wealth*, Augusta M. Kelley, New York, 1965, p. v.

2   V. Pareto, quoted in E. Roll, *History of Economic Thought*, Faber, London, 1973, p. 453.

3   H. George, *Progress and Poverty*, Robert Schalkenback, New York, 1966 (1879), p. 224.

4   M. Friedman and R. Friedman, *Free to Choose*, Penguin, Harmondsworth, 1980, ch. 1.

5   For further discussion of this issue, see G. Harcourt, *The Social Science Imperialists*, Routledge & Kegan Paul, London, 1982, pp. 223–328.

6   C. Ferguson, *The Neoclassical Theory of Production and Distribution*, Cambridge University Press, Cambridge, 1969.

7   For more on Joan Robinson's contributions to political economy, see G. C. Harcourt and P. Kerr, *Joan Robinson*, Palgrave Macmillan, Basingstoke and New York, 2009.

23   Economic Welfare and Neoliberalism

1   As with everything in economics, there are exceptions. The so-called hog cycle is an example of dynamic disequilibrium in neoclassical economics. Consumer demand for bacon rises; the price of bacon rises, so farmers rear more pigs; eventually there is excess supply, so the price plunges; this stimulates demand, but discourages farmers from keeping pigs. Continual oscillation of prices rather than stable equilibrium prevails in these market conditions.

2   A. C. Pigou, *The Economics of Welfare*, Macmillan, London, 1920.

3   For further discussion, see S. K. Nath, *A Perspective of Welfare Economics*, Macmillan, London, 1973; and A. Sen, Introduction, in *Choice, Welfare and Measurement*, Basil Blackwell, Oxford, 1982. For more than everything you want to know about welfare economics, see K. J. Arrow, A. K. Sen, and K. Suzumura (eds), *Handbook of Social Choice and Welfare*, Elsevier, Oxford, 2 vols, 2002 and 2005.

4   A formal statement of the principle is R. Lipsey and K. Lancaster, 'The General Theory of Second Best', *Review of Economic Studies*, vol. 24, 1956–57, pp. 11–32. For a more readable interpretation of the principle, see P. Ormerod, *The Death of Economics*, Faber & Faber, London, 1994, pp. 82–4.

5   There are other blind alleys in welfare economics, too. Of particular note is the problem of constructing a social welfare function to show the preference ordering for a whole community. One might think this could be done by the aggregation of individual preferences (utility functions); however, according to Kenneth Arrow's impossibility theorem, this cannot be done because, among other things, of the problem of intransitivity in preference ordering. According to Arrow, the only social welfare function that ranks outcomes consistently is that of a dictatorship. This conclusion, being unpalatable to liberals, has led to the abandonment of the notion of an identifiable social welfare function. D. T. Slesnick, reviewing this and other problems in welfare theory, concludes that

'this left a gap between what theorists felt was a suitable framework for applied welfare economics and what policy analysts needed to provide a complete and consistent assessment of policies'. Indeed it did. See D. T. Slesnick, 'Empirical Approaches to the Measurement of Welfare', *Journal of Economic Literature*, vol. 36, no. 4, December 1998, p. 2139.

6   Quoted in M. A. Lutz, *Economics for the Common Good: Two Centuries of Economic Thought in the Humanist Tradition*, Routledge, London, 1999, p. 122.

7   'Neoliberalism' is the most widely used term. 'Economic rationalism' is a term that has been widely used in Australia, and 'economic fundamentalism' is the term used in New Zealand. For a general analysis of the development and influence of neoliberalism, see D. Harvey, *A Brief History of Neoliberalism*, Oxford University Press, Oxford, 2005. On the gulf between free market mythology and the history of capitalist development in practice, with particular reference to the USA, see M. Perelman, *Railroading Economics: The Creation of the Free Market Mythology*, Monthly Review Press, New York, 2006.

8   See P. Self, *Government by the Market? The Politics of Public Choice*, Macmillan, Basingstoke, 1993, chs 1–3.

9   J. Buchanan, *Liberty, Market and the State: Political Economy in the 1980s*, Wheatsheaf Books, Brighton, UK, 1986, p. 256.

10 For further discussion of this awkward link between welfare theory and neoliberalism in practice, see P. Self, *Rolling Back the Market: Economic Dogma and Political Choice*, Macmillan, Basingstoke, 2000, ch. 3; and L. Orchard and H. Stretton, *Public Goods, Public Enterprise, Public Choice*, St Martin's Press, New York, 1994.

11 D. Cahill, 'Actually Existing Neoliberalism and the Global Financial Crisis', *Labour and Industry*, vol. 20, no. 3, April 2010, pp. 298–316.

12 Articles questioning the basic assumptions of welfare economics, such as the presumption that higher incomes and more status goods are conducive to happiness, include R. A. Esterlin, 'Income and Happiness: Towards a Unified Theory', *Economic Journal*, vol. 111, no. 473, July 2001, pp. 465–86; and B. Cooper, C. Garcia-Penalosa, and P. Funk, 'Status Effects and Negative Utility Growth', *Economic Journal*, vol. 111, no. 473, July 2001, pp. 642–65; see also G. F. De Martino, *Global Economy, Global Justice: Theoretical Objections and Policy Alternatives to Neoliberalism*, Routledge, London, 2000, chs 1 and 2. We return to these issues in Chapter 42.

24   Economy and Society

1   W. Lazonick, *Business Organisation and the Myth of the Market Economy*, Cambridge University Press, Cambridge, 1991, p. 8.

2   See, for example, N. Smelser and R. Swedberg (eds), *Handbook of Economic Sociology*, Princeton University Press, Princeton, 2nd edn, 2005.

3   The professional association of institutional economists based in the USA is called the Association for Evolutionary Economics. On the character of evolutionary economics, see G. Hodgson, *Economics and Evolution: Bringing Life Back into Economics*, University of Michigan Press, Ann Arbor, 1993. For a dialogue between an institutionalist and a Marxist regarding how best to study economic evolution, see W. H. Dugger and H. J. Sherman, *Reclaiming Evolution: A Dialogue between Marxism and Institutionalism on Social Change*, Routledge, London, 2000.

4   See S. Berger and G. Dore (eds), *National Diversity and Global Capitalism*, Cornell University Press, Ithaca, 1996; J. R. Hollingsworth and R. Boyer (eds), *Comparing Capitalisms: The Embeddedness of Institutions*, Cambridge University Press, Cambridge, 1997; R. D. Whitley, *Divergent Capitalisms: The Social Structuring and Change of Business Systems*, Oxford University Press, Oxford, 1999; and P. A. Hall and D. W. Soskice, *Varieties of Capitalism: The Institutional Foundations of Comparative Advantage*, Oxford University Press, Oxford, 2003.

5   See R. Swedberg, *Max Weber and the Idea of Economic Sociology*, Princeton University Press, Princeton, 1998; and J. N. Baron and M. T. Hannan, 'The Impact of Economics on Contemporary Sociology', *Journal of Economic Literature*, vol. 32, no. 3, September 1994, pp. 1111–46.

6   On the origins and history of institutional economics, see R. Lekachman, *A History of Economic Ideas*, McGraw-Hill, New York, 1976, chs 12 and 13.

7   See J. K. Galbraith, *The Age of Uncertainty*, BBC, London, 1977, ch. 2.

8   This theme is further explored in chapter 28. For further discussion of the nature and influence of Veblen's ideas, see R. Tilman, *The Intellectual Legacy of Thorstein Veblen: Unresolved Issues*, Greenwood Press, Westport, 1996.

25   A Dissident Tradition in Economics

1   See D. Fusfeld, *The Age of the Economist*, Addison-Wesley, Reading, 1999, ch. 8.

2   The problem—from an institutional economics perspective—is that econometrics has become tied to particular economic theories. An obvious example is computerised general equilibrium models, based on the Walrasian conception of the market economy, as outlined in Chapter 23. Contrary to Mitchell's empiricist inclination, the theory here determines what is measured, and the quantitative work tends to be largely a demonstration of the theory. Of course, such models may be appraised according to the accuracy of their predictions, but this process usually leads to minor modifications of the econometric model's specifications rather than to a rejection of the underlying theory. Mitchell will probably be turning in his grave. For some further reflections on the relationship between econometrics and political economy, see F. Stilwell, 'Barro and Beyond', *Journal of Economic and Social Policy*, vol. 3, no. 2, Winter 1999, pp. 221–8.

3   See, for example, K. Cowling and R. Sugden, *Transnational Monopoly Capitalism*, Oxford University Press, Oxford, 1987. The authors argue that the traditional definition of the firm, according to ownership, is not appropriate in the circumstances of modern industry, where firms can exercise control over other, nominally independent, firms. A broadened definition of the firm based on 'effective strategic control' is advocated.

4   R. L. Heilbroner, *An Inquiry into the Human Prospect*, W. W. Norton, New York, 1974, p. 132.

5   For a summary of key themes in the theory of circular and cumulative causation, see G. Argyrous, 'Economic Evolution and Cumulative Causation', in G. Argyrous and F. Stilwell (eds), *Readings in Political Economy: Economics as a Social Science*, Tilde University Press, Melbourne, 3rd edn, 2011, pp. 144–51. For fuller expositions of its historical development, see P. Toner, *Main Currents in Cumulative Causation: The Dynamics of Growth and Development*, Macmillan, Basingstoke, 1999, and S. Berger (ed.), *The Foundations of Non-Equilibrium Economics: the Principle of Circular and Cumulative Causation*, Routledge, London and New York, 2009.

6   N. Kaldor, 'The Irrelevance of Equilibrium Economics', *Economic Journal*, December 1972, vol. 82, no. 328, pp. 1237–55.

7   G. Myrdal, *An American Dilemma*, Harper & Brothers, New York, 1944.

8   R. Nurske, Some Aspects of Capital Accumulation in Under-developed Countries, commemoration lecture, Cairo, 1952.

9   G. Myrdal, *Economic Theory and Underdeveloped Regions*, Methuen, London, 1957, p. 27.

10   On urban bias, see the classic study by M. Lipton, *Why Poor People Stay Poor: Urban Bias in World Development*, Avebury, Aldershot, 1988.

11   G. Argyrous in G. Argyrous and F. Stilwell, op. cit., pp. 144–51.

12   See J. Phillimore, 'Neo-Schumpeterian Economics: Political Possibilities and Problems', *Journal of Australian Political Economy*, no. 42, December 1998, pp. 48–74, or the shorter version, 'Neo-Schumpeterian Economic Policy', in G. Argyrous and F. Stilwell (eds), op. cit., 2011, pp. 292–9. More generally, on the significance and influence of Schumpeter, see H. Hanusch (ed.), *The Legacy of Joseph A. Schumpeter*, Edward Elgar, Cheltenham, 1999.

13   See, for example, O. E. Williamson, *The Economic Institutions of Capitalism*, Free Press, New York, 1985; and R. Langlois (ed.), *Economics as a Process: Essays in the New Institutional Economics*, Cambridge University Press, Cambridge, 1986.

14   O. E. Williamson, *Markets and Hierarchies: Analysis and Anti-trust Implications: A Study in the Economics of Internal Organisation*, Free Press, New York, 1975, p. 20.

15 G. M. Hodgson, 'The Return of Institutional Economics', in N. Smelser and R. Swedberg (eds), *Handbook of Economic Sociology*, Princeton University Press, Princeton, NJ, 1994, p. 70. On the critique of 'new' institutionalism, see also J. Mulberg, *Social Limits to Economic Theory*, Routledge, London, 1995, ch. 5.

16 On new growth theories, see P. M. Romer, 'The Origins of Endogenous Growth Theory', *Journal of Economic Perspectives*, vol. 8, no. 4, Winter 1994, pp. 3–22. For contributions to a more institutionalist interpretation of path dependence in the growth process, see P. Garrouste and S. Ionnides (eds), *Evolution and Path Dependence in Economic Ideas*, Edward Elgar, Cheltenham, 2001.

26   Economic Power

1   J. K. Galbraith, *The Anatomy of Power*, Corgi Books, London, 1985, p. 23.

2   ibid., p. 24.

3   id.

4   Galbraith's clearest statement of the imperatives of technology is *The New Industrial State*, Penguin, Harmondsworth, 1972, ch. 2.

5   ibid., p. 31.

6   See, for example, H. Thompson, 'The Social Significance of Technological Change', *Journal of Australian Political Economy*, no. 8, July 1980, pp. 57–68.

7   Galbraith used this term in *Economics and the Public Purpose*, Andre Deutsch, London, 1974, p. 285, in a rather different way: to denote the case for more public control over 'unduly weak industries and unduly strong ones'.

8   *The New Industrial State*, p. 86.

9   J. K. Galbraith, 'The State and the Good Society', in G. Argyrous and F. Stilwell (eds), *Readings in Political Economy: Economics as a Social Science*, Tilde University Press, Melbourne, 3rd edn, 2011, p. 278.

10 W. M. Dugger argues that the relative autonomy of the technostructure was characteristic of the 1950s and 1960s; but, squeezed by the creation of a market for corporate control, power was effectively shifted back to the shareholders from the 1970s; see W. M. Dugger, 'The Great Retrenchment and the New Industrial State', *Review of Social Economy*, vol. 50, Winter 1992, pp. 453–71.

11 J. K. Galbraith, *The Affluent Society*, Penguin, Harmondsworth, 1962, p. 107.

12 *Economics and the Public Purpose*, pt 3.

13 *The New Industrial State*, p. 216.

14 J. K. Galbraith, 'Economics as a System of Belief', in *A Contemporary Guide to Economics, Peace and Laughter*, Andre Deutsch, London, 1971; extract in E. L. Wheelwright and F. Stilwell (eds), *Readings in Political Economy*, vol. 2, ANZ Book Co., Sydney, 1976, pp. 32–43.

15 J. K. Galbraith, *The World Economy Since the Wars*, Sinclair-Stevenson, London, 1994, p. 1.

16 *The Affluent Society*, p. 206.

17 J. K. Galbraith, *American Capitalism: The Concept of Countervailing Power*, Penguin, Harmondsworth, 1952, ch. 9.

18 *Economics and the Public Purpose*, pt 5.

19 J. K. Galbraith, 'The State and the Good Society', in G. Argyrous and F. Stilwell (eds), *Readings in Political Economy: Economics as a Social Science*, Tilde University Press, Melbourne, 3rd edn, 2011, p. 279.

20 ibid., p. 275.

21 *The New Industrial State*, ch. 25.

22 J. K. Galbraith, *The Culture of Contentment*, Houghton Mifflin, Boston, 1992.

23 J. K. Galbraith, in Argyrous and Stilwell, op. cit., p. 278.

24 ibid., p. 278.

25 ibid., p. 279.

26 id.

27 ibid., p. 280. Research by US political sociologist Fred Block also confirms the importance of government in fostering innovation: see F. Block and M. R. Keller (eds), *State of Innovation: The US Government's Role in Technology Development*, Paradigm Publishers, Boulder, 2010.

28 J. K. Galbraith, in Argyrous and Stilwell, op. cit., p. 280.

29 *Economics and the Public Purpose*, p. 223.

30 ibid., pp. 277, 283.

27   Economic and Social Reform

1 See R. Alford and R. Friedland, *Powers of Theory: Capitalism, the State and Democracy*, Cambridge University Press, Cambridge, 1985.

2 The USA is somewhat exceptional in this regard.

3 J. K. Galbraith, *The Anatomy of Power*, Corgi Books, London, 1985, p. 42.

4 A. Okun, *Equality and Efficiency: The Big Trade-off*, Brookings Institution, Washington DC, 1975, p. vii.

5 These phrases appear as the titles of two books: B. Jessop, *The Capitalist State: Marxist Theories and Methods*, Martin Robertson, Oxford, 1982; and R. Miliband, *The State in Capitalist Society*, Quartet Books, London, 1973.

6 L. S. Moss, review of M. A. Lutz, *Economics for the Common Good*, in *Economic Journal*, vol. 111, no. 469, February 2001, pp. 129–31.

7 Fusfeld, op. cit., pp. 102–3.

8 For a pioneering contribution to developing an understanding of these issues, see I. Gough, *The Political Economy of the Welfare State*, Macmillan, London, 1979; see also N. Barr, *The Economics of the Welfare State*, 4th edn, Oxford University Press, Oxford, 2004; and N. Kildal and S. Kutile, *Normative Foundations of the Welfare State: the Nordic Experience*, Routledge London, 2004. A comprehensive compendium of contributions to analysis of the welfare state is R. E. Goodwin and I. C. D. Mitchell (eds), *The Foundations of the Welfare State*, 3 vols, Edward Elgar, Cheltenham, 2000. On challenges to the welfare state, see A. B. Atkinson, *The Economic Consequences of Rolling Back the Welfare State*, MIT Press, Cambridge, Mass., 1999.

9 G. Myrdal, *The Political Element in the Development of Economic Thought*, Simon & Schuster, New York, 1969, p. xii.

10 F. Block, 'Reinventing Social Democracy for the 21st Century', *Journal of Australian Political Economy*, no. 67, June 2011, pp. 5–25.

11 P. J. O'Rourke, *Eat the Rich: A Treatise on Economics*, Pan Macmillan, Sydney, 1998, p. 56.

12 J. O'Connor, *The Fiscal Crisis of the State*, St Martin's Press, New York, 1973.

13 G. Dow, 'Policy Matters in Political Economy', in G. Argyrous and F. Stilwell (eds), *Readings in Political Economy: Economics as a Social Science*, Tilde University Press, Melbourne, 3rd edn, 2011, pp. 64–70.

14 D. Fusfeld, *The Age of the Economist*, Addison Wesley, New York, 2002, pp. 100–2.

15 Dow, op. cit., p. 68.

16 List shared one experience with Karl Marx: he was expelled from his native Germany for excessive forthrightness in his journalism. For discussion of List, see W. O. Henderson, *Friedrich List: Economist and Visionary*, Frank Cass, London, 1983.

17 See L. Weiss, *The Myth of the Powerless State: Governing the Economy in a Global Era*, Polity Press, Cambridge, 1998.

18 Dow, op. cit., p. 70.

28   Corporate Globalisation

1 See, for example, K. Ohmae, *The Borderless World: Power and Strategy in the Interlinked Economy*, HarperBusiness, New York, 1999. A more carefully reasoned contribution, emphasising potentially progressive aspects of globalisation, is G. Kitching, *Seeking Social Justice through Globalization: Escaping a Nationalist Perspective*, University of Philadelphia Press, Philadelphia, 2001.

2 See, for example, P. Hirst and G. Thompson, *Globalization in Question: The International Economy and the Possibilities of Governance*, Polity Press, Cambridge, 2nd edn, 1999; R. Went,

Globalisation: Neoliberal Challenge, Radical Responses, Pluto Press, London, 2000; M. Della Ginsta, U. S. Kambhampati, and R. Wade (eds), *Critical Perspectives on Globalisation*, Edward Elgar, Cheltenham, 2006; and W. Bello, 'Globalisation in Retreat?', in G. Argyrous and F. Stilwell (eds), *Readings in Political Economy: Economics as a Social Science*, Tilde University Press, Melbourne, 2011, pp. 4–7.

3   The most substantial of these contributions is G. J. Crough and E. L. Wheelwright, *Australia: A Client State*, Penguin, Melbourne, 1982. On Wheelwright's other studies in political economy, see P. O'Hara, 'Contributions of E. L. Wheelwright to Political Economy: Public Scholar, Economic Power and Global Capitalism', *History of Economics Review*, no. 51, Winter 2010, pp. 24–42.

4   G. Buckman, *Globalization: Tame It or Scrap It?*, Zed Books, London and New York, 2004, p. 36.

5   See UNCTAD, *World Investment Report 2009: Transnational Corporations, Agricultural Production and Development*, UNCTAD, New York and Geneva, 2009, p. xxi.

6   G. Buckman, op. cit., p. 37.

7   ibid., p. 37.

8   ibid., p. 16.

9   Crough and Wheelwright, op. cit., p. 13.

10   On the footloose character and destabilising effect of the transnationals, see H-P. Martin and H. Schumann, *The Global Trap: Globalisation and the Assault on Prosperity and Democracy*, Zed Books, London, 1997, ch. 4. On understanding global business more generally, see G. Ietto-Gillies, *Transnational Corporations and International Production: Concepts, Theories and Effects*, Edward Elgar, Cheltenham, 2005.

11   The classic reference on this topic is F. Froebel, J. Heinrichs, and O. Kreye, *The New International Division of Labour*, Cambridge University Press, Cambridge, 1980.

12   See, for example, R. Fagan and M. Webber, *Global Restructuring*, Oxford University Press, Melbourne, 2nd edn, 1999; and T. Bramble, 'Solidarity Versus Sectionalism: The Social Tariff Debate', *Journal of Australian Political Economy*, no. 48, December 2001, pp. 73–114.

13   On transfer pricing, see G. J. Crough and E. L. Wheelwright, op. cit., pp. 143–7.

14   D. Peetz, *Unions in a Contrary World: The Future of the Australian Trade Union Movement*, Cambridge University Press, Melbourne, 1998.

15   This view is particularly associated with British (transnational?) sociologist Leslie Sklair; see *The Transnational Capitalist Class*, Blackwell, Oxford, 2001; see also W. K. Carrol, *The Making of a Transnational Capitalist Class: Corporate Power in the 21st Century*, Zed Books, London, 2010.

16   Crough and Wheelwright, op. cit., passim.

17   N. Hertz, *The Silent Takeover: Global Capitalism and the Death of Democracy*, Heinemann, London, 2003, p. 88.

18   S. Holland, *The Global Economy: From Meso to Macroeconomics*, Weidenfeld & Nicolson, London, 1987, pp. xiii–xiv.

19   See, for example, R. Bryan and M. Rafferty, *The Global Economy in Australia: Global Integration and National Economic Policy*, Allen & Unwin, Sydney, 1999. A subsequent work by the same authors is *Capitalism With Derivatives: A Political Economy of Financial Derivatives, Capital and Class*, Palgrave Macmillan, Basingstoke, 2006.

20   E. L. Wheelwright, *Capitalism, Socialism or Barbarism? The Australian Predicament. Essays in Contemporary Political Economy*, ANZ Book Co., Sydney, 1978.

21   J. Stiglitz, *Globalization and its Discontents*, Penguin, London, 2002, p. 187. Stiglitz was awarded the Nobel Prize in Economic Sciences in 2001.

22   R. Peet, *Unholy Trinity: The IMF, World Bank and WTO*, Zed Books, London and New York, 2003, p. 200; see also A. Buira (ed.), *Challenges to the World Bank and the IMF*, Anthem Press, London, 2003. For a critical consideration of a recent bilateral trade agreement proposal, see J. Kelsey (ed.), *No Ordinary Deal: Unmasking the Trans-Pacific Free Trade Partnership Agreement*, Allen & Unwin, Sydney, 2010.

23   The former interpretation is presented by R. Catley, *Globalising Australian Capitalism*, Cambridge University Press, Melbourne, 1996, p. 222.

24 See K. R. Cox (ed.), *Spaces of Globalisation: Reasserting the Power of the Local*, Guilford Press, New York, 1997; and J. Mander and E. Goldsmith (eds), *The Case Against the Global Economy and for a Turn Toward the Local*, Sierra Club Books, San Francisco, 1996.

25 An example of an effective campaign, contesting the proposed Multilateral Agreement on Investment (MAI), is described in J. Goodman and P. Ranald (eds), *Stopping the Juggernaut*, Pluto Press, Sydney, 2000. For more general discussion of social movements contesting the globalisation of capital, see A. Starr, *Naming the Enemy: Anti-corporate Social Movements Confront Globalisation*, Zed Books, London, 2000; J. Goodman (ed.), *Protest and Globalisation*, Pluto Press Australia, Sydney, 2002; W. F. Fisher and T. Ponniah, *Another World is Possible: Popular Alternatives to Globalisation at the World Social Forum*, Zed Books, London, 2003; and W. Bello, *Deglobalisation: Ideas for a New World Economy*, Zed Press, London, 2004.

29 The Disillusioned Defence of Capitalism

1 This self-perpetuating character of unemployment is sometimes labelled hysteresis. It may be interpreted as one illustration of the principle of circular and cumulative causation discussed in Chapter 25.

2 See M. Watts and W. Mitchell, 'The Costs of Unemployment in Australia', *Economics and Labour Relations Review*, vol. 11, no. 2, December 2000, pp. 180–97.

3 On the Great Depression, see J. K. Galbraith, *The Great Crash*, Deutsch, London, 50th anniv. edn, 1980; and T. E. Hall and J. D. Ferguson, *The Great Depression*, University of Michigan Press, Ann Arbor, 1998.

4 See J. Robinson, 'Marx, Marshall and Keynes: Three Views of Capitalism', in E. L. Wheelwright and F. Stilwell (eds), *Readings in Political Economy*, vol. 1, ANZ Book Co., Sydney, 1976, pp. 147–59.

5 Critics of Keynes sometimes contend he simplified and/or misrepresented the prevailing economic orthodoxies; see S. Kates, *Say's Law and the Keynesian Revolution: How Macroeconomics Lost its Way*, Edward Elgar, Cheltenham, 1998. Of course, cutting through to the essence of the prevailing orthodoxies is usually a precondition for pushing them aside and moving on.

6 A. C. Pigou, *Theory of Unemployment*, Macmillan, London, 1933, p. 252.

7 It is pertinent to note that Keynes did not seek to establish a link between his macro theory and the micro theories of imperfect competition being developed at Cambridge University (by Joan Robinson) at the same time. This kept the primary focus on the aggregate level of economic activity and its management—but at the expense of having a more comprehensive analysis of the capitalist economy.

8 J. M. Keynes, *The General Theory of Employment, Interest and Money*, Macmillan, London, 1936, p. 131.

9 D. Fusfeld, *The Age of the Economist*, Addison-Wesley, Reading, Mass., 1999, p. 127.

10 R. O'Donnell, 'Keynes's Socialism: Conception, Strategy and Espousal', in C. Sardoni and P. Kriesler (eds), *Keynes, Post-Keynesianism and Political Economy: Essays in Honour of Geoff Harcourt*, vol. 3, Routledge, London and New York, 1999, p. 165.

30 Constructing a Keynesian Model

1 For a political economic reinterpretation of the circular flow model, see E. Nell, 'Economics: The Revival of Political Economy', in R. Blackburn (ed.), *Ideology in Social Science*, Fontana, London, 1972, pp. 76–95; extract in G. Argyrous and F. Stilwell (eds), *Economics as a Social Science: Readings in Political Economy*, Pluto Press, Sydney, rev. edn, 2003, pp. 189–97.

2 For an analysis of investors' confidence and the associated instability and cyclical patterns in the economy, drawing also on the ideas of Michal Kalecki, see J. Courvisanos, *Investment Cycles in Capitalist Economies*, Edward Elgar, Cheltenham, 1996.

3 'Irrational exuberance' is a modern term, with echoes of 'animal spirits', describing volatile behaviour in share markets; see R. Shiller, *Irrational Exuberance*, Broadway Books, New York, 2001.

31   Instability in a Monetary Economy

1   In estimating the money supply and in formulating monetary policy, various definitions of money are used (for example, M1, M2, M3), according to which classes of liquid assets are included with cash. In this chapter, for ease of exposition, cash is taken to be synonymous with money (that is, M1).

2   This does not mean that only money can function as a means of exchange. Local Area Trading Schemes (LETS) have been developed as systems of exchange that help to combat unemployment, foster social reciprocity, and strengthen local communities. The problems of barter are avoided by the adoption of a common unit of value, without recourse to money in the form of notes and coin.

3   G. Argyrous, 'The Economics of the General Theory', in G. Argyrous and F. Stilwell (eds), *Readings in Political Economy: Economics as a Social Science*, Tilde University Press, Melbourne, 3rd edn, 2011, pp. 164–171.

4   The use of the term 'speculators' should not necessarily be taken to imply a distinct class of people separate from ordinary citizens. Anyone seeking the best rate of return on his or her savings would wisely consider different types of financial assets and their likely changes in value. Of course, some people (and institutions) have much more surplus funds to use for such purposes than others. Such people also usually have a higher propensity to switch assets based on day-to-day changes in market prices. They can reasonably be considered central to the processes of speculation.

5   There is a separate body of post-Keynesian economic analysis examining the possibility of endogenous money supply; that is, changes in the supply of money through the banking system in direct response to changes in the conditions of demand for money, depending on the level of investment. See L. R. Wray (ed.), *Money, Financial Instability and Stabilization Policy*, Edward Elgar, Cheltenham, 2006.

6   There is one circumstance where this policy does not work. If virtually all savings are currently being held as cash (that is, liquidity preference is high), an increase in the money supply may not cause the interest rate to fall. So there will be no stimulus to investment. This is the problem known as the liquidity trap, where interest rates have hit rock bottom and investment remains stagnant. Monetary policy is usually said to be of no avail in these circumstances. However, a public sector-led recovery is still possible. If the central bank provides low-interest loans to the government and the government then spends the money on job creation and public works, economic expansion can occur.

7   On this post-Keynesian view of endogenous money, see R. Guttman, *How Credit Money Shapes the Economy: The US in a Global System*, Sharpe, London, 1994. The quotation by Galbraith comes from a review of this book in *Journal of Economic Literature*, vol. 33, no. 4, December 1995, p. 1989.

8   J. Hartley, reviewing D. Laidler, *Fabricating the Keynesian Revolution*, Cambridge University Press, Cambridge, 1999, in *Journal of Economic Literature*, vol. 37, no. 4, December 1999, p. 1799.

9   The LM curve in Box 31.1 becomes steeper to the right because more money is held for transactions and precautionary purposes as national income rises, so the equilibrium interest rate (needed to balance the supply and demand for money) must rise. The curve becomes vertical when the whole of the existing money supply is held for transactionary and precautionary purposes. This limit represents the highest level of real income that can be financed by the existing money supply. For a brief but insightful comment on the limitations of this IS/LM model, see D. E. Moggridge, *Keynes*, Macmillan, Basingstoke, 1986, Appendix, pp. 165–7.

10   Chapter 36 returns to these issues.

11   J. M. Keynes, *The General Theory of Employment, Interest and Money*, Macmillan, London, 1936, p. 159.

12   ibid., p. 376.

32   Macroeconomic Policy

1   A discussion of measures to address unemployment, explicitly linked to a social democratic perspective on the state, is provided by G. Dow, P. Boreham, and M. Leet, *Room to Manoeuvre: Political Aspects of Full Employment*, Melbourne University Press, Melbourne, 1999.

2   J. K. Galbraith, *Economics and the Public Purpose*, Houghton Mifflin, New York, 1973, p. 21.

3   R. O'Donnell, 'Keynes's Socialism: Conception, Strategy and Espousal', in C. Sardoni and P. Kriesler (eds), *Keynes, Post-Keynesianism and Political Economy: Essays in Honour of Geoff Harcourt*, vol. 3, Routledge, London and New York, p. 169.

4   For discussion of this tendency in Australia, see J. Dullard and D. Hayward, 'The Democratic Paradox of Public Choice Theory: The Case of the Costello Cuts', *Journal of Australian Political Economy*, no. 42, December 1998, pp. 16–47.

5   Some political economists advocate a general long-term policy of running the lowest achievable interest rates; see H. Stretton, *Political Essays*, Georgian House, Melbourne, 1987, pp. 37–47. Others advocate linking monetary policy, specifically low-interest loans to the government from the central bank, to higher levels of government expenditure on job creation and infrastructure provision.

6   For discussion of how financial deregulation worked out in the Australian context, see J. Spoehr, *From Lending Binge to Credit Squeeze: The Failure of Bank and Finance Sector Deregulation*, United Trades and Labour Council, Adelaide, 1990.

7   J. M. Keynes, *The General Theory of Employment, Interest and Money*, Macmillan, London, 1936, p. 372.

8   For discussion of the Accord, see the various contributions to K. Wilson, J. Bradford, and M. Fitzpatrick (eds), *Australia in Accord*, South Pacific Publishing, Melbourne, 2000.

9   Keynes, op. cit., p. 378.

10 For further discussion of historical lessons from the Swedish experience, see G. Dow, 'The Swedish Model and the Anglo-Saxon Model: Reflections on the Fate of Social Democracy in Australia', *Economic and Industrial Democracy*, vol. 12, no. 4, November 1991, pp. 515–26.

11 For further discussion of the proposed Tobin tax, see M. ul Huq, I. Kaul, and I. Grunberg (eds), *The Tobin Tax: Coping with Financial Volatility*, Oxford University Press, Oxford, 1996; and H. Patomaki, *Democratising Globalisation: The Leverage of the Tobin Tax*, Zed Books, London, 2001. For a more critical view on the Tobin tax proposal, see R. Bryan and B. Rafferty, *Capitalism with Derivatives: A Political Economy of Financial Derivatives, Capital and Class*, Palgrave Macmillan, Basingstoke, 2006, pp. 188–192.

33   The Keynesian Legacy

1   J. M. Keynes wrote this in a letter to George Bernard Shaw dated 1 January 1935, quoted in M. Stewart, *Keynes and After*, Penguin, Harmondsworth, 1972, p. 12.

2   See R. M. Collins, *The Business Response to Keynes, 1929-1964*, Columbia University Press, New York, 1981.

3   J. K. Galbraith, *The Age of Uncertainty*, BBC, London, 1977, p. 221. The New Deal of President Franklin D. Roosevelt in the USA was a more positive example, putting people to work in socially beneficial jobs. Beginning in 1933, this was 'primal Keynesianism' before Keynes's theory was fully developed and published. Thus, 'in the end Keynesian economics was to justify policies already in vogue'; E. R. Canterbery, *The Literate Economist*, HarperCollins, New York, 1995, p. 158.

4   In the UK, a national health system was set up by the first Labour government after the Second World War. In Australia, the introduction of a universal public health system had to wait until the election of a Labor government in 1972. In the USA, a more limited, insurance-based national health system was introduced by the Obama administration in 2010.

5   E. Jones, *Was the Post-War Keynesian?*, Working Paper no. 131, Department of Economics, University of Sydney, October, 1989.

6   See, for example, R. Sutcliffe, 'Keynesianism and the Stabilisation of Capitalist Economies', in F. Green and P. Nore (eds), *Economics: An Anti-Text*, Macmillan, London, 1977, pp. 163–81.

7   M. Bleaney, *The Rise and Fall of Keynesian Economics*, Macmillan, London, 1985, pp. 131–54; see also R. Leeson, *The Eclipse of Keynesianism: The Political Economy of the Chicago Counter-Revolution*, Macmillan, Basingstoke, 2001.

8   See W. J. Barber, 'Chile con Chicago: A Review Essay', *Journal of Economic Literature*, vol. 23, no. 4, 1985, pp. 1941–8.

9   M. Friedman, 'The Methodology of Positive Economics', in M. Friedman (ed.), *Essays in Positive Economics*, University of Chicago Press, Chicago, 1953, pp. 3–43.

10   N. G. Mankiew, 'The Inexorable and Mysterious Trade-off between Inflation and Unemployment', *Economic Journal*, vol. 111, no. 471, May 2001, p. 59; see also David Laidler's review of the collected works of A. W. Phillips in the same journal (no. 472, June 2001, p. 526). Laidler notes that, by drawing a curve through the scatter, Phillips was 'unintentionally providing an empirically based functional relationship for others to interpret as a policy menu'. As a result, 'Phillips' name will forever be associated with damaging fine tuning policies whose many pitfalls his own work was designed to reveal and warn against'. Moreover, as P. J. Kurwin had earlier noted, Phillips recognised the existence of loops causing the expansion and contraction paths to differ, so the dynamic instability in the unemployment–inflation trade-off was acknowledged from the start; see P. J. Kurwin, *Inflation*, Macmillan, London, 1976. A comprehensive compilation of contributions by Phillips is presented by R. Leeson (ed.), *A. W. H. Phillips: Collected Works in Contemporary Perspective*, Cambridge University Press, Cambridge, 2000.

11   See G. Argyrous, 'Government Budgets: A Surplus of Funds, a Deficit of Logic', in G. Argyrous and F. Stilwell (eds), *Readings in Political Economy: Economics as a Social Science*, Tilde University Press, Melbourne, 3rd edn, 2011, pp. 319–25.

12   See F. Stilwell, *Changing Track: A New Political Economic Direction for Australia*, Pluto Press, Sydney, 2000, ch. 6.

13   For discussion of the NAIRU, see the special symposium in *Journal of Economic Perspectives*, vol. 11, no. 1, Winter 1997, especially J. K. Galbraith (Jnr), 'Time to Ditch the NAIRU', pp. 93–108.

14   J. B. de Long, 'The Triumph of Monetarism?', *Journal of Economic Perspectives*, vol. 14, no. 1, Winter 2000, pp. 83–94. On de Long's reasoning, 'new Keynesian' economics is a misnomer: it should really be called 'new monetarism'.

15   See J. B. Taylor, 'Teaching Modern Macroeconomics at the Principles Level', *American Economic Review*, vol. 90, no. 2, 2000, pp. 90–4; and B. S. Bernanke and F. S. Mishkin, 'Inflation Targeting. A New Framework for Monetary Policy?' in *Journal of Economic Perspectives*, vol. 11, no. 2, Spring 1997, pp. 97–116.

16   On rational expectations, see L. Thurow, *Dangerous Currents: The State of Economics*, Oxford University Press, Oxford, 1983, ch. 6.

17   See J. E. Hartley, *The Representative Agent in Macroeconomics*, Routledge, London, 1997; and T. Sargent, *Bounded Rationality in Macroeconomics*, Clarendon Press, Oxford, 1993. The work of Robert Lucas pushes this emphasis on the micro foundations of macroeconomics to an (anti-Keynesian) extreme. In his own words, 'Progress in economic thinking means getting better and better abstract analogue economic models, not better verbal observations about the world'; R. Lucas, 'Methods and Problems in Business Cycle Theory', *Journal of Money, Credit and Banking*, vol. 12, 1980, pp. 696–715, cited (approvingly) by V. V. Chari, 'Nobel Laureate Robert E. Lucas, Jr., Architect of Modern Macroeconomics', *Journal of Economic Perspectives*, vol. 12, no. 1, Winter 1998, pp. 171–86.

18   For assessments of these policies in Australia, see J. Quiggin, *Great Expectations*, Allen & Unwin, Sydney, 1996; and T. Anderson, 'The Meaning of Deregulation', *Journal of Australian Political Economy*, no. 44, December 1999, pp. 5–21. For discussion of what policies could put the emphasis back on solving unemployment, see S. Bell (ed.), *The Unemployment Crisis in Australia: Which Way Out?*, Cambridge University Press, Melbourne, 2000.

19   See, for example, W. F. Mitchell and J. Muyksen, *Full Employment Abandoned*, Edward Elgar, Cheltenham, 2008.

20   P. Sraffa, *The Production of Commodities by Means of Commodities*, Cambridge University Press, Cambridge, 1960. For an introduction to this enigmatic theory, see Y. Varoufakis, *Foundations of Economics: A Beginner's Companion*, Routledge, London, 1998, pp. 191–200.

21   One book putting Sraffa's work forward as superior to either neoclassicism or Marxism is S. Keen, *Debunking Economics*, Zed Books, Sydney, 2004.

22   M. Kalecki, 'Political Aspects of Full Employment', in J. Osiatynski (ed.), *Collected Works of Michal Kalecki*, vol. 1, Clarendon, Oxford, 1990; reprinted in G. Argyrous and F. Stilwell (eds), *Readings in*

Political Economy: Economics as a Social Science, Tilde University Press, Melbourne, 3rd edn, 2011, pp. 180–183; see also, Kalecki's *Economics Today*, in Z. Sadowski and A. Szerworski (eds), Routledge, London, 2003.

23   A. Eichner, *The Megacorp and Oligopoly*, Cambridge University Press, Cambridge, 1976.

24   See, for example, F. Lee, *Post Keynesian Price Theory*, Cambridge University Press, Cambridge, 1998.

25   H. Minsky, *Stabilizing an Unstable Economy*, Yale University Press, New Haven, 1986.

26   P. A. O'Hara (ed.), *Encyclopedia of Political Economy*, Routledge, London, 1999, p. 434.

27   For fuller discussion of post-Keynesian economics, see P. O'Hara (ed.), *Encyclopedia of Political Economy*, Routledge, London, 1999, pp. 880–7; J. King, *Conversations with Post Keynesians*, St Martin's Press, New York, 1995; L. R. Wray, 'The Continuing Legacy of John Maynard Keynes', in F. Forstater and L. R. Wray (eds), *Keynes for the Twenty-first Century: The Continuing Relevance of the General Theory*, Palgrave Macmillan, Basingstoke, 2008, pp. 1–20; and P. Kriesler, 'Post Keynesian Economics', in G. Argyrous and F. Stilwell (eds), op. cit., pp. 164–171.

28   This characterisation of the Keynesian state is by S. Holland, *The Global Economy*, Weidenfield & Nicolson, London, 1987, p. 1.

34   A Radical Reconstruction

1   There are some modern political economists who, continuing to operate within the analytical traditions we have considered, see no need for a synthesis of this sort. Marxist economists, such as those contributing to the journal *Monthly Review*, are generally of the view that what is required is the further development and application of Marxism in the context of contemporary capitalism. On the other hand, some post-Keynesian and institutional economists prefer to have no truck with the Marxian analysis, seeing its basis in value theory as an obstacle to empirical study. Some of the most interesting work in modern political economy is concerned with exploring fruitful interconnections between Marxian and non-Marxian perspectives; see, for example, S. Tsuru, *Institutional Economics Revisited*, Cambridge University Press, Cambridge 1993; and P. A. O'Hara, *Marx, Veblen and Contemporary Institutional Political Economy: Principles and Unstable Dynamics of Capitalism*, Edward Elgar, Cheltenham, 2000. On the competing currents flowing into modern political economy, also see B. Clark, *Political Economy: A Comparative Approach*, Praeger, Westport, 1998; and W. K. Tabb, *Reconstructing Political Economy: The Great Divide in Economic Thought*, Routledge, London, 1999.

2   It even features in postmodern Marxism; see J. K. Gibson-Graham, S. Resnick, and R. Wolff (eds), *Re/Presenting Class: Essays in Postmodern Marxism*, Duke University Press, Durham, 2001.

3   For discussion of work–life balance, see B. Pocock, *The Work/Life Collision*, Federation Press, Sydney, 2003

4   See Chapter 37.

5   For further discussion of behavioural economics, see A. A. Schmid, *Conflict and Cooperation: Institutional and Behavioural Economics*, Blackwell, Oxford, 2004; and G. Argyrous and F. Stilwell (eds), *Readings in Political Economy: Economics as a Social Science*, Tilde University Press, Melbourne, 3rd edn, 2011, pp. 251–69.

35   Economy and Environment

1   D. Attenborough, *The State of the Planet*, television series, BBC, 2000.

2   D. Meadows et al., *The Limits to Growth*, Earth Island, London, 1972; see also D. Meadows, J. Randers, and D. Meadows, *The Limits to Growth: The 30 Year Update*, Earthscan, London, rev. edn, 2005.

3   An important publication, giving official international status to the concern over global environmental issues, was *The World Commission on Environment and Development, Our Common Future*, Oxford University Press, Oxford, 1987.

4   See Chapter 8, nn. 1 and 3.

5   For discussion of this contested concept, see H. Daly, *Beyond Growth: The Economics of Sustainable Development*, Beacon Press, Boston, 1996; S. Beder, *The Nature of Sustainable Development*, Scribe, Newham, 2nd edn, 1996; J. Bowers, *Sustainability and Environmental Economics: An*

Alternative Text, Addison Wesley Longman, London, 1997; E. Neumayer, *Weak versus Strong Sustainability: Exploring the Limits of Two Opposing Paradigms*, Edward Elgar, Cheltenham, 2010; and G. J. Paton, *Seeking Sustainability: On the Prospect of an Ecological Liberalism*, Routledge, London and New York, 2011.

6   These four categories are adapted from I. Lowe, 'Ecologically Sustainable Development', *Consuming Interest*, Australian Consumers Association, June–July 1991; see also Diesendorf and Hamilton (eds), *Human Ecology, Human Economy: Ideas for an Ecologically Sustainable Future*, Allen & Unwin, Sydney, 1997, ch. 3.

7   This change of terminology was officially adopted in July 2000.

8   See, for example, P. Hawken, *The Ecology of Commerce: A Declaration of Sustainability*, Phoenix, London, 1995. For a critique of the market-based policies that follow from this type of analysis, see S. Beder, *Environmental Principles and Policies: An Interdisciplinary Approach*, UNSW Press, Sydney, 2006.

9   See Diesendorf and Hamilton, op. cit., ch. 12.

10 C. Hamilton, T. Hundloe, and J. Quiggin, *Ecological Tax Reform in Australia*, Discussion Paper no. 10, Australia Institute, Canberra, April 1997.

11 For discussion of the influence of vested economic interests in transport, see one of the first textbooks on environmental issues by a political economist: M. Edel, *Economies and the Environment*, Prentice Hall, Englewood Cliffs, 1973, ch. 6.

12 For discussion of claims and counterclaims about the Los Angeles experience, see B. C. Snell, 'American Ground Transport: A Proposal for Restructuring the Automobile, Truck, Bus and Rail Industries', Part 4A, Appendix to Part 4, *Hearings Before the Sub Committee on Antitrust and Monopoly of the Committee on the Judiciary*, United States Senate, 1974; and P. Mees, *A Very Public Solution: Transport in the Dispersed City*, Melbourne University Press, Melbourne, 2000, pp. 42–5.

13 This need not be an absolute impediment to achieving a shift from private to public transport; see Mees, op. cit., passim.

14 C. Hamilton, *Scorcher: The Dirty Politics of Climate Change*, Black Inc., Melbourne, 2007.

15 S. Beder, *Free Market Missionaries: The Corporate Manipulation of Community Values*, Earthscan, London, 2006.

16 K. Boulding, Environmental Quality: Discussion, *Papers and Proceedings of the American Economic Association*, May 1971, p. 169.

17 The ACTU–ACF report, *Green Gold Rush*, and other estimates of potential growth in green jobs are discussed in A. Pearce and F. Stilwell, 'Green Collar Jobs: Employment Impacts of Climate Change Policies', *Journal of Australian Political Economy*, no. 62, December 2008, pp. 120–38.

18 See H. Masterman-Smith, 'Green Collaring a Capital Crisis?', *Labour and Industry*, vol. 20, no. 3, April 2010, pp. 317–30.

19 On the concept of common heritage capital, see A. F. Anderson, *Challenging Newt Gingrich*, Tom Paine Institute, Eugene, 1996, pp. xvii–xx.

20 For an example of an attempt to move beyond conventional approaches to environmental economics and construct an ecological political economy, see F. P. Gale and R. M. M'Gonigle, *Nature, Production, Power: Towards on Ecological Political Economy*, Edward Elgar, Cheltenham, 2000; and, with more attention to the politics of addressing the threat of climate change, see M. Diesendorf, *Climate Action: A Campaign Manual for Greenhouse Solutions*, UNSW Press, Sydney, 2009; and the special issue of the *Journal of Australian Political Economy* on 'Challenging Climate Change', no. 66, Summer 2011.

36   Technology, Industry, Work

1   E. Nell, *The General Theory of Transformational Growth: Keynes after Sraffa*, Cambridge University Press, Cambridge, 1998.

2   M. Castells, *The Information City*, Basil Blackwell, Oxford, 1989, and *The Rise of the Network Society*, Blackwell, Cambridge, MA, 1997. For a more sceptical view on the new economy, see R. Boyer, 'Is a Finance-Led Growth Regime a Viable Alternative to Fordism?', *Economy and Society*, vol. 29, no. 1,

February 2000, pp. 111–45. Critical assessments of how the potential of new technologies is distorted in practice are to be found in R. W. McChesney, E. M. Wood, and J. B. Foster (eds), *Capitalism and the Information Age*, Monthly Review Press, New York, 2000.

3   L. Thurow, *The Future of Capitalism*, Nicholas Brealey, London, 1997.

4   This argument is put by G. Zappala, 'The Economic and Social Dimensions of the New Economy', *Australian Journal of Social Issues*, vol. 35, no. 4, November 2000, pp. 317–32. See also M. Ford, *The Lights in the Tunnel: Automation, Accelerating Technology and the Economy of the Future*, Acculant Publishing, 2009.

5   D. Munro, 'The Knowledge Economy', *Journal of Australian Political Economy*, no. 45, June 2000, p. 9.

6   H. Braverman, *Labor and Monopoly Capital: The Degradation of Work in the Twentieth Century*, Monthly Review Press, New York, 1975; see also Box 14.1.

7   This distinction between a regime of accumulation and a mode of social regulation is characteristic of the regulation school of political economy based in France; see R. Boyer, *The Regulation School: A Critical Introduction*, Columbia University Press, New York, 1990; and R. Boyer and Y. Saillard (eds), *Regulation Theory: The State of the Art*, Routledge, London, 2001.

8   The classic exposition of this view is that of M. J. Piore and C. Sabel, *The Second Industrial Divide*, Basic Books, New York, 1984.

9   For a fuller description of these features of post-Fordism, see R. Murray, 'Fordism and Post-Fordism', in S. Hall and M. Jacques (eds), *New Times*, Lawrence & Wishart, London, 1990, pp. 38–53; on Fordism and post-Fordism in practice, see M. Koch, *Roads to Post-Fordism: Labour Markets and Social Structures in Europe*, Ashgate, Aldershot, 2006.

10   See, for example, D. Harvey, *The Condition of Postmodernity*, Basil Blackwell, Oxford, 1990; S. Lash and J. Urry, *Economics of Signs and Space*, Sage Publications, London, 1994; and S. Zukin, *Cultures of Cities*, Blackwell, Oxford, 1995.

11   For a critical perspective on the various currents in explanations of post-Fordism and regional development, see A. Amin and K. Robbins, 'The Mythical Geography of Flexible Accumulation', *Environment and Planning: Society and Space*, vol. 8, 1990, pp. 7–34.

12   On new industrial spaces, see A. J. Scott, *New Industrial Spaces: Flexible Production, Organisation, and Regional Development in North America and Western Europe*, Pion, London, 1988; and B. T. Asheim, 'Industrial Districts: The Contributions of Marshall and Beyond', in G. L. Clark, M. P. Feldman, and M. S. Gertler (eds), *The Oxford Handbook of Economic Geography*, Oxford University Press, Oxford, 2000, pp. 413–31.

13   A positive view of these possibilities was presented by J. Mathews, *The Culture of Power*, Pluto Press, Sydney, 1988, and in the reply by Mathews to his critics in *Journal of Australian Political Economy*, no. 30, December, 1992, pp. 91–128.

14   See, for example, I. Campbell, 'The Australian Trade Union Movement and Post-Fordism', *Journal of Australian Political Economy*, vol. 26, 1990, pp. 1–26; and B. Harrison, *Lean and Mean: The Changing Landscape of Corporate Power in the Age of Flexibility*, Guilford Press, New York, 1994.

15   R. Reich, *The Work of Nations*, Simon & Schuster, London, 1993.

16   H.-P. Martin and H. Schumann, *The Global Trap: Globalisation and the Assault on Democracy and Prosperity*, Zed Books, London, 1997.

17   On developments in establishing shorter working weeks, see A. Hayden, *Sharing the Work, Sparing the Planet*, Zed Books, London, 1999, ch. 7.

18   C. Sanne, *The (Im)possibility of Sustainable Lifestyles: Can We Trust the Public Opinion and Plan for Reduced Consumption?*, Working Paper no. 63, Urban Research Program, Australian National University, Canberra, August 1998.

19   Australia Institute, *Redistributing Work: Solutions to the Paradox of Overwork and Unemployment in Australia*, Discussion Paper no. 7, Australia Institute, Canberra, June 1996.

20   A. Gorz, *Paths to Paradise*, Pluto Press, London, 1985, and *Reclaiming Work: Beyond the Wage-Based Society*, Polity Press, London, 1999.

21   See F. Stilwell, 'Speculation or Productive Investment?', *Journal of Australian Political Economy*, no. 23, August 1988, pp. 25–44. The following arguments draw from this source.

22 One estimate is that about one in 70 foreign exchange deals actually reflects needs arising from international trade and commerce; see D. Richardson, *Client Memorandum*, Department of Parliamentary Library, Information and Research Services, Canberra, 18.6.1999.

23 Bank for International Settlements, *Triennial Central Bank Survey: Foreign Exchange Derivatives Market Activity in 2007*, online at <www.bis.org/publ/rpfxf07t.htm>.

24 S. Melman, *Profits Without Production*, Knopf, New York, 1983.

25 ibid., p. xiii; see also B. Frankel, 'Financialisation: How New Financial Forms of Economic Government Are Reshaping the Politics of Redistribution', in S. Bell (ed.), *Economic Governance and Institutional Dynamics*, Oxford University Press, Melbourne, 2002.

26 M. Hudson, 'Quantitative Easing is Fracturing the Global Economy', *Global Research*, 1.11.2010; reprinted in *ERA Newsletter*, Economic Reform Australia, vol. 3, no. 51, January 2011, pp. 10–22.

27 T. Philippon, The Evolution of the US Financial Industry from 1860 to 2007, Working Paper, New York University, 2008.

28 B. Frankel, 'Financialisation', in S. Bell (ed.), *Economic Governance and Industrial Dynamics*, Oxford University Press, Melbourne, 2002, pp. 78.

29 G. Dow, 'Neoliberal Corporate Governance of the Australian Economy', in S. Bell (ed.), op. cit., p. 67.

30 D. Gordon, T. Weisskopf, and S. Bowles, *The Imperilled Economy*, URPE, New York, 1987; extract in G. Argyrous and F. Stilwell (eds), *Economics as a Social Science: Readings in Political Economy*, Pluto Press, Sydney, 1st edn, 1996, pp. 256–9.

37   Class, Gender, Ethnicity

1 D. Ricardo, *On the Principles of Political Economy and Taxation*, Dent, London, 1962 (1817).

2 See A. K. Sen, *Inequality Reexamined*, Clarendon Press, Oxford; Russell Sage Foundation, New York, 1995. For discussion of the importance of inequality in different currents of political economic thought, see J. C. Myers, *The Politics of Equality: An Introduction*, Zed Books, London, 2010.

3 A significant early contributor to this tendency was A. Okun, *Equality and Efficiency: The Big Tradeoff*, Brookings Institution, Washington, 1975.

4 Marx developed a different position in *Theories of Surplus Value*, Lawrence & Wishart, London, 1951, ch. 17, p. 6, where he refers to 'the continual increase in numbers of the middle classes ... situated midway between the workers on one side and the capitalists and landowners on the other'. On this point, see also T. Bottomore, *Theories of Modern Capitalism*, George Allen & Unwin, Boston, 1985. Bottomore seeks to reconcile the two views of Marx in terms of a distinction between the 'tendency' and 'counter-tendencies', akin to the Marxian analysis of the tendency of the rate of profit to fall and the counteracting forces to push in the opposite direction.

5 See F. Stilwell and K. Jordan, *Who Gets What? Analysing Economic Inequality in Australia*, Cambridge University Press, Melbourne, 2007, ch. 3.

6 For evidence on these economic inequalities in Australia, see J. Shields, 'Setting the Double Standard: Chief Executive Pay the BCA Way', *Journal of Australian Political Economy*, no. 56, December 2005, pp. 299–324.

7 This analysis is adapted from E. O. Wright, *Class, Crisis and the State*, New Left Books, London, 1978. For other works by the same author, see *Classes*, Verso, London, 1985; *Class Counts: Comparative Studies in Class Analysis*, Cambridge University Press, Cambridge, 1997; and 'Understanding Class: Towards an Integrated Analytical Approach', *New Left Review*, no. 60, November–December 2009, pp. 101–16.

8 A. Gramsci, *Selections from the Prison Notebooks of Antonio Gramsci*, Q. Hoare and G. Smith (eds and trans), Lawrence & Wishart, London, 1971; see also D. Foracs (ed.), *A Gramsci Reader*, Lawrence & Wishart, London, 1988, and R. Crompton, F. Devine, M. Savage, and J. Scott, *Reviewing Class Analysis*, Blackwell, Oxford, 2002.

9 See N. Hollier (ed.), *Ruling Australia: the Power, Privilege and Politics of the New Ruling Class*, Overland, in conjunction with Australian Scholarly Publications, Melbourne, 2004.

10 J. K. Gibson-Graham, S. Resnick, and R. Wolff (eds), *Re/Presenting Class: Essays in Postmodern Marxism*, Duke University Press, Durham, 2001.

11 For an introduction to writings on political economy from a gender perspective see G. Argyrous and F. Stilwell (eds), *Readings in Political Economy: Economics as a Social Science*, Tilde University Press, Melbourne, 3rd edn, 2011, pp. 213–233, and references cited therein.

12 On patriarchy, see S. Walby, *Theorising Patriarchy*, Blackwell, Oxford, 1989; and K. Pritchard Hughes (ed.) *Contemporary Australian Feminism*, Addison, Wesley, Longman Australia, South Melbourne, 1997.

13 See F. Blau and R. Ehrenberg (eds), *Gender and Family Issues in the Workplace*, Russell Sage Foundation, New York, 1997, especially the chapter by Goldin. For a fuller discussion of social reproduction from a feminist perspective, see also N. Folbre, *Who Pays For the Kids? Gender and the Structure of Constraint*, Routledge, London, 1994.

14 One of the leading contributions to this type of analysis was the article by A. Game and R. Pringle, 'Production and Consumption, Public versus Private', in D. H. Broom (ed.), *Unfinished Business: Social Justice for Women in Australia*, Allen & Unwin, Sydney, 1984, pp. 65–79. For further discussion of the relationship between women's work in the two spheres, see N. Folbre and J. A. Nelson, 'For Love or Money—or Both?', *Journal of Economic Perspectives*, vol. 14, no. 4, Fall 2000, pp. 123–40.

15 For discussion of the neglect of women's work in the calculation of national income, see M. Waring, 'A Woman's Reckoning', in G. Argyrous and F. Stilwell (eds), *Readings in Political Economy: Economics as a Social Science*, Tilde University Press, Melbourne, 3rd edn, 2011, pp. 214–218.

16 For a specific example of the bias against women's domestic contributions, see J. Smith and L. Ingham, 'Breastfeeding and the Measurement of Economic Progress', *Journal of Australian Political Economy*, no. 47, June 2001, pp. 51–72.

17 See A. Summers, *Damned Whores and God's Police*, Penguin, Melbourne, 2nd rev. edn, 2002, ch. 12.

18 Important research on gender and work in Australia was pioneered by A. Game and R. Pringle, *Gender at Work*, George Allen & Unwin, Sydney, 1983; R. Pringle, *Secretaries Talk*, Verso, London, 1989; and R. Pringle, *Sex and Medicine*, Cambridge University Press, Cambridge, 1998.

19 See A. Hochschild, *The Managed Heart: The Commercialisation of Human Feeling*, University of California Press, Berkeley, 2003.

20 F. Stilwell and K. Jordan, *Who Gets What? Analysing Economic Inequality in Australia*, Cambridge University Press, Melbourne, 2007, p. 129.

21 See G. Meagher, 'Evaluating Women's Work: NSW Nurses and Professional Rates', *Journal of Australian Political Economy*, no. 34, December 1994, pp. 77–102; and E. Sorensen, *Comparable Worth: Is It a Worthy Policy?*, Princeton University Press, Princeton, 1994.

22 It is notable, for example, that Australia elected its first female Prime Minister, Julia Gillard, in 2010.

23 J. K. Galbraith, *Economics and the Public Purpose*, Houghton Mifflin, New York, 1973, p. 233.

24 A radical feminist perspective, by contrast, emphasises gender inequalities as a more pervasive feature of all patriarchal societies.

25 See P. Griffiths, 'The Political Economy of Racism', in Argyrous and Stilwell, op. cit., pp. 37–43.

26 G. Becker, *The Economics of Discrimination*, University of Chicago Press, Chicago, 2nd edn, 1971. Becker was awarded the Nobel Prize in Economic Sciences in 1992.

27 M. Friedman, *Capitalism and Freedom*, University of Chicago Press, Chicago, 1962, p. 108.

28 See M. N. Leiman, *Political Economy of Racism*, Westview Press, Boulder, 1993; E. H. Tuma, *The Persistence of Economic Discrimination: Race, Ethnicity and Gender*, Pacific Books, Palo Alto, 1995; and K. J. Arrow, 'What Has Economics to Say about Racial Discrimination?', *Journal of Economic Perspectives*, vol. 12, no. 2, Spring 1998, pp. 91–100.

29 For an example of this opposition to 'reverse discrimination', see M. Friedman, 'A comment on SWEP' (the American Economic Association's Committee on the Status of Women in the Economics Profession), *Journal of Economic Perspectives*, vol. 12, no. 4, Fall 1998, pp. 197–9; see also B. R. Bergman, *In Defence of Affirmative Action*, HarperCollins, New York, 1996; and H. J. Holzer and D. Neumark (eds), *The Economics of Affirmative Action*, Edward Elgar, Cheltenham, 2004.

30 See C. Taylor, 'The Politics of Recognition', in A. Gutman (ed.), *Multiculturalism*, Princeton University Press, New Jersey, 1994, pp. 23–73; and N. Fraser, 'From Redistribution to Recognition? Dilemmas of Justice in a "Post-Socialist" Age', *New Left Review*, no. 212, July–August 1995, pp. 68–93.

38   The Political Economy of the State

1   An example of this position, introduced in chapter 27, is G. Dow, P. Boreham, and M. Leet, *Room to Manoeuvre: Political Aspects of Full Employment*, Melbourne University Press, Melbourne, 1999.

2   A strong statement of this view is M. Friedman and R. Friedman, *Free to Choose*, Penguin, Harmondsworth, 1980: extract in G. Argyrous and F. Stilwell (eds), *Readings in Political Economy: Economics as a Social Science*, Tilde University Press, Melbourne, 3rd edn, 2011, pp. 119–124.

3   See also G. Dow, 'Policy Matters in Political Economy', in Argyrous and Stilwell, op. cit., pp. 64–70.

4   For a little more on Fabianism, see B. Burkitt, *Radical Political Economy: An Introduction to Alternative Economics*, Wheatsheaf Books, Brighton, UK, 1984, ch. 6.

5   R. H. Tawney, *Equality*, Unwin Books, London, 1964. Tawney argued strongly for an assault on economic inequality, notwithstanding the vested interests opposed to any such program of reform.

6   S. Holland, *The Socialist Challenge*, Quartet Books, London, 1975.

7   A. Gorz, *Reclaiming Work: Beyond the Wage-Based Society*, Polity Press, London, 1999, p. 8.

8   K. Marx and F. Engels, *Manifesto of the Communist Party*, Foreign Languages Publishing House, Moscow, 1960 (1848), p. 66–7.

9   The classic debate in the Marxist literature on the state was that between Nicos Poulantzas and Ralph Miliband; for a brief summary, see D. Gold, C. Lo, and E. O. Wright, 'Recent Developments in Marxist Theories of the Capitalist State', in E. L. Wheelwright and F. Stilwell (eds), *Readings in Political Economy*, vol. 1, ANZ Book Co., Sydney, 1976, pp. 260–5. For a more modern, less structuralist interpretation of the state, see M. Konings, 'Renewing State Theory', *Politics*, vol. 30, no. 3, 2010, pp. 174–82.

10   This relationship between capital accumulation and legitimisation was a major political economic theme established by J. O'Connor, *The Fiscal Crisis of the State*, St Martin's Press, New York, 1973.

11   A focus on the influence of freemasonry is not a normal feature of Marxist analysis. It is mentioned in this context as an example of an institutionalised process of preferment. For further discussion of how it works, see S. Knight, *The Brotherhood: The Secret World of the Freemasons*, Granada, London, 1984; and M. Baigent and R. Leigh, *The Temple and the Lodge*, Guild Publishing, London, 1989.

12   See, for example, R. Bryan and M. Rafferty, *The Global Economy in Australia: Global Integration and National Economic Policy*, Allen & Unwin, Sydney, 1999; and D. McNally, *Global Slump: The Economics and Politics of Crisis and Resistance*, PM Press, Oakland, 2011.

13   G. Baldelli, *Social Anarchism*, Penguin, Harmondsworth, 1972, p. 19.

14   D. C. Mueller, *Public Choice*, Cambridge University Press, Cambridge, 1979, p. 105; see also G. D. Myles, *Public Economics*, Cambridge University Press, Cambridge, 1995; and D. C. Mueller (ed.), *The Economics of Politics*, Edward Elgar, Cheltenham, 2001.

15   See L. Orchard and H. Stretton, *Public Goods, Public Enterprise, Public Choice*, St Martin's Press, New York, 1994; and P. Self, *Government by the Market*, Macmillan, London, 1993. For a less-than-riveting dialogue between a proponent of public choice theory and an advocate of a more substantial role for the state and public finance, see J. A. Buchanan and R. A. Musgrave, *Public Finance and Public Choice: Two Contrasting Views*, MIT Press, Cambridge, MA, 2000.

16   Self, op. cit., p. 209.

17   E. Jones, 'Economics and the Neglected Spirit of Reform', *Journal of Australian Political Economy*, no. 35, June, 1995, p. 84.

18   An example is the green bans movement that saved Sydney from more environmentally damaging urban renewal in the 1970s; see M. Burgmann and V. Burgmann, *Green Bans: Red Union*, UNSW Press, Sydney, 1998.

39   Why Do Economists Disagree?

1   This notion originates from K. Boulding, *The Image*, University of Michigan Press, Ann Arbor, 1956; see also E. Jones, 'Methodology in Economics: An Introduction', in E. L. Wheelwright and F. Stilwell (eds), *Readings in Political Economy*, vol. 1, ANZ Book Co., Sydney, 1976, pp. 275–9.

2   A standard reference on these epistemological issues is A. Chalmers, *What Is This Thing Called Science?*, University of Queensland Press, St Lucia, 3rd edn, 1999; see also A. S. Eichner (ed.), *Why Economics*

is Not Yet a Science, M. E. Sharpe, New York, 1983, and J. B. Davis (ed.), *Recent Developments in Economic Methodology*, Edward Elgar, Cheltenham, 2006.

3   W. S. Jevons, 1888, quoted in B. Toohey, *Tumbling Dice: The Making of Modern Economic Policy*, Heinemann, Melbourne, 1994, p. 12.

4   E. Jones, 'Positive Economics or What?', *Economic Record*, vol. 53, September 1975, pp. 350–63.

5   See, for example, R. Bhaskar, M. Archer, A. Collier, T. Lawson, and A. Norrie (eds), *Critical Realism: Essential Readings*, Routledge, London, 1998; and S. Fleetwood, *Critical Realism in Economics: Development and Debate*, Routledge, London, 1999.

6   M. Friedman, *Essays in Positive Economics*, University of Chicago Press, Chicago, 1953, pp. 3–43.

7   A view of knowledge as socially constructed has also had widespread influence in other social sciences through the work of French philosopher Michel Foucault. See M. Foucault, *Power/ Knowledge: Selected Interviews and Other Writings, 1972-7*, Colin Gordon (ed. and trans.), Pantheon Books, New York, 1980.

8   A. J. Scott, 'Economic Geography: The Great Half-century', in G. L. Clark, M. P. Feldman, and M. S. Gertler (eds), *The Oxford Handbook of Economic Geography*, Oxford University Press, Oxford, 2000, p. 34.

9   T. Barnes, *Logics of Dislocation: Models, Metaphors and the Meanings of Economic Space*, Guilford Press, New York, 1996, p. 95.

10   C. Mouffe, 'Rorty's Pragmatic Politics', *Economy and Society*, vol. 29, no. 3, August 2000, pp. 439–53; see also R. Rorty, *Truth and Progress*, Cambridge University Press, 1998, and *Philosophy and Social Hope*, Penguin, Harmondsworth, 1999.

11   See D. McCloskey, *The Rhetoric of Economics*, University of Wisconsin Press, Madison, 1985.

12   There are many currents in postmodernism, so generalisation is difficult. For further discussion of the impact of postmodernism, see P. M. Rosenau, *Post-Modernism and the Social Sciences*, Princeton University Press, Princeton, 1992; and J. Sanbonmatsu, 'Postmodernism and the Politics of Expression', in S. Lilley (ed.), *Capital and its Discontents*, PM Press, Oakland, CA, 2011, pp. 201, 220–36.

13   For example, the original R. G. Lipsey, *An Introduction to Positive Economics*, Weidenfeld & Nicolson, London, 1979; and various subsequent editions and nation-specific adaptations, such as R. G. Lipsey and K. A. Chrystal, *Principles of Economics*, Oxford University Press, Oxford, 2000.

14   The classic exposition of this view is G. Myrdal, *The Political Element in the Development of Economic Theory*, Simon & Schuster, New York, 1969.

15   F. M. Watkins, *The Age of Ideology: Political Thought, 1750 to the Present*, Prentice Hall, Englewood Cliff, 1964; see also R. Bronk, *Progress and the Invisible Hand: The Philosophy and Economics of Human Advance*, Warner Books, London, 1998.

16   This position is argued by F. Stilwell, *Changing Track: A New Political Economic Direction for Australia*, Pluto Press, Sydney, 2000, ch. 3.

17   See, for example, R. Leach, *Political Ideologies: An Australian Introduction*, Macmillan, Melbourne, 1993.

18   See P. Feyerabend, *Against Method: Outline of an Anarchistic Theory of Knowledge*, London, Verso, 3rd edn, 1993.

40   A Level Playing Field for Economic Ideas?

1   For an attempt to defend what mainstream economists do in practice, notwithstanding the persistence of neoclassical principles in the curriculum, see D. Coyle, *The Soulful Science: What Economists Do and Why it Matters*, Princeton University Press, Princeton and Oxford, 2007.

2   Personal communication with an academic economist at a British university.

3   See G. J. Butler, E. Jones, and F. Stilwell, *'Political Economy Now! The Struggle for Alternative Economics at the University of Sydney*, Darlington Press, Sydney, 2009, ch. 9.

4   See R. H. Frank, T. D. Gilovich, and D. T. Regan, 'Does Studying Economics Inhibit Cooperation?', *Journal of Economic Perspectives*, vol. 7, no. 2, Spring 1997, pp. 159–71. It is also interesting to note that a survey of American economics graduate students (cited by A. J. Field, book review, *Journal*

of Economic Literature, vol. 36, no. 1, March 1998, p. 229), reported only 3 per cent of students as thinking it important for an economist to have knowledge about the real world. Another empirical study of students' attitudes indicated that the study of economics prioritises straightforward profit maximisation over more complex concerns with conflicting interests and ethics; see A. Rubinstein, 'A Sceptic's Comment on the Study of Economics', *Economic Journal*, vol. 116, no. 510, March 2006.

5   M. Pusey, *Economic Rationalism in Canberra: A Nation-building State Changes Its Mind*, Cambridge University Press, Cambridge, 1991.

6   M. Pusey, 'The Impact of Economic Ideas as Public Policy in Australia', in G. Argyrous and F. Stilwell (eds), *Economics as a Social Science: Readings in Political Economy*, Pluto Press, Sydney, 1st edn, 1996, p. 229.

7   W. Parsons, *The Power of the Financial Press*, Rutgers University Press, New Brunswick, 1990, cited in B. Toohey, *Tumbling Dice: The Story of Modern Economic Policy*, Heinemann, Melbourne, 1994, p. 216.

8   D. Hallin, *The Uncensored War: The Media and Vietnam*, University of California Press, Los Angeles, 1986, cited in Toohey, op. cit., p. 218.

9   On bias in journalism, see also R. W. McChesney, 'Journalism, Democracy and Class Struggle', *Monthly Review*, vol. 5, no. 6, November 2000, pp. 1–15.

10 R. Cockett, *Thinking the Unthinkable: Think-tanks and the Economic Counter-Revolution, 1931–83*, HarperCollins, London, 1995.

11 In Australia the principal example is The Australia Institute, based in Canberra, whose publications have been cited in previous chapters of this book.

12 See P. Sheldon and L. Thornthwaite, *Employer Associations and Industrial Relations Change*, Allen & Unwin, Sydney, 1999, for discussion of these institutions in Australia.

13 Their meetings also provide focal points for antiglobalisation protests, such as those that occurred in Seattle in 1999 and in numerous other cities since then (see Box 3.1).

14 Even that is disputable. The argument of F. Hayek is that the real strength of a competitive market system is not its allocative efficiency or other equilibrium properties, but its anarchic character, which fosters risk taking and innovation. See Y. Varoufakis, *Foundations of Economics: A Beginner's Companion*, Routledge, London, 1998, pp. 189–90.

15 An early exploration of the soulful corporation idea was C. Kaysen, 'The Social Significance of the Modern Corporation', *American Economic Review*, May 1957, p. 314. Although it didn't catch on in the economic discipline, it persists as a theme in the business management literature; see, for example, J. Batten and T. Fetherston (eds), *Social Responsibility: Corporate Governance Issues*, Elsevier, 2003.

16 J. K. Galbraith, 'Power and the Useful Economist', *American Economic Review*, March 1973, p. 1.

41   W(h)ither Capitalism?

1   K. Marx and F. Engels, *Manifesto of the Communist Party*, Foreign Languages Publishing House, Moscow, 1960 (1848), p. 68. For a recent analysis of why class inequalities continue to deepen and cause crises, see D. Dowd, *Inequality and the Global Economic Crisis*, Pluto Press, London and New York, 2009.

2   R. Heilbroner, *An Inquiry into the Human Prospect*, W. W. Norton, New York, 1974, p. 76.

3   The following chapter explores the connection between happiness and material progress; see also R. Bronk, *Progress and the Invisible Hand: The Philosophy and Economics of Human Advance*, Warner Books, London, 1998, ch. 9; R. Kuttner, *Everything for Sale: The Virtues and Limits of Markets*, Knopf, New York, 1998; and R. Layard, 'Happiness and Public Policy: a Challenge to the Profession', *Economic Journal*, vol. 116, no. 510, March 2006, pp. C24–C33.

4   Marx and Engels, op. cit., p. 67.

5   See F. Stilwell, *Changing Track: A New Political Economic Direction for Australia*, Pluto Press, Sydney, 2000, ch. 8.

6   R. A. Esterlin, *Growth Triumphant: The Twenty-first Century in Historical Perspective*, University of Michigan Press, Ann Arbor, 1996.

7   H. Minsky's analysis, briefly mentioned in Chapter 33, is particularly relevant in this context.

8   Admittedly, this is a tricky distinction between redistributive and transformative activities. Most struggles have a local and specific focus, but contain the potential for wider impacts. Treating struggles about production relations as more important than struggles about distribution is not necessarily implied. We all do what we can. For an article reasserting the strength of class consciousness, see P. Sweezy and H. Magdoff, 'Socialism: A Time to Retreat?', *Monthly Review*, vol. 52, no. 4, September 2000, pp. 1–7.

9   The view that dispossessed people comprise the principal source of challenge to the existing social order is not novel. It was one of the renowned claims of philosopher Herbert Marcuse, in the penultimate paragraph of his book *One Dimensional Man*, Sphere Books, London, 1968, pp. 200–1.

10   See J. O'Connor, 'Environmental Crisis: an Eco-Marxist Perspective', in G. Argyrous and F. Stilwell (eds), *Readings in Political Economy: Economics as a Social Science*, Tilde University Press, Melbourne, 2011, pp. 202–206; and J. B. Foster, *The Ecological Revolution: Making Peace with the Planet*, Monthly Review Press, New York, 2009.

11   The following analysis is partly reproduced from Stilwell, op. cit., ch. 10, where it is more fully developed. See also A. MacEwan, *Neo-Liberalism or Democracy? Economic Strategy, Markets and Alternatives for the 21st Century*, Zed Books, London, 2005; and H. Shutt, *Beyond the Profits System: Possibilities for a Post-Capitalist Era*, Zed Books, London, 2010.

12   For debates about market socialism, see D. McNally, *Against the Market: Political Economy, Market Socialism and the Marxist Critique*, Verso, London, 1993; and P. Bardhan and J. Roemer, *Market Socialism*, Oxford University Press, Oxford, 1993.

13   See T. Ramsey and C. Lloyd, 'Infrastructure Investment for Full Employment: A Social Democratic Program of Funds Regulation', *Journal of Australian Political Economy*, no. 65, Winter 2010, pp. 59–88.

14   On the case for cooperatives, see R. Mathews, *Jobs of Our Own: Building a Stakeholder Society*, Pluto Press, Sydney, 1999.

15   'With most problems nowadays, the economic answers are only political questions'; J. Robinson, *Collected Economic Papers II*, Basil Blackwell, Oxford, 1980, p. 275.

42   A Happy Ending?

1   R. Layard, 'What Is Happiness? Are We Getting Happier?', in *Happiness: Has Social Science a Clue?*, Lecture 1, Lionel Robbins Memorial Lectures 2002–03, London School of Economics and Political Science, London, 4 March, 2003, p. 14.

2   This chapter draws substantially on evidence and arguments previously developed in F. Stilwell and K. Jordan, *Who Gets What? Analysing Economic Inequality in Australia*, Cambridge University Press, Melbourne, 2007, ch. 9.

3   J. Hirata, *Happiness and Economics: Enriching Economic Theory with Empirical Psychology*, <http://johannes-hirata.de/research_master.htm>, 2001, accessed 25 May 2005.

4   R. Gwynne, *Maslow's Hierarchy of Needs*, <http://web.utk.edu/~gwynne/maslow.htm>, 1997, accessed 25 May 2005; J. de Graaf, D. Wann & T. H. Naylor, *Affluenza: The All-Consuming Epidemic*, 2nd edn, Berrett-Koehler, San Francisco, 2005.

5   R. Veenhoven, *Conditions of Happiness*, Kluwer, Dordrecht, Netherlands, 1984.

6   C. Hamilton, 'The Politics of Affluence', *Arena Magazine*, no. 64, April–May, p. 43. The problems of affluence have been extensively probed in other works by Hamilton and researchers at the Australia Institute in Canberra: see, for example, C. Hamilton, 'Consumer Capitalism', in G. Argyrous and F. Stilwell (eds), *Readings in Political Economy: Economics as a Social Science*, Tilde University Press, Melbourne, 3rd edn, 2011, pp. 18–20; C. Hamilton, *Growth Fetish*, Allen & Unwin, Sydney, 2003; and C. Hamilton and R. Denniss, *Affluenza: When Too Much Is Never Enough*, Allen & Unwin, Sydney, 2005.

7   ibid., p.44.

8   R. Layard, op. cit., p. 14.

9   R. Layard, 'Income and Happiness: Rethinking Economic Policy', in *Happiness: Has Social Science a Clue?*, Lecture 2, Lionel Robbins Memorial Lectures 2002–03, London School of Economics and Political Science, London, 4 March, 2003, p. 4.

10   R. Frank, *Luxury Fever: Why Money Fails to Satisfy in an Era of Excess*, The Free Press, New York, 1999.

11   E. Diener and M. Seligman, 'Beyond Money: Towards an Economy of Well-being', *Psychological Science in the Public Interest*, vol. 5, no. 1, 2004; R. Layard, *Happiness: Lessons from a New Science*, Penguin, New York, 2005.

12   R. Frank, op. cit.

13   R. Layard, op. cit., p. 4. Similar results have been found in other industrialised countries.

14   R. Layard, 'What is Happiness? Are We Getting Happier?', in *Happiness: Has Social Science a Clue?*, Lecture 1, Lionel Robbins Memorial Lectures 2002–03, London School of Economics and Political Science, London, 3 March, 2003, p. 13.

15   ibid., see also R. Layard, *Happiness: Lessons from a New Science*, Penguin, New York, 2005.

16   R. Wilkinson and K. Pickett, *The Spirit Level: Why More Equal Societies Almost Always Do Better*, Allen Lane, London, 2009.

17   The argument that shifting income from rich to poor would increase total utility was developed by A. C. Pigou (see *The Economics of Welfare*, 4th edn, Macmillan, London, 1946). As noted in Chapter 23 of this book, subsequent neoclassical economists argued that the conclusion was illegitimate because it assumed the possibility of making interpersonal comparisons of utility.

18   Cited in R. Frank, op. cit., p. 122.

19   A. E. Clark and A. J. Oswald, 'Satisfaction and Comparison Income', *Journal of Public Economics*, vol. 61, no. 3, 1996, pp. 359–81.

20   J. Hirata, *Happiness and Economics: Enriching Economic Theory with Empirical Psychology*, <http://johannes-hirata.de/research_master.htm>, 2001, accessed 25 May 2005, p. 36.

21   B. Heady and M. Wooden, 'The Effects of Wealth and Income on Subjective Well-being and Ill-being', *Economic Record*, vol. 80, s. 1, 2004, pp. S24–S33.

22   A. E. Clark and A. J. Oswald, 'Satisfaction and Comparison Income', *Journal of Public Economics*, vol. 61, no. 3, 1996, pp. 359–81.

23   R. Layard, 'Income and Happiness: Rethinking Economic Policy', in *Happiness: Has Social Science a Clue?*, Lecture 2, Lionel Robbins Memorial Lectures 2002–03, London School of Economics and Political Science, London, 4 March, 2003.

24   R. Frank, op. cit.

25   T. Veblen, *The Theory of the Leisure Class*, Unwin Books, London, 1970.

26   F. Hirsch, *Social Limits to Growth*, Routledge & Kegan Paul, London, 1977.

27   C. Hamilton and R. Denniss, *Affluenza: When Too Much is Never Enough*, Allen & Unwin, Sydney, 2005; see also J. de Graaf, D. Wann, and T. H. Naylor, *Affluenza: the All-Consuming Epidemic*, 2nd edn, Barrett-Koehler Publishers, San Francisco, 2005; and O. James, *The Selfish Capitalist: Origins of Affluenza*, Vermilion, London, 2008.

28   See R. Frank, op. cit.

29   See, for example, C. Hamilton and R. Denniss, Tracking Well-being in Australia: The Genuine Progress Indicator 2000, *Discussion Paper no. 35*, Australia Institute, Canberra, December 2000.

30   Illustrative outcomes (based on somewhat different calculations of the GPI) were shown in previous editions of this book.

31   J. Stiglitz, A. Sen, and J.-P. Fitoussi, *Report by the Commission on the Measurement of Economic Performance and Social Progress*, 2010, available at <www.stiglitz-sen-fitoussi.fr>. A document showing how the Australian Treasury has partially incorporated such concerns into its strategic framework is *Strategic Framework 2010-11*, Australian Treasury, 2010. See also P. A. Lawn and M. Clarke (eds), *Sustainable Welfare in the Asia–Pacific: Studies Using the Genuine Progress Indicator*, Edward Elgar, Cheltenham, 2008. Finally, for further discussion of the issues introduced in this chapter, see R. Gittins, *The Happy Economist: Happiness for the Hard-Headed*, Allen & Unwin, Sydney, 2010.

Index

Bold entries denote boxes.